BUSINESS POLICY AND STRATEGY

CONTRIBUTING AUTHORS

ALONZO, MARTIN V.
ANSOFF, H. IGOR
APPLEBAUM, STEPHEN H.
BENKE, RALPH L., JR.
CAPLAN, ROBERT H., III
CLELAND, DAVID I.
COWEN, SCOTT S.
DAVIS, JAMES V.
DAY, GEORGE S.
DEAN, BURTON V.
GALBRAITH, JAY R.
GORONZY, FRIEDHELM
GRAY, EDMUND R.
HALL, WILLIAM K.
HANAN, MACK
HAY, ROBERT
HULBERT, JAMES M.
KING, WILLIAM R.
KINNUNEN, RAYMOND M.
LOHRASBI, ARDESHIR
LORANGE, PETER
MacMILLAN, IAN C.
MINTZBERG, HENRY
MURRAY, EDWIN A., JR.
NAOR, JACOB
PAVAN, ROBERT J.
PITTS, ROBERT A.
RINGBAKK, KJELL-ARNE
ROMAN, DANIEL D.
SCHEIN, EDGAR H.
SEED, ALLEN H., III
SHIRLEY, ROBERT C.
STEINER, GEORGE A.
STEVENSON, HOWARD H.
STRAUSS, GEORGE
TOY, NORMAN E.
TURNER, ROBERT C.
VANCIL, RICHARD F.
WHALEY, WILSON M.
WHEELWRIGHT, STEPHEN C.
WILLIAMS, ROBERT A.
WILSON, IAN H.
YOSHINO, M. Y.

EDMUND R. GRAY, EDITOR
Louisiana State University

BUSINESS POLICY AND STRATEGY:

SELECTED READINGS

AUSTIN PRESS
EDUCATIONAL DIVISION OF
LONE STAR PUBLISHERS, INC.
P.O. BOX 9774
AUSTIN, TEXAS 78766

Library of Congress Card Number 78-59402

ISBN: 0-914872-12-5

Printed in the United States of America

TO: NANCY AND KELLY

CONTENTS

PART II
STRATEGY IMPLEMENTATION

G. STRATEGIC CONTROL AND EVALUATION

PREFACE

When writing the preface to the first edition of this book over a decade ago, I quoted William Starbuck's famous definition: "Business Policy is a course which appears near the end of a student's curriculum bearing the title 'Business Policy'." With this bit of sarcasm he was emphasizing the fact that there was almost no agreement on the content of this course. However, in the past ten years or so the field of Business Policy has developed greatly and taken definition. Currently, there is a more or less generally accepted framework that centers around the concept of corporate strategy pioneered at the Harvard Business School.

Today, as in the past, most Business Policy courses are taught primarily by the case method but the series of cases used tend to be organized so as to lead the student through the analyses involved in the several subparts of the corporate strategy concept. In addition to providing a useful pedagogical structure, the strategy framework has generated significant research and sub-theory. Most of this information is housed in a variety of scholarly and professional journals. Hence, a major purpose of this book is to present under a single cover a selection of the best of this literature.

The primary organization of this book follows the usual corporate strategy framework, i.e., Strategy Formulation and Strategy Implementation. The first section is further, somewhat arbitrarily divided into three subsections: Basic Concepts in Strategy and Strategic Planning, Critical Inputs to Strategy Making, and Key Areas of Strategic Concern. The Implementation section is subdivided into four areas: Organization for Strategy Implementation, Top Level Leadership and Motivation, Processes and Systems for Strategy Implementation, and Strategic Control and Evaluation. The individual selections have been chosen to represent a balance between classic and relatively recent articles; reports of research results, and theory and "how-to" articles.

I see this book as serving two principal functions.

First, it may be used as a supplementary text in a Business Policy course where the instructor desires a balance between case analysis and readings and discussion of theory and research results. Second, it could be utilized as a primary text in a course where the instructor wishes to emphasize the literature in the field. Suggested additional readings are furnished at the end of each section to aid the instructor and the student in pursuing this objective.

I am very grateful to the authors of the included selections and their publishers for the permission to reprint. In order to preserve the integrity of the author's ideas, each article is reprinted in its entirety. To me this seems preferable to the presentation of excerpts as is sometimes done in books of this type.

I would also like to express my appreciation to A. J. Lerager for his encouragement and support in this endeavor and Mrs. Gloria Armistead for her help in preparing the manuscript. Of course, the responsibility for the selection and organization of the materials is mine.

E.R.G.

I

STRATEGY FORMULATION

SECTION A.

BASIC CONCEPTS IN STRATEGY AND STRATEGIC PLANNING

1

Strategy-Making in Three Modes*

HENRY MINTZBERG

HOW DO ORGANIZATIONS make important decisions and link them together to form strategies? So far, we have little systematic evidence about this important process, known in business as *strategy-making* and in government as *policy-making*. The literature of management and public administration is, however, replete with general views on the subject. These fall into three distinct groupings or "modes." In the *entrepreneurial* mode, found in the writings of some of the classical economists and of many contemporary management writers, one strong leader takes bold, risky actions on behalf of his organization. Conversely, in the *adaptive* mode, described by a number of students of business and governmental decision-making, the organization adapts in small, disjointed steps to a difficult environment. Finally, the proponents of management science and policy science describe the *planning* mode, in which formal analysis is used to plan explicit, integrated strategies for the future.

I shall begin by describing each mode as its proponents do, in simple terms and distinct from the other two. Considered in this way, each may appear to be a naive reflection of the complex reality of strategy-making. But taken as a set of three, as I shall do in subsequent sections, to be combined and alternated by managers acting under different conditions, these modes constitute a realistic and useful description of the strategy-making process. To illustrate this point, I shall cite studies of the strategy-making

---

behaviors of a number of very different kinds of organizations--hotels, hospitals, car dealerships, modeling agencies, airports, radio stations, and so on. Finally, I shall discuss some important implications for strategic planning.

THE ENTREPRENEURIAL MODE

The entrepreneur was first discussed by early economists as that individual who founded enterprises. His roles were essentially those of innovation, of dealing with uncertainty, and of brokerage. The entrepreneur found capital which he brought together with marketing opportunity to form, in the words of Joseph Schumpeter, the well-known Harvard economist, "new combinations."

In a recent book called *The Organization Makers*, Orvis Collins and David Moore present a fascinating picture of those independent entrepreneurs, based on a study of 150 of them. The authors trace the lives of these men from childhood, through formal and informal education, to the steps they took to create their enterprises. Data from psychological tests reinforce their analysis. What emerges are pictures of tough, pragmatic men driven from early childhood by a powerful need for achievement and independence. At some point in his life, each entrepreneur faced disruption ("role deterioration"), and it was here that he set out on his own.

> What sets them apart is that during this time of role deterioration they interwove their dilemmas into the projection of a business. In moments of crisis, they did not seek a situation of security. They went on into deeper insecurity...[1]

A number of management writers view the entrepreneurial mode of strategy-making not only in terms of creating new firms but in terms of the running of ongoing enterprises. Typical of these is Peter Drucker, who writes in a recent article:

> Central to business enterprise is...the entrepreneurial act, an act of economic risk-taking. And business enterprise is an entrepreneurial institution....Entrepreneurship is thus central to function, work and performance of the executive in business.[2]

What are the chief characteristics of the entrepreneurial mode of strategy-making as described by economists and management writers? We can delineate four:

1. *In the entrepreneurial mode, strategy-making is dominated by the active search for new opportunities.* The entrepreneurial organization focuses on opportunities; problems are secondary. Drucker writes: "Entrepreneurship requires that the few available good people be deployed on opportunities rather than frittered away on 'solving problems'."[3] Furthermore, the orientation is always active rather than passive. Robert McNamara, when he was Secretary of Defense, stressed the active role for the government administrator:

> I think that the role of public manager is very similar to the role of a private manager; in each case he has the option of following one of two major alternative courses of action. He can either act as a judge or a leader. In the former case, he sits and waits until subordinates bring him problems for solution, or alternatives for choice. In the latter case, he immerses himself in the operations of the business or the governmental activity...
>
> I have always believed in and endeavored to follow the active leadership role as opposed to the passive judicial role.[4]

2. *In the entrepreneurial organization, power is centralized in the hands of the chief executive.* Collins and Moore write of the founder-entrepreneur: "The entrepreneurial personality...is characterized by an unwillingness to 'submit' to authority, an inability to work with it, and a consequent need to escape from it."[5] In the entrepreneurial mode, power rests with one man capable of committing the organization to bold courses of action. He rules by fiat, relying on personal power and sometimes on charisma. Consider this description of an Egyptian firm:

> The great majority of Egyptian-owned private establishments...are organized closer to the pattern of the Abboud enterprises. Here the manager is a dominant individual who extends his personal control over all phases of the business. There is no charted plan of organization, no formalized procedure for selection and development of managerial personnel, no publicized system of wage and salary classifications.
>
> ...authority is associated exclusively with an individual...

> Abboud is the kind of person most people have in mind when they discuss the successful Egyptian entrepreneur.[6]

But while there may be "no charted plan of organization," typically one finds instead that strategy is guided by the entrepreneur's own vision of direction for his organization--his personalized plan of attack. Drucker writes:

> Every one of the great business builders we know of--from the Medici and the founders of the Bank of England down to IBM's Thomas Watson in our days--had a definite idea, indeed a clear "theory of the business" which informed his actions and decisions.[7]

3. *Strategy-making in the entrepreneurial mode is characterized by dramatic leaps forward in the face of uncertainty.* Strategy moves forward in the entrepreneurial organization by the taking of large, bold decisions. The chief executive seeks out and thrives in conditions of uncertainty, where his organization can make dramatic gains. The entrepreneurial mode is probably most alive in the popular business magazines such as *Fortune* and *Forbes* which each month devote a number of articles to the bold actions of manager-entrepreneurs. The theme that runs through these articles is what has been referred to as the "bold stroke," the courageous move that succeeds against all the odds and all the advice.

4. *Growth is the dominant goal of the entrepreneurial organization.* According to psychologist David McClelland, the entrepreneur is motivated above all by his need for achievement. Since his organization's goals are simply the extension of his own, we can conclude that the dominant goal of the organization operating in the entrepreneurial mode is growth, the most tangible manifestation of achievement. *Fortune* magazine came to this conclusion in a 1956 article about the Young Presidents' Organization entitled "The Entrepreneurial Ego":

> Most of the young presidents have the urge to build rather than manipulate. "Expansion is a sort of disease with us," says one president. "Let's face it," says another. "We're empire builders. The tremendous compulsion and obsession is not to make money, but to build an empire." The opportunity to keep on pushing ahead is, indeed, the principal advantage offered by the entrepreneurial life.[8]

In summary, we can conclude that the organization operating in the entrepreneurial mode suggests by its actions that the environment is malleable, a force to be confronted and controlled.

THE ADAPTIVE MODE

The view of strategy-making as an adaptive process has gained considerable popularity since the publication of two complementary books in 1963. Charles Lindblom and David Braybrooke wrote *A Strategy of Decision* about policy-making in the public sector, while Richard Cyert and James March published *A Behavioral Theory of the Firm* based on empirical studies of decision-making.

Lindblom first called this approach "the science of 'muddling through'," later "disjointed incrementalism."[9] The term "adaptive" is chosen here for its simplicity. As described by Lindblom, the adaptive policy-maker accepts as given a powerful status quo and the lack of clear objectives. His decisions are basically remedial in nature, and he proceeds in small steps, never moving too far from the given status quo. In this way, the policy-maker comes to terms with his complex environment.

Cyert and March's strategy-maker, although working in the business firm, operates in much the same fashion. Again, his world is complex and he must find the means to cope with it. Cyert and March suggest that he does so in a number of ways. He consciously seeks to avoid uncertainty, sometimes solving pressing problems instead of developing long-run strategies, other times "negotiating" with the environment (for example, establishing cartels). Furthermore, because the organization is controlled by a coalition of disparate interests, the strategy-maker must make his decisions so as to reduce conflicts. He does this by attending to conflicting goals sequentially, ignoring the inconsistencies:

> Just as the political organization is likely to resolve conflicting pressures to "go left" and "go right" by first doing one and then the other, the business firm is likely to resolve conflicting pressures to "smooth production" and "satisfy customers" by first doing one and then the other.[10]

Four major characteristics distinguish the adaptive mode of strategy-making:

1. Clear goals do not exist in the adaptive organization; strategy-making reflects a division of power among members of a complex coalition. The adaptive organization is caught in a complex web of political forces. Unions, managers, owners, lobby groups, government agencies, and so on, each with their own needs, seek to influence decisions. There is no one central source of power, no one simple goal. The goal system of the organization is characterized by bargaining among these groups, with each winning some issues and losing others. Hence, the organization attends to a whole array of goals sequentially, ignoring the inconsistencies among them. The organization cannot make decisions to "maximize" any one goal such as profit or growth; rather it must seek solutions to its problems that are good enough, that satisfy the constraints.

2. *In the adaptive mode, the strategy-making process is characterized by the "reactive" solution to existing problems rather than the "proactive" search for new opportunities.* The adaptive organization works in a difficult environment that imposes many problems and crises. Little time remains to search out opportunities. And even if there were time, the lack of clear goals in the organization would preclude a proactive approach:

> ...if [the strategy-makers] cannot decide with any precision the state of affairs they want to achieve, they can at least specify the state of affairs from which they want to escape. They deal more confidently with what is wrong than with what in the future may or may not be right.[11]

Furthermore, the adaptive organization seeks conditions of certainty wherever possible, otherwise it seeks to reduce existing uncertainties. It establishes cartels to ensure markets, negotiates long-term purchasing arrangements to stabilize sources of supply, and so on.

3. *The adaptive organization makes its decisions in incremental, serial steps.* Because its environment is complex, the adaptive organization finds that feedback is a crucial ingredient in strategy-making. It cannot take large decisions for fear of venturing too far into the unknown. The strategy-maker focuses first on what is familiar, considering the convenient alternatives and the ones that differ only slightly from the status quo. Hence, the organization moves forward in incremental steps, laid end to end in serial fashion so that feedback can be received and the course adjusted as it moves along. As Lindblom notes, "...policy-making is typically a never-ending process of successive steps in which continual nibbling is a substitute for a good bite."[12]

4. *Disjointed decisions are characteristic of the adaptive organization.* Decisions cannot be easily interrelated in the adaptive mode. The demands on the organization are diverse, and no manager has the mental capacity to reconcile all of them. Sometimes it is simply easier and less expensive to make decisions in disjointed fashion so that each is treated independently and little attention is paid to problems of coordination. Strategy-making is fragmented, but at least the strategy-maker remains flexible, free to adapt to the needs of the moment.

Lindblom provides us with an apt summary of the adaptive mode:

> Man has had to be devilishly inventive to cope with the staggering difficulties he faces. His analytical methods cannot be restricted to tidy scholarly procedures. The piecemealing, remedial incrementalist or satisficer may not look like an heroic figure. He is nevertheless a shrewd, resourceful problem-solver who is wrestling bravely with a universe that he is wise enough to know is too big for him.[13]

THE PLANNING MODE

In a recent book, Russel Ackoff isolates the three chief characteristics of the planning mode:

> 1. Planning is something we do in advance of taking action; that is, it is *anticipatory decision-making*....
> 2. Planning is required when the future state that we desire involves a set of interdependent decisions; that is, a *system of decisions*....
> 3. Planning is a process that is directed toward producing one or more future states which are desired and which are not expected to occur unless something is done.[14]

Formal planning demands rationality in the economist's sense of the term--the systematic attainment of goals stated in precise, quantitative terms. The key actor in the process is the analyst, who uses his scientific techniques to develop formal, comprehensive plans.

The literature of planning is vast, and is growing rapidly. Much of the early writing concerned "operational planning"--the projecting of various budgets based on the given strategies of the organization. More recently, attention has turned to the planning of organizational strategies themselves, the more significant and long-range concerns of senior managers. Two techniques have received particular attention--strategic planning in business and planning-programming-budgeting system (PPBS) in government.

George Steiner has written what up to this point is the definitive book on business planning, entitled *Top Management Planning*. The general prescriptive flavor of the planning literature is found throughout this book. For example, "plans can and should be to the fullest possible extent objective, factual, logical, and realistic in establishing objectives and devising means to attain them."[15] Steiner outlines a stepwise procedure for business planning which begins with three studies: (1) fundamental organizational socioeconomic purpose, (2) values of top management, and (3) evaluation of external and internal opportunities and problems, and company strengths and weaknesses. Strategic plans are then devised, and these lead to the formulation of medium-range programs and short-range plans. In Steiner's opinion, comprehensive planning is important because it simulates the future, applies the systems approach, prevents piecemeal decision-making, provides a common decision-making framework throughout the company, and so on.

In PPBS, the focus is on the budget rather than the general plan (although a budget is, of course, one type of plan). The steps in the process are, by now, well known--the determination of overall governmental goals and objectives, the generation of program proposals to achieve these, the evaluation of these proposals in terms of costs and benefits, the choice of a group of proposals that will satisfy the objectives while not overextending the resources, and the translation of these into five-year and one-year budgets for implementation.

We can delineate three essential features of the planning mode:

1. *In the planning mode, the analyst plays a major role in strategy-making.* The analyst or planner works alongside the manager, and assumes major responsibility for much of the strategy-making process. His role is to apply the techniques of management science and policy analysis to the design of long-range strategies. A U. S. Senator notes the reasons for this:

> I am convinced that we never will get the kind of policy planning we need if we expect the top-level officers to participate actively in the planning process. They simply do not have the time, and in any event they rarely have the outlook or the talents of the good planner. They cannot explore issues deeply and systematically.

> They cannot argue the advantages and disadvantages at length in the kind of give-and-take essential if one is to reach a solid understanding with others on points of agreement and disagreement.[16]

2. *The planning mode focuses on systematic analysis, particularly in the assessment of the costs and benefits of competing proposals.* Formal planning involves both the active search for new opportunities and the solution of existing problems. The process is always systematic and structured. As one business planner wrote recently:

> No doubt much of top-level management is unscientific. But by applying a systematic, structured approach to these problems, we have a better basis for analyzing them. We may identify more specifically the challenges and needs in the situation and see how they are interrelated.[17]

Formal planning follows a stepwise procedure in which particular attention is paid to the cost-benefit evaluation of proposals, where the planning methodology is best developed. The planner tests proposals for feasibility, determines their efficiency (or economic value), and relates them to each other. The planner deals best with conditions known to the management scientist as "risk"--where the uncertainty can be expressed in statistical terms. Conditions of certainty require no planning; those of pure uncertainty cannot be subjected to analysis.

3. *The planning mode is characterized above all by the integration of decisions and strategies.* Ackoff notes that "the principal complexity in planning derives from the interrelatedness of decisions rather than from the decisions themselves."[18] But this interrelatedness is the key element in planning. An organization plans in the belief that decisions made together in one systematic process will be less likely to conflict and more likely to complement each other than if they were made independently. For example, planning can ensure that the decision to acquire a new firm complements (or at least does not conflict with) the decision to expand the product line of an existing division. Thus, strategic planning is a process whereby an organization's strategy is designed essentially at one point in time in a comprehensive process (all major decisions made are interrelated). Because of this, planning forces the organization to think of global strategies and to develop an explicit sense of strategic direction.

To conclude, the planning mode is oriented to systematic, comprehensive analysis and is used in the belief that formal analysis can provide an understanding of the environment sufficient to influence it.

The upper part of Table 1-1 presents in summary form the characteristics of the three modes of strategy-making, while Figure 1-1 depicts these three modes in graphic form. The first figure shows the taking of bold steps consistent with the entrepreneur's general vision of direction. In the second figure, we see a purely adaptive organization taking incremental steps in reaction to environmental forces, while the third figure indicates a precise plan with a specific, unalterable path to one clear end point.

THE DETERMINATION OF MODE

What conditions drive an organization to favor one mode of strategy-making over the others? We may delineate a number of characteristics of the organization itself, such as its size and the nature of its leadership, and features of its environment, such as competition and stability. These are discussed below and are summarized in the lower portion of Table 1-1.

The *entrepreneurial* mode requires that strategy-making authority rest with one powerful individual. The environment must be yielding, the organization oriented toward growth, the strategy able to shift boldly at the whim of the entrepreneur. Clearly, these conditions are most typical of organizations that are small and/or young. Their sunk costs are low and they have little to lose by acting boldly. Young organizations in particular have set few precedents for themselves and have made few commitments. The way is open for them to bunch a number of key decisions at an early stage and take them in entrepreneurial fashion. This behavior may also be characteristic of the organization in trouble--it has little to lose by acting boldly, indeed this may be its only hope. In a study of the Montreal radio industry, one student concluded that the less successful stations were predisposed to adopt an entrepreneurial approach in order to catch up and displace the leader (whose behavior was primarily adaptive).

To satisfy the condition of centralized power, the organization must be either a business firm (often with the owner as chief executive), or an institutional or governmental body with a powerful leader who has a strong mandate. The entrepreneurial mode is often found with charismatic leadership. Charles de Gaulle could have been characterized as an entrepreneur at the head of government.

Use of the *adaptive* mode suggests that the organization faces a complex, rapidly changing environment and a divided coalition of influencer forces. Goals cannot be agreed upon unless they are in "motherhood" form and non-operational

TABLE 1-1.
CHARACTERISTICS AND CONDITIONS OF THE THREE MODES

Characteristic	Entrepreneurial	Adaptive Mode	Planning Mode
Motive for Decisions	Proactive	Reactive	Proactive & Reactive
Goals of Organization	Growth	Indeterminate	Efficiency & Growth
Evaluation of Proposals	Judgmental	Judgmental	Analytical
Choices made by	Entrepreneur	Bargaining	Management
Decision Horizon	Long Term	Short Term	Long Term
Preferred Environment	Uncertainty	Certainty	Risk
Decision Linkages	Loosely Coupled	Disjointed	Integrated
Flexibility of Mode	Flexible	Adaptive	Constrained
Size of Moves	Bold Decisions	Incremental Steps	Global Strategies
Vision of Direction	General	None	Specific
Condition for Use			
Source of Power	Entrepreneur	Divided	Management
Objectives of Organization	Operational	Non-Operational	Operational
Organizational Environment	Yielding	Complex, Dynamic	Predictable, Stable
Status of Organization	Young, Small or Strong Leadership	Established	Large

(they cannot be quantified). Here we have a clear description of the large established organization with great sunk costs and many controlling groups holding each other in check. This is typical of most universities, of many large hospitals, of a surprising number of large corporations, and of many governments, especially those in minority positions or composed of coalitions of divergent groups. Indeed, the American system of government has been expressly designed to create conditions of divided power, and it is, therefore, not surprising that Charles Lindblom, the chief proponent of the adaptive approach, is a student of the U. S. public policy-making process.

In order to rely on the *planning* mode, an organization must be large enough to afford the costs of formal analysis, it must have goals that are operational, and it must face an environment that is reasonably predictable and stable. (This last point inevitably raises the comment that planning is most necessary when the environment is difficult to understand. This may be true, but the costs of analyzing a complex environment may be prohibitive and the results may be discouraging. As one Latin American chief executive commented: "Planning is great. But how can you plan--let alone plan long-term--if you don't know what kind of government you'll have next year?"[19])

The above conditions suggest that formal comprehensive planning will generally be found in business firms of reasonable size that do not face severe and unpredictable competition and in government agencies that have clear, apolitical mandates. NASA of the 1960's is a prime example of extended use of the planning mode in government. Its goal was precise and operational, its funding predictable, its mission essentially apolitical in execution. The communist form of government with its five-year plan is another good example. The power system is hierarchical, goals can be made operational, the home environment can be controlled and made more or less stable and predictable (at least as long as the crops are good).

FIGURE 1-1. PATHS OF THE THREE MODES

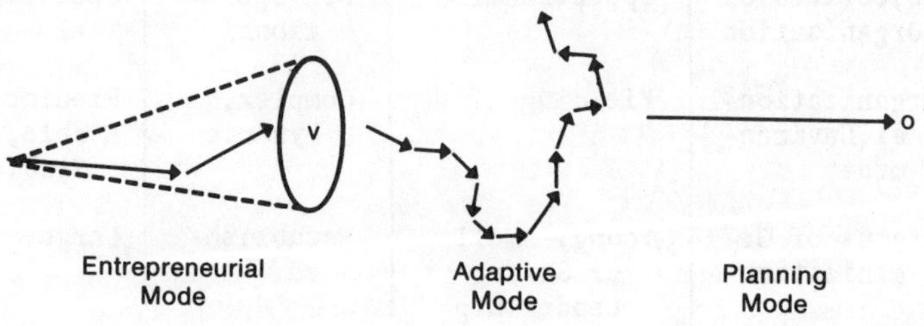

MIXING THE MODES

What is the relationship between our three abstractions and strategy-making reality? Clearly, few organizations can rely on a pure mode. More likely, an organization will find some combination of the three that reflects its own needs. Management students at McGill University have examined a number of business and public organizations according to these three modes, and they have uncovered a variety of ways in which organizations mix these modes. I shall discuss four combinations below, citing examples from these studies to illustrate each.

Combination 1: *Mixing the pure modes.* As we have seen, the literature tends to delineate three modes which are quite distinct in their characteristics. This trichotomy provides a convenient starting point for analysis; however, we cannot preclude the existence of other modes that mix their characteristics. Indeed, studies have revealed various combinations of the modes. We have, for example, found a number of adaptive entrepreneurs. One owned a car dealership. Reluctant to delegate authority but unable to achieve further growth without doing so, he was content to hold power absolutely, like the entrepreneur, but to avoid risk and move in incremental steps, like the adaptive strategy-maker.

We can find the two other combinations of the pure modes as well. In entrepreneurial planning, the organization takes bold, decisive steps in terms of a systematic plan for growth, while in adaptive planning the organization reaches a specific goal through a flexible path. Herbert Simon describes an example of adaptive planning found in nature:

> We watch an ant make his laborious way across a wind-and wave-molded beach. He moves ahead, angles to the right to ease his climb up a steep dunelet, detours around a pebble, stops for a moment to exchange information with a compatriot. Thus he makes his weaving, halting way back to his home....[His path] has an underlying sense of direction, of aiming toward a goal....He has a general sense of where home lies, but he cannot foresee all the obstacles between. He must adapt his course repeatedly to the difficulties he encounters....[20]

Combination 2: *Mixing modes by function.* Within single organizations, we have found different modes in different functional areas. One group of students carefully studied all departments of a large downtown hotel, and found evidence of all three modes. Where operations were largely routinized and predictable, as in housekeeping and the front office, the planning mode was used. In marketing, where there was room for imagination and bolder action, the hotel tended to act in an entrepreneurial fashion, while in the personnel department, which faced a complicated labor market, the mode was clearly adaptive.

Another group studied a modeling agency and found that in the area of fashion it was forced (as were all its competitors) to adapt to the dictates of the hautes couturieres of Paris, while it was free to be entrepreneurial or to plan in the areas of marketing and operations. Clearly, different parts of an organization can employ those modes which best fit their particular situations.

COMBINATION 3: *Mixing modes between parent and subunit.* Neil Withers, a member of a group studying the Montreal International Airport (which comes under the purview of the Canadian Department of Transport), became interested in the relationship between a parent organization and its subunit (a division, a subsidiary, an agency, and so on). The question he addressed was: If the parent uses a particular mode, what limitations does that impose on the subunit (assuming, of course, that there is not enough decentralization to allow the subunit to operate independently)? Withers considers all nine possible combinations in which each could use one of the three modes, and he draws some interesting conclusions.

Figure 1-2 shows the use of the adaptive mode by both parent and subunit--a situation Withers refers to as "muddling through times two." In this case, the subunit merely follows the path of the parent, adapting to its incremental moves, and following a slightly more varied and lagged path. Withers concludes that the adaptive mode is, in fact, always an acceptable one for the subunit, no matter what the mode of the parent.

Withers believes "entrepreneurial duets"--whereby both parent and subunit employ the entrepreneurial mode--to be "the worst possible combination." The subunit is subjected not only to its own bold moves but to the unexpected bold moves of the parent. The disruption may prove intolerable. One is led to conclude that no centralized organization is big enough for two entrepreneurs. Sooner or later one must make a bold, unexpected move that interferes with the other. (In contrast, another group described a decentralized social work agency where strategy-making was largely in the hands of the social workers. They were all entrepreneurs, acting independently to initiate original programs and seeking approval from the main office whose behavior was described as adaptive.)

FIGURE 1-2. MUDDLING THROUGH TIMES TWO

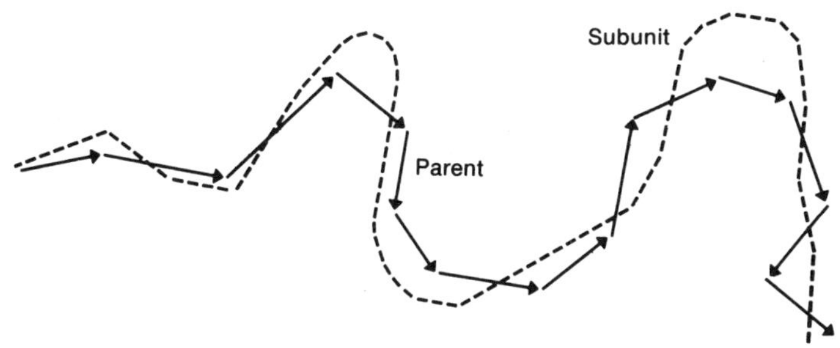

Finally, Withers considers the conditions under which the subunit can plan. Figure 1-3 shows a situation where the subunit plans while the parent organization adapts. The subunit at time t_1 anticipates the trend of the parent's strategy and plans accordingly.

Up to time t_2, no difficulties are incurred, and the subunit continues to extrapolate. But soon the parent's direction begins to change, and the subunit finds itself in conflict with the parent. According to Withers, "The use of planning in this uncertainty may not yield sufficiently improved results over [adapting] to justify the cost of planning and the long-term commitment of resources." Withers concludes that subunit planning will work only if the parent plans and if the two planning centers are properly coordinated.

FIGURE 1-3. PLANNING IN AN ADAPTIVE ENVIRONMENT

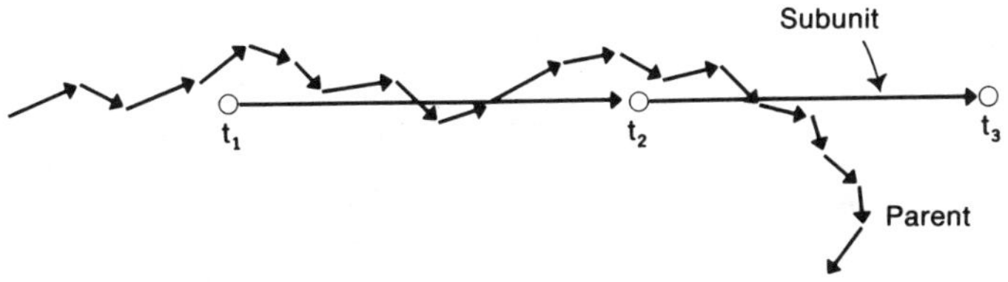

Combination 4: *Mixing modes by stage of development.* A number of writers have described the growth of organizations in terms of three or four basic stages--generally corresponding to a life cycle beginning with youth and ending with maturity. It appears that we can characterize the various stages by the mode of strategy-making employed.

Generally, the young organization is entrepreneurial--it has few committed resources, it stands to lose little and to gain much by taking bold steps, leadership tends to be charismatic, and there is much spirit associated with its mission. This is the period of expansion and growth. But each new strategic decision commits additional resources, and gradually the organization locks itself into specific strategies, bureaucratic structures, and demanding pressure groups. The adaptive mode sets in. For example, one group of students studied a Montreal hospital which began in a most entrepreneurial fashion, with dramatic innovations in design and operation. Some time later, when the hospital was established, the provincial government took over increasing control of its budgets and by the time of the study these students felt that the adaptive mode was most descriptive of this organization's strategy-making behavior.

The adaptive mode may signal the final stage of maturity, or the conditions may be such that an organization can attempt to regenerate itself through a new period of entrepreneurship. In fact, it appears that the way to turn around a large, adaptive organization requiring major change is to bring in an entrepreneurial leader. Only by consolidating power in the hands of one strong newcomer will it be possible to override the established factions and the entrenched attitudes.

Some organizations appear to develop cyclical patterns in which periods of entrepreneurship are alternated with periods of adaptiveness. They make a set of bold changes in order to grow, then settle down to a period of stability in which the changes are consolidated, later embark on a new period of growth, and so on. Perhaps in some cases these follow economic cycles--an entrepreneurial mode in an expanding economy, an adaptive mode during recession.

Some time ago, I interviewed the president of a hotel chain who traced his firm's strategy through to the third distinct cycle of change and consolidation. The first stage of growth, as a real estate firm, involved the purchase of a number of older downtown hotels as property investments. Later, realizing the potential of investments, the firm entered a period of consolidation in which the properties were developed into an efficient hotel chain. Having reached this point after some years, a second wave of entrepreneurial growth began. First the firm became public in order to obtain expansion capital and then it entered into a major expansion program involving primarily the construction of a chain of modern motor hotels. Toward the end of the program, the firm found that its financial resources were overextended, partly due to higher expansion costs than anticipated. Again growth was halted while the firm consolidated its new units, concentrating on making them efficient, and waiting until its financial reserves were sufficient to begin to grow again. About three years later, at the time of the interview, cycle three has just begun, this time with the emphasis on the construction of larger downtown hotels.

Such an approach to strategy-making may, in fact, be a sensible one. It proceeds on the assumption that it is better to keep the modes distinct, concentrating fully on one mode at a time rather than mixing them and having to reconcile the different styles of strategy-making.

Other organizations, as they mature, tend to use the planning mode--the development of new strategies by controlled, orderly change. As these organizations grow large, they commit more and more of their staff resources to planning. Indeed, this is the thesis of John Kenneth Galbraith who claims, in *The New Industrial State*, that large business firms are controlled by the planners (the "technostructure") who use their techniques to enable the firms in turn to control their markets.

Our studies have not covered these large firms, but analyses of the strategy-making behaviors of a diverse array of smaller organizations--airlines, brokerage firms, universities, race tracks, cultural centers--suggest that virtually all start in the entrepreneurial mode, most later shift to an adaptive mode, and some move on to planning or back to entrepreneurship in their maturity.

IMPLICATIONS FOR STRATEGIC PLANNING

What can we conclude from this description of strategy-making? One point merits special emphasis. *Planning is not a panacea for the problems of strategy-making.* As obvious as this seems, there is little recognition of it in planning books or by planners. Instead, one finds a focus on abstract, simple models of the planning process that take no cognizance of the other two modes of strategy-making. Little wonder then that one finds so much frustration among formal planners. Rather than seeking panaceas, we should recognize that the mode used must fit the situation. An unpredictable environment suggests use of the adaptive mode just as the presence of a powerful leader may enable the organization to best achieve its goals through the entrepreneurial mode.

Some situations require no planning, others only limited planning. Often the planning mode can be used only when mixed with the others. Most important, planners must recognize the need for the manager to remain partially in the adaptive mode at all times. Crises and unexpected events are an important part of every strategy-maker's reality. Conventional planning requires operational goals which managers cannot always provide (the coalition may simply not agree on anything specific). Furthermore, it must be recognized that good planning is expensive, it often requires unrealistic stability in the environment, and, above all, it is the least flexible of the strategy-making modes. All this is not to conclude that planning is useless; rather, it suggests that the planner must become more realistic about the limitations of his science.

Often there is a need to redesign the formal planning process. Adaptive planning would differ from conventional planning in a number of important respects. The plans would be flexible so that the manager could adjust as the future unfolded itself. He would be able to time his moves accordingly--to begin construction on the new plant when interest rates fall, to reorganize the structure after certain executives retire. The plans would also provide for different options--alternate locations for a new plant depending on impending state legislation, different possible acquisition strategies depending on the success of recent acquisitions, and so on. In other words, like the path of the ant described earlier, strategic plans would specify end points and perhaps alternate routes, but they would also leave the manager with the flexibility necessary to react to his dynamic environment.

In addition, the planner could draw up a series of contingency plans to help the manager deal with any one of a number of possible events that could have a sudden, devastating effect on the organization. He could also be prepared to "plan in the realtime," that is, to apply his analytical techniques quickly for the manager who faces an unforeseen crisis. By preparing in this way, planners can more closely adapt themselves to the realities of strategy-making.

FOOTNOTES

[1]O. Collins and D. G. Moore, *The Organization Makers* (New York: Appleton, Century, Crofts, 1970), p. 134.

[2]P. F. Drucker, "Entrepreneurship in the Business Enterprise," *Journal of Business Policy*, (1:1, 1970), p. 10.

[3]*Ibid.*, p. 10.

[4]Quoted in C. J. Hitch, *Decision-Making for Defense*

(Berkeley: University of California Press, 1967).

[5]Collins and Moore, *op. cit.*, p. 45.

[6]F. Harbison and C. A. Myers, *Management in the Industrial World* (New York: McGraw-Hill, 1959), pp. 40-41.

[7]Drucker, *op. cit.*, p. 5.

[8]S. Klaw, "The Entrepreneurial Ego," *Fortune* (August, 1956), p. 143.

[9]See C. E. Lindblom, "The Science of 'Muddling Through'", *Public Administration Review* (19, 1959), pp. 79-88; C. E. Lindblom and David Braybrooke, *A Strategy of Decision* (New York: Free Press, 1963); C. E. Lindblom, *The Intelligence of Democracy* (New York: Free Press, 1965); and C. E. Lindblom, *The Policy-Making Process* (Englewood Cliffs, N. J.: Prentice-Hall, 1968).

[10]R. M. Cyert and J. G. March, *A Behavioral Theory of the Firm* (Englewood Cliffs, N. J.: Prentice-Hall, 1963), p. 118.

[11]Lindblom, *op. cit.*, (1968), p. 25.

[12]*Ibid.*, p. 25.

[13]Lindblom, *op, cit.*, (1968), p. 27.

[14]R. L. Ackoff, *A Concept of Corporate Planning* (New York: Wiley Interscience, 1970), pp. 2-5.

[15]G. A. Steiner, *Top Management Planning* (New York: Macmillan, 1969), p. 20.

[16]Quoted in R. N. Anthony,*Planning and Control Systems: A Framework for Analysis* (Boston: Harvard Graduate School of Business Administration, 1965), p. 46-47.

[17]M. F. Cantley, "A Long-range Planning Case Study," *OR Quarterly* (20, 1969), pp. 7-20.

[18]R. L. Ackoff, *op. cit.*, p. 3.

[19]Quoted by H. Stieglitz, *The Chief Executive and His Job* (New York: National Industrial Conference Board, Personnel Policy Study Number 214, 1969), pp. 46-47.

[20]H. A. Simon, *The Sciences of the Artificial* (Cambridge, Massachusetts: MIT Press, 1969), pp. 23-24.

STUDENT REVIEW QUESTIONS

1. What are the three modes of strategy making identified by Mintzberg?
2. What does Lindblom mean when he talks about "disjointed incrementalism"?
3. What factors seem to be important in determining the mode of strategy making a particular organization will use?
4. What combination of "mixed modes" does Mintzberg identify?
5. Discuss the statement "planning is not a panacea for the problems of strategy making."
6. Why is growth probably the dominant goal of the entrepreneurial organization?
7. Discuss the differences in the locus of power in organizations using the three modes.

2

The Critical Role of Top Management in Long-Range Planning*

GEORGE A. STEINER

THERE IS NO substitute for long-range planning in the development of profitable and healthy organizations. It is not, of course, the only requirement, but it is a major one. Too few companies, particularly the smaller and medium-sized ones, and too few government organizations try or do effective long-range planning.

In examining many long-range planning programs, I have come to two major conclusions. First, the fundamental concept of an effective long-range planning program is deceptively simple. Second, creating and maintaining a first-rate long-range planning program is deceptively difficult and demands, for its success, devoted attention by chief executives. I should like to discuss these two points, but first I should like to say a few words about the importance of effective long-range planning.

IMPORTANCE OF LONG-RANGE PLANNING

There exists in some business and government quarters surprising resistance to developing systematic and comprehensive planning. Naturally there are a great many reasons for such resistance, but failure to grasp the significance of effective planning is more important than it should be.

Several years ago, Mr. S. C. Beise, then president of

*George A. Steiner, "The Critical Role of Top Management in Long-Range Planning," *Arizona Review* (April, 1966), pp. 1-8. Reprinted by permission.

the Bank of America, observed that for many years before World War II commercial banks did not aggressively seek savings deposits. As a result, the industry did not involve itself importantly in the related field of real estate financing. After World War II building boomed and little financial firms grew dramatically to fill the home financing need. Mr. Beise commented:

> Today these once-small savings and loan companies constitute a big industry in the United States and have given banks stiff competition for savings funds. The commercial banking industry today has made a strong comeback in the fields of savings and real estate lending, but due to its lack of foresight some twenty years ago, the banking industry gave birth to one of its own biggest competitors. I believe the industry has learned its lesson well, and it is one every industry and company should note.[1]

A recent study of the thirteen fastest growing companies in the United States revealed that all give high priority to long-range planning and manage to inspire most levels of managers to think about the future.[2]

Not only are more companies discovering the advantages of comprehensive and effective planning programs, but governments are developing organized long-range planning programs. This movement is particularly rapid among Western European governments and some developing nations. Last August President Johnson dramatically announced that the planning-programming-budgeting system introduced into the Pentagon by Secretary McNamara must be applied throughout the government.

There are many reasons why systematic and structured long-range planning is considered so important by progressive business and non-business organizations. Effective planning prevents ad hoc decisions, random decisions, decisions that unnecessarily and expensively narrow choices for tomorrow. Effective planning gives an organization a structural framework of objectives and strategies, a basis for all decision making. Lower-level managers know what top management wants and can make decisions accordingly. But there are also ancillary benefits. An effective planning organization, for example, provides a powerful channel of communications for the people in an organization to deal with problems of importance to themselves as well as to their organization.

It is difficult to exaggerate the importance of effective comprehensive planning to an organization. It has, for many companies, provided that margin needed for outstanding growth and profitability.

A CONCEPTUAL MODEL OF LONG-RANGE PLANNING

A conceptual model of planning at a sufficiently low level of abstraction is a guide in establishing a complete system. The words *long-range planning* are useful in emphasizing a time dimension to planning. In describing an effective planning program, however, I prefer to speak of comprehensive, corporate or total planning.

Planning in this sense may be described from four points of view. First, a basic generic view of planning as dealing with the futurity of present decisions. This means that current decisions are made in light of their long-range consequences. It means also that future alternatives open to an organization are examined and decisions made about preferred alternatives. On this basis, guidance is provided for making current operating decisions. There are also many other conceptual views of planning; one concept, for example, recognizes planning as reasoning about how you get from here to there.

Planning is also a process. It is a process which establishes objectives; defines strategies, policies and sequences of events to achieve objectives; defines the organization for implementing the planning process; and assures a review and evaluation of performance as feedback in recycling the process.

Planning may be considered from a third point of view--namely, as a philosophy. Planning has been described as projective thought, or "looking ahead." Planning in this sense is an attitude, a state of mind, a way of thinking.

Finally, planning may be viewed in terms of structure. Long-range planning, as the term is typically used in the business world, refers to the development of a comprehensive and reasonably uniform program of plans for the entire company or agency, reaching out over a long period of time. It is an integrating framework within which each of the functional plans may be tied together and an overall plan developed for the entire organization.

Broadly, this structure includes four major elements (Figure 2-1). The first consists of strategic plans. These are a loose, written and unwritten set of major objectives, strategies and policies. The second is a detailed, uniform and a rather complete medium-range set of plans (two to seven, but generally five years) covering major areas or organizational activity. The third part is short-term plans and budgets. The fourth structural part consists of planning studies which frequently are projections of things to come. A government agency, for example, may make a study of future revenues and demands for funds. A public utility may make population projections for its area. An automobile company may study changing consumer tastes, likely competitor moves and developing automotive technology. Such forecasts are not plans. The results of such studies, however, are impor-

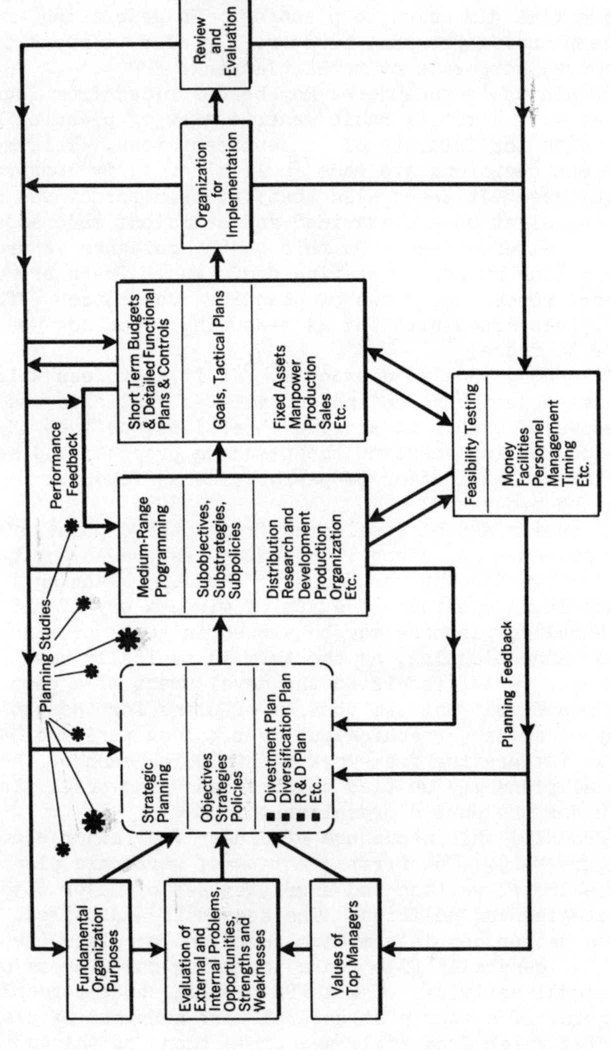

FIGURE 2-1. A STRUCTURE AND PROCESS OF BUSINESS PLANNING

tant in actually making plans.

Long-range planning as the term is typically used in the business world does not refer so much to the future span of time covered as to the idea of management grappling systematically with future opportunities, problems and alternative courses of action. Many companies typically have the pattern of plans and the concepts of planning already defined. This can be and often is called long-range planning. But I prefer other words to describe this structure.

LONG-RANGE PLANNING IN LARGE AND SMALL BUSINESSES

All companies plan ahead in some degree. But not all have the sort of concept and structure noted here. While statistics on this subject are rather poor, I think it is probably true that close to a majority of the largest companies throughout the world have some sort of overall business planning program and a staff assigned to help executives do the work. Two years ago I held a research seminar at the Palais de Fontainebleau, France, to discuss strategic business planning. About one hundred directors of corporate planning or top line managers of the largest multinational corporations of the world were present. One of the surprising conclusions reached at the seminar was that, despite the great surface diversities of planning among these companies, there was a large degree of comparability among basic planning definitions, principles, procedures and structures.[3]

There are relatively fewer numbers of medium and small-sized companies with comprehensive planning programs, but their numbers are growing. They are beginning to realize that, despite their limited resources, they have about the same fundamental planning requirements as the larger companies. Their salvation is not to ignore the problem but to develop shortcuts and rough-cut techniques for dealing with it.[4] There are many ways for a small company to get outside help at a reasonable price. Local banks can give advice. Many consulting agencies are available. Even professors are sometimes handy as consultants. Placing on his board of directors some persons who can contribute to long-range planning may also be attractive to a small businessman.

Systematic and reasonably well-structured planning programs are required by all organizations to survive and progress in the most healthy and effective manner. This is not something that only large companies need and are able to do. The requirement for effective planning exists for small companies, trade associations, industrial development agencies and for governments.

Professor Frank Gilmore of Cornell University presents the necessity for better planning in small businesses with this warning:

> The swing to strategic planning in large organizations constitutes a serious threat to small business management. It challenges one of the important competitive advantages which the small company has enjoyed--being faster on its feet than the larger company in adapting to changing conditions. It is perfectly clear that mere adaptation in the short run will no longer suffice. Trends must henceforth be made, not simply coped with.[5]

His point, of course, is that strategic planning among small businesses and smaller nonprofit organizations must accompany the better planning of the larger organizations. Smaller organizations can plan ahead systematically and continuously. First, however, there must be a recognition by the chief executive that this is possible. Then the smaller organization must devise ways and means to perform planning at a cost under benefit.

Naturally, different organizations go about meeting their planning responsibilities in different ways. Many big corporations have a large central planning staff reporting to the chief executive through a senior vice president. Each of the divisions of such a company may also have a planning staff. At the other extreme are the very small firms where the chief executive does almost all the planning. As firms increase in size, the chief executive may get help by hiring a special assistant, by using his vice presidents in ad hoc advisory planning committees or by using his vice presidents and functional officers as a permanent planning staff to help him develop plans.

In a similar fashion, basic principles essential for effective planning apply to all organizations--large and small, profit and nonprofit. Precisely how the principles are applied, however, does differ among organizations and among problems and over time.

Of cardinal importance in creating and maintaining useful comprehensive planning programs is the role played by chief executives.

TOP MANAGEMENT'S KEY ROLE IN PLANNING

There can and will be no effective long-range planning in any organization where the chief executive does not give it firm support and make sure that others in the organization understand his depth of commitment. Yet one competent observer finds:

> Probably the single most important problem

> in corporate planning derives from the belief of some chief operating executives that corporate planning is not a function with which they should be directly concerned. They regard planning as something to be delegated, which subordinates can do without responsible participation by chief executives. They think the end result of effective planning is the compilation of a "Plans" book. Such volumes get distributed to key executives, who scan the contents briefly, file them away, breathe a sigh of relief, and observe, "Thank goodness that is done--now let's get back to work."[6]

This, of course, shows a lack of understanding of the planning task and the responsibility of the top executive. Another competent observer says the matter is not so much a lack of understanding but abdication of responsibility. Professor O'Donnell has said:

> I think one of the outstanding facts about corporate planning at the present is that the presidents of corporations have been ducking their jobs....They seem to be following the practice of setting in a fuzzy way some objectives to be accomplished in the future and establishing a committee, with the staff help of a planning group, to come up with a plan for achieving the objectives. From this point until the plan is presented to him, the president almost abdicates his responsibilities. When the plan is placed on his desk it is often too late for him to exert much influence on it.[7]

It is essential that the chief executive assume primary responsibility for his organization's long-range planning. When he hires an assistant to help him, or establishes a planning staff, he is merely extending his reach. These people are helping him do *his* job. This is a recognition that the world is too large for one man to grasp completely, and that to the extent he can get others to help him he will be more able to examine a wider range of threats to and opportunities for his organization.

Issues concerning the role of the chief executive in the development of plans are subtle and complex. I participated in one conference with chief executives where the major focus was on the relationship of the president with his staff in the development of corporate plans. These executives were dedicated to the idea of comprehensive planning but were uncertain about many matters relating to their participation. The range of alternatives is very wide. Effective planning, for example, requires that the top executive "buy it." He must believe in planning as being important to the success of his enterprise. He must give more than "lip service" to the effort. He must feel committed, and his support must be visible to others in the corporation. By his actions the chief executive will set the psychological climate in which planning is done.

How an executive does these things will depend upon his style of management, the way his company is organized, the personalities involved and his own sense of commitment. For example, if the chief executive devotes most of his attention to short-range problems, this emphasis will not be lost on his subordinates. Even if he is interested in long-range planning, can he find the time to do it properly? I agree partly with Senator Jackson for example, when, speaking about the federal government, he observed:

> ...I am convinced that we never will get the kind of policy planning we need if we expect the top-level officers to participate actively in the planning process. They simply do not have the time, and in any event they rarely have the outlook or the talents of the good planner. They cannot explore issues deeply and systematically. They cannot argue the advantages and disadvantages at length in the kind of give-and-take essential if one is to reach a solid understanding with others on points of agreement and disagreement.[8]

While this observation does have an important element of truth in it for a large government department or a large multinational business, it has much less for a small enterprise where the chief executive must plan if any planning is to be done. But even in the largest companies and government agencies the chief executives must get involved in the substance of planning. If they do not they will clearly be abdicating one of their major responsibilities. At the very least they will be captives of their planning staffs and thereby lose some element of control of their enterprises.

But the question still exists: how shall the chief executive participate in the substance of planning? There is no simple answer. For the first planning effort, the chief executive of any organization--large or small, profit or nonprofit--ought to be deeply involved. Once the planning program has gotten on a solid footing, with periodic cycling, general understanding and acceptance, the chief executive will know more clearly at what points and how much of his participation is required. If a company, for example, has just begun the planning process and is pounding out long-range objectives, the chief executive should be intimately involved. Once those objectives are established, he must help make and approve strategies to reach them. When this work is done, he may get involved in subsequent cycles of planning only with selected changes in specific objectives and strategies. Both he and his staff will know better with experience what these points are. There is no ready answer for any chief executive, however, to the question of when and how much he can delegate to and rely upon his staff--both line and functional--what are, in the end, his planning responsibilities.

It is not enough that the chief executive participate in the planning exercise. His relationship to it must be visible to others in the organization. By various methods open to him, the chief executive must have others know about and understand his interest in the process.

DEVELOPING THE PLAN

It is a major responsibility of the chief executive to see that the proper planning system is developed and maintained. In this effort, of course, he will have help from subordinates--both line managers and their staffs. But it is his responsibility to make sure that the system is appropriate to his enterprise, and that it is done at a cost (using this word broadly) under benefit which produces optimum values.

Many years ago I had the job of helping an organization develop its first comprehensive planning program. In preparing procedures and suggesting roles of people in the organization I ran into grave difficulties. People were not sure of their responsibilities, or did not want to assume the responsibility I suggested. Different people wanted to do different things which did not necessarily mesh. There were also other points of dispute. To solve the entire problem I prepared a letter for the signature of the chief executive which set forth the essential elements of the planning program, how it should be developed and who was responsible for what. This worked like a charm. From that day to this the top executives of that company have watched over the planning process. It is an outstanding system.

I am not saying, of course, that chief executives must get enmeshed in all the grubby details of a total planning program. What I do say is they must see that the job of planning the plan is done, that it is appropriate and put into operation.

Clarification of roles of participants in the planning process is important and raises complex issues. For example, since corporate planning staffs are direct aids to the chief executive he must see that their roles are clear and generally understood.

A staff, for example, which fails to distinguish between strategic planning and tactical planning may lose top management if it gets too deeply involved in the details of tactical planning. Top management is interested in both strategic and tactical planning, but principally strategic planning. I once knew a staff that simply could not get itself out of the morass of details involved in short-range tactical planning. It was not long before the top management and its planning staff stopped talking to one another. There have been managers who simply could not differentiate between their responsibilities for strategic as distinguished from short-range tactical planning. Their concentration on the latter got them involved in a sort of Gresham's law of planning: short-range planning tends to drive out long-range planning.

Subtle problems of staff role arise in the development of strategic plans by central planning staffs and plans and operations of divisions. Long-range plans made in one area of a company often make sense only when considered in light of other areas and of the company as a whole. In this light, corporate planning staffs inevitably get involved in this interrelationship. Their role in modification of plans to relate better to the company as a whole may result in bitter conflict with line officers if large issues are involved. No matter how clear staff roles may be this sort of conflict will arise. It is less likely to arise and less likely to be serious if roles are clearly specified and understood.

There is no question about the fact that planning should not be separated from doing. Upon examination, however, this is not as simple as it sounds. In the strategic planning area, for example, plans may be developed for divisional execution, and the divisions may not have much if any participation in their preparation. Even with close line and staff interrelations at central office headquarters, staff inevitably will make decisions. The mere choice of alternatives to present to line managers, for example, may implicitly be decision-making by staff. Problems of drawing a line of demarcation between staff and line decision-making, and planning and operations, vary from case to case in the development of plans, and from time to time. There can be no simple formula. But efforts to clarify staff role can prevent unnecessary conflict.

Even when the staff role is clear, however, difficult problems of relationships may arise. In larger companies with comprehensive planning programs, corporate functional staffs, including long-range planning staffs, review divisional plans at the request of top management. Plans are submitted up the line, but staffs help line managers review them. In one instance a president asked his director of long-range planning to review the plans of a powerful division manager. The president insisted upon a rigorous examination of the plans because of the substantial capital outlays sought by the divisional manager. The planner did so and provided the rationale for rejecting the plans. He was not very happy about his role. He had been cultivating this divisional manager for a long time in order to develop a better planning program in his division and to arrange better communications to help them both do a better planning job. Now the divisional manager felt he had been double-crossed. The corporate planner will have problems in rebuilding his lines of communication with this division.

The planning process is complex. There must be understanding of authority, responsibility, procedures and timing. The chief executive is responsible for seeing that this need is met.

BASIC DECISIONS ON PLANS

Comprehensive planning done with and on behalf of top management should result in operating decisions. Without decisions the planning process is incomplete. Failure to take action on prepared plans, or continuous vacillation, will weaken staff efforts. People simply will not be motivated to exert the energy, develop the creativity and use the imagination needed to make quality plans if top management ignores them or cannot seem to act upon them.

In one company I know, one month after a five-year long-range plan had been developed for the first time and approved by top management, the president announced a flat seven percent budget cut for all division budgets. This was his method to reduce costs. The announced reason was the need to bring costs within the year's anticipated revenues. With this announcement, the longer-range projects naturally were abandoned and the benefits of long-range planning cast in grave doubt.

The extent to which divisional line managers make decisions in light of strategic corporate plans raises a different type of problem. In come companies the connection between the corporate strategic plan and the divisional intermediate-range plans is very close. The two may, in effect, be prepared together. In one small company of about five hundred people making a variety of electronics equipment, there was a planning program where strategic plans were developed for the company as a whole and the divisions tied their sub-strategies and detailed long-range plans clearly and closely into the corporate plan. These were intermeshed because the two were done by about the same people and at about the same time. In other instances, the corporate strategic plan constitutes an umbrella under which the divisional plans are made but the interrelationship between the two is rather loose.

A somewhat different type of problem arises very subtly if divisional managers think that corporate planning staffs are making plans for them to execute. It can arise if chief executives do not get involved in the planning and accept staff recommendations without much or any reservation. In such cases divisional managers are likely to take this position to the corporate staff: "You made the plans, now execute them. Don't ask me to."

One of the major attributes of comprehensive corporate planning is that the structure, especially when written, permits managers down the organizational chain to make decisions with a reasonable degree of certainty they are in line with the objectives sought by higher level management. Naturally, if decisions made throughout an organization do not relate to the planning program, it will not be long before the planning program disappears.

This, of course, does not mean blind devotion to plan. Depending upon circumstances, it may be wise for a manager to make decisions which are very different than those planned. Flexibility must be injected into planning. There are a number of techniques to do this. One major method is for the chief executive to inject a philosophy and understanding of flexibility into the planning and operational decision-making process.

In sum, chief executives have an important role in assuring that decisions throughout the organization are made in light of plans and evolving circumstances--not blindly, not without reference to plans, but related meaningfully within a planning framework.

PLANNING TAKES TIME

While conceptually simple, a comprehensive long-range planning program for a large organization cannot be introduced overnight and expected to produce miraculous results immediately. Several years ago I calculated that about five years were required for a medium-sized or large company to develop an effective comprehensive planning system.[9] This was confirmed by another study.[10] Since there is so much more known today about how to develop effective comprehensive planning programs, it is possible to reduce this time span. Much depends upon the organization and what is going on inside it.

Among most initial efforts to develop comprehensive long-range planning programs with which I have been familiar, the first effort did not produce much of immediate substantive value. Yet, all those involved felt the effort worthwhile. This was so, I found, because the effort introduced a new point of view into the company which appeared to have important possibilities in future planning. It also was seen as a focal point for communicating in a common language about major problems. There are many other reasons why managements have been pleased with the first attempt at long-range planning even though it did not provide immediate substantive values. But first efforts do not always provide important bases for immediate decision.

An effective planning program of one company cannot be lifted intact and applied to another. While the fundamental process and structure may be removed from one company to another, the details of operation will vary. Furthermore, since an organization is a living, dynamic institution in a rapidly changing environment, the procedures for planning change.

RESUME

Two major underlying considerations in the development of effective long-range planning are, first, understanding of an operational conceptual model of plans, and second, understanding and acceptance by the chief executive of his role in creating and maintaining quality planning.

George Humphrey used to say that the best fertilizer ever invented was the footsteps of the farmer. Similarly, the best assurance of effective planning in an organization is the active participation of the chief executive in doing it.

FOOTNOTES

[1]S. C. Beise, "Planning for Industrial Growth: An Executive View," remarks before the Milan Conference on Planning for Industrial Growth, sponsored by Stanford Research Institute, 1963, mimeographed.

[2]Jack B. Weiner, "What Makes a Growth Company?" *Dun's Review and Modern Industry*, November, 1964.

[3]See George A. Steiner and Warren M. Cannon, eds., *Multinational Corporate Planning* (New York: The Free Press, Spring, 1966).

[4]For suggestions about how to do this, see Roger A.

Golde, "Practical Planning for Small Business," *Harvard Business Review,* September - October, 1964; Myles L. Mace, "The President and Corporate Planning," *Harvard Business Review,* January - February, 1965; and Raymond M. Haas, Richard I. Hartman, John H. James and Robert R. Milroy, *Long-Range Planning for Small Business,* Bureau of Business Research, Graduate School of Business, Indiana University, 1964.

[5]Frank F. Gilmore, "Strategic Planning's Threat to Small Business," mimeographed, 1966.

[6]Mace, *op. cit.,* p. 50.

[7]George A. Steiner, ed., *Managerial Long-Range Planning* (New York: McGraw-Hill Book Co., Inc., 1963), p. 17.

[8]Henry M. Jackson, "To Forge a Strategy for Survival," *Public Administration Review,* Vol. XIX (Summer, 1959), p. 159.

[9]Steiner, *op. cit.,* p. 19-21.

[10]R. Hal Mason, "Organizing for Corporate Planning," Proceedings of the Long-Range Planning Service Client Conference, February 7-9, 1962, Menlo Park, Calif., Stanford Research Institute.

STUDENT REVIEW QUESTIONS

1. What does Steiner mean when he talks about long-range planning? What are the four points of view from which planning may be described?
2. Why is long-range planning important?
3. What does Steiner consider top management's proper role in long-range planning?
4. What is the goal of comprehensive planning?
5. Sketch out a model of a formal planning process.

3

Strategic Planning in Diversified Companies*

RICHARD F. VANCIL

PETER LORANGE

THE WIDELY ACCEPTED THEORY of corporate strategic planning is simple: using a time horizon of several years, top management reassesses its current strategy by looking for opportunities and threats in the environment and by analyzing the company's resources to identify its strengths and weaknesses. Management may draw up several alternative strategic scenarios and appraise them against the long-term objectives of the organization. To begin implementing the selected strategy (or continue a revalidated one), management fleshes it out in terms of the actions to be taken in the near future.

In smaller companies, strategic planning is a less formal, almost continuous process. The president and his handful of managers get together frequently to resolve strategic issues and outline their next steps. They need no elaborate, formalized planning system. Even in relatively large but undiversified corporations, the functional structure permits executives to evaluate strategic alternatives and their action implications on an ad hoc basis. The number of key executives involved in such decisions is usually small, and they are located close enough for frequent, casual get-togethers.

Large, diversified corporations, however, offer a different setting for planning. Most of them use the product/market division form of organizational structure to permit decentralized decision making involving many responsibility-center managers. Because many managers must be involved in decisions requiring coordinated action, informal planning is almost impossible.

Our focus in this article is on formal planning processes in such complex organizations. However, the thought processes in undertaking planning (as described in the opening paragraph) are essentially the same whether the organization is large or small. Therefore, even executives whose corporate situation permits informal planning may find that our delineation of the process helps them clarify their thinking. To this end, formalizing the steps in the process requires an explanation of the purpose of each step.

THREE LEVELS OF STRATEGY

Every corporate executive uses the words *strategy* and *planning* when he talks about the most important parts of his job. The president, obviously, is concerned about strategy; strategic planning is the essence of his job. A division general manager typically thinks of himself as the president of his own enterprise, responsible for its strategy and for the strategic planning needed to keep it vibrant and growing. Even an executive in charge of a functional activity, such as a division marketing manager, recognizes that his strategic planning is crucial; after all, the company's marketing strategy (or manufacturing strategy, or research strategy) is a key to its success.

These quite appropriate uses of strategy and planning have caused considerable confusion about long-range planning. This article attempts to dispel that confusion by differentiating among three types of "strategy" and delineating the interrelated steps involved in doing three types of "strategic planning" in large, diversified corporations. (Admittedly, although we think our definitions of strategy and planning are useful, others give different but reasonable meanings to these words.)

The process of strategy formulation can be thought of as taking place at the three organizational levels indicated in Exhibit 3-1: headquarters (corporate strategy), division (business strategy), and department (functional strategy). The planning processes leading to the formulation of these strategies can be labeled in parallel fashion as corporate planning, business planning, and functional planning. We have to define these notations briefly before constructing the framework of the planning process:

- *Corporate planning and strategy*--Corporate objec-

EXHIBIT 3-1.

STRUCTURE OF A DIVISIONALIZED CORPORATION

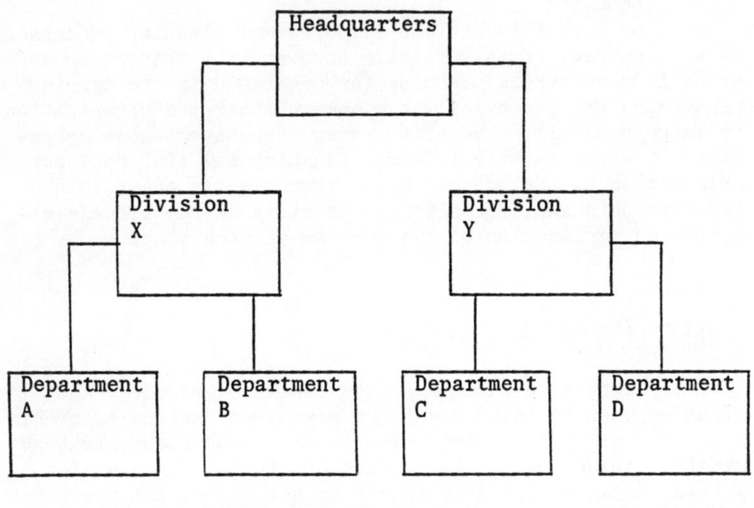

tives are established at the top levels. Corporate planning, leading to the formulation of corporate strategy, is the process of (a) deciding on the company's objectives and goals, including the determination of which and how many lines of business to engage in, (b) acquiring the resources needed to attain those objectives, and (c) allocating resources among the different businesses so that the objectives are achieved. (See the Appendix at the end of this chapter for definitions of *objectives* and *goals* as used in this article.)

- *Business planning and strategy*--Business planning, leading to the formulation of business strategy, is the process of determining the scope of a division's activities that will satisfy a broad consumer need, of deciding on the division's objectives in its defined area of operations, and of establishing the policies adopted to attain those objectives. Strategy formulation involves selecting division objectives and goals and establishing the charter of the business, after delineating the scope of its operations vis-à-vis markets, geographical areas, and/or technology.

Thus, while the scope of business planning covers a quite

homogeneous set of activities, corporate planning focuses on the portfolio of the divisions' businesses. Corporate planning addresses matters relevant to the range of activities and evaluates proposed changes in one business in terms of its effects on the composition of the entire portfolio.

- *Functional planning and strategy*--In functional planning, the departments develop a set of feasible action programs to implement division strategy, while the division selects--in the light of its objectives--the subset of programs to be executed and coordinates the action programs of the functional departments. Strategy formulation involves selecting objectives and goals for each functional area(marketing, production, finance, research, and so on) and determining the nature and sequence of actions to be taken by each area to achieve its objectives and goals. Programs are the building blocks of the strategic functional plans.

Obviously, these levels of strategy impinge on each other to some extent--for example, the corporation's choice of business areas overlaps the scope of division charters, and the delineation of the markets by the division can dictate, at the department level, the choice of strategy in the marketing function. But the distinction remains valid and useful.

THREE-CYCLE SYSTEM

An important point to note about the planning process is that it requires formal interaction among the managers at different times. The more formal aspects--business planning, functional planning, and budgeting--are a way of organizing the interaction among managers at different levels in the hierarchy; one way of conceptualizing the planning process is as a series of meetings where executives are trying to arrive at decisions about actions to be taken. In each meeting, obviously, the basic question being addressed is the same: "What should we do?"

A detailed answer to that question is best developed by breaking it into a series of more specific questions dealt with in several meetings. These questions include: What are the objectives and goals of our company? What sort of environment can we expect to operate in? What businesses are we in? What alternative strategies could we pursue in those businesses? What other businesses should we enter? Should we make entry through an acquisition or through our research? What is the best combination of existing and new businesses to achieve corporate goals? What programs should the divisions undertake? What should each division's operating budget be?

The series of agreements among individuals in the corpo-

EXHIBIT 3-2. STEPS IN

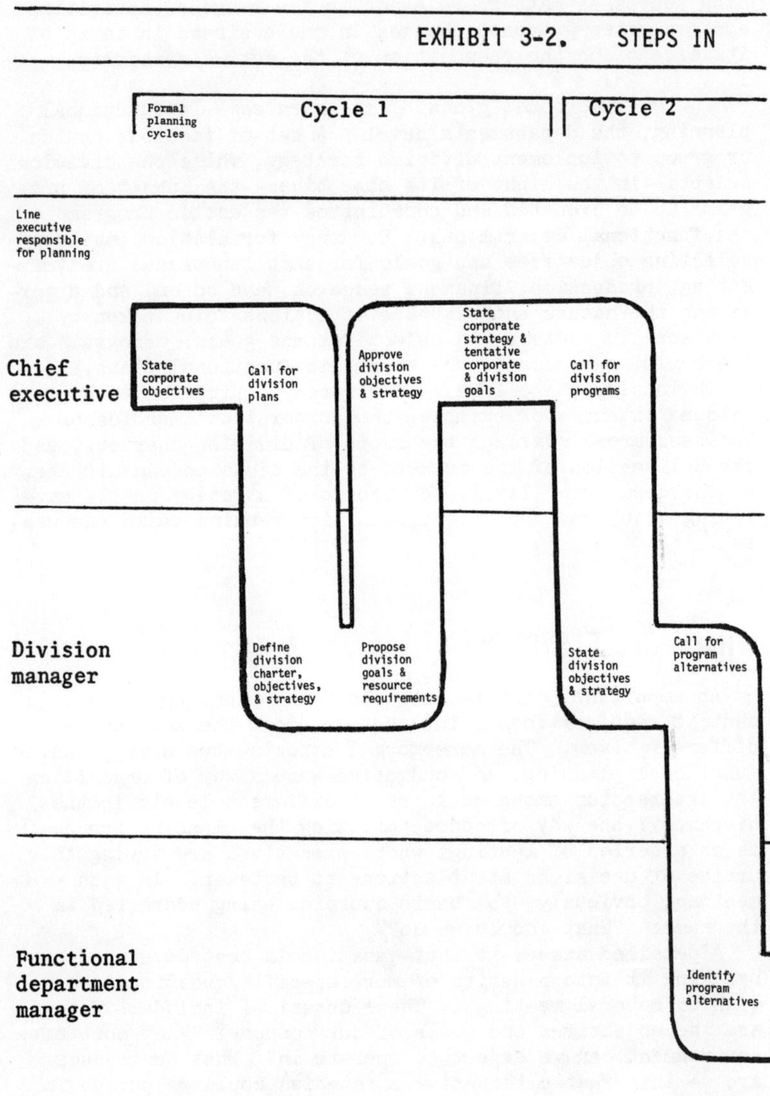

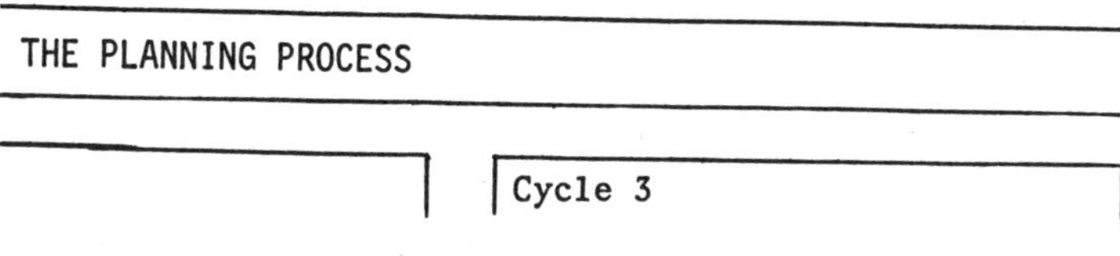
THE PLANNING PROCESS
Cycle 3

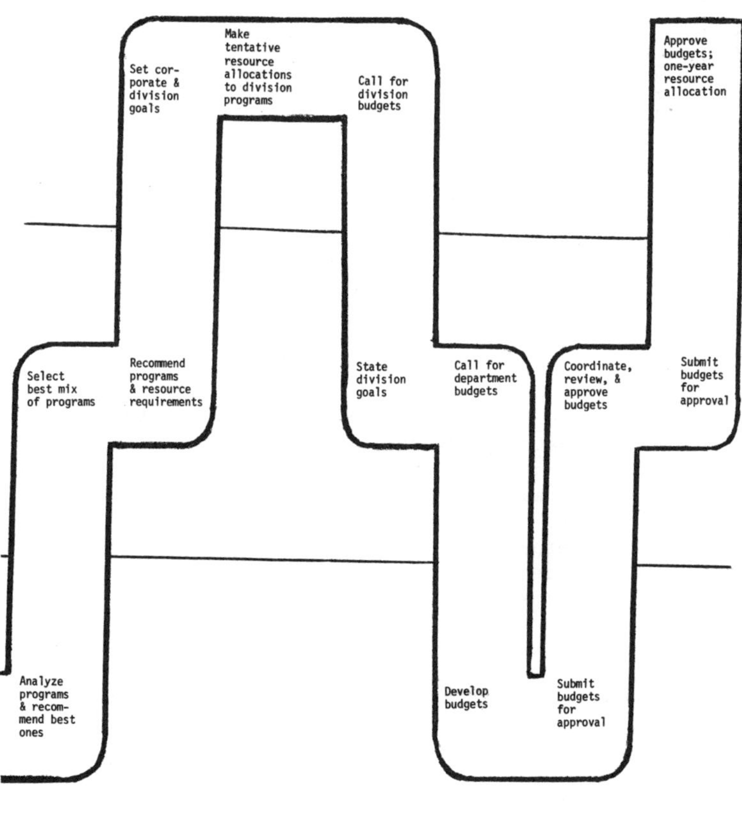
Set corporate & division goals
Make tentative resource allocations to division programs
Call for division budgets
Approve budgets; one-year resource allocation
Select best mix of programs
Recommend programs & resource requirements
State division goals
Call for department budgets
Coordinate, review, & approve budgets
Submit budgets for approval
Analyze programs & recommend best ones
Develop budgets
Submit budgets for approval

rate hierarchy begin on a very broad level and then are framed in progressively more detailed terms. The options are numerous in the early stages of this ordering process but narrow gradually to the final choice: a set of specific goals (budgets) for each responsibility center in the corporation. Initially, only a small group of corporate executives is involved in the process; later, more and more managers at lower levels become involved. The process eventually engages all the managers who must be committed to making the strategy work.

The reason companies adopt a complex planning process such as that shown in Exhibit 3-2 is made clear by the example of a multibillion-dollar, diversified corporation, headquartered in Europe and multinational, which had a well-established budgeting process but found "negotiating" the final budget in the closing months of each year to be difficult. The company was divisionalized, but it had decentralized very little initiative for examining strategic options.

Top management, increasingly uneasy over its ability to resolve all the strategic issues implicit in the budget, decided to ask the divisions to prepare formal five-year plans for its approval before drawing up the final corporate budget. The controller's department was to coordinate the preparation of the detailed plans. The company moved from a one-cycle planning system to a two-cycle system, as shown in Exhibit 3-3. The result was a flood of paper work and very little strategic thinking on the division managers' part.

When top management reviewed the first set of five-year plans--a 20-pound packet of neat notebooks--it decided the results were unacceptable. It made suggestions to the divisions and requested a new set. This process was repeated no fewer than five times during the summer and early fall before all sides reached agreement and the budgeting could proceed.

After this experience corporate management agreed that the procedure needed much improvement. So in the following year the company installed a three-cycle system. The first step required no comprehensive financial projections; instead, each division manager was asked to identify three or four strategic issues for presentation and discussion at headquarters. Agreement on those issues set the stage for orderly functional planning and budgeting, which had been so cumbersome before.

An important point to note about Exhibit 3-2 is its demarcation vertically, by cycles, and also horizontally, by activities at the three managerial levels. The degree of involvement at these levels is different in each planning cycle.

In the first cycle, corporate executives and division managers are primarily involved. A division manager draws his functional subordinates into discussions about the unit's strategy, but the functional manager's role usually remains

EXHIBIT 3-3.

EXAMPLES OF ONE-, TWO-, AND THREE-CYCLE PLANNING PROCESSES

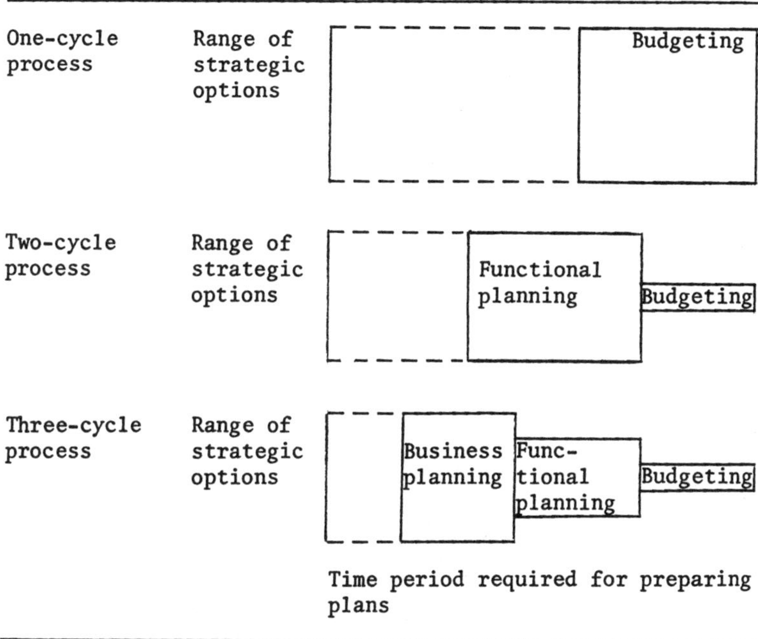

informal. At this point the division manager regards the strategy as "his"; then, seeking the head office's endorsement, he formalizes it for better communication.

Once the division's strategy is set, the second cycle begins; here functional managers play a much more important part. In both that cycle and the budgeting cycle, they have the primary responsibility for developing detailed programs and budgets. The division manager and his staff are involved more or less actively in these two cycles, while top management limits itself to a review of division proposals.

Exhibit 3-2, of course, makes no pretense of depicting the planning process as it is universally practiced; it is only illustrative. Nor is the process as neat and orderly as it appears here. For one reason, the process does not start from scratch each year; the previous year's efforts feed into the first cycle. Moreover, while managers plan, the world keeps turning; so during a cycle events may oblige them to hold many meetings involving two levels.

FIRST CYCLE

The first cycle of a formal planning process serves a dual purpose: (1) to develop a tentative set of agreements between corporate management and the division managers about overall strategy and goals, and thereby (2) to provide focus for the more detailed planning in the next cycle. The process of reaching these initial agreements requires three discrete activities: establishing corporate objectives, drawing up division charters, and setting corporate goals. The ensuing discussion centers on these activities in a hypothetical (but representative) corporation whose fiscal year corresponds with the calendar year.

ESTABLISHING CORPORATE OBJECTIVES

In the initial dialogue between corporate and division management--starting in early February--the two groups form a statement of the corporation's purpose and objectives. Naturally, its scope and the degree of detail provided vary greatly from one company to another. Company X prepares a detailed statement, starting this year with the general assertion that it is a "systems-oriented, high-technology, multinational, and socially conscious company."

The principles set out mainly for strategic planning include breakthrough strategies (such as "seek projects, internal or external, waiting for application rather than invention"), resource management (such as "continuous emphasis on market orientation as opposed to product orientation"), financing ("utilization of the borrowing power of subsidiaries to escape the provisions of the debentures and foreign investment regulations"), public relations ("genuine concern for the quality of life, inside and outside the company"), acquisitions, joint ventures, licensing ("export and import technology in the form of licenses or joint ventures, including third countries"), and so on.

The preparation of such a statement gives division managers guidance as they begin strategic planning for their businesses. So as a minimum the statement must include the intended company policies for allocating resources among the divisions. In effect, such policies constitute a statement of strategy for the entire corporation--although many businessmen are uncomfortable using the term "strategy" in such an abstract sense. Therefore, the delineation of an explicit statement of corporate strategy is often deferred until the final step in the first cycle.

Whether corporate strategy should be enunciated early or

late in the planning process depends primarily on the degree of diversity in the company's businesses. In general, the more diverse the corporation, the less feasible it is to develop an explicit, cohesive strategy for its businesses and, therefore, the more desirable it is to make the resource allocation policies explicit at an early stage. On the other hand, less diversified companies frequently delay preparing a strategy statement until the division heads have developed strategic proposals for their own businesses. Many large corporations are divisionalized, but not so many are highly diversified. The more common practice is to delay the definition (or redefinition) of corporate strategy until it can be stated in fairly explicit terms.

DRAWING UP DIVISION CHARTERS

In mid-March headquarters calls on each division manager to (a) write or review the "charter" of his division, specifying the scope of its activities and his objectives for the business as he defines it, and (b) propose a strategy for the business and a tentative set of goals for the coming year.

Giving the initiative to the division manager at this step challenges him to think strategically about the scope of his activities and then propose a charter broad enough to permit him to contribute significantly to achieving corporate objectives. Formalizing this step in the planning process is an important device by which corporate management widens the horizons of division heads. An explicit charter also serves two secondary purposes: (1) it increases the likelihood of clear agreement between the top executives and the division manager about the scope of his activities, and (2) it reduces the risk of redundant efforts or competition between divisions.

Establishing a division's charter is not a discrete activity; it is inextricably connected to the task of identification and analysis of alternative strategies that exploit the charter selected. Obviously, the decision based on this analysis is crucial because the long-term performance of any division is a function of the strategy it adopts, and the performance of the company as a whole is likewise a function of the strategies of its particular businesses.

Although the initiative for identifying and analyzing strategic options lies with the division manager, guidelines that headquarters gives him for presentation of his proposals affect the way he pursues the task. Increasingly common is a request by corporate management that when he proposes a strategy and specifies goals, at the same time he also presents a statement of the alternative strategies which he has evaluated and rejected. The intent is not to permit the head office to second-guess the division manager's thinking, but to ensure that he used strategic thinking in arriving at his recommendations.

In mid-May, four to ten weeks after headquarters presents its request for division proposals, the unit's manager presents his recommendations to the corporate management group. The presentation consists at least of an integrated proposal for the division's charter, its objectives, the strategy to be pursued, and tentative goals. The recommendations may also include a general statement of the action programs that would be developed to implement the strategy (developed in more detail in the second cycle) and a crude estimate of the resources that would be required. Detailed financial data are usually not included at this step because such information is not necessary to evaluate the strategy and because the effort of preparing it may go to waste if the recommendations are modified.

In the ensuing discussions, which extend over several meetings in late spring, corporate management and each division chief work toward reaching an agreement about the appropriate division strategy and goals.

SETTING CORPORATE GOALS

By the middle of June top management has prepared an explicit statement of corporate strategy and goals. In some companies this document is, in effect, a set of decisions on how resources are to be allocated among the divisions, as well as a forecast of the results expected from each. In most cases, however, the statement is not intended to constitute a final resource allocation decision; rather, it is designed to provide feedback to the division managers about the corporate implications of the agreed-on business strategies. The presentation and discussion of corporate strategy and goals are also commonly used as a device to initiate the second cycle of the planning process.

The sum of the recommended division goals is likely to be inadequate to achieve the goals envisioned by headquarters for the entire organization. In trying to close this "planning gap," corporate management has only three choices:

1. It can improve division performance by pressing, during the review of division recommendations, for more aggressive strategies and more ambitious goals.
2. It can divert company resources into more promising businesses. This move may give rise to an acquisition program.
3. It can decide that the corporate goals are unrealistic and scale them down.

The fact that the corporation's goals normally are more

or less the sum of those division goals sought by top management implies that headquarters is concerned with rather minor adjustments of this portfolio of goals. If so, the first cycle of formal planning has the salutary effect of providing an annual "mid-course correction" to the trajectory of the combined businesses. Momentum is a factor in the continued success of a diversified corporation--as with a rocket headed for the moon--and a wise chief executive does not dissipate it needlessly. Rather, he nudges the bundle of energies represented by his division managers, trying to make minor adjustments early enough to be nondisruptive and at the same time affect the corporation's position several years ahead.

Occasionally--perhaps inevitably--a major corporate shift is necessary, affecting one of its businesses. Care must be taken to isolate the effect on the remaining businesses. In late spring a couple of years ago, for example, top management of a major diversified corporation went through its usual review of division strategic plans. One operation, created to develop a substantial new business for the corporation, presented its usual story: "Buying market share in this high-technology business is very expensive, breakeven is still two or three years away, and additional investment of several hundred million dollars is required. But the eventual profits will be enormous."

The division's management concluded that it was progressing about as expected and that its strategy was sound, and it recommended continued aggressive investment. With minor modifications, top management approved the proposal. Three months later the company abruptly announced that the business would be discontinued and the investment written off.

Poor planning? Obviously, the decision to enter the business was a mistake. But implementation of that decision, and the planning done to minimize the investment exposure without compromising the chances for success, were probably sound. There are two important lessons here about the process of corporate planning:

1. Strategic decisions--like this divestment--are not made in accordance with some precise timetable. They are made whenever top management reaches the conclusion that interference in a unit's affairs is necessary.
2. Formal planning procedures are *not* intended to facilitate strategic decisions such as this--if only because a division manager rarely recommends the disposal of his operation. Rather, formal corporate strategic planning has the more modest, if no less crucial, purpose of seeking to optimize the collective thrust

of the continuing businesses.

Approving a division's strategic plan but closing the unit three months later is not hypocrisy or poor planning. The ax is much more merciful than the slow strangulation of providing inadequate resources. In the meantime, until the ax falls, division management must prove the viability of its business. For its part, headquarters must not fail to recognize the difference between a sound plan and a sound business. A sound plan deserves approval, but only top management can decide whether the business is sound enough to continue implementation of that plan.

SECOND CYCLE

The second planning cycle also has two purposes. First, each division head and his functional subordinates should reach tentative agreement on the action programs to be implemented over the next few years. Second, the involvement of functional managers in the long-range planning process should deepen and sharpen the strategic focus of the business and thus provide a better basis for the even more detailed budgeting task to follow.

The division manager in Company X initiates the functional planning process in the middle of June after reaching tentative agreement with top management about his organization's charter, objectives, strategy, and goals. In the first planning meeting with subordinates, he briefly reviews the corporate/division dialogue that has just concluded and describes the approved division objectives and strategy.

At this time he usually does not make explicit the sales or profit goals, even though tentative agreement on targets has been reached. There are two reasons for dealing in generalities at this point. First, being specific might constrain the thinking of the functional managers, who have the chance in this cycle to make a creative contribution toward achieving the division's objectives. Second, division goals will become final only when corporate management has approved the unit's programs and allocated resources to implement them.

Long-range planning by functional managers is conceptually a simple process, being limited by the tentative agreements reached in the first cycle. It is operationally more complex than the planning activity in the first cycle, however, since it requires substantially more detailed plans and involves many more people. The purpose of such "programming"--so called because the activity focuses on specific programs--is to translate the division's externally oriented business strategy into an internally directed, coordinated set of activities designed to implement it. Inasmuch as the resources available for implementation are always limited, programming must help ensure their optimal use.

Obviously, the scope, magnitude, and duration of a program depend on the nature of the goal. In the broadest sense, a product division of a diversified corporation might be conceived of as a "program." The division manager's goal may be stated in simple financial terms and extend over several years, and his discretion may be constrained only by a charter for his product line and the availability of corporate resources. In such a situation, the division program may be international in scope, almost unlimited in breadth of product line, and may involve hundreds of millions of dollars in expenditures. At the other end of the spectrum, the sales manager for a district in the northeast region of that division may have been charged with improving market penetration by 10% over the next 18 months. His actions also fulfill the definition of a program.

FORMALIZED PROGRAMMING

The need to formalize the programming process grows as functional interdependence in the business increases and as more time is required to evaluate the effectiveness of alternative functional plans. Formalization is designed to improve the specification of programs and the matching of programs and goals.

The charter and strategy for the business and the objectives and goals that top management has set for it limit the functional manager's strategic planning. Within those constraints, however, he may still enjoy very broad discretion concerning the best course to take. His challenge is to devise more effective ways to combine the available resources in order to achieve his goals. A useful way to look at the specification of programs is in terms of the chronology for involvement of the functional departments. In a typical manufacturing enterprise there are four types of programs to be developed:

1. *Existing revenue programs*--An example is the development of a set of marketing programs for the existing product lines.
2. *New revenue programs*--Planning the development and introduction of new products is an example.
3. *Manufacturing programs*--Typically, sales forecasts by product line are furnished to the manufacturing function, which develops the programs necessary to meet the revenue goals in the marketing programs.
4. *Support programs*--Managers of other functional support activities, such as admin-

istration, may also get involved in the development of programs.

The programming process, even when formalized, is inevitably haphazard because it requires repeated interaction among the departments. The intended result is a plan that is integrated like the two sides of a coin. On one side is the set of action programs and on the other a coordinated statement of the resources needed by each functional manager to execute his part of the program.

A major purpose of the formal programming process is to review the ongoing programs to see whether they can be expected to fulfill the goals for which they were designed. Or, if more effective programs have been devised, the existing ones must be modified or discontinued. At the same time, some "old" programs may be nearing completion, the new ones will need approval if the goals are to be met. Programming also involves coordination of functional activities to ensure that the selected programs can be implemented efficiently. Each functional department must understand the implications of a set of programs for its own activities, and the department manager must accept the tasks assigned him and the resources to be made available to him.

In our mythical Company X, after much analysis and discussion the division manager and his functional subordinates finally agree by the end of August on a set of programs to recommend to headquarters. This time, in contrast to the first, a more elaborate presentation is in order and a large number of managers--corporate and division, line and staff--may attend.

THIRD CYCLE

The third cycle of the formal planning process needs little explanation. Naturally, throughout the planning process top managers and division executives often discuss the allocation of resources among the divisions. But it becomes the focus of attention in the last step of the second cycle,when the divisions have completed their program proposals and sent them to the head office for approval. At this point (mid-September at Company X), decisions on allocation of resources can be made, subject to final approval when the detailed budgets are submitted (in mid-November). These general points are worth making here:

- Resource allocation is almost always a very informal, unstructured process, heavily dependent on the skill in advocacy and political weight of the executives concerned. Since it is also a continuous process, by the end of the second cycle the risk of serious mismatch between programs and resources is unlikely--if headquarters/division communications have been good.

- Although programs may have an expected life of several years, resources are usually allocated for only one year at a time. Whether top management will make a commitment to meet next year's needs will depend on the scale and timing flexibility of the program in the competition for resources.

- Although resource allocation to projects is based on a perception of the desirability of each, corporate planning attempts to ensure that each also fits into a portfolio of undertakings.

RAISING THE ODDS

The formal long-range planning process in large, diversified corporations is both simple and complex. Conceptually, the process is very simple--a progressive narrowing of strategic choices--although it may involve many steps along that path. Operationally, the process is far more complex than the activities we have described because the formal part of the process is only the tip of the iceberg. Good strategic planning can take place only when qualified managers engage in creative thinking--and creativity, by definition, cannot be produced on a schedule.

Yet there is little doubt that formalizing the planning process is worthwhile; it ensures that managers at all levels will devote some time to strategic thinking, and it guarantees each of them an audience for his ideas. While formal strategic planning cannot guarantee good ideas, it can increase the odds sufficiently to yield a handsome payoff.

APPENDIX

It is worth differentiating between *objectives* and *goals*, since these terms are used separately here.

OBJECTIVES are general statements describing the size, scope, and style of the enterprise in the long term. They embody the values and aspirations of the managers, based on their assessment of the environment and of the capabilities and health of the coproration. For example, the financial objective of a large, diversified, multinational corporation might be to rank in the top 10% worldwide in compound rate of growth in earnings per share.

GOALS are more specific statements of the achievements targeted for certain deadlines. At the corporate level these statements are likely to include such aspects as sales, profits, and EPS targets. Annual budgets constitute goals at all levels in the organization.

STUDENT REVIEW QUESTIONS

1. What are the different levels at which strategy formulation occurs in the divisionalized organization? Explain briefly the differences among them.
2. Identify and explain the three cycles Vancil and Lorange say are involved in the planning process.
3. Explain what Vancil and Lorange mean when they talk about goals and objectives. What are the differences between the two terms? Do their definitions agree with your own?
4. How are the different levels of the organization involved in the three cycles Vancil and Lorange identify?

4

How to Design a Strategic Planning System*

PETER LORANGE

RICHARD F. VANCIL

EVERY BUSINESS CARRIES on strategic planning, although the formality of that process varies greatly from one company to the next. Conceptually, the process is simple: managers at every level of a hierarchy must ultimately agree on a detailed, integrated plan of action for the coming year; they arrive at agreement through a series of steps starting with the delineation of corporate objectives and concluding with the preparation of a one- or two-year profit plan. However, the *design* of that process--deciding who does what, when--can be complex, and it is vital to the success of the planning effort.

A strategic planning system is nothing more than a structured (that is, designed) process that organizes and coordinates the activities of the managers who do the planning. No universal, off-the-shelf planning system exists for the simple and obvious reason that companies differ in size, diversity of operations, the way they are organized, and managers' style and philosophy. An effective planning system requires "situational design"; it must take into account the particular company's situation, especially along the dimensions of size and diversity.

While providing in this article some guidelines for designing strategic planning systems, we caution the reader to

---

*Reprinted with permission from the *Harvard Business Review*, September - October, 1976, recognize that, for the reasons just stated, such generalizations can be treacherous. We do not aspire to prescribe a planning system for your organization; you must do the tailoring.

But some useful generalizations are possible, particularly in distinguishing between large companies and small ones and between highly diversified companies and less diversified ones. Size and diversity of operations generally go hand-in-hand, although exceptions to that rule are common. Several of the large airlines, for example, are in one business, and a number of mini-conglomerates with sales of less than $100 million have divisions in disparate industries.For convenience here, we shall talk about companies as "small" or "large," defining those labels in terms of the typical characteristics shown in Exhibit 4-1.

EXHIBIT 4-1.

CHARACTERISTICS OF "SMALL" AND "LARGE" COMPANIES

	"Small" Companies	"Large" Companies
Annual sales	Less than $100 million	More than $100 million
Diversity of operations	In a single industry	In two or more different industries
Organization structure	Functional departments	Product divisions
Top executives' expertise in industries in which company operates	Greater than that of functional subordinates	Less than that of divisional subordinates

While your company may not neatly match either set of characteristics, an understanding of why an effective strategic planning system is different in these two types of companies may enable you to design a system that fits your situation. We should note that the characteristics of small companies also describe a "typical" division in a large, diversified business. Therefore, division managers in such companies can follow our discussion at two levels simultaneously: (1) in their role as a part of the corporate planning process, and (2) in their strategic planning role for their own "small" businesses.

There are six issues on which a choice must be made while designing a strategic planning system. With each issue the proper choice for large companies will be different in most cases from the one for small companies. The issues are: communication of corporate performance goals, the goal-setting process, environmental scanning, subordinate managers' focus, the corporate planner's role, and the linkage of planning and budgeting. We shall describe each of these issues in turn and briefly discuss why the design choice differs in the two corporate settings.

COMMUNICATION OF CORPORATE GOALS

A common roadblock in designing a formal planning system occurs when second-level managers ask headquarters for guidelines to focus the preparation of their strategic plans. These managers, uncertain how to tackle the assignment, may ask, implicitly or explicitly, "Tell us where you want us to go and the performance you expect from us, and we'll give you a plan of how to achieve it." These questions are not unreasonable, but acceding to them may violate the very purpose for undertaking strategic planning. To determine how goals should be communicated and how specific they should be is an important matter in planning system design.

When the president of *a small company* (or the general manager of a division of a diversified company) initiates the strategic planning process, he shares with his functional subordinates his thoughts about the objectives and strategy of the business. In most situations, however, he does not make explicit his performance goals. Instead, he asks his functional managers to devise a set of action programs that will implement the strategy of the business in a manner consistent with its objectives. In a pharmaceutical company that we observed, the R&D, manufacturing, and marketing functions jointly proposed a series of possible programs for developing various new drugs and modifying existing ones. But often, of course, this "programming" process involves only a single department.

Usually, the managers concerned realize that there is no need to anticipate the results of their planning efforts by trying to establish goals before establishment and evaluation of the programs. This would be time-consuming and burdensome and might also create false expectations among the functional managers.

The programming process is oriented much more toward analysis of alternative actions than toward establishment of corporate goals, primarily because the functional managers involved in programming tend (properly) to have a parochial point of view. They have a somewhat shorter time horizon than the president and focus their attention on their own areas of the business. The president is the one who selects the action programs for achieving the goals he has set for the business. Functional managers do not need to know the president's performance goals, only that he wants the managers to recommend the best set of programs.

Because of its action orientation, the programming process usually lacks continuity from one year to the next. The objectives and strategy of the business may remain the same, but each year it is necessary to reexamine all existing programs and try to devise new ones. As a consequence, even though the programming activity commonly uses a three- to five-year time horizon, management pays little attention to the tentative goals established in the preceding year. Instead, the focus is on the current situation, the best set of action programs now, and the development of an achievable goal for the forthcoming year.

The diversity of the portfolio of businesses in *large companies* is often so great that it limits top management's capacity for in-depth perception and familiarity with each business. Consequently, management has to rely on the relatively unconstrained inputs from the divisions.

Division managers do heed corporate guidance in the form of broad objectives, but as a rule top management should delay development of a statement of performance goals for the corporation. Usually, a division manager is in a better position to assess the potential of his own business if he is unbiased by corporate expectations. Delay also permits the top executives to change their approach to the task. In the absence of a formal strategic planning process, top management may have developed explicit goals for itself; but it cannot be sure of the appropriateness of the goals when viewed in the context of a set of independently arrived-at divisional goals. Divisional recommendations stimulate a better job of corporate goal setting.

GOAL-SETTING PROCESS

From the division manager's viewpoint, should he or corporate management set the division's goals? This issue is sometimes cast as a choice between "top-down" and "bottom-up" goal setting. Actually, of course, management at both levels must agree on divisional goals. An important issue, however, remains: Which level in the hierarchy should initiate the process? In a homogeneous company, the same issue arises concerning the general manager and functional managers. The design of the planning system can strongly influence how this issue is resolved.

The goals that emerge from the programming process in *a small company* are tied to an approved set of action programs. Until the president has decided on the programs, no functional manager can set goals for his sphere of activity. Selection of a set of action programs, therefore, more or less automatically determines the performance goals for each functional unit. In many small companies--such as the pharmaceutical concern we spoke of--a "package" of action programs spells out the functional goals for every department, because of the interdependence of all the departments.

In a sense then, functional goal setting is a top-down process. The functional managers propose action programs, but the president with his business-wide perspective determines the programs and goals for his functional subordinates.

In *a large company* with a relatively diversified group of businesses, "capacity limitations" at the corporate level dictate a more or less bottom-up approach. The divisions initiate much of the goal setting, since it requires intimate knowledge of the industry-specific set of business conditions.

Establishing an effective corporate-divisional goal-setting climate in a large company is not easy. For the first year or two of a formal planning effort, the best approach in most situations is to allow the initiative for recommending divisional goals to rest with the division manager. This approach gives him support in running his business and encourages strategic thinking at the divisional level.

Later, after the corporate and divisional managers have gained experience in hammering out a mutually agreeable set of divisional goals, the division manager's annual proposal for divisional goals will become more constrained than in the early years. In a divisionalized, consumer goods manufacturer we know of, the first years of carrying on the planning process were viewed frankly as a learning experience for division managers in making plans operational as well as for top management in learning to appreciate the strategic problems of each business of the company.

The cumulative experience of negotiating the goal setting over the years improves the effectiveness of the process. Corporate management can help nurture this development by creating a system that maintains a proper top-down/bottom-up balance. One way to achieve this balance is by withholding an explicit statement of corporate goals for the first year or two, while requiring the division manager to recommend goals for his division.

ENVIRONMENTAL SCANNING

A strategic planning system has two major functions: to develop an integrated, coordinated, and consistent long-term plan of action, and to facilitate adaptation of the corporation to environmental change. When introducing and developing such a system, companies commonly concentrate on its integrative aspects. The design of the system, however, must also include the function of environmental scanning to make sure that the planning effort also fulfills its adaptive mission.

Corporate management, of course, provides subordinates with a set of forecasts and assumptions about the future business environment. Since each manager, initially at least, draws the strategic plans for his sphere of responsibility more or less independently of his counterparts, all managers must have access to the **same** set of economic and other environmental forecasts.

Environmental scanning in *small companies* is a strategically oriented task that can go far beyond the mere collection of data about markets, competitors, and technological changes. A company that, for example, enjoys a large share of the market for a product used by middle- and upper-income teenagers and young adults may devote considerable effort in analyzing demographic trends and changes in per capita income. A fairly accurate forecast of market size five years hence is possible to make and would be useful in appraising the potential for the company's growth.

The task of monitoring detailed environmental changes in *large companies* is too difficult to be performed by top management alone. Division management, therefore, is expected to study the external environment that may be relevant to their particular businesses. In these circumstances, headquarters typically provides only a few environmental assumptions--mainly economic forecasts.

Environmental scanning may play another important role in large companies that are interested in diversification through acquisitions. In one diversified electronics and high-technology company that set out to decrease its dependence on defense contracts, the vice president in charge of planning spent most of his time searching for acquisition opportunities. After establishing close ties with the investment community and certain consultants, he spread word of his company's intentions.

SUBORDINATE MANAGERS' FOCUS

In a strategic planning effort, where should the second-level managers direct their attention? What roles do the division manager, functional manager, and top management play? We shall consider these questions in terms of whether plans should be more quantitative or more qualitative, more concerned with financial detail or with strategic analysis.

Preparation of a functionally coordinated set of action programs for *a small company* may require a great deal of cross-functional communication. Much of this interchange is most efficiently expressed in dollar or other quantitative terms, such as numbers of employees, units of product, and square feet of plant space. Use of financial or quantitative data is appropriate for two reasons: (1) it helps each functional manager understand the dimensions of a proposed program and forces him to think through the implications of executing it; (2) it permits the president to select more confidently the set of programs to be implemented. The pharmaceutical company previously referred to, for instance, focuses on the funds flows that might be expected from the various strategic programs suggested by the functional departments.

In practice, the financial and quantitative aspects of functional planning become progressively detailed as the programming process continues, culminating in very specific plans that constitute the operating budget.

In a diversified *larger company,* top management wants each division to adopt a timely strategic outlook and division management to focus primarily on achieving that outlook. Particularly during the early years of the planning program, division managers should be permitted to develop as much financial detail in support of their proposals as they think desirable. As a result, they may generate more financial detail than necessary for strategic business planning. After a year or two, therefore, the corporate requirements for financial detail to support division proposals should be made explicit--and should be explicitly minimal.

Division managers should be asked to shift the focus of their efforts to identification and analysis of strategic alternatives, using their expertise to estimate quickly the financial implications. This focus has been a goal from the beginning, of course, but it is difficult to achieve at the outset. Failing to shift the focus is an even greater danger; the planning activity becomes a "numbers game" and never achieves its purpose.

Considering that the division manager may never have seen, much less prepared, long-range financial projections for his business, drawing them up should be a useful activity. Such projections help him lengthen the time horizon of his thinking; they oblige him to make his intuitive economic model of the business more explicit, which in turn enables him to forecast changes in financial performance. As a result, a division manager's initial planning efforts tend to be financially oriented and, in many respects, analogous to long-range budgeting. Corporate management should design the requirements of the system to mitigate the pressures that initiation of formal planning poses for a division manager.

One important caveat for the chief executive of a large company: he should never allow himself to get so involved in the development of business plans that he assumes the division managers' planning job. A situation that we investigated concerned the newly appointed president of a multinational company in the consumer products business, whose experience was mainly in marketing. He could not resist "helping" one of his divisions develop a detailed, more aggressive marketing plan. Such interference often inhibits the division from coming up with a realistic plan to which it can commit itself. In this case, quiet resistance effectively shelved the president's ideas.

CORPORATE PLANNER'S ROLE

A major issue in the design of the planning system is where the corporate planner fits. Strategic planning is a line management function; a sure route to disaster is to have plans produced by staff planners and then issued to line managers. Strategic planning is essentially a people-interactive process, and the planner is only one in the cast of characters involved. If the process is to function effectively, he must clearly understand his proper role. The corporate planner's function in small and large companies is quite different.

In *a small company* (or a product division of a large company), the planner performs the function of staff planning assistant to the president (or the general manager). While coordinating the planning activities of the functional managers, he concerns himself with the president's problem of selecting the best set of action programs. Only the president--and his planning assistant--has a business-wide perspective of the choices, and the assistant must do the bulk of the analysis.

Cast in this role, the planner may become a very influential member of the president's (or the general manager's) executive team. If he uses his power sensitively, he need not lose effectiveness with his peers running the functional departments. They can appreciate the necessity for cross-functional analysis of program alternatives. Managing the planning process is an almost incidental role for the assistant, since he merely formalizes the analysis that leads to a coordinated set of action programs.

In *a large company*, the corporate planner's organizational status can have significant symbolic value in conveying to division managers the importance of formal strategic planning and the difference between it and conventional budgeting. The planner's role initially is that of a catalyst, encouraging line managers to adopt a strategic orientation. He helps corporate management do a better job of resource allocation among the divisions, partly by assisting the division managers in strategic planning for their businesses. But he must not succumb to the temptation to become more involved in formulating the plans, or he may lose his effectiveness.

System maintenance and coordination is the planner's primary function as the planning effort matures; he monitors its evolution and maintains consistency. His tasks differ greatly from the mainly analytical role of the planner in the small company.

LINKAGE OF PLANNING AND BUDGETING

The steps in a typical planning system represent an orderly, gradual process of commitment to certain strategic alternatives. Each step is, theoretically at least, linked to those preceding. In financial terms, this linkage may be quite explicit; for instance, a division's profit forecast prepared in the first planning cycle may become the profit commitment for next year's operating budget. Although few companies expect to achieve this financial linkage in narrowing the choices, all the parties involved in the process should understand the intended relationship between the cycles.

How fast this narrowing should be is a situational design question that depends on the particular corporate setting. A tight linkage between planning and budgeting indicates that more strategic commitments have been made at an earlier stage. A loose linkage, on the other hand, implies that the narrowing process is slower and will occur mainly late, in the budgeting stage of the process.

Exhibit 4-2 shows examples of slow versus rapid narrowing profiles. Notice that a company that does little narrowing in the early stages faces the task of considering a large number of strategic issues in the budgeting stage. This implies that either the company is equipped with an adequate organization to process an immense and "peaky" budgeting workload, or it will neglect some choices altogether, with the likely result that the quality of its allocation decisions suffers.

A *small company* with little diversity in its operations may wish to adopt an early or rapid narrowing process, since the functional and corporate executives involved are thoroughly familiar with the strategy of the few businesses in question. Then functional managers can proceed directly to the development of action programs to continue implementation of that strategy. Quantitative financial linkage between the selected programs and the resulting budgets is feasible, and "tight" linkage of this type is common practice.

In *a large company,* linkage is usually looser and the narrowing process more gradual. During the start-up phase top management should give division managers plenty of time to devote to strategic thinking about their businesses--but the lower-level executives must remember to differentiate that activity from long-range budgeting, with its related requirement of divisional performance fulfillment.

As the system matures, however, management can gradually accelerate the narrowing process without jeopardizing the

EXHIBIT 4-2.

SLOW VERSUS RAPID NARROWING PROFILES IN THE PLANNING PROCESS

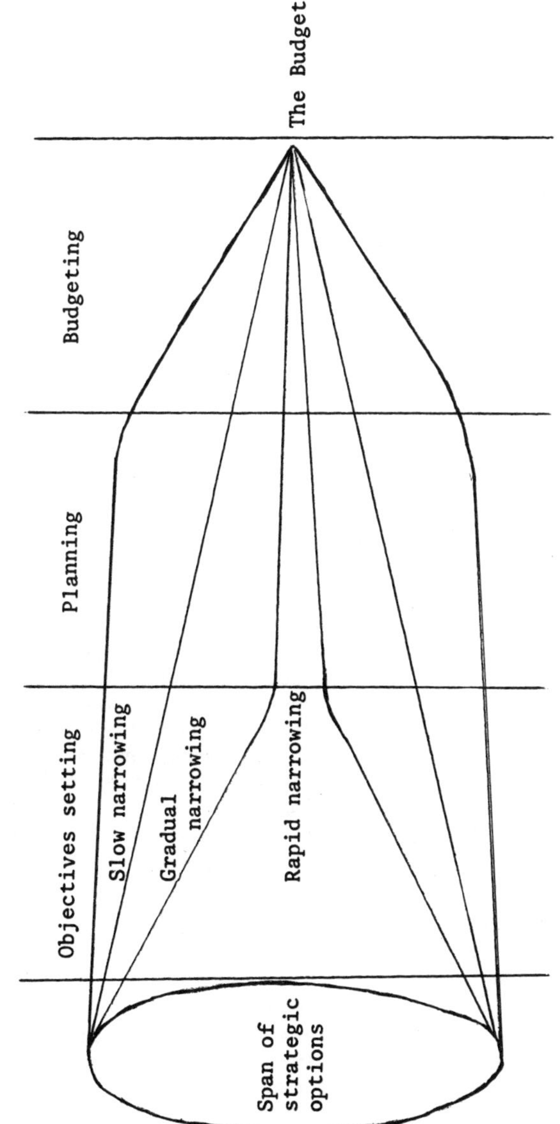

creative aspect of planning. A natural result of this progress is a more precise definition of the linkage between the planning cycle and the budgeting cycle. A large producer of heavy equipment we know of, for instance, has "tightened up" the linkage between planning and budgeting. The top executives believe that this development is a natural consequence of their increasingly cohesive strategic points of view.

EVOLVING SYSTEMS

In sum, significant differences exist between the planning procedures used in the two types of companies we have examined. The issues that management must address, and our attempt to delineate what is good practice in small and large companies, are summarized in Exhibit 4-3.

In companies that are not very diversified and are functionally organized--as well as product units of diversified corporations--top management carries on the strategic thinking about the future of the business. In such companies, a formal process to help organize that reflective activity is frequently unnecessary, in view of the few managers involved. Instead, formal strategic planning focuses on the development and review of innovative action programs to implement the strategy. The planning system reflects that focus: goal setting is top-down, linkage to the budget is tight, and the staff planning officer plays a major role as cross-functional program analyst and environmental scanner.

In companies that operate in several industrial sectors and are organized into product divisions, initiating a formal strategic planning process is a major task. The first year or two of such an effort must be viewed as an investment in fostering a planning competence among division managers; the payoff in better decisions at the corporate level must wait until the system matures.

If the planning system is to survive as more than an exercise in pushing numbers into the blank spaces on neatly designed forms, it must evolve rapidly along several dimensions. A mature system, however, can be invaluable, helping both corporate and divisional executives make better and better-coordinated strategic decisions.

Any company--indeed, any organization--is a dynamically evolving entity whose situational setting is subject to change. Accordingly, to remain effective, the design of the planning process is a continuous task requiring vigilance and insight on the part of management.

EXHIBIT 4-3.

APPROACHES TO PLANNING SYSTEM DESIGN ISSUES

Issues	Situational Settings		
	"Small" Companies	"Large" Companies	
		New Planning System	Mature Planning System
Communication of corporate goals	Not explicit	Not explicit	Explicit
Goal-setting process	Top-down	Bottom-up	"Negotiated"
Corporate-level environmental scanning	Strategic	Statistical	Statistical
Subordinate managers' focus	Financial	Financial	Strategic
Corporate planner's role	Analyst	Catalyst	Coordinator
Linkage of planning and budgeting	Tight	Loose	Tight

STUDENT REVIEW QUESTIONS

1. What is a strategic planning system to Lorange and Vancil?
2. What are the major functions of a strategic planning system?
3. Explain the difference between a slow and a rapid narrowing of strategic options.
4. Do Lorange and Vancil advocate "top-down" or "bottom-up" goal setting? Explain your answer.
5. How do Lorange and Vancil explain the corporate planner's role?

5

Managing Strategic Surprise by Response to Weak Signals*

H. IGOR ANSOFF

If we could first know where we are and whither we are tending, we could better judge what to do and how to do it.
Abraham Lincoln, 1858

Everything (before the Arab oil embargo) is history....The future is a whole new game.
Irving Shapiro, Du Pont Company, 1975

Neither past experience nor academic training has prepared many younger managers for such reversal in the approach to business planning and operation.
John T. Hackett, Cummings Engine Company, 1975

THE PARADOX OF strategic military surprise has been a familiar phenomenon throughout recorded human history. From the Trojan Horse to Pearl Harbor to the Yom Kippur war, nations and armies have been confronted with sudden crises, in spite of ample information about enemy intentions.

THE PROBLEM

The recent "petroleum crisis" was a comparable event in the industrial world: large and important firms were suddenly confronted with a major discontinuity, although advance forecasts of Arab action were not only publicly available, but on the day of the surprise, were to be found on the desks of some of the surprised managers. Because of its pervasive scope, the petroleum crisis highlighted the danger of strategic business surprises. But such surprises had overtaken numerous firms, one by one, from the early 1950's --enough of them to provide material for a *Fortune* book titled *Corporations in Crisis*.

In the aftermath, it was argued that these corporations were caught unaware because they lacked modern forecasting and planning systems. But in the 1970's a majority of the firms caught by the petroleum crisis had such systems. In the mid-1960's, the management of one of the world's largest conglomerates proudly displayed its planning and control. A week after the public display, the same management made a red-faced admission of two multimillion-dollar surprises: a major overrun in its office furniture division and another in its shipbuilding division.

The American automotive industry, a leader in modern planning and control, was certainly unprepared for the forceful congressional position on automotive safety. And a bare four years later it was again "surprised" by the success of the small car. Such events need little support from the voluminous literature on futurology to predict that discontinuities and surprises will occur with increasing frequency. If, as experience suggests, modern planning technology does not insure against surprises, the technology needs to be extended to provide such insurance. An exploration of such extension is the purpose of this article.

THE NATURE OF STRATEGIC SURPRISE

Figure 5-1 plots, against time, the growth of a firm which can be measured by any one of the common yardsticks, such as sales, profits, or rate of interest (ROI). The middle line shows smooth extrapolation of past experience into the future. The two branching curves, a threat and an opportunity, show a significant departure, a *strategic discontinuity* from the past. In principle, such discontinuities can be anticipated by available forecasting techniques. Given enough warning, the firm should be able to avert the threat or seize the opportunity.

In fact, firms often fail to anticipate and suddenly discover that a fleeting opportunity has been missed or that survival of a product line is threatened. Typically, at the "moment of truth," neither the causes nor the possible re-

FIGURE 5-1.

IMPACT OF THREAT/OPPORTUNITY

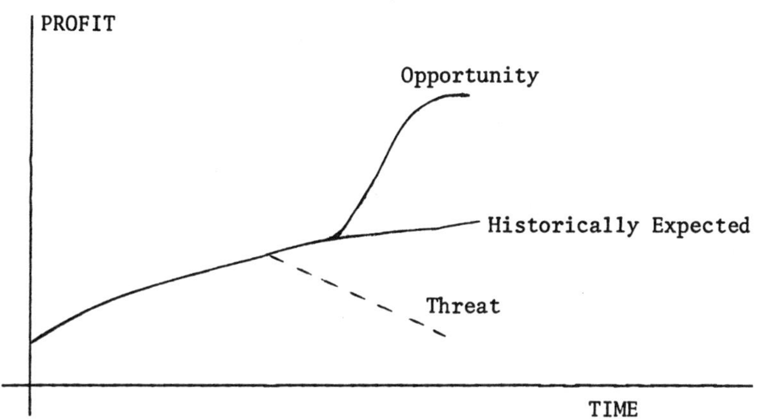

sponses are clear; the firm confronts an unfamiliar and often threatening event. Such events are *strategic surprises:* sudden, urgent, unfamiliar changes in the firm's perspective which threaten either a major profit reversal or loss of a major opportunity.

A firm that wishes to prepare for strategic surprises has two options. The first is to develop a capability for effective *crisis management*--fast and efficient, *after-the-fact* responsiveness to sudden discontinuities. A useful prototype is a firefighting company; unable to predict or control occurrence of fires, it prepares itself, through repeated practice, to respond quickly and effectively to a whole range of different alarms. The second approach is to treat the problem *before-the-fact* and thereby minimize the probability of strategic surprises--to prepare in such a way that a strategic discontinuity loses its suddenness, urgency, and unfamiliarity.

Both approaches deserve management attention: before-the-fact strategic preparedness because it is the more efficient approach, crisis preparedness because even the best advance efforts do not assume immunity from surprises. Each approach deserves full treatment; in this article, however, we shall limit our attention to before-the-fact strategic preparedness.

LIMITATIONS OF ENVIRONMENTAL INFORMATION

There is now a well-developed technology, called *strate-*

gic planning, for converting environmental information about strategic discontinuities into concrete action plans, programs, and budgets. But to date strategic planning has had little success in dealing with surprises. One major reason is that strategic planning is overly demanding for input information. To be useful in strategic planning, information must satisfy two conditions. First, it must be available early enough to permit time for preparation of plans and programs. For example, a firm that takes five years to develop a new product needs a forecasting horizon of seven to ten years. Second, if strategic plans and programs are to be made, the content of the forecast must be adequate to permit the planners to estimate the impact on the firm, to identify specific responses, and to estimate the potential profit impact of these responses.

In both strategic planning literature and practice, an assumption is usually made that both timeliness and content conditions can be satisfied, that the forecaster can meet the needs of the planner. This expectation is not unreasonable when planning is concerned with "logical," incremental development of historical trends. Curves fitted to past experience can be smoothly extrapolated into a relatively distant future.

But when a potential surprise originates in an alien technology, with a previously unknown competitor, with a new political coalition, or with a new economic phenomenon, simple extrapolation will not suffice. In such cases these will be either discontinuous departures from past growth trends or, at least, sharp changes in the curvature of past growth curves. The firm planners can have longer range for forecasts from the forecasters, but they must be willing to put up with content that becomes increasingly vague as the time horizon is extended. Or they can wait for originally vague information to become specific.

Thus, the recent phenomenon of stagflation is still imperfectly understood. The workings of the economy appear to have undergone a structural change which the economists have so far failed to explain. The simple question of when and how the current recession will come to an end has become difficult to answer except in very general and contradictory terms. In responding, firms have a choice of either basing their plans and actions on these generalities or waiting until the mechanism of recovery becomes clearer. Acting now implies taking risks on imperfect knowledge; waiting courts the danger of being late in important decisions that have long lead times, such as diversification, geographic expansion, and capital investment.

The timeliness of the firm's response depends on two variables: the rapidity with which the threat/opportunity, such as stagflation, affects the firm's growth and profits, and the amount of time needed by the firm to plan and effect the response. Since the 1950's these two variables have been on a collision course. The rate of environmental change has accelerated, and the firm's response has been made slower by growing size, complexity, and geographic diversification.

Thus, there is an apparent paradox: if the firm waits until information is adequate for strategic planning, it will be increasingly surprised by crises; if it accepts vague information, the content will not be specific enough for thorough strategic planning. A solution to this paradox is to change the approach to the use of strategic information. Instead of letting the strategic planning technology determine the information needs, a firm should determine what planning and action are *feasible* as strategic information becomes available in the course of the threat/opportunity. Early in the life of a threat, when the information is vague and its future course unclear, the responses will be correspondingly unfocused, aimed at increasing the strategic flexibility of the firm. As the information becomes more precise, so will the firm's response, eventually terminating in a direct attack on the threat or an opportunity. But the prior buildup of flexibility will make this attack or opportunity occur earlier, and the attack will be better planned and executed.

We might call this *graduated response through amplification and response to weak signals*,[1] in contrast to conventional strategic planning that depends on strong signals. Such a practical method for planning a graduated response can be developed. The first task is to explore the range of weak signals that can be typically expected from a strategic discontinuity.

STATUS OF KNOWLEDGE

The threat information typically required in strategic planning for evaluating the impact of threats/opportunities (TO's) gives the impression of being imperfect because of the uncertainties in both the occurrence and the probable course of the threat. A closer look shows that while uncertain, this is very *content-rich* information: the threat has to be well enough understood to compute the possible profit consequences, the responses well enough developed to estimate both their costs and their countereffects on the threat.

It is reasonable to expect this much knowledge from a threat/opportunity which arises from a familiar prior experience. This will be the case when a competitor introduces a new marketing approach, a new product, or a new pricing strategy. But when the T/O is discontinuous (such as the impact of laser technology on land surveying or of large-scale integration on electronic components), then in the early stages, the nature, impact, and possible responses are unclear. Frequently it is not even clear whether the discontinuity will develop into a threat or an opportunity. Thus, when a threat/opportunity first appears on the horizon, we must be prepared for very vague information, which will progressively develop and improve with time. This progression may be characterized by successive *states of knowledge*. These are illustrated in Table 5-1, where level five, the

TABLE 5-1. STATES OF IGNORANCE UNDER DISCONTINUITY

States of Knowledge / Info Content	(1) Sense of Threat/ Opportunity	(2) Source of Threat/ Opportunity	(3) T/O Concrete	(4) Response Concrete	(5) Outcome Concrete
Conviction that discontinuities are impending	YES	YES	YES	YES	YES
Source of discontinuity identified	NO	YES	YES	YES	YES
Characteristics, nature, gravity, and timing of impact understood	NO	NO	YES	YES	YES
Response identified timing, action, programs, budgets can be identified	NO	NO	NO	YES	YES
Profit impact and consequences of response are computable	NO	NO	NO	NO	YES

For those who wish to relate this table to the terminology of statistical decision theory, we should note that the information in each state of knowledge may be certain, uncertain, or risky in the sense of definitions commonly used in the theory. The focus in the table is on illustrating the variability of content and not in the state of uncertainty. The dimension of uncertainty can be easily added at right angles to the table, thus creating a cube of possible states of information. In this cube, the states of information, treated in statistical decision theory, would be included in slice number 5.

highest state of knowledge, contains exactly the information required for strategic planning. Enough is known to compute both the probable profit impact of the discontinuity and the profit impact of the response.

At the other extreme, level one is the highest state of ignorance that can be of use to management. As the "No's" show, all that is known is that some threats and opportunities will undoubtedly arise, but their shape and nature and source are not yet known. In today's "political and economic fog of uncertainty"[2] many firms find themselves in exactly such a state of ignorance. Having experienced shocks of change in the recent past, managers are convinced that new ones are coming, but they cannot identify the source.

States of knowledge on level two improve matters somewhat. For example, in the early 1940's, it was generally recognized by physicists that solid-state physics had great potential for the electronics industry. But the invention of the specific discontinuity, the transistor, was still several years off. The source of the threat was clear, but not the threat itself. When the transistor was invented by Shockley and his team, the knowledge was raised to state three, but at the outset, the ramifications of the inventions were unclear, as were the defensive and aggressive responses that different firms were eventually to make.

When the firms developed and made the initial responses and knowledge was raised to level four, the eventual investments and profits were not yet visible. Pioneering firms were investing boldly into the new technology with little experience to guide them, in high hopes that their entrepreneurial risks would pay off. State five was not reached until knowledge of crystal yields and manufacturing process costs was sufficient to make reasonable predictions of the ultimate technology and its profitability. But by then the leaders were entrenched and those who originally held back had to pay a high cost of entry into the industry.

PRACTICAL THREAT/OPPORTUNITY ANALYSIS

As indicated by the growing number of "Yes's" in Table 5-1, ignorance is reduced and information is enriched as a threat/opportunity evolves from state one to state five. As this evolution takes place, and as the management is trying to decide when and how to respond, the question of crucial importance is the time remaining before the impact on the firm passes a critical profit benchmark. For a threat this benchmark may be the level of loss beyond which the firm's survival is threatened; for an opportunity the point beyond which the cost of "climbing on the bandwagon" can no longer be recovered through profits.

Each threat and opportunity will pass through the respective stages of Table 5-1, some more quickly than others.

Furthermore, each T/O will impact on different parts of the firm with varying strength. Therefore, we need a process for a systematic examination of T/O's and their impacts on the firm. The process described here is an extension of a well-known technique called *impact analysis*.

The first step is to compile a list of *strategic issues:* major environmental trends and possible events that may have a major and discontinuous impact on the firm. Today, most firms would list such issues as petroleum politics, stagflation, technology of energy generation, changing consumer attitudes, changing attitudes toward work, government regulation of business, and a growing demand for worker participation in decisions. Many of the strategic issues are shared by all firms, but each firm would find important issues which are specific to its industrial setting. Thus, firms in the automotive business would certainly add automotive safety legislation as a major strategic issue.

The second step is to estimate the impact of each issue on the firm. In the early days of strategic planning this was done by examining the impact on each self-contained organizational unit, division, or subsidiary. After a time it became apparent that unit-by-unit analysis gives a confusing picture of the future, particularly when a division has a number of product lines and operates in many markets.

Recently, an alternative approach has emerged which, instead of using an "inside out" organizational perspective on the firm's world, takes an "outside in" view. This is done by subdividing the environment into relatively independent *strategic business areas* (SBA's), each of which has distinctive trends, threats, and opportunities. (Recent strategic resource shortages, as well as sociopolitical pressures on the firm, focus attention on strategic resource areas and strategic influence areas. Thus, a complete analysis of threats and opportunities would include these two in addition to strategic business areas. However, we can illustrate the method of analysis by confirming our attention to the latter.)

For firms operating in a single homogeneous geographic area the SBA's will be synonymous with major product lines. But for geographically diversified firms, a geographic subdivision may be necessary. Thus, for example, a firm selling color television sets in North America, Europe, and South America would recognize three distinctive SBA's because of differences in the maturity of the markets, the political and competitive environments. For firms whose product line is based on different technologies, a technological subdivision may be further necessary. If television manufacturers make both tube and integrated circuit sets, the respective products will have different growth prospects, stages of maturity, and strategic vulnerabilities in each of the geographic areas. Thus, to understand the future of the color television product line it may be necessary to construct as many as six significantly different SBA's.

Once the SBA's are identified, estimates are made of the impact of the strategic issues on each SBA. Four dimensions are: identification of the impact as a threat, or opportunity, or both; magnitude of the impact (measured by the probable range of loss or gain in the profit currently derived from the SBA); timing of the critical profit benchmark (using the range from the earliest to the latest possible moment); and identification of the present state of knowledge about the threat.

The precision and range of these estimates will depend on the state of knowledge. They will be more vague for emerging threats/opportunities and more precise for well-developed ones. Similarly, the methodology usable for estimation will vary. In lower levels of knowledge, simple judgment or expert opinion techniques such as Delphi will have to be used. In later stages, a variety of quantitative modeling and forecasting techniques become usable.

Table 5-2 shows the results of impact estimation through a simple example of a firm with one major threat/opportunity

TABLE 5-2. THREAT/OPPORTUNITY ANALYSIS

Strategic Business Area	Profit Contribution	State of Knowledge: Sense of Threat/Opportunity	Source of Threat/Opportunity	T/O Concrete	Response Concrete	Outcome Concrete
SBA_1	50%		Type of impact:→ T Timing:→ 3-5 yrs. Profit impact:→ 0.2-0.5			
SBA_2	30%	T/O 10-15 yrs. 0.0-0.2				
SBA_3	15%				Opportunity→ O_F generated by the firm:	1-2 yrs. 2.5-3.0
SBA_4	5%	0 4-8 yrs. 2.0-5.0				
Status Environmental Awareness						

for each of its four SBA's. Immediately adjacent to the SBA column is the percentage of the firm's profit that it contributes.

As seen in the table, the range of the timing and profit impact estimates becomes wider as ignorance increases. Thus, the impact on SBA_2, which is ten to fifteen years off, may turn into either a threat or an opportunity, but it is clear that the impact is likely to be very serious. Clearly this discontinuity needs close watching. On the other hand, the profit estimates for the opportunity in SBA_3 can be estimated within a narrow range of both occurrence and impact.

ALTERNATIVE RESPONSE STRATEGIES

Just as we have expanded the states of information to include poorer knowledge, we need to enlarge the repertoire of responses to permit weaker responses. This is shown in Table 5-3, where management options are subdivided into two groups: responses that change the firm's relationship with the *environment* and responses that change the *internal dynamics and structure* of the firm. For each group there are three progressively stronger strategies: one that enhances the firm's awareness and understanding; one that increases the firm's flexibility; and one that directly attacks the threat/opportunity. Thus the table provides a total of six response strategies.

The strongest *external action* strategy, as its name implies, mounts a direct counteraction against identified threats of opportunities. It proceeds through selection of

TABLE 5-3. ALTERNATIVE RESPONSE STRATEGIES

Response Strategies / Domain of Response	Direct Response	Flexibility	Awareness
Relationship to Environment	External action (strategic planning & implementation)	External flexibility	Environmental awareness
Internal Configuration	Internal awareness (contingency planning)	Internal flexibility	Self-awareness

the type of counteraction, preparation of programs and budgets, and implementation of the latter. The end result is a threat averted or an opportunity captured in the firm of an enhanced potential for future profits. Selection of the best counteraction is the object of strategic planning.[3]

Internal readiness strategy matches the skills, structure, and resources of the firm to the demands of specific counteraction, creating a state of preparedness for external action. In strategic planning internal readiness is commonly referred to as strategy implementation, implying that preparedness must await selection of the course of action that it will support. The prescribed sequence is: strategic planning to internal preparation to action in the environment. But many of the preparedness measures can be successfully carried out in state three, as soon as the shape of the impending T/O becomes concrete and before strategic planning and external action become possible. Thus, the firm's response can be accelerated by reversing the sequence to internal preparedness to strategic planning to action in the environment.

The earliest possible response to an opportunity/threat is offered by the pair of *awareness strategies*, shown in the right column of Table 5-3. In most firms a degree of environmental awareness is provided through economic forecasting, sales forecasting, and analysis of competitive behavior. But all of these measures are extrapolative, based on a smooth extension of the past into the future, and do not provide information about strategic discontinuities. To broaden the awareness to include discontinuities, the firm must add special types of environmental analysis, such as environmental monitoring, technological forecasting, sociopolitical forecasting, and threat/opportunity analysis. Starting all of these activities in the firm requires no concrete information about threats/opportunities. Thus, the highest state of ignorance, a sense of threat, is adequate to justify a program for enhancing the firm's environmental awareness. A sense of threat is also adequate for starting many of the self-awareness measures, such as capacity audits, strength/weakness analysis, and financial modeling of the firm.

The *flexibility strategy* shown in the middle column of Table 5-3 differs from the direct action strategies in that its end product is an enhanced *potential* for the firm's future, rather than tangible changes in profits and growth. The *external flexibility* substrategy is concerned with positioning the firm in the environment in a way that satisfies two criteria: satisfactory *average potential* for profitability over the long term and adequate diversification of the firm's position to assure *coping with deviations* from the expected average—capture of attractive major opportunities and minimization of catastrophic reversals.

Formulation of the external flexibility strategy (commonly known as position strategy) is part of the strategic planning process, where it is usually assumed to require level-five information input. But measures such as balance of technological, business, and political-geographical risks can be substantially planned *and implemented* if the state of knowledge is not better than level two, long before the nature of the threat becomes concrete.

Logistic flexibility is concerned with configuring the resources and capabilities of the firm to permit quick and efficient repositioning to new products and new markets, whenever the need arises. One important element is the flexibility of the managers, including awareness of the environment, psychological readiness to face unpleasant and unfamiliar events, ability to solve unfamiliar problems, and creativity. Another element is the flexibility of the managerial systems and structure to permit expeditious and flexible response to change. A third element is the flexibility of logistic resources and systems--resource liquidity, diversification of work skills, modular capacities, and so forth.

Unlike external flexibility, *internal flexibility* received relatively little attention from strategic planners. But recent history shows it to be a crucial ingredient in strategic preparedness. In the area of managerial flexibility, the preparation of managers for strategic thinking and action is now recognized as essential and vital if the firm is to anticipate and deal with the growing turbulence of the environment. Without it, efforts to introduce strategic planning typically encounter strong resistance to planning.

Flexibility of the logistic resources has received even less attention than managerial flexibility. A major reason is the fact that the idea of flexibility runs contrary to the fundamental principle of the Industrial Age, which holds that maximum profitability is to be gained through the maximum possible specialization of facilities and machinery and through largest possible capacity, maximum capital-labor substitution, and longest possible production runs.

Application of this principle invariably leads to special-purpose, capital-intensive investments. In the recent past principle-maximum specialization has been repeatedly compromised when expensive specialized factories were made prematurely obsolete by unexpected technological changes or when the length of production runs was cut short by shrinking product life cycles. In the coming years, as strategic change accelerates, logistic flexibility will become increasingly important. As with external flexibility, the mere knowledge of the sources of threats/opportunities is sufficient to start a rigorous program of logistic preparedness.[4]

The preceding discussion shows that if management is receptive to weak signals, much can be done long before the threat becomes tangible and concrete. The possibilities are summarized in Figure 5-2, in which the shaded portions represent the areas of feasible response. As seen in the figure, all of environmental awareness measures, all of internal flexibility, and a substantial portion of external flexibility can be put in place before the threat becomes clear and definite. In our earlier example, this means that electronic component manufacturers could have attained a high state of readiness for coping with the transistor before the transistor was invented!

FIGURE 5-2. FEASIBLE RANGES OF RESPONSE STRATEGIES

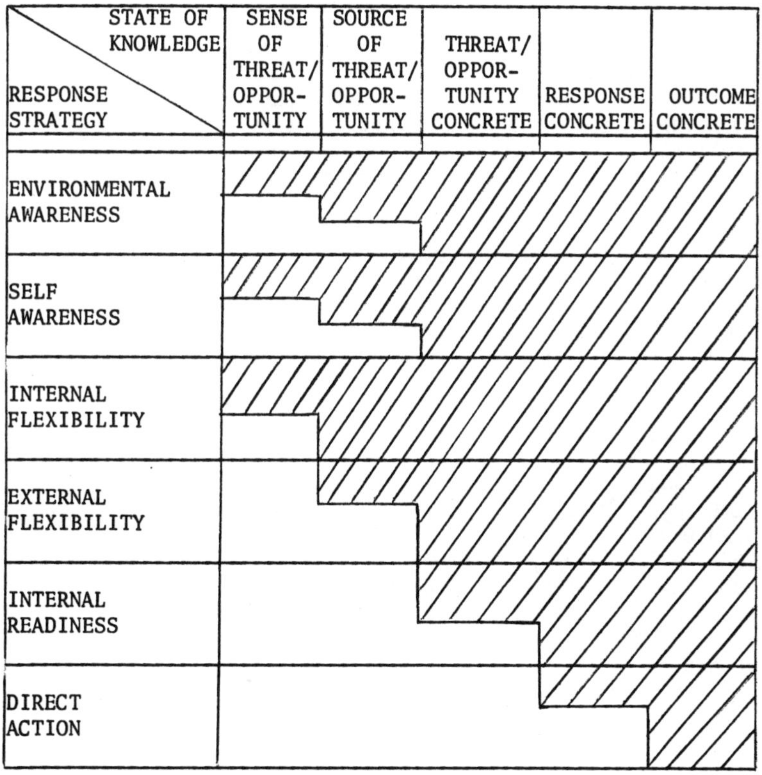

STATE OF KNOWLEDGE / RESPONSE STRATEGY	SENSE OF THREAT/ OPPOR-TUNITY	SOURCE OF THREAT/ OPPOR-TUNITY	THREAT/ OPPOR-TUNITY CONCRETE	RESPONSE CONCRETE	OUTCOME CONCRETE
ENVIRONMENTAL AWARENESS					
SELF AWARENESS					
INTERNAL FLEXIBILITY					
EXTERNAL FLEXIBILITY					
INTERNAL READINESS					
DIRECT ACTION					

As Figure 5-2 shows, for direct response strategy it is necessary to have a good idea of the threats that one is proposing to attack. But even here, a sufficiently clear idea of the origin and shape of a threat is sufficient to launch a substantial percentage of internal readiness measures, including acquisition of necessary technological, production, and marketing skills, new product development, and development of sources of supply.

Even direct external action need not, and *in practice*

frequently does not, await information that makes possible reliable cash- and profit-flow calculations. This is where entrepreneurial risk takers become differentiated from cautious followers. Adventurous firms will typically launch their entry into a new industry at level four, before the technology, market, and competition are well enough defined to permit such calculations. More conservative firms will prefer to wait on the sidelines until the "ball game" is better defined.

DYNAMICS OF RESPONSE

Each of the six response strategies makes a complementary contribution to the firm's ability to handle strategic discontinuities. Each requires a different length of time for implementation. The total length of time for mastering a particular threat/opportunity depends on the prior preparedness of the firm, the vigor with which the firm responds, and the sequence in which the respective strategies are put in place.

As mentioned previously, conventional strategic planning proceeds from direct response, to flexibility, to awareness. Figure 5-2 and preceding discussion suggest that the reverse sequence--awareness to flexibility to direct response--enables the firm to start response much earlier, and finish earlier, utilizing weak signals. Figure 5-3 illustrates the

FIGURE 5-3. DYNAMICS OF INTERNAL RESPONSE

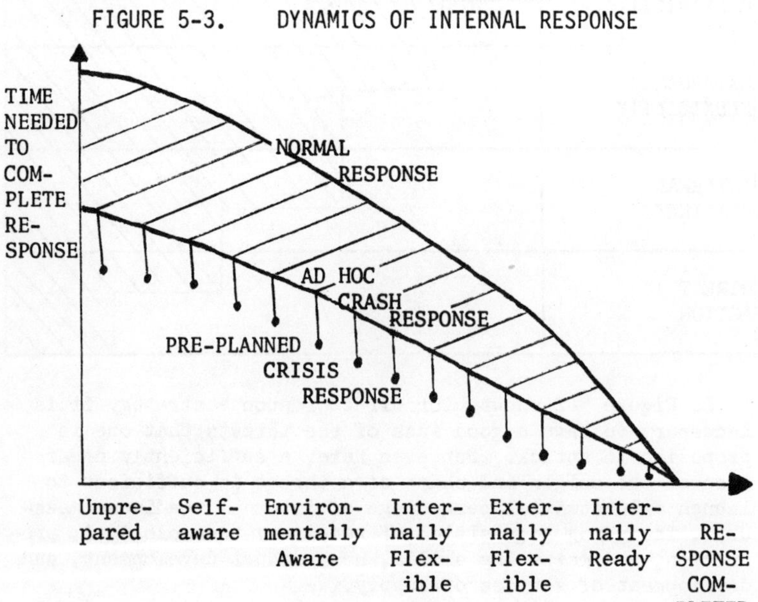

dynamics of the firm's response, using this latter sequence. The vertical scale shows the time needed by the firm to complete the response, that is, to eliminate or stabilize operating losses or to make viable a new opportunity. The horizontal scale lists the states from which it may start. The curves show the obvious advantage of prior readiness: the better prepared the firm when it starts, the less time it will need to complete the response.

The upper curve of Figure 5-3 traces the *normal response* in which the threat/opportunity is treated routinely by existing processes, structure, systems, and procedures. The lower solid curve, the *ad hoc crash response*, shows the time savings that can be effected when everything possible is done to speed up the response--normal rules and procedures are suspended, other priorities are pushed into the background, organizational lines are crossed, activities are duplicated, overtime is incurred, and so forth.

The mere "pulling out of the stops," implying an ad hoc improvisation when a crisis looms, is not the only emergency procedure open to the firm. If, in spite of best efforts to anticipate threats/opportunities, the firm still expects to be confronted with sudden, fast-developing threats, investment in a program of training in *crisis management* is worthwhile in much the same way that a firefighting company invests in a capability to fight unexpected types of fires. The result will be to lower the response time required to the level labeled *preplanned crisis response*, thus increasing the capability for handling strategic surprises.

The envelope of response times defined by the three curves in Figure 5-3 will of course differ among firms and from one discontinuity to another. Size, complexity, and rigidity of structure will lengthen the response times, and the nature of the threat/opportunity will be equally influential. Important factors will be the size of the discontinuity as well as its degree of unfamiliarity, both of which determine the magnitude of the response effort. Thus, again, a procedure is needed that will translate the theoretical curves of Figure 5-3 into practical application.

PRACTICAL PREPAREDNESS DIAGNOSIS

Reference to Figure 5-2 shows that the respective states of knowledge will differ from SBA to SBA. Consequently, the range of possible responses will also differ. Thus, the first step is to determine the feasible responses for each SBA-threat/opportunity combination.

Continuing with the example of Table 5-2, we have chosen SBA_1, which had a single, clearly visible threat (T/O concrete stage). A reference to the feasibility table of Figure 5-2 shows that five of the six response strategies are feasible in this advanced stage of information. This is recorded as "F" or "I" (infeasible) in the second column of Figure 5-4.

FIGURE 5-4. PREPAREDNESS DIAGNOSIS: SBA_1

	FEASIBILITY	STATUS	RELATIVE IMPORT	CRASH		NORMAL	
				TIME	COST	TIME	COST
Self-awareness	F	0% ●—— 100% 	VH	3		6	
Environmental awareness	F	 ————●—	H	1		2	
Internal Flexibility	F	 ●——————	H	2		4	
External Flexibility	F	 ——●————	L	4		8	
Action Readiness	F	 ———●———	M	2		4	
Action	I		VH	2		4	
Completed Response	X	0% ———●—— 100% 	X	4 Yes	4.0	8 Yes	1.0

The next step is to diagnose the firm's current state of readiness in each of the feasible strategies; the result is shown in column three of Figure 5-4. Letting 100 percent represent the maximum that can be done to respond to the T/O in the current state of ignorance, the entry is an estimate of the current readiness in each of the categories.

The roughly 15-percent entry for self-awareness suggests that, while the threat is concrete enough, the firm has done relatively little to determine the usefulness of its own capability for dealing with the threat. This might have been the case in the example of a vacuum tube firm which, having learned about the existence of the transistor, has not made the effort to analyze that applicability of its technology and organization to the emerging transistor industry. On the other hand, that firm appears to be well advanced in understanding the market, the potential competition, and the future of the transistor.

To continue with the example, the low rating on the internal flexibility shows that the firm's resources and facilities are highly specialized, and external flexibility shows that the firm's profits are largely dependent on its vacuum tube business and that it is therefore threatened by new technology.

The next and critical step is to estimate the time the firm will need to carry the state of readiness to 100-percent level for each of the preparedness categories. The estimate is made category by category for both normal and crash responses. In the last line of Table 5-2 a summary estimate is made of four to eight years for completed responses. In our example this might have meant divesting from the vacuum tube SBA, narrowing to a market in which the tube will continue to be competitive, or making a successful entry into the transistor business.

The final step in readiness diagnosis is to estimate the cost-effectiveness of the total response. The cost of the response is shown in the last line of the table as a fraction of the percentage of current profits contributed by the SBA (see Table 5-2). If, as shown in Figure 5-4, a crash program will cost four times the current contributed profits, and if the response will prevent a loss of 0.2 to 0.5 of this profit, the investment will amortize itself in eight to twenty years. The cost-effectiveness is low, which suggests that the threat be written off and allowed to run its course. On the other hand, the normal response (if it turns out to be timely enough), costing 1.0, will be cost-effective, because the amortization period will be only two to five years.

OPPORTUNITY-VULNERABILITY PROFILE

The preceding discussion suggests two conclusions. First, the decision to respond should not be based on response costs alone, nor on the amount of profit loss or gain that is at stake. Rather, it should be based on the return on the costs incurred. We used the simple but useful payback measure of this return. With better data (particularly in the advanced states of knowledge), other measures can be employed. By doing this, "throwing of good money after bad" is avoided, especially when the threat looms large and the temptation is to attack it, no matter what the costs.

Second, the selection of the counteraction, in the range between normal and crash response, cannot be made independently of the timing of the threat. A comparison of the timing is provided by the opportunity-vulnerability profile,

FIGURE 5-5. OPPORTUNITY-VULNERABILITY PROFILE

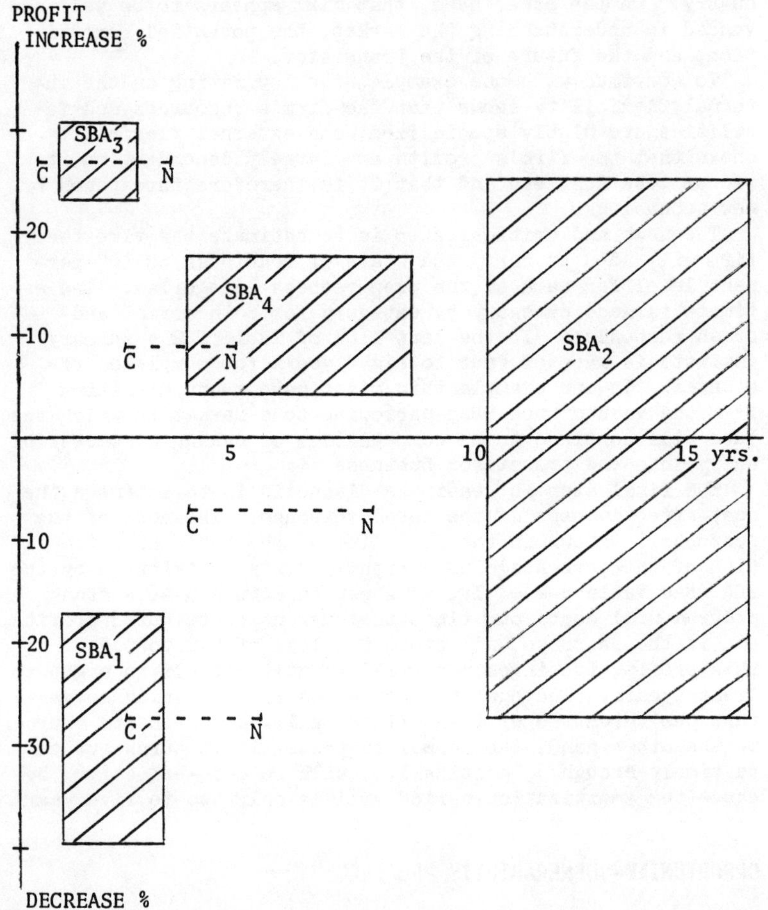

shown in Figure 5-5, which combines the results of the threat/opportunity analysis and the readiness diagnosis. The respective shaded rectangles enclose the "regions of probable impact" on the respective SBA's. Rectangles below the horizontal axis spell potential losses in profitability due to threats; those above indicate gains offered by opportunity. The height of the rectangle spans the probable range of loss/gain, the base spans the probable times when the discontinuity will reach the critical benchmark level of the firm. Both dimensions are obtained from the threat/opportunity analysis in Table 5-2.

The horizontal dotted lines in Figure 5-5, obtained from

the readiness diagnosis (Figure 5-4), span the time of probable completion of successful response. Thus, the normal response for SBA_3 would be late, but the firm can assure itself of capturing the opportunity through a crash program. SBA_2 is "safe"; normal response will capture it, provided the firm continues to monitor the development of the contingency. SBA_1 is in trouble because even a crash response may be late; it looks like a "surprise" in the making.

These examples show that timing of the threat does not by itself determine the priority of the respective responses. The priorities are determined in part by the *urgency* derived from comparing the timing of the threat with the time needed for response. Thus, in our example, both SBA_1 and SBA_3 are expected to reach critical impact at about the same time. But, because of the longer response time needed, SBA_1 must be handled on an all-out crisis-response basis, while a moderately urgent response will suffice for SBA_4. The priorities also are determined in part by the potential *cost-effectiveness* of the responses determined in the manner discussed in the preceding section.

The opportunity profile also provides an overall perspective of significant strategic changes in the firm's future. The firm needs to check the impact of SBA_1, because if unchecked, a minimum of 15 percent and a maximum of 40 percent of the profit will be lost. Since, at best, timely arresting of this threat will be difficult, the crash response must be used. The firm also must make an effort to capture the opportunity in SBA_3, as an offsetting insurance. Further, if the firm wishes to capture the attractive opportunity in SBA_4, it needs to start right away to avoid a crash response later. Only SBA_2 seems to call for no immediate aggressive action. But its potential impact is so great that a vigorous monitoring program should be spotlighted on the strategic issues that give rise to this T/O.

A SYSTEM FOR MANAGING STRATEGIC ISSUES

Selection of one response cannot be made independently of others, because they all lay claim on the time, managerial energy, and financial, human, and physical resources of the firm. The totality of the T/O's must be considered, in light of the continual changes in the environmental challenges, threats, and opportunities. And, given the evolving state of knowledge in each of them, the totality must be considered in a dynamic, changing perspective. Consideration of this totality should be made a part of a flexible and responsive management system. Such a system, which we shall call a *strategic issue management system (SIM)*, is shown in the somewhat complicated Figure 5-6.

The upper part of each box identifies the involvement by four groups of actors: the planning staff, general manage-

FIGURE 5-6.

STRATEGIC ISSUE MANAGEMENT SYSTEM (SIM)

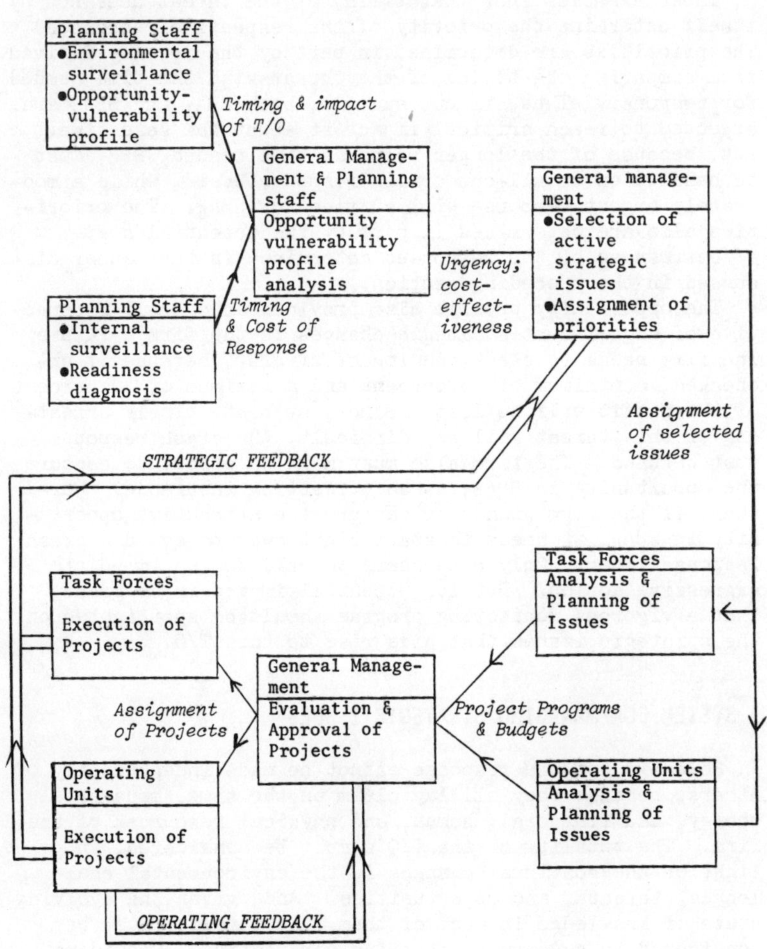

ment, task forces (drawn, as necessary, from all parts of the firm), and operating units. The lower part of the box described the function performed in the successive stages of the process: the planning staff detects, tracks, and analyzes strategic issues; general management keeps up to date the list of important strategic issues, assigns specific issues for planning, approves the plans , and monitors the execution; and task forces and/or operating units plan and execute specific projects.

One distinctive feature of strategic issue management is its organizational flexibility. The general management groups involved may be the top management in small or medium-sized firms or several groups scattered through a large corporation. Both the planning and implementation of strategic issues are determined not by the organizational structure but by the nature of the problem involved. Whenever a problem cuts across organizational units or requires special attention, ad hoc task forces are set up. The same task force may plan and execute, or the executive may be assigned, in part or in whole, to the permanent organizational units.

Another distinctive feature, not readily evident from the figure, is the *real time* character of the process. It follows no fixed planning calendar; rather, the surveillance is continuous, strategic issue list updating is both periodic and triggered by appearance of major T/O's, and planning execution is ongoing throughout the year, with completed projects being succeeded by new ones.

A third distinctive feature, because the system responds to weak signals, is the special attention to the two different types of feedback shown in Figure 5-6--operating and strategic. The results obtained from executing the project are interpreted in two ways: first, to judge whether the programs and budgets are being followed (the operating feedback); and second, to determine whether the strategic issue has been well identified, whether it deserves the priority assigned to it, and whether the action strategy has been well chosen (strategic feedback).

When the issues arise from vague incipient trends, stratetic feedback dominates and guides progressive redefinition of the response. In later stages of T/O, the focus naturally shifts to operating feedback. Thus, the *gradual response permits gradual commitment on the part of the management.*

Finally, strategic issue management is an action, and not a purely planning, system, The results of implementation feed directly back to management groups that originally selected and authorized the issues. Planning and implementation are not separated. An issue is not "resolved" until it is dropped from the list or concrete changes are produced in the profitability and growth of the firm.

STRATEGIC ISSUES AND STRATEGIC PLANNING

Strategic issue management is an expansion and extension of a planning technique of strategic issue analysis, which has emerged in practice in the past few years. Our expansion has been to admit weak signals as a basis of decision making, and the extension was from a purely planning to a total action system.

Strategic issue management overcomes a basic shortcoming of the strategic planning technology which has become increasingly evident in practice--the inability of strategic planning to handle quickly and efficiently individual fast-developing threats and opportunities. The reasons for this are several: the dependence of strategic planning on strong signals, which delays the recognition of a strategic issue; the rigidity of the planning calendar, including six- to nine-month delays between initiation and completion of the planning cycle; and organizational inflexibility of the strategic planning system, which cannot effectively handle strategic issues that simultaneously affect more than planning units. When an issue fails to fit into the perspective of a single unit, both its planning and implementation tend to "fall between the chairs."

In summary, preoccupation with system and organizational dynamics of the planning process leads to an inability to cope with the dynamics of rapidly developing threats and opportunities. In computer terminology, strategic planning is an off line process as compared to the real time character of strategic issue management. But in return for the real time responsiveness, strategic issue management incurs the penalty of lack of comprehensiveness. It is essentially an opportunistic approach that fails to capture the totality of the firm's future perspective. An examination of the strategic issue list reveals the potential threats and opportunities, but it offers little information about where the firm as a whole is headed.

If, for example, all of the firm's SBA's are in the state of maturity or decline, it is dangerous to use strategic issue management without adjoining strategic planning to it. SIM will focus attention on dealing with contingencies, whereas the need is for a fundamental realignment of the firm's strategic thrust. Thus, strategic issue management is a complement, rather than a replacement for strategic planning. The salient features of each are summarized in Table 5-4, which shows that the choice of one or the other, or both, depends on the strategic environment of the firm.

1. A firm that is in a relatively surprise-free environment, but whose basic business prospects are unsatisfactory because of market saturation, technological obsolescence, or change in the structure of demand, needs to engage in comprehensive strategic planning. A firm that seeks large-scale diversification from a position of strength would do

likewise; so would a firm that needs a fundamental rebalance of its strategic business areas.

2. A firm whose growth prospects appear satisfactory, but whose environment is strategically turbulent, may confine itself to strategic issue management. Today this would apply, for example, to the ball bearing industry, where Japanese competition is changing the market structure, the computer industry, where technology is changing rapidly, or the pharmaceutical industry, where both technology and societal relations are turbulent.

3. Firms that face both a fundamental realignment of the strategic thrusts and a turbulent, surpriseful environment would benefit from combining both strategic planning and strategic issue analysis into a comprehensive strategic management system.[5]

TABLE 5-4.

COMPARISON OF STRATEGIC PLANNING AND STRATEGIC ANALYSIS

STRATEGIC PLANNING	STRATEGIC ISSUE ANALYSIS
Deals with firm's total strategy	Deals with probable discontinuities
Focused on products-market-technology	Embraces discontinuities from all sources
Applicable when major strategic reorientation is desired	Applicable when insurance against surprises is desired
Responds to strong signals	Responds to weak signals
Strategic information needs derived from decisions	Feasible decisions determined by available information
Prepared periodically	A continuous process
Organization-focused	Problem-focused

ANTICIPATING RESISTANCE TO PLANNING

In the preceding pages we have developed a conceptual framework and a practical procedure by which a firm in a turbulent environment can cope with weak signals, thus minimizing the chances of surprise. The result is a new planning approach, which must be accepted and used by practicing managers to become effective. However persuasive and practical the approach, neither its acceptance nor its use can be taken for granted. To do so would be to disregard the numerous instances when similarly logical approaches encountered resistance to planning and were either rejected or emasculated by the using organizations.

To gain acceptance for this particular approach, it is necessary to assure within the firm a climate of openness to strategic risk and preparedness to face unfamiliar and threatening prospects. The creation of such a climate of strategic decisiveness is as complex and difficult a problem as the one discussed here. Therefore, we have explored decisiveness in two separate articles.[6,7]

These articles argue that management in most firms lacks the necessary strategic decisiveness to accept a system such as strategic issue management or genuine strategic planning. An attempt to introduce such a system is highly likely to encounter resistance and possible rejection. In a strategic crisis, strategic thinking and action will be the last resort, after historically suceessful operating remedies have been exhausted.

Enhancing strategic decisiveness involves making changes in decision-making technology, systems, information, distribution of power, and above all, in the risk attitudes and values of managers who are key to the strategic response. Thus, strategic decisiveness is an organizational state of mind--a culture--as well as a distinctive competence. The process of cultural change is difficult and requires special understanding and skills. But technology for inducing organizational change exists, has been described in voluminous literature, and has been successfully tested in practice.[8]

In the application of this technology, a typical "chicken and egg" problem arises: should strategic decisiveness be built up first, or should the new system be introduced? In most cases it is possible to join the two change processes in a single program of organizational transformation in which the new system and the new problem-solving skills are used as a vehicle for bringing about behavioral changes.[9]

FOOTNOTE REFERENCES

[1]W. W. Bryant (Manager, TEO Central, Phillips, Eindhoven, Holland), personal communication.

[2]Leslie Smith (Chairman of the BOC Limited, London), personal communication.

[3]For each of the six response strategies, a series of alternative types of counteractions can be enumerated. See H. Igor Ansoff, "Managing Surprise and Discontinuity: Strategic Response to Weak Signals," Working Paper 75-21 (April 1975), European Institute for Advanced Studies in Management.

[4]A detailed listing of possible measures for external and internal awareness, as for external and internal flexibility, can be found in Ansoff, *op. cit.*

[5]One of the potential by-products of such combination is an acceleration of strategic planning processes; see Ansoff, *op. cit.*

[6]H. Igor Ansoff, J. Eppink, and H. Gomer, "Management of Surprise and Discontinuity: Problems of Management Decisiveness," Working Paper 75-29 (July 1975), European Institute for Advanced Studies in Management.

[7]H. Igor Ansoff, "Enhancing Managerial Decisiveness in the Face of Strategic Turbulence," forthcoming.

[8]H. Igor Ansoff, R. Hayes, and R. Declerck, "From Strategic Planning to Strategic Management," in *From Strategic Planning to Strategic Management* (London: John Wiley & Sons, 1976).

[9]Pierre Davous and James Deas, "Design of a Consulting Intervention for Strategic Management," in *From Strategic Planning to Strategic Management, op. cit.*

STUDENT REVIEW QUESTIONS

1. What is a "strategic surprise"?
2. What are the two options Ansoff identifies for firms wishing to prepare for "strategic surprises"?
3. To be useful for strategic planning, what two conditions must information satisfy?
4. Expalin the steps involved in Threat/Opportunity Analysis.
5. Discuss briefly the alternative response strategies Ansoff identifies.
6. Compare strategic planning and strategic issue analysis as explained by Ansoff. Do you agree?

REFERENCES FOR ADDITIONAL STUDY

Ansoff, H. Igor, "The Concept of Strategic Management," *Journal of Business Policy*, Summer 1972.

Bales, Carter F., "Strategic Control: The President's Paradox," *Business Horizons*, August 1977.

Cohen, K. J. and R. M. Cyert, "Strategy Formulation, Implementation, and Monitoring," *Journal of Business*, July 1973.

Emshoff, James R. and Ian I. Mitroff, "Improving the Effectiveness of Corporate Planning," *Business Horizons*, October 1978, pp. 49-60.

Gerstner, Louis V., "Can Strategic Planning Pay Off?", *Business Horizons*, December 1972.

Kinnunen, Raymond M., "Hypothoses Related to Strategy Formulation in Large Divisionalized Companies", *Academy of Management Review*, October 1976.

Litschert, Robert J. and T. W. Bonham, "A Conceptual Model of Strategy Formulation," *The Academy of Management Review*, April 1978.

Lunneman, Robert E. and John D. Kennell, "Short-Sleeve Approach to Long-Range Plans," *Harvard Business Review*, March-April 1977.

Mason, R. Hall; Jerome Harris; and John McLaughlin, "Corporate Strategy: A Point of View," *California Management Review*, Spring 1971.

Mazzolini, Renato, "European Corporate Strategies," *The Columbia Journal of World Business*, Spring 1975.

Newman, William H., "Shaping the Master Strategy of Your Firm", *The California Management Review*, Spring 1967.

Quinn, James Brian, "Strategic Goals: Process and Politics," *Sloan Management Review*, Winter 1976.

Salveson, Melvin E., "The Management of Strategy," *Long-Range Planning*, February 1974.

Steiner, George and Hans Schollhommer, "Pitfalls in Comprehensive Long-Range Planning: A Comparative Multi-National Survey," *Long-Range Planning*, April 1975.

Steiner, George A., "How to Improve Your Long-Range Planning," *Managerial Planning*, September-October 1974.

Steiner, George A., "Rise to the Corporate Planner," *Harvard Business Review*, September-October 1970.

Thune, Stanley S. and Robert J. House, "Where Long-Range Planning Pays Off," *Business Horizons*, August 1970.

Vancil, Richard F., "Strategy Formulation in Complex Organizations," *Sloan Management Review*, Winter 1976.

Wrapp, H. Edward, "Good Managers Don't Make Policy Decisions," *Harvard Business Review*, September-October 1967.

SECTION B.

CRITICAL INPUTS TO STRATEGY MAKING

6

Information for More Effective Strategic Planning*

WILLIAM R. KING

DAVID I. CLELAND

NEARLY EVERY TEXTBOOK on strategic, or long-range, planning describes the strategic planning process in terms of strategic information as well as planning activities. For instance, the simple strategic planning process of Figure 6-1 shows a variety of information inputs to the 'choice' activities which comprise the process. Among these informational inputs are assessments of the organization's strengths and weaknesses, competitive information, and environmental opportunities and risks--all of which are referred to in the figure as 'strategic data bases.'

Despite the general agreement which exists in the literature and among planning professionals concerning the need for such informational inputs to strategic planning, we have found that the information which is implicitly defined in Figure 6-1 is often either:

not explicitly gathered and evaluated, or
gathered, but not made a substantive part
of the strategic choice process.

Thus, while all planners, and most managers, appear to pay lip service to the idea that these informational input are critical parts of the overall strategic planning process, there is a little evidence that they actually play such a role.

The authors can, for instance, point to a company which

---

*From *Journal of Long Range Planning*, Vol. 10, February, 1977, pp. 59-64. Reprinted by permission.

FIGURE 6-1. STRATEGIC DATA BASES

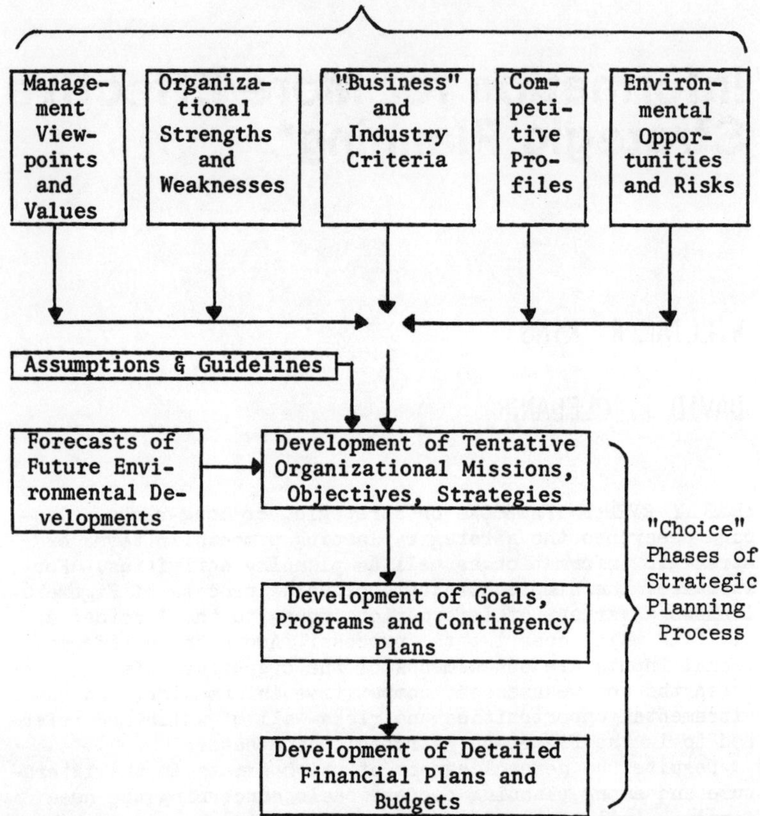

(This diagram, in part, utilizes ideas which are explained in *Corporate Strategy: A Synthesizing Concept for General Management* by John H. Grant. This is an unpublished research paper at the Graduate School of Business, University of Pittsburgh, 1975.)

---

employed two staff people for 6 months to develop a 'competitive data base' which was to be used in the planning process. When their efforts reached fruition, they had created a room full of carefully crossfiled documents which were made no use of in planning because the data was 'too voluminous' and 'too difficult to use'. Subsequent evaluation of these competitive data resulted in the production of a very thick loose-leaf book which was put to little use for the same reasons.

In this article, we seek to illustrate an entity--referred to as a 'strategic data base' (SDB)--which can be developed in a form which makes it useful for directly supporting the strategic planning process. In doing so, we also describe the process through which strategic data bases are developed. These strategic data base development processes thereby become intrinsic parts of the overall planning process.

The specific SDBs and processes described here are largely taken from actual experience with business firms, although the illustrations are disguised and simplified for security and expositional purposes.

DEVELOPING STRATEGIC DATA BASES

Strategic data bases are concise statements of the *most significant* strategic items related to various clientele/or environments which affect the organization's strategic choices. As such, they are the mechanisms through which the current situation and future opportunities are assessed. The strategic data bases shown in Figure 6-1 reflect the influence of various forces--the environment, competitors, top management, the 'business' in which the organizations operates, as well as the organization itself--on the strategic options which are available.

These strategic data bases are essential to developing meaningful answers to the first basic question which must be asked in any planning process. 'Where are we?' Such a basic question is often reacted to by managers with one of two extreme positions--either the question is regarded to be a foolish one since, 'we obviously know where we are', or it is regarded as being adequately answered only by collecting voluminous data on all of the many aspects of the organization's status.

The approach adopted here is a middle ground between these extremes which emphasize the development of strategic data bases--*objective collections of data which are manageable, and therefore useful, in the planning process.* These 'strategic data bases' represent the *major conclusions regarding the environment and the organization's clientele;* these conclusions having been evaluated to be the *most important* such informational inputs to be considered in the planning process.

The evaluations of the vast quantities of data which form the raw input for the development of strategic data bases should be performed by task forces, or teams of managers representing diverse interests within the organization. *In this way, the organization can be assured that the evaluation does not represent one narrow point of view, or only the parochial viewpoint of analysts.*

These teams of managers, supported by staff, may be charged with arriving at *conclusions* concerning a *specified number* (usually from 10 to 15) of the *most important* factors affecting the future of the organization in a specified area. The development of conclusions on the 10-15 most important organizational strengths and weaknesses can be, as any experienced manager knows, a difficult task, when it involves managers representing various organizational interests and points of view. *Developing a 20-page list of strengths and weaknesses could be accomplished relatively easily, but a list of the 10-15 most significant ones involves analysis and negotiation.* This is so both because of the judgments which are involved and the potential organizational impact which such a list can have through the strategic choice process.

It is useful to contrast this participative process for developing strategic inputs to the planning process with the one more commonly used to prepare the informational inputs to planning. This common approach relies on staff analysts, who gather data and prepare documents which are to serve as background information supporting planning activities and choices. Because the planners and analysts who perform these tasks often have neither the managerial expertise nor the authority to make the significant choices which are involved in any information evaluation process, the typical output of such an exercise is a document which seems to have been prepared on the basis of 'not leaving anything out'.

Such an emphasis on ensuring that nothing relevant is omitted rather than on attempting to distinguish the most relevant information from the mass of less relevant and the irrelevant serves only to perpetuate the existing state of affairs regarding the informational support provided to managers at all levels: the manager is deluged with irrelevant information, while at the same time, he is unable to find elements of information which are crucial to his function.[1]

Conversely , the proposed process focuses on charging task forces, which are made up of managers representing various of the parochial interests within the organization,with gathering and evaluating the data in each of a number of areas and *choosing*--through the consensual process that guides most task force decision making--those that are the most important to the development of the organization's strategy.

Thus, the 'strategic data bases' represent 'information' rather than 'data' in the sense that large quantities of data have been evaluated and condensed to a form which can feasibly be used in the strategic planning process. Thus, with the SDB approach, there is a greater likelihood that some of the information which is so universally regarded as being important to strategic planning will actually become an integral part of the strategic planning process.

Moreover, a secondary benefit which is invariably realized from the SDB approach must not be overlooked. The participative process of developing SDBs will usually involve a variety of middle-level managers from each of the organization's functional units. The SDB development process is thereby a way of involving middle managers in the 'strategic thinking' of the total organization long before they might normally become so involved by virtue of their operational job responsibilities. Thus, the SDB approach serves as a *training ground for the development of those elusive 'strategic thinking' abilities* which are so necessary to successful top-level management.

Since the best way to elaborate on the SDB concept is through illustration, we shall provide a detailed description of those data bases described in Figure 6-1. While these strategic data bases are somewhat generic, they also represent those with which we have worked in our consulting activities. Thus, others will most surely prove to be useful in other organizations and situations.

STRENGTH AND WEAKNESS STRATEGIC DATA BASE

A 'strength and weakness strategic data base' is a candid and concise statement of the most significant strengths and weaknesses of the organizations. While most planners would agree in principle that such a 'data base' should importantly guide strategic choice, there is little evidence to suggest that many organizations have explicitly developed strength-weakness data bases or made effective use of them. For instance, a major U. S. electrical manufacturer who got into public housing and then land development businesses might have been deterred from doing so if the organization's weakness in the basic skills necessary for success in that area had been explicitly enumerated for all to see.

Table 6-1 shows a strength-weakness strategic data base for one business unit of a major conglomerate. This summary list was displayed on the first page of a 'strength and weakness' planning guidebook which was prepared for use in the planning process. The remainder of the book contained exhibits which explained and elaborated on these conclusions.

Some of the items in Table 6-1 might be thought of as simply items describing the status of the firm, or as problems that need to be corrected, rather than weaknesses. However, in the firm's detailed explanations of these areas in their planning guidebook, they were treated as weaknesses that must guide strategic decisions, rather than merely as problems to be overcome. For instance, the details relevant to the 'low market share' weakness emphasized the strategies which were precluded as a result of low market share rather than emphasizing low market share merely as a deficiency to be corrected. In this way, attention was directed toward the *strategic implications of each strength and weak-*

ness rather than to the familiar sort of exhortations for the firm to 'do better by increasing market share'.

Two of the entries in the Strength-Weakness Table refer to the firm's 'image'. These indicate that the firm believes that its customers perceive it positively in terms of its technical superiority and (perhaps) negatively in terms of the relatively high price of its products. Such 'image assessments' are commonly incorporated into statements of corporate objectives as well as into strength-weakness analyses. Yet often, as in this instance, the firm is to some degree uncertain of just how it is perceived. In this instance, the company was not certain if its high technical quality was perceived as justifying its relatively higher price.

Such a resolution of the image situation in a state of partial uncertainty is a common, and valuable, kind of outcome of strategic data base development efforts. It points up the need for information that is more detailed and specific than that which the firm currently possesses. This result can lead to an *ad hoc* study or to the development of a more detailed information system that will provide the firm with the answers that it wants and the understandings that it needs to do effective strategic planning.

TABLE 6-1.
ILLUSTRATIVE STRENGTH AND WEAKNESS DATA BASE

Major strengths	Major Weaknesses
Technical expertise in centrifugal area	Low market share
International sales force	Lack of product standardization
Heavy machining capability	Poor manufacturing non-fragmented product line
Business systems	Poor labor relations
Puerto Rico facilities	Weak domestic distribution network
Technically superior image among customers	High price image (?)

The key difference between 'strategic data bases' and the more detailed data bases which are important to information systems can now be made quite clear in the context of this illustration. 'Data bases' such as that of Table 6-1 require significantly more *evaluation* in their preparation than do the data bases which are commonly a part of computerized information systems.

Table 6-1 is the result of an evaluative process which has begun with the compilation of a long list of potential strengths and weaknesses and proceeded, through the efforts of a task force composed of upper-middle managers from all functional units of the firm, to evaluate those strengths and weaknesses which are most crucial in the determination of the firm's strategy. This concise list can then be referred to in the later phases of the planning process to suggest strategies, to aid in identifying relatively good and poor strategies, and to guide the development of plans for implementing the chosen strategies.

BUSINESS AND INDUSTRY CRITERIA STRATEGIC DATA BASE

One informational input to planning which is widely recognized to be important, but rarely made into an explicit element of the planning process, is the key element of *'what it takes to be successful in this business.'* There are critical elements of 'business sense' in any activity, and while successful top executives may have a good feel for these elements, a rational planning process will make the elements, a rational planning process will make the elements explicit and available to all planning participants. Such planning inputs help to guide the choices which are made just as do the strength and weakness analyses.

For instance, the 'business criteria' which one might specify as being the keys to success in the military weapons system industry could be:

A strong research and development capability;
A commitment to using project management systems;
A strong field marketing effort closely tied in with customer organizations;
An ability to deal effectively with a relatively few knowledgeable customers;
An ability to identify and track emerging technological and market opportunities over long periods leading to consummation of sales;
Willingness to commit substantial company resources to study and prepare bids on government proposals.

In a consumer-oriented industry the requirements for success might include such factors as:

Standardization of product line components;
High volume production runs;
Highly dispersed marketing and service centers;
Low technology;
Development of a recognized brand name.

The 'Business and Industry Criteria' SDB may be developed by a team in much the same fashion as discussed previously. Their work will probably involve more interviewing of top executives and less formal data gathering than will the work of the developers of the stregnth-weakness data base, but ultimately, data will have to be developed to substantiate, if possible, the beliefs of top executives about the factors that are critical to success.

The format used by one company to present all of their 'data bases' is appropriate here as well--a one-page summary of the data base along with substantiating details in the form of a booklet.

COMPETITIVE STRATEGIC DATA BASE

Competition is the most apparent, and probably least understood, element of the organizational environment. In developing a competitive SDB, the organization must take care to avoid the inherent problems associated with the belief of some individuals that nothing useful can actually be discovered concerning competitors, the reality of the voluminous material which can actually be obtained concerning competitors, and the ethical considerations which quickly come to the surface.

We have dealt with these issues elsewhere.[2] Here, we can merely indicate the broad insights concerning competition which can be used as guidance for the planning process in the form of a strategic data base.

For instance, competitors who are identified to be outperforming the organization can be identified and their significant actions and strategies can be cataloged and analyzed. Several major issues must be addressed with regard to competition:

First--who are the several most threatening competitors?

Second--what are the strengths and weaknesses of the competition?

Third--what is believed to be the strategy (and associated risks) of the competition?

Fourth--what resources (financial, plant, and equipment, managerial know-how, marketing resources, and technical abilities) are at the competition's disposal to implement his strategies?

Fifth--do any of these factors give the competition a distinctly favorable position?

The evaluation of competition is, in a sense, a mirror image of the strengths and weaknesses of the organization itself. The competitor's ability to conceive and to design has to be evaluated. This evaluation should concentrate on his products and their design, as well as on his ability to innovate in the creation, production, and marketing of his products. Evaluation of a competitor's resources must be done in a fashion which emphasizes what each can be expected to accomplish rather than solely on the resources that are available.

ENVIRONMENTAL OPPORTUNITIES AND RISKS STRATEGIC DATA BASE

A wide variety of other-than-competitive environmental information can provide valuable inputs to the strategic choice process. Every organization has environmental opportunities and risks related to customers, government agencies and other 'regulators' of the organization. Profiles of some important organizational clientele can be maintained and culled of their saliencies to provide input to planning in a fashion similar to that done for competitors. This idea is particularly valuable in the case of major customers, who may be viewed in much the same way as a competitor for analytic and informational purposes.

Often, environmental risks and opportunities may be reduced to a series of specific questions, and hopefully, answers which can guide planning. Amara and Lipinski[3] have illustrated such questions as:

> Will there be widespread nationalization of industry?
>
> What is the possibility of the development of large industry/government cartels in the United States, particularly with respect to foreign markets?
>
> What dominant changes are likely to take place in the attitudes of the labor force--both supervisory and nonsupervisory?
>
> Is consumerism a fad? And, if not, what directions is it likely to take in the next decade?
>
> In what ways may the activities of multinational corporations be subject to increasing regulation?

Illustrative answers to such questions are also provided by Amara and Lipinski in a concise form which is adaptable for use in guiding the planning process:[4]

> ...Rail transport (both freight and passenger) is likely to be fully nationalized by 1985; all other industries (including energy-related) will remain in private hands. Financial services (insurance, banking, securities) and consumer goods industries will undergo the greatest regulatory changes.
>
> ...Any major shift toward industry/government cooperative arrangements (as in Japan) is highly unlikely in the near future.
>
> ...Workplace discontent will intensify con-

siderably. Much of this will be due to the entrance into the labor force of the baby bulge of the late 1950s and the peculiar set of problems associated with this age group. Work incentives in the future will emphasize greater freedom of choice regarding surroundings, dress, and a decision-making role in forming teams and structuring work functions. This change involves democratization to some degree, but not of business decisions. A reversal of economic prosperity will markedly reduce the importance of psychological rewards to employees.

...Consumerism is not a fad. The scope of consumer protection measures will widen in the next few years; mandatory product performance guarantees are quite possible, and regulation requiring industry-wide common performance indicators and detailed reporting of product testing results is very likely.

...The rate of growth of multinational corporations will slow somewhat in the next decade, and multinational corporations can anticipate more international controls, both from regional codes and from global organizations. However, it is unlikely that capital controls will be bothersome to multinational corporations.

The environmental data base can, as well, entail a section dealing with general areas of opportunity which are perceived to emanate from the environment. For instance, in a business related to recreation, the increasing availability of leisure time, which can be projected from a temporal analysis of union contract provisions regarding the length of the work-week and vacation durations, might well be identified as a basic environmental opportunity for consideration.

The risks associated with these 'opportunities' should be delineated so that they are not viewed with the proverbial rose-colored glasses or treated as established facts subsequently in the planning process. For instance, increased vacation durations among blue-collar workers might translate into increased sales of paints and other home repair items long before it affects sales of vacation homes.

MANAGEMENT VIEWPOINTS AND VALUES STRATEGIC DATA BASE

It is well understood that top management's viewpoints

and values play an important role in guiding the organization. While this is completely proper, it is often not explicitly spelled out in the organization's strategic choice process. This is not to say that a 'management viewpoints and values' guidebook be provided in the same fashion as might be done for strengths and weaknesses, environmental opportunities and risks and business criteria, and the other SDBs, but it is also important that the organization not be misled into considering alternatives that have little chance to be viewed positively by top management. Participative strategic planning is a time-consuming activity and clearly, the effort should be focused in directions satisfying the practical constraints, which reflect top management views, as well as more formal resource and legal constraints. If these constraints become apparent only *after* the planning process has been conducted, it will have been wasteful and the negative effect on managerial morale will be severe. There are few more disheartening situations for a manager than to feel that he is involved in high-level decisions regarding the future of the organization only to discover that recommendations on which he has spent considerable time and effort have been rejected because they violate constraints that he was not told about.

Ackoff[5] has used the term 'stylistic objectives and constraints' to describe this sort of qualitative statement about what the organization will do and what it will not do. He illustrates stylistic constraints as (paraphrased):

(1) The company is not interested in any government-regulated business.
(2) The businesses into which we may go must permit entry with modest initial investments but eventually permit large investments to be made.
(3) The technology of any new businesses should be directly related to that used in current businesses.

However, the idea of 'management values and viewpoints' clearly is broader than that which is implied by these examples. For instance, it includes the *social responsibility* viewpoint of top management. Do they feel that the organization should pursue a broad multifacted social purpose, or do they believe that the broad social good is best served if each institution seeks only a narrow range of objectives which best suits its expertise? If, in the case of a business firm, top management believes that profit-seeking does create the greatest social benefit that the firm itself can feasibly produce,[6] this belief must be translated into operational terms to guide the strategic planning process.

The general aggressive versus the defensive posture of the organization is another guide to the planning process which can only be specified by top management. If the posture is to be defensive, much time can be wasted in considering aggressive strategies which will ultimately be 'shot down' by top management review. If the general posture is stated in advance, it serves to make the planning process more efficient and more productive.

Some top executives might be reluctant to spell out their personal ideas in such a way that they will formally constrain the planning process. Their fear in doing so reflects an unwillingness to appear to be making the organization into their personal image. However, most managers recognize the appropriateness of having the personal philosophy of top management play a role in guiding the organization's direction. Indeed, most experienced managers realize that chief executives often have as a major personal objective the making of *a distinctive personal impact* on the organization. Therefore, if the 'rules of the game' are made clear in advance, few managers will object or be disheartened; if they are not, difficulties are almost certain to ensue.

If strategic planning were solely the function of top management, this would not be a problem; but such is not the case. Therefore, a 'management viewpoints and values' SDB can play an important role in initiating a participative strategic planning process. For instance, its essence can be conveyed in a memo or letter from the chief executive which serves as a cover letter for the planning guidelines which are promulgated to initiate the planning process. Such a cover can treat, in some detail, those constraints and emphases which are to play a major role in the strategic decisions which are to be made. In this fashion, a happy medium may be struck between the extremes of burying such guidelines in the minds of top managers and requiring that they be spelled out in the formal terms that are suggested for the other strategic data bases.

FOOTNOTES

[1]See R. L. Ackoff,"Management Misinformation Systems," *Management Science*, pp. B147-B156, December (1967), for a full exposition of this situation.

[2]David I. Cleland and William R. King, "Competitive Business Intelligence Systems," *Business Horizons*, December (1975).

[3]Roy Amara and Andrew Lipinski, "Strategic Planning: Penetrating the Corporate Business", p. 3, Institute for the Future, Paper P-30, November (1974).

[4]*Ibid.*, p. 4.

[5]R. L. Ackoff, *A Concept of Corporate Planning*, pp. 28-29, John Wiley (1970).

[6]See P. F. Drucker, *The Age of Discontinuity*, Harper & Row (1968), and the writings of many conservative economists, such as Milton Friedman, for the rationale for this viewpoint.

STUDENT REVIEW QUESTIONS

1. What are strategic data bases?
2. Explain why King and Cleland say "the manager is deluged with irrelevant information" using common planning practices.
3. What is the key difference between strategic data bases and typical information systems data bases?
4. Briefly discuss the development of the strengths and weaknesses data base discussed in the article.

7

Factors in Corporate Growth*

FRIEDHELM GORONZY

EDMUND R. GRAY

SINCE WORLD WAR II there has been great interest in planning for corporate growth. Current management literature abounds with books and articles on long-range or strategic planning.[1] Although this interest in planning for the future growth and prosperity of the firm is relatively new among scholars and practitioners in the field of management, it has long been a subject of intense interest to economists and related researchers.

Recent management writers concerned with this area have emphasized such subjects as:

1. the importance of long-range corporate planning,
2. the methodology for long-range planning,
3. the organization for long-range planning, and
4. the problems of implementing long-range plans.

In short, these writers have stressed the "why" and "how" of long-range corporate planning. Economists, on the other hand, have tended to take a more detached and objective view. Their focus has been the objective factors in the external and internal environment of the firm which influence and limit growth of the firm.

It is important that senior management in general and long-range planners in particular have a working knowledge of these factors because they provide some basic explanations of corporate growth. The task of the planner, as we

*From *Management International Review*, 1974/4-5, pp. 75-85. Reprinted by permission.

see it, is to mold a corporate strategy that will allow the firm to adjust to a basically hostile environment and thus survive by growing at a satisfactory rate. These objective factors afford the planner a starting point for identifying and understanding the principal opportunities for and limitations to the growth of his firm. In other words, they provide him with a framework (albeit a sketchy one) from which he can commence to shape his firm's growth strategy. The situation is analogous to that of the doctor who uses his knowledge of the theory of biological growth, at least indirectly, as a starting point in planning a child's health program. The theory does not dictate what he will prescribe but is essential background knowledge for understanding what he is doing and why.

Similarly, a planner needs a basic theoretical framework. The objective growth factors presented here provide this although they clearly do not represent a comprehensive theory. On the contrary, they are fragmentary and in some instances conflicting. They do represent, however, the best thinking on the subject of corporate planner's mental "data bank".

The purpose of this article is to review and examine the principal objective growth factors identified by scholars. The factors to be examined may be divided conveniently into three groups:

1. external factors,
2. internal factors, and
3. motives of management.

Each of these will be discussed in turn.

EXTERNAL FACTORS

Classical and neo-classical price theory economists view the firm as a reactor to market conditions. Changes in market forces lead to certain reactions on the part of the firm. Hence, environmental changes are viewed as the starting points of growth; they act as the stimili which present the opportunity for growth without the help of which the company is fighting against difficult if not impossible odds.

The origins of the environmental changes which provide opportunity for growth fall into four broad categories[2]:

1. *Social* -- e.g., changes in the age composition of the population, increasing leisure demands, and rising educational levels.

2. *Economical* -- e.g., increasing incomes, rising labor costs, and changing foreign competition.

3. *Political* -- e.g., vacilating defense spend-

ing, government subsidies, and business regulations.

4. *Technological* -- e.g., technological breakthroughs, and innovation spin-off.

These environmental changes produce opportunities for various types of expansion. Some of the primary expansion routes are summarized below.

Purely quantitative expansion -- the energies and abilities of management are concentrated on the existing product or products. The expansion path follows a given demand curve and the size of the market and legal restrictions are the principal constraints. It is this mode of growth, which frequently is called market penetration, that has been so thoroughly analyzed by economists. Large franchise operations in the United States such as McDonald's Hamburgers and Kentucky Fried Chicken furnish salient examples of market penetration.

Product-mix changes -- the range of products and models made by similar processes and sold in similar markets is enlarged. Growth is achieved through greater product differentiation and market segmentation.[3] The Coca Cola Company has achieved this by coming out with the new soft drink, Fresca. Another illustration of this mode of growth is Beecham, which originally produced McClean's regular flavor toothpaste and later added McClean's peppermint flavor toothpaste.

Qualitative expansion -- the increasing complexity of the environment may demand new technologies to meet demands which have been with us for a long time. For example, techniques for measuring weight and distances have become increasingly sophisticated over time.[4] Also, the advent of color television has opened entirely new expansion vistas for the television industry which had been witnessing a diminishing market potential.

Technological advancement -- new technologies also may rise to meet entirely new demands. The integrated circuit industry, for example, which was virtually non-existent prior to 1960 has grown to become a billion dollar industry.[5]

Complementary products -- in some areas the market may demand complementary products, e.g., washers and dryers.[6] This method of expansion also has been well-explored by early economists.

Conglomerate expansion -- here companies move into entirely new (to the company) product areas. It is almost always achieved through acquisition or merger. In the 1950's and

'60's, this mode of expansion was dominant. Firms such as Ling-Temco-Vought, Georgia-Pacific and Litton Industries represent salient examples of the conglomerate type industrial giant.

Often several growth factors influence the history of a company. For example, American Photocopy played a leading role in developing a wet copier in order to create and meet a new demand. Later, competition from dry copiers forced it to abandon the wet copying technology. Moreover, the firm had to make qualitative improvements on the dry copying technology in order to remain successful in the business it had helped to create.

The above considerations depict the firm basically as a reactor to changing external forces. The environment provides the opportunity for growth but also sets the external limits to expansion. Economists view these forces as only a partial explanation of company growth, however. Internal factors must also be considered.

INTERNAL FACTORS

Economists trace the internal factors which influence enterprise growth to two major sources: economies of scale and outlay, and motives of top management. The economies that result from large scale production have been a favorite subject of inquiry by economists for many years. The many facets of this area and the controversy that surrounds it make it difficult to deal with in abbreviated form. Only the more significant issues, therefore, will be considered here.

The motives of top management as a growth factor have only recently begun to receive attention. This area is still in an embryonic state and its theories are constantly being modified and new managerial motives or combinations of motives are being proposed to explain managerial behaviour.

ECONOMIES OF SCALE

Economists analyze economies of scale by means of long-run cost curves which usually take the form of an envelope curve (See Figure 7-1). Three cases are generally distinguished: 1. increasing long-run cost curves (decreasing returns to scale, diminishing marginal productivity), 2. constant long-run cost curves (constant returns to scale, constant marginal productivity), 3. decreasing long-run cost curves (increasing returns to scale, increasing marginal productivity).

Empirical verification of the actual nature of the cost curves is exceedingly difficult and the little evidence

FIGURE 7-1.

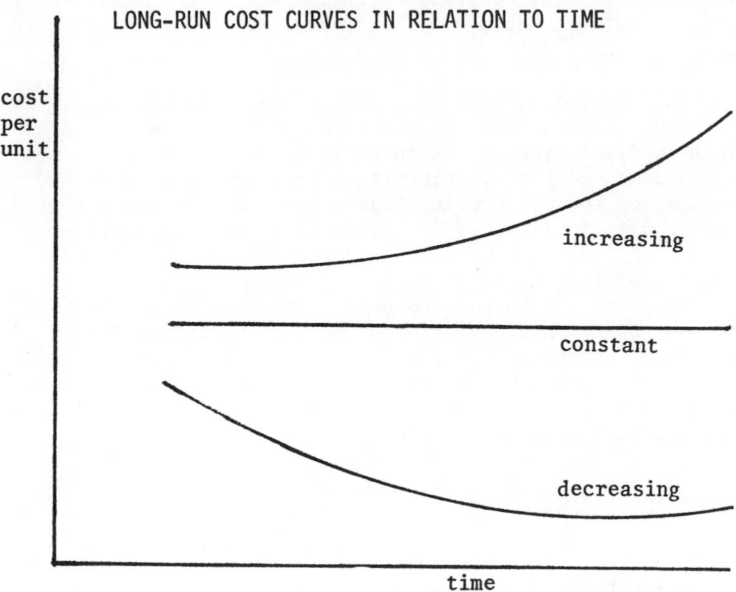

available is contradictory. There appears to be general agreement, however, that constant long-run cost curves do not exist in the real world. If they did, any size firm would be optimum--the smallest to the largest. Our discussion, therefore, is concerned with the question of whether long-run cost curves are decreasing or increasing. Let us examine the reasons advanced for decreasing long-run cost curves first.

In describing reasons for decreasing long-run cost curves two contrasting assumptions may be isolated--constant factor proportions and variable factor proportions. Constant factor proportions means that the ratio of factors of production (land, labor, capital and management) remain constant for all levels of production. Since some factors of production come in discrete amounts (e.g.--machinery) small firms cannot fully utilize these factors. Consequently, there is a powerful incentive to expand to utilize fully these special resources. The balance of all productive factors for optimum efficiency may be determined by Babbage's "Principle of multiples"[7]. This principle is, of course, related to the modern concept of production line balancing and can most easily be explained by a simple example. Assume that a product is produced by three consecutive operations. The first is a hand process where a craftsman can turn out forty units per week. The second is an automatic process where 1,000 units per week can be produced. The third process requires a semi-automatic machine and 300 units per week can be produced. Here, the lowest common multiple that will employ craftsmen and special machinery to full capacity (a multiple of 40, 300, and 1,000) is 3,000 units--requiring 3 automatic machines, 10 semi-automatic machines, and 75 craftsmen. Similarly, the next level of efficient expansion is to 6,000 units.

The variable factor proportion assumption represents a more typical real-world situation. It states that the optimal factor proportions vary with output. Five major reasons for increasing returns to scale consistent with this assumption have been put forward. There are:

1. the six-tenths factor,
2. the principle of massed or pooled reserves,
3. the principle of bulk transactions,
4. quality changes through increasing size, and
5. the learning curve.

These will be briefly examined in turn.

The six-tenths factor gets its name from the geometric relationship between surface and volume which states that the surface increases only by a factor of 2/3 to the change in volume. In similar fashion, output per unit of capital investment tends to increase with size. Engineers, especially in chemical processing plants, have found this rule of thumb a useful short-cut method of estimating the relationship between investment in plant and changes in production capacity.[8] Of course, the actual numerical value of the "six-tenths" factor varies considerably according to the nature of the project, but clearly there are economies of the large scale plant as Figure 7-2 shows.

The principle of massed reserves is simply the economic application of the statistical probability theory which states that the greater the number of items involved the more likely are deviations in their amounts to cancel out and leave actual results nearer the expected results. For example, breakdown of machines occur less than proportionately to the number of machines employed, smaller percentage stocks have to be maintained for products which sell in large volumes than those which have a lower level of demand, i.e., the increase in finished goods inventory is less than proportionate to the expansion of sales. Hence, again it follows that a larger scale of operation lead to economies.[9]

The principle of bulk transactions is well known. It is illustrated by the fact the administrative costs of dealing in large quantities is sometimes no greater (and in any case, is less than proportionately greater) than those of dealing in smaller quantities. Therefore, the per unit cost becomes smaller with large quantities. A purchasing agent or salesman may spend no more time and effort in negotiating a $10,000 order than he does a $100 order. Similarly, the

FIGURE 7-2.

PLANT COST AS A FUNCTION OF PLANT CAPACITY

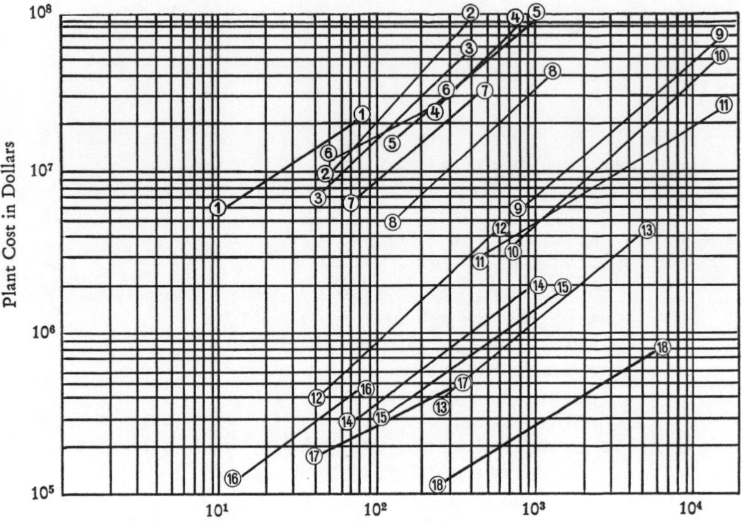

(Source: H. C. Chilton, "Six-Tenths Factor Applies to Complete Plant Costs", *Chemical Engineering* April, 1960, p. 112)

Curve No.	Product or Process	Capacity Basis	Slope
1	Magnesium via ferrosilicon	Product	0.62
2	Butadiene ex butylenes	Product	1.02
3	Aluminum ingot	Product	0.90
4	TNT	Product	1.01
5	Synthetic ammonia	Product	0.81
6	Styrene	Product	0.53
7	GR-S copolymer	Product	0.82
8	Aviation gasoline	Product	0.88
9	Complete refinery including catalytic cracking	Crude charge	0.75
10	Catalytic cracking, topping, feed preparation, gas recovery, polymerization	Crude charge	0.88
11	Topping and thermal cracking	Crude charge	0.60
12	Contact sulphuric acid ex smelter gas	Product	0.91
13	Two coil crude oil cracking	Crude charge	0.82
14	Solvent dewaxing of lube oil	Lube fraction charge	0.74
15	Solvent extraction of lube oil	Lube fraction charge	0.68
16	Catalytic desulphurization of gasoline	Gasoline charge	0.81
17	NaOH purification via ammonia	NaOli product	0.48
18	Atmospheric crude oil topping	Crude charge	0.62

machine set-up costs for large and small production runs typically is about the same.[10]

The notion that quality improvements occur as a result of larger size may be demonstrated by showing that expansion normally results in the use of more specialized machinery and labor. This specialization is accompanied by significant quality improvements and results in lower unit costs.[11]

The learning curve theory also asserts that large production runs lead to reduction in manufacturing time and hence cost per unit. The savings are attributed to the learning of the production workers and technical improvements in the production system which come from greater experience with the operation. The extent of the unit time reduction through learning depends on labor content of the job. The technical improvements are often small tools and fixtures or changes in procedure that reduce costs independently of the economies of the big machine. Figures 7-3 and 7-4 give examples of such cost improvements. Of course, with time the incremental time savings become less and less and eventually become insignificant. However, the slope of the learning curve can have a major influence on the competitive position of the firm.[12]

INCREASING LONG-RUN COST CURVES

Two primary reasons are given for increasing long-run cost curves:

1. increasing costs of administration, and
2. rising distribution costs.

Economists argue that cost of administration increases with size--at least beyond some optimal size. The rationale is that as a firm grows, specialization and division of labor become greater and the cost of coordinating these specialized groups and individuals increases disproportionately.[13] Moreover, it is suggested that even without excessive specialization the problems of coordination become proportionately greater as the work force multiplies. Graicunas, for example, has asserted that as a superior's subordinates multiply arithmetically his coordination problems increase geometrically.[14]

Although it probably is true that there are increasing costs of administration, it is equally clear that more sophisticated management techniques are increasing the optimal organizational size. For example, greater organizational decentralization, more effective use of delegation and increasing improvements in information technology are helping managers effectively manage rapidly growing firms.

Rising distribution costs is the second persuasive reason given for a rising long-run cost curve. Transportation and sales promotion costs are the principal factors here. For example, as a firm grows the cost of procuring resources

FIGURE 7-3.

MAN-HOURS PER UNIT OF OUTPUT IN U.S. BASIC STEEL INDUSTRY--SUGGEST LEARNING CURVE DECLINE 1935-1955

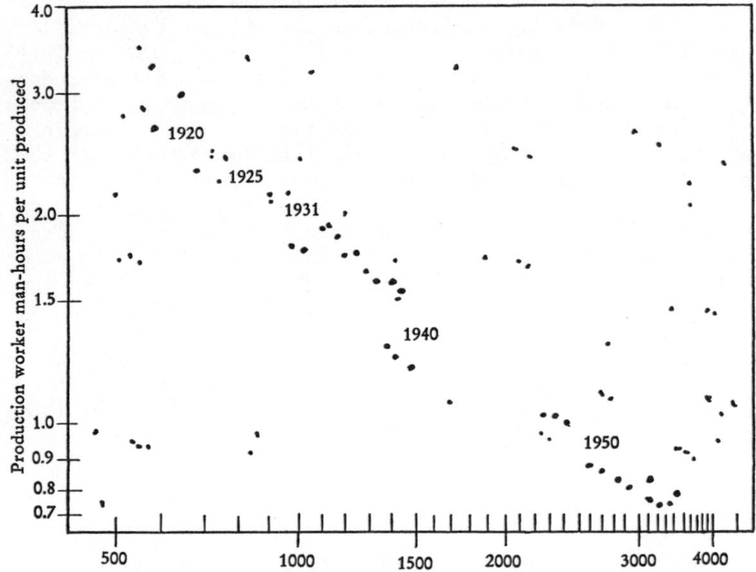

Source: *Bulletin 1200*, Washington, U. S. Department of Labor Statistics, September 1956, and other sources (From: Winfred B. Hirschmann, "Profit from the Learning Curve", *Harvard Business Review*, Jan.-Feb., 1964, p. 135)

will probably increase because the needed resources are seldom available locally in the required amounts and in acceptable quality. Furthermore, large firms typically serve geographically dispersed markets and this, of course, results in rising transporation costs. In industries with bulk products (e.g., cement) this factor is especially significant. For most industries, however, this factor does not seem to be critical.

Advertising costs represent another important category of rising distribution costs. Advertising in competitive industries at lower levels of scales may lead to increased sales and thus enable larger scale manufacturing with accompanying lower unit costs.

In an oligopolistic situation, with extremely large firms, however, advertising may be simply a defensive action with each firm trying to maintain its market share. Hence, sales

FIGURE 7-4.

FINAL ASSEMBLY OF AN ELECTRO-MECHANICAL PRODUCT

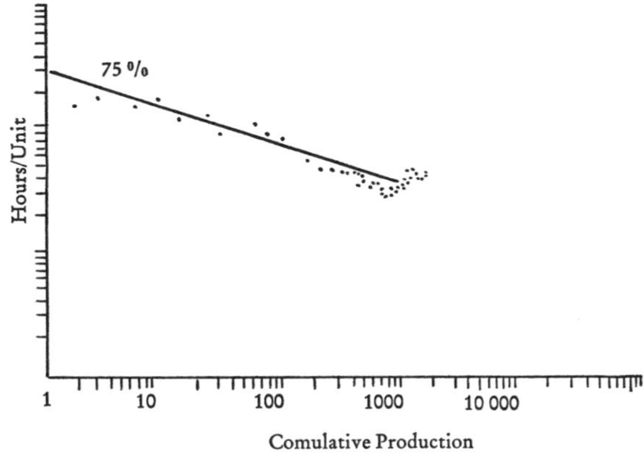

Source: Richard Conway and Andrew Schultz, "The Manufacturing Progress Function", *Journal of Industrial Engineering*, Jan. - Feb., 1959, p. 45.

promotion becomes an added cost as is largely the case in automobile, oil and airline industries.

Theoretically the question of whether the long-run cost curve is decreasing or increasing turns on the concept of the optimal size of the firm. In other words, up to the point of optimal size, economists argue, returns to scale are increasing; after optimal size is reached returns to scale decreasing. Empirically, the point of optimal size has never been determined. It is safe to conclude, however, that this point is different for each industry and each firm; and, in addition, it probably varies over time and with the ability of management. The important thing for planners to realize is that there are two conflicting sets of internal influences being exerted on the firm--one encouraging expansion and the other working against it. The critical problem, of course, is to determine which is dominant at a given time.

MOTIVES OF TOP MANAGEMENT

With the separation of ownership and management the motives of corporate managers have come under closer scrutiny. An important finding in this connection is the fact that executive compensation is more closely correlated with the size of the business enterprise than any other factor.[15] This phenomenon has prompted many new "managerial" theories of the firm. These theories of firm behaviour are based on the assumption that self-interested managers will behave so as to improve their own welfares first and then attend to the welfare of the owners of the firm and other interested parties. Because growth is rewarding to top management in terms of compensation, prestige, power, and job security, many managers seek growth for its own sake and not necessarily because it leads to improved profits. Based on this assumption, Baumol hypothesizes an objective of scales maximization subject to a minimum profit constraint.[16] Monsen and Downs assume that managers attempt to maximize their lifetime incomes.[17] Marris views management as a growth maximizer subject to a security constraint. In the development of his theory Marris shows that growth can be accelerated through the employment of debt but that too much leverage may endanger the financial structure of the firm under adverse conditions. Furthermore, the retention of earnings for growth purposes may not always be the most prudent course of action because too high a retention ratio can increase the danger of a raid or take-over. Hence, the security motive causes management to adopt policies of safe growth: reasonable leverage, high returns on productive assets and avoidance of excess liquidity. All this will reduce the probability of a raid and serve to enhance management's security.[18]

Williamson has proposed a managerial theory of the firm that emphasizes managerial discretion when profits are above a certain minimum level. Management, he asserts, will increase and strengthen the personnel in the firm even to the detriment of profits if times are good. A reservoir of personnel is necessary for future expansion and expansion, in turn, is of personal value to management.[19]

Elliot Jaques has developed an interesting behavioural theory which has bearing here. Jaques spent many years investigating the work capacity of individuals and found that capacity tends to grow over the life span of an individual. Consequently, firms with a relatively young layer of top management will have to expand in order to create positions with greater responsibility for these men. Otherwise these men will outgrow their job and leave if they have no opportunity to advance.[20] It has been suggested, in fact, that this theory may explain, to a great degree, the phenominal expansion of such prominent growth companies as Texas Instrument, Ling-Temco-Vought, Litton Industries, and Xerox.

RÉSUMÉ

In summary, it can be seen that although management scholars have, in recent years, been placing great emphasis on long-range or strategic planning for future growth, researchers in other academic fields, especially economics, have been pondering this area for a much longer period of time. Management writers have tended to stress the "how to" of growth planning. The economists and other scholars discussed above have focused on objective factors in the environment of the firm. These objective factors may be placed in three primary categories:

1. external factors,
2. internal factors, and
3. managerial motives.

The external factors are basic market conditions which provide the opportunity for growth and put limits on growth potential. The internal factors tend to focus on the question of whether the long-run cost curve is decreasing or increasing. Albeit no definite empirical evidence is available, a *priori* reasoning suggest that the curve decreases up to a point (the optimal size of the firm) and then increases as the firm grows larger. The optimal size, of course, will vary from firm to firm. Finally, managerial motives present the most recent focus for economists interested in understanding firm growth. The theories evolving from this focus substitute some form of growth incentive for the controversial profit maximization motive.

Hopefully, the above discussion will give corporate planners a better conception of how the objective outside observer has viewed the problem of corporate growth and thus provides useful background input into long-range planning process.

FOOTNOTES

[1]See, for example: E. Kirby Warren, *Long-Range Planning: The Executive Viewpoint*, Englewood Cliffs, N. J.: Prentice-Hall, Inc.; George A. Steiner, *Top Management Planning* (New York: MacMillan, 1969); Myles L. Mace, "The President and Corporate Planning," *Harvard Business Review*, January - February, 1965.

[2]Robert B. Young, "Keys to Corporate Growth," *Harvard Business Review*, November - December, 1961, pp. 53-54.

[3]H. U. Baumberger, *Die Entwicklung der Organisationsstruktur in wachsenden Unternehmen* (Bern: Paul Haupt, 1951), pp. 11-12.

[4]Roland S. Edwards and Harry Townsend, *Business Enterprise: Its Growth and Organization* (London MacMillan, 1958),

pp. 47-49.

[5] *Ibid.*, pp. 50-51.

[6] *Ibid.*, pp. 54-55.

[7] Edith T. Penrose, *The Theory of the Growth of the Firm* (New York: John Wiley, 1959), pp. 18-20.

[8] H. C. Chilton, "Six-Tenths Factor Applies to Complete Plant Costs," *Chemical Engineering*, April, 1960, pp. 112-114.

[9] Florence, *op. cit.*, pp. 17-18.

[10] *Ibid.*, p. 16 .

[11] H. Speight, *Economies and Industrial Efficiency*, (London: McMillan, 1962), pp. 45-47.

[12] Herbert G. Hicks and Friedhelm Goronzy, "Notes on the Nature of Standards", *Academy of Management Journal*, Dec., 1966, pp. 281-293.

[13] William H. Starbuck, "Organizational Growth and Development," in James G. March (ed.) *Handbook of Organizations* (Chicago: Rand McNally & Co., 1965), pp. 458-459.

[14] V. A. Graicunas, "Relationship in Organization," *Bulletin of the International Management Institute* (Geneva: International Labor Office, 1933), in L. Gulick and L. Urwick (eds.), *Papers on the Science of Administration* (New York: Institute of Public Administration, 1937), pp. 181-187.

[15] D. R. Robert, *Executive Compensation* (Glencoe, Illinois: The Free Press, 1959).

[16] William J. Baumol, *Business Behaviour, Value and Growth* (New York: Harcourt, Brace and World, 1967).

[17] R. J. Monsen and A. Downs, "A Theory of Large Managerial Firms," *The Journal of Political Economy*, June, 1965, pp. 221-236 .

[18] Robin Marris, *The Economic Theory of Managerial Capitalism* (Glencoe, Illinois: The Free Press, 1964).

[19] Oliver E. Williamson, *The Economics of Discretionary Behaviour: Managerial Objectives in a Theory of the Firm* (Englewood Cliffs, N.J.: Prentice-Hall, 1964).

[20] Elliot Jaques, *Measurement of Responsibility* (Cambridge, Mass.: Harvard University Press, 1956).

STUDENT REVIEW QUESTIONS

1. Explain the difference between the approach to planning for corporate growth of management scholars and of economists.
2. What do Goronzy and Gray see as the primary task of the planner?
3. Explain the differences between quantitative and qualitative expansion. Give an example of each.
4. What is the six-tenths factor?
5. Explain the learning curve theory.
6. Explain briefly the major reasons given for increasing long-run cost curves.
7. What impact do the motives of top management have on growth?

8

Defining Corporate Strengths and Weaknesses*

HOWARD H. STEVENSON

INTRODUCTION

BUSINESS ORGANIZATIONS HAVE certain characteristics--strengths--which make them uniquely adapted to carry out their tasks. Conversely they have other features--weaknesses--which inhibit their ability to fulfill their purposes. Managers who hope to accomplish their tasks are forced to evaluate the strengths and weaknesses of the organization over which they preside. Many managers may not think in terms of "defining strengths and weaknesses." However, the evaluations which they make in determining areas for action reflect judgments of their organizations' capabilities related to either a competitive threat or a belief about what "ought to be."

Many corporate activities are aimed at helping a manager to understand what his own unit and the other units with which he comes into contact are doing well or poorly. Internally gathered information provides data for evaluating the performance of parts of the organization. Externally supplied information provides an understanding of the company's place in its competitive spectrum. It has become common for business organizations to formalize such information into a "resource evaluation program," a "capability profile," or other formally communicated assessments.

---

*From *Sloan Management Review*, Spring, 1976, pp. 51-68. Reprinted by permission.

Although many organizations have undertaken such studies, the results have often been difficult to integrate into an effective planning cycle. Many of the statements which emerged were either of the "motherhood" type or else did not readily lead to operational decisions. The research for this article examined some of the characteristics which create these operational difficulties.

RESEARCH METHODOLOGY

Defining strengths and weaknesses is viewed by management theorists as an important prelude to the development of an organizational commitment to strategic purpose.[1] In the book *Business Policy: Text and Cases,* the authors identify the following four components of strategy:[2]

- Market opportunity,
- Corporate competences and resources,
- Personal values and aspirations,
- Acknowledged obligations to segments of society other than stockholders.

These components are integrated into an overall program of strategy formulation. One such process model is shown in Figure 8-1.

Other writers clearly put the objective appraisal of strengths and weaknesses high on the list of necessary activities for a company which desires to grow.[3] Almost all work available has emphasized the normative aspects of the resource evaluation process. Even those authors examining practice have to a large extent focused on the formal methods by which the evaluation process is carried out.

The study which this article presents examined the process from the viewpoint of output. Fifty managers from six companies were asked for their evaluation of the corporate strengths and weaknesses and the reasons underlying those evaluations. The sample was structured so that it provided a relatively broad representation of managers within an organization. The dimensions shown in Table 8-1 were studied. From analysis of the 191 responses examined, typologies were constructed and an evaluation was made of the consistencies of responses.

The companies selected were:

- PAPERCO -- a diversified paper converter,
- AMERICAN INK -- a specialty chemical producer,

FIGURE 8-1.

A PROCESS MODEL OF STRATEGY FORMULATION

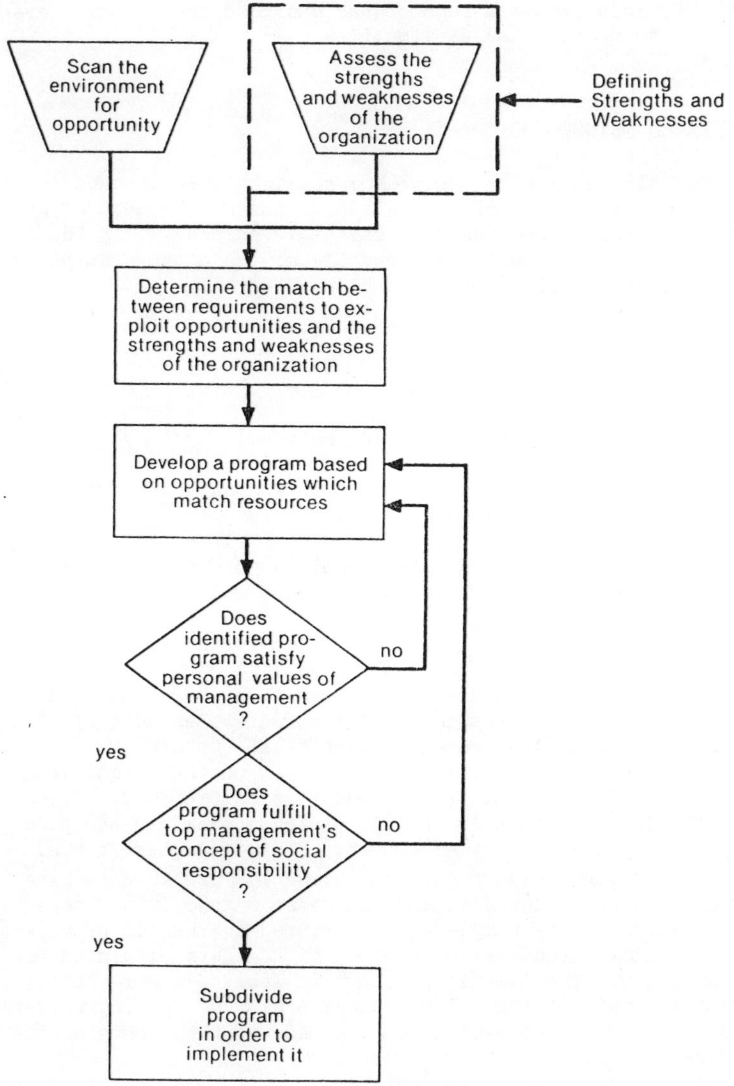

TABLE 8-1. STEPS IN THE PROCESS OF ASSESSING STRENGTHS AND WEAKNESSES

Which attributes can be examined?	What organizational entity is the manager concerned with?	What types of measurements can the manager make?	What criteria are applicable to judge a strength or a weakness?	How can the manager get the information to make these assessments?
Organizational structure Major policies Top manager's skills Top manager's experience Information system Operation procedures Planning system Employee attitudes Manager's attitudes Union agreements Technical skills Research skills New product ideas Production facilities Demographic characteristics of personnel Distribution network Sales force's skill Breadth of product line Quality control procedures Stock market reputation Knowledge of customer's needs Market domination	The corporation Groups Divisions Departments Individual employees	Measure the existence of an attribute Measure an attribute's efficiency Measure an attribute's effectiveness	Historical experience of the company Intracompany competition Direct competitors Other companies Consultants' opinions Normative judgments based on management's understanding of literature Personal opinions Specific targets of accomplishment such as budgets, etc.	Personal observation Customer contacts Experience Control system documents Meetings Planning system documents Employees Subordinate managers Superordinate managers Peers Published documents Competitive intelligence Board members Consultants Journals Books Magazines Professional meetings Government economic indicators

- HITECH -- an integrated electronic manufacturer,
- PUMPCO -- a heavy machinery manufacturer,
- NATIONAL GAS -- a manufacturer of gas products and transmission equipment,
- ELECTRICO -- an electrical equipment manufacturer.

Despite other differences these companies had a strong commonality in their product lines. Annual sales of the selected companies ranged from $200 million to over $2 billion.

The results of the study brought into serious question the value of formal assessment approaches. It was found that an individual's cognitive perceptions of the strengths and weaknesses of his organization were strongly influenced by factors associated with the individual and not only by the organization's attributes. Position in the organization, perceived role, and type of responsibility so strongly influenced the assessment that the objective reality of the situation tended to be overwhelmed. In addition, there were wide variations among standards of measurement and criteria for judgment employed.

Few members of management agreed precisely on the strengths and weaknesses exhibited by their companies. To facilitate further analysis the responses were classified within twenty-two categories. These categories were further reduced into five major groups as follows.

General Category	Includes These Attributes
Organization	Organizational form and structure Top management interest and skill Standard operating procedures The control system The planning system
Personnel	Employee attitude Technical skills Experience Number of employees
Marketing	Sales force

	Knowledge of the customer's needs Breadth of the product line Product quality Reputation Customer service
Technical	Production facilities Production techniques Product development Basic research
Finance	Financial size Price-earnings ratio Growth pattern

The individual attributes listed are neither mutually exclusive nor collectively exhaustive in partitioning each of the general categories. They do, however, represent the focal point of the responses from among the managers interviewed.

ANALYSIS OF STRENGTHS AND WEAKNESSES REPORTED

The list of attributes identified by the managers interviewed is notable both for the factors which have been included and for those which were not mentioned. Also important is the overall distribution of responses among each of the general categories and the individual attributes. Absent from the list were such items as: quality control procedures, channels of distribution, relationships with unions, share of market data, characteristics of the customers, growth rate of the industries in which the company is participating, purchasing and contract administration techniques, and competitive relationships.

The most obvious feature of the overall distribution of responses is the relatively equal importance attached to each of the general categories of attributes. Marketing related attributes were the subject of 26.7 percent of the responses, and technical, organizational, and personnel related attributes each accounted for over 20 percent. Since one might have predicted that the relationship to markets and customers would have been most important to the companies studied, its lack of dominance comes as a surprise. This is especially true given that over 48 percent of the responses came from managers with a marketing background. The overall distribution of the responses is shown in Table 8-2.

TABLE 8-2.

THE RELATIVE IMPORTANCE OF ATTRIBUTES IDENTIFIED AS STRENGTHS AND WEAKNESSES (ALL MANAGERS)

General Category	Percent of Response
Organizational	22.0%
Personnel	21.5
Marketing	26.7
Technical	22.0
Financial	7.9

The study indicates that there are a variety of influences impinging upon the manager as he analyzes the strengths and weaknesses of his corporation. These influences are shown diagrammatically in Figure 8-2.

FIGURE 8-2. FACTORS WHICH INFLUENCE A MANAGER IN DEFINING STRENGTHS AND WEAKNESSES

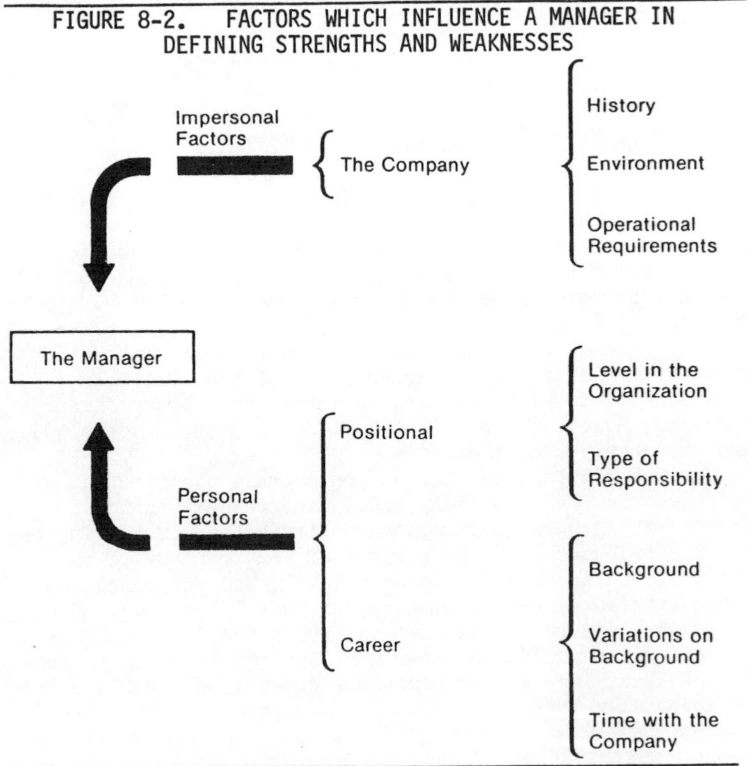

As would be expected the distribution of responses differed from company to company. The pattern of responses among the companies is shown in Table 8-3.

TABLE 8-3.

THE ATTRIBUTES EXAMINED IN RELATION TO THE COMPANIES STUDIED

	PAPERCO	AMERICAN INK	HITECH	PUMPCO	OVERALL
Organizational	30.4%	16.5%	18.2%	20.0%	22.0%
Personnel	36.2	7.7	27.3	30.0	21.5
Marketing	15.9	36.3	45.5	10.0	26.7
Technical	14.5	29.7	-	25.0	22.0
Financial	2.9	9.9	9.1	15.0	7.9
	100.0%	100.0%	100.0%	100.0%	100.0%
Number of Responses	69	91	11	20	191

Some generalizations of particular interest can be drawn from this small sample. It would appear that the following statements are true.

- There are some aspects of a company that are of concern in all companies.

- Managers within any company examine a broad range of attributes. There is no consensus on "the corporation's strengths and weaknesses."

Attributes of Common Concern

One of the interesting phenomena observed was that there were many attributes which received roughly equal consideration from all companies. There was not a statistically significant difference among the attributes examined by the companies. Evidence of the interest of the company in a particular type of problem was shown by a tendency to examine additional attributes of the same category.

The clearest examples of this phenomenon were the "organization" and "marketing" categories. Within these categories, there were similar responses for some individual attributes, for example, organizational form. This attribute was mentioned in the following percentages of responses: 7.2 percent for PAPERCO; 5.5 percent for AMERICAN INK; 5.6 percent for HITECH; and 5.0 percent for PUMPCO. The wide variation between companies in examining the "organizational" category arose as people in PAPERCO examined the other organizational attributes, such as top management, standard procedures, the control system, and the planning system.

Managers in all companies were concerned with the attributes listed in Table 8-4. Variations arose as the managers examined other attributes which affected their companies' strengths and weaknesses in the organizational, personnel, marketing, technical and financial categories.

TABLE 8-4. ATTRIBUTES OF COMMON CONCERN TO THE COMPANIES STUDIED (PERCENTAGE OF ALL RESPONSES FROM THE MANAGERS CITING ATTRIBUTES)

	PAPERCO	AMERICAN INK	HITECH	PUMPCO
Organizational Form	7.2%	5.5%	5.6%	5.0%
Attitudes	18.8	4.4	9.1	15.0
Technical Skills	13.0	1.1	18.2	10.0
Breadth of Line	10.1	7.7	15.5	5.0
Growth Pattern	1.4	3.3	5.0	10.0
Percentage of Total Response for Company	37.7%	22.2%	36.9%	45.0%

The Range of Concern

The broad range of attributes examined in each company should at once be a comfort and a warning signal to those interested in the process of defining strengths and weaknesses. PAPERCO managers evaluated seventeen of the twenty-two categories. AMERICAN INK managers had at least one response in each category. Even in the companies where only three or four executives were questioned, more than half of the list of twenty-two attributes were cited as being either a strength or a weakness.

This broad dispersal of responses indicated the situation that one staff manager stated: "My job is to worry about certain aspects of the company's business. To cover others with real meaning, you can talk to some other people." There was apparently an effective, if informal, division of the effort of "scanning the internal environment." The managers assumed certain territories upon which they felt qualified and responsible for judgment. These territories did not overlap; therefore, a majority of the important aspects of the company's existence was surveyed for relative strengths or weaknesses.

Most attributes were found to be both strengths and weaknesses. The results of the definition process were therefore ambiguous. The dynamic reasons underlying this difficulty were perhaps best expressed by the planning director at NATIONAL GAS who said:

> We have a formal system to develop a list of corporate strengths and weaknesses. We held a two-day planning session with our top corporate officers in which we were to review the results of the formal planning process including the list of strengths and weaknesses. Unfortunately, or perhaps fortunately, we found the list to offer only a very marginally useful guide to action. The "yes, but" phenomenon took hold. We found that by the time we got through discussing the strengths on the list, we weren't so certain that they were that strong. Conversely, the weaknesses were, upon examination, not so weak.

The resolution of the process of defining strengths and weaknesses into a list often did not produce the expected results. Further management judgment needed to be applied in order to develop a meaningful guide to action.

Although the strengths which a manager identifies depend in part upon his company affiliation, it is also apparent that certain characteristics of the manager's position influence his evaluations. Level in the organization, type of responsibility, functional background, time with the company and variations in background were all studied as possible explanatory variables. The results indicated that only level in the organization and type of responsibility were significantly related to the attributes which a manager cited as being strengths or weaknesses.

Importance of the Manager's Level in the Organization

The traditional theory of organization rests on the differentiation of responsibility within a hierarchical structure. With this as a framework, the hypothesis is that the attributes which are cited as strengths and weaknesses will vary by organizational level within a company. The results of the study show variations which are consistent from company to company. Table 8-5 shows variations among the overall sample in the attributes examined as they were related to the organizational level of the respondent. The organizational levels are defined as follows: level one is presidents and board chairmen; level two reports to either the company president or board chairman; level three is two steps removed; and level four is three or more steps removed from the company's executive officers.

Table 8-5 suggests several tentative conclusions. The level of responsibility is connected with the type of attribute cited. Personnel attributes, for example, are of increasing concern as the level of responsibility goes up.

TABLE 8-5.
THE RELATIONSHIP BETWEEN THE CATEGORY OF ATTRIBUTE EXAMINED AND THE MANAGER'S ORGANIZATIONAL LEVEL

	One	Two	Three	Four	Overall
Organizational	25.0%	17.3%	24.2%	26.9%	22.0%
Personnel	32.1	22.7	17.7	15.4	21.5
Marketing	10.7	28.0	33.9	23.1	26.7
Technical	7.1	24.0	21.0	34.6	22.0
Financial	25.0	8.0	3.2		7.9
Percentage of Total Response by Level	14.7%	39.3%	32.5%	13.6%	100.0%

This finding is consistent with the frequently made statement that the problems of managers at higher levels of responsibility increasingly become questions of the management of people. Comments have often been heard that judgments have to be made on the basis of whether the person is right for the job rather than on other more measurable dimensions. An interesting aspect of the citation of personnel attributes is that an individual's technical skills and experience tended to be examined equally at all levels. The consideration of attitudes of the individual, on the other hand, was definitely an increasing function of the organizational level of the examiner. The incidence of citation by levels of personnel attitudes as strengths or weakness is shown in Table 8-6.

TABLE 8-6.
CONCERN FOR PERSONNEL ATTITUDES BY ORGANIZATIONAL LEVEL (PERCENTAGE OF RESPONSES DEALING WITH ALL ATTRIBUTES)

	Organizational Level				
	One	Two	Three	Four	Overall
Attitudes	21.4%	12.0%	6.5%	7.7%	11.0%

Technical attributes exhibited the opposite pattern from that observed in the personnel attributes. Managers at higher levels were less concerned with the technical aspects of running the business. This finding is consistent with the traditional theory. Among the four attributes which comprise the technical category, only facilities and basic research were cited at all by the top management personnel (level one). Techniques and product development were of roughly equal concern to each of the other three levels. Facilities were of increasing concern to the lower levels of management. These detailed trends appear in Table 8-7.

TABLE 8-7.
CONCERN FOR TECHNICAL ATTRIBUTES BY LEVEL
(PERCENTAGE OF ALL RESPONSES AT EACH LEVEL)

	Organizational Level				
	One	Two	Three	Four	Overall
Facilities	3.6%	4.0%	8.1%	11.5%	6.3%
Techniques	-	8.0	8.1	7.7	6.8
Product Development	-	9.3	4.8	11.5	6.8

The financial attributes were of more interest to higher organizational levels. The concern for the price-earnings ratio and growth pattern was confined to the executive officers and their immediate subordinates. The only element of the financial category which was of concern to lower levels was the ability and willingness of the corporation to serve as a source of funds.

The organizational category showed no clear-cut pattern. There was approximately equal concern for the organizational aspects at all levels of the company. The control system, planning system, and the interest and skills of top management were not cited with any clearly identifiable pattern according to organizational level. These attributes were of importance to particular individuals for a variety of reasons identified with their job responsibility, such as planning vice-president or assistant controller. It is of interest to note, however, that some of the particular attributes cited among the organizational categories varied distinctly and predictably by level. The attributes of organizational categories varied distinctly and predictably by level. The attributes of organizational form and standard operating procedures fit nicely with conventional wisdom. Table 8-8 shows that organizational form was a concern of higher management while standard operating procedures were a concern to primarily the lowest level of management.

The marketing category showed no clear pattern, other than a slight tendency for the attributes to be of more concern to the lower levels, three and four,than to the upper levels of management. The specific attributes exhibited no recognizable pattern.

Another result of examining strengths and weaknesses by level is the apparent difference in perceptions of where a company is strong and where it may be weak according to the level of the evaluator within the company. Overall a pattern of greater optimism exists at higher organizational levels. One explanation for the trend is that the further down in an organization a manager is, the more levels there are above him to point to his mistakes and the weaknesses surrounding him. His comments reflect these evaluations.

TABLE 8-8.
CONCERN FOR ORGANIZATIONAL ATTRIBUTES BY LEVEL OF RESPONSIBILITY (PERCENTAGE OF ALL RESPONSES AT EACH LEVEL)

	Organizational Level				
	One	Two	Three	Four	Overall
Organizational Form	10.7%	2.7%	9.7%	-	5.8%
Standard Procedures	-	4.0	1.6	15.4%	5.2

The overall pattern of recognizing more strengths than weaknesses at higher levels was not consistent among all categories of attributes. Some categories were perceived differently at the different levels of management. The organizational elements were increasingly perceived as strengths the higher the level of the respondent. Marketing and financial attributes were perceived more positively by lower levels of management. Personnel and technical attributes also had slight tendencies toward more positive ratings by lower levels of management. Table 8-9 shows these results.

It appears that the manager's organizational level influences both his choice of which attributes to examine and his perception of them as either strengths or weaknesses. This effect is quite consistent across company boundaries, confirming the influence of the changing organizational perspective upon what is at least theoretically an objective exercise.

TABLE 8-9.
PERCENTAGE OF RESPONSES IDENTIFYING CATEGORY AS A STRENGTH AT EACH ORGANIZATIONAL LEVEL

	Organizational Level				
	One	Two	Three	Four	Overall
Organizational	85.7%	38.4%	83.3%	28.6%	42.9%
Personnel	66.7	58.8	27.3	50.0	51.2
Marketing	66.7	57.1	86.7	66.7	70.6
Technical	50.0	55.5	38.4	44.4	47.6
Financial	14.3	66.7	100.0	-	46.7

Strengths Were Judged Differently than Weaknesses

- Historical — Historical Experience of the Company; Intracompany Comparisons; Budgets
- Competitive — Direct Competition; Indirect Competition; Other Companies
- Normative — Consultants' Opinions; Management's Understanding of Management Literature; Rules of Thumb; Opinion

The impact of the use of differing criteria is striking. Strengths are judged by different criteria than weaknesses. As shown in Table 8-10, 90 percent of historical criteria are used to identify a strength while only 21 percent of normative criteria are used to identify a strength.

TABLE 8-10.
THE ASSOCIATION OF SPECIFIC CRITERIA WITH IDENTIFICATION OF STRENGTHS AND WEAKNESSES

	Strengths	Weaknesses
Historical	90%	10%
Competitive	67	33
Normative	21	79

The nature of the criteria determines whether they will

be used for judging strengths or weaknesses. The utilization of the historical criteria for judging strengths occurs because managers are constantly searching for improvements in problem areas which they have previously identified. The base from which these improvements are made then becomes the standard by which the current attributes of the organization are judged. The converse is true with respect to weaknesses. The organization's current position is only a step on the way to where the managers wish it were. The gap is then measured between the current position and the goal which reflects a normative judgment of what ought to be. This relationship is depicted in Figure 8-3.

FIGURE 8-3.

CRITERIA USED TO JUDGE AN ATTRIBUTE

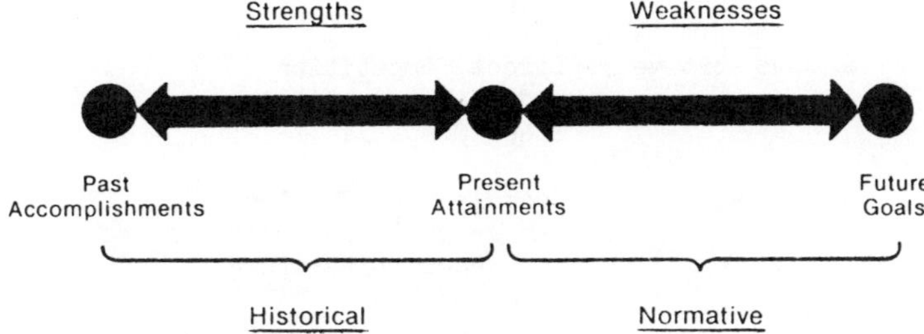

The same differentiation carries over to the relationship between the criteria employed and the attribute examined. It is evident that managers have developed models against which they test the strengths or weaknesses of their organization. These models reflect both the historical position and a normative sense of the possible.

This differentiation was especially critical for organizational questions. Every individual attribute within the organizational category was judged at least 50 percent of the time according to normative standards. The almost total absence of competitive judgment is noticeable. It seems apparent that the managers were not comfortable in comparing their companies' organizational attributes with other companies' characteristics. They contented themselves with comparisons to "what was in the past" or "what should be." The specific use of the judgmental criteria for the individual organizational attributes is shown in Table 8-11.

TABLE 8-11.
THE RELATIONSHIP BETWEEN SPECIFIC ORGANIZATIONAL ATTRIBUTES AND THE CRITERIA EMPLOYED

	Historical	Competitive	Normative
Organizational Form	27.3%	9.1%	63.6%
Top Management	50.0	-	50.0
Standard Procedures	25.0	-	75.0
Control System	9.1	-	90.9
Planning System	-	-	100.0
Overall	23.8%	2.4%	73.8%

(Row Percentages Sum to 100%)

CONCLUSIONS OF THE STUDY

The research study which this article presents was exploratory in the broadest sense of the word. The aim of the study was to provide insights and to develop understanding of a complex measurement process. No effort was made to test scientifically formulated propositions. Several generalizations emerge from the study.

- Managers tend to treat strengths differently from weaknesses.

- The underlying steps in the process of defining strengths and weaknesses are similar in all the companies studied. The particular factors which are examined and the criteria for judgment vary according to the operational requirements of the business and its history.

- The manager's position and responsibility in the organization are crucial influences on the way in which he carries out the process of defining strengths and weaknesses.

- There is no single type of measurement or criterion relevant to the measurement of all attributes as strengths and weaknesses.

The results show that traditional notions about strengths and weaknesses are in need of further examination. The factors studied reflect upon the difficulty of establishing meaningful procedures for the transmission and evaluation of lower-level managers' analysis of strengths and weaknesses. The "adding of apples to oranges" syndrome is all too prevalent.

In addition to the procedural difficulties which emerged in the study of the process, several situational factors contriubted to difficulties encountered by managers in implementing a program for defining corporate strengths and weaknesses. The factors resulted from general causes: the need for situational analysis, the need for self-protection, the desire to preserve the status quo, and the problems of definition and computational capacity. Each of these problems was observed not from statistical data but from analysis of anecdotal evidence.

The most common single complaint of managers who did not feel that the definition of strengths and weaknesses was meaningful was that they had to be defined in the context of a problem. One manager stated his opinion succinctly.

> I think that our people attempt to make honest appraisals of the organization's capability. We have some people who think that they can move fast and run any business and others who are committed to staying with the present course. Each honestly believes that he has made a realistic appraisal of the company's capabilities.
>
> As I see it, the only real value in making an appraisal of the organization's capabilities comes in the light of a specific deal--the rest of the time it is just an academic exercise. We have to ask ourselves if we have the marbles to put on the table when a deal is offered.

Although convinced of the need for evaluation and action this manager did not believe in the efficacy of a priori definitions which were not related to a specific situation.

SUGGESTIONS FOR MANAGERS

The process of defining strengths and weaknesses should ideally require the manager to test his assumptions and to analyze the status quo in relationship to the requirements for future success given the competition and the changing environment. The analysis performed by managers is rarely so dispassionate. There is a great tendency toward inertia.

On other occasions, managers are faced with the necessity of recommending changes which include abolition of organizational subunits. There is tremendous pressure to identify the problem with personalities or environmental conditions rather than in a fashion which would prejudice the existence of a whole organizational subunit. Often the definition of the problem prescribes the solution. Managers are aware of this connection and shy away from making definitions which contribute to inevitable change.

Managers cannot and do not explore every existing or potential attribute in order to arrive at new evaluations of the corporation's strengths and weaknesses. They must make choices and decide when they are sufficiently certain. They can then examine areas about which there is less certainty or for which the payoff of an accurate assessment is larger.

The results of the study lead to suggestions for improvement of the process of defining strengths and weaknesses. The manager should:

- Recognize that the process of defining strengths and weaknesses is primarily an aid to the individual manager in the accomplishment of his task.
- Develop lists of critical areas for examination which are tailored to the responsibility and authority of each individual manager.
- Make the measures and the criteria to be used in evaluation of strengths and weaknesses explicit so that managers can make their evaluations against a common framework.
- Recognize the important strategic role of defining attributes as opposed to efficiency of effectiveness.
- Understand the difference in the use of identified strengths and identified weaknesses.

Overall, the assessment of strengths and weaknesses is an important element of strategic planning. The actual items being evaluated are not specific occurrences; rather they are directions, strategies, overall policy commitments, and past practices. The conscious process of defining the strengths and weaknesses of a firm provides a key link in a feedback loop. It allows managers to learn from the success or failure of the policies which they initiate. According to Wiener:

> ...feedback is a method of controlling a system by reinserting into it the results of its past performance....If... the information which proceeds backward from the performance is able to change the general method and pattern of per-

FIGURE 8-4.

FEEDBACK LEARNING MODEL OF DEFINING STRENGTHS AND WEAKNESSES

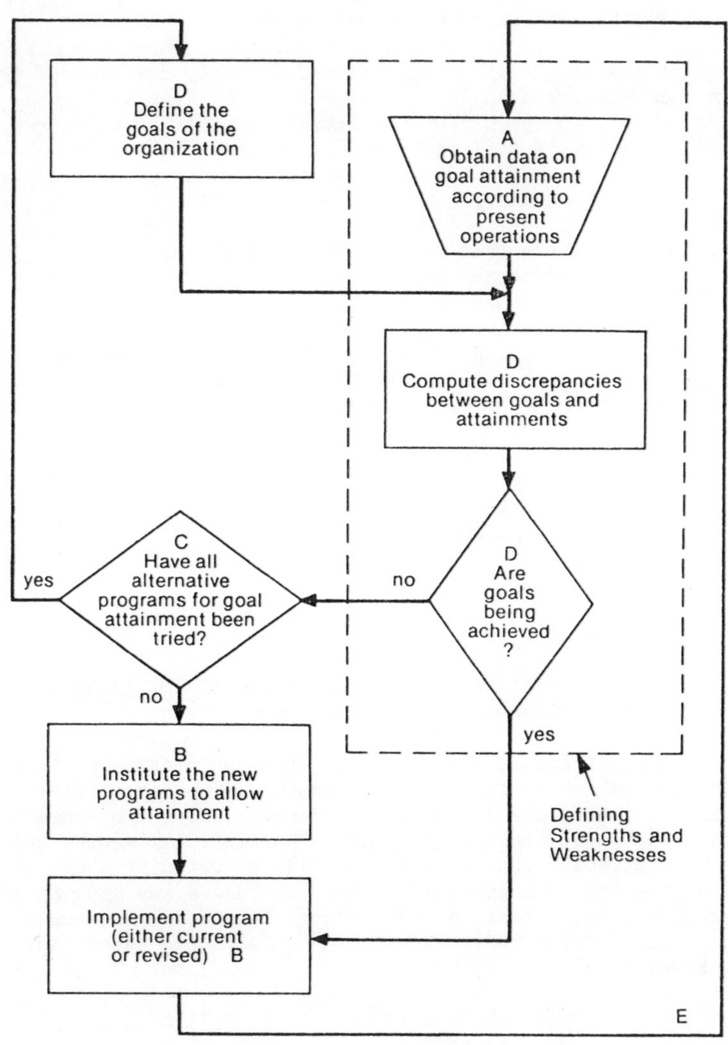

> formance, we have a process which may well be called learning.[4]

Figure 8-4 illustrates a strategic planning system which emphasizes the feedback learning aspects of defining strengths and weaknesses. The features of the model include: an input channel (A), output devices (B), a memory device (C), selection rules (D), and a channel for recycling (E) so that the system can receive inputs about its outputs. The comparison of attainments with goals using normative, competitive, or historical judgment criteria forms the central focus of the feedback loop.[5]

This system should be contrasted with the traditional strategic planning process shown earlier in Figure 8-1. In that system the definition of strengths and weaknesses was not part of a closed loop. It was an input, a hurdle goal which each new opportunity had to clear. Once past this initial barrier, the planning process left the definition of corporate strengths and weaknesses alone until a new opportunity was presented.

The research for this article shows that organizational acceptance of the necessity of a process of defining strengths and weaknesses depends on whether the information gathered can be integrated meaningfully into the manager's individual strategic planning efforts. Definitions of strengths and weaknesses generally applicable for whole organizations were not found. However, there appear to be definitions which can aid the individual manager in doing his own job. The use of a formal assessment program developed from the budgeting process seems unlikely to succeed because the information gathered at one organizational level is not directly additive with information from other levels. A program which carefully defines the relevant attributes to be examined and which imposes rigorous and consistent criteria may provide important assistance in the strategic planning process.

FOOTNOTES

[1]P. Selznick. *Leadership in Administration.* New York: Harper & Row, 1957, p. 143.

[2]E. P. Learned, C. R. Christensen, K. R. Andrews, and W. D. Guth. *Business Policy: Text and Cases.* Homewood, Ill.: Richard D. Irwin, 1965, p. 21.

[3]H. I. Ansoff, *Corporate Strategy,* New York: McGraw-Hill, 1956, p. 92. R. J. Cordiner, *New Frontiers for Professional Managers,* New York: McGraw-Hill, 1956, pp. 95-98.

P. Drucker, *Managing for Results*, New York: Harper & Row, 1964, p. 313, *et. seq.* R. A. Golde, "Practical Planning for Small Businesses," *Harvard Business Review*, September - October, 1964, p. 147. T. Leavitt, *Innovations in Marketing*, New York: McGraw-Hill, 1965, p. 176. H. A. Simon, D. W. Smithburg, and V. A. Thompson, *Public Administration*, New York: Knopf, 1950, p. 24.

[4]N. Wiener, *The Human Use of Human Beings: Cybernetics and Society*, Garden City, N. Y.: Doubleday & Company, 1954, p. 58.

[5]For further discussion about the requirements of a learning system see H. Leavitt, *Managerial Psychology*, Chicago: University of Chicago Press, 1964, p. 77, *et. seq.*

STUDENT REVIEW QUESTIONS

1. Explain the research methodology employed by Stevenson.
2. What factors influenced the managers in the study in defining strengths and weaknesses? Which were the significant factors?
3. Explain the statement by Stevenson that "managers utilize differing criteria in defining corporate strengths and weaknesses."
4. How does Stevenson say the assessment of strengths and weaknesses should be used in strategic planning?

9

Should You Take Business Forecasting Seriously ?*

ROBERT C. TURNER

"FORECASTING IS BUNK, and all forecasters are charlatans!" So argue some well-informed people, including some first-rate economists. Nevertheless, business decision makers, especially in large firms, often have enough confidence in business forecasts to rely heavily on them in their own planning. Further, economic forecasts have become an integral part of government policymaking, as a quick persual of budget documents, the President's economic reports, papers of the Congressional Budget Office, and other documents will reveal. After nearly four decades of forecasting, teaching and writing about forecasting, and studying other people's forecasts, I have come to some conclusions on this issue that may be helpful to business managers.

Business forecasting is probably as old as the study of economics itself, but its technical quality and apparently its respectability have grown over time--in spite of a forecasting disaster in 1973-1974. Prior to the development of the national income accounts in the late 1930s, forecasting was severely limited by lack of data, although the work of Wesley C. Mitchell and later of Arthur F. Burns on measuring business cycles and identifying leading economic time series provided a useful tool. It is perhaps significant that the *1953 Economic Report of the President,* prepared by the Council of Economic Advisers, was the first such report to make an overt forecast. Even that forecast, however, was not a "cold turkey" forecast, complete with a GNP model, but rather a diagnosis of deficiencies in aggregate demand that were likely to develop later in the year and in 1954. It concluded that "this analysis might seem to strike a note of pessimism. Yet the Council believes that, while real problems are visible, the high objective of uninterrupted economic stability and growth is attainable if proper and adequate adjustments in private and public policies are made."[1]

The 1953 report was followed by assiduous avoidance of overt forecasts by the Council of Economic Advisers during the Eisenhower administration. Not until the 1960s did the Council again go openly into the forecasting business. Perhaps it is significant that in contrast to the 1953-1961 years, which produced three recessions, the Kennedy-Johnson years covered a period when it was possible for the Council to forecast, correctly as it turned out, only rising business activity. It is politically difficult for a government agency, especially an authoritative one like the Council, to predict an impending downturn.

Throughout this period, a growing number of nongovernment persons went into the forecasting business, and in the late 1960s and early 1970s, an explosion of forecasting services occurred. These organizations--universities, spin-offs from universities, consulting firms, brokerage houses, large commercial banks, and others--typically employed elaborate econometric models supported by high-capacity computers. Today, a number of such forecasting services are available, plus a variety of other forecasting services of a less econometric sort. The latter include several solo practitioners who can convince enough people that they have a unique capacity for prescience to make a comfortable living in the forecasting business. Most large businesses now subscribe to one or more forecasting services, usually for a substantial fee, and rely heavily on them for their own in-house forecasts. A limited number of these forecasts are made available to the financial press so that nonsubscribers may sense the tenor of professional forecasts and be guided by them.

EXOGENOUS VERSUS ENDOGENOUS

Economic activity is determined by two broad categories of influences. One is autonomous or exogenous events--forces external to the economy that cause changes in economic variables. The economist *qua* economist has no special competence for forecasting such events. Any informed person can normally predict, within a tolerable margin of error, short-run events or changes in some exogenous factors, such as population change, continuity of our political institutions, and broad technological trends. But many important exogenous events are quite unpredictable, especially as to their timing--for example, the oil embargo and the ensuing massive price increase, crop failures, and abnormal weather. Occasionally even some of the normally predictable happenings spring surprises.

The other category of influences is endogenous events--the interactions of economic variables themselves. This type of influence is within the province and presumably the competence of the economic forecaster. Examples are consumer responses to a change in disposable income, investor responses to changing interest rates, and international trade responses to changing relative price levels. Computerized models are a valuable tool for tracing out these interactions as they have manifested themselves in the past. Even here, however, economists simply do not have enough knowledge of how this highly diverse and complex economy really functions, and data are not available to quantify accurately some of the important parameters in their theories (for example, inflation anticipations). Moreover, economic relationships and responses are forever changing, so that past performance is not always an accurate guide to future behavior. Further, the participants in the economic process are human beings; at times they may react in quite atypical, even apparently irrational, ways--collectively as well as individually. For example, sometimes consumers respond to an increase in the inflation rate by accelerating their buying in order to get the jump on higher prices. At other times they balk at the higher prices and refuse to buy, especially if they view the accelerated inflation rate as an advance signal of an increased likelihood of unemployment or a substantial erosion of their ability to achieve future real savings goals.

Despite the difficulty of predicting completely exogenous events and the limited reliability of past endogenous relationships, the forecaster must face up to the problem and produce the best possible forecast. There are two means of dodging at least a part of the problem. One is to assume away major exogenous changes by postulating that so-and-so will (or will not) happen. In this event, the forecast is only as valid as the assumption or set of assumptions underlying it. If the assumptions later prove to be wrong, then "all bets are off." The other is to produce two, three, or four forecasts, based on as many sets of assumptions. The user of the forecast can use his own judgment as to which set of assumptions he thinks is most probable. This device is in a sense a cop-out, but it is useful for certain purposes. First, if the alternative sets of assumptions seem to span the range of possible exogenous events, the alternative forecasts provide some guidance as to the upper and lower limits of economic activity. This information, however limited, is often in itself of value. Second, if the exogenous events are subject to control (for example, the enactment of a tax cut), the alternative forecasts provide guidance as to the need for and probable effects of the exogenous event.

The environment for economic forecasting is far less favorable than it was a decade or two ago because exogenous events are playing a far more influential role than they formerly did. To be sure, some exogenous events--wars, the weather, crop failures--are nothing new. But other types of exogenous events have assumed increasing importance for many reasons, of which three obviously are major.

GOVERNMENT INTERVENTION

Government is playing a far more interventionist role than it once did. Large increases in government expenditures and taxes, plus the use of fiscal policy for economic purposes, have introduced a new exogenous element in forecasting. The Federal Reserve, which in the early years of the system operated under the "real bills" doctrine and therefore did not, in the main, play an activist role, has become a major factor in the economy. Other governmental interventionist actions, such as pollution controls, health and safety controls, energy legislation, interference in the pricing process, welfare, and employment programs, have added different types of exogenous influences. The business forecaster has to be a prescient political scientist before he can begin his forecast.

INTERNATIONALIZATION OF ECONOMIC FORCES

The days when the U. S. economy was relatively isolated from other economies of the world are gone. The economic world is now highly interdependent, and events abroad can have major influences on economic activity at home. The oil embargo is a dramatic example but by no means the only one. Economic policies in Japan, Germany, and other industrialized nations have an impact on business activity in the United States. Even some of the minor countries can jolt economic activity in the United States; nationalization of production on control of export prices of raw materials (bauxite in Jamaica, for example) must be factored into the forecast. Moreover, it is becoming increasingly obvious that inflation is quickly transmitted from one country to another--including the United States. Hence, the rate of world inflation must also be factored into the forecast.

CHANGING STRUCTURE OF THE ECONOMY

Any forecasting technique is based on certain functional relationships that are assumed to be reasonably stable--an assumption that is valid only if the structure of the economy does not undergo substantial change. But the structure of the economy *has* changed substantially over the past two or three decades. For structural reasons, price competition, especially at the manufacturing level, is not nearly as pervasive as it once was. Wage rates, which once tended to decline with a declining demand for labor (especially in the 1930s), are now quite inflexible on the downside. According to prevailing theory at least, consumption was almost exclusively a function of disposable income. The aggregate supply function--the line of relationship between wage rates (or prices) and real output at successively higher levels of aggregate demand--could once be conceived as an essentially horizontal line. That line would rise only in response to rising marginal costs, up to the point of capacity real output, whereupon it would angle sharply upward. In other words, an increase in aggregate demand would lead primarily to an increase in real output, and only to a minor degree in prices, up to the point where the economy was operating at capacity. This assumed functional relationship was probably reasonably accurate a few decades ago. But the structure of the economy today is such that inflationary consequences occur long before the capacity barrier is reached. In general, it was once reasonably safe to assume that the endogenous relationships within the economy would work out, as logic suggested they should, in a highly competitive, flexible, and responsive economy.

Whether this assumption was ever fully valid is debatable, but today it is clearly of limited validity. The structural rigidities introduced into the economy by concentrations of economic power in both business and labor--with and without government support--are too numerous and too well known to explain here. Their net effect, however, is that many economic responses that once were largely endogenous in character have become largely exogenous. Wage rates are often changed, for example, not because of changes in the demand for labor but because of union power. And union wage rates set a precedent for nonunion wage rates. Investment decisions are based not only on the cost of capital but also on the need to retain the desired share of the market, anticipation of inflation, and expected government policies. Moreover, major exogenous events, if they are perceived to be long-lasting, can themselves alter functional relationships. The quadrupling in the price of oil, for example, has altered the production function (the relationship between the firm's alternative inputs and its output) in numerous industries. It certainly affected consumer spending-saving responses in 1974 and 1975. As exogenous shocks become more frequent, endogenous relationships become less dependable.

A COUNTERBALANCING INFLUENCE?

Another change that serves to make the forecaster's job

easier is the great improvement in the quantity and quality of data needed for forecasting.[2] Data improvements have been accompanied by major advances in the theoretical underpinnings of economic model building--although there is far from unanimous opinion as to which body of theory is "the truth." Further, the fact that government is committed in the Employment Act of 1946 to maintaining "maximum production, employment, and purchasing power" may make government policy more predictable--in some situations. However, other policy considerations often take precedence over economic stability--unintentionally, perhaps, but effectively nonetheless. Examples are environmental programs, programs to improve social equity, balance of payments considerations, and national defense. And pure politics sometimes interferes with rational economic policymaking.

The growing importance of exogenous events seems to outweigh the favorable changes just discussed. Forecasting is treacherous business because the exogenous events are so numerous and so unpredictable. The forecaster is on relatively safe ground if he limits his horizon to a span of time short enough that no major exogenous event is likely to come along--hence the old saying, "If you must forecast, forecast often." I suspect that the reliability of a forecast varies inversely with the square of the length of time from the date of the forecast to the period being forecasted.

CHANGING RELATIONSHIPS

A problem in forecasting already referred to briefly is the fact that even in the absence of exogenous events, endogenous relationships do not stay put. This is a problem for all forecasters, judgmental or econometric, but it is especially troublesome for large econometric models.

THE ROLE OF ECONOMETRIC MODELS

The essence of such models is the identification of reasonably consistent economic relationships over a past period of time. Quantification (reduction to equations) of these relationships is the principal advantage of econometric models. To the extent that the equations remain valid, the computerized model can solve mathematical problems beyond the capabilities of the human brain. But such quantification is also the biggest liability of econometric models. Development of an econometric model requires large expenditures of time and money. Once a model is programmed into the computer, it is a cumbersome job to change it. The retroactive revision by the Department of Commerce of some important time series, for example, may force recomputation of dozens of equations and indeed of the entire model. Or simply realization that some previously quantified relationship does not seem to be behaving properly may require a reexamination of the entire model. A governor of the Federal Reserve Board has pointed out the way in which the board's model for forecasting growth in the money supply, which had worked moderately well prior to 1974, produced numbers that were "far wide of the mark" in subsequent years.[3]

It is probably correct to say that every model is out of date the day that it is put into the computer. The most recent (and therefore most relevant) data on which it was based were, at best, one to three months old and were probably preliminary data, subject to later revision. And rarely does an examination of past relationships fully explain the variance in components of the model. Further, no model, however complex, can encompass the full panoply of economic relationships. I know of no model that could have assessed the impact of a quadrupling in the price of oil.

For these reasons, most econometric model builders do not depend entirely on the model--even given the assumptions as to exogenous events. They adjust the figures to reflect intuitive judgment as to what makes sense. Or they modify the model's output to incorporate, in a judgmental way, some new development that is not covered by the equations.

THE ROLE OF JUDGMENTAL MODELS

Purely judgmental forecasting methodologies usually use simple, noncomputerized models and lack the precision and coverage of the econometric models. Perhaps the simplest is a tabulation of the components of gross national expenditure by the usual categories. The forecaster pulls together all the information he can about each of the components, uses his good judgment to evaluate this information, plugs in numbers, and then adds them up. Numerous revisions may be necessary until the model seems to be internally consistent. A preferable if somewhat more difficult methodology also forecasts judgmentally the income side of the accounts, and then tests the two sides against each other for consistency. Adjustments are made to remove inconsistencies and to yield a zero or negligible statistical discrepancy.

Judgmental models do offer one advantage. It is relatively easy for the forecaster to incorporate into his model recent unexpected exogenous events or recent changes in endogenous relationships that he discerns, perhaps intuitively. Moreover, coming from an experienced forecaster, a judgmental sensing of endogenous relationships is sometimes more reliable than an equation. For example, what will the spending-versus-saving mood of consumers be during the forecast period? In other words, what will the saving rate be? An equation based on past performance can tell us what it "ought" to be, but an experienced and sensitive forecaster may be able to outguess the equation. True, as just noted, econometric model builders do introduce judgmental elements into their forecasts, but when they do they cease to be "pure" econometric forecasters. They compromise the presumed objectivity of the econometric model.

THE ROLE OF LEADING INDICATORS

A third forecasting technique is the use of leading indicators, published monthly by the Department of Commerce. The leading indicators are economic time series that in the past have moved fairly consistently in advance of general business activity, measured by the reference cycle as originally developed by the National Bureau of Economic Research. The leading indicators offer one practical advantage to the non-economist forecaster: They are empirically derived, and no underlying theory is required. However, they suffer from several disadvantages. They depend heavily on preliminary data for the previous few months. Retroactive revisions of the basic series a month or two later may, indeed often do, reverse the signals. Even after averaging the leading series, they exhibit many a wiggle, and it is not until some months after the event that one is able to differentiate between a mere wiggle and a real turn, by which time the direction of the economy may be obvious. The leads vary widely, from none at all to a year or more. It is not much help to be informed that, according to recent signals, a turn in business activity is probably *sometime* within the year or so. They sometimes give false signals. Paul Samuelson is reported to have said that stock prices (one of the leading indicators) have correctly forecasted "eight of the last five" recessions. And finally, they are focused on turning points; the magnitude of the ensuing decline (or upturn) can be inferred only by adding the information supplied by the empirically derived indicators to an analysis that is based on a theory of the functioning of the economy.

Although the leading indicators are not a substitute for comprehensive analysis, they are a useful adjunct to forecasting. They must be used with judgment. The forecaster must look behind each indicator to see why it behaved the way it did. Is the change a random one, the result of a temporary circumstance, or indicative of some fundamental development?

SOURCES OF ERROR

It should be clear that any method of forecasting is more of an art than a science. Michael K. Evans of Chase Econometrics was reported in the *Wall Street Journal* as having said that his forecasts are about 50 percent judgment and about 50 percent model. Even more important, the role of exogenous events is currently so heavy that even with the best of judgment errors are inescapable, especially if the forecast extends very far into the future.

But this is only part of the problem. Users of forecasts should keep in mind other sources of error when they look at a set of forecast figures:

Ideological Bias. Forecasters are, after all, human beings with value systems. However objective they try to be, they are inevitably influenced by their value systems. Some are chronic pessimists; the world is going to hell, they believe, perhaps because of increasing governmental intervention. Some are chronic optimists and look upon active stabilization efforts by government with favor. Some see in a tax cut a stimulus to the economy; others see a worsening of inflation with devastating economic effects.

Provincialism. Every forecaster is also influenced by the environment in which he lives and works. The New York forecaster is likely to be heavily influenced by developments in the financial markets; the forecaster in Detroit by developments in the automobile industry; in an agricultural area, by the farm situation. The forecaster employed by an industrial company is likely to look at the world through the windows of his own company and attribute to the economic world at large trends that are peculiar to his company.

Oversensitivity. Too many forecasters hover and quiver over the most recent statistics so intently that they cannot see the underlying trends. A one-month reversal of an important time series (for example, manufacturers' new orders) is interpreted as a harbinger of doom--or boom. The fact is that the U. S. economy is characterized by an enormous momentum. Rarely, unless some major exogenous event comes along, does the economy make abrupt reversals of direction. Indeed, any forecaster can make a good statistical record simply by extrapolating the direction of the economy in the past quarter into the next quarter; but he would have to limit his forecasts to one or two quarters into the future.

Insensitivity. Some forecasters forecast by sheer extrapolation and are unable to detect developing changes in underlying economic forces until long after the event. The most difficult job in forecasting is identifying an impending turn, partly because so often turns are caused by unpredictable exogenous events. But, at the least, a competent forecast identifies and quantifies endogenous developments that may cause a turn. If the forecast fails to examine and explain these potentialities, it is suspect.

Imputation of Rhythm. There is no such thing as a business "cycle," if by cycle we mean something that is inevitably rhythmical in character. The fact that business activity has been advancing for X consecutive months, which is substantially longer than the average recovery period in the past, tells us nothing about the future. Obviously, every advance will eventually come to an end. But the U. S. economy is evolving and changing. Forecasting cannot be done by the calendar.

There are, to be sure, successive stages in a recovery period. The typical sequence is usually an increase in consumer buying, including housing, then a step-up in inventory accumulation, with a rise in capital formation bringing up the rear. But even this sequence is not dependable. There is no escaping a diagnosis of the forces at work in the economy to determine, as best one can, how soon the rise (or decline) in business activity will be reversed.

Simplism. Though their number has decreased in recent years, a few forecasters still claim to be able to divine the economic future by following a single variable or relationship. Some simplistic examples include sun spots, the length of women's skirts, the demand for big versus little dogs, and astrology. Single indicators that command more attention in some circles are changes in the money supply, variations in unit labor costs, automobile production, and the shape of the securities yield curve, among others. No one of these elements could be the dominant determinant shaping the future. Our economy is too complex for that.

Intentional Bias. Forecasting can be slanted intentionally one way or the other for either of two purposes. One is to forecast better business conditions than one actually expects in the hope that the forecast will prove to be a self-fulfilling one. Authoritative forecasts *are* used by private decision makers, and an optimistic forecast may nudge them into taking actions that would raise the level of business activity. Or a decidedly negative forecast may be avoided because it could trigger a decline that would not otherwise have occurred. The Council of Economic Advisers faces a dilemma: Its public responsibility almost precludes it from making a decidedly negative forecast, and one has to read between the lines of the council's forecasts to discern the full import of their diagnoses.

At the one extreme, forecasters in either business or labor organizations who do not like current government (or private) policy may forecast dire consequences, in the hope that they will frighten policymakers into taking steps of which the forecasters approve. One can usually detect such forecasts by considering the source and the one-sided tenor of the forecast analysis.

The Self-Defeating Forecast. Some forecasts, not so much of economic activity in general as of specific economic sectors, may induce action that will make the forecast come untrue. For example, if the Department of Agriculture reports in the spring that corn plantings are below normal and forecasts that a short crop (and consequent higher prices) is in prospect, this may simply induce farmers to pour on more fertilizer and boost their yields. Or a forecast of developing excess capacity in some industry may induce companies in that industry to stretch out or postpone their capacity expansion programs. These "boomerang" effects are not common and are hard to detect, but they do occur.

Forecasts Relying Heavily on Government Policy. Finally, the forecast may see trouble ahead but concludes that a particular action by government will handle the problem. Uninterrupted expansion can therefore be anticipated. Our large economy is subject to a host of influences, domestic and foreign. Decision makers, large and small, do not always respond to government stimuli or constraints as they are supposted to. Government can exert a heavy influence, but its powers are limited--by lack of adequate knowledge of economic behavior, by the time-consuming character of the governmental process, by the simple fact that there are no governmental tools to solve some of the most important economic problems, and by pure politics. Further, it has been argued that government stabilization actions, to the extent that they are anticipated, are discounted well ahead of the action and thus have little or no effect when they actually occur. For example, a tax cut in 1978, which is widely anticipated, may have most of its effects in the early months of the year. To the extent that such anticipatory response is a reality, a forecast based on the premise that government will change the future course of the economy by taking action at a future date will prove to be correspondingly in error.

If there is one lesson we should have learned in the past decade, it is that the U. S. economy has a mind and a momentum of its own, and that about all that government can do is to change the course of the economy moderately and, we hope, either prevent or correct extremes of economic performance.

This recital of the problems and shortfalls of short-run forecasting may have led the reader to conclude that all forecasts are worthless and should be ignored. Such is not my intent. Careful analytical and objective forecasts by competent forecasters are worth attention. Their record, especially in the past two decades, has been quite respectable, except when an unpredictable exogenous event has shocked the economy, as in late 1973 and early 1974. Forecasts by competent economists are certainly far superior to sheer extrapolation, hunch, or intuitive judgments by persons inexperienced and unskilled in the forecasting art. Most of the time, the better forecasts provide, within a tolerable margin of error, an adequate basis for business planning.

My purpose, then, in writing this article was to alert readers to both the limits and potentialities of forecasting, and to assist them in recognizing a good forecast when they see one. Business forecasting is unavoidable. Every business decision involves a forecast, implicit or explicit, because every business decision pertains to the future. Although business decision makers should neither accept any forecast as infallible nor rely exclusively on it, they would be well advised to give forecasts done by competent and objective economists a significant weight in their own planning.

FOOTNOTES

[1]One member of the Council, John D. Clark, did not approve in principle the presenting of a forecast in the report and dissented specifically from the forecast of the other two members, of which the present writer was one. He therefore disassociated himself from the analysis and policy discussion of that portion of the report.

[2]Data are also becoming available more promptly, but this is a mixed blessing. The forecaster has more current information, which facilitates forecasting, but the frequent revisions of the most recent figures sometimes require a major revision of the forecast.

[3]J. Charles Partee, "The State of Economic Forecasting," *Business Horizons* (October, 1976), p. 26.

STUDENT REVIEW QUESTIONS

1. Explain the differences between Exogenous and Endogenous factors.
2. Discuss briefly the major exogenous events Turner believes are increasingly important.
3. What is a "judgmental model"? Are judgmental models of any use?
4. Explain briefly what is meant by the following sources of errors.
    a. Ideological bias
    b. Oversensitivity
    c. Simplism
    d. Intentional bias

10

Technological Forecasting in the Decision Process*

DANIEL D. ROMAN

INTRODUCTION

THE NEW TECHNOLOGY

COMPANIES IN THE United States are spending billions of dollars each year to research and develop new products. Technological expansion has vital economic, sociological and political implications.

The economic impact of technology is so great that some industries derive most of their current business from products which did not exist 20 years ago.[1] A study of 11 industries indicated that somewhere from 46 to 100 percent of anticipated short-term corporate growth could be sttributed to new products.[2] It is now commonplace for major companies to derive 50 percent or more of current sales from products developed and introduced in the past 10 years.[3]

In a dynamic technology there must be recognition of potential human and capital obsolescence. Productive utilization of new knowledge will affect the demand and supply of present skills and new occupations not yet identifiable will emerge. Additionally, it is reasonably safe to assume that technological pressures will encourage increased interdisciplinary communication.

It is difficult to isolate the economic, sociological and political consequences of technology. It is obvious that economic and sociological factors could not be disassociated from political factors. It is also difficult to do justice

---

*From *Academy of Management Journal*, June, 1970, pp. 127-138. Reprinted with permission.

to the full range of economic, sociological and political possibilities in a paper of this nature. However, recognition of the extent and direction of technological expansion can help provide the means to minimize disruption, lead to an orderly transition and assist in maximizing the positive aspects of technology.

The impact of technical developments such as lasers, jet aircraft, atomic energy and communication devices, to name a few, has been significant. On the horizon are such developments as new rapid transit systems, mechanical devices to replace human organs,[4] undersea farming and mining, economically useful desalinization of sea water, new synthetic materials for ultra-light construction, automatic language translators, and reliable weather forecasts. Other major technological breakthroughs are not so remote as to preclude planning for integration of these developments.[5]

As we move into a "post industrial society" phase, science and technology will be a compelling force for change.[6] In some environments managers must be alert and plan to compensate for change; in other situations a prime managerial function is to instigate technological change.[7]

In either case the manager must be aware of technological impact and be sensitive to the need for more precise planning for the future. Technological forecasting has been a response to this need.

TECHNOLOGICAL FORECASTING

TECHNOLOGICAL FORECASTING--A DISTINCTION

Technological forecasting, as distinct from general forecasting activity, has been described as "the probabilistic assessment, on a relatively high confidence level, of future technology transfer."[8] According to Jantsch, technology transfer is usually a complex process taking place at different technology transfer levels. These levels can be segregated into development and impact levels and are composed of vertical and horizontal technology transfer components. Vertical transfer of technology progresses through a discovery phase, a creative phase, a substantiate phase, a development phase and an engineering phase. The engineering phase leads to a functional, technological system that could involve a hardware product, a process, or an intellectual concept. Jantsch feels that the extension of the vertical transfer by substantial subsequent horizontal technology transfer represents technological innovation.[9]

Cetron essentially supports Jantsch's definition. He cautions that a technological forecast is not a picture of what the future will bring; it is a prediction, based on confidence, that certain technical developments can occur within a specified time period with a given level of resource allocation. According to Cetron, "the foundation underlying technological forecasting is the level that individual R & D events are susceptible to influence." The periods where these events occur, if they are possible, can be significantly affected by the diversion of resources. Another fundamental of technological forecasting is that many futures can be achieved and the route to these occurrences can be determined.[10]

EXPLORATORY AND NORMATIVE FORECASTING

It is important to recognize the two fundamental types of technological forecasts--exploratory and normative. The exploratory technological forecast starts from the existing base of knowledge and proceeds to the future on the assumption of logical technological progress. Exploratory technological forecasting is passive and primarily an analysis and reporting of anticipations. As a simple illustration, technological development in electronics can be cited. Starting with the post World War II period, transistors have evolved from an expensive and qualitatively unpredictable commodity to a modestly priced, reliable component. If exploratory forecasting were used in the 1940's to target in on this phase of technology, it would have been possible to predict increasing availability, lower price and more extensive use of transistors. The anticipations suggested would have been miniaturization of electronic systems and the potential for a vast number of new products resulting from application, such as portable radios, home appliances, etc.

It would seem that most industrial firms could effectively use exploratory forecasting. Reasonable identification of emerging technology and analysis of technological implications could provide clues for the firm as to competition, possible expansion of existing product lines, related product lines--which the firm should ease into, and new product areas where a foothold could provide a competitive edge. In short, a look into the future would enable better planning, more effective use of resources and considerable avoidance of human and capital obsolescence.

Normative forecasting represents a different approach; it is mission- or goal-oriented. As distinct from exploratory forecasting, normative forecasting is an active or action-directed process.

In the normative method, future objectives are identified exclusive of the fact that technological gaps may currently exist that might act as constraints to attainment of these technological objectives. Normative technological forecasting can provide incentive to technological progress by focusing on the problems to be surmounted and solved. Perhaps the supersonic transport (SST) can be used to demonstrate normative forecasting. At a given time the state of the art for aircraft technology can be determined. It is decided that a need will exist five years from the base period for an aircraft incorporating the SST specifications. On a logical technological progression using exploratory forecasting some technical advancements can be predicted. However, technical gaps appear which indicate that the SST will not be an evolutionary development by the time the need or market will require the product. There are many problems beyond the technical expertise of this author which must be surmounted but some examples could be the development of materials necessary to make flying at supersonic speeds economical, safe and technically feasible.[11] Also, ways must be found to cope with sonic booms so the SST can be used over land routes.

In normative forecasting situations, the analyst works backward from the planned mission operational date and determines the technical obstacles. Normative forecasting could act as a directional force to channel effort and resources. In the example used, these resources would be diverted to solving such problems as the sonic boom or developing new materials. Since resources are limited, normative forecasting could be used in deciding priorities and decisions could be made in conjunction with cost effectiveness studies to determine whether the mission requirements are as critical as presented, are possible within the stipulated time and if the ultimate accomplishment of the mission is worth the resource expenditure.

Normative forecasting has been used primarily by the military, but industrial organizations could possibly use it. With the normative approach, the firm could examine the market potential, explore the technical feasibility, look at its expertise in the area, estimate the cost to accomplish product development and then decide whether the project should be undertaken.

Jantsch contends that presently the most difficult technological forecasting problem is establishing the correct time-frame in normative forecasting. In exploratory forecasting difficulty exists in conceiving an end-effect in the future due to the time covered, but it is relatively simple to prognosticate compared to the normative forecast difficulties. In the normative method the forecast is predicated on objectives, requirements, and sociological factors; the problem is the assumption that present requirements or anticipations are representative of the future.[12]

METHODOLOGIES OF TECHNOLOGICAL FORECASTING

Technological forecasting methods range from naive intuitive approaches to ultra sophisticated procedures.[13] Most of the methods are academic with limited practical adoption.

Essentially, the methods can be refined to intuitive, extrapolative and correlative, and logical sequence or network type techniques.

Intuitive forecasting, the most common method employed, can be done individually by genius forecasting or by consensus. Generally this method represents an "educated guess" approach. It can vary from a very naive approach in a localized situation to a broad sampling and consensus of authoritative opinion. Delphi, the best known method under this classification, was developed by Olaf Helmer of the Rand Corporation.

A plethora of methods exist which are essentially variations of PERT. Relevance trees, graphic models, Planning-Programming-Budgeting Systems (PPBS), Mission networks, Decision Trees and Systems Analysis all use network construction to derive technological forecasts.

If numbers are any criteria it would seem that after some variation of Delphi, the network technique is the most popular avenue to technological forecasting. Networks help in identifying and establishing a logical pattern from an existing point to an anticipated goal. An intuitive method, regardless of individual technological perception, might ignore or minimize a significant obstacle to technological attainment. On the other hand, the network system is vulnerable in that all critical events might not be recognized, parallel technology might be ignored or unknown, information may be inaccurate, fragmentary, or misinterpreted (leading to wrong conclusions) and, finally, optimism or pessimism might permeate the forecast.

After examining the multitude of techniques available for technological forecasting, the author is of the opinion that while some methods appear quite scientific on the surface, minute examination almost invariably shows reliance on non-quantifiable and subjective factors before reaching conclusions. Additionally, the rationale of seemingly more sophisticated methods is often difficult to follow and the cost compared to ultimate value of the forecast could also be questioned, all of which might explain the popularity of the Delphi method or its derivatives.

TECHNOLOGICAL FORECASTING AS A MANAGEMENT TOOL

SOME GENERAL OBSERVATIONS

Technological forecasting as an organized management concept is relatively new. The model depicted in Figure 10-1 shows how technological forecasting might be integrated into the management process. Objectives which represent the initial *raison d'etre* generally become fluid as the organization moves through its operational life cycle. The degree

FIGURE 10-1.

OBJECTIVES (raison d'etre) → output

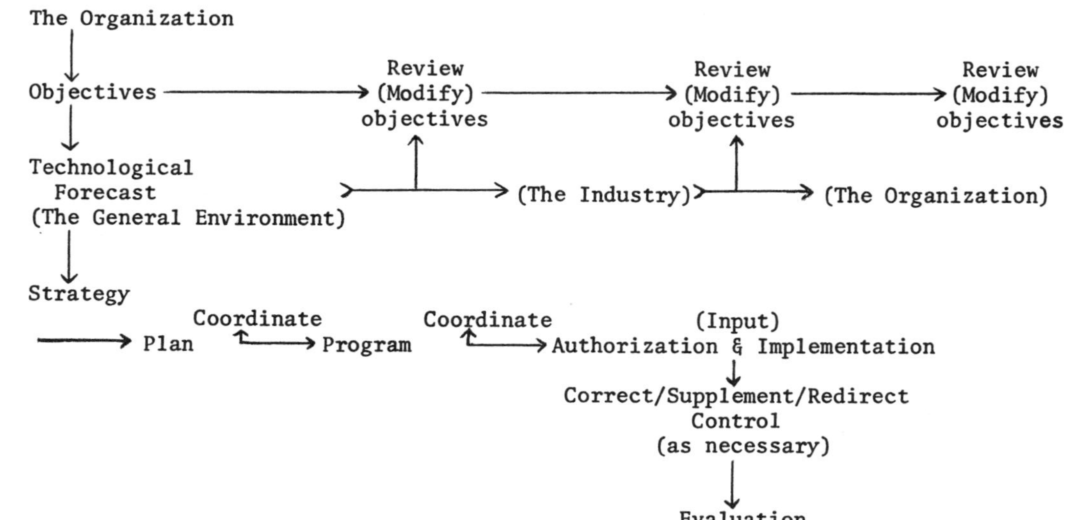

of modification of objectives and the extent of operational flexibility can be dictated by external and internal factors.

In the model, technological forecasting is shown as a prelude to operational activity. Technological forecasting, depending on the nature of the operation, can encompass the universe or it can be used to focus on a relatively small segment of the universe. It can be used by management in probing the general environment and then be refined to help in determining the implications for the industry and the specific organization. As each technological phase is explored, objectives should be reviewed and modified for compatibility with potential accomplishment. From this, procedure strategy can be derived to guide planning, programming, authorization, implementation, control and evaluation.

ADVANTAGES AND APPLICATION

The incorporation of technological forecasting into the process of management is an extension of existing methodology. In the past it would appear that management has often intuitively drifted in this direction. Evidence can be advanced to support this contention from the information in Table 10-1 which shows a condensation of the time gap from innovation to application.

TABLE 10-1.

Innovation	Year of Discovery	Year of Application
Electric motor	1821	1886
Vacuum tube	1882	1915
Radio broadcasting	1887	1922
X-ray tubes	1895	1913
Nuclear reactor	1932	1942
Radar	1935	1940
Atomic bomb	1938	1945
Transistor	1948	1951
Solar battery	1953	1955
Stereospecific rubbers & plastics	1955	1958

SOURCE: Seymour L. Wolfbein, "The Pace of Technological Change and the Factors Affecting It," *Manpower Implications of Automation*, Papers presented by U. S. Department of Labor at the O.E.C.D. North American Regional Conference on Manpower Implications of Automation (Washington, D. C.: December 8-10, 1964), p. 19.

To be useful, technological forecasting does not have to

be precise. If an innovation can be identified, and if the innovation can be translated into constructive action within a reasonable and discernible time frame, it can substantially contribute to the decision-making process.

Often, long-term commitments are undertaken on the basis of short-term technology. In many cases inability to anticipate technology leads to built-in obsolescence. Attendant to obsolescence are high modification costs to update facilities and operations, difficulty in selling change to entrenched interests and failure to exploit market potential.

An illustration of potential benefit from technological forecasting would be in product development. The technological forecasters have not yet developed the precise refinement of being able to localize specific innovations within a technological continuum. However, most technologies follow an "S" shaped curve and evaluation of existing and anticipated status of the technology can be meaningful in the decision to undergo or forego investment in product development. The technical scope, cost and time to develop a new product may be attractive or unattractive after technological forecasting information is assembled.

Generally, technological forecasting can assist management in several ways. It can represent an organized approach to a selective search for information. It can provoke thought by expanding horizons. It can help provide perspective and facilitate interdisciplinary communication. It can encourage operational sensitivity. It can assist management in determining the magnitude of anticipated change and provide a basis for estimating costs and requirements for people, facilities, equipment, etc. It can aid in giving direction to product development and market penetration. It can assist in recognizing competition and other possible restraints such as natural resources or technological limitations. It can be used to help determine sociological and economic trends.

LIMITATIONS

Several limitations to technological forecasting should be apparent to the discerning reader. The fact that limitations exist in technological forecasting just as there are limitations in other techniques should not discourage management; awareness should lead to more critical and productive application.

Information may be the greatest limitation to contributive technological forecasting. The information problem is extensive. For instance: What information is needed? How much information is required? Is the information accurate? Have related and unrelated disciplines been explored for possible information transfer or possible technological fallout?

Information interpretation is a vital ingredient in technological forecasting. No mechanical process presently exists which will evaluate the information in terms of available technical solutions, cost and value, product applicability and market potential. Human judgment is a factor in interpreting information and interpretation can be colored by optimism or pessimism and courage or conservatism. Information analysis can also differ due to the competence of the analyst and his functional orientation. Augmenting the difficulties cited is the fact that often pertinent information may not be available due to security restrictions and trade secrets. The unavailability of essential information may negate the entire process by establishing the technological forecast on incomplete or erroneous premises.

Forecasting is far from an exact science, so much so that standard methods and procedures have not been generally established. Although the literature abounds with methodology, in practice, it appears that variations of the Delphi technique and network construction are most commonly used. More exact and understandable techniques must be developed which are practical and provide management with reasonable confidence in their accuracy. However, a standard method may not be feasible since each organization based on its size and mission must develop forecasting techniques to suit its own operational environment.

Another limitation is that unanticipated discovery can lead to demand for a family of products which were previously inconceivable. Good examples are the transistor and the laser. A major discovery can instigate derived demand for related and supporting products and technology and give rise to satellite industries.[14]

Quinn points out that the interaction of many technological breakthroughs could lead to unforeseen prospects which would have a negating effect on all forecasts. He says,

> Similarly, one cannot at present anticipate specifically how biological studies of cellular and molecular coding will interact with extremely high-polymer investigations which are beginning to produce synthetic molecules with many of the characteristics of living organisms. In such advanced areas one can only recognize that there is a strong probability of potential interactions which will increase the importance of both fields, and therefore do more extensive research or monitor such activities more closely.[15]

ORGANIZING FOR TECHNOLOGICAL FORECASTING

Many functions survive in organizations because of defensive management attitudes. Most managements desire a progressive image and as a consequence may install publicized new techniques without really embracing the concept. Utilization failures can often be attributed to management's unwillingness to get involved with things about which they are not familiar, and subsequently have misgivings about. Contributing to this attitude are the practitioners who lose themselves in technique and take little or no pains to translate their work into understandable terms and useful concepts which management would be willing to implement. This represents a very real threat to expanded management acceptance of technological forecasting.

A review of the literature leaves the impression of enamorment with technique. This can be disastrous if substance is sacrificed for method.

SOME ORGANIZATIONAL CONSIDERATIONS

There are several factors management must consider before commiting itself to technological forecasting. It must look at the type of operation in which it is involved. Is the organization in a technologically sensitive environment? Is the organization a leader or follower in its operational environment? Are operations large and diverse enough to justify commitment to a technological forecasting activity? How extensive a commitment should be made in terms of people, facilities and budget? Would management want sporadic technological forecasts on an informal basis or would there be formal reviews at set intevals? The answer to the last question could dictate the extent of commitment management is willing to make and the type of people it will have to train or recruit. In line with the aforementioned, management will have to select people with compatible skills to achieve technological forecasting objectives. Does management want a group of specialists in a range of technical areas? Does management want a group composed of multiviewed individuals with broad perspective and minimal functional allegiance? Or is a combination of generalists and specialists more desirable? The range of possibilities is not exhausted because management can use in-house functional specialists in concert with management types to act as a technological forecasting advisory board. Finally, management may not want any internal commitment and may prefer to use outside specialists or consulting organizations to bring in fresh views to reconcile against internal prognostications.

ORGANIZATIONAL LOCATION

Technological forecasting can be a function or an activity within a function. Several organizational affiliations appear logical such as placement in long-range planning, marketing, materials management or in the research and development group. Technological forecasting can also be elevated to functional status with independent identity.

There are no clear cut answers or universal solutions to organizational location of technological forecasting. Strong arguments can be advanced for affiliation with each of the functions indicated or for independent status. The ultimate answer of placement might be dictated by factors such as functional utilization of the technological forecast or management's orientation. Functional affiliation may lead to high utilization but it can also mean that the technological forecasting activity is functionally captive and narrow in its perspective. A danger in this situation is that technological forecasting may be slanted to support the functional parent rather than provide general direction more compatible with the objectives of the total organization.

There are some compelling advantages to having technological forecasting as an independent operation and functional entity if the size and scope of the organization warrants technological forecasting. As a non-captive operation it can be used by management for organizational checks and balances and as a directional force in assessing the validity of long-range planning and objectives. It can help in determining what emphasis to place in research and development and to give management insight into the reality of marketing goals. What must be guarded against if technological forecasting has functional independence is excessive cost generated by operational practice inconsistent with the organization's need and capacity.

CONCLUSIONS

Several significant theories and techniques have been incorporated into management practice in the past quarter of a century. Often these ideas have been accepted without critical examination. Adoption without adequate evaluation has, in many instances, initially led to disillusionment and obscured the true value. Uncritical acceptance and over commitment frequently can be attributed to the disciples of innovations who oversell a concept. The fact that all tools are not applicable in all situations, or, where applicable, have differing degrees of utility should not minimize the potential contribution. Management must recognize that no single panacea exists and must judiciously exploit ideas with consideration of the operational environment.

Technological forecasting as a formal concept can be traced back to the mid-1940's. Its present structure and direction took shape around 1960.[16] To date the greatest application and methodology development has been military-oriented. The military services have had encouraging success and indications are for intensification of effort in this area.

The idea of technological forecasting is relatively unknown in business circles. Professor Bright has probably been the most active disciple in promoting technological forecasting to industry. Indications are that inroads are being made. There has generally been enthusiastic reception from those industrial executives exposed to technological forecasting.

Technological forecasting in proper context should seriously be considered as an addition to the management process. As Jantsch so aptly stated,

> Technological forecasting is not yet a science but an art, and is characterized today by attitudes, not tools; human judgment is enhanced, not substituted by it. The development of auxiliary techniques, gradually attaining higher degrees of sophistication (and complexity) since 1960, is oriented towards ultimate integration with evolving information technology.[17]

FOOTNOTES

[1]*Investing in Scientific Progress*, 1961-1970, Report NSF 61-27 (Washington, D.C.: National Science Foundation, 1961), p. 7.

[2]*Management of New Products, 4th ed.*,(New York: Booz, Allen and Hamilton, Inc., 1964), p. 6.

[3]*Ibid.*, p. 2, and Report of the Joint Economic Committee, U. S. Congress, 88th Congress, 2nd session, (1964), p. 56.

[4]In the November 1969 issue of *Industrial Research* there is an interesting discussion of the potential use of glassy materials in product design, specifically glass that won't clot blood which could be used for producing artificial organs.

[5]Olaf Helmer, *Social Technology* (New York-London: Basic Books, Incorporated, 1966), pp. 56-57, and "New Products--Setting a Time Table," *Business Week* (May 27, 1967), pp. 52-61. Bright identifies seven technological trends: (1) increasing capability in transportation, (2) increased mastery of energy, (3) increased ability to control the life of animate and inanimate things, (4) increased ability to alter the characteristics of materials, (5) extension of man's sensory capabilities, (6) growing mechanization of physical activities, and (7) increasing mechanization of intellectual processes. James R. Bright, "Directions of Technological Change and Some Business Consequences," appearing in *Automation and Technological Change*, Report of the Assembly Jointly Sponsored by Battelle Memorial Institute and the American Assembly (May 9-11, 1963), pp. 9-22. Also, P. Michael Sinclair, "10 Years Ahead," *Industrial Research* (January 1969), pp. 68-72. Also, William O. Craig, "The Technology of Space--Earth," *Transportation & Distribution Management* (October 1969), pp. 22-26.

[6]Editorial, "Managing Technology," *Science and Technology* (January 1969), pp. 72-73.

[7]Marvin J. Cetron and Alan L. Weiser, "Technological Change, Technological Forecasting and Planning R&D--A View From the R&D Manager's Desk," *The George Washington Law Review*, Vol. 36, No. 5, (July 1968), p. 1079.

[8]E. Jantsch, *Technological Forecasting in Perspective*, (Paris: Organization for Economic Cooperation and Development, 1967), p. 15.

[9]*Ibid.*

[10]M. Cetron, "Prescription for the Military R&D Manager: Learn the Three Rx's," unpublished paper presented to The NATO Defense Research Group Seminary on Technological Forecasting and its Application to Defense Research (Teddington, Middlesex, England: (November 12, 1968), p. 2.

[11]One such material emerging as a possibility is boron filament which has remarkable strength for its weight. See "Tough Featherweight Plays Hard to Get," *Business Week* (November 15, 1959), p. 38.

[12]Jantsch, *op. cit.*, pp. 29-32.

[13]Extensive treatment of technological forecasting methodologies can be found in: M. J. Cetron, *Technological Forecasting* (New York: Gordon and Breach, 1969), Jantsch, *op. cit.*, and J. R. Bright (Ed.), *Technological Forecasting For Industry and Government* (Englewood Cliffs, N.J.: Pren-

tice-Hall, Inc., 1968).

[14]J. B. Quinn, "Technological Forecasting," *Harvard Business Review* (March-April 1967), pp. 101-103.

[15]*Ibid.*, p. 102.

[16]Jantsch, *op. cit.*, p. 17.

[17]*Ibid.*

STUDENT REVIEW QUESTIONS

1. Explain what Roman means by the term "technological forecasting."
2. Define exploratory technological forecasting and normative technological forecasting. Explain the difference between them.
3. How does Roman say technological forecasting can assist management?
4. What are some of the organizational considerations that must be examined before management begins to use technological forecasting?
5. What are some of the methodologies Roman identifies as currently employed in technological forecasting?

11

Socio-Political Forecasting: A New Dimension to Strategic Planning*

IAN H. WILSON

AS WITH ANY current fancy, there is the danger that management's romance with socio-political forecasting will turn out to be a short-lived affair, weakened by lack of substantive contribution to business planning and crushed by the exaggerated claims of a few enthusiastic proponents.

This would be a pity, if it happened. The need for this new dimension to strategic planning is real and, to a large extent, recognized by managers. What is mainly lacking is an armory of analytical tools and techniques that are available to, say, economic and technological forecasting. And these take time, skill and discipline to develop. Now is the time, then, for a serious evaluation--by managers and forecasters alike--of the progress to date, the potential to be realized, and the programs of research and action to be implemented.

SOCIAL CHANGE AND THE NEED FOR FORECASTING

The instincts of those pioneering companies which turned, in the late Sixties, toward some experimentation with social forecasting were right. Something basic *is* changing on the social scene, something that will have profound impact on business, something to which business needs time to adjust. And the hope was, and is, that this forecasting will provide the necessary lead time for companies to develop their "strategies of adjustment."

---

*Reprinted by permission from the July, 1974, issue of the *University of Michigan Business Review*, published by the Graduate School of Business Administration.

What are these changes? It is perhaps misleading, in an age and world of discontinuous change, to single out any one particular trend but, for purposes of this article, we can focus on the phenomenon of changing societal values and expectations and the resulting increased politicizing of our economy.

The years 1965-70 were a watershed in U. S. history. The analogy is apt for, since then, the streams of our social thinking have started to flow in quite different directions. We need only consider the changing values inherent in our new perceptions about the right relationship between man and woman, the majority and minorities, the individual and institutions, the economy and ecology, business and society. Among the consequences of these value shifts will be a rewriting of society's "charter of expectations" of corporate performance, and a shaking of what I have termed the "seven pillars of business," those basic values that we have up to now considered to be eternal verities undergirding our business system--growth; technology; profit; private property (as it applies to corporations); managerial authority; "hard work"; company loyalty.

Clearly, expectations are on the march and institutions must scurry to keep up with them. By 1970 it was obvious that business could no longer be satisfied with a complacent "other things being equal" formulation to cover the areas of its planning that lay outside traditional economic and technological forecasting. The impact of the various "movements" of the period broke suddenly and forcefully on the unprotected flanks of many companies, causing major disruptions in their plans of action. Lacking strategies to deal with these unexpected forces, companies were forced back on hastily improvised tactics that did little more than stave off one assault before another came.

Such a course of reluctant and belated *re*action is the antithesis of corporate enterprise and initiative on which companies pride themselves and which is an essential prerequisite for the future vitality and legitimacy of the corporation. If business is to reverse this situation and engage in *pro*active strategies to deal with changing social and political forces, it seems logical to conclude that it must, as one condition for success, expand its forecasting system to include these new factors.

A CRITIQUE OF OBJECTIONS

Up to this point there would most probably be general agreement with this line of reasoning: the need is apparent and managers are aware, if not of the rewards for success, at least of the penalties for failure. Where uncertainty, and perhaps disagreement, sets in is over the feasibility, scope and effectiveness of any formal venture into socio-political forecasting. The feeling is widespread that there is a basic incompatibility between the "soft" data of social and political analyses and the "hard" data of economic and technological forecasting: that the key strategic issues for business will be almost exclusively economic and financial; and that there is no satisfactory way of making socio-political forecasting contribute effective inputs into the strategic planning process.

Yet experience suggests that each one of these assumptions is subject to rebuttal. And the rebuttals are, of course, inter-linked in their rationale.

First, the "hardness" of economic and technological forecasting data seems to be an assumption based on the fact that these data can be more easily quantified. Just how "hard" the data really may be is subject to question when one considers, for instance, the record in economic forecasting. This is said, *not* to damn economic forecasting, but simply to call in question the validity of this alleged dichotomy between "hard" and "soft" data. Forecasts may, in *any* classification, be "right" or "wrong"--which is surely an important and valid difference. But I think we should lay to rest any objection to socio-political forecasting that is based on a supposed incompatibility of data with the more traditional inputs to corporate planning.

A somewhat similar dichotomy appears to underlie the second objection which states, in effect, that the central issues for business will remain economic (market conditions, costs of labor and materials, etc.) and financial (cash flow, availability of capital, etc.), while social and political factors will be peripheral. Admittedly, the rebuttal involves a somewhat circular argument: namely, socio-political forecasting so far undertaken indicates the key importance to business of certain social and political issues which, in turn, argues the case for more such forecasting in the future. For instance, a priority analysis of social pressures on the corporation, undertaken in 1972 for the Public Issues Committee of General Electric's Board of Directors, highlighted the following as key corporate issues of the future:

1. Constraints on corporate growth--a spectrum of issues ranging from national growth policy through economic controls and environmental protection to questions of antitrust policy and industrial structure.
2. Corporate governance--including matters of accountability, personal liability of managers and directors, board representation, and disclosure of information.
3. Managing the "new work force"--dealing

with the growing demands for job enlargement, more flexible scheduling, more equality of opportunity, greater participation and individualization.

4. External constraints on employee relations--the new pressures from government (EEO, health and safety, "federalization" of benefits), unions (coalition bargaining) and other groups (class-action suits, "whistle-blowing").
5. Problems and opportunities of business-government partnership--including a redefinition of the role of the private sector in public problem-solving.
6. "Politicizing" of economic decision-making--the growing government involvement in corporate decisions through consumerism, environmentalism, industrial reorganization, inflation control, etc.

It is quite beside the point to argue whether this (or some comparable) listing of issues is *more* or *less* important than economic, financial and technological issues. All that is needed is agreement that they are, and will be, *as* important and central to a corporation, and therefore deserve the same careful forecasting, monitoring and analysis that we now give to the state of the economy, the growth (or decline) of markets and the flow of funds.[1]

What, then, of the third objection? Are socio-political forecasts and analyses doomed forever to be interesting "coffee-table studies" and nothing more? Is it really true that there is no way of placing them in the mainstream of corporate planning? Here perhaps the best answer is provided by our early and, I think, promising experience at General Electric.

SOCIO-POLITICAL FORECASTING AT GENERAL ELECTRIC

Socio-political forecasting emerged as a separate operation in General Electric in May, 1967, with the establishment of Business Environment Studies (BES) in the corporate-level Personnel and Industrial Relations component. (In retrospect, there is some organizational logic to the fact that this "people-oriented" forecasting grew up in the "people function" of the corporation.) At that time, with social and political change already starting to accelerate, it seemed to us that the Relations function of the business was in as much need of a forecasting operation and a futures dimension, in order to do an intelligent job of long-range planning, as were the marketing and technical functions of the company.

Personnel and industrial relations policies and practices are no exception to the general rule of institutional inertia. Indeed, the probability is that systemic change occurs more slowly here than in other areas of the business, if for no other reason than that it is inherently more sensitive and difficult a task to deal with people than with technologies. In this area above all, therefore, companies need lead time for strategies of adjustment. 1967 was, in other words, not too soon to be thinking about the relations policies that might be needed in 1974.

The area of our search lay in the broad sweep of social, political and economic trends in the United States over the next ten years or so (our original time-horizon was 1980). The tasks of the new BES operations were to identify and monitor these trends; to analyze them to determine their implications for relations planning and, hopefully, to catalyze those strategies of adjustment of which I have written. The last element of the task is, in a sense, the crucial one, for there is little point to gaining lead time if it is not put to good use.

The initial BES effort was a broad survey of the whole prospective business environment of the Seventies. In an effort to "make sense of change," to see a pattern in the kaleidoscope of prospective events, the BES group viewed social change as the interaction of eight developing forces for change:

1. Increasing affluence
2. Economic stabilization
3. Rising levels of education
4. Changing attitudes toward work and leisure
5. Increasing pluralism and individualism
6. Emergence of the post-industrial society
7. Growing interdependence of institutions
8. The urban/minority problem

This broad survey can be likened to a single 360° sweep of the early warning system radar, revealing a number of ill-defined "blips" on the screen. If left there, the survey might justifiably have been relegated to the "interesting, but ineffective" category of studies.

It was, however, only a beginning. It provided us with a frame of reference and a perspective on the future. More important, it established the priorities for more detailed studies and analyses. To continue the radar analogy, these subsequent studies examined the "blips" on the screen in greater detail in an effort to determine the exact nature, trajectory and impact points of the incoming "missiles." It was these studies (for example, on the future minority environment; women's rights in the Seventies, prospects for inflation) that, by focusing more sharply on specific policy implications, started to make the hoped-for contribution toward making personnel and industrial relations planning a more proactive affair. One indicator: whereas the minority study (1969), though focusing on the future, barely enabled us to keep pace with events, the women's rights study (1970) gave us enough of a jump on events that our own affirmative action guidelines on equal employment opportunity for women were published a year before the Federal guidelines.[2]

A "FOUR-SIDED FRAMEWORK" FOR PLANNING

Two years' experience with this new venture convinced us of its potential value to personnel relations planning. However, it became increasingly clear that many of the questions raised by our studies simply could not be answered within the framework of the personnel function. The implications of trend-analysis spilled over into matters of the social purpose of business, the structure and governance of the corporation, business-government relationships, production processes and market orientation. They could fit comfortably in only one frame of reference--corporate planning as a whole.

It would, however, have to be a different type of corporate planning from the past. Typically, corporate planning has based its strategies on inputs derived from economic forecasting (predictions about GNP, consumer and government spending, savings and investment, market analyses, etc.) and technological forecasting (assessments of "state of the art" developments, expected outputs from one's own and competitors' laboratories). The planning parameters of the past (and present) can, therefore, be conceptually represented by the model in Figure 11-1. Certainly these inputs have been, and will continue to be, vital to the planning process: change--and, therefore, forecasting--in these fields is becoming more complex and more needed. However, these inputs, our studies suggested, would no longer suffice, as the "exposed flanks" in this diagram might lead one to guess.

The typical business now finds itself the focal point for a bewildering array of external forces that impact on it from every angle. The larger the company, the more likely is this to be true. There is virtually no major trend in the social, political and economic arena, at home and abroad, that does not affect in some way the operations or future growth of the large corporation. To create an "early warning system" on only two fronts--economic and technological--is, therefore, apt to leave a company highly vulnerable to attack from an unexpected quarter. Managers have been too ready to pretend that other factors were adequately covered by generalized assessments of the conventional and obvious political events--war, an election, or international trade agreements--or to rely on the caveat "other things being

FIGURE 11-1.

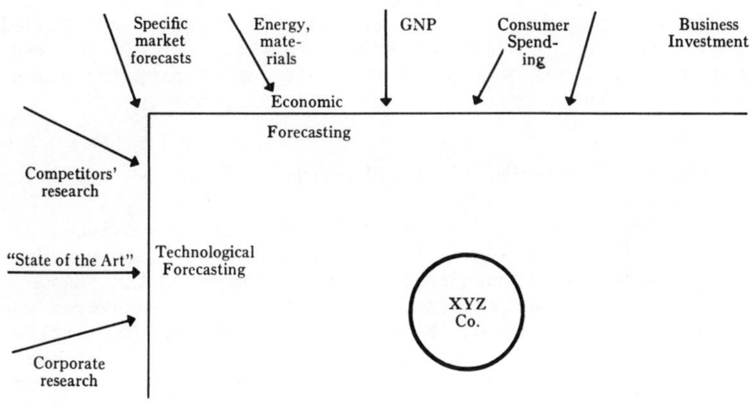

equal," which in the circumstances of today is a highly unsatisfactory (and unbusiness-like) treatment of vital factors.

If we have learned one lesson from the disruptions of accelerating change in the past decade, we should by now have recognized that "other things" have an uncomfortable habit of *not* being "equal." To look no further than at the outbursts in our cities and on our campuses, at the surge of a heightened ecological consciousness, at the proliferation of legislation on product safety, equal employment opportunity and occupational health, it should be obvious that social moods, personal attitudes, and political action have become dynamic and determinative forces for business.

The planning model for the future, therefore, will be more nearly represented by the four-sided framework illustrated in Figure 11-2.

An approximation of this model was, in fact, incorporated as one element in the revamping of General Electric's strategic planning system in 1970. The starting point for the planning cycle is now the long-term environmental forecast. This establishes the basic premises from which can be deduced the strategies and policies that are likely to produce the best "fit" between the company and the future business environment. And it is in this larger context of environmental forecasting that socio-political forecasting finds its natural place.

FIGURE 11-2.

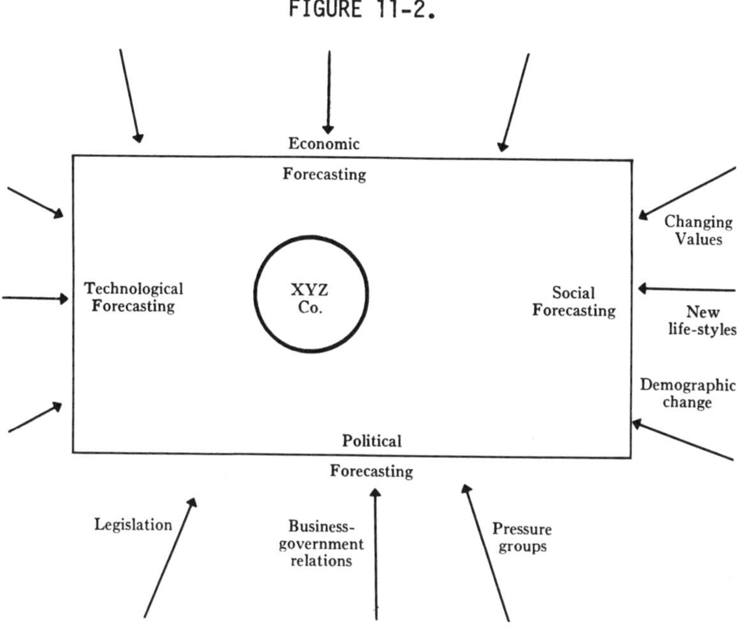

SOME KEY ELEMENTS IN THE PROCESS

Socio-political forecasting is nothing if not an art. By any standard, it is still far from being a science. However, even lacking the precision and instruments of science, it is evolving its own beginning processes, methodologies and discipline. Four key elements in the process bear examination:

1. *Continuous and comprehensive monitoring.* The paradox of forecasting in what Max Ways once called an "era of radical change" is that it becomes at once more necessary and more difficult. In a relatively stable society, in which tomorrow will predictably be pretty much like today, forecasting is relatively easy; but, by the same token, it is scarcely necessary since today's way of doing things will still be valid tomorrow. The more rapid, complex and pervasive change becomes, the more essential it is to try to "get a fix on the future." But, of course, the difficulties of forecasting increase geometrically with the number of sources of change.

The salient characteristics of a good monitoring system are continuity and comprehensiveness. A non-repetitive scanning of the environment ("We did our 1980 study in 1970--and that's it!") will soon become an erroneous input to planning. Even a long-term forecast requires continuous updating, granted the rapidity of change and the present state of the art.

Whether the monitoring is actually done by company personnel or outside consultants remains a matter of choice. Probably the best self-operated system is, in fact, an industry-wide effort among life insurance companies, under the leadership of the Institute of Life Insurance (ILI). Their Trend Analysis Program (TAP) operates on the basis of a matrix, one axis of which is categories of publications (general press, business publications, academic journals, etc.), the other being segments of the environment (social change, technology, politics, etc.). "Monitors" are nominated to the Program by individual companies, and each is then assigned to a particular cell of the matrix to monitor a publication (or a set of them) for evidence of trends in that segment of the environment. Monitors' reports are collected, analyzed and synthesized into periodic reports by ILI, which distributes them to participating companies.

Most companies will find it imperative to supplement their own efforts, either by participating in a cooperative effort such as TAP or by purchasing monitoring services from outside organizations. Among the better known organizations are the Hudson Institute (Corporate Environment Program), the Futures Group ("Scout"), Institute for the Future ("Project Aware") and Daniel Yankelovich, Inc. ("Monitor," "Corporate Priorities")--However achieved, comprehensiveness must be a goal--and there is a large environment to monitor.

2. *Analyzing for critical business implications.* However the monitoring is done, the critical job of particularizing the findings to significance for a single company must, I think, be done internally. Only in this way can it become part of the thinking process of the management system of that company.

Here I would like to stress the importance of seeing *patterns* in trends and events. It is not sufficient merely to identify and monitor hundreds, maybe thousands, of separate items of change; to do only that would saturate the planning system with data. I appreciate that there is a very fine dividing line between objectively trying to find patterns in the trends, and subjectively imposing one's own pattern on them. Nevertheless, I think we must make this attempt and tread this fine line. I stress this need to see patterns in change because of its importance in enabling us to:

a. see the significance of isolated events;
b. analyze the cross-impacts of one trend on another (or others);
c. improve management's understanding of the probable future course of events.

Bringing the generalized forecast down to specific implications for a particular business may prove to be the most difficult part of all. We are all most apt to be blind in matters that closely affect us. But however difficult the exercise may be, we must make a thorough-going and conscientious effort to answer, in precise terms, the crucial questions: "What does this trend mean for me? For my work? For my company?" This exercise may be particularly difficult for managers because many of the implications will seem to challenge and even undermine some of their basic assumptions and values. These implications are, therefore, most apt to be set aside as mistaken interpretations, as "unthinkable," or as inconsistent with past experience and future forecasts along "traditional" lines. Yet it is precisely these seeming "wild cards" that our research must seek to uncover and evaluate.

3. *Developing tools and techniques.* As already noted, socio-political forecasting lacks the armory of analytical tools and techniques possessed by older forecasting disciplines. Trend projections, Delphi forecasting, scenarios, and "cross-impact analysis" are useful starts on forecasting methodologies, but the need for more tools remains great. With an acute awareness of their limitations and relative lack of sophistication, I offer for consideration two tools that we have found to be of some value.

(a) Probability-Diffusion Matrix

In predicting developments over a decade it is more meaningful to talk in terms of degrees of relative probability, than of certainty or "inevitability." In the final analysis, assigning probability to a trend or future event is a matter of judgment after weighing the known data and cross-checking with informed opinion. A further cross-check can be run by plotting the predictions along a probability axis so that their relative positions are made apparent.

It is also helpful to assess the probable "diffusion" of a trend or event--that is, the extent to which it is uniformly distributed over the population to which it applies (world, U. S. A., an industry, etc.) or relatively confined to a segment of that population. Again, plotting the predictions along a diffusion axis makes explicit, in a coordinated fashion, the relative weightings assigned in separate judgments.

Combining these two axes into a probability/diffusion matrix, as is done in Figure 11-3, serves as a check on the internal consistency of a relatively large number of predictions, from two viewpoints. By itself, such a matrix adds little to a scientific approach to environmental forecasting, but it does provide a way of looking at the future that may perhaps be helpful.

FIGURE 11-3. PROBABILITY/DIFFUSION MATRIX FOR EVENTS AND TRENDS OCCURRING IN U.S. AND WORLD BY 1980

Diffusion ↓ / Probability →	Low				Probability				High
High	Thermo-nuclear war						3+% inflation		
						35-hr. work week			Rising level of education
Diffusion									
					Retire-ment at 55				3.5–5% unem-ployment
		Detroit-type riots					More business-government partnerships		
			Strikes outlawed						$3,600 per capita income
Low							Regional conflicts		

The plottings made in this matrix are largely for purposes of illustration, and not to be taken as final judgments. To the extent that they provoke debate, they will have at least demonstrated the value of making judgments clearly explicit so that planned action can more surely be taken.

(b) "Values Profile":

As we have already noted, changes in value systems may be the major determinants of social and political trends in the future, and business planning would be well advised to try to get a fix on these changes as one essential element in its forecasting system. One way of systematizing analysis of value trends is to develop a "values profile" (Figure 11-4). Like the probability/diffusion matrix, this chart should be viewed, not as a precise scientific measurement, but merely as a useful way of looking at the future. Like the matrix, too, it contains plottings that are meant to be indicative--pointing the way to a more comprehensive study--rather than definitive.

To point up the possible attitudinal changes as dramatically as possible, the chart has been made up of contrasting pairs of values (to a greater or lesser extent, that is, enhancement of one value implies a diminution of the other--e.g., war vs. peace; conformity vs. pluralism). Each society and generation has tended to seek its own new balance between these contrasting pairs, with the weight shifting from one side to the other as conditions and attitudes change.

The chart also emphasizes the value changes likely to be most prevalent among the trend-setting segment of the population (young, well-educated, relatively affluent, "committed"). These are the people among whom companies recruit the managerial and professional talent they require.

The chart presents two value profiles--one representing the approximate balance struck by these trend-setters in 1969 (when our initial study was undertaken) between each pair of values; the other indicating the hypothetical balance that might be struck in 1980. It is important to stress that the chart attempts to predict value changes, *not* necessarily events. Even though trend-setters may value, say, arms control agreements, events may lag behind their influence (e.g., due to political thinking of the electorate as a whole) or lie outside their control (e.g., regional wars among developing nations).

4. *Integrating with other forecasts.* The essence of environmental forecasting, as has been mentioned, is the integration of the various conventional and non-conventional types of forecasting. The four-sided framework implies only four sets of inputs to the process; but this is merely a conceptual approach, and ideally the number should be higher.

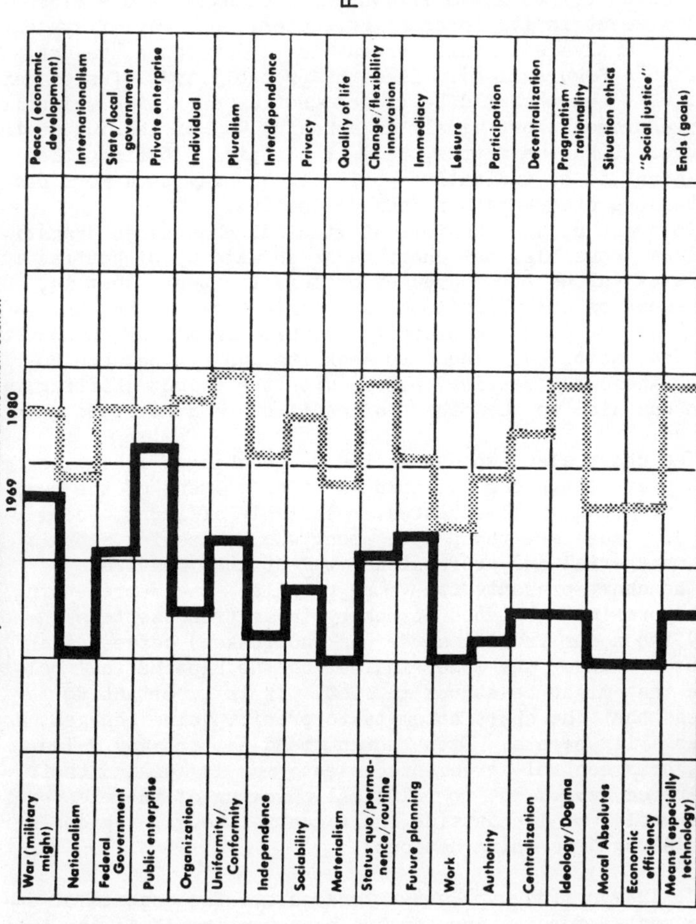
Profile of Significant Value-System Changes: 1969-1980
as seen by General Electric's Business Environment section
1969
1980
War (military might)
Nationalism
Federal Government
Public enterprise
Organization
Uniformity/Conformity
Independence
Sociability
Materialism
Status quo/permanence/routine
Future planning
Work
Authority
Centralization
Ideology/Dogma
Moral Absolutes
Economic efficiency
Means (especially technology)
Peace (economic development)
Internationalism
State/local government
Private enterprise
Individual
Pluralism
Interdependence
Privacy
Quality of life
Change/flexibility innovation
Immediacy
Leisure
Participation
Decentralization
Pragmatism/rationality
Situation ethics
"Social justice"
Ends (goals)
1969 Values Profile
1980 Values Profile

FIGURE 11-4.

When the long-term environmental forecast was first undertaken in 1971 for our strategic planning, the number of initial inputs was set at nine (see Figure 11-5)--geopolitical/defense, international economic, social, political, legal, economic, technological, manpower and financial. In each of these, separate "tunnel visions" of specific aspects of the future we tried to (a) give a brief historical review(1960-70) as a jumping-off point for our analysis of the future; (b) analyze the major future forces for change--a benchmark forecast for 1970-80; (c) identify the potential discontinuities, i.e., those events which might have low probability, but high significance for General Electric; and (d) raise the first-order questions and policy implications suggested by these forecasts.

FIGURE 11-5.

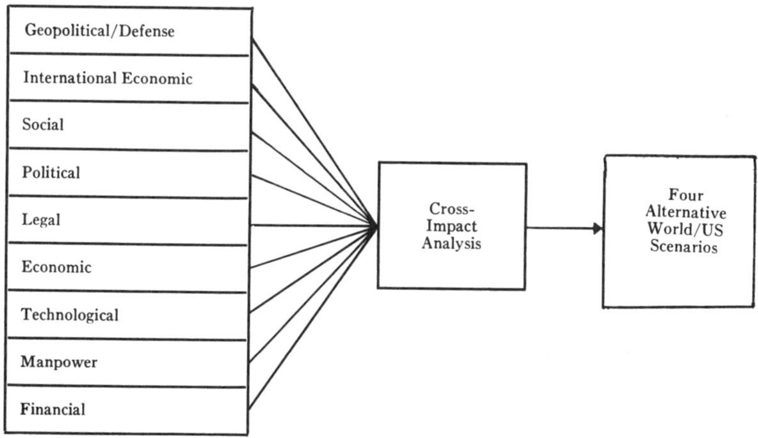

These were, by definition, *segmented* views of the future, and so inadequate as a final product. We proceeded to a "cross-impact analysis," selecting from the hundreds of trends/events in those nine environmental "slices" the 75 or so that had the highest combined rating of probability and importance. (Some events that were quite probable had little significance for General Electric; while others of low probability would have critical importance for the Company, should they occur.) On these 75 trends/events, we performed the sort of cross-impact analysis developed by Theodore J. Gordon, asking "If event A occurs, what will be the impact on the other 74? Will the probability of their occurrence increase? Decrease? Remain the same?" In effect, this process enabled us to build sets of "domino chains," with one event triggering another, and then to construct a small number of consistent configurations of the future.

The final step in the environmental forecasting process was the development of scenarios as an integrative mechanism for our work, pulling together the separate forecasts of the nine "slices," and blending quantitative and qualitative data. I must stress that we developed multiple scenarios; we did *not* take a single view of the future. In fact, we ended up with four possibilities:

---A benchmark forecast, which combined the "most probable" developments from the nine environmental "slices."

---Three variants which, in effect, were derived from varying combinations of discontinuities.

Significantly, I think, we rated even the benchmark forecast no more than a 50 percent probability. That, at least, is a measure of our own uncertainty about the future.

CONCLUSION

When all is said and done, of course, the element of chance or surprise will always remain. Indeed, one certain prediction is that managers will have to learn how to live with, and manage, uncertainty. However, within a framework of four (or nine) environmental parameters, business plans can be formulated with greater assurance that the major predictable environmental factors have been taken into consideration. With anything less, an otherwise sound strategy will remain vulnerable to the new discontinuities of our age.

FOOTNOTES

[1]One overclaim that must be guarded against is the reasoning that political decisions will be the major determinants of the economy, and that political forecasting is *the* crucial input to planning. As in any system, it is the interaction of *all* trends and factors that determines the outcomes, so I would argue that it is futile to argue for the primacy of any *one* type of forecasting.

[2]Even this could not, of course, guarantee immunity from EEOC complaints and lawsuits as recent events have demonstrated.

STUDENT REVIEW QUESTIONS

1. Why does Wilson consider the years 1965-70 so important?
2. Contrast what Wilson calls the "planning model of the past" with the "planning model of the future."
3. Explain what Wilson means when he stresses the importance of "seeing patterns in trends and events."
4. Name and briefly explain two tools Wilson says have shown value in socio-political forecasting.
5. Briefly describe socio-political forecasting at General Electric.

12

Values in Decision Making: Their Origin and Effects*

ROBERT C. SHIRLEY

ALL MANAGERS, especially those at the highest levels of organizations, are keenly aware of the fact that few major decision issues have obvious solutions. The decision issue of corporate strategy is a case in point. Strategy refers to the product-market scope, objectives, and major plans of action for any firm. The formation of strategy is a complex and iterative process, involving consideration of a myriad of environmental opportunities and constraints in relation to organizational resources and abilities. The role of *judgment* in strategic decision-making has long been recognized, primarily due to three major factors:

1. All information related to the numerous external forces operative in any situation cannot possibly be gathered, assimilated, and evaluated.
2. The information which can be collected and evaluated is frequently imperfect.
3. The large number of variables related to strategic decisions cannot be "modeled" in the sense of establishing precise functional relationships which provide deterministic outputs or "correct" decisions.

Thus, the role of judgment in strategic decisions has been legitimized due to incomplete and imperfect information about all relevant variables and their interrelationships. Nonetheless, the tendency is to assume that judgment is (or

---

*From *Managerial Planning,* January/February, 1975, pp. 1-5. Reprinted by permission.

should be) exercised in a very objective manner, i.e., final determination of the most feasible economic strategy for the firm will be based upon a "rational" assessment of whatever information happens to be available. This is a glaring misconception of the strategic decision-making process; the fact that these and similar decisions inevitably depend on evaluation of imperfect information indicates that "subjective" judgment plays an important role, i.e., judgment which is not wholly a function of objective analysis. It thus should be recognized that the *personal values* of top managers are an integral component of strategic decisions; moreover, it will be argued below that such values *should* be reflected and satisfied by decisions on major issues such as corporate strategy.

CULTURALLY DERIVED VALUES

A personal value can be viewed as one's "conception of the desirable." Edward Spranger identified six major kinds of value orientations which are useful for distinguishing among types of men:[1]

1. *Theoretical* (dominant intellectual interest in an empirical and rational approach to systematic knowledge).
2. *Economic* (orientation toward practical affairs, the production and consumption of goods, the uses and creations of wealth).
3. *Aesthetic* (dominant interest in the artistic, in form, symmetry, and harmony).
4. *Social* (primary value is the love of people and warmth of human relationships).
5. *Political* (dominant orientation toward power, influence, and recognition).
6. *Religious* (primary orientation toward unity and creation of satisfying and meaningful relationship to the universe).

The above types of values may be viewed as "culturally derived." As noted by Guth and Taguiri, values are transmitted to a person "through his parents, teachers, and other significant persons in his environment who, in turn, acquired their values in similar fashion."[2] These culturally derived values serve as guiding principles for decision making in our everyday life. Being such an integral and active component of one's personality structure, it is logical to reason that such values will also serve as guiding principles in making decisions on organizational issues for which no predetermined "correct" solution exists.

As the success of any business firm is generally measured by economic criteria,[3] the tendency has been to impute dominant economic values or orientations to decision-makers.

Although little research has been done in this area, the results to date reveal enormous individual variations among the value structures of U. S. executives--some have dominant economic values, while others may be primarily oriented to the aesthetic, political, social, theoretical, or religious.[4] Granted that these individual variations exist, what may be the nature of their respective influences on decision issues such as corporate strategy? Or, to put it another way, how might executives with different value structures differ in their general perceptions of the most desirable course of action for the firm?

Obviously, the executive with dominant economic values would tend to emphasize strategic opportunities which promise the greatest increases in growth and/or profitability of the firm. On the other hand, an executive with dominant aesthetic values would be more prone to eschew any profitable opportunities which require, for example, "cheapening" the design of a product and thus detracting from the firm's image as the quality producer in the industry. An executive with dominant social values may well veto profitable opportunities which threaten to upset interpersonal relationships within the organization (assuming, of course, that a reasonable return on investment is being earned with the present strategy). The individual with dominant social values would also be more favorable toward strategies which are "socially responsible" than others who are *primarily* concerned with increasing the profitability of the firm. An individual with a dominant political (power) orientation will tend to emphasize those opportunities which promise to increase the various indicators of the size of a firm (e.g., sales volume, total assets, total employees), while an executive with a primary orientation toward the theoretical may be more prone to emphasize long-range research and development activities at the expense of short-run economic returns. Finally, strategic opportunities will likely be evaluated by the highly religious person in terms of their moral implications for the "nature of man" vis a vis his Creator and the total universe. The highly religious person might also evaluate opportunities in terms of ethical criteria which are generally thought to be beyond the rightful concern of businessmen, i.e., those ethics which are more philosophical or religious in nature than those related to everyday business practice (e.g., fair trade, independent determination of prices).

The above examples indicate that, consciously or unconsciously, our culturally derived personal values may serve as criteria for choice among competing strategic alternatives--assuming, of course, that all the alternatives satisfy minimum economic criteria for the perpetuation of the firm. The following section discusses the manner in which our organizationally derived values may exert a similar type of influence.

ORGANIZATIONALLY DERIVED VALUES

A second classification of values may be viewed as "organizationally-derived." Within this general classification, it is possible to identify five major types of values:

1. PRODUCTION (dominant value is cost reduction, operating efficiency, commitment to schedules, work simplification, and certainty and stability of operations).
2. RESEARCH AND DEVELOPMENT (primary orientation toward innovation, design ingenuity, "scientific challenge," discovery of new knowledge, and technical superiority of products over those of competitors.)
3. MARKETING (dominant value is increased sales volume and market share).
4. FINANCIAL (dominant value is profits return on investment, efficient cash flows, safety of assets, orderly records).
5. PERSONNEL (greatest emphasis is on organizational stability and worker satisfaction and development).

These types of values have been termed organizationally derived, as they tend to be associated with one's major role grouping within an organization. Thus, different functional area personnel tend to have different "conceptions of the desirable" for their firm insofar as product mix, customer designation, product characteristics and quality, priority of objectives, and the like are concerned. Specific market opportunities would be perceived entirely differently by the various functional area personnel due to the differences in dominant or primary orientations among them. Different criteria would be applied to the same opportunities for the firm, whether consciously or not, logically resulting in disagreement over the efficacy of various decision outcomes. An example of the manner in which this may arise is discussed below.

CASES OF CONFLICTING VALUES

The following two case examples illustrate instances where culturally and organizationally derived values have contributed to conflict and disagreement among top managers.

CASE 1--CONFLICT AMONG CULTURALLY DERIVED VALUES

Consider the case of a brewery located in the midwestern section of the United States. The brewery was founded in 1862 and soon established itself as the top producer of premium draught beer over a two-state area. This reputation was enhanced over the years as further improvements in brewing techniques were developed and implemented. In 1964, however, the brewing industry turned to packaged (canned and bottled) beer and found immediate consumer acceptance. By the mid-1960's, over 80 percent of national beer consumption was in canned and bottled beer; the brewery in question, however, continued to emphasize premium draught beer in the face of declining sales and despite numerous market surveys which indicated consumer preferences for packaged beer. A strategy session was called by the president and included, in addition to himself, the vice presidents of sales, production, and finance. The subject: What should be the future product-market scope (basic strategy) of the firm in light of the changing preference of beer consumers?

Three basic alternatives were advanced by the executives:

1. The sales vice president was in favor of switching to cans and concentrating on retail grocery outlets and packaged-liquor stores. He pointed out that this change in basic strategy would reflect consumer preferences and offered the greatest potential for increasing sales volume in the local area. He presented detailed statistics to support his proposal, including information to show that national markets were beyond the firm's capabilities at the present time.
2. The production vice president (brewmaster) argued against the alternative just noted. He was strongly of the conviction that "packaged beers taste as differently from draught beer as cabbage tastes from sauerkraut. Can or bottle it and it is no longer the real thing." He favored maintaining the firm's present strategy of producing and selling premium draught beer in the two-state area.
3. The president felt that the firm should expand nationally with both canned and draught

> beer and that his personal skill in advertising would enable him to at least match the greater resources devoted to advertising by the national brands. Selective exploitation of restricted market areas would be necessary until a greater capital base was established; the accumulation of such efforts over the years to come would result in the brewery's becoming truly national in scope.

Examination of the alternatives reveals the influence of three differing value orientations on perceptions of the *same basic set of market data.* The sales vice president exhibits a dominant economic orientation via emphasis on the strategy which "offered the greatest potential for increasing sales volume"; the production vice president's alternative of maintaining the status quo appears to result from his concern over the aesthetic nature (quality and taste) of the product; and finally, the president's proposed strategy exhibits a tendency toward a political or power orientation via emphasis on the firm's becoming "truly national in scope."

CASE 2--CONFLICT AMONG ORGANIZATIONALLY DERIVED VALUES

The fact that most top management decision-making groups are composed of functional area vice presidents creates a situation of potential conflict among organizationally derived values. Lawrence and Lorsch provide rich examples of such potential in their discussion of differentiation and integration in organizations.[5] In the following excerpt from their book, imagine that the sales manager and the research scientist are vice presidents of marketing and research and development, respectively, and that the integrator is the chief executive of the firm:[6]

> In the plastics organization we might find a sales manager discussing a potential new product with a fundamental research scientist and an integrator. In this discussion the sales manager is concerned with the needs of the customer. What performance characteristics must a new product have to perform in the customer's machinery? How much can the customer afford to pay? How long can the material be stored without deteriorating? Further, our sales manager, while talking about these matters, may be thinking about more pressing current

> problems. Should he lower the price on an existing product? Did the material shipped to another customer meet his specifications? Is he going to meet this quarter's sales targets?
>
> In contrast, our fundamental scientist is concerned about a different order of problems. Will this new project provide a scientific challenge? To get the desired result, could he change the molecular structure of a known material without affecting its stability? What difficulties will he encounter in solving these problems? Will this be a more interesting project to work on than another he heard about last week? Will he receive some professional recognition if he is successful in solving the problem? Thus our sales manager and our fundamental scientist not only have quite different goal orientations, but they are thinking about different time dimensions--the sales manager about what's going on today and in the next few months; the scientist, how he will spend the next few years.

It is obvious from the above example that the two individuals are applying quite different criteria in evaluating the feasibility of a new product proposal. The fact that many alternative strategies available to a given firm are economically sound permits the intrusion of these organizationally derived values, in addition to the fact that the "correct" decision solution at this level, however defined, is never known in advance. If a proposed alternative satisfies *both* sets of criteria being employed in the above example, then obviously little disagreement will occur. When one considers that the problem is usually compounded by the presence of other functional specialties (at least production and finance) in evaluation of decisions affecting the total firm, however, the potential for considerable disagreement and conflict exists.

THE RESOLUTION OF CONFLICTING VALUES

The preceding illustrations raise the issue of how to resolve conflicting values in the process of decision making. Although there is no easy answer to such conflict, several comments can be made. First, we must be *aware* of our own values and the manner in which they affect our decisions. Such an awareness will better enable us to distinguish between the rational or objective features of our own proposals and those features which reflect our personal "conceptions of the desirable." This awareness of our own values and their influence should also make us more tolerant of the personal values inherent in proposals made by others;[7] developing such an awareness and understanding is thus the first step towards resolution of conflicting values. Second, it should be noted that although one value orientation may be dominant in an individual, other values are also possessed by that same person. Thus it may be possible to appeal to these "lower-order" values in an attempt to effect some sort of compromise when disagreement over future strategy or other decision issues occurs.

Third, we should be aware of the tendency to exaggerate value differences between ourselves and others; as shown by Guth and Taguiri's study, there is frequently a tendency to inaccurately attribute dominant value orientations to individuals based on our stereotypes of their particular organizational roles.[8] Those researchers found, for example, that scientists and research personnel attributed higher economic and political value scores to a group of executives than the executives actually indicated for themselves. Similarly, the executives attributed higher theoretical values to the research personnel than the latter indicated for themselves. Thus there may be more "common ground" for agreement than is apparent at first glance.

Fourth, we should recognize that this type of conflict is healthy for the firm. The assessment of decision alternatives from several different value perspectives lends another dimension to the advantage of obtaining a "diversity of inputs" in decisions of major importance. Such advantage is usually couched in terms of obtaining a diversity of *technical* inputs from different functional areas of expertise. It appears that a diversity of *value* inputs would contribute greatly toward illumination of the more subtle elements of decisions--namely, the extent to which the decision outcomes may be congruent with the value structures of those who will bear primary responsibility for decision implementation.

Finally, it is particularly important that the chief executive of a firm maintain a workable balance among the various types of values--both those which are culturally derived and those which emanate from organizational role groupings. As noted by Katz, there can be no "separate, permanent, 'general management' set of values and criteria."[9] To effectively integrate the various cultural and organizational orientations in a manner which will ensure enterprise success and personal commitment *simultaneously* remains the responsibility of the chief executive. Thus it is mandatory that this individual carefully examine his own innate bias and compensate for it in the attempt to reconcile value conflicts among his immediate subordinates.

CONCLUDING REMARKS

It should be emphasized that the principal task of top managers is to develop a strategy which is *economically viable*. Yet, many alternative strategies available to a given firm are economically sound; this fact, in conjunction with the fact that perfect information about the consequences of the alternatives is never available, permits a great deal of latitude for integrating personal values of top managers into the final strategic decisions. This is desirable; to the extent that such values may be reflected in decisions, the greater the degree of personal commitment which will be attached to them. Everyone is familiar with the emphasis which has been placed on the satisfaction of lower-level employee needs in an organizational setting; in fact, human considerations have frequently outweighed technical considerations in the design of operative work processes in some organizations. It is no different to argue that the design of corporate strategy should provide for satisfaction of executive needs and wants in order to inspire commitment and stimulate motivation.

Obviously, top management must first design alternative strategies which satisfy whatever economic criteria are necessarily employed as future performance standards; rather than stopping at this point(as is usually the case), however, the alternatives should be further evaluated in terms of their motivational consequences, i.e., the extent to which they satisfy the "conceptions of the desirable" held by key personnel. To the extent that economic values are dominant throughout the upper management levels, it will be unnecessary to modify the maximum economic strategy designed initially; to the extent that other-than-economic values are dominant, however, then it would be worthwhile to examine how the strategy may be modified to "fit" those other values without unduly sacrificing the economic viability of the firm. Such an approach thus focuses on satisfactory economic returns as the first priority but gives *explicit* recognition to the fact that corporate strategy must also serve as a stimulus to organizational effort and personal commitment.

FOOTNOTES

[1]Edmund P. Learned, et. al., *Business Policy*, (Homewood, Ill: Richard D. Irwin, Inc., 1969), p. 324. The authors' summary of the six value orientations is based on Spranger's more elaborate discussion in his book *Types of Men*, translated by P. Pigors (Halle, Germany: Niemeyer, 1928).

[2]William D. Guth and Renato Taguiri, "Personal Values and Corporate Strategy," *Harvard Business Review* (September-October, 1965), p. 125

[3]This obviously remains true today and for the near future, although growing public dissatisfaction with profits as the primary criterion for business success may eventually result in "social performance" indicators. This movement in itself represents a shift in the personal values of the larger society.

[4]Guth and Taguiri, *op. cit.*,pp. 126-127.

[5]Paul R. Lawrence and Jay W. Lorsch, *Organization and Environment* (Homewood, Illinois: Richard D. Irwin, Inc., 1969).

[6]*Ibid.*, pp. 134-135.

[7]This point is developed more fully in Learned, et. al., *op. cit.*, p. 325.

[8]Guth and Taguiri, *op. cit.*, pp. 130-131.

[9]Robert L. Katz, *Cases and Concepts in Corporate Strategy*, (Englewood Cliffs: Prentice Hall, Inc., 1970), p. 19.

STUDENT REVIEW QUESTIONS

1. Explain what Shirley means by values.
2. Would executives with different value structures tend to make different decisions? Give a few examples to illustrate your answer.
3. Compare culturally derived variables with organizationally derived variables. Which are more important?
4. In what ways does Shirley indicate we can help resolve the problem of conflicting values?
5. Shirley says that the chief executive of the organization must "maintain a workable balance among the various types of values." Explain what he means by this. Do you agree?

13

Social Responsibilities of Business Managers*

ROBERT HAY

EDMUND R. GRAY

THE CONCEPT OF THE social responsibility of business managers in recent years has become a popular subject of discussion and debate within both business and academic circles. Nevertheless, a look back through business history reveals that people have always held some concept of the responsibility owed by business management to society. It is the contention here that concepts of social responsibility have moved through three distinct phases.

HISTORIC PHASES

PHASE I--PROFIT MAXIMIZING MANAGEMENT

The Phase I concept was the belief that business managers have but one single objective--to maximize profits. The only constraint on this pursuit was the legal framework within which the firm operated. The origin of this view may be found in Adam Smith's *Wealth of Nations*. Smith believed that each individual business man acting in his own selfish interest would be guided by an "invisible hand" to promote the public good. In other words, the individual's drive for

*From *Academy of Management Journal*, March, 1974, pp. 135-143. Reprinted by permission.

maximum profits and the regulation of the competitive market place would interact to create the greatest aggregate wealth for a nation and therefore the maximum public good. In the United States this view was widely accepted throughout the nineteenth century and the early part of the twentieth century. Its acceptance rested not solely on economic logic, but also on the goals and values of society.

America in the nineteenth and first half of the twentieth century was a society of economic scarcity. Hence, economic growth and the accumulation of aggregate wealth were primary national goals. The business system, with its emphasis on maximum profit, was seen as a vehicle for eliminating economic scarcity. In the process, employee abuses such as child labor, starvation wages, and unsafe working conditions could be tolerated. Moreover, few questions were raised with regard to expending natural resources, polluting the streams and the land. There was little concern about urban problems, unethical advertising, unsafe products, and poverty problems of minority groups.

The profit maximization view of social responsibility, moreover, complemented the Calvinistic philosophy which pervaded nineteenth and early twentieth century American thinking. Calvinism stressed that the road to salvation was through hard work and the accumulation of wealth. It then logically followed that a businessman could demonstrate his diligence (and thus his godliness) and accumulate a maximum amount of wealth by adhering to the discipline of profit maximization.

PHASE II--THRUSTEESHIP MANAGEMENT

Phase II, which may be labeled the trusteeship concept, emerged in the 1920s and 1930s. It resulted from structural changes both in business institutions and in society. According to this concept, corporate managers were responsible not simply for maximizing stockholder wealth but also for maintaining an equitable balance among the competing claims of customers, employees, suppliers, creditors, and the community, as well as the stockholders. In this view, the manager was seen as a trustee for the various contributor groups to the firm rather than simply an agent to the owners (2).*

The two structural trends largely responsible for the emergence of the newer view of social responsibility were: (a) the increasing diffusion of ownership of the shares of American corporations and (b) the development of a pluralistic society. The extent of the diffusion of stock owner-

*Numbers in parentheses refer to the alphabetical listing of References at the end of the chapter.

ship may be highlighted by the fact that by the early 1930s the largest stockholders in corporations such as American Telephone and Telegraph, United States Steel, and the Pennsylvania Railroad owned less than one percent of the total shares outstanding of these companies (1). Similar dispersion of stock ownership existed in most other large corporations. In such situations management typically was firmly in control of the corporation. Except in rare circumstances the top executives were able to perpetuate themselves in office through the proxy mechanism. If an individual shareholder was displeased with the performance of the firm, he had little recourse other than to sell his stock. Hence, although the stockholder's legal position was that of an owner--and thus a principal-agent relationship existed between the stockholder and the managers--his actual position was more akin to bondholders and other creditors of the firm. Given such a situation, it was only natural to ask the question, "To whom is management responsible?" The trusteeship concept provided an answer. Management was responsible to all the contributors to the firm, i.e., stockholders, workers, customers, suppliers, creditors, and the community.

The emergence of a largely pluralistic society reinforced the logic of the trusteeship concept. A pluralistic society has been defined as "one which has many semi-autonomous and autonomous groups through which power is diffused. No one group has overwhelming power over all others, and each has direct or indirect impact on all others" (5). From the perspective of business firms, this translated into the fact that exogenous groups had considerable impact upon and influence over them. In the 1930s the major groups exerting significant pressure on business were labor unions and the federal government. Today the list has grown to include numerous minority, environmental, and consumer groups, among others. Clearly, one logical approach to such a situation is to consider the firm as having responsibility to each interested group, with management's task being to reconcile and balance the claims of the several groups.

PHASE III--"QUALITY OF LIFE" MANAGEMENT

Phase III, which may be called the quality of life concept of social responsibility, has become popular in recent years (4). The primary reason for the emergence of this concept is the very significant metamorphosis in societal goals which this nation is experiencing. Up to about the middle of this century, society's principal requirement of business was that it produce increasing amounts of goods and services and thus continuously raise the standard of living of the American people. The fact that the U. S. had become the wealthiest society in the history of the world was testimony to the business establishment's success in meeting this expectation.

In the process, however, the U. S. has become what John Galbraith calls an "affluent society" in which the aggregate scarcity of basic goods and services is no longer the fundamental problem. Other social problems, however, have developed as direct and indirect results of economic success. Thus, there are pockets of poverty in a nation of plenty, deteriorating cities, air and water pollution, defacement of the landscape, and a disregard for consumers, to mention only a few prominent social problems. The mood of the country seems to be that things have gotten out of balance, that economic abundance in the midst of a declining social and physical environment does not make sense. As a result, a new set of national priorities, which stress the quality of life, appears to be emerging.

Concomitant with the new priorities, societal consensus seems to be demanding that business, with its technological and managerial skills and its financial resources, assume broader responsibilities--responsibilities that extend beyond the traditional economic realm of the Phase I concept or the mere balancing of the competing demands of the sundry contributors and pressure groups of the Phase II concept. The socially responsible firm under Phase III reasoning is one that becomes deeply involved in the solution of society's major problems.

PERSONAL VALUES

Values are the beliefs and attitudes of a person which form his frame of reference. They help to determine the behavior which an individual displays. All managers have a set of values which affect their decisions, but the values are not the same for each manager; however, once they are ingrained in a manager, they do not change except over a considerable period of time. It is possible to group these values in terms of the general patterns of behavior which may characterize the three styles of managers--the profit maximizer, the trusteeship style, and the quality of life style of management.

values for:

PHASE I

The Phase I profit maximizing manager has a personal set of values which reflects his economic thinking. He believes that raw self-interest should prevail in our society. His values dictate that "what is good for me is good for my country." Therefore, he rationalizes that making as much profit as is possible would be good for society. He bends every effort to become as efficient as possible and to make as much money as he can. To him, money and wealth are the most important goals of life.

In the pursuit of maximum profit, the manager's actions toward his customers would be reflected in a *caveat emptor* philosophy. "Let the buyer beware" would characterize his decisions and actions in dealing with his customers. He would not necessarily be concerned with product quality, safety, or sufficient and truthful information about his products and services. His views toward his employees would be stated as, "Labor is a commodity to be bought and sold in the market place." His chief accountability would be to the owners of the business, and chances would be good that he would be the owner or part owner of the organization.

To the profit maximizer technology would be very important. Machines and equipment would rank high on his scale of values. Materialism would characterize his philosophy.

Social values would not dominate his thinking. In fact, he would believe that employee personal problems should be left at home. The economic man should be separated from the social man or family man. His own leadership style would be as rugged individualist. "I am my own boss, and I will manage my business as I please." His values regarding minority groups would dictate that Blacks and Indians and foreigners are inferior to whites and that they should be treated accordingly.

His political values would be based on the doctrine of laissez faire. "That government is best which governs the least" would characterize his thinking. As a result, any dealing with politicians and governments would be foreign and distasteful to him.

His belief about the environment would be stated: "The natural environment controls the destiny of man. Therefore, use it to protect your interests before it destroys you. Do not worry about the physical environment because there are plenty of natural resources which you can use."

Aesthetic values to the profit maximizer would be of minimal concern. In fact, he would say, "Aesthetic values? What are they?" He would have very little concern for the arts and cultural aspects of life. He would hold musicians, artists, entertainers, and social scientists in low regard.

The values that a profit maximizing manager held were commonly accepted in the economic textbooks of the 1800s and early 1900s, although they obviously did not apply to all managers of those times. It is easy to see how these values would conflict with the values of those characterized by the quality of life and the trusteeship styles of management.

PHASE II

The Phase II trusteeship manager recognizes that self-interest plays a large role in his actions, but he also reccognizes the interests of those people who contribute to his organization--customers, employees, suppliers, owners, creditors, government, and community. He thus operates from self-interest plus the interests of other groups. He states "What is good for G. M. is good for our country." He is a profit satisficer; that is, he balances the profits of the owners and the organization with the wages for employees, taxes for the government, interest for the creditors, and so forth. Money is important to him, but so are people, because his values tell him that satisfying people's needs is a better goal than just making money.

In balancing the needs of the various contributors to the organization, the trusteeship manager deals with the customers as the chief providers of revenue to the firm. His values tell him not to cheat the customers because cheating is not good for the firm. He is concerned with providing sufficient quantities of goods as well as sufficient quality at the right time and place for customer satisfaction. He views employees as having certain rights which must be recognized; they are more than a mere commodity to be traded in the marketplace. His accountability as a manager is to owners as well as customers, employees, suppliers, creditors, government, and the community.

To the trusteeship style of manager technology is important, but so are people. Technological innovation is to be commended because new machines, equipment, and products are useful in creating a high standard of living for people. Materialism is important, but so is humanism.

His political values are reflected in a recognition that government and politics are important, but he views government and politics as necessary evils. He distrusts both, recognizing that government serves as a threat to his existence if his firm does not live up to laws such as those passed in the 1930s.

His environmental beliefs are stated as follows: "Man can control and manipulate his environment. Therefore, let him do it for his benefit and incidentally for society's benefit."

The social values which he holds are more liberal than those held by the profit maximizer. He recognizes that employees have several needs beyond their economic needs. They have a desire for security and belongingness as well as for recognition. He knows that he is an individualist, but he also knows the value of group participation in managing the business. He views minority groups as having their place in society, but "their place is usually inferior to mine. Minority group members are usually not qualified to hold their jobs, but that is not my fault."

Aesthetic values are not alien to the trusteeship manager, but "they are not for our firm although someone has to support the arts and cultural values."

PHASE III

In contrast to the values of the profit maximizer and the trustee manager are those of the Phase III quality of life manager. He believes in enlightened self-interest. He agrees that selfish and group interests are important, but that society's interests are also important in making decisions. "What is good for society is good for our company" would be his opinion. He agrees that profit is essential for the firm, but that profits in and of themselves are not the end objectives of the firm. As far as money and wealth are concerned, his set of values would tell him that money is important but people are more important than money.

In sharp contrast to *caveat emptor* in dealing with customers, his philosophy would be *caveat venditor*, i.e., let the seller beware. The company should bear the responsibility for producing and distributing products and services in sufficient quantities at the right time and place with the necessary quality, information, and services necessary to satisfy customers' needs. The Phase III manager would recognize the dignity of each employee, not treating him as a commodity to be bought and sold. Accountability as a manager is to the owners, to the other contributors to the business, *and* to society in general.

Technological values would be important, but people would be held in higher esteem than machines, equipment, computers, and esoteric products. He would be a humanist rather than a materialist.

His political values would dictate that government and politicians are necessary contributors to the quality of life. Rather than resist government, he would state that business and government must cooperate to solve society's problems.

The social values of a quality of life manager indicate that a person cannot be separated into economic man or family man. The philosophy would be, "We hire the whole man and all of his problems." The manager would recognize that group participation rather than rugged individualism is a determining factor in his organization's success. His values regarding minority groups are different from the other managers. His view is: "Blacks, Indians, and foreigners are people as you and I are. They need support and guidance like any other person."

Man must preserve the environment, not for environment's sake alone, but for the benefit of people who want to lead a quality life. As far as aesthetic values are concerned, the Phase III manager recognizes that the arts and cultural values reflect the lives of people whom he holds in high regard. His actions would support the aesthetic values by committing resources to their preservation.

The contrast among the three sets of values creates an awareness of the differing ideologies of managerial decision makers. (See Table 13-1.) A managerial set of values is important because values determine the decisions the manager makes. They are the norms for managerial statements of an organization's objectives. They determine the managerial policies that an organization follows in trying to accomplish these objectives. They determine the strategies and tactics which are used. They become the standards upon which the manager judges whether some action is right or wrong. They are the filters which a manager unconsciously uses to sort out one alternative from another. They determine the tones of his **actions**.

TABLE 13-1. COMPARISON OF MANAGERIAL VALUES

Phase I *Profit Maximizing Management*	*Phase II* *Trusteeship Management*	*Phase III* *Quality of Life Management*
	Economic Values	
1) Raw self-interest	1) Self-interest 2) Contributors' interest	1) Enlightened self-interest 2) Contributors' interests 3) Society's interests
What's good for me is good for my country.	What's good for GM is good for our country.	What is good for society is good for our company.
Profit maximizer	Profit satisficer	Profit is necessary, but. . . .
Money and wealth are most important.	Money is important, but so are people.	People are more important than money.
Let the buyer beware. (*caveat emptor*)	Let us not cheat the customer.	Let the seller beware. (*caveat venditor*)
Labor is a commodity to be bought and sold.	Labor has certain rights which must be recognized.	Employee dignity has to be satisfied.
Accountability of management is to the owners.	Accountability of management is to the owners, customers, employees, suppliers, and other contributors.	Accountability of management is to the owners, contributors, and society.
	Technology Values	
Technology is very important.	Technology is important but so are people.	People are more important than technology.
	Social Values	
Employee personal problems must be left at home.	We recognize that employees have needs beyond their economic needs.	We hire the whole man.
I am a rugged individualist, and I will manage my business as I please.	I am an individualist, but I recognize the value of group participation.	Group participation is fundamental to our success.
Minority groups are inferior to whites. They must be treated accordingly.	Minority groups have their place in society, and their place is inferior to mine.	Minority group members are people as you and I are.
	Political Values	
That government is best which governs least.	Government is a necessary evil.	Business and government must cooperate to solve society's problems.
	Environmental Values	
The natural environment controls the destiny of man.	Man can control and manipulate the environment.	We must preserve the environment in order to lead a quality life.
	Aesthetic Values	
Aesthetic Values? What are they?	Aesthetic values are okay, but not for us.	We must preserve our aesthetic values, and we will do our part.

THE CURRENT STATE

The concept of social responsibility has gone through the three distinct phases described above--each corresponding to a described set of managerial values. Each new phase did not replace the earlier phase, but rather it was superimposed on it. Thus, a modern view of social responsibility would to some degree incorporate essential parts of all three phases of the concept. It would encompass not only a deep commitment to social problems, but also an understanding of the firm's responsibility to its contributors and, most importantly, a realistic comprehension of the need for profit as an essential prerequisite for operating at higher levels of social responsibility.

In today's business world and academic community there are people who subscribe to all three phases of the social responsibility concept. One rather vocal group follows the logic of Milton Friedman, who believes that Phase I logic still prevails (4). He feels that a corporate manager is an agent of the stockholders and any diversion of resources from the task of maximizing stockholder wealth amounts to spending the stockholders' money without their consent. Moreover, he argues that government, not business, is the institution best suited to attacking social problems. Although this position typically is supported vigorously by its proponents, in practice it often breaks down because of the extreme difficulty in drawing a line between spending the stockholders' money for charity and spending it in the enlightened self-interest of the firm.

Probably the majority of business managers today adhere to a Phase II concept of social responsibility. They understand the pluralistic nature of our society and are generally committed to being equitable in dealing with the various contributors to the firm and the concerned outside pressure groups. Typically, these businessmen emphasize good wages and good working conditions and being fair and forthright in dealing with their customers and suppliers.

A growing number of academicians and business executives, however, appear to be accepting the Phase III concept of social responsibility. A number of our largest corporations, such as IBM, Chase Manhattan Bank, Xerox, Eli Lilly, and Coca-Cola are becoming involved in major social action programs.

It must not be forgotten, however, that managers are constrained in their actions by the economic needs of their companies. Profit and positive cash flow are still the *sine qua non* for all firms. Thus, the top management of a large profitable corporation has much greater latitude in the social area than does the manager of a small marginal operation, although even small firms can make a contribution to a better quality of life through social action programs. But in small as well as large companies, executives cannot afford to jeopardize their firm's financial position in the name of social involvement.

Boise Cascade Corporation, for example, promoted a minority enterprise in the heavy construction industry. The venture resulted in a pretax loss of approximately $40 million to Boise Cascade. As a result, the corporation's stock price plummeted 60 points and, undoubtedly, there was much serious soul searching within the organization. The point is that a business firm is still fundamentally an economic entity and must be concerned first with its own economic well-being. True, the public does expect business to become socially involved, but not at the expense of its primary mission, that of making a profit and thereby contributing to a healthy and vigorous economy.

In summary, currently there is a three-way split or schizophrenia in business and academic circles over the subject of business management's social responsibility. This disagreement among those who study, teach, and practice business has contributed greatly to public confusion and disenchantment concerning the role of business in today's society. Despite this confusion and disenchantment, the public views business as the most productive and efficient institution in society and therefore as a major resource in the struggle to solve society's great social problems. Since business as an institution exists only because it is sanctioned by society, it is inevitable that business managers will fall in line with society's expectations. Hence, the modern concept, Phase III, of business' social responsibility will be increasingly accepted by businessmen in the future.

REFERENCES

1. Berle, Adolph A., and Gardiner C. Means. *The Modern Corporation and Private Property,* (New York: Macmillan, 1932), p. 47.

2. Bowen, Howard R. "Business Management: A Profession," in William T. Greenwood, *Issues in Business and Society,* 2nd ed. (Boston: Houghton-Mifflin, 1971).

3. Committee for Economic Development. *Social Responsibilities of Business Corporations* (New York: Research and

Business Policy Committee, CED, June, 1971).

4. Friedman, Milton. "The Social Responsibility of Business Is to Increase Its Profits," *The New York Times Magazine*, September 13, 1970, pp. 122-126.

5. Steiner, George A. *Business and Society* (New York: Random House, 1971), pp. 70-71.

STUDENT REVIEW QUESTIONS

1. Explain the relationships between the three phases of social responsibility and the social environments in which they emerged.
2. What do Hay and Gray mean by a "pluralistic society"?
3. Discuss briefly how a manager's personal values (Phase I, II, or III) will be reflected in his actions.
4. Compare and contrast the ideas of Milton Friedman with John Galbraith. Which do you agree with?
5. How would you describe the current state of social responsibility?

REFERENCES FOR ADDITIONAL STUDY

Abouzeid, Kamal M. and Charles N. Weaver, "Social Responsibility in the Corporate Goal Hierarchy," *Business Horizons*, June, 1978.

Bright, James R., "Evaluating Signals of Technological Change," *Harvard Business Review*, January-February, 1970.

Davis, Keith, "Social Responsibility is Inevitable," *California Management Review*, Fall, 1976.

Fahey, Llam, and William R. King, "Environmental Scanning for Corporate Scanning," *Business Horizons*, August, 1977.

Goeldner, C. R., and Laura M. Dirks, "Business Facts: Where to Find Them," *Business Topics*, Summer, 1976.

Gorry, G. Anthony, and Michael S. S. Morton, "A Framework for Management Information Systems," *Sloan Management Review*, Fall, 1971.

Guth, William D. and Renato Tagiuri, "Personal Values and Corporate Strategy," *Harvard Business Review*, September-October, 1965.

Hall, William K., "Forecasting Techniques for Use in the Corporate Planning Process," *Managerial Planning*, November-December, 1972.

Hussey, David E., "The Corporate Appraisal: Assessing Company Strengths and Weaknesses," *Long Range Planning*, December, 1968.

Rippe, Richard D., "The Integration of Corporate Forecasting and Planning, *Columbia Journal of World Business*, Winter, 1976.

Sawyer, George C., "Social Issues and Social Change:

Impact on Strategic Decisions," *MSU Business Topics*, Summer, 1973.

Steiner, George A., "Social Policies for Business," *California Management Review*, Winter, 1972.

Thurston, Philip H., "Make TF Serve Corporate Planning," *Harvard Business Review*, September-October, 1971.

Tipgos, Manuel A., "Structuring a Managerial Information System for Strategic Planning," *Managerial Planning*, January-February, 1975.

Vogt, Richard J., "Forecasting as a Management Tool," *University of Michigan Business Review*, January, 1970.

Wall, Jerry, "What the Competition is Doing: Your Need to Know," *Harvard Business Review*, November-December, 1974.

Warren, E. Kirby, "The Capability Inventory: Its Role in Long Range Planning," *Management of Personnel Quarterly*, Winter, 1965.

Weidenbaum, Murry L., "The Role of Economics in Business Planning," *MSU Business Topics*, Summer, 1962.

White, George R., and Margaret B. W. Graham, "How to Spot a Technological Winner," *Harvard Business Review*, March-April, 1978.

SECTION C.

KEY AREAS OF STRATEGIC CONCERN

14

Strategic Planning in a Turbulent International Environment*

KJELL-ARNE RINGBAKK**

MULTINATIONAL STRATEGIC PLANNING has never been more needed and at the same time more difficult and frustrating than to-day. Executives involved in international business are acutely aware of how government and politically motivated actions have emerged as critical forces in the international system.

Recent developments in the negotiation of social compacts, demands for indigenization, nationalization of key industries, national planning, the emergence of state-owned enterprises, and global redistribution of wealth and power are powerful forces for change in the world economy. Successful multinational corporate planning for the fourth quarter century must be increasingly environmental, strategic, and political in orientation. At stake is no less than the multinational corporation itself.

The purpose of this article is to review those developments in the multinational corporate environment supporting the spectacular growth of foreign direct investments and multinational corporations since World War II, to assess some of the current changes fundamentally altering the premises for multinational corporate planning, and to identify some implications for international executives involved in strategic planning and management.

---

*From *Journal of Long-Range Planning*, June, 1976, pp. 2-11. Reprinted by permission.

**This article is based on research which was funded by the Amos Tuck School of Business Administration. The author is working with several international enterprises on strategic planning and management questions.

The late 1960s and early 1970s mark a turning point for international business where a long period of *steady state* has been jolted by turbulence and discontinuities. We find it useful to think of the 1945 to 1970 period as the third quarter century. In so doing many of the generalizations made in the subsequent sections generally hold true.*

THE THIRD QUARTER CENTURY BUSINESS ENVIRONMENT

Although many business enterprises had significant commitments overseas and by most definitions were multinational by World War II, the *large-scale rise* has taken place since the war. For the purpose of this analysis we treat the modern multinational corporation as a product of the post World War II international environment in line with the proposition that *the multinational is not a cause but a symptom or an effect of the international system.* This is also the rationale for emphasizing the characteristics of the system itself viewing this as a prerequisite for understanding the challenges facing international executives today.[1]

The evolution of foreign direct investments and multinational corporations since World War II has taken place within an environment displaying a set of clear characteristics.

GEOPOLITICS

Geopolitically, the period following the war was characterized by general stability and only gradual or limited change. The U. S. dominance in the international political economy produced a set of known alliances and thus friendly areas business could rely on. The ideology-based cold war produced its own stability where areas 'off limit' to U. S. business were identified and known. Official lists of strategic goods placed clear restrictions on what products could be traded. Most favoured nation status affected international trade and investment opportunities in part by restricting credit and tariff terms. Embargoes determined which countries could not be traded with at all. From a corporate point this meant limited and often predictable political risks.

The Marshall Plan which started in 1948 stimulated not only large-scale exports of food stuffs, capital goods, and consumer products from the United States, but it also fostered European measures for selfhelp. The German 'Wirt-

---

*In this paper we for convenience of presentation focus on U.S.-based multinationals while recognizing that the same forces are worldwide exerting similar pressures on non-U.S. based MNCs.

schaftswunder', or economic miracle, is a prime and well-known example. The currency and economic reforms introduced in mid-1948 replaced state planning and controls by the 'social market economy' concept.[2]

The reconstruction and accompanying growth provided immense opportunities for exports to Germany and later direct investments in marketing and local manufacturing.

Motivated by humanitarian and anti-communist ideas, the U.S. made large-scale commitments to aid and development programmes throughout the third quarter century. This contributed to the economic and political preconditions favouring the overseas expansions of U. S. firms.

> "Europe's rehabilitation, a management job of an unprecedented order, calls for an unprecedented effort. What is required is a giant transformation of healthy economic blood into a shock-struck continent. The job must be done either on grounds of Christian duty or on grounds of egotistic self-preservation; but it must be done. And the only country that can do the job is America."[3]

The gap between the industrialized 'North' and underdeveloped 'South' implied that both purchasing power and effective demand were concentrated in the more developed countries (MDCs). The planning and strategy implications of this were that market-based investments were made in MDCs while investments in exploration and subsequent production of natural resources were made in LDCs. In the course of the third quarter century the less developed countries, contrary to popular belief, did not become very important markets for most multinational corporations. In personal interviews international executives have pointed out that as they begin to analyse the fourth quarter century multinational environment, many less developed country markets are at best of marginal interest to them. In some instances these international executives say they would prefer *not* to do business within the LDCs in part due to political risk, general uncertainty, and the prospects for no more than marginal returns. Peter F. Drucker in a study referring to confidential data strongly supports this point.[4]

The geopolitical conditions favoured U. S. overseas involvement. A review of the writings in a management journal such as *Fortune* during the second half of the 1940s reveals great concern with global problems and the future of America. The articles frequently appealed to U. S. enterprises to become more directly involved in support of the American ideals and U. S. foreign policy. Many of the writings stress not only moral obligations but helped create a new awareness of overseas opportunities and threats. The appeal in some instances were very direct:

> "The U.S. must lend some of its capital and its capital goods, to be sure. But it must also, if it is really to lead the way to world freedom, lend the world some of its industrial knowhow. Americans with the needed knowledge and resourcefulness must go over the earth, as investors and managers and engineers, as makers of mutual prosperity, as missionaries of capitalism and democracy."[5]

In the same article[6] the writer admonishes U. S. corporations, experienced managers and professionals, and 'the young men, the ex-GIs and the college boys dreaming of fortune and adventure' to go overseas to serve as 'front-line soldiers and batallions in the battle for freedom'.[7]

RESOURCES

Ready access to natural resources was another important driving force facilitating the internationalization of business. The energy needs following World War II produced large-scale investments in oil exploration and production in the Middle-East and Latin America. The resulting supply and ready availability of low cost energy exerted an important influence on strategies for product design, process and technology choices, and on location and transportation decisions. Likewise, the availability of low-cost plentiful raw materials permitted the adoption of standardized production methods and the use of specialized plant and equipment in pursuits of production efficiencies and economies of scale. For example, the plastic industry, synthetic fibres, and fertilizers have gained their importance in part due to the development of large-scale highly automated facilities dependent on inexpensive petroleum based inputs. It is difficult to envision that these and many other products would have gained their importance if energy had cost not $1.50 a barrel but more than seven times as much.

During the post-World War II period vertically integrated multinational corporations headquartered in MDCs dominated much of the global resource exploitation. These multinationals pursued startegies which initially were acceptable or at least tolerated by both the resource-using and resource-producing countries. However, as resource conflicts have emerged many of these multinationals have found themselves caught 'between the dog and the lamp post'.

ECONOMICS

The international *economic* situation following World War II also supported international corporate expansion. The reconstruction in Europe and Japan and the commitment to economic growth created a multitude of business opportunities. The American economy came out of World War II vastly stronger than any other country. American corporations enjoyed significant technological leads. They possessed the differentiated products and the necessary production capacity. They were experienced in mass production and mass marketing. They were hence well positioned to take advantage of the demands developing overseas. In the immediate post-World War II period the U. S. firms built up strong export positions.

The Bretton Woods Conference in 1944 had produced important agreements on the establishment of the International Monetary Fund and on the future international monetary system promising exchange stability and convertibility. The General Agreement on Tariffs and Trade in parallel promised a freeing of international trade and a stimulation of the international economy. Tariffs were to be reduced, quantitative restrictions were to be eliminated, and countries agreed to refrain from using the beggar-thy-neighbour policies characteristic of the pre-war period. Until growth came under scrutiny and attack by the late 1960s, the international economic environment supported corporate internationalization.

INSTITUTIONAL FRAMEWORK

During the third quarter century the evolving international institutional framework was an added driving force. The development of an international infrastructure and particularly the improvements in international transportation and communications systems facilitated the flows of products, services, technology, and information. Whereas in 1935 an Imperial Airways flight from Great Britain to India took 5 days, after the introduction of DC8s and Boeing 707s in the late 1950s the same trip could be undertaken in 1 day.

The large-scale economic integration producing blocs such as the European Economic Community (EEC), the European Free-Trade Association (EFTA), and the Latin American Free-Trade Association (LAFTA) helped create larger economic units and markets where mass production and mass marketing expertise were needed. They also offered the prospects for a redefinition of national trade and business boundaries.

The development of international sources of funds such as Eurodollars, Eurobonds, and Eurocurrencies made the growing multinational corporation less dependent on restrictive national monetary policies and institutions. The growth in multinational banking may initially have been motivated by 'following the customer'. Multinational banks and consortia during this period became an important force satisfying the financing needs stemming from multinational expansion.

ATTITUDES AND PERCEPTIONS

Throughout the third quarter century the *attitudes* toward international business and foreign direct investments were generally favourable. MDCs and LDCs alike in the post-war were ready to play host to the foreign investors.*

A major reason was the lack of viable alternatives. These investments were perceived as suitable means for closing international economic, technical, and capital gaps. Foreign investments also contributed to national ends such as growth and employment.

In negotiating the foreign entry, decision makers in the host country tended to focus on short-term benefits rather than long-term costs. The emphasis was on transfers of capital and technology, the building of new plants and equipment, the employment of workers, and the stimulus to economic activities. The subsequent evolution of multinational corporations, their future size and dominance, and their eventual threat to national sovereignty were not anticipated or of major concern although earlier investment by U. S. companies in Europe had created some opposition. 'America has invaded Europe not with armed men, but with manufactured goods. Its leaders have been captains of industry and skilled financiers whose conquests are having a profound effect on the lives of the masses from Madrid to St. Petersburg.' Thus wrote F. A. McKenzie in 1902 in a book entitled, *The American Invaders*. However, in the later 1940s and 1950s thoughts such as these were not foremost on politicians' minds.

From a United States perspective the overseas growth by the large corporations was frequently perceived supportive of and rarely in conflict with foreign policy objectives.

> "As the U. S. has demonstrated, the methods of production and exchange developed in the Industrial Revolution have, for the first time in history, made it a realistic possibility for every human being to have the basic necessities and comforts of life, and most of the people of the world know it.

---

*Japan was an important exception to this. After the war, regulations and requirements by the Japanese authorities made direct investment difficult or impossible in that country.

> The Communist revolution can probably be halted only by revival of the Industrial Revolution in war-devastated lands, and advancement of it in the lands whose people have only begun to enjoy its abundance.
>
> The U. S. possessing industrial production roughly equal to that of all the rest of the world, is alone capable of producing and exporting the machinery and skills required to do this."*

In sum, the quarter century after World War II was rich in opportunities for U. S. managers wanting to expand operations outside their home markets. In the immediate post-war period one set of favourable preconditions existed due to the rebuilding and reconstruction efforts. As of the mid-1950s and throughout the 1960s policies pursuing economic growth produced a new set of driving and only select restraining forces. Corporations responded aggressively by pursuing their own growth objectives and strategies. However, a review of the multinational corporate environment and its prospects as we enter the fourter quarter century suggests significant changes are taking place. Note that in the following we are *not* making predictions about the fourth quarter century *per se*. Instead we are focusing on current forces for change and what appears to happen to the trends and parameters discussed above. The readers could therefore use this as a basis for developing their own historical analysis and to derive parameters most important for their situation.

THE FOURTH QUARTER CENTURY ENVIRONMENT

A comparison of the past with the emergent multinational corporate environment is summarized in Table 14-1. In the realm of *geopolitics* stability has been replaced by new conflicts, a breakdown of the old alliances, and the emergence of new centres of power. Detente and the subsequent push for East-West trade have reduced the old ideological division between the United States and the U.S.S.R.[8]

At the same time, however, resource-based conflicts have emerged as a new central geopolitical and economic issue. In raw materials and resource trades, a century-long trend has abruptly been reversed with abundance replaced by scarcity. While physical shortages do not appear to be an imminent problem, politically motivated shortages are very likely to be with us well into the fourth quarter century. One obvi-

*The U.S. Situation, *Fortune*, XXXV, 6, June (1947).

TABLE 14-1. CHANGES IN THE MULTINATIONAL CORPORATE ENVIRONMENT

PARAMETERS	THIRD QUARTER CENTURY (WW II--early 1970s)	FOURTH QUARTER CENTURY (Early 1970s---)
Geopolitics	1. General political stability	1. Breakdown of old alliances, nationalism, new conflicts
	2. Ideologically based Cold War	2. Resource-based 'economic war'
	3. U. S. dominance in international political economy	3. Erosion of U. S. pre-eminence and superiority
	4. North-South gap	4. Food, population, Fourth World Problems Interdependence with shifting locus of power
Resources	5. Ready availability of low cost energy	5. Uncertain availability but high cost
	6. Ready access to raw materials	6. Resource nationalism and cartels
	7. MDC-controlled exploration, exploitation	7. LDC and resource-rich controlled production
Economics	8. Reconstruction in Europe and Japan	8. Preventing Malthusian prophesies of doom
	9. Economic growth objectives	9. Socio-Ecological balances
	10. Closing international gaps	10. Problematique: Multivariant, Interactive, Global
	11. 'Limits to Growth' unknown	11. Conserving resources

	12. GATT: promising free international trade	12. Bilateralism, regionalism, and barter
	13. IMS: offering monetary stability	13. Breakdown of Bretton Woods system
Institutional Framework	14. International communications and transportation	14. Improved communications and transportation
	15. International banking and financial markets	15. More prudent and controlled developments
	16. Eurodollars, Eurobonds, Eurocurrencies	16. Currency cocktails, shifting currency strength
	17. EEC, EFTA, LAFTA, COMECON ANCOM	17. OPEC, IBA type political-economic organization
Foreign Investments	18. Long tradition of portfolio investments	18. Foreign dominance or influence resisted
	19. Open host environments welcoming direct investment as means to close gaps	19. Restrictive host environments scrutinizing existing and new foreign investments
	20. Home country tolerance for export of capital, technology, and management	20. Home country concern with export of jobs and loss of national economic welfare
	21. Emphasis on short-term benefits, discounting long-term costs	21. Perception that costs exceed benefits and that MNC is a threat to sovereignty
	22. Direct investments a means to national ends	22. Important gaps are closed and direct investments have served primary purpose
	23. Minor government involvement or interference	23. Extensive government involvement in national planning and management of economic affairs

ous consequence of this reversal is that MNCs and MDCs alike are becoming dependent on resource rich countries with different objectives and ideologies.

The case of OPEC has demonstrated well how political, ideological, and economic objectives are pursued simultaneously in a blend different from what has been perceived acceptable in the industrialized North. In addition to quadrupling the price of oil, placing embargoes on select countries, and blacklisting companies for economic dealings with Israel, some OPEC members have devised ambitious plans for national development, downstream investments in petro-related industries, and they have used part of their petro-dollar surplus to buy real assets and negotiate part ownership of companies such as Daimler Benz or Krupp in Germany, and in Pan Am or real estate in the United States.[9]

In addition to OPEC, a number of resource cartels have been formed or are in preparation.[10]

While these resource or commodity cartels have experienced difficulties during the 1974-1975 recession, uncertain availability and higher cost for energy and natural resources can be anticipated in the years ahead. Resource nationalism has been intensifying worldwide and is not confined to the LDCs. After the discovery of oil in the North Sea, the Norwegian and British governments have developed very aggressive resource policies and have been negotiating to extract the maximum benefit for themselves. In the span of one decade, Norway has become oil rich, has rejected membership in the EEC, and has become known as 'the blue-eyed Arabs of the North'.[11]

Countries such as Canada and Australia traditionally enjoying the reputation as free and open host countries have as of the early 1970s become very restrictive and conscious about potential conflicts between foreign interests and their own economic welfare and priorities.[12]

Many observers suggest the resource-rich countries will seek further controls over the total production of natural resources and thus their own destiny as part of their efforts to 'redress existing imbalances and shortcomings'. A review of some LDC objectives reveals the following aspirations:

(1) Increase the LDC proportion of the World Gross Product from the present 7 to 25 percent by the year 2000;
(2) Incrase the real gross national product by 8 percent/year;
(3) Form additional resource cartels;
(4) More processing and domestic value added to raw materials before exporting;
(5) Nationalizing those sectors where multinational corporations play too large a role;
(6) Increase the transfer of real resources from

> more developed countries through special taxes and assessments on all raw materials.[13]

The pressing problems of food, population, and the survival of the **fourth** world are adding new tensions within the geopolitical picture. According to some analyses, food resources may become so inadequate during the next quarter century that we invariably will experience a reversal of present birth and death rates and a return to the Malthusian prophesies of doom.[14]

The forces unleashed by the transition from resource abundance to resource scarcities are contributing to further reduction in geopolitical stability and invite--and frequently *necessitate*--government involvement and regulation.

The new interdependencies in the global system make partial analysis insufficient. We have now come up against a new 'problematique' which is multivariant, interactive, and increasingly global calling for strategies at macro and micro levels aimed at conserving resources, recycling, and preserving or restoring socio-ecological balances.[15]

To master national destinies in face of this new reality governments are playing new and more active economic roles. One example is the multibillion dollar trade agreements signed by heads of state signifying that important strategic decisions have been lifted from the corporate to the government level. When the Shah of Iran signs a $3-5 billion deal with the French government or a $15 billion agreement with the U. S., that has far reaching implications for corporate planning and strategy.[16]

Within the new global system the range of viable national economic and political objectives has become much greater than before. As a consequence the process of allocating resources has become much more political. This has placed added premium on understanding the political dimension of the business environment. A senior U. S. official has warned of a 'new nationalism' on each side of the Atlantic in which 'countries as a defensive move tend to export problems to other nations without regard for the real interdependence in the system. Growth, interdependence, and comparative advantages have led to a broadening of goals which in turn have produced new demands for fulfillment and solutions which frequently are internationally incompatible. What we need is more international compromise and new international structure for dialogue'.[17]

The lacking progress in multilateral trade negotiations during the late 1960s and early 1970s reveals the basic mismatch between the problems, the goals, and the institutional framework and mechanisms necessary for effective resolution. Fragmentation rather than unity appears to be the hallmark of international affairs today.[18]

> "It has been convenient for a genera-

> tion to consider the world as divided between the rich, powerful, and industrialized developed countries and the poor, weak, and industrially backward developing countries whose only hope for salvation rested on greatly increased aid from richer nations.
> "That old assumption has been abruptly altered by the unwelcome trinity of global inflation, recurrent materials shortages, and the huge increase in oil prices imposed by the OPEC cartel. The resulting sharp shifts of economic power are not only transforming the structure of international finance but creatin a new order of relationships between industrial countries and poor countries and among the poor ones themselves."[19]

Fundamental changes of the kind characterizing the fourth quarter century have not only added uncertainty and complexity to the multinational environment, they have also impacted directly on the relationship between the multinational corporation and home and host countries alike. Attitudes toward foreign direct investments, international production, and multinational corporations, have begun to reverse and the free investments climate of the past is being replaced by suspicion, restrictions, and new constraints and regulations. Foreign economic dominance is resisted, resented, and no longer tolerated. Host countries are scrutinizing existing and new foreign direct investments in efforts to align private to public interests. Existing contracts are renegotiated and in many instances cancelled. New contracts are no longer based on terms dictated by the MNC but on the principle of maximizing the benefits for the host countries by extracting the most favourable terms from the foreign investor.[20]

In *home* countries multinational corporations have likewise become subject to novel pressures and scrutiny. Multinationals are attacked by home country groups for exporting technologies and thereby reducing home country comparative advantage, exporting jobs, exploiting the lower labor costs in other countries notably LDCs and more recently East-European countries, contributing to the unfavourable balance of payments by exporting less and importing more, while allocating capital to international rather than domestic investments.

What the attacks bring out is the basic disharmony between the sovereignty of the nation state and the efficiency-seeking multinational corporation. As the old gaps in standards of living, technology, capital, and management have been reduced or closed, the original purpose of the foreign direct investment as far as the host country is concerned has been served. Consequently, a reassessment of multinationals and the value of foreign investments is taking place worldwide.

Critics have done an excellent job of analysing and attacking multinational for their costs and negative sides.[21]

The defenders are at best providing a meek rebuttal and have been doing a poor job in bringing out the true benefits of foreign direct investments and multinational corporations.[22] This has done much to shape the new attitudes towards multinationals.

In Table 14-2 we have summarized the changing attitudes towards multinational corporations proposing that a number of important preconditions are reversing and growing negative. Multinational corporations are viewed with less enthusiasm and a new hostility in home as well as host countries. This can in part be attributed to the size, dominance, and power modern multinationals represent. In light of strengthening values and concerns with corporate giantism and the potential for misuse of power, it is difficult to envision a steady growth for the supergiants in the future. *Externally* new barriers are likely to be erected to prevent some of this super growth from continuing. In different parts of the world antitrusters are seeking to break up companies with too much market or economic power. *Internally* managers are experiencing that their multiproduct, multimarket, multiunit, multitechnology, multigeography, and multi-everything corporations have almost become too difficult to manage. In interviews managers in various multibillion dollar corporations have expressed concern about their ability to plan and control present operations. Some have in their planning recognized this multidimensionality and size problem to be a real constraint in the years ahead.[23]

Until recently multinational corporations were largely a product of the more developed countries of Europe and North America. This is beginning to change as a function of the strengthening aspirations of other countries and regimes. Japan's international commitments have boomed through joint ventures and large-scale projects involving consortia of corporations, banks, and trading houses--frequently also including the government of Japan and the government of the host country as well. Japanese alternatives to the western multinational should be anticipated in the years ahead.[24]

Established or evolving competitive structures will also be upset by other newcomers. Communist countries have displayed clear interests in expanding their participation in international business.[25]

Some resource-rich countries such as Venezuela or Iran have sought control of their economic destiny through more direct participation in economic affairs. New partnerships between the resource-rich and multinationals are blooming. Initially these are manifested through negotiated transfers

TABLE 14-2. CHANGING ATTITUDES TOWARDS MULTINATIONAL CORPORATIONS

Country	Third Quarter Century	Fourth Quarter Century
U.S.A.	Supportive as home country Open to foreigners Relatively free and unregulated	Regulation and controls proposed More protective and closed Select Xenophebia; less freewheeling
Canada	Very open and free Actively seeking investments	Very restricted: 'Buy back Canada' Harsh scrutiny. Reduced dependence on the U.S.
Western Europe	Generally supportive as home Open to foreigners Some concern with 'American Challenge'	European company law Restricted, selectively closed Government support or outright nationalization
Japan	Almost totally regulated Recent moderation Strict government supervision Few Japanese MNCs	Capital liberalization More Japanese overseas investments Macro–Micro ventures as alternative to MNC Trading houses as multinational systems organizers
Australia	Open, free Actively seeking investments	Temporary restrictions Resource nationalism: 'Buy back the farm'
Communist	No entry Politics guiding economics	Select opportunities but uncertain Government partner Economics more important
LDCs	Open and free	Reversals, re-negotiations Indigenization Nationalism
Resource-Rich	Open and free	Unpredictable Extortionist

of production facilities previously owned by the multinationals. In line with their interest in forward integration and downstream investments, some resource-rich countries are planning their own multinationals through joint ventures and foreign direct investments.[26]

In Table 14-3 we have summarized some of the common demands placed on foreign investors by host countries. While this list by no means is exhaustive, it points to substantive changes in the ways MNCs and subsidiaries should be managed. Applied in the extreme, these demands may *negate* the benefits and advantages multinationals can offer. Nationalistic politicians who are proponents of the most extreme localization have a confined constituency and pursue ethnocentric and not geocentric policies. The consequences of the changing environmental preconditions, the new attitudes towards foreign investment and ownership, and demands such as the ones presented here must receive much more top management attention.

By indigenization we refer to all the processes by which the foreign direct investor can localize so that the foreign-ness will diminish and eventually disappear. This implies changes in management structure, more local autonomy, and less dependence on foreigners. One consequence of this is that the MNC cannot operate as an efficiency-seeking system the way it has in the past. Instead, new criteria must be factored into the decision processes to adapt to present and emerging local demands.

TABLE 14-3. HOST COUNTRY DEMANDS ON MNCs

Indigenization

- Locals in management, technical positions, on board of directors
- Participation in ownership
- Localize decision-making
- Less dependence on foreigners

Technology transfer

- Upgrade quality of investments and jobs
- Education and training for local mastery of skills
- Local R & D, develop indigenous technology

Strategy adaptation

- Reinvestment of earnings, less repatriation
- Local sourcing of supplies, parts, components
- Local manufacturing
- Increased exports to third and home markets
- Local control
- Subordinating to national plans, policies, and interests
- Avoid dominating industries or regions
- Limited access to natural resources
- Maximize net contribution to society through backward integration, higher local value added

In the realm of technology transfers, host countries again are placing stronger demands on MNCs to upgrade the quality of investments and jobs. They are quite legitimately pressing for more education and training of locals so they in turn can master the technologies and skills involved. Through more localized R & D MNCs are expected to help in the development of indigeneous technology adapted to actual factor of production conditions.

A series of demands for strategy adaptation also reflect the changing power balance and strengthening host country position. This could be viewed as part of the indigenization process since the end result is to make the local operations function as if they were full-fledged local corporations or entities.

Implications for Multinational Corporate Planning

If we accept the premise that the multinational corporation is a product or consequence of the conditions in the multinational corporate environment, then our analysis raises fundamental questions about the future of the multinationals. The forces for change and new reality we have begun to sketch for the period ahead implies far-reaching changes and upsets in those preconditions having produced the multinational growth to date. Just as free international trade came to an end during an earlier period, we may now be witnessing the beginning of a similar end for free international production and free overseas expansion by corporations. Past preconditions and relationships have been upset. In multinational strategic planning new forces for change have to be reckoned with. For many managers this has produced frustration and anxiety as past experience and solutions have been rendered irrelevant or inadequate. Past environmental surveillance and planning approaches frequently have been found wanting or insufficient to identify the right problems--not to mention the right solutions.

Since many of the new challenges arise from the turbulence in the multinational corporate environment, it is necessary to evolve a more comprehensive, multidimensional *concept of what the relevant corporate environment really is*. More attention and resources must be devoted to multinational environmental surveillance in order to understand the interdependencies in the system. Environmental sensitivity analysis holds one prospect whereby managers are able to identify the half dozen or so parameters making or breaking a given strategy. The old maxim was never more true: 'You understand the environment and the future only to the extent you study it.' While planning during periods of steady state emphasized the development and implementation of plans, planning in a turbulent environment requires a shift in emphasis to monitoring assumptions and premises guiding the planning processes.

To the extent the future multinational corporate environment is characterized by greater uncertainty, complexity, and reduced predictability, management must develop deeper, more explicit, and more specific assumptions to assess existing and map new strategies.

It is a truism that the rise of the multinational corporation has passed a threshold level where the actions of these supergiants induce autochtomous processes for change in the environment. As a result new anti-MNC forces have developed placing limits on future multinational growth and raising questions about the future of the multinational corporation itself. We appear to have entered a period where a true world economy is emerging but where the nation state as a political unit is no longer the optimal economic unit. Through the globalization of production, modern corporations have replaced traditional trade between sovereign nation states. This is part of the source of the new conflict and restraints multinational corporate planning must explicitly incorporate.

In planning ahead it may be useful to view the multinational corporation as we know it today as a transitory phenomenon. Elsewhere we have suggested that corporations grow through a life-cycle and that we in the years ahead will see increasing numbers of multinationals evolve into *anational corporations*.[27]

Likewise, in planning ahead managers might use the worst or the most pessimistic scenario as the acid test in evaluating strategic alternatives. If a company cannot meet the most stringent demands being proposed today, the new commitment of corporate resources should probably not take place.

CONCLUSION

While corporate planning in the past was marketbased and concerned with growth and profitability in terms such as return on investments or assets, planning in the years will have to be much more politically oriented and sensitive to societal and national priorities. To live up to these challenges, international executives and enterprises will have to display increasing corporate flexibility, entrepreneurship, contingencies, and above all corporate statesmanship. To accomplish this, we must develop a broader and richer language of multinational strategic management. We need to assess past conventions and practices in light of the emergent forces for change. By viewing today's state of affairs *not as normalcy but a transient phase,* we in multinational management should not be planning for more of the same. Instead, we need to understand the dynamic relationship between the MCE, strategic options, and corporate response.

Whilst much planning in MNCs to date has been action-oriented and efficiency-seeking, the new reality of the fourth quarter century calls for new approaches and ways. A review of current practice reveals that many MNCs use planning constructs and models that do not fit the current situation. Instead their multinational corporate planning is merely a 'refined extension of organized corporate planning as developed for the third quarter century reality. A first step towards progress, therefore, is *substantial organizational unlearning* to discontinue wrong or poor practices. This requires both a historical and future-oriented perspective. In the post World War II period we have gained enough experience with corporate planning, the multinational environment, and the functioning of MNCs to begin using a broader and richer multinational strategic management language.

This paper has in part sought to demonstrate the need for such a change. Work with select international enterprises shows they have recognized this and are beginning to change behaviour accordingly. Many MNCs, however, employ traditional planning and strategy concepts as if the conditions of the third quarter century MCE will continue to exist. Our analysis indicates this will not be the case.

A good starting point for the requisite unlearning and attainment of new perspective is to study the evolution of the multinational environment and its impact on corporate strategy and structure. By asking some new questions about the meaning and possible consequences of indigenization, industrial democracy, the Law of the Sea conference, resource cartels modified after OPEC, or the changing attitudes towards MNCs, it becomes clear that multinational strategic planning and management are more important than ever. The key to progress does not lie in formal planning systems or the use of so-called sophisticated management technology. The key is developing international managers with more environmental sensitivity and understanding--with empathy for the aspirations and demands by the multinational stakeholders MNCs in the future must serve.

FOOTNOTES

[1]For a description of some European cases and patterns, see Charles Wilson, *The History of Unilever*, London (1954); W. J. Reader, *Imperial Chemical Industries: A History*, London (1970); F. C. Gerretson, *The History of Royal Dutch*, Leiden (1953); Lawrence G. Franko, "The Origins of Multinational Manufacturing By Continental European Firms," *Business History Review*, pp. 277-302, Autumn (1974); Christopher Tugendhat, *The Multinationals*, Eyre & Spottiswoode,

London (1971), particularly Chapter 1.

For an empirical study of the evolution of U. S. big business, see Alfred Chandler, *Strategy and Structure, Chapters in the History of Industrial Enterprise,* The MIT Press, Cambridge, Mass., 1962. In his study Chandler demonstrates how the move overseas by U. S. corporations must be interpreted within the broader evolution from small single-product and single-market functional entities to large diversified enterprises.

Mira Wilkins has produced two detailed accounts of the American business move abroad: *The Emergence of Multinational Enterprise: American Business Abroad from the Colonial Era to 1914,* Harvard University Press, Cambridge, Mass. (1970); *The Maturing of Multinational Enterprise: American Business Abroad from 1914 to 1970,* Harvard University Press, Cambridge, Mass. (1974); The internationalization of Japanese business which is a much more recent phenomenon is described by M. Y. Yoshino, "The Multinational Spread of Japanese Manufacturing Investments Since World War II," *Business History Review,* pp. 357-381, Autumn (1974).

[2]The chief architect of this economic reform has written a fascinating account of the circumstances surrounding the German reconstruction. Ludwig Erhard, *Prosperity Through Competition,* Thames & Hudson, London (1958).

[3]"Europe: From Freedom to Want, the Destitute Continent in Shock of Liberation Waits for Transfusion of U. S. Health," *Fortune,* XXXI, No. 5, pp. 109-115, May (1945).

[4]Peter F. Drucker, "Multinationals and Developing Countries: Myths and Realities," *Foreign Affairs,* pp. 21-34, October (1974).

[5]The U. S. opportunity, by advancing the industrial revolution at home and abroad, we may win new prosperity for ourselves and freedom for the world. "Needed: Adventurous Business Men," *Fortune,* XXXV (6), 83, June (1947).

[6]*Idem.,* pp. 189 and 192.

[7]While *Fortune* magazine may not have reflected actual feelings, U. S. businessmen clearly got moral support and stimulus for overseas expansion. Writings such as these may therefore have created some of the 'ideological preconditions' for international corporate growth.

[8]For a discussion of how one author sees *detente* aiding multinational corporations, see: Robert Scheer, *America After Nixon: The Age of the Multinationals,* McGraw-Hill, New York (1975).

[9]C. N. Stabler,"Infusion Confusion: Foreign Capital, a Key to Rise of Early U. S., Now Stirs Misgivings," *The Wall Street Journal,* 5 March (1975). Todd E. Fandell, "Off the Brink: $300 Million Rescue of Pan Am by Iran Is About to Be Effected," *The Wall Street Journal,* 13 May (1975); "The Defi OPEC," *The Economist,* pp. 85-89, 8 December (1974); "OPEC: The Economics of the Oil Cartel," *Business Week,* pp. 71-81, 13 January (1975); Louis Kraar, "The Shah Drives to Build a New Persian Empire," *Fortune,* pp. 145-149ff, October (1974); Daniel Yergin, "The Economic, Political, Military Solution," *The New York Times Magazine,* pp. 10-11ff, 16 February (1975).

[10]C. Fred Bergsten, "The New Era in World Commodity Markets," *Challenge,* pp. 34-42, September-October (1974).

[11]Harold Burton Meyers, "'Blue eyed Arabs', Scramble for the Riches of the North Sea," *Fortune,* pp. 140-145, June (1973).

[12]"Trudeau's Balancing Act: Economic Nationalism--With Continued U. S. Ties," *Business Week,* pp. 60-65, 30 November (1974); John E. Cooney,"Clampdown by Canadians on Investing by Aliens Alarms Multinational Firms," *The Wall Street Journal,* 7 May (1975); Charles L. Coltman, III, "The Economic Outlook for Australia," *Columbia Journal of World Business,* pp. 69-72, Spring (1974).

[13]"LDC's Stake Out Ambitious Economic Goals," *Business International,* p. 91, 21 March (1975).

[14]Alvin Toffler, *The Eco-Spasm Report,* Bantam Books (1975); Lester R. Brown and Erik P. Eckholm, "Food and Hunger: The Balance Sheet," *Challenge,* pp. 12-24, September/October (1974).

[15]Barbara Ward and Rene Dubos, "Only One Earth: The Care and Maintenance of a Small Planet," *Columbia Journal of World Business,* pp. 13-25, May/June (1972).

[16]"Iran Will Spend $15-Billion in U. S. Over Five Years," *The New York Times,* 5 March (1975).

[17]Author's note from Ambassador William D. Eberle's speech, "Europe and the Trans-Atlantic Questions," at the third *European Management Symposium* in Davos, Switzerland, 1-9 February (1973).

[18]Grenzen dicht, *Der Spiegel,* No. 12, pp. 67-68, March (1975).

[19]Irving S. Friedman, "The New World of the Rich-Poor

and the Poor-Rich," *Fortune,* p. 244, May (1975).

[20]The following titles from recent *Business International* weekly reports reflect the current state of affairs: "Watching the Watchdog: How Companies Fared with Canada's Investment Agency in its First Year," pp. 121-122, 128, 18 April (1975). "What to Expect and How to Cope in Iran," p. 5, 3 January (1975). "A New Ballgame in Brazil: What It Means...," pp. 116-117, 11 April (1975). "Venezuela--The Next Five Years, Petrofunds Fueling Inflation--and Expectations, Tight Ground Rules for Foreign Investment, No Upvaluation for the Bolivar," pp. 84-85, 14 March (1975). "Indonesia--The Next Five Years, Increasing Restrictions on Foreign Investment, GNP Growth of 9% for 1975-79, Booming Oil Earnings," pp. 36-37, 31 January (1975). "What Foreign Firms Can--and Cannot--Do in Venezuela," p. 7, 3 January (1975).

[21]Ronald E. Müller, "National Instability and Global Corporations: Must They Grow Together?", *Business and Society Review,* pp. 61-72, October (1974). Michael P. Sloan, "When Transnational Corporations Sneeze, The World Catches Cold," *Business and Society Review,* pp. 55-60, October (1974); Elizabeth R. Jajer, "The Changing World of Multinationals," *AFL-CIO American Federationists,* pp. 17-24, September (1974); C. Fred Bergsten, "Coming Investment Wars?",*Foreign Affairs,* pp. 135-152, October (1974); Stefan H. Robock, "The Case for Home Country Controls Over Multinational Firms," *Columbia Journal of Business,* pp. 75-79, Summer (1974).

[22]International Chamber of Commerce, *Realities Multinational Enterprises Respond on Basic Issues,* London (1974); Robert W. Gardner, "Why Caterpillar Speaks Out," *Industry Week,* 178, 78-81, August (1973).

[23]For one discussion supporting the contention that corporations can continue their growth, see Edward R. Bagley, *Beyond the Conglomerates,* Amacom, New York (1975).

[24]Morihisa Emori, "Japanese General Trading Companies: Their Function and Roles," January (1971), unpublished paper; Sumitomo: "How the Keiretsu Pulls Together to Keep Japan Strong," *Business Week,* pp. 43-48, 31 March (1975).

[25]Thomas A. Wolf, "New Frontiers in East-West Trade," *European Business,* pp. 26-35, Autumn (1973).

[26]"Qatar is Ready to Buy 40% of Ethylene Plant to be Built in France," *The Wall Street Journal,* 25 February (1975); Charles N. Stabler, "Analysis are Tracing Where Some Oil Funds are Being Invested," *The Wall Street Journal,*

30 December (1974).

[27]Kjell-Arne Ringbakk, "Multinational Corporations and Foreign Policy," in *Selected Mid-Term Problems in U. S. Foreign Policy*, Dartmouth College, Public Affairs Center, December (1974).

STUDENT REVIEW QUESTIONS

1. Briefly explain the geopolitics of the third quarter century.
2. Generally, what were the attitudes toward international business and foreign investment during this period?
3. How has the environment for multinationals changed in the fourth quarter century?
4. What is the attitude of many host countries to the MNC's?
5. What implications does Ringbakk see for MNC managers of the present and future?
6. What solutions does he propose?

15

Corporate Strategy for Combating Inflation*

MARTIN V. ALONZO**

AMAX's strategies for combating inflation encompass investing, financing, operating and planning policies. Before I discuss these strategies, however, I think it is necessary to go back to the formation of the modern-day AMAX because these strategies developed as a product of the company's formation. In 1957, the American Metal Company and the Climax Molybdenum Company merged to form American Metal Climax, Inc., now called AMAX. The American Metal Co. was a mining finance company holding equity positions in several copper and base metal companies and conducted a trading operation in these metals. The Climax Molybdenum Co. operated a molybdenum mine in Colorado. Before the merger, these two companies had combined assets of $250 million. Today, AMAX is a diversified natural resource company with $3 billion in assets.

In the early 1960's, Ian MacGregor, who recently retired as chairman and chief executive officer of AMAX, was given the responsibility for developing the company's investment strategy. He concluded inflation would be a long-term structural problem facing the world. He reached this conclusion because he believed the dynamics created by the political and social policies in the United States and the

---

*From *Management Accounting,* March, 1978, pp. 57-60. Copyright © 1978 by National Association of Accountants, New York. Reprinted by permission.

**Martin V. Alonzo is vice president and controller, AMAX, Inc., Greenwich, Conn. This article is based on an address by Mr. Alonzo at a meeting of The Conference Board on December 13, 1977, devoted to the theme, "Corporate Strategy for Combating Inflation."

Free World could not effectively combat inflation. These political and social forces causing inflation have not changed since the early 1960's. In fact, I think it is fair to say they have increased.

INVESTMENT STRATEGY

An investment strategy was created to explore for, buy and develop natural resources and build capital facilities as a hedge against inflation. A comparison of the company's assets and their composition at the end of 1960 and September, 1977, is a good snapshot of this strategy:

	Dec.31,1960		Sept.30,1977	
	Amount	%	Amount	%
Cash	$ 82MM	26	$ 130MM	4
Property, plant & equipment	83	27	1,954	65
Total Assets	310	100	2,991	100

Our property account of $1.9 billion does not give true recognition to our most important asset--mineral reserves in the ground, which are stated on the books at nominal amounts. Our cash account would be $778 million today, rather than $130 million, if we maintained the same percentage of our total assets in cash as we did in 1960. We would have invested an additional $648 million in cash where the rate of return in the money markets is less than the inflation rate applicable to capital goods.

Our strategy led to the following investments. We entered the aluminum business in 1963, built an aluminum smelter in the mid-1960's and expanded the business until we sold a one-half interest in 1974 to Mitsui & Co. In the late 1960's we acquired the rights to substantial bauxite reserves in the Kimberleys, Western Australia. We have continued to expand the business whenever the environmentalists allow us to build capacity. In 1969, we started production from a 50%-owned lead-zinc mine in Missouri. Also, in 1969, our first shipments of iron ore were made to Japan from the Mt. Newman Joint Venture in Western Australia in which we have a 25 percent participation. Today, this is one of the largest high-grade iron ore mines in the world. Our studies in the late 1960's also focused on energy and the declining reserves of oil and gas. Therefore, in 1969 we acquired the Ayrshire Collieries Corp., which then produced about 11 million tons of steam coal. In 1977, this operation, now called the AMAX Coal Co., was the third largest bituminous coal producer in the U. S. and will produce about 28 million tons of coal. Our energy studies also resulted in investments in Dutch North Sea and the Texas Offshore area where we have found substantial gas reserves. In 1971 we acquired an interest in a Canadian potash mine and in 1973 became a producer of primary copper through the acquisition of a one-half interest in an operation in Arizona. In 1976, we started up the Henderson molybdenum mine in Colorado which cost more that $500 million to develop. Our investments will total $2 billion in the years 1974-77. This amount approximates our net property and plant account today.

The second aspect of our investment strategy has to do with timing. Recessionary periods offer opportunities to negotiate better engineering, construction and labor contracts than can be negotiated when the economy is overheated. In addition, the availability of skilled labor and productivity is better during such economic periods. Also, once we start a project we continue construction through the ups and downs of the economic cycle. Delays only guarantee higher capital costs because of inflation, reduced productivity and demobilization and remobilization costs. For example, we experienced three recessions during the 10 years it took to develop the Henderson molybdenum mine prior to its start-up in 1976. Each time we analyzed our position and decided to continue the project development. Recessionary periods or periods of over-supply for a particular metal or mineral offer excellent buying opportunities if you have faith in the future. The acquisition of our potash interest in Canada is a good example of this strategy. We acquired the interest during the tail end of an over-supply period at a bargain price. One year later the same transaction could not have been consummated.

The third aspect of our investment strategy is that we are prepared to buy used facilities. If purchased properly, the rehabilitation cost will result in the total cost of the facility being substantially less than the cost of a new plant. Also, environmental problems are reduced. The purchases of our nickel refinery in Braithwaite, La., and electrolytic zinc plant in Sauget, Ill., in the early 1970's are good examples of this strategy. The fourth aspect of our strategy is to look for "buys" in the stock market. An example of this strategy was the acquisition of the coal company in 1969. Today, probably the best asset acquisitions are in the stock market. Why build facilities if you can buy them below cost? The fifth aspect of our investment strategy is that we are prepared to forecast higher future selling prices to justify new investment.

FINANCING STRATEGY

Our financing strategy is coordinated with our investment strategy and our views on inflation. A comparison of the composition of the liability and equity side of the company's balance sheet at the end of 1960 and September 1977 is again a good snapshot of our strategy to combat inflation:

	Dec.31, 1960 Amount	%	Sept. 30, 1977 Amount	%
Short-term borrowings	--		$ 40MM	1.3
Current maturities of long-term debt	$ 1MM	.3	19	.6
Long-term debt	10	3.2	705	23.6
Production payments	--		180	6.0
Deferred taxes	3	1.0	81	2.7
Total liabilities and equity	310	100	2,991	100

At September 30, 1977, including non-capitalized equipment leases, our ratio of total long-term financial obligations to total capital was 36.0% compared with 4.0% at the end of 1960. Our policy is to maintain this long-term obligation to total capital ratio between 30 to 40% and in recent years it usually has been about 35%. The policy is to borrow as much long-term debt as we can for as long as we can. In essence we are going short the dollar. We hope to repay, and in fact have been repaying, these borrowings in cheaper dollars.

We do not defer capital investment because we think interest rates may be too high or they may go down in a year or two. If you go through the calculations you will determine that the increase in capital costs due to inflation exceeds the savings from a possible reduction in the interest rate.

In our lease financing transactions we retain the residual equipment values. I think many lessees who surrendered their residual values in prior years are unhappy today as they recompute their financing costs based on inflated equipment values.

We have avoided the temptation to borrow Swiss francs or Deutsche marks at lower interest rates than U. S. dollar borrowings and as a result have probably saved some money over the long run. This policy results from our views of the political and social forces in the United States which are debasing the value of the dollar.

OPERATING STRATEGY

We have developed several operating policies to combat inflation. The company has used the LIFO inventory valuation method at least since 1960. At December 31, 1976, 71 percent of our product inventories were on a LIFO basis.

During periods of over-supply the company has voluntarily built up substantial inventory positions after evaluating forecasted market conditions, escalating production costs, financing costs, and its overall cash requirements. For example, during the recession of 1971-72 the company increased its molybdenum inventory to almost 60 million pounds by the end of 1972. This was equivalent to one year's production at that time. We estimated that the market would turn around by 1975 and that the additional inventory buildup would represent the cheapest-cost molybdenum we could ever produce. Our calculations indicated the profit from the sale of this additional inventory would substantially exceed the financing costs. By the end of 1975 our inventory was reduced to 33 million pounds after purchasing and selling 26 million pounds of GSA moly.

Long-term purchase contracts extending beyond the year 2000 were executed several years ago for the purchase of a raw material basic to one of our operations. The formula for computing the purchase price fixes the amount applicable to the recovery of the plant investment at historical cost. This purchase contract was executed during a recession which was affecting both parties--the purchaser and seller--which are in the same industry. However, our investment strategy resulted in taking a long position while the seller took a short position. Needless to say our purchase price for this product today is below the current market price.

Steam coal is sold to utilities under long-term contracts running for the life of the mine which may be from 15 to 30 years. At the time we acquired the Ayrshire Collieries Co. in 1969 its sales contracts did not have adequate provisions to recover escalating costs and it had no provision to maintain the purchasing power of the profit margin in real terms. Since then, we have improved the provisions to recover escalating costs and introduced the concept of indexing the profit margin to maintain its purchasing power in new contracts.

In developing new technology we are trying to design away from energy-based processes because we think the cost of energy will escalate faster than other materials. For example, we are working on a sulfuric acid-based process to produce nickel rather than an ammonia-based process which is available from other companies.

We apply the GNP deflator and the wholesale price index to our operating results to try to measure our performance in real terms. For example, we convert current selling prices to real prices back to 1950. We convert the current earnings of a business to its purchasing power in a base year we consider to be normal for that business. These computations with which we are experimenting are conducted as separate exercises and are not built into our reporting system. When we finalize our replacement cost numbers for plant and equipment investment, we will begin to measure ROI on replacement cost rather than historical cost. In addition, we deflate our annual net income, earnings per share and common dividend per share. If you have not made these per share computations for your company, I suggest you do so. The results can be startling and I think you will have a better appreciation of why your stock price and the Dow Jones average are at their current levels.

PLANNING

We prepare a five-year corporate plan and our major mining operations prepare a 10-year plan. As you would expect, we inflate our capital and operating costs. Selling prices are forecast based on projected supply-demand conditions for the particular metal or mineral. However, it is difficult for an operating executive to forecast increasing operating costs and level, or even worse, declining selling prices during a period of over-supply. Therefore, the forecast for selling prices tends to have an optimistic upward bias at times. The operating divisions also prepare an uninflated income statement so that a comparison can be made with the inflated statement.

One reason we inflate our five-year plan is to determine the magnitude of our financing requirements. We announced last year our investment program would approximate $2 billion in the five-year period 1977-81. Included in this amount was more than $300 million of inflation. The projections also indicated that by 1981, our working capital requirements would increase by $100 million due to inflation. Therefore, at the end of five years, inflation increased the financing requirements $400 million and this amount represented about 65 percent of the net financing to be raised during this period after repayments.

SUMMARY

In summary, we think inflation is a long-term structural problem facing the world. In fact, national and international institutions are actively at work trying to prevent deflation. Therefore our strategy to combat inflation has been to invest more than our cash flow each year and to cover the cash deficit with long-term borrowings and equity when necessary.

STRATEGY FOR BEATING INFLATION

Investment
- Explore, buy and develop natural resources and build capital facilities as a hedge;
- Take advantage of recessionary periods and negotiate better engineering, construction and labor contracts;
- Be prepared to buy used facilities;
- Look for "buys" in the stock market;
- Forecast higher future selling prices to justify new investment;

Financing
- Borrow as much long-term debt as you can for as long as you can;
- In lease-finance transactions retain residual equipment values.

Operating
- Use LIFO inventory valuation method;
- During periods of over-supply increase inventory;
- Negotiate long-term purchase contracts;
- In new technology development, design away from energy-based processes because of anticipated escalating energy costs;
- Measure performance in real terms by converting operating results via use of GNP deflator and wholesale price index.

STUDENT REVIEW QUESTIONS

1. Why does Alonzo believe a company must have a strategy to combat inflation?
2. Why does AMAX often purchase used facilities?
3. What does Alonzo mean when he says "we are going short the dollar"?
4. Briefly explain AMAX's strategy for combating inflation.
5. Has AMAX's strategy worked?

16

Why Corporate Marriages Fail*

ALLEN H. SEED, III

TEN REASONS WHY CORPORATE MARRIAGES FAIL:

1. Unfamiliar territory--a field of endeavor that we know nothing about.
2. Sick situation--business in trouble looking for angel.
3. Sickness at home--acquisition to solve own problem.
4. Artificial rationalization--absence of real operating fit.
5. Personality mismatch--people incompatible with one another.
6. Insufficient investigation--failure to ask all the right questions.
7. Overexpectations--pitfalls, risks, and capital requirements not properly appraised.
8. Clumsy integration--acquiring management tries to remake business too quickly.
9. Instant prosperity--acquired management "goes fishing" after the deal is closed.
10. Uncontrollable factors--the unpredictable external world that makes the best of deals go sour.

MANY EXECUTIVES HAVE FOUND that courting, marrying, and living with new businesses can involve the same misunderstandings, traumatic experiences, pitfalls, and risks of failure

*From *Financial Executive,* December, 1974, pp. 56-62. Reprinted by permission.

that are associated with the relationship between man and wife. Of course, many corporate marriages end up in well-publicized wedded bliss. However, the divorce rate (one divestiture for every three acquisitions) is high enough to suggest that corporate combinations--even if undertaken in the best of faith--are hazardous undertakings. One might also ask, if the corporate divorce rate is one in three, how many other marriages are simply tolerated but really fall short of initial expectations?

This high potential for failure is born out by my own experience. Of the dozen or so sales or acquisitions that I have participated in over the past 20 years, I would recommend that less than half be done over again if it were possible to turn back the clock. Each case that fell short of expectations looked like an attractive business undertaking at the time, but as it turned out, for one reason or another, matters did not develop as planned.

My comparison of corporate marriages with the more familiar domestic condition is meant to be more than a literary device. The activities of attraction, flirtation, courting, marriage, living together, and divorce are common to both institutions and are similar in many respects. So, too, are the emotions involved: love, hate and even lack of interest. Both institutions share many of the same characteristics of human behavior because they are both significant events of major importance to the principles involved. Both institutions can also fail, and many of the reasons for failure have characteristics in common.

1. UNFAMILIAR TERRITORY

One fundamental business truism, often learned the hard way, is that each field of business is unique. Various businesses share certain management, administrative, and financial characteristics in common; but sales, marketing, and technological characteristics and ways of doing business vary widely from one field of business to another. The successful operators seem to know the peculiarities of their business, their people, their industry, and their trade. They generally know intuitively what motivates their consumers and they are able to respond intelligently to changing circumstances. The candy business is different from the toiletry business, apparel is different from cosmetics, hobbies and crafts is different from toys and games, greeting cards is different from giftware, process machinery is different from farm machinery, and consumer finance is different from insurance.

The trouble comes when someone in one field acquires a company in another field and tries to run it like the parent. Many skills are transferable, but there is no substitute for the capabilities that are developed from spending a lifetime in an industry.

The odds of success can be increased if this is borne in mind by the management of the acquiring company.

2. SICK SITUATION

Some individuals and firms are "business doctors" who specialize in acquiring and "turning around" sick situations. However, most successful operating-oriented company managements do a very poor job of this. Most sick situations simply get sicker.

Companies for sale are usually in worse shape than the seller would have one believe or even one's pre-acquisition investigation would indicate. So a company that seems to be slightly ill is probably quite ill, and one that seems to be moderately ill is probably dying. Moreover, declining situations develop a certain momentum that is difficult to arrest and turn around.

The skills and operating methods that work in successful companies generally do not apply in sick companies. Most successful managers are "business builders." They do not like to fire people and cut back the organization; they do not want to work 12 hours a day, seven days a week; they like to pay their bills when due and do not like stalling off creditors; they do not like disposing of unused capacity and inventory at fire sale prices. In short, saving a sick situation is for most organizations an incompatible, disagreeable, grubby undertaking that offers long odds of success.

3. SICKNESS AT HOME

All too often corporate marriages are made to dress up a balance sheet, to show continuing growth, to acquire management, or to solve other internal problems. Although Accounting Principles Board Opinion No. 16 has limited many accounting abuses and current stock market conditions have substantially reduced the value of the legal tender used to acquire quick remedies for illnesses at home, the practice has not been altogether eliminated.

The current low price/earnings multiples of certain diversified companies testify to the hazards of trying to buy instant earnings or a stronger financial position. In the two situations that I know of where a company attempted to buy management, the acquired management is no longer associated with the combined companies.

In so far as possible, the partners in a prospective marriage should be equally healthy. Making a successful marriage generally adds to the work of both partners and, if the acquiring company is ill, an acquisition is likely to make the illness more acute.

4. ARTIFICIAL RATIONALIZATION

Several large manufacturing and forest product companies rationalized entering the home building business through acquisition in the late '60s. Their rationalization was based on their capital resources, mass production skills, building product interests, and land holdings. Nevertheless, many of these companies subsequently found that the financial requirements of home building are quite different than those of manufacturing and that the capital of one business couldn't be used for the other. In fact, when the 1970 credit crunch arrived the capital requirements of the acquired company proved to conflict with those of the parent in many cases. The style of management of each business was different, and it was found that mass production skills do not lend themselves to home building. Moreover, the building product interests and land holdings of certain forest product companies were not found to be compatible with the needs of the builder. Yet, the rationalization for entering the home building business seemed quite logical to a number of sophisticated managers and directors.

Management can rationalize almost any course of action it decides to embark upon. The financial community is full of "stories," and the marketing world is laden with "concepts."

Some stories and concepts are very real and have constructively changed the direction of certain businesses. These usually result from enlightened, hard-nosed, objective-setting, and imaginative strategic planning. The acquisition is a step towards implementing this plan. However, too often the managements of other businesses decide who they want to buy and rationalize this decision.

The basic question is, "What can the prospective bride do for us and what can we do for her?" Neither growth for its own sake nor a highfalutin' concept is a sufficient answer. If the answer cannot be translated into operating "nuts and bolts," then a marriage may be on its way to trouble.

5. PERSONALITY MISMATCH

The partner in charge of acquisitions for a leading New York investment banking firm told me the reason he would put at the top of the list of why corporate marriages fail is "people." He said that 80 percent of his time is spent solving personality problems. Of particular importance, he said, the principals involved have to like each other because they have to work with each other for a long time.

However, beyond individual personalities, each company has a distinct corporate personality of its own. This personality is often a reflection of the personality, background, and business attitudes of the chief executive officer; but it is also a function of the size of the business, its stage of development, and the industry involved.

Large companies are usually professionally managed and they tend to operate in a highly structured fashion. They disperse responsibility for decision making; they employ many specialists; they move slowly and use formal budget, planning, performance evaluation, salary administration techniques, etc. Smaller companies, on the other hand, are generally entrepreneurial in their orientation. They are run by a few key people, they move quickly, have few staff specialists, little overhead, and few formalized record-keeping systems. Few small businesses can afford the staff specialization and detailed planning and control procedures that are common to larger companies. Many of the planning and control techniques that are used by larger businesses could be adapted for smaller businesses, but many acquirers try to install their ways of doing business and systems without modification.

Many other personality factors must be considered as well. Some businesses are run by young "hard chargers" who would be uncomfortable in a restrictive, conservative environment.

Pay and employment practices vary widely among businesses. Businesses with relatively high compensation levels and fringe benefits can often not afford to absorb businesses that pay close to minimum wages and few fringes.

Ethical standards vary, as do approaches toward research, product, quality, and pricing in the trade and the marketplace.

The important point is not that these differences exist but rather, to the extent they reflect differences in underlying attitude and style of management, they can lead to conflict, unhappiness,and an unsuccessful corporate marriage.

6. INSUFFICIENT INVESTIGATION

The seller generally knows a great deal more about what he has to sell than the buyer knows about what he is buying. Thus, even under the best of circumstances, the seller has a substantial advantage over the buyer.

The buyer, of course, can investigate the company he is buying, but too often his investigation is limited to maintain confidentiality or he does not allow enough time to do a thorough job.

Many corporate brides have been lost as a result of dilatory decision making, but I've never heard anyone say that they made a mistake by overinvestigating a proposed acquisition.

More importantly, the thoroughness of an investigation is not so much a product of the amount of data that is gathered as it is an ability to identify the key issues and ask all of the right questions.

Acquisition checklists are useful in assuring that all of the needed routine information is obtained, but they are generally of little help in identifying the soft spots, risks, and possible unexploited opportunities that are part and parcel of each acquisition candidate. Nor do such checklists generally help in sorting out the critical factors on which the future success of the business depends.

Answers to these critical questions usually are most effectively obtained from the trade and others in the industry.

Knowledgeable people in the trade (generally at the day-to-day buying level) can usually give a fairly realistic appraisal of the condition of an acquisition candidate's product line, its level of service, competitive position, quality of sales management, and field personnel. They can also tell what competition is doing, and that is important. Each industry has a grapevine, and many times a competitor will tell more about a business than the principals of the company itself.

Too often, too, an evaluation of a company tends to focus on the company itself rather than on the dynamics of the marketing and competitive environment in which it is operating. As a result, the acquirer often develops a very complete picture of the company, but only a sketchy picture of its prospects because he really doesn't understand what is going on in the marketplace and in the competition.

7. OVEREXPECTATIONS

It is very easy to "fall in love" with a deal, as many executives have found. One is attracted to all of the virtues of the intended and tends to overlook the faults. In the course of courting and selling the prospect, it is natural to identify with the prospect. He becomes a friend and one shares his hopes and aspirations.

Moreover, each prospective acquisition usually has a sponsor within the acquiring company, and it becomes his role to "sell the deal" to his associates. This responsibility makes the individual concerned an "advocate," rather than an objective analyst.

As a result, the tendency is often to accept overoptimistic sales and earnings forecasts and underestimate the problems associated with integrating the business and achieving the forecasts.

I have seldom seen a set of five-year projections from an acquisition candidate where each succeeding year was not substantially better than the one before it. Unfortunately, the records of most publicly held companies show that such performance is the exception rather than the rule.

One solution to the problem of overexpectations is to

provide each potential acquisition candidate with a "devil's advocate," logically the chief financial officer. This avoids placing the candidate's sponsor in the schizophrenic position of having to both "sell the deal" and evaluate the plans and projections that are prepared.

Another solution is to engage an outsider to evaluate the situation's potential. The outsider has no allegiance to the deal and may be in a more objective position to judge the outlook for the business than could an insider.

8. CLUMSY INTEGRATION

An unfortunate aftermath of many corporate marriages is the "conquering army syndrome." It usually involves middle managers rather than top managers and goes something like this: "We bought you so we are better than you are...our ways of doing business are better than yours and our systems are better than yours....We know best...."

Some managers give orders, make requests, and take actions with little regard to the reaction involved. In their eagerness to exercise their responsibilities, they demoralize the acquired organization, distract it from the work of "running the store," and ignore all of the reasons why the company was an attractive bride in the first place.

"Be sensitive, go slow, have a plan" is, therefore, my counsel. Remember that the management of the acquired company is generally under great stress. Management of the acquired company hopes for the best, but fears the worst. Every memo, contact, phone call, and request is gleaned for clues and hidden meanings and is magnified way out of proportion. Insecurity prevails.

Integration problems are magnified when a U. S. company acquires a European company or vice versa. Not only are substantial geographical distances and differences in language, laws, and currency involved; but, most importantly, there are often immense differences in cultural background and management techniques. Under these circumstances, particular sensitivity is required.

Most experienced acquirers minimize their contacts with the newly acquired company, Some changes are inevitable, but they are made slowly, carefully, and deliberately. Unimportant changes (like conforming administrative and certain reporting procedures) are postponed. The disposition to "help" is avoided unless it is clearly called for and needed. The newly acquired management is trusted, encouraged, and rewarded for superior performance.

9. INSTANT PROSPERITY

A common result of corporate matchmaking is that the owners of the acquired business are made "rich men." They may have had a good income beforehand, but now they have something they can put into the bank. They don't *have* to work.

This change in the personal financial position of the owners of a business can change their working habits. Before the sale they may have devoted long hours each day to the business. Now there is a tendency to "go fishing," travel, and enjoy some of the benefits from the sale. The old entrepreneurial spirit is just now what it used to be.

Although there is no cure for this, it can be avoided by careful evaluation and by recognizing the realities of the situation. It can be curbed through the use of incentive arrangements and by offering new challenges to the principals involved.

10. UNCONTROLLABLE FACTORS

Despite careful planning, investigation, and analysis, even the best-laid plans can fall apart as a result of unforeseen circumstances.

The energy crisis severely curtails prospects for recreational vehicle manufacturers; droughts crumble the hopes of farm machinery companies, and a money crunch raises havoc in the home building or consumer finance business.

I recall one manufacturer of wallets, belts, and other personal leather goods which was acquired in late 1971. We checked the history of leather prices and found that leather had historically been one of the most stable commodities. However, immediately following the closing, cattle production declined for a number of economic reasons, and leather prices took off. Fortunately, the company involved was able to compensate for some of these cost increases with price increases, but the fact remains that earnings fell short of expectations.

There is a strong element of luck in corporate acquisitions. Some corporate marriages would have worked out had not such and such happened. Other corporate marriages worked out because it did. Some say that men of vision are able to foresee the impact of uncontrollable factors. Perhaps this is so, but even the most successful acquirers will admit to being wrong a certain percentage of the time.

The acquisition of other companies should be an important component of a strategy for corporate growth. The successes of ITT, Textron, Beatrice Foods, W. R. Grace, Harsco, Warner Lambert, American Home Products, and many others have proven this. But corporate marriage, even if undertaken for the soundest of business reasons, is a high-risk course that offers the promise of marital bliss on the one hand and recriminations and the possibility of unhappiness or divorce on the other.

STUDENT REVIEW QUESTIONS

1. Why do mergers often fail when one of the partners is sick?
2. Explain the statement "at the top of the list of why corporate marriages fail is people".
3. How useful does Seed believe checklists are for investigating an organization? Why?
4. What is the "conquering army syndrome"?
5. Why does Seed advocate use of a "devil's advocate" for each potential acquisition?

17

The Strategic Divestment Decision*

JAMES V. DAVIS

MANAGEMENT PERIODICALS HAVE of late been reflecting the increasing attention corporate managers are paying to the difficult problem of divestment.[1] The purpose of this paper is to outline conceptually a planning and analytical framework for dealing with divestments.

The discontinuance or sale of a product, product line or part or all of an operating division means a reallocation of resources within the firm. As Table 17-1 suggests, this reallocation can be accomplished in a variety of ways to achieve different managerial objectives. Strategic divestment decisions should be made to support the long-term goals of the firm by converting assets into more profitable uses.

Certain strategic divestments can be accomplished solely within the firm. An unsatisfactory operation may be shut down and the market value of the assets recovered for investment elsewhere in the business. If the firm is engaged in a series of integrated operations, return on investment may be improved by, for example, allocating more resources to manufacturing and less to retailing if manufacturing is relatively more profitable. The firm also has the option of selling a product or an entire subsidiary to an independent company.

Financial divestment decisions, at least in the short run, are made to improve the firm's balance sheet by providing additional liquidity and by converting an investment in a wholly-owned subsidiary to an investment with a market value in a partially-owned subsidiary. (Since the purpose of this

---

*From *Journal of Long Range Planning*, February, 1974, pp. 15-18. Reprinted by permission.

TABLE 17-1. TYPES OF DIVESTMENT DECISIONS

	INTERNAL TO THE FIRM	EXTERNAL TO THE FIRM
Strategic Divestment	(1) Shut-down of operations. (2) Reallocation of resources among a series of ongoing integrated operations	Sale of a product, product line,or part or all of a division to an independent company
Financial Divestment	Issuance of stock in a subsidiary to firm's own shareholders	Sale of a stock interest in a subsidiary to the general public

paper is to examine the role that divestment of existing operations should play in the strategic planning process, no further mention will be made of financial divestment. Business periodicals have often lumped the different forms of divestment under a single label. It is useful to distinguish them for analytical purposes.)

PLANNING FOR DIVESTMENT

There are numerous reasons why a corporation might choose to liquidate or sell some part of its business activities. Unsatisfactory profit performance, lack of management, pressure from short- and long-term lenders to lighten the debt load of the parent company, and the requirement for more cash to support higher growth aspects of the business are a few of the more significant ones.

When the reasons for a specific divestment occasionally are made public, however, it is striking how often it appears that the decision was forced on management. What is required is a change in the management culture that will make routine divestment analysis acceptable. Managerial recognition of its ability to improve ROI through planned divestment should help. The fact that funds secured for divested product lines may form an important component of the financially mobile resources available to a firm may be an important consideration, especially to those entrepreneurially minded companies that aggressively search for new opportunities and attempt to seize those that randomly present themselves.[2]

A number of criteria may be utilized to identify divestment candidates. These include:

- Position on product life-cycle curve
- Profitability
- Market position.

Of particular usefulness is the concept of a product life-cycle curve for it can be utilized to evaluate the firm's portfolio of products. The life-cycle curve in Figure 17-1 indicates the present life-cycle position of each product or service as estimated by management. It is the stage of the life cycle the product is in rather than its exact position which is important.

Any product in the decline stage of its life cycle should probably be divested. Initial market feedback on new product introductions will suggest others. What is less commonly recognized is that a firm with too many of its products in the growth stage may have insufficient capital to adequately support all of them. Divestment of one product may provide the funds to properly support the others.

The other criteria mentioned are obvious ones. Low profitability may suggest divestment. Poor market penetration will do the same. Whatever the criteria, and the relative weights assigned to them, the important concept is the periodic survey of the firm's products with divestment as a clearly articulated managerial option that may be exercised.

For large multi-division firms, the Boston Consulting Group has developed a useful way to conceptualize possible targets for divestment. All of a firm's product lines or divisions are classified according to their market share and

FIGURE 17-1. TYPICAL PRODUCT LIFE-CYCLE CURVE

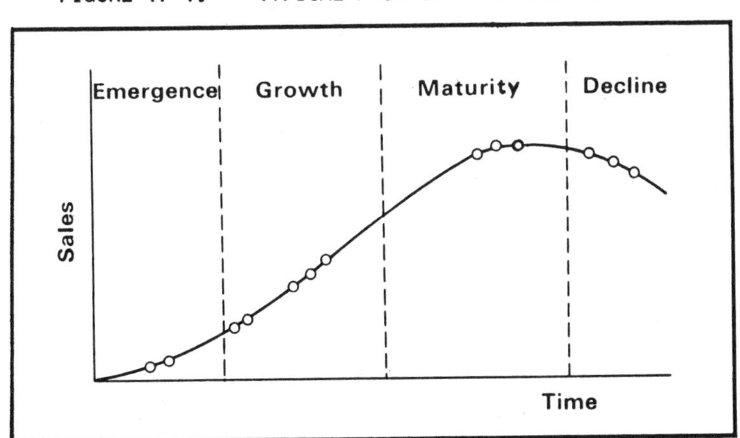

FIGURE 17-2. PRODUCT MATRIX

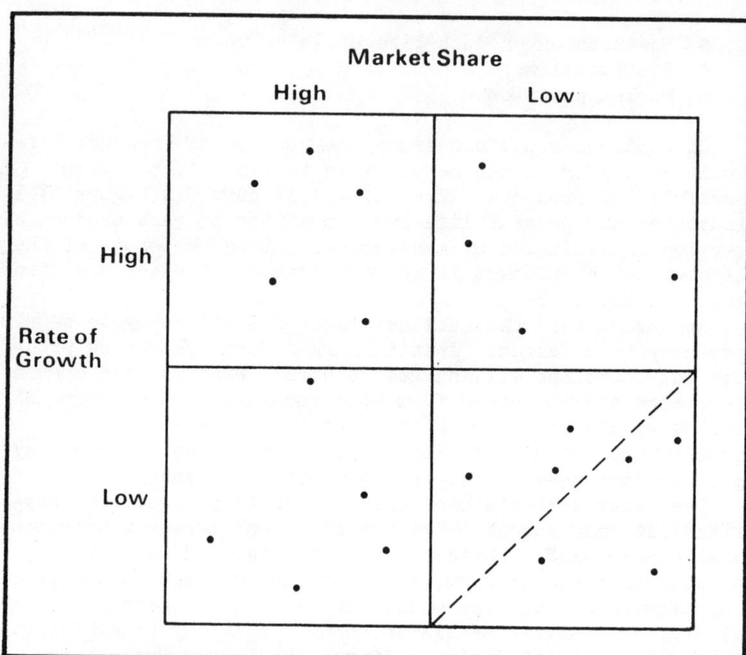

their rate of market growth. An illustration of this approach is shown in Figure 17-2. The upper left-hand box in this figure depicts those product lines or divisions which are characterized by high market share and high growth. These activities will need to be supported by heavy investment. The lower left-hand box shows operations that will generally be providing substantial amounts of cash for investment elsewhere in the firm; they have a substantial share of the market but a low growth rate.

Classified in the upper right-hand box are the operations with a low market share but high growth potential. They should either be supported with sizable amounts of investment capital or be discarded.

The product lines or divisions that fall into the lower right-hand box are of most interest to us. Here are the ones with low market share and low growth potential. These are the corporation's candidates for divestment. The high priority divestment targets would be those product lines or divisions to the right of the dashed 45-degree line.

Implicit in this approach is that market share and rate of growth are correlated with profitability. Again, the portfolio aspects of the firm's businesses must be explicitly considered.

DIVESTMENT ANALYSIS

A diagrammatic approach to identifying proper divestment candidates is presented in Figure 17-3. A trigger mechanism as part of the overall strategic planning process starts the identification process. A product review committee which periodically examines each product or division in terms of its contribution to corporate objectives provides a reasonable trigger.

If a combination of the planning profile developed above is utilized, products may be evaluated using the criteria of profitability and market growth. Products that fail to meet

FIGURE 17-3. THE DIVESTMENT DECISION PROCESS

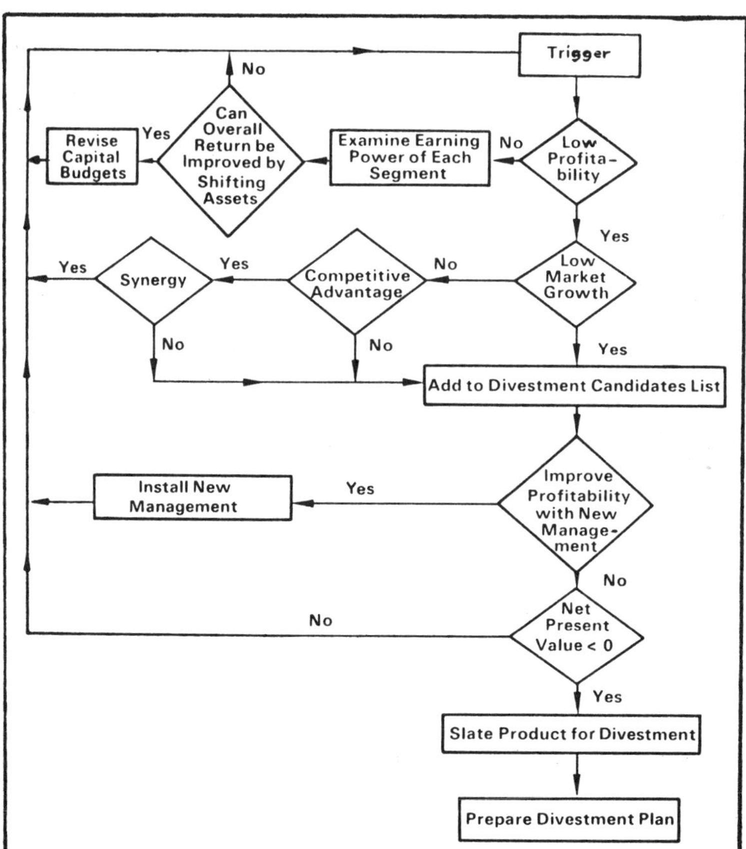

these internal standards are designated as possible divestments. In addition, products which meet the growth criteria but do not offer the promise of competitive advantage or expected synergy are also identified as possible divestments.

Management may begin at this point and often does, a search for ways to shore up even the most troubled division. New management may be an alternative as well as new marketing approaches or a change in the channels of distribution. The internal criteria for the corporate problem child may be revised downward.[3]

An integral stage in this process is the financial analysis that relates future profitability of each product line to the market value of the assets which could be freed for other purposes if the product line were discontinued. If the product line fails this future profitability test utilizing a default free discount rate in a new present value analysis, the product is listed for divestment. Preparation of the divestment plan then commences.

Analytic approaches to divestment problems have not received the same attention that analysis of new ventures has. In large measure, this has been due to the perceived importance of new ventures to corporate growth and in part through a failure to appreciate the importance of the divestment decision.

In two earlier articles Shillinglaw has outlined the scope of the problem.[4] There are three major areas that may cause difficulty in the analysis: (1) revenue effects, (2) cost effects, and (3) investment commitments.

Most of the revenue effects are familiar. Deletion of a product line may not result in total loss of revenue because substitute products from other lines may capture some of the business. If a product line complementary to other product lines is dropped, however, the resulting sales reduction may be larger than for the deleted line.

Cost effects will also vary with the nature of the product. The decision to sell one product line may result in elimination of variable factory cost plus some fixed cost. Selling cost may also be reduced. Almost certainly some fixed cost will be truly 'fixed' and cannot be avoided by abandonment. Certain central office staff functions are an example.

Traditional accounting practices have come under increasing criticism in recent years because of the irrelevance of the data generated for managerial decision making. Nowhere are the shortcomings highlighted quite so well as in divestment decisions. Cost accumulation procedures may make it virtually impossible to unscramble the costs associated with a certain product line. And once the going-concern assumption has been dropped, the recorded values for plant and equipment and land may be close to meaningless.

What matters for divestment decisions are what the assets will bring when sold. This means that the market values of both current assets (inventory particularly may be a problem) and fixed assets are critical. The company can take bids to help determine the value of its fixed assets for sale; more likely it will rely on internally generated estimates of market worth.

After the different adjustments have been made, it is then simple to use a discounted cash flow technique like net present value to determine whether the future cash proceeds that will be lost are worth less than the recoverable value of the assets to be sold. Alternatively the problem could be stated as follows: the decision not to divest is the same as the decision to invest the recoverable value of the assets. In this case, the future proceeds must justify the continued commitment of the assets.

(Management decisions would be improved if specific evaluation of the possibilities for future disinvestment were considered at the time a new product was evaluated. The return-risk characteristics of particular new ventures may be significantly altered as a result.[5])

HOW TO WIN ACCEPTANCE FOR DIVESTMENT ANALYSIS

While it would appear that routine divestment analysis should be part of the strategic planning process, there is considerable evidence to indicate that it is not. This is because the divestment decision is one of the few decisions that forces the executive to say: "I was wrong." In large part because this is something that is understandably difficult for any executive to admit, mature managers have described "the decision to divest and the implementation of it ...as (1) the single most unpalatable decision a company manager has to make, (2) one of the most significant decisions in terms of short- and long-range profitability, (3) the one business move where emotion is more likely to prevail over judgment, (4) and a business maneuver usually made late and most often undertaken without adequate study."[6]

What procedures can a firm introduce to encourage the analysis of divestment opportunities? I would suggest the following:

(1) Making the study of divestment alternatives a component part of the analyses carried out for new products. This should help to make consideration of divestment later more acceptable by formally acknowledging it as a possible outcome from the beginning. Adoption of this step will also lead to better decision-making by recognizing that front-end divestment analyses will affect which products are finally introduced.

(2) Revising the firm's management information

system. Even if managers were inclined toward conducting divestment analyses, the time and expense involved in assembling the relevant data would discourage most. The introduction of double-coded accounts is one way to begin to achieve this objective.

(3) Changing the compensation plan for managers. Compensation plans based on the meeting of sales objectives or short-range profitability goals are not likely to encourage the identification of potential divestments. Compensation plans which do in part measure how effectively a manager utilizes corporate capital will help.

(4) Adopting the analytical process proposed in this paper. It will be familiar to the individuals who now perform the capital budgeting function in the firm, and they will have no difficulties in relating to it.

(5) Establishing a procedure for routine review of the firm's existing products and services. Product review committees are one possibility.

The real key to improving divestment procedures will be the recognition by an executive team that divestment constitutes sound management practice. This recognition may make it feasible for a manager to admit the implicit sunk costs in a product line or division that has turned sour.

FOOTNOTES

[1]See, for example, Robert H. Hayes, "New Emphasis on Divestment Opportunities," *Harvard Business Review*, Vol. 50 (July-August, 1972), pp. 55-64; Richard H. Hillman, "How to Redeploy Assets," *Harvard Business Review*, Vol. 49 (November-December, 1971), pp. 95-103; Alex C. Hutchinson, "Planned Euthanasia for Old Projects," *Long Range Planning*, Vol. 4, (December, 1971), pp. 17-22; and Arthur Bettauer, "Strategy for Divestments," *Harvard Business Review*, Vol. 45 (March-April, 1967), pp. 116-24.

[2]Donaldson has developed this point in his recent book. See Gordon Donaldson, *Strategy for Financial Mobility*, pp. 277-280, 289-290. Irwin, Homewood, Illinois (1971).

[3]See, for example, the discussion in Peter Hilton, *Planning Corporate Growth and Diversification*, pp. 113-115.

McGraw-Hill, New York (1970). This paragraph is not meant to suggest that a product line has to be formally catalogued as a divestment candidate before its problems are addressed by management. Rather it suggests that this process is likely to be intensified as application of formal criteria highlight the product line's shortcomings.

[4]Gordon Shillinglaw, "Residual Value in Investment Analysis, and Profit Analysis for Abandonment Decisions," in *The Management of Corporate Capital* (Edited by Ezra Solomon), pp. 259-268, 269-281. Free Press, Glencoe (1959). The discussion that follows is based on the second of these articles.

[5]Alexander A. Robichek and James C. Van Horne, "Abandonment Value and Capital Budgeting," *Journal of Finance*, Vol. 22, (December, 1967), pp. 577-589.

[6]P. Hilton, *op. cit.*, p. 112.

STUDENT REVIEW QUESTIONS

1. What are the various ways in which divestments can be handled?
2. How can the product-life-cycle concept be used in planning?
3. Diagram a product matrix and explain how it might be useful for product planning.
4. What are some of the areas that cause difficulty in analyzing the divestment decision?
5. Why is divestment analysis not generally a part of the strategic planning process? Should it be?

A Profits-Oriented Approach to Project Selection*

WILSON M. WHALEY**

ROBERT A. WILLIAMS**

IT IS CLEAR TODAY that R&D must be justified as a profit-generating activity. We know that R&D can be evaluated in business terms. And we also know that it must be, in order to earn management support, for the contributions made by R&D are evaluated by top management according to the same criterion used for the rest of the organization--profitability. This one fact provides the basis for all of the technical planning methods which are useful in industry. Technical planning is planning for profit,but the application of scientific and engineering skills rather than manufacturing or merchandising skills. Therefore, the planning needs to be done according to business and financial principles. Since the most important act in the planning of R&D is the selection of projects, it follows that project selection must be on the basis of profit potential.

ORIENTED R&D PROJECTS

Industrial research and development is applied science and engineering; its projects should be oriented toward useful end results which are hoped to be profit generating.

---

*From *Research Management,* September, 1971, pp. 25-36. Reprinted by permission.
**This article is based on a paper presented at the national meeting of the American Institute of Chemical Engineers, December, 1970.

Unoriented exploration has a very low probability of generating profit because the world of technology is just too large for much of it to be relevant. It is usually not realized that applied research can be just as long-range and sophisticated as academic research. The only difference is that one has a commercial motive and the other does not.

There are two general categories of projects: process-oriented and product-oriented. Differentiation between the two categories is not always readily apparent because it is often necessary to perfect a process to produce a new or improved product. Conversely, process improvement projects sometimes lead to product improvements. However, we find it appropriate to view a project as product-oriented if it is likely to produce products that are different in the marketplace and, therefore, have an effect on sales income. Process-oriented projects are considered to be those that do not have a direct impact on the marketplace, but exert their effect either directly or indirectly by cost reduction in the manufacturing operation.

Before a project idea can be evaluated and selected, it must be phrased in meaningful and precise terms. That is accomplished by stating it as a specific objective relating to its ultimate end-use application. In other words, the project objective is results oriented rather than devoted to technical methodology or interim accomplishments. It has been found best to set tangible and pragmatic targets (objectives) first, and then direct suitable technological efforts toward reaching them. Thomas Edison was an eminent practitioner of that research philosophy, and much of his success can be attributed to that fact.[1] Use of the term "edisonian" in the usual disparaging fashion is an unwarranted insult to the successful manager of industrial R&D.

Project evaluation centers first around the objective rather than the technical aspects. If the project has been well conceived, the objective should not change as the project moves along toward completion. Technical approaches often change, and at those times it will be important to determine which approach offers the best economic result. A project objective must be tangible, explicit and controlling. It must also relate to the commercial environment, because the project's value can only materialize by the ultimate application of the technical accomplishment to a commercial exploitation. In industry no credit can be gained from a technical success which is a commercial failure.

Process-oriented objectives should state specifically what is to be done; e.g., improve operating efficiency by five percent or lower waste materials by twenty percent or reduce labor content by ten cents per pound, etc. Product-oriented objectives should express a definite goal in terms of product specifications. If this is not done, it will be impossible to develop valid marketing projections. Without a clear objective, it will also be difficult to determine whether the technical effort has met its objective.

PROJECT EVALUATION CRITERIA

The confusion and indecision usually present in the evaluation of R&D project ideas are primarily due to the multiplicity of pertinent criteria and influences. The total set of criteria, and their relative importance, vary from company to company. A representative set is given here just as an example. As will be shown later, their rational use for project evaluation can be rather straightforward.

Corporate Objectives and Attitudes:

1. Guidelines--may occur as written business objectives, but if not they can be learned by asking questions. These are broad-brush guidelines, often including social and legal boundaries.
2. Desire for innovation--only real if it includes willingness to invest money.
3. Patience and long-range commitment.
4. Courage in risk taking.

Corporate Capabilities:

1. Marketing capabilities--scope, type, volume, philosophy.
2. Product introduction--refine or introduce "as is".
3. Position relative to competitor--may have to copy their product.
4. The state of the required technology--a long-range effort may be necessary.

R&D Policies:

1. Technical risk--maximum acceptable.
2. Project size--maximum and minimum.
3. Outside research--contract research, consultants, purchased technology.

Economic Factors:

1. R&D Costs--includes pilot plant and engineering.
2. Commercialization costs--includes facilities capital and market-development capital.
3. Commercial value--includes cost reduction and increased sales income.
4. Profitability--minimum limits are already set by corporate policy in terms of standard financial calculations.

Although cognizance will be taken of all these criteria, primary emphasis is given to economic justification. Economic evaluation and performance are at the heart of any business enterprise, and it is essential that they also provide the core of the project-evaluation system.

DEVELOPMENT OF ECONOMIC EVALUATIONS

Economic evaluations encompass a broad field extending from superficial "back-of-the-envelope" projections to an all-out effort involving many man-months of time and a wide range of talents. As applied to research and development projects, economic studies should commence when the project-selection process begins and continue on an up-date basis through the entire life span of the project, with the techniques and input data becoming more and more refined as the project moves closer to a technical and commercial success.

Since our aim here is to cope with the selection phase of project management, attention is concentrated on the preliminary screening and selection rather than on the follow-up effort. However, even in the intitial selection phase, the evaluation effort should increase as the potential cost of a project increases. For example, initiation of a project may involve purchase of special equipment, often with considerable cost. In this case, a rather thorough analysis is important, and is justified during the initial selection process. In all cases, it is false economy to attempt to avoid the expense of project analysis. This expenditure can be shown to yield the highest return of any monies spent.

It is a popular misconception that the world abounds with valuable project ideas, and one's only problem is finding the time to get to them. In reality, a careful examination of the real value of most ideas reveals that the majority are not attractive based upon expected dollar value. This should come as no big surprise, since it has been estimated that perhaps one in sixty proposed projects reaches commercial reality.[2] It is also a known phenomenon that the closer a project gets to technical and commercial reality, the lower the value becomes. A careful analysis of the value prior to initiation will reduce this "will-o'the-wisp" effect.

As mentioned, we are striving to determine a potential dollar value for a successful commercialization of the project's objective, where the value represents gross (before taxes) profit expected. It is, of course, an easy step to translate from gross into net profit, but it is easier to equate process-oriented (cost reduction) value to product-oriented (increased sales) value if we use the gross-profit relationship.

Screening of cost-reduction projects is a much easier task than determination of product-oriented value, since cost reduction is primarily an intra-company activity. For example, if we can effect a $100,000 per year reduction in operating costs by realization of a project objective, the value increase is $100,000 per year, since this is an inverse relationship and adds directly to gross profit. On the other hand, product value is a more difficult item to determine, because increased sales income does not translate directly into increased gross profit. It is necessary to do a more thorough examination of the complete economic equation (manufacturing costs, overhead allocations, volume considerations, and pricing) in order to arrive at a gross-profit projection.

On the surface, it would seem that cost-reduction projects are therefore the most promising areas for concentrating R&D effort, since a dollar saved is a dollar earned, and it is necessary to effect perhaps five-to-fifteen dollars in increased sales to realize one dollar in gross profit from product-oriented projects.[3] It can also be argued that cost-reduction projects involve lower risk than product-oriented projects. Nevertheless, a company will never display adequate growth through pursuit of process-related R&D alone, but only through a well-balanced program of both project types. It is often pointed out that for most companies, well over 50 percent of today's sales dollar is generated by new products and improved products which did not exist ten years ago.

It is apparent that even at the project-selection phase, we must have a well-organized communications network which can identify and supply input data in a timely manner. Input for evaluating cost-reduction projects will primarily come from manufacturing areas. Product-related evaluations must rely upon marketing data as well as manufacturing input. Therefore, R&D cannot function in terms of product-oriented project selection without proper ties with corporate marketing groups. Such groups must be willing and qualified to project the market impact of product-oriented effort from the initiation point. Far too often, marketing input data are not solicited until a project is well under way.

PROJECT RATING EQUATIONS

Once the value of the project objective has been estimated, it is necessary to associate it with the cost (both R&D and commercialization) plus the risk and the probability of success. In attempting to cope with these three factors, it should be realized that both value and cost relate to tangible measurements, whereas risk is strictly an intangible criterion.

The real secret to a workable selection system deals with the ability to bring these three factors together into a meaningful relationship. Many man-years of effort have been devoted to this problem, and there are numerous proposed methods and equations that attempt to define this relationship in such a manner as to produce a rating or priority index, which can be compared with other projects, thus yielding a listing of "best to worst." Examples of such rating equations are:

Industrial Research Institute[4]

$$I = \frac{PN}{C}$$

Carl Pacifico[5]

$$R = rdpc\ \frac{SA\sqrt{L}}{C_1}$$

Sidney Sobelman[6]

$$Z = P_1 \left[T + T \left(1 - t/\bar{t}\right) \right] - C_2 \left[t + \bar{t} \left(1 - T/\bar{T}\right) \right]$$

Whaley & Williams

$$W = \frac{V^2 - (RC_3)}{RC_3}$$

(In our search for project selection techniques, we have examined many index and rating schemes. This example is one of many which we developed and analyzed.)

Where:

I = index of relative value
W = priority index
Z = product worth
P = over-all probability of commercial attainment
N = estimated net return for an arbitrary five-year period
C = estimated future research costs
rdpc = cumulative probability of success for research, development, process and commercialization
S = estimated average annual sales volume in units
A = estimated average unit profit
L = estimated life of the project in years
C_1 = total estimated cost of R&D effort on project
P_1 = estimated average net profit per year
T = estimated actual profit life
$\bar{T}$ = profit life of average project
C_2 = estimated average annual development cost
t = estimated time to develop the project
$\bar{t}$ = time required to develop average project
V = over-all numerical index value rating

R = numerical index rating for combined risk factors
C_3= numerical index rating for combined cost factors

While these methods are perhaps interesting in a somewhat academic way, they do not provide a practical means of selecting projects. They are empirical and do not relate adequately to standard financial practices; therefore, they are not suitable for presentation to top management. In addition, they bring into play an additional risk factor, since they actually represent stochastic approaches to the problem. Instead of searching for a selection method that relies upon an abstract numerical index, we propose to rely on the conventional, easily understood financial methods, and devise a practical selection system within which to utilize those methods.

Selection of projects on the basis of their financial potential implies that the measurement of that potential must be related to:

1. Returns of invesment
2. Cash flow
3. Payout

These are standard economic tools and do not require further explanation in this discussion. However, one comment is appropriate. R&D costs are normally included in cash flow and payout estimates, but not in return on investment, since ROI depicts a measurement of commercial performance at a point in time subsequent to the expenditure of R&D funds. However, we suggest that the projected R&D costs be included as an expense in the ROI calculation, by averaging them over the expected useful life of the technology.

When we consider that only part of the total R&D program will prove to be commercially successful, it is necessary to make an allowance for this in the ROI estimate. Each organization will have its own average estimate. Activated projects should have sufficient value such that, if successful, they would yield an ROI sufficient to absorb the R&D costs of the unsuccessful efforts. A highly efficient selection process should greatly reduce this burden of project failures.

SOME BASIC GUIDELINES

Before proceeding to the selection system itself, the following basic points are emphasized:

1. Selection should be based upon the understanding that only a portion of the projects initiated will reach commercial reality. For this reason it is advisable to risk rejecting a potentially good project rather than risk undertaking a project with a low probability of success. In project selection, the aim is to allocate a limited resource

(R&D manpower and money) to a presumably unlimited resource (project opportunities). Rejecting a promising project does not, therefore, have the same damaging effect as undertaking a questionable project.

2. The tangible criteria (i.e., value and cost) should be examined independently of the risk aspect, since risk may be controlled by revising the approach or manpower assignment if the value/cost relationship is attractive.

3. Give careful consideration to the commercialization costs of projects. In most cases, these costs far outweigh the R&D expenses.

4. Be sure that the time span of the R&D effort is not out of line with the need. If the project will require two years, then the need must be related to conditions likely to exist two-plus years hence. Many a project has reached a technical success only to find the need vanished.

5. Remember that risk increases with time lapsed. Long-range projects are thus of greater risk and must have a greater payoff.

6. Although R&D is sometimes directed by corporate management to undertake a project, it is still the responsibility of technical management to evaluate the project carefully. Passage of time often obscures the initiator of the effort, and it is only clear in the end whether the project was a success or failure.

7. The key to the final justification of R&D expenditures centers around the selection of projects which meet the needs of the company. It is imperative that R&D management be cognizant of corporate management's objectives and attitudes relative to diversification, maintenance of current product lines, long-range versus short-range effort, and limitation of funds and resources. All of these factors must be understood if project selection is to function in a meaningful and efficient manner.

8. In many organizations, R&D management is preoccupied with the unrewarding task of making project-evaluation decisions by subjective and intuitive methods. Those decisions should derive logically from objective analyses as described here, allowing management to perform its proper function of managing the R&D machinery and assuring that the required results are forthcoming.

9. So-called mandatory projects may be occasionally required as a result of government regulations, for example. This type of project is not a matter of choice and does not enter into the selection process.

10. Technical service of a routine nature requested by non-R&D groups should be performed when practicable, and the requestor may be billed for the cost; project selection is unnecessary.

11. Exploratory research without tangible goals can be budgeted as a small percentage of the total effort.

TEN-STEP SYSTEM

With these guidelines in mind, the ten-step procedure for project selection is now presented:

1. Develop a checklist of criteria defining the bounds within which the R&D organization will function. These are the essentially intangible criteria mentioned previously (corporate objectives and attitudes, corporate capabilities, broad timing considerations, social and legal considerations).

2. As project opportunities are presented for consideration, determine whether they meet the qualitative criteria of acceptability. This is a simple checklist operation and is not time-consuming. Those which do not qualify are dropped from further consideration. (decision point)

3. Estimate the value in dollars of the projects which pass the first decision point, utilizing previously discussed methods. The value estimate is independent of risk or cost of the project and deals only with the objectives. At this point, the estimate of value does not require great accuracy, but it must be realistic.

4. Establish a minimum-value level which is commensurate with the size of the corporation. Measure each project's value against the established minimum and reject those which fall below it. Most managements are looking for a breakthrough or big developments which will have an appreciable impact upon the business. (Decision Point)

5. Assign the surviving R&D projects and objectives to appropriate segments of the R&D department for establishment of technical approaches. This should be given major emphasis through the line organization and should employ all available resources to assure that the best approach or approaches are proposed for each project. At the same time, the technical experts should develop an expression of the probability of success to be expected from each technical approach.

6. Establish an estimated R&D cost to carry out the technical approach. If there are alternative approaches, it is advisable to study the economic merits of each relative to selecting the most economical and/or the one which should be pursued first.

7. Compare projected costs with established maximum-tolerable costs for R&D projects. Projects which are too costly in comparison with the total R&D budget should not be undertaken. However, allow for management override at this point. (decision point)

8. Examine the surviving projects for the cost of commercial application of each objective in the context of the technical approach chosen. Projects implying commercialization costs greater than the company is willing to incur are eliminated. (decision point)

9. Develop standard financial analyses for the remaining projects using the best data obtainable. There would normally be included:
   (1) Return on investment (ROI)
   (2) Cash flow (discounted or not)
   (3) Payback time
   (4) Production cost

10. Make final decision concerning each project:
   (1) Approve
   (2) Reject (but retain data for future use as technology/market situations change)
   (3) Send back for rework to determine whether a better technical approach is possible. These decisions are made within the normal corporate guidelines for investments. (decision point)

ADVANTAGES OF THE PROCEDURE

1. Provides methodology and data which are understandable by merchandising, manufacturing and management personnel. Enables them to analyze suggested projects according to their own viewpoints, and thus to make meaningful judgments with full knowledge of the relevant facts.

2. Establishes a straightforward, consistent and factual approach, uncomplicated by esoteric manipulations or theories, and reasonably free from private opinion.

3. Allows each project to be evaluated separately and objectively, rather than relative to other projects.

4. Eliminates unacceptable projects by a progression of steps (i.e., each potential project is reviewed several times and from different viewpoints). Assures that the considerable effort involved in applying financial techniques (step 9) is devoted to projects already shown to have some merit.

5. Incorporates a feedback mechanism whereby financially weak projects can be reviewed, if desired, with the aim of improving their technical approach and economics. Gives the technical team clues to where the cost problems are located.

6. Documents and communicates the business justification for each accepted project, thus lending incentive and stimulation to the project team as well as to the commercialization effort. Permits the project team to make more rational selection of alternative technical approaches on the basis of economic attractiveness.

7. Facilitates justification of total R&D effort by simple addition of the profitability statements of the individual projects. This in turn validates budget requests for the R&D department.

INITIATION OF R&D PROJECTS

It is advisable to maintain a distinct line of demarcation between the project selection phase of research management and the subsequent project-initiation phase. The ideal situation exists when there are many more selected and approved projects than available manpower can undertake. Under those conditions, the most promising and profitable projects can be initiated first, with proper allowance for the skills of the persons available at the time. Also, a backlog of approved projects will prevent the occurrence of idle time or make-work situations. In addition, the pressure of a project backlog will lead to more rapid and conclusive performance on existing projects.

If project initiation is not a separate phase, there is a tendency to get started on every project with at least a token effort as soon as it is selected and approved. This inevitably leads to a greater project load in each group than the technical personnel can cope with efficiently. Each project should be initiated only when there are available the number and types of people required for an optimum effort.

In some cases, the project backlog may contain a project of such great priority and profitability that it will be tempting to initiate it with personnel obtained from active projects of lesser value. The less valuable projects would thus be either reduced in effort or deferred altogether. This is an acceptable practice if carried out with adequate thought and if done infrequently. Irresponsibility in this regard can lead to an unproductive turmoil.

There will be times when a backlog of selected and approved projects can be a distinct advantage to organizational planning. The backlog of unstarted projects is an excellent justification for requesting increases in personnel, facilities, scope, or outside contract funds.

Before a project is actually initiated, a suitable project leader should be selected. His first task will be to redefine the technical approach as a series of distinct phases (if this has not already been done). Such phases should be based on a rational division of effort, as: exploratory, feasibility, research, development, prototype, engineering, pilot plant, in-plant trials, market tests,etc.

For each phase planned, a well-defined target (milestone, checkpoint) must be identified so that it is always clear where each phase is headed and when it has arrived. The extent of the phasing adopted depends largely on the size and scope of the project. Very large or very complex projects can be much more efficiently pursued through application of a planning aid such as PERT or CPM. Even a smaller project can benefit from those techniques if the initial inputs are manifold and there are multiple technical approaches or contributions.

In some R&D organizations, project work is implemented by functional project teams.[7] The actual organization chart of such a research department has little effect on the staffing of each project team. Thus, the functional project team system assembles a team of men having exactly the skills needed for each individual project regardless of where the men normally reside in the physical organization. A project team might in this way be composed of a physicist, a polymer chemist, a chemical engineer, and a specialist in injection molding, although they report through different line management channels and do not usually work together.

The gathering of such diverse skills can often result in much more effective project implementation than the older alternative of placing projects in stable organizational groups which always work together on a variety of projects. The functional project team system is recommended for the following reasons:

1. Assures that all required skills will be available to the team.
2. Provides for periodic changes in the composition of the team (array of skills) as the project progresses through various phases (e.g., research to development to engineering to commercialization).
3. Avoids the stagnation of thinking which has been observed after about four to five years in groups of people who work together constantly.[8]
4. Overcomes the common problem of trying to transfer a project from one organizational group to another. It is historically difficult to arouse the interest of a development group in a subject which originated with an organizationally distant research group. Hence, the oft-quoted "not-invented-here" (NIH) phenomenon, a problem recognized by all R&D administrators.
5. Permits continuity of project leadership or transfer of project leadership, as the situation demands, but in any case without destruction of the project team and its momentum.

The procedures for project selection and initiation which we have presented here represent the best thoughts and observations of a great many people who have studied the subject over a period of years. Many of the principles and concepts are not original with us, but we have attempted to collect, organize, and present them in a uniquely straightforward manner as a practical, practicable system for R&D management. We are firm in our belief that use of such a system would greatly enhance the contributions of R&D to corporate profits, potentially with the full understanding and support of corporate management.

FOOTNOTES

[1]Josephson, M., "Edison," McGraw-Hill, New York (1963).

[2]*Management of New Products*, Booz, Allen & Hamilton, Inc., 1960.

[3]*Fortune*, May, 1970, p.201.

[4]Heyel, Carl, ed., "Handbook of Industrial Research Management," 2nd edition, Reinhold Publishing Corp., New York (1968), p. 162.

[5]Dean, Burton V., *AMA Research Study 89*, American Management Association, Inc., New York (1968).

[6]Kiefer, David M., ed., *Chemical & Engineering News*, March 23, 1964, pp. 88-109.

[7]Middleton, C. J., *Harvard Business Review*, March-April, 1967, pp. 73-82.

[8]Pelz, Donald C. and Andrews, Frank M., "Scientists in Organizations," J. Wiley & Sons, Inc., New York (1966), pp. 240-260.

STUDENT REVIEW QUESTIONS

1. Distinguish between the two categories of projects identified by Whaley and Williams.
2. How practical do the authors believe project rating equations to be? Why? Do you agree?
3. What types of financial analyses may be used for evaluating potential projects?
4. Why do the authors recommend that the project selection phase and the project initiation phase be kept separate?
5. Why is the functional project team recommended for project work?

19

SBU's: Hot, New Topic in the Management of Diversification*

WILLIAM K. HALL

IT STARTED IN 1971 in the executive offices at General Electric, the world's most diversified company. Corporate management at GE had been plagued during the 1960s with massive sales growth, but little profit growth. Using 1962 as an index of 100, dollar sales grew to 180 by 1970; however, earnings per share fluctuated without growth between 80 and 140, while return on assets fell from 100 to 60. Thus, in 1971, GE executives were determined to supplement GE's vaunted system of management decentralization with a new, comprehensive system for corporate planning.

The resulting system was based upon the new concept of strategic business units--SBUs, as they are now commonly called. Not only did this new system change the direction of planning at GE; it subsequently affected the corporate strategies and the planning processes in hundreds of other diversified firms around the world as well.

The SBU concept of planning is an intuitively obvious one, based on the following principles:

> The diversified firm should be managed as a "portfolio" of businesses, with each business unit serving a clearly defined product-market segment with a clearly defined strategy.
>
> Each business unit in the portfolio should develop a strategy tailored to its capabilities and competitive needs, but consistent with the overall corporate capabilities and needs.

---

*From *Business Horizons,* February, 1978, pp. 17-25.

> The total portfolio of business should be managed by allocating capital and managerial resources to serve the interests of the firm as a whole--to achieve balanced growth in sales, earnings, and asset mix at an acceptable and controlled level of risk. In essence, the portfolio should be designed and managed to achieve an overall corporate strategy.

As might be expected, the successful implementation of this intuitive approach provides a number of complex management choices and challenges. As a result, a heightened understanding of the benefits and costs of the SBU approach to the management of diversification is essential to the practice of general management. The objective of this article is to add to this understanding by summarizing the principles behind the SBU approach, and by examining the alternatives, benefits, and problems encountered to date in its successful implementation.

A LOOK AT TRADITIONAL PLANNING

In order to put the SBU concept of planning into a proper context, it is necessary to review briefly the traditional planning and resource allocation processes in large, diversified firms. These traditional processes grew out of the massive movement toward divisionalization and decentralization during the period 1920-1965. This movement began as a response to growth, diversity, and overall complexity in the large, diversified firm. In essence, the movement was essential, as one general manager put it, "to tailor responsibilities down to the size where a general manager could get his arms around them."

As the decentralized, divisionalized structure matured in the 1960s, formal planning became a way of life in the well-managed, diversified firm. Typically, the approach was initiated with the delineation of overall corporate mission, objectives, targets, and environmental assumptions. These were disseminated annually to the various divisions, where plans, projections, and sub-unit targets were developed as a response to these guidelines. Then a delicate, iterative process of "bottom up--top down" negotiation and consensus-seeking eventually resulted in an "approved plan" for the upcoming planning period.

This approach to formal planning had a number of advantages:

> It forced divisional managers to be explicit in their target-setting and goal-seeking, often on a profit center or investment center basis.

It allowed the corporate entity to add up the divisional pieces in advance, adjusting resource allocations and pushing divisions toward different targets when discrepancies against corporate objectives arose.

It allowed the development of sophisticated control systems to project, measure, and interpret deviations from the planned divisional results.

At the same time, however, this approach to planning and control was not without deficiencies. Divisional plans were frequently either overly optimistic or overly pessimistic. Depending upon the corporate "culture," they typically were based on one of three scenarios: extrapolated results, a philosophy that "next year things will get better," or a philosophy that "it's better to plan things a little conservatively so that we come out looking good at the end." Often, management commitment to plans was incomplete--either at the corporate or divisional level. Variances were frequently explained by unforeseen external factors, inadequate divisional resources, or deficiencies in the target-setting process itself. The total corporate plan, formed by adding up the divisional plans, often left corporate management without a clear grasp of either divisional or corporate strategy. Moreover, division plans were frequently approved (or rejected) without an explicit understanding of the strategy behind the plans or the risks and opportunities associated with this strategy. As one divisional general manager commented, "Planning without an understanding of corporate strategy was a lot like throwing darts in a darkened room."

In short, the traditional corporate plan almost always contained notebooks full of facts, figures, and forecasts, but it frequently failed to digest these in a way that provided key insights into strategies and business success factors at both the divisional and the corporate levels. The result, for many firms, was a decade of "profitless growth."

THE SBU ALTERNATIVE

In an attempt to deal with inadequacies in its traditional planning process, General Electric, guided by a task force of senior general managers and assisted by a team of management consultants, developed the SBU alternative to corporate planning. This process, now applied under a variety of names and in a variety of ways in other diversified firms, is almost always based on four steps:

identification of strategic business elements, or units;

strategic analysis of these units to ascertain their competitive position and long-term product-market attractiveness;
strategic management of these units, given their overall positioning;
strategic follow-up and reappraisal of SBU and corporate performance.

IDENTIFYING SBUs

The fundamental concept in the identification of SBUs is to identify the discrete, independent product-market segments served by the firm. In essence, the idea is to decentralize on the basis of strategic elements, not on the basis of size or span of control. This can be accomplished, as one general manager observed, by "identifying natural business units which correspond to the degrees of freedom a manager has available to compete."

Thus, within GE, nine groups and forty-eight divisions were reorganized into forty-three strategic business units, many of which crossed traditional group, divisional, and profit center lines. For example, in three separate divisions, food preparation appliances were merged as a single SBU serving the "housewares" market. A very small part of the Industrial Components Division was broken out as a separate SBU, serving a distinct industrial product-market niche in the machine tool industry. Within Union Carbide, another firm adopting the SBU approach, fifteen groups and divisions were decomposed into 150 "strategic planning units," and these were then recombined into nine new "aggregate planning units."

Ideally, an SBU should have primary responsibility and authority for managing its basic business functions: engineering, manufacturing, marketing, and distribution. In practice, however, traditions, shared facilities and distribution channels, manpower constraints, and business judgments have resulted in significant deviations from this concept of autonomy. In General Foods, for instance, strategic business units were originally defined on a product line basis, even though several products served overlapping markets and were produced in shared facilities. Later, these product-oriented SBUs were redefined into menu segments, with SBUs like breakfast food, beverage, main meal, dessert, and pet foods targeted toward specific markets, even though these, too, shared common manufacturing and distribution resources.

The General Foods example, and examples from many other firms adopting the SBU concept, point out that identification and definition are ultimately managerial decisions reflecting philosophical and pragmatic resolutions of the question: "What are our businesses and what do we want them to be?" As one general manager succinctly put it, "In our company an SBU ultimately becomes whatever subdivision corporate management wants it to be."

STRATEGIC POSITIONING

The subsequent process of positioning an SBU is typically driven by two criteria: long-term attractiveness of the product-market segment served by the SBU, and the SBU's competitive position (business strength) within that product-market segment. A conceptual 2 x 2 matrix illustrating this positioning is shown in the following figure:

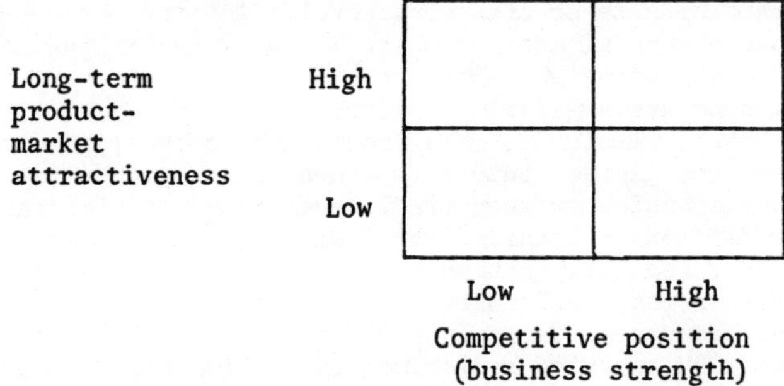

Here again, the scales of measurement and the precision of measurement along both scales vary significantly in practice. Since the choice of a measurement scale is more important than the degree of detail in measurement along the chosen scale, it will be discussed in some detail.[1]

Long-Term Product-Market Attractiveness. Two distinctive philosophies have evolved in ranking SBUs on this dimension. The first uses a single measure, almost always defined as the long-term projected real growth rate of the product-market segment.[2] (The split between high and low growth rates is sometimes arbitrarily set at 10 percent; other times it is set at the level of growth of the economy as a whole or at the level of growth of some sector of the economy.) Support for the growth rate definition of product-market attractiveness is clearly based upon a life cycle theory. With such a theory, attractive product-market segments are those

---

[1]I have seen primarily 2 x 2 matrices, although 3 x 3 and 4 x 4 matrices are used in some organizations.

[2]In a few cases, I have also seen projected long-term return on assets used as a measure of segment attractiveness.

in the development or "take-off" stage, and less attractive segments are in maturity or decline. Ideally, the long-term growth rate measures life cycle position and, hence, long-term product-market attractiveness.

The second methodology for assessing product-market attractiveness uses a set of measures, some qualitative and others quantitative. There, the choice of measures and the actual assessment of SBU position against these meaures can be made at the SBU level, the corporate level, or jointly. In corporate practice, I have seen all of these possibilities being utilized. At General Electric, for example, SBU product-market attractiveness is determined by examining and projecting ten criteria: segment size, segment growth rate (units and real dollars), competitive diversity, competitive structure, segment profitability, and technological, social, environmental, legal, and human impacts.

Competitive Position (Business Strength). As in the case of assessing long-term attractiveness, two alternative philosophies have evolved for ranking competitive position. Here again, the first is based on a single measure, generally defined as segment share or as segment share relative to competition.[3] Support for this single factor concept comes from the theory of experience curves, an approach to strategy formulation developed by the Boston Consulting Group.[4]

This theory suggests that the unit costs of production, marketing, and distribution drop proportionately (in real terms) each time total output (experience) doubles. This decrease in unit costs presumably comes from learning effects, scale effects, substitution of lower cost factor inputs, redesign, and technology. Thus, if one believes that costs in an SBU are on an experience curve, it follows that there should be strong relationships between high market share (experience), lower costs, and higher profitability.[5] In essence, high market share (or relative market share) becomes a surrogate measure of business strength relative to competition within the product-market segment.

In many firms, however, the market-share--experience-curve approach to assessing competitive position is viewed

---

[3]Relative share is defined as the ratio of the SBU's dollar sales in the product-market segment to the dollar sales of the SBU's major competitor (or in some cases, competitors).

[4]See, for example, the article by Hedley, "A Fundamental Approach to Strategy Development," *Long Range Planning*, (December, 1976), pp. 2-11.

[5]See Buzzell, "Market Share: Key to Profitability," *Harvard Business Review*, (January - February, 1975), for an empirical study lending some support to this hypothesis.

as overly simplistic or even erroneous. In this regard, a number of arguments have emerged:

> The competition with the most experience may be the "oldest" competitor. If this older firm has dedicated plant and equipment, it may not be able to exploit new, cost-reducing technology as rapidly as an emerging competitor.
>
> Shared experience obtained from other related product-market segments may be as important as accumulated output in lowering costs. (That is, experience cannot be measured independently for each product-market segment).
>
> External factors, technology breakthroughs, and other events may be as important as accumulated output in lowering (or in raising) costs.

In those firms that have either partially or totally rejected the experience-curve rationale, multiple measures of business strength have emerged. These measures are generally a mixture of qualitative and quantitative factors, and, depending upon the company, they can be defined and assessed either at the corporate or at the SBU level. At General Electric, for example, competitive position is evaluated on the following dimensions: segment size and SBU growth rate, share, profitability, margins, technology position, skill or weaknesses, image, environmental impact, and management.

Strategic handling. The strategic plan for an SBU is ultimately derived from its position with respect to long-term attractiveness (potential) and competitive position. Four combinations are possible.

Low potential/low position. An SBU in this category is clearly an unattractive member of the firm's portfolio for both the short run and long run. Furthermore, an infusion of resources to improve position will still leave the SBU in a low-potential segment. In essence, the SBU in this category is unworthy of major future commitments.

In the evolving jargon of the field, this "low/low" SBU is typically given the title of "cash trap," "mortgage," or "dog." Regardless of the title, the recommended strategic handling is always the same--manage the SBU to maximize short-term cash flow. In some cases this strategy can be accomplished through closing the SBU down or through rapid divestiture. In other cases, it can be handled by "harvesting" cash from the operation through ruthless cost cutting, short-term pricing policies, and sometimes through giving up market share and growth opportunities that absorb short-term cash.

Low potential/high position. Here an SBU is serving an unattractive product-market segment from a position of strength. Typically called a "bond" or "cash cow" in SBU parlance, the recommended strategic handling is to "milk" the entity for cash, although without the aggressiveness with which one would handle a "dog." The idea of selective cash "milking" is to preserve market position while generating dollars in an efficient fashion to support other, growth-targeted elements of the portfolio. Carefully targeted growth segments, stabilized pricing, differentiated products, selective cost reduction, less creative marketing, and selective capital investment are all means of achieving this goal.

High potential/low position. SBU elements in this category are typically termed "question marks," "problem children," or "sweepstakes" competitors. These elements are in an awkward position, for if they do not strengthen their competitive position, someone will almost certainly attack their product-market segment aggressively. Yet, the costs of strengthening their competitive position may not warrant the effort.

Thus, these elements are in a "get up or get out" strategic handling situation. Rigorous planning alternatives must be generated, evaluated, and costed. And then, the SBUs in this category must be moved, either upward or out of the firm's portfolio through divestiture or consolidation.

High potential/high position. SBUs in this category would seem to have the best classification. As "stars" or "savings accounts," these represent the businesses that must be groomed for the long run. As such, they should be given the resources and corporate support to grow faster than the market segment in sales, profits, and cash flow.

The recommended strategic handling of portfolio SBU elements can be summarized as follows:

> Dogs and cash cows are managed for short-term cash flow. Over the long run, dogs are divested or eliminated, while cash cows ultimately become dogs as their competitive position declines.
>
> Question marks must either get into the star category or get out of the portfolio. In the first case, they should make the move with carefully developed strategic plans so that major risk elements are identified and contained.
>
> Stars are short-run cash consumers and are managed for long-term position. Over the long run, as their segment attractiveness ultimately declines, they will become cash cows, generating cash to support the next round of stars.

STRATEGIC FOLLOW-UP AND REAPPRAISAL

In most explanations of the SBU process, the typical discussion stops after an explanation of SBU identification, classification, and handling. Unfortunately, failure by corporations to exploit the last element--follow-up and reappraisal--has probably resulted in most of the frustrations and failures encountered with the SBU process to date. To be successful, the SBU process must be iterative and ongoing, incorporating strategic planning and reappraisal, as well as managerial control.

Strategic Planning. Simply saying that a business is a star or cash cow will not make anything happen. Once a decision on strategic handling has been reached in this regard, detailed strategic goals and action plans must be evaluated and implemented. Such planning clearly offers alternatives; as one manager put it, "Some companies forget that there's more than one kind of cow." Detailed analysis and conceptual thinking are both required here, focusing on key success factors and major risk elements apt to be encountered along the way.

Strategic Reappraisal. A one-time evaluation and stragegic positioning are also insufficient. In most companies in which SBUs are successful, strategic reappraisal is routinely conducted on an annual or biannual basis. In one large company, for instance, each SBU manager must completely reassess his competitive position and strategy in an annual presentation before corporate management. Simultaneously, a staff review group will present and evaluate alternatives to this positioning on a total portfolio basis.

In other organizations, such as GE, reappraisal is initiated when a strategic "trigger point"--an external factor projected to have a significant impact on SBU performance--occurs. One GE manager described this system as follows: "For each business unit we require that management identify the sensitivity to these key external factors. These sensitivities must be identified in advance, and specific contingency plans must be ready in advance. Thus, we at least face the future with our eyes open!"

Managerial Control. Senior managers in many large firms also argue that the SBU approach to the management of diversification requires major changes in systems for budgeting, capital appropriation, measurement, reward, and managerial development. One general manager described the problem in his firm as follows: "To me it makes little sense to go through a sophisticated SBU analysis and then continue to allocate capital simply on discounted rate of return. Moreover, it makes even less sense to continue to measure and reward SBU management on annual performance against a profit budget."

Very little information is available on the modifications in managerial control that accompany the SBU concept.[6] However, General Electric has provided some interesting information on their systems in public sources.

> SBU control systems with GE are based on key success indicators (called business screens). For each SBU, performance measurements are monitored on five broad criteria: market position, competive position, profitability/cash flow, technological position, and external trigger points. Standards for each criteria are set and weighted differently, depending upon how the SBU is categorized. In addition, a "quality of performance" ranking is maintained as a measure of how well individual SBU managers have attained their standards of performance. As one GE manager put it, "the maturity of our SBU planning process could be measured when we began to bridge the gap between budgeting and the strategic plan."
>
> The measurement and reward of managerial performance was perhaps the biggest shift in the revised GE system. Under the previous system of reward, GE had compensated key managers on the basis of residual earnings--controllable profits during the planning period less a charge for corporate services and capital. Under the SBU system, however, SBU managers in different sectors of the matrix are measured and compensated differentially according to a bonus schedule, as shown in the table.

SBU Classification	*Current Performance (Residual Income)*	*Future Performance (Strategy)*	Other *Factors*
Invest/Grow	40%	48%	12%
Selectivity	60	28	12
Harvest/Divest	72	16	12

Clearly, SBU elements with an invest-and-grow classification are being rewarded on the basis of long-term (strategic) contributions. While GE has recognized the difficulty of such a long-term appraisal, key managers in the company agree that an invest-and-grow manager can be evaluated and

---

[6]Recently, Richard Bettis and I initiated a research project at the University of Michigan on these issues.

rewarded on the quality of his long-run strategy through a careful appraisal of his manpower plans, facilities plans, action programs, and competitive evaluation. As one GE manager described the system, "Of course, it has measurement problems, but so do most good compensation systems. In the end, I'm convinced that our revised executive incentive compensation system is the key that will make the SBU process work."

> Management development in GE has also shifted to reflect differential needs in differential business elements. Invest-and-grow business managers are developed to foster entrepreneurial characteristics. Cash cow (selectivity) business managers are developed to take sophisticated and hard looks at their businesses, and harvest and divest managers are developed with a heavy orientation toward experience, operations, and cost-cutting.

The philosophy behind the GE management systems is a classical one: Effective strategy implementation decisions will be made only if managerial selection, appraisal, and incentives are consistent with the strategy and with the planned results. As one manager in a large, diversified company recently observed, "Most firms have gone only half way with the SBU concept--they position their product-market segments and then go right on rewarding and promoting managers on traditional criteria. In the end the companies which make the SBU concept work will be those which change all management systems; developing and rewarding SBU managers differentially depending upon their SBU position and the strategic handling which is appropriate for their element of the portfolio."

PITFALLS IN SBU ANALYSIS

FAILURE TO GO ALL THE WAY

As discussed above, the failure to tie all management systems to the SBU approach is frequently a key pitfall in SBU analysis. In addition, there is the ever-present danger that short-term perturbations in the economy may drive invest-and-grow managers away from the long-term orientation required by the SBU approach. One senior manager commented on this problem as follows: "The 1974-1975 recession came when many companies were moving onto the SBU system. Unfortunately, indiscriminate cost cutting and cash conservation caused many of these firms to cover their heads with a blanket, going back to the 'good old ways' of doing business. In the end, the good companies of the 1980s will be those that stayed with their strategies during the recession--repositioning themselves in the short run to strengthen themselves for the long run."

DOCTRINAIRE APPROACHES

There is a wide variety of alternatives for identifying product-market segments, for evaluating these segments, and for developing an SBUs strategy vis-à-vis competition. The application of a single methodology in a doctrinaire fashion is likely to create dissension, confusion, and misleading results. SBU-based planning, even more than traditional corporate planning, must be conducted to generate "multi-business insights"--that is, to learn more about one's businesses than the competitor knows about his. As one manager succinctly observed, "The real payback from SBU planning is an intangible one--it comes slowly as you develop a strategic understanding of your businesses and your portfolio."

TRANSITION COSTS

Both the measurable and the hard-to-measure costs of moving from the traditional corporate planning process to the portfolio planning process must also be considered. Managers who have risen through the ranks of a firm to positions of leadership in groups and divisions are not apt to "jump for joy" when they are reorganized and retitled "dogs," "cows," or "question marks." Moreover, their subordinates are apt to be even more unsure as they assess their future employment, career development, and promotion prospects. One middle manager in a business redefined as a cash cow commented on this problem:

> I spent two years in an MBA program learning how to run a business as a profit/investment center. Now, suddenly I'm told to manage my department as a cash center.
>
> Then the corporation turns down a major expansion proposal from our division, reallocating investment funds to another set of businesses. I don't understand it, I don't like it, and I really wonder what my future looks like with the XYZ company.

In addition to these costs of managerial adjustment, there is some question as to whether traditionally trained managers can manage cows or dogs at all. A related question is whether or not a firm can develop and keep the diversified managerial talent necessary for managing diversified portfolio elements. And finally, "going all the way" with SBU implementation involves the high costs of adding new managerial systems or organization, planning, and control.

Transition costs can (and are) being handled in part by executive development programs within companies and within management education institutions. While these programs are useful--perhaps even essential--to a company shifting to the SBU philosophy, management transition takes time and involves some painful reallocations. It remains to be seen how much time and pain will be incurred as organizations shift and how many of these organizations will be able to endure these transition costs. The key issue, as one middle manager put it, will be "to convince managers that there are other ways to heaven than a star."

NEW VENTURES AND R&D

A fourth unresolved problem with the SBU approach to date involves corporate strategies toward new ventures and research and development--that is, toward the businesses of the future.

In theory, it would appear that R&D in a cash cow should be eliminated or restricted to short-term projects generating cost reductions. It is possible that a major R&D effort in a cow could result in major new markets or products that could ultimately turn the cow into a star (or lengthen the life during which the cow continues to generate cash). However, failure to maintain a competitive advantage in R&D within a cow could give competitors market leadership, accelerating, in effect, the cow's movement toward the dog category.

SBU theory would also seem to indicate that new ventures, R&D, and acquisition-merger policies should be directed at potential stars. The question is, how does one identify future stars in business segments where the firm has little or no experience, and should one develop these business segments internally or through acquisition-merger?

Determining the role of new technology and searching for stars of the future that are outside of the firm's existing portfolio are difficult--in theory and in practice. In essence, while the SBU philosophy has provided new insights into the management of existing businesses, new concepts are needed for managing additions to the portfolio effectively.

SBUs IN NONDIVERSIFIED FIRMS

It is obvious that SBU analysis has evolved as a powerful concept in the management of diversification. Still, while diversification has been a major trend throughout world corporations for the past quarter-century, many large, nondiversified businesses--even entire corporations--remain, in effect, single SBUs.

The question must be asked: Are there any concepts that

would aid in strategy formulation within a nondiversified firm? Clearly there are some:

consideration of resegmenting the existing single product-market segment into new segments to gain improved competitive position and segment attractiveness;

consideration of using cash flow from the existing single product-market segment to develop new stars--either through acquisition or through internal development (that is, manage the base business as a cow to feed the stars of the future).

While these ideas have conceptual merit, they are not without problems. Resegmentation takes time, money, and managerial skill. Diversification does also, and diversification raises the additional question of direction. Unfortunately, it is uncommon for the nondiversified firm to possess simultaneously all three elements--time, money, and skill in shifting strategies. Even when these three factors are present to some degree, reinvestment decisions in the base business tend to claim priorities on these scarce resources.

This strategic dilemma of the maturing, nondiversified firm is a major challenge to management and to society. While SBU analysis aid in understanding the dilemma, it has not as yet provided the conceptual framework to aid in the resolution.

There is little question that formal SBU analysis--identification, positioning, handling, and follow-up--provides new insights into the management of diversification. While the total number of diversified firms adopting some variant of this approach is unknown, one estimate is that 20 percent of the "Fortune 500" manufacturing firms are utilizing the concept. And while after only five years of experience it is too early to assess its impact, some testimonials provide a feel for preliminary management reaction:

General Electric: "GE is growing rapidly as a result of its strong financial controls and marketing strategies....Two basic failures--an absence of strategic planning and a dearth of financial controls have brought [their major domestic competition] to an [unfortunate] pass."[7]

Mead Paper: "Our track record for earnings won't validate it, but we will make this thing (SBU analysis) work. You can't help but improve

---

[7]"The Opposites: GE Grows While Westinghouse Shrinks," *Business Week* (January 31, 1977), pp. 60-66.

> a company if you get rid of the losers and step up the winners. Our program is the common thread running through the company."[8]
>
> *Union Carbide:* "Business strategies that reflect the category assigned to the business have been developed for each strategic planning unit....At present, about 60 percent of Union Carbide's total sales is concentrated in businesses in growth categories. For the period 1975 to 1979, about 80 percent of forecasted (capital) expenditures has been allocated to these businesses."[9]
>
> *Armco Steel:* "We [now] know the businesses we should pursue aggressively, those to maintain at the current level, and those to deemphasize or phase out. We can set goals that are reasonable...as they are attractive. And, importantly, we can have confidence in achieving our goals."[10]

However, the concept of portfolio management, like any other concept, must continue to evolve and mature as a philosophy for the effective management of diversification. And this evolution must come to grips with a number of issues that still are not fully resolved: tailoring and restructuring planning and control systems, avoiding doctrinaire approaches, and effectively managing transition costs. In addition, the handling of research and development and new ventures, as well as the application of the SBU concept to the nondiversified firm, provide major challenges to both business and business research.

There is little question, however, that the SBU approach to the management of diversification will leave a major mark--just as the movement to divisionalization and decentralization did twenty-five years ago. As one senior executive put it, "SBU analysis makes planning discontinuous.... It forces general managers to develop competitive and multibusiness insights at a strategic level....And in the uncertain, rapidly changing world of the 1980s, this kind of strategic planning will become a way of life."

---

[8] J. W. McSwiney, Chairman, in "Mead's Technique to Sort Out the Losers," *Business Week,* (March 11, 1972), pp. 124-127.

[9] *1975 Annual Report,* Union Carbide Corporation, p. 6.

[10] C. W. Verity, Chairman, in "Why a Portfolio of Businesses?" *Planning for Corporate Growth,* Planning Executives Institute (December, 1974), pp. 54-60.

STUDENT REVIEW QUESTIONS

1. Explain briefly the SBU concept of planning.
2. How are SBU's identfied?
3. Develop a 2 x 2 matrix that identifies the position of an SBU. Explain how the matrix can aid in decision making.
4. Explain what the following terms mean in relation to SBU's:
    a. dog
    b. cash cow
    c. problem children
    d. stars
5. What implications does the SBU concept have for managers and management development?

20

Diagnosing the Product Portfolio*

GEORGE S. DAY

HOW TO USE SCARCE CASH AND MANAGERIAL RESOURCES FOR MAXIMUM LONG-RUN GAINS

THE PRODUCT PORTFOLIO approach to marketing strategy formulation has gained wide acceptance among managers of diversified companies. They are first attracted by the intuitively appealing concept that long-run corporate performance is more than the sum of the contributions of individual profit centers or product strategies. Secondly, a product portfolio analysis suggests specific marketing strategies to achieve a balanced mix of products that will produce the maximum long-run effects from scarce cash and managerial resources. Lastly the concept employs a simple matrix representation which is easy to communicate and comprehend. Thus it is a useful tool in a headquarters campaign to demonstrate that the strategic issues facing the firm justify more centralized control over the planning and resource allocation process.

With the growing acceptance of the basic approach has come an increasing sensitivity to the limitations of the present methods of portraying the product portfolio, and a recognition that the approach is not equally useful in all corporate circumstances. Indeed, the implications can sometimes be grossly misleading. Inappropriate and misleading applications will result when:

---

*Reprinted from *Journal of Marketing*, Vol. 41, No. 2 (April, 1977), pp. 29-38, published by the American Marketing Association, by permission.

- The basic *assumptions* (especially those concerned with the value of market share dominance and the product life cycle) are violated,
- The *measurements* are wrong, or
- The *strategies* are not feasible.

This article identifies the critical assumptions and the measurement and application issues that may distort the strategic insights. A series of questions are posed that will aid planners and decision-makers to better understand this aid to strategic thinking, and thereby make better decisions.

WHAT IS THE PRODUCT PORTFOLIO?

Common to all portrayals of the product portfolio is the recognition that the competitive value of market share depends on the structure of competition and the stage of the product life cycle. Two examples of this approach have recently appeared in this journal.[1] However, the earliest, and most widely implemented is the cash quadrant or share/growth matrix developed by the Boston Consulting Group.[2] Each product is classified jointly by rate of present or forecast *market growth* (a proxy for stage in the product life cycle) and a measure of *market share dominance*.

The arguments for the use of market share are familiar and well documented.[3] Their basis is the cumulation of evidence that market share is strongly and positively correlated with product profitability. This theme is varied somewhat in the BCG approach by the emphasis on relative share--measured by the ratio of the company's share of the market to the share of the largest competitor. This is reasonable since the strategic implications of a 20% share are quite different if the largest competitor's is 40% or if it is 5%. Profitability will also vary, since according to the experience curve concept the largest competitor will be the most profitable at the prevailing price level.[4]

The product life cycle is employed because it highlights the desirability of a variety of products or services with different present and prospective growth rates. More important, the concept has some direct implications for the cost of gaining and/or holding market share:

- During the *rapid growth stage*, purchase patterns and distribution channels are fluid. Market shares can be increased at "relatively" low cost by capturing a disproportionate share of incremental sales (especially where these sales come from new users of applications rather than heavier usage by existing users).

- By contrast, the key-note during the *maturity stage* swings to stability and inertia in distribution and purchasing relationships. A substantial growth in share by one competitor will come at the expense of another competitor's capacity utilization, and will be resisted vigorously. As a result, gains in share are both time-consuming and costly (unless accompanied by a breakthrough in product value or performance that cannot be easily matched by competition).

PRODUCT PORTFOLIO STRATEGIES

When the share and growth rate of each of the products sold by a firm are jointly considered, a new basis for strategy evaluation emerges. While there are many possible combinations, an arbitrary classification of products into four share/growth categories (as shown in Exhibit 20-1) is sufficient to illustrate the strategy implications.

LOW GROWTH/DOMINANT SHARE (CASH COWS)

These profitable products usually generate more cash than is required to maintain share. All strategies should be directed toward maintaining market dominance--including investments in technological leadership. Pricing decisions should be made cautiously with an eye to maintaining price leadership. Pressure to over-invest through product proliferation and market expansion should be resisted unless prospects for expanding primary demand are unusually attractive. Instead, excess cash should be used to support research activities and growth areas elsewhere in the company.

HIGH GROWTH/DOMINANT SHARE (STARS)

Products that are market leaders, but also growing fast, will have substantial reported profits but need a lot of cash to finance the rate of growth. The appropriate strategies are designed primarily to protect the existing share

EXHIBIT 20-1. THE CASH QUADRANT APPROACH TO DESCRIBING THE PRODUCT PORTFOLIO*

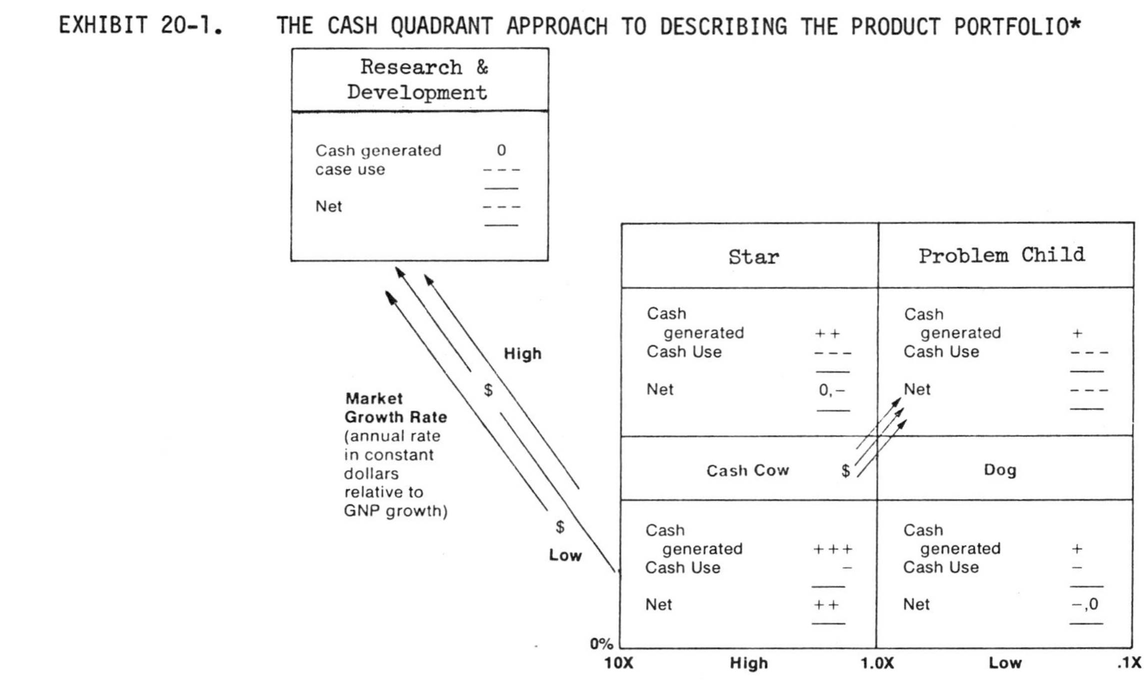

*Arrows indicate principal cash flows.

level by reinvesting earnings in the form of price reductions, product improvement, better market coverage, production efficiency increases, etc. Particular attention must be given to obtaining a large share of the new users or new applications that are the source of growth in the market.

LOW GROWTH/SUBORDINATE SHARE (DOGS)

Since there usually can be only one market leader and because most markets are mature, the greatest number of products are usually at a cost disadvantage and have few opportunities for growth at a reasonable cost. Their markets are not growing, so there is little new business to compete for, and market share gains will be resisted strenuously by the dominant competition.

The slower the growth (present or prospective) and the smaller the relative share, the greater the need for positive action. The possibilities include:

1. Focusing on a specialized segment of the market that can be dominated, and protected from competitive inroads.
2. Harvesting, which is a conscious cutback of all support costs to some minimum level which will maximize the cash flow over a foreseeable lifetime--which is usually short.
3. Divestment, usually involving a sale as a going concern.
4. Abandonment or deletion from the product line.

HIGH GROWTH/SUBORDINATE SHARE (PROBLEM CHILDREN)

The combination of rapid growth and poor profit margins creates an enormous demand for cash. If the cash is not forthcoming, the product will become a "Dog" as growth inevitably slows. The basic strategy options are fairly clear-cut; either invest heavily to get a disproportionate share of the new sales or buy existing shares by acquiring competitors and thus move the product toward the "Star" category or get out of the business using some of the methods just described.

Consideration also should be given to a market segmentation strategy, but only if a defensible niche can be identified and resources are available to gain dominance. This strategy is even more attractive if the segment can provide an entrée and experience based from which to push for dominance of the whole market.

OVERALL STRATEGY

The long-run health of the corporation depends on having some products that *generate* cash (and provide acceptable reported profits), and others that *use* cash to support growth. Among the indicators of overall health are the size and vulnerability of the "Cash Cows" (and the prospects for the "Stars," if any), and the number of "Problem Children" and "Dogs." Particular attention must be paid to those products with large cash appetites. Unless the company has abundant cash flow, it cannot afford to sponsor many such products at one time. If resources (including debt capacity) are spread too thin, the company simply will wind up with too many marginal products and suffer a reduced capacity to finance promising new product entries or acquisitions in the future.

The share/growth matrix displayed in Exhibit 10-2 shows how one company (actually a composite of a number of situations) might follow the strategic implications of the product portfolio to achieve a better balance of sources and uses of cash. The *present* position of each product is defined by the relative share and market growth rate during a representative time *period*. Since business results normally fluctuate, it is important to use a time period that is not distorted by rare events. The *future* position may be either (a) a momentum forecast of the results of continuing the present strategy, or (b) a forecast of the consequences of a change in strategy. It is desirable to do both, and compare the results. The specific display of Exhibit 10-2 is a summary of the following strategic decisions.

- Aggressively *support* the newly introduced product A, to ensure dominance (but anticipate share declines due to new competitive entries).

- Continue present strategies of products B and C to ensure *maintenance* of market share.

- Gain share of market for product D by investing in *acquisitions*.

- Narrow and modify the range of models of product E to *focus* on one segment.

- *Divest* products F and G.

EXHIBIT 20-2.

BALANCING THE PRODUCT PORTFOLIO

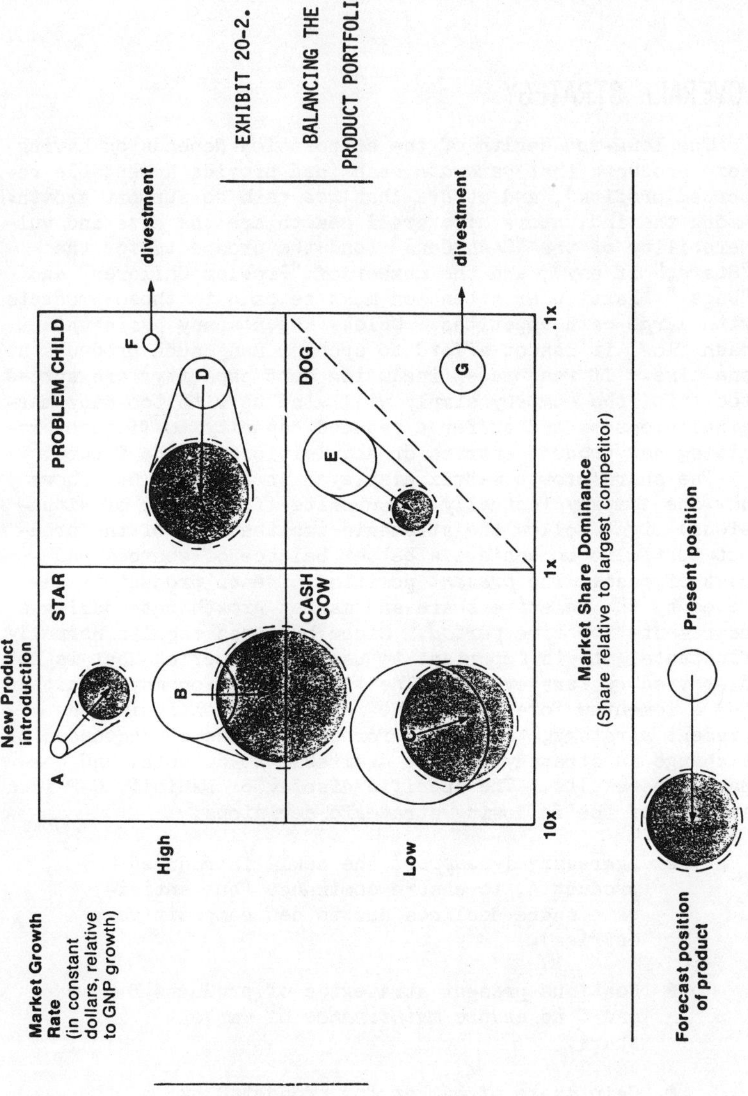

PITFALLS IN THE ASSUMPTIONS

The starting point in the decision to follow the implications of a product portfolio analysis is to ask whether the underlying assumptions make sense. The most fundamental assumptions relate to the role of market share in the businesses being portrayed in the portfolio. Even if the answers here are affirmative one may choose to not follow the implications if other objectives than balancing cash flows take priority, or there are barriers to implementing the indicated strategies.

WHAT IS THE ROLE OF MARKET SHARE?

All the competitors are assumed to have the same overhead structures and experience curves, with their position on the experience curve corresponding to their market share position. Hence market share dominance is a proxy for the *relative* profit performance (e.g., GM vs. Chrysler). Other factors beyond market share may be influential in dictating *absolute, profit performance (e.g., calculators versus cosmetics).*

The influence of market share is most apparent with high value-added products, where there are significant barriers to entry and the competition consists of a few, large, diversified corporations with the attendant large overheads (e.g., plastics, major appliances, automobiles, and semiconductors). But even in these industrial environments there are distortions under conditions such as:

- One competitor has a significant technological advantage which can be protected and used to establish a steeper cost reduction/experience curve.

- The principal component of the product is produced by a supplier who has an inherent cost advantage because of an integrated process. Thus Dupont was at a cost disadvantage with Cyclohexane vis-à-vis the oil companies because the manufacture of the product was so highly integrated with the operations of an oil refinery.[5]

- Competiors can economically gain large amounts of experience through acquisitions or licensing, or shift to a lower (but parallel) cost curve by resorting to offshore production or component sourcing.

- Profitability is highly sensitive to the

rate of capacity utilization, regardless of size of plant.

There are many situations where the positive profitability and share relationship becomes very tenuous, and perhaps unattainable. A recent illustration is the building industry where large corporations--CNA with Larwin and ITT with Levitt--have suffered because of their inability to adequately offset their high overhead charges with a corresponding reduction in total costs.[6] Similar problems are also encountered in the service sector, and contribute to the many reasons why services which are highly labor-intensive and involve personal relationships must be approached with extreme caution in a product portfolio analysis.[7]

There is specific evidence from the Profit Impact of Market Strategies (PIMS) study[8] that the value of market share is not as significant for consumer goods as for industrial products. The reasons are not well understood, but probably reflect differences in buying behavior, the importance of product differentiation and the tendency for proliferation of marginally different brands in these categories. The strategy of protecting a market position by introducing line extensions, flankers, and spin-offs from a successful core brand means that product class boundaries are very unclear. Hence shares are harder to estimate. The individual brand in a category like deodorants or powdered drinks may not be the proper basis for evaluation. A related consequence is that joint costing problems multiply. For example, Unilever in the U.K. has 20 detergent brands all sharing production facilities and marketing resources to some degree.

WHEN DO MARKET SHARES STABILIZE?

The operating assumption is that shares tend toward stability during the maturity stage, as the dominant competitors concentrate on defending their existing position. An important corollary is that gains in share are easier and cheaper to achieve during the growth stage.

There is scattered empirical evidence, including the results of the PIMS project, which supports these assumptions. Several qualifications must be made before the implications can be pursued in depth:

- While market share *gains* may be costly, it is possible to mismanage a dominant position. The examples of A&P in food retailing, and British Leyland in the U.K. automobile market provide new benchmarks on the extent to which strong positions can erode unless vigorously defended.

- When the two largest competitors are of roughly equal size, the share positions may continue to be fluid until one is finally dominant.

- There are certain product categories, frequently high technology oriented, where a dominant full line/full service competitor is vulnerable if there are customer segments which do not require all the services, technical assistance, etc., that are provided. As markets mature this "sophisticated" segment usually grows. Thus, Digital Equipment Corp. has prospered in competition with IBM by simply selling basic hardware and depending on others to do the applications programming.[9] By contrast, IBM provides, for a price, a great deal of service backup and software for customers who are not self-sufficient. The dilemma for the dominant producer lies in the difficulty of serving both segments simultaneously.[10]

WHAT IS THE OBJECTIVE OF A PRODUCT PORTFOLIO STRATEGY?

The strategies emerging from a product portfolio analysis emphasize the balance of cash flows, by ensuring that there are products that use cash to sustain growth and others that supply cash.

Yet corporate objectives have many more dimensions that require consideration. This point was recognized by Seymour Tilles in one of the earliest discussions of the portfolio approach.[11] It is worth repeating to avoid a possible myopic focus on cash flow considerations. Tilles' point was that an investor pursues a balanced combination of risk, income, and growth when acquiring a portfolio of securities. He further argued that "the same basic concepts apply equally well to product planning." The problem with concentrating on cash flow to maximize income and growth is that strategies to balance risks are not explicitly considered.

What must be avoided is excessive exposure to a specific threat from one of the following areas of vulnerability:

- The economy (e.g., business downturns).
- Social, political, environmental pressures.
- Supply continuity.
- Technological change.
- Unions and related human factors.

It also follows that a firm should direct its new product search activities into several different opportunity areas, to avoid intensifying the degree of vulnerability. Thus many companies in the power equipment market, such as Brown Boveri, are in a quandry over whether to meet the enormous resource demands of the nuclear power equipment market, because of the degree of vulnerability of this business compared to other possibilities such as household appliances.

The desire to reduce vulnerability is a possible reason for keeping, or even acquiring, a "Dog." Thus, firms may integrate backward to assure supply of highly leveraged materials.[12] If a "Dog" has a high percentage of captive business, it may not even belong as a separate entity in a portfolio analysis.

A similar argument could be used for products which have been acquired for intelligence reasons. For example, a large Italian knitwear manufacturer owns a high-fashion dress company selling only to boutiques to help follow and interpret fashion trends. Similarly, because of the complex nature of the distribution of lumber products, some suppliers have acquired lumber retailers to help learn about patterns of demand and changing end-user requirements. In both these cases the products/businesses were acquired for reasons outside the logic of the product portfolio, and should properly be excluded from the analysis.

CAN THE STRATEGIES BE IMPLEMENTED?

Not only does a product portfolio analysis provide insights into the long-run health of a company; it also implies the basic strategies that will strengthen the portfolio. Unfortunately, there are many situations where the risks of failure of these strategies are unacceptably high. Several of these risks were identified in a recent analysis of the dangers in the pursuit of market share.[13]

One danger is that the company's financial resources will not be adequate. The resulting problems are enormously compounded should the company find itself in a vulnerable financial position if the fight were stopped short for some reason. The fundamental question underlying such dangers is the likelihood that competitors will pursue the same strategy, because they follow the same logic in identifying and pursuing opportunities. As a result, there is a growing premium on the understanding of competitive responses, and especially the degree to which they will be discouraged by aggressive action.

An increasingly important question is whether government regulations will permit the corporation to follow the strategy it has chosen. Antitrust regulations--especially in the U.S.--now virtually preclude acquisitions undertaken by large companies in related areas. Thus the effort by ITT to acquire a "Cash Cow" in Hartford Fire and Indemnity Insurance was nearly aborted by a consent decree, and other moves by ITT into Avis, Canteen Corp., and Levitt-have been divested by court order at enormous cost. Recent governmental actions--notably the *ReaLemon* case--may even make it desirable for companies with very large absolute market share to consider reducing that share.[14]

There is less recognition as yet that government involvement can cut both ways; making it difficult to get in *or out of* a business. Thus, because of national security considerations large defense contractors would have a difficult time exiting from the aerospace or defense businesses. The problems are most acute in coutnries like Britain and Italy where intervention policies include price controls, regional development directives and employment maintenance which may prevent the replacement of out-moded plants. Unions in these two countries are sometimes so dedicated to protecting the employment status quo that a manager may not even move employees from one product line to another without risking strike activity.

The last implementation question concerns the viability of a niche strategy, which appears at the outset to be an attractive way of coping with both "Dogs" and "Problem Children." The fundamental problem, of course, is whether a product or market niche can be isolated and protected against competitive inroads. But even if this can be achieved in the long-run, the strategy may not be attractive. The difficulties are most often encountered when a full or extensive product line is needed to support sales, service and distribution facilities. One specialized product may simply not generate sufficient volume and gross margin to cover the minimum costs of participation in the market. This is very clearly an issue in the construction equipment business because of the importance of assured service.

PITFALLS IN THE MEASURES

The "Achilles' Heel" of a product portfolio analysis is the units of measure; for if the share of market and growth estimates are dubious, so are the interpretations. Skeptics recognize this quickly, and can rapidly confuse the analysis by attacking the meaningfulness and accuracy of these measures and offering alternative definitions. With the present state of the measurements there is often no adequate defense.

WHAT SHARE OF WHAT MARKET?

This is not one, but several questions. Each is controversial because they influence the bases for resource allocation and evaluation within the firm:

- Should the definition of the product-market be broad (reflecting the generic need) or narrow?

- How much market segmentation?

- Should the focus be on the total product-market or a portion served by the company?

- Which level of geography: local versus national versus regio-centric markets?

The answers to these questions are complicated by the lack of defensible procedures for identifying product-market boundaries. For example, four-digit SIC categories are convenient and geographically available but may have little relevance to consumer perceptions of substitutability which will influence the long-run performance of the product. Furthermore, there is the pace of product development activity which is dedicated to combining, extending, or otherwise obscuring the boundaries.

Breadth of Product-Market Definition? This is a pivotal question. Consider the following extremes in definitions:

- Intermediate builder chemicals for the detergent industry *or* Sodium Tri-polyphosphate.

- Time/information display devices *or* medium-priced digital-display alarm clocks.

- Main meal accompaniments *or* jellied cranberry.

Narrow definitions satisfy the short-run, tactical concerns of sales and product managers. Broader views, reflecting longer-run, strategic planning concerns, invariably reveal a larger market to account for (a) sales to untapped but potential markets, (b) changes in technology, price relationships, and supply which broaden the array of potential substitute products, and (c) the time required to present and prospective buyers to react to these changes.

Extent of Segmentation? In other words, when does it become meaningful to divide the total market into sub-groups for the purpose of estimating shares? In the tire industry it is evident that the OEM and replacement markets are so dissimilar in behavior as to dictate totally different marketing mixes. But how much further should segmentation be pushed? The fact that a company has a large share of the high-income buyers of replacement tires is probably not strategically relevant.

In general the degree of segmentation for a portfolio analysis should be limited to grouping those buyers that share situational or behavioral characteristics that are strategically relevant. This means that different marketing mixes must be used to serve the segments that have been identified, which will be reflected in different cost and price structures. Other manifestations of a strategically important segment boundary would be a discontinuity in growth rates, share patterns, distribution patterns and so forth when going from one segment to another.

These judgments are particularly hard to make for geographic boundaries. For example, what is meaningful for a manufacturer of industrial equipment facing dominant local competition in each of the national markets in the European Economic Community? Because the company is in each market, it has a 5% share of the total EEC market, while the largest regional competitor has 9%. In this case the choice of a regional rather than national market definition was dictated by the *trend* to similarity of product requirements throughout the EEC and the consequent feasibility of a single manufacturing facility to serve several countries.

The tendency for trade barriers to decline for countries within significant economic groupings will increasingly dictate regio-centric rather than nationally oriented boundaries. This, of course, will not happen where transportation costs or government efforts to protect sensitive industry categories (such as electric power generation equipment), by requiring local vendors, creates other kinds of barriers.

MARKET SERVED VERSUS TOTAL MARKET?

Firms may elect to serve only just a part of the available market; such as retailers with central buying offices or utilities of a certain size. The share of the market served is an appropriate basis for tactical decisions. This share estimate may also be relevant for strategic decisions, especially if the market served corresponds to a distinct segment boundary. There is a risk that focusing only on the market served may mean overlooking a significant opportunity or competitive threat emerging from the unserved portion of the market. For example, a company serving the blank cassette tape market only through specialty audio outlets is vulnerable if buyers perceive that similar quality cassettes can be bought in general merchandise and discount outlets.

Another facet of the served market issue is the treatment

of customers who have integrated backward and now satisfy their own needs from their own resources. Whether or not the captive volume is included in the estimate of total market size depends on how readily this captive volume can be displaced by outside suppliers. Recent analysis suggests that captive production--or infeeding--is "remarkably resilient to attack by outside suppliers."[15]

WHAT CAN BE DONE?

The value of a strategically relevant product-market definition lies in "stretching" the company's perceptions appropriately--far enough so that significant threats and opportunities are not missed, but not so far as to dissipate information gathering and analysis efforts on "long shots." This is a difficult balance to achieve, given the myriads of possibilities. The best procedure for coping is to employ several alternative definitions, varying specificity of product and market segments. There will inevitably be both points of contradiction and consistency in the insights gained from portfolios constructed at one level versus another. The process of resolution can be very revealing, both in terms of understanding the competitive position and suggesting strategy alternatives.[16]

MARKET GROWTH RATE

The product life cycle is justifiably regarded as one of the most difficult marketing concepts to measure--or forecast.

There is a strong tendency in a portfolio analysis to judge that a product is maturing when there is a forecast of a decline in growth rate below some specified cut-off. One difficulty is that the same cut-off level does not apply equally to all products or economic climates. As slow growth or level GNP becomes the reality, high absolute growth rates become harder to achieve for all products, mature or otherwise. Products with lengthy introductory periods, facing substantial barriers to adoption, may never exhibit high growth rates, but may have an extended maturity stage. Other products may exhibit precisely the opposite life cycle pattern.

The focus in the product portfolio analysis should be on the long-run growth rate forecast. This becomes especially important with products which are sensitive to the business cycle, such as machine tools, or have potential substitutes with fluctuating prices. Thus the future growth of engineered plastics is entwined with the price of zinc, aluminum, copper and steel; the sales of powdered breakfast beverages depends on the relative price of frozen orange juice concentrate.

These two examples also illustrate the problem of the self-fulfilling prophecy. A premature classification as a mature product may lead to the reduction of marketing resources to the level necessary to defend the share in order to maximize net cash flow. But if the product class sales are sensitive to market development activity (as in the case of engineered plastics) or advertising expenditures (as is the case with powdered breakfast drinks) and these budgets are reduced by the dominant firms then, indeed, the product growth rate will slow down.

The growth rate is strongly influenced by the choice of product-market boundaries. A broad product type (cigarettes) will usually have a longer maturity stage than a more specific product form (plain filter cigarettes). In theory, the growth of the individual brand is irrelevant. Yet, it cannot be ignored that the attractiveness of a growth market, however defined, will be diminished by the entry of new competitors with the typical depressing effect on the sales, prices and profits of the established firms. The extent of the reappraisal of the market will depend on the number, resources, and commitment of the new entrants. Are they likely to become what is known in the audio electronics industry as "rabbits," which come racing into the market, litter it up, and die off quickly?

PITFALLS FROM UNANTICIPATED CONSEQUENCES

Managers are very effective at tailoring their behavior to the evaluation system, *as they perceive it.* Whenever market share is used to evaluate performance, there is a tendency for managers to manipulate the product-market boundaries to show a static or increasing share. The greater the degree of ambiguity or compromise in the definition of the boundaries the more tempting these adjustments become. The risk is that the resulting narrow view of the market may mean overlooking threats from substitutes or the opportunities within emerging market segments.

These problems are compounded when share dominance is also perceived to be an important determinant of the allocation of resources and top management interest. The manager who doesn't like the implications of being associated with a "Dog," may try to redefine the market so he can point to a larger market share or a higher than average growth rate. Regardless of his success with the attempted redefinition, his awareness of how the business is regarded in the overall portfolio will ultimately affect his morale. Then his energies may turn to seeking a transfer or looking for another job, and perhaps another prophecy has been fulfilled.

The forecast of market growth rate is also likely to be manipulated, especially if the preferred route to advancement and needed additional resources is perceived to depend on association with a product that is classified as "Star." This may lead to wishful thinking about the future growth prospects of the product. Unfortunately the quality of the review procedures in most planning processes is not robust enough to challenge such distortions. Further dysfunctional consequences will result if ambitious managers of "Cash Cows" actually attempt to expand their products through unnecessary product proliferation and market segmentation without regard to the impact on profits.

The potential for dysfunctional consequences does not mean that profit center managers and their employees should not be aware of the basis for resource allocation decisions within the firm. A strong argument can be made to the effect that it is worse for managers to observe those decisions and suspect the worst. What will surely create problems is to have an inappropriate reward system. A formula-based system, relying on achievement of a target for return on investment or an index of profit measures, that does not recognize the differences in potential among business, will lead to short-run actions that conflict with the basic strategies that should be pursued.

ALTERNATIVE VIEWS OF THE PORTFOLIO

This analysis of the share/growth matrix portrayal of the product portfolio supports Bowman's contention that much of what now exists in the field of corporate or marketing strategy can be thought of as contingency theories. "The ideas, recommendations, or generalizations are rather dependent (contingent) for their truth and their relevance on the specific situational factors."[17] This means that in any specific analysis of the product portfolio there may be a number of factors beyond share and market growth with a much greater bearing on the attractiveness of a product-market or business; including:

- The contribution rate.
- Barriers to entry.
- Cyclicality of sales.
- The rate of capacity utilization.
- Sensitivity of sales to change in prices, promotional activities, service levels, etc.
- The extent of "captive" business.
- The nature of technology (maturity, volatility, and complexity).
- Availability of production and process

opportunities.

- Social, legal, governmental, and union pressures and opportunities.

Since these factors are situational, each company (or division) must develop its own ranking of their importance in determining attractiveness.[18] In practice these factors tend to be qualitatively combined into overall judgments of the attractiveness of the industry or market, and the company's position in that market. The resulting matrix for displaying the positions of each product is called a "nine-block" diagram or decision matrix.[19]

Although the implications of this version of the product portfolio are not as clear-cut, it does overcome many of the shortcomings of the share/growth matrix approach. Indeed the two approaches will likely yield different insights. But as the main purpose of the product portfolio analysis is to help guide--but not substitute for--strategic thinking, the process of reconciliation is useful in itself. Thus it is desirable to employ both approaches and compare results.

SUMMARY

The product portfolio concept provides a useful synthesis of the analyses and judgments during the preliminary steps of the planning process, and is a provocative source of strategy alternatives. If nothing else, it demonstrates the fallacy of treating all businesses or profit centers as alike, and all capital investment decisions as independent and additive events.

There are a number of pitfalls to be avoided to ensure the implications are not misleading. This is especially true for the cash quadrant or share/growth matrix approach to portraying the portfolio. In many situations the basic assumptions are not satisfied. Further complications stem from uncertainties in the definitions of product-markets and the extent and timing of competitive actions. One final pitfall is the unanticipated consequences of adopting a portfolio approach. These may or may not be undesirable depending on whether they are recognized at the outset.

Despite the potential pitfalls it is important to not lose sight of the concept; that is, to base strategies on the perception of a company as an interdependent group of products and services, each playing a distinctive and supportive role.

FOOTNOTES

[1]Bernard Catry and Michel Chevalier, "Market Share Strategy and the Product Life Cycle," *Journal of Marketing*, Vol. 38, No. 4 (October, 1974), pp. 29-34; and Yoram Wind and Henry J. Claycamp. "Planning Product Line Strategy: A Matrix Approach," *Journal of Marketing*, Vol. 40, No. 1 (January, 1976), pp. 2-9.

[2]Described in the following pamphlets in the *Perspectives* series, authored by Bruce D. Henderson, "The Product Portfolio" (1970), "Cash Traps" (1972) and "The Experience Curve Reviewed: The Growth-Share Matrix or the Product Portfolio." (Boston Consulting Group, 1973). By 1972 the approach had been employed in more than 100 companies. See "Mead's Technique to Sort Out the Losers," *Business Week*, (March 11, 1972), pp. 124-30.

[3]Sidney Schoeffler, Robert D. Buzzell and Donald F. Heany, "Impact of Strategic Planning on Profit Performance," *Harvard Business Review*, Vol. 52 (March-April, 1974), pp. 137-45; and Robert D. Buzzell, Bradley T. Gale and Ralph G. M. Sultan, "Market Share--A Key to Profitability," *Harvard Business Review*, Vol. 53 (January-February, 1975), pp. 97-106.

[4]Boston Consulting Group, *Perspectives on Experience* (Boston: 1968 and 1970), and "Selling Business a Theory of Economics," *Business Week*, September 8, 1974, pp. 43-44.

[5]Robert B. Stobaugh and Philip L. Towsend, "Price Forecasting and Strategic Planning: The Case of Petrochemicals," *Journal of Marketing Research*, Vol. XII (February, 1975), pp. 19-29.

[6]Carol J. Loomis, "The Further Misadventures of Harold Geneen," *Fortune*, June, 1975.

[7]There is incomplete but provocative evidence of significant share-profit relationships in the markets for auto rental, consumer finance, and retail securities brokerage.

[8]Same as reference 3 above.

[9]"A Minicomputer Tempest," *Business Week*, January 27, 1975, pp. 79-80.

[10]Some argue that the dilemma is very general, confronting all pioneering companies in mature markets. See Seymour Tilles, "Segmentation and Strategy," *Perspectives*

(Boston: Boston Consulting Group, 1974).

[11]Seymour Tilles, "Strategies for Allocating Funds," *Harvard Business Review,* Vol. 44 (January-February, 1966), pp. 72-80.

[12]This argument is compelling when $20,000 of Styrene Monomer can affect the production of $10,000,000 worth of formed polyester fiberglass parts.

[13]William E. Fruhan, "Pyrrhic Victories in Fights for Market Share," *Harvard Business Review,* Vol. 50 (September-October, 1972), pp. 100-107.

[14]See Paul N. Bloom and Philip Kotler, "Strategies for High Market-Share Companies," *Harvard Business Review,* Vol. 53 (November-December, 1975), pp. 63-72.

[15]Aubrey Wilson and Bryan Atkin, "Exorcising the Ghosts in Marketing," *Harvard Business Review,* Vol. 54 (September-October, 1976), pp. 117-27. See also, Ralph D. Kerkendall, "Customers as Competitors," *Perspectives* (Boston: Boston Consulting Group, 1975).

[16]George S. Day and Allan D. Shocker, *Identifying Competitive Product-Market Boundaries: Strategic and Analytical Issues* (Boston: Marketing Science Institute, 1976).

[17]Edward H. Bowman, "Epistemology, Corporate Strategy, and Academe," *Sloan Management Review* (Winter, 1974), pp. 35-50.

[18]The choice of factors and assessment of ranks is an important aspect of the design of a planning system. These issues are described in Peter Lorange, "Divisional Planning: Setting Effective Direction," *Sloan Management Review* (Fall, 1975), pp. 77-91.

[19]William E. Rothschild, *Putting It All Together: A Guide to Strategic Thinking* (New York: AMACOM, 1976).

STUDENT REVIEW QUESTIONS

1. Discuss the four product portfolio strategies Day examines.
2. What are some conditions that may distort the value of market share?
3. What does Day say is the objective of a product portfolio strategy?
4. Day calls the units of measurement the "Achilles' Heel" of product portfolio analysis. Explain what he means by this.
5. What are some of the problems involved in using the product life cycle concept?
6. Explain what is meant by the statement "much of what now exists in the field of corporate or marketing strategy can be thought of as contingency theories."

21

Reflecting Corporate Strategy in Manufacturing Decisions*

STEVEN C. WHEELWRIGHT

IN SPITE OF THE FACT that manufacturing frequently accounts for the majority of a firm's human and financial assets, top management often overlooks the role that operations can play in accomplishing corporate objectives. The problem is not that top management ignores manufacturing, but rather that marketing and finance are expected to play a major role in formulating corporate plans, with manufacturing simply reacting to those plans as best it can. This failure to consider manufacturing to be a key resource in realizing corporate objectives seldom represents an explicit decision to restrict it to a reactive role. The reasons for such shortsightedness and its consequences have been described by Wickham Skinner:**

> Top management unknowingly delegates a surprisingly large portion of basic policy decisions to lower levels in the manufacturing area. Generally, this abdication of responsibility comes about more through a lack of concern than by intention. And it is partly the reason that many manufacturing policies and procedures developed

---

*From *Business Horizons*, April, 1978, pp. 64-72.

**Wickham Skinner, "Manufacturing--Missing Link in Corporate Strategy," *Harvard Business Review* (May-June, 1969), pp. 136-145; and "The Focused Factory," *Harvard Business Review* (May-June, 1974), pp. 113-121.

> at lower levels reflect assumptions about corporate strategy which are incorrect or misconstrued.
>
> The conventional factory produces many products for numerous customers in a variety of markets, thereby demanding the performance of a multiplicity of manufacturing tasks all at once from one set of assets and people. Its rationale is "economy of scale" and lower capital investment.

Unfortunately, even a company that recognizes these problems and has first-rate managers to work on them faces a major challenge in establishing procedures to ensure that manufacturing decisions mesh with corporate plans and goals. While operating decisions may make sense individually, they may not work cumulatively to reinforce the corporate strategy. The basic problem is that most decisions, particularly those in manufacturing, require trade-offs among various criteria. All too often the trade-offs that are made in such decisions reflect priorities that are internally inconsistent or that run counter to corporate strategy. Management needs a procedure for developing and implementing plans that support and reinforce corporate strategy.

Research and experience suggest that it is not enough just to communicate strategy throughout the organization. Some intermediate mechanism is needed for translating strategy into a form directly applicable to manufacturing decisions. One approach that several firms have applied utilizes a set of criteria that are appropriate for evaluating operations decisions. When the company assigns weights to these criteria that reflect the priorities of corporate strategy, these priorities can be used to ensure that trade-offs associated with operation decisions are consistent with strategy. This approach has been successfully used both by corporate manufacturing staff and by line management charged with making improvements in manufacturing decision-making.

The remainder of this article describes and illustrates this approach. The major emphasis is on implementing proven concepts so that the problems cited earlier can be avoided and the full strategic potential of manufacturing can be realized. As a starting point, four typical production decisions are described, and for each one the course of action initially selected by manufacturing management is indicated. The modifications in those decisions that resulted when a broader corporate perspective was considered are then examined. Following these illustrations of what it means to have manufacturing decisions reinforce corporate strategy, a conceptual framework is described that assists managers to accomplish systematically that desired congruence. Finally, two alternative procedures are presented for implementing that framework. In the first, the corporate manufacturing staff takes the initiative; in the second, line management.

SOME INAPPROPRIATE DECISIONS

In each of the following decision situations, manufacturing management had identified those actions they thought would be most appropriate. However, a subsequent review of each decision's compatibility with corporate goals and strategy indicated that a different course of action would be more appropriate. These four situations suggest the range of operating decisions which are typically made independently, but which have a major cumulative impact on the corporation's success in accomplishing its overall strategy.

SITUATION A: MAJOR EQUIPMENT PURCHASE

Production output was approaching the capacity of a major piece of equipment at a wholly owned subsidiary of a diversified company. This subsidiary sold 85 percent of its output to other divisions within the corporation. The other 15 percent, which represented outside sales, was an important source of profits for the subsidiary because of the transfer price arrangement established for corporate business and because the in-house business was at the low-priced end of the market. It was agreed that the division would soon need new equipment, and management was about to propose a multipurpose machine. This equipment offered more capacity per dollar invested than other alternatives and promised a chance to expand outside business and thereby increase return on investment. The only question appeared to be whether to buy the new machine at once or to delay the purchase for a year.

As a first step in taking a broader view of this decision, division management determined that the goal for the subsidiary was to be a low-cost source of supply to the corporation for that particular product. Other firms were potential suppliers, but top management had originally established this subsidiary to obtain low-cost materials for specialized, high-volume needs.

Review indicated that purchase of the proposed machine was not the best decision if the subsidiary was to work only for the parent company in the future. The subsidiary's outside customers put quality ahead of cost, but corporate customers emphasized cost. The proposed multipurpose machine would raise the cost on corporate business because of its cost structure. Also, because of the natural desire to utilize expensive equipment as fully as possible, it would probably lead to less emphasis on sales to corporate customers (and on costs) and more emphasis on outside sales (and quality) in order to utilize the equipment's full capability.

SITUATION B: QUALITY CONTROL BUDGET

This company had grown substantially over several years but had recently noted that indirect and overhead costs were growing more rapidly than sales. Management was concerned that these costs were getting out of line. As part of the annual budgeting procedure, manufacturing management proposed that the quality control area be rationalized and streamlined to bring its costs more in line with what they had been historically. The plan was to use more final product sampling (and less components testing) to cut quality control cost per unit.

A broader examination of this situation revealed that the company's products were selling at a premium price with an image of quality and high reliability. In fact, when the use of the product was examined for the major customer segment, it became apparent that the cost of a motor breakdown for even a single day was more than the price of a new motor. Manufacturing concluded that quality had to be maintained and given top priority. Component reliability was identified as an integral part of quality because of the modular product design and customer maintenance procedures. As a result of this review, management decided that more, not less, quality control per unit was appropriate, and that reductions in overhead and indirect costs would have to come from areas other than quality.

SITUATION C: LABOR NEGOTIATIONS

In six months, the major production facility of a manufacturer of a perishable consumer product (shelf life about three months) would face its first labor contract renewal. The corporate labor relations staff, whose policy had always been one of firmness, considered the existing contract most attractive and wanted to keep the new contract equally favorable to the company. Unfortunately, the union had recently been agitating among employees, emphasizing that the existing contract, unlike most other contracts in that region and industry, had no cost-of-living adjustment clause. A group of employees had become vocal in demands for a substantial "catch-up" adjustment in the new contract. It was assumed that when the contract expired in six months, the normal procedure of having the corporate labor relations staff handle negotiations would be followed. That staff had already recommended that as much extra inventory as possible should be built up in anticipation of a three-to-four-week strike. Given current capacity constraints and the perishable nature of the product, manufacturing had indicated that no more than three weeks of finished goods inventory could be accumulated by the time the current contract expired.

A more thorough examination of this situation indicated

that the market was growing at about 60 percent annually and that there were two other major firms in the business. This company and its two competitors each had about the same market share and were seeking to build national distribution as quickly as possible. In addition, recent studies of similar products and their economies suggested that there might only be room for two major firms once the growth rate began to slow. Manufacturing concluded that to achieve reliable, uninterrupted supply was the key task of production if corporate goals were to be met. Consequently, manufacturing decided to take an active role in urging labor relations to open negotiations early and, if at all possible, to resolve the contract issues before a strike became inevitable.

SITUATION D: MAJOR CAPACITY EXPANSION

The established manufacturer of a branded household product suddenly found its market growing rapidly, severely taxing its outdated production process. An engineering firm had been hired to develop process equipment that would improve the consistency of the product and provide substantial productivity improvement. A new process design had been completed and, although the equipment was new to this application, it was based on known technologies from other fields. To meet the coming year's substantially increased capacity requirements, manufacturing management planned to replace the old production process with the new one. This promised twice the output per square foot of plant and per employee, with an investment per unit of capacity that was slightly lower than for the old equipment. The new process appeared to more than meet cost goals, and manufacturing management was planning to move ahead with it as quickly as possible.

In this situation, a broader look at the corporate strategy and the environment identified the critical role of additional capacity. There was no contingency plan in the event that the new production process met unexpected startup problems, a fact that signaled danger. Further investigation indicated that the cost of excess capacity was minimal compared with the product's gross margin of almost 50 percent, and the maintenance of 30 percent excess capacity would add only 1 or 2 percent to product cost. Management concluded that if the firm was unable to meet all of the demand for its products, the penalty would not only be a loss in market share but a waste of advertising dollars equivalent to the capital investment required for 30 percent idle capacity. Manufacturing concluded that the new process might be appropriate in the longer term; initially, however, it should be added as excess capacity, not as a replacement for the existing process.

A CONCEPTUAL FRAMEWORK

The four decisions described above illustrate a range of situations where individual decisions must be reviewed in the context of corporate goals and strategy if those decisions are to have the desired reinforcing effect. In each instance, manufacturing management thought it had identified the appropriate action; yet a more comprehensive strategic review indicated that a major change in that action was needed. These situations suggest the need to develop a framework that triggers such a review, establishes company-specific criteria to be applied in that review, and provides a means of using those criteria effectively.

The ability of a company's manufacturing function to reinforce corporate strategy is determined by a number of decisions over an extended period of time. Understanding these decisions is the first step in using them to accomplish corporate goals. The following are among the most important factors in determining whether a firm's manufacturing actions will be truly supportive:

Facilities. The rationalization and focus of individual plants and their sizes and locations are major manufacturing commitments. These decisions are often the most visible examples of manufacturing strategy selection, in that options are often first defined at this point.

Choice of Process. A major set of manufacturing decisions concerns the matching of the company's choice of equipment and processes with its products' characteristics and competitive pressures. Choices must be made regarding the degree of automation, the level of product-line specificity, and the degree of interconnectedness among different stages in the process.

Aggregate Capacity. Both type of capacity and the timing of capacity changes are important elements in this category. Should the production rate be level or should it chase demand? Should overtime, second shift, or subcontracting be used for peak capacity requirements?

Vertical Integration. The number of production and distribution stages to be managed by a single firm, and the balance and relationships between vertically linked stages, are cirtical manufacturing decisions with an impact on corporate strategy.

Manufacturing Infrastructure. Molding the bricks, mortar, equipment, and people into a coordinated whole requires that the firm specify policies for production planning and control, quality control, inventory and logistic systems, and work-force management. Labor policies and materials-management procedures are important related topics.

Interface with Other Functions. Manufacturing must work closely with the other corporate functions. The operations manager and the manufacturing executive must facilitate these relations while balancing them against their own priorities.

These six choices determine corporate strategy in a company's manufacturing operations. They are the points at which key trade-offs are made. If they are to support corporate aims, they must consistently reinforce the desired competitive focus and goals--a simple achievement in firms in which the chief executive is involved in all decisions of significance. In larger firms with functional or divisionalized structures, a systematic effort is needed to insure this consistency. This effort is particularly critical as products and businesses grow, develop, or shrink, requiring change in the corporate strategy and in the manufacturing decisions to support that change.

Unfortunately, simply giving manufacturing management a statement of the corporate objectives and strategy is not particularly effective in achieving this desired consistency in decision making. The gap between operating decisions and their impact on corporate strategy is just too great. Some intermediate step is needed.

Manufacturing decisions reflect trade-offs among different performance criteria. Thus, identifying these criteria and prioritizing them has proven effective in bridging this gap. The most important performance criteria are the following:

Efficiency. This criterion encompasses both cost efficiency and capital efficiency and can generally be measured by such factors as return on sales, inventory turnover, and return on assets.

Dependability. The dependability of a company's products and its delivery and price promises is often extremely difficult to measure. Many companies measure it in terms of the "percent of on-time deliveries."

Quality. Product quality and reliability, service quality, speed of delivery, and maintenance quality are important aspects of this criterion. For many firms this is easy to measure by internal standards, but as with the other criteria, the key is how the market evaluates quality.

Flexibility. The two major aspects of flexibility changes are in the product and the volume. Special measures are required for this criterion, since it is not generally measured.

The four situations described earlier illustrate how an initially narrow view may lead to decisions that are not most appropriate for the corporation as a whole. As is frequently the case, in three of those four situations manufacturing management erred initially in assuming that the appropriate trade-offs were those that minimized the production cost per unit. A broader perspective for the last three situations indicated that the single criterion of lowest cost did not identify the best overall decision for those companies.

Every corporate situation is unique; no single procedure will guarantee that manufacturing decisions always reinforce corporate strategy. However, utilizing this framework that seeks to establish manufacturing priorities has been helpful in many situations. A first step in implementing the framework for an individual company is to answer two important questions: *Who* will apply the framework? *When and where* in existing planning and decision-making procedures will it be applied?

Among those who might take responsibility for applying the framework are the division general manager, the director of the corporate manufacturing staff, the division controller, and the division's director of manufacturing. These positions can be grouped into two main categories--line and staff. The division general manager and the director of manufacturing represent line management; the corporate manufacturing manager or a member of the controller's office represents staff. Who can best assume this responsibility depends on the organization of the company and its normal split of staff and line assignments. Even when a staff group facilitates and shepherds the application of this framework, it is always necessary to have the understanding and commitment of line management to make the framework useful.

When and where the implementation of this framework should be monitored depends largely on established management and decision-making procedures. For one company, the most logical time might be the annual budgeting or planning cycle. For another, it might best be incorporated in the periodic corporate review of divisional plans or in the division general manager's quarterly review of operations. How the framework can be used most effectively will depend both on the organization's motivation and management philosophy and on the manager (line or staff) most willing to take responsibility for seeing that significant progress is made.

APPLYING THE FRAMEWORK

Two separate applications of this conceptual framework will illustrate the range of approaches available for its implementation. The first was developed by a corporate manufacturing staff seeking to improve annual manufacturing plans. The second was designed and implemented by a vice president of manufacturing.

A STAFF APPROACH

The corporate manufacturing staff of a large diversified company with several autonomous divisions was concerned that manufacturing was not achieving its potential as a competitive weapon. Historically, the manufacturing staff had consisted of fewer than a dozen people whose major task was to make sure that requests for major capital appropriations were "complete." While the staff's charter continued to call for a limited staff, the vice-president who had recently been put in charge of the group wanted to move quickly to help division manufacturing managers take a more active role in the accomplishment of corporate strategy.

As a first step in this direction, he decided that all the divisions had a similar problem: developing annual manufacturing plans consistent with marketing and product strategies. Subsequently, corporate manufacturing assumed responsibility for communicating the framework and concepts related to manufacturing performance priorities and for having each division's manufacturing manager make them operational.

Two major objectives motivated corporate manufacturing's pursuit of this framework in the company. First, the corporate staff wanted to provide the different manufacturing managers from each of the operating divisions with a common set of concepts and language. It was felt that the corporate manufacturing staff and top management, who are not familiar with the technical problems, pressures, and issues facing manufacturing management, would be better able to review and evaluate operations decisions if they mastered these concepts.

A second objective was to help operating managers recognize the specific competitive decisions faced by their division. This could then help such managers make manufacturing decisions and formulate action plans consistent with corporate and division strategies and objectives.

The staff's approach in accomplishing these goals consisted of two phases. The first phase was a two-day seminar for thirty-five key manufacturing and distribution managers selected from all of the company's divisions. The first step was to introduce the framework presented in Figure 21-1. Thereafter, through a variety of case studies, the manufacturing managers were able to see the concepts applied to different situations.

The second phase applied the framework to each of the individual operating units as a part of their annual five-year planning process. After the division's operating plan had been drafted, manufacturing management met for a day with the corporate manufacturing staff. Their purpose was to review the draft plan and to examine the interaction between anticipated operating decisions and the division's strategy. These follow-up sessions consisted of four steps, as illus-

FIGURE 21-1. MANUFACTURING STRATEGY AND OPERATING DECISIONS

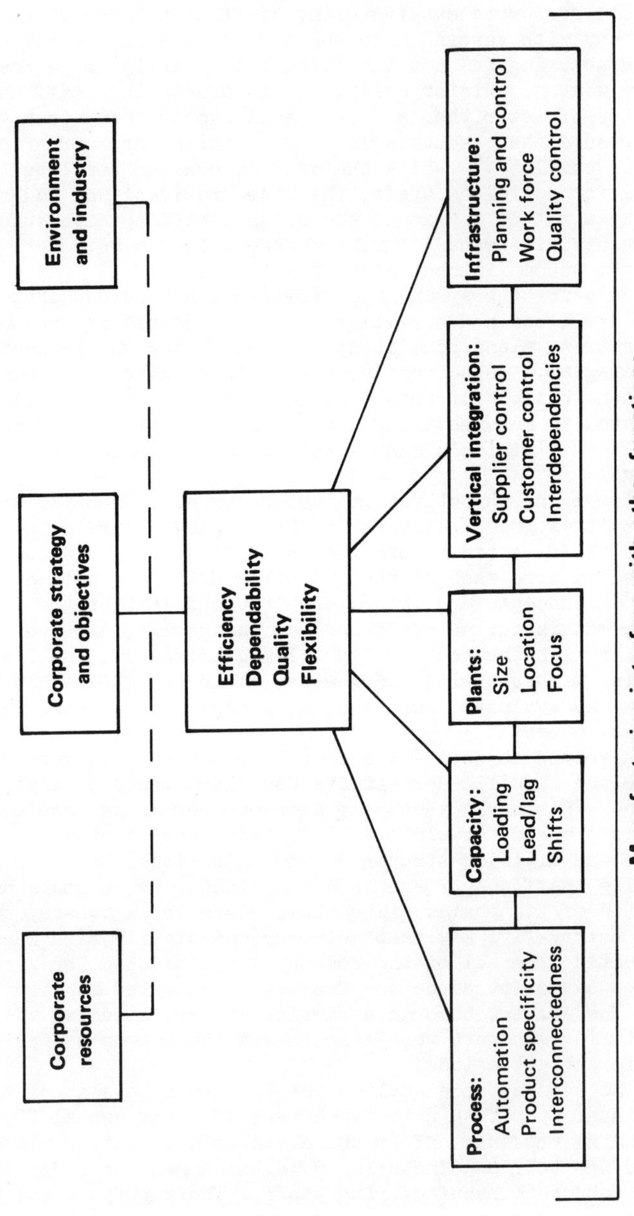

trated in Figure 21-2.

Step 1 defined the basic business units of the division--those product-market groupings for which the division had a homogeneous strategy and for which a single set of priorities for the manufacturing performance criteria would be appropriate. Step 2 defined the four performance criteria for that division's manufacturing and marketing setting, determining what constituted quality, flexibility, cost, and dependability. Step 3 identified for each business unit the priorities customarily assigned to the four performance criteria. Identification was accomplished through a review of past manufacturing decisions and the relative emphasis those had given to each criterion. Future priorities for each business unit were also identified during this part of the session. Step 4 identified the key operating decisions to be made in the coming years and evaluated those using the performance priorities specified in Step 3.

FIGURE 21-2. APPLICATION OF MANUFACTURING CRITERIA BY CORPORATE MANUFACTURING STAFF

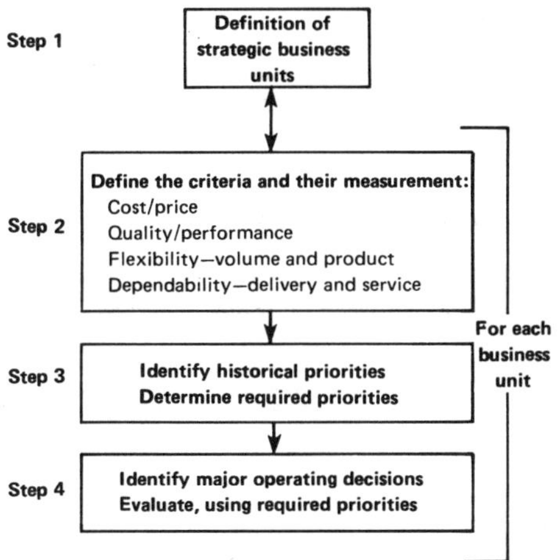

In several instances, this process did no more than reinforce the actions tentatively planned by manufacturing management. In other instances, however,the priorities suggested that the proposed decisions should be altered so that actions would better reinforce the division's strategy and have the desired cumulative effect. Situations A, C, and D described earlier were among the proposed decisions that were reviewed and subsequently revised as a result of this

TABLE 21-1. CURRENT AND REQUIRED PRIORITIES AS ASSESSED BY VICE-PRESIDENTS (VP)* AND MANUFACTURING MANAGERS (MM)*

	Cost		*Quality*		*Dependability*		*Flexibility*	
	VP	*MM*	*VP*	*MM*	*VP*	*MM*	*VP*	*MM*
PRODUCT 1								
As is	42	44	17	15	25	26	16	15
Should be	28	46	24	16	31	26	17	12
Needs more (less)	(14)	2	7	1	6	0	1	(3)
PRODUCT 2								
As is	26	20	37	43	24	22	13	15
Should be	26	30	36	38	26	20	12	12
Needs more (less)	0	10	(1)	(5)	2	(2)	(1)	(3)
PRODUCT 3								
As is	34	36	27	28	23	19	16	17
Should be	34	38	29	24	24	20	13	18
Needs more (less)	0	2	2	(4)	1	1	(3)	1
PRODUCT 4								
As is	24	34	30	22	19	17	27	27
Should be	39	44	20	25	23	15	18	16
Needs more (less)	15	10	(10)	3	4	(2)	(9)	(11)
PRODUCT 5 (Parts)								
As is	45	37	21	14	18	31	16	18
Should be	22	31	24	13	35	35	19	21
Needs more (less)	(23)	(6)	3	(1)	17	4	3	3

*Criteria totals for VP and MM for each priority = 100.

exercise.

A LINE MANAGEMENT APPROACH

A second situation where the framework of Figure 21-1 proved effective did not involve any staff support. It was initiated and guided by the vice-president of manufacturing. The company, which manufactured four major industrial products and a line of spare parts, had found itself capacity-constrained for some time. Production bottlenecks were frequent, and manufacturing had been under substantial pressure to improve its performance and its support of the company's goals.

The motivation for this particular application came from the vice-president of manufacturing, who had recently attended a two-week seminar on manufacturing in corporate strategy. Upon returning, he was asked, half jokingly, to tell some of the other members of top management what he had learned. He decided to respond by discussing the use of manufacturing priorities to support corporate strategy. He also wanted to determine the appropriate priorities for his own operations and to review major operating decisions.

The first step in his approach was to have company vice-presidents individually assess current manufacturing priorities. This was done by defining the four criteria described in the accompanying box and having them distribute points among these criteria. The assessment form identified the company's five separate business units and requested that 100 points be allocated for historical (as is) priorities and 100 points for required (should be) priorities for each. (The split into five product categories had been used frequently as part of the planning process.)

As might be expected reponses from the vice-presidents varied considerably. To reconcile the differences, discussion sessions were held among all of the members of top management. The result was a consensus as to past priorities and required priorities for each of the company's five business areas, as shown in Table 21-1. This step identified a number of areas in need of a change in emphasis so that manufacturing and its performance priorities would be most supportive of the corporate strategy.

Some of the actions that resulted from the identification of major differences in historical and required emphasis included the following:

> Product 1 should have modest increases in quality and dependability at the expense of manufacturing cost efficiencies.
>
> Products 2 and 3 should have no significant changes in manufacturing.
>
> Product 4 should have a significant im-

Elements of Manufacturing Strategy as Defined by the Vice-President of Manufacturing

Cost. This criterion refers to low cost or even lowest possible cost, including cost of capital employed. This would imply minimum wages, particularly for hourly but also supervision. The amount of supervision would be determined by cost minimization rather than maintenance of quality or dependability levels. Capital equipment selections would be based on acquiring specialized machinery to produce at the lowest cost and would produce parts to the loosest possible acceptable tolerance levels. Equipment would be replaced only when completely worn out and would likely be overhauled once or twice prior to actual replacement. Inventories would be maintained at the minimum level needed to avoid idle shop time but would not necessarily be based upon needs for customer service levels. Emphasis of this criterion maximizes return and minimizes investment.

Quality. This criterion focuses on maintaining high levels of quality. High levels of quality can be defined as significantly higher than competitive products and sufficiently high to support sale of the product based upon its high quality, even if its price is unfavorable with respect to competition. Examples of primary emphasis on quality would be Mercedes automobiles and Hewlett-Packard calculators.

Dependability. This refers primarily to meeting all delivery commitments for new orders and parts. It includes not only the capability to stock products, but also the ability to manufacture replacement parts quickly.

Flexibility. Flexibility refers to the ability to make significant changes in manufacturing volumes and/or products. It entails high responsiveness to either increases or decreases in customer demand in the short term (substantially less than one year). It also may be related to flexibility to changes in product design such as the acquisition of new product lines and/or the significant modification of existing product lines.

provement in manufacturing cost efficiencies at the expense of quality and flexibility.

Product 5 (parts) should have a significant increase in dependability at the expense of manufacturing cost efficiencies.

As a follow-up, the vice-president of manufacturing used the same approach with the manufacturing department heads who reported to him; the results are also shown in the table. This second application of the framework convinced the vice-president of manufacturing that his manufacturing managers were motivated primarily by the desire to achieve a high degree of cost efficiency. Since manufacturing's action plan was based on consensus reached by top management, the vice-president of manufacturing sought to convince his manufacturing subordinates that it was an appropriate plan of action since it was reached at the policy level in the company.

The vice-president was very satisfied with the results he obtained from this process and concluded that his manufacturing people had gained a better understanding of the corporate strategy for each major product segment. He also felt that their ability to use the policies derived from this priority-setting procedure would continue to grow. Situation B described earlier is typical of the impact that this approach has had on his company.

In both of the companies described above, the managers involved found the establishment and application of priorities for manufacturing performance measures to be extremely valuable. This was particularly the case in the second example, where all of the vice-presidents had reached a consensus on the priorities for manufacturing. A significant reduction in the conflict resulted between manufacturing and marketing because both areas agreed on a common direction. The exercise also proved to have very useful organizational development benefits, many of which were greater than those obtained from programs designed only for organizational development purposes.

Upon reflection, the corporate manufacturing staff in the first situation felt its approach would have been strengthened had there been feedback to marketing for comment and appraisal. While they were uncertain how best to handle that, given their role as a staff group, they did agree that such marketing involvement should be obtained in future applications.

In both instances, there was some skepticism at the outset about the benefits obtainable from such an approach. In the first case, even the company's president had reservations in the beginning about the value of the exercise. After seeing its results, however, the president subsequently sought to make such an approach a more integral part of the company's annual planning and budgeting process. In the second case, the priorities are being used on an ongoing basis to help both staff and line management more adequately review division operating plans and ensure that major decisions submitted for corporate approval reflect appropriate priorities.

The four decision situations described initially illustrate how the establishment of manufacturing performance priorities allow such individual decisions to be made quickly and effectively in a manner that supports corporate strategy. Also, for those decisions already consistent with corporate strategy, the reinforcement gained through use of these priorities can often advertise their usefulness and appropriateness to other members of top management. By making these concepts an integral part of a company's planning and decision-making processes, manufacturing can realize its own strategic potential. Rather than simply being reactive to others' plans, manufacturing can itself be part of the plan.

STUDENT REVIEW QUESTIONS

1. Why does manufacturing often play a secondary role in corporate strategy decisions?
2. Explain briefly one of the situations given in the article.
3. What factors determine the corporate strategy in a manufacturing operation?
4. What are the most important performance criteria Wheelwright identifies? Explain each briefly.
5. Diagram the framework Wheelwright develops and briefly explain how it can be useful for developing manufacturing strategy.

22

Strategy and Flexibility in the Smaller Business*

IAN C. MACMILLAN

IN SMALL BUSINESSES the owner *IS* the business. Unlike the large enterprise where a large number of people's livelihood and aspirations must be achieved by the survival and profitability of the enterprise, the small business is there to satisfy the needs and wants of one man or at most a very small group of people. The 'death' of a specific small enterprise is therefore not as serious for the manager/owner as for a large one provided that 'death' has been recognized as inevitable and an alternative has been planned for, and provided that the owner/manager has a truly adventurous and entrepreneurial personality.

KEY ADVANTAGES OF THE SMALL BUSINESS

What are the key advantages of the small business? Conceptually, for an adventurous entrepreneur, they should be (1) Mobility, (2) Unanimity, (3) Innovative potential, (4) Size of Investment and (5) Commitment. Each will be discussed.

UNANIMITY

Since the small business has at most a very small group of managers and few personnel, there is far less discussion and political manoeuvring when decisions must be made. The control of the company is in the hands of the owner/manager.

---

*From *Journal of Long Range Planning,* June, 1976, pp. 62-63. Reprinted by permission.

His decisions dominate the enterprise and so the decision making which takes place is virtually unanimous. There is little question of management by coalition.

MOBILITY

Since the decision making is virtually unanimous, this gives rise to high mobility. The company can change direction fast, respond to change quickly. The small firm does not have the lumbering inertia of the large one, where a change in direction involves considerable redeployment of resources in the face of resistance by the members of the organization. Key personnel need not be persuaded and convinced that the new direction is necessary and 'management by debate' is eliminated.

INNOVATION POTENTIAL

The small business can be far more innovative due to its unanimity and mobility.

With a large organization any innovative ideas must be sold to a vast number of people whose cooperation is essential but who may have entirely different attitudes to the direction the firm must take. In a small business the only person to convince is the owner/manager and perhaps a very small group of others.

SIZE OF INVESTMENT AND SCALE OF FIXED COSTS

If the business is small then the investment *should* be small and fixed costs should be small in absolute terms. A small investment means that break-even should be achieved at low volumes. This gives the small firm the opportunity of catering profitably for small market segments, and profitable but low volumes can be disposed of before market saturation occurs. A large firm with large fixed costs and investment cannot afford to compete on this basis.

COMMITMENT

The owner/manager is *totally* committed to the firm as long as it is *his* firm.

STRATEGIC IMPLICATIONS FOR SMALL BUSINESSES

What are the strategic implications of these advantages for the strategy of a small business?

If we are to take advantage *of* these advantages simultaneously this implies:

That fixed costs and investment in fixed assets

be kept to a minimum:

By investing in fixed assets we reduce mobility and, because fixed investments are expensive, we need larger volumes and hence larger markets to make a good return. The same argument applies to fixed costs.

That we keep the business small enough to be run by as few levels of management as possible:

If the business cannot be operated by one level of management then it is desirable to have no more than two levels, so that the lowest level is continuously interacting with the highest. Any more levels of management detract from the advantages of unanimity and commitment (one could say almost geometrically).

That the owner/manager devotes most of his creative time to scanning the future for new opportunities:

These opportunities should satisfy the following requirements:

(a) They should not require high investment.
(b) They should promise high initial payoff in a relatively small concentrated market, but need *not* have high payoffs over the long term.
(c) Their product/market scope should be within the capability and/or expertise of the owner/manager.
(d) They should give the entrepreneur the opportunity to continue interacting with the environment.

The primary limitation on the size of the business is the owner/manager's ability to run the business with as few assistants as possible yet still be able to devote substantial time to finding and exploiting new opportunities.

That the ongoing, current business be programmed as far as possible: to give the manager time to devote his attention to finding new opportunities.

This is perhaps best accomplished by employing a competent administrator--competent to the task of administering a *small* business, not a large one. His/her cost should therefore not be high.

That before the business is started, the conditions under which it will be discontinued be clearly formulated:

Before the business is launched the owner/manager should clearly bear in mind that:

(a) If it is a failure, he will waste money and effort trying to shore it up if he is not careful. Explicit levels of satisfactory performance must be established and the business ruthlessly demolished if these aspirations are not achieved.

(b) If it is a moderate success he can expect competition from other small businessmen, and the point at which he is going to sell out to some potential competitor wishing to enter the field must be clearly defined.

(c) If it is a great success it will attract the attention of the large companies. The point at which he will sell out to them, or even go to them with an offer, must be clearly formulated. Once they have taken over control the small businessman can still benefit from future growth by opting for part cash/part shares as payment.

The philosophy behind (b) and (c) above is that *small* businesses, if kept small and mobile, have a high chance of survival and *large* businesses have a high chance of survival but it is the small, growing business that has the highest fatality rate, as the business becomes larger the owner/manager loses his total control over the situation (losing the advantage of unanimity), his time becomes more and more absorbed by day-to-day crises (losing the advantage of innovation potential), he is forced to invest more heavily (losing the advantages mobility and investment size) and then it grows to the point where more and more people who are not totally committed become involved (losing the advantage of commitment). By persisting with a growing company without selling out to a larger company *he is eroding all his initial advantages*.

The counter argument that this philosophy means we would then never get large businesses, is rejected. There *are* already large businesses,and it is these businesses to whom the owner/manager should sell. It is they who have the reserves to absorb the growing pains.

That the small businessman must make long-term plans. If he is to adhere to the above strategies the owner/manager must have a clear idea when the opportunities he envisages for the future will materialize,their expected scope and potential, and plan his resource deployments, his phasing out of one activity and phasing in of the other, just as carefully as a large firm carries out its long-term planning.

CONCLUSION

In conclusion it may be stated that a strategy for a small business is essential. It differs from the strategy for a large business in that the owner and the business are virtually one, so that as long as the owner benefits, the survival of the business is not of importance. The strategy of the small business should therefore be composed of a long linked series of short-term plans which take advantage of the small business's mobility, unanimity, commitment, innovative potential and deliberately restricted investment in fixed assets.

STUDENT REVIEW QUESTIONS

1. Explain how mobility is one of the major advantages of the small business.
2. How can the small size of investment and fixed cost be a key advantage.
3. Why does the small business want to maintain the fewest levels of management possible?
4. Explain MacMillan's statement that "it is the small growing business that has the highest fatality rate...."
5. Do small businesses need a strategy?

REFERENCES FOR ADDITIONAL STUDY

Bloom, Paul N. and Philip Kotler, "Strategies for High Market Share Companies," *Harvard Business Review*, November-December, 1975.

Bright, Willard M., "Alternative Strategies for Diversification," *Research Management*, July, 1969.

Catry, Bernard and Michael Chevalier, "Market Share Strategy and the Product Life Cycle," *Journal of Marketing*, October, 1974.

Cooper, Arnold C. and Dan Schendel, "Strategic Responses to Technological Threats," *Business Horizons*, February, 1976.

Gilmore, Frank F., "Formulating Strategy in Smaller Companies," *Harvard Business Review*, May-June, 1973.

Gray, Edmund R., and H. Baird Green, "Cash Throw-Off: A Resource Allocation Strategy," *Business Horizons*, June, 1976.

Hedley, Barry, "Strategy and the 'Business Portfolio'", *Long Range Planning*, February, 1977.

Heskett, James L., "Logistics--Essential to Strategy," *Harvard Business Review*, November-December, 1977.

Levitt, Theodore, "Marketing Myopia," *Harvard Business Review*, July-August, 1960.

MacAvoy, Robert E., "New Rules for Strategy and Planning," *Management Review*, June, 1976.

Pryor, Millard H., "Planning in a Worldwide Business," *Harvard Business Review*, January-February, 1965.

Randle, C. Wilson, "Selecting the Research Program: A

Top Management Function," *California Management Review*, Winter, 1960.

Seed, Allen H., "Needed: Strategies to Improve Cash Flow," *Management Review*, March, 1975.

Singhvi, Surenda S., "A Conceptual Framework for Planned Growth," *SAM Advanced Management Journal*, October, 1974.

Skinner, Wickham, "Manufacturing--Missing Link in Corporate Strategy," *Harvard Business Review*, May-June, 1969.

Souder, William E., "Budgeting for R&D," *Business Horizons*, June, 1970.

Tincher, William R., "Yardsticks for Evaluating Corporate Acquisitions," *Management Review*, October, 1964.

Toan, Arthur B., Jr., "The Impact of Corporate Policy on Cash Flow," *Financial Executive*, November, 1963.

Wallender, Harvey W., "A Planned Approach to Divestment," *Columbia Journal of World Business*, Spring, 1973.

II

STRATEGY IMPLEMENTATION

SECTION D.

ORGANIZATION FOR STRATEGY IMPLEMENTATION

23

Matrix Organization Designs: How to Combine Functional and Project Forms*

JAY R. GALBRAITH

EACH ERA OF MANAGEMENT evolves new forms of organization as new problems are encountered. Earlier generations of managers invented the centralized functional form, the line-staff form, and the decentralized product division structure as a response to increasing size and complexity of tasks. The current generation of management has developed two new forms as a response to high technology. The first is the free-form conglomerate; the other is the matrix organization, which was developed primarily in the aerospace industry.

The matrix organization grows out of the organizational choice between project and functional forms, although it is not limited to those bases of the authority structure.[1] Research in the behavioral sciences now permits a detailing of the choices among the alternate intermediate forms between the project and functional extremes. Detailing such a choice is necessary since many businessmen see their organizations facing situations in the 1970's that are similar to those faced by the aerospace firms in the 1960's. As a result, a great many unanswered questions arise concerning the use of the matrix organization. For example, what are the various kinds of matrix designs, what is the difference between the designs, how do they work, and how do I choose a design that is appropriate for my organization?

The problem of designing organizations arises from the choices available among alternative bases of the authority structure. The most common alternatives are to group together activities which bear on a common product, common

---

*From *Business Horizons*, February, 1971, pp. 29-33.

customer, common geographic area, common business function (marketing, engineering, manufacturing, and so on), or common process (forging, stamping, machining, and so on). Each of these bases has various costs and economies associated with it. For example, the functional structure facilitates the acquisition of specialized inputs. It permits the hiring of an electromechanical and an electronics engineer rather than two electrical engineers. It minimizes the number necessary by pooling specialized resources and time sharing them across products or projects. It provides career paths for specialists. Therefore, the organization can hire, utilize, and retain specialists.

These capabilities are necessary if the organization is going to develop high technology products. However, the tasks that the organization must perform require varying amounts of the specialized resources applied in varying sequences. The problem of simultaneously completing all tasks on time, with appropriate quality and while fully utilizing all specialist resources, is all but impossible in the functional structure. It requires either fantastic amounts of information or long lead times for task completion.

The product or project form of organization has exactly the opposite set of benefits and costs. It facilitates coordination among specialties to achieve on-time completion and to meet budget targets. It allows a quick reaction capability to tackle problems that develop in one specialty, thereby reducing the impact on other specialties. However, if the organization has two projects, each requiring one half-time electronics engineer and one half-time electromechanical engineer,the pure project organization must either hire two electrical engineers--and reduce specialization--or hire four engineers (two electronics and two electromechanical)--and incur duplication costs. In addition, no one is responsible for long-run technical development of the specialties. Thus, each form of organization has its own set of advantages and disadvantages. A similar analysis could be applied to geographically or client-based structures.

The problem is that when one basis of organization is chosen, the benefits of the others are surrendered. If the functional structure is adopted, the technologies are developed but the projects fall behind schedule. If the project organization is chosen, there is better cost and schedule performance but the technologies are not developed as well. In the past, managers made a judgment as to whether technical development or schedule completion was more important and chose the appropriate form.

However, in the 1960's with a space race and missile gap, the aerospace firms were faced with a situation where both technical performance and coordination were important. The result was the matrix design, which attempts to achieve the benefits of both forms. However, the matrix carries some costs of its own. A study of the development of a matrix design is contained in the history of The Standard Products Co., a hypothetical company that has changed its form of organization from a functional structure to a matrix.

A COMPANY CHANGES FORMS

The Standard Products Co. has competed effectively for a number of years by offering a varied line of products that were sold to other organizations. Standard produced and sold its products through a functional organization like the one represented in Figure 23-1. A moderate number of changes in the product line and production processes were made each year. Therefore, a major management problem was to coordinate the flow of work from engineering through marketing. The coordination was achieved through several integrating mechanisms:

Rules and procedures. One of the ways to constrain behavior in order to achieve an integrated pattern is to specify rules and procedures. If all personnel follow the rules, the resultant behavior is integrated without having to maintain on-going communication. Rules are used for the most predictable and repetitive activities.

Planning processes. For less repetitive activities, Standard does not specify the procedure to be used but specifies a goal or target to be achieved, and lets the individual choose the procedure appropriate to the goal. Therefore, processes are undertaken to elaborate schedules and budgets. The usefulness of plans and rules is that they reduce the need for on-going communication between specialized subunits.

Hierarchical referral. When situations are encountered for which there are no rules or when problems cause the goals to be exceeded, these situations are referred upward in the hierarchy for resolution. This is the standard management-by-exception principle. This resolves the nonroutine and unpredictable events that all organizations encounter.

Direct contact. In order to prevent top executives from becoming overloaded with problems, as many problems as possible are resolved by the affected managers at low levels by informal contacts. These remove small problems from the upward referral process.

Liaison departments. In some cases, where there is a large volume of contracts between two departments, a liaison department evolves to handle the transactions. This typically occurs between engineering and manufacturing in order to handle engineering changes and design problems.[2]

The Standard Products Co. utilized these mechanisms to integrate the functionally organized specialties. They were effective in the sense that Standard could respond to changes in the market with new products on a timely basis, the new products were completed on schedule and within budget, and the executives had sufficient time to devote to long-range planning.

FIGURE 23-1.

STANDARD'S FUNCTIONAL ORGANIZATION

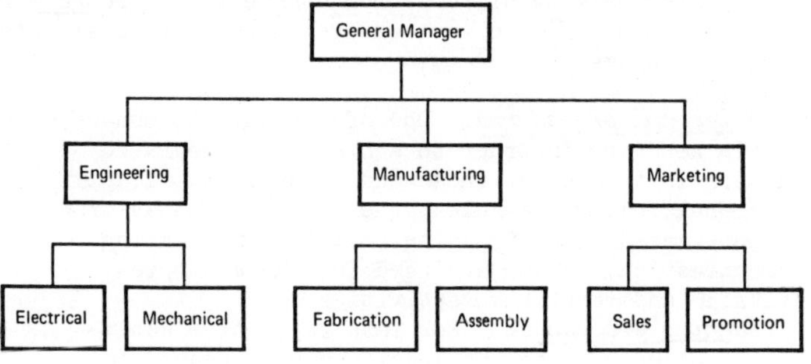

MATRIX BEGINS EVOLUTION

A few years ago, a significant change occurred in the market for one of Standard's major product lines. A competitor came out with a new design utilizing an entirely new raw material. The initial success caused Standard to react by developing one of their own incorporating the new material. They hired some specialists in the area and began their normal new product introduction activities. However, this time the product began to fall behind schedule, and it appeared that the product would arrive on the market at a time later than planned. In response, the general manager called a meeting to analyze the situation.

Task Force. After a briefing, it was obvious to the general manager and the directors of the three functions what was happening. Standard's lack of experience with the new material had caused them to underestimate the number and kinds of problems. The uncertainty led to a deterioration in usefulness of plans and schedules. The problems affected all functions, which meant that informal contacts and liaison processes were cumbersome; therefore, the majority of the problems were referred upward. This led to overloads on the directors of the functions and the general manager, which in turn added to the delays. Thus, the new situation required more decision making and more information processing than the current organization could provide.

The directors of engineering and manufacturing suggested that the cause of the problem was an overly ambitious schedule. More time should have been allowed for the new product; if realistic schedules were set, the current coordination processes would be adequate. They proposed that the schedules be adjusted by adding three to six months to the current due dates, which would allow more time to make the necessary decisions.

The director of marketing objected, reporting that the company would lose a good percentage of the market if the introduction was delayed. A number of big customers were waiting for Standard's version of the new product, and a delay would cost the company some of these customers. The general manager agreed with the marketing director. He proposed that they should not change the schedule to fit their current coordination processes, but that they should introduce some new coordination mechanisms to meet the scheduled due dates.

The group agreed with the general manager's position and began to search for alternative solutions. One of the solution requirements suggested was to reduce the distance between the sources of information and the points of decision. At this point the manufacturing director cautioned them about decentralizing decisions. He reminded them of previous experiences when decisions were made at low levels of the engineering organization. The data the decision makers had were current but they were also local in scope; severe problems in the manufacturing process resulted. When these decisions were centralized, the global perspective prevented these problems from developing. Therefore, they had to increase decision-making power at lower levels without losing the inputs of all affected units. The alternative that met both requirements was a group with representation from all the major departments to enter into joint decisions.

The group was appointed and named the "new product task force." It was to last as long as cross-functional problems occurred on the new product introduction. The group was to meet and solve joint problems within the budget limits set by the general manager and the directors; problems requiring more budget went to the top management group. The purpose was to make as many decisions as possible at low levels with the people most knowledgeable. This should reduce the delays and yet ensure that all the information inputs were considered.

The task force consisted of nine people; three, one from each function, were full-time and the others were part-time.

They met at least every other day to discuss and resolve joint problems. Several difficulties caused them to shift membership. First, the engineering representatives were too high in the organization and, therefore, not knowledgeable about the technical alternatives and consequences. They were replaced with lover level people. The opposite occurred with respect to the manufacturing representatives. Quite often they did not have either information or the authority to commit the production organization to joint decisions made by the task force. They were replaced by higher level people. Eventually, the group had both the information and the authority to make good group decisions. The result was effective coordination: coordination = *f* (authority x information).

Creation of the task force was the correct solution. Decision delays were reduced, and collective action was achieved by the joint decisions. The product arrived on time, and the task force members returned to their regular duties.

Teams. No sooner had the product been introduced than salesmen began to bring back stories about new competitors. One was introducing a second-generation design based on improvements in the raw material. Since the customers were excited by its potential and the technical people thought it was feasible, Standard started a second-generation redesign across all its product lines. This time, they set up the task force structure in advance and committed themselves to an ambitious schedule.

Again the general manager became concerned. This time the product was not falling behind schedule, but in order to meet target dates the top management was drawn into day-to-day decisions on a continual basis. This was leaving very little time to think about the third-generation product line. Already Standard had to respond twice to changes initiated by others. It was time for a thorough strategy formulation. Indeed, the more rapid the change in technology and markets, the greater the amount of strategic decision making that is necessary. However, these are the same changes that pull top management into day-to-day decisions. The general manager again called a meeting to discuss and resolve the problem.

The solution requirements to the problem were the same as before. They had to find a way to push a greater number of decisions down to lower levels. At the same time, they had to guarantee that all interdependent subunits would be considered in the decision so that coordination would be maintained. The result was a more extensive use of joint decision making and shared responsibility.

The joint decision making was to take place through a team structure. The teams consisted of representatives of all functions and were formed around major product lines. There were two levels of teams, one at lower levels and another at the middle-management level. Each level had defined discretionary limits; problems that the lower level could not solve were referred to the middle-level team. If the middle level could not solve the problem, it went to top management. A greater number of day-to-day operating problems were thereby solved at lower levels of the hierarchy, freeing top management for long-range decisions.

The teams, unlike the task force, were permanent. New products were regarded as a fact of life, and the teams met on a continual basis to solve recurring interfunctional problems. Task forces were still used to solve temporary problems. In fact, all the coordination mechanisms of rules, plans, upward referral, direct contact, liaison men, and task forces were used, in addition to the teams.

Product Managers. The team structure achieved interfunctional coordination and permitted top management to step out of day-to-day decision making. However, the teams were not uniformly effective. Standard's strategy required the addition of highly skilled, highly educated technical people to continue to innovate and compete in the high technology industry. Sometimes these specialists would dominate a team because of their superior technical knowledge. That is, the team could not distinguish between providing technical information and supplying managerial judgment after all the facts were identified. In addition, the specialists' personalities were different from the personalities of the other team members, which made the problem of conflict resolution much more difficult.[3]

Reports of these problems began to reach the general manager, who realized that a great number of decisions of consequence were being made at lower and middle levels of management. He also knew that they should be made with a general manager's perspective. This depends on having the necessary information and a reasonable balance of power among the joint decision makers. Now the technical people were upsetting the power balance because others could not challenge them on technical matters. As a result, the general manager chose three technically qualified men and made them product managers in charge of the three major product lines.[4] They were to act as chairmen of the product team meetings and generally facilitate the interfunctional decision making.

Since these men had no formal authority, they had to resort to their technical competence and their interpersonal skills in order to be effective. The fact that they reported to the general manager gave them some additional power. These men were successful in bringing the global, general manager perspective lower in the organization to improve the joint decision-making process.

The need for this role was necessitated by the increasing differences in attitudes and goals among the technical, production, and marketing team participants. These differences are necessary for successful subtask performance but interfere with team collaboration. The product manager allows collaboration without reducing these necessary differences. The cost is the additional overhead for the product management salaries.

Product Management Departments. Standard Products was now successfully following a strategy of new product innovation and introduction. It was leading the industry in changes in technology and products. As the number of new products increased, so did the amount of decision making around product considerations. The frequent needs for tradeoffs across engineering, production, and marketing lines increased the influence of the product managers. It was not that the functional managers lost influence; rather, it was the increase in decisions relating to products.

The increase in the influence of the product managers was revealed in several ways: First, their salaries became substantial. Second, they began to have a greater voice in the budgeting process, starting with approval of functional budgets relating to their products. The next change was an accumulation of staff around the products, which became product departments with considerable influence.

At Standard this came about with the increase in new product introductions. A lack of information developed concerning product costs and revenues for addition, deletion, modification, and pricing decisions. The general manager instituted a new information system that reported costs and revenues by product as well as by function. This gave product managers the need for a staff and a basis for more effective interfunctional collaboration.

In establishing the producet departments, the general manager resisted requests from the product managers to reorganize around product divisions. While he agreed with their analysis that better coordination was needed across functions and for more effective product decision making, he was unwilling to take the chance that this move might reduce specialization in the technical areas or perhaps lose the economies of scale in production. He felt that a modification of the information system to report on a product and a functional basis along with a product staff group would provide the means for more coordination. He still needed the effective technical group to drive the innovative process. The general manager also maintained a climate where collaboration across product lines and functions was encouraged and rewarded.

THE MATRIX COMPLETED

By now Standard Products was a high technology company; its products were undergoing constant change. The uncertainty brought about by the new technology and the new products required an enormous amount of decision making to planreplan all the schedules, budgets, designs, and so on. As a result, the number of decisions and the number of consequential decisions made at low levels increased considerably. This brought on two concerns for the general manager and top management.

The first was the old concern for the quality of decisions made at low levels of the organization. The product managers helped solve this at middle and top levels, but their influence did not reach low into the organization where a considerable number of decisions were made jointly. They were not always made in the best interest of the firm as a whole. The product managers again recommended a move to product divisions to give these low-level decisions the proper product orientation.

The director of engineering objected, using the second problem to back up his objection. He said the move to product divisions would reduce the influence of the technical people at a time when they were having morale and turnover problems with these employees. The increase in joint decisions at low levels meant that these technical people were spending a lot of time in meetings. Their technical input was not always needed, and they preferred to work on technical problems, not product problems. Their dissatisfaction would only be aggravated by a change to product divisions.

The top management group recognized both of these problems. They needed more product orientation at low levels, and they needed to improve the morale of the technical people whose inputs were needed for product innovations. Their solution involved the creation of a new role--that of subproduct manager.[5] The subproduct manager would be chosen from the functional organization and would represent the product line within the function. He would report to both the functional manager and the product manager, thereby creating a dual authority structure. The addition of a reporting relation on the product side increases the amount of product influence at lower levels.

The addition of the subproduct manager was intended to solve the morale problem also. Because he would participate in the product team meetings, the technical people did not need to be present. The subproduct manager would participate on the teams but would call on the technical experts within his department as they were needed. This permitted the functional department to be represented by the subproduct manager, and the technical people to concentrate on strictly technical matters.

Standard Products has now moved to a pure matrix organization as indicated in Figure 23-2. The pure matrix organization is distinguished from the previous crossfunctional forms by two features. *First,* the pure matrix has a dual authority relationship somewhere in the organization. *Second,* there is a power balance between the product management and functional sides. While equal power is an unachievable razor's edge, a reasonable balance can be obtained through enforced collaboration on budgets, salaries, dual information and reporting systems, and dual authority relations. Such a balance is required because the problems that the organization faces are uncertain and must be solved on their own merits--not on any predetermined power structure.

FIGURE 23-2.

STANDARD'S PURE MATRIX ORGANIZATION

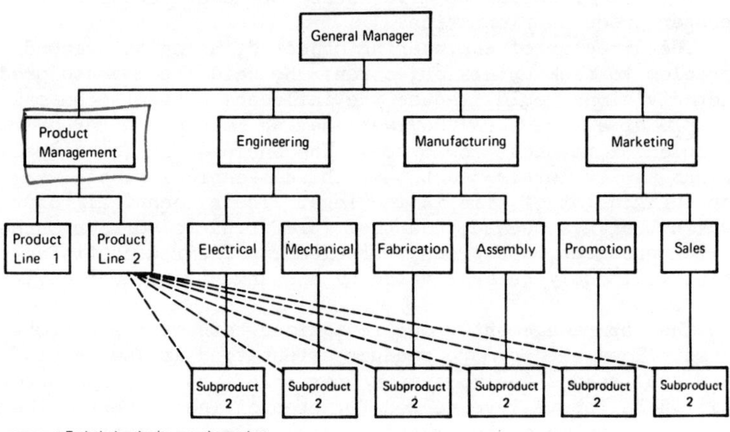

Thus over a period of time, the Standard Products Co. has changed from a functional organization to a pure matrix organization using dual authority relationships, product management departments, product teams at several levels, and temporary task forces. These additional decision-making mechanisms were added to cope with the change in products and technologies. The changes caused a good deal of uncertainty concerning resource allocations, budgets, and schedules. In the process of task execution, more was learned about the problem causing a need for rescheduling and rebudgeting. This required the processing of information and the making of decisions.

In order to increase its capacity to make product relevant decisions, Standard lowered the level at which decisions were made. Coordination was achieved by making joint decisions across functions. Product managers and subproduct managers were added to bring a general manager's perspective to bear on the joint decision-making processes. In addition, the information and reporting system was changed in order to provide reports by function and by product. Combined, these measures allowed Standard to achieve the high levels of technical sophistication necessary to innovate products and simultaneously to get these products to the market quickly to maintain competitive position.

HOW DO I CHOOSE A DESIGN?

Not all organizations need a pure matrix organization with a dual authority relationship. Many, however, can benefit from some cross-functional forms to relieve top decision makers from day-to-day operations. If this is so, how does one choose the degree to which his organization should pursue these lateral forms? To begin to answer this question, let us first lay out the alternatives, then list the choice determining factors.

The choice, shown in Figure 23-3, is indicated by the wide range of alternatives between a pure functional organization and a pure product organization with the matrix being half-way between. The Standard Products Co. could have evolved into a matrix from a product organization by adding functional teams and managers. Thus there is a continuum of organization designs between the functional and product forms. The design is specified by the choice among the authority structure; integrating mechanisms such as task forces, teams and so on; and by the formal information system. The way these are combined is illustrated in Figure 23-3. These design variables help regulate the relative distribution of influence between the product and functional considerations in the firm's operations.

The remaining factors determining influence are such things as roles in budget approvals, design changes, location and size of offices, salary, and so on. Thus there is a choice of integrating devices, authority structure, information system, and influence distribution. The factors that determine choice are diversity of the product line, the rate of change of the product line, interdependencies among subunits, level of technology, presence of economies of scale, and organization size.

PRODUCT LINES

The greater the diversity among product lines and the greater the rate of change of products in the line the

the greater the pressure to move toward product structures.[6] When product lines become diverse, it becomes difficult for general managers and functional managers to maintain knowledge in all areas; the amount of information they must handle exceeds their capacity to absorb it. Similarly, the faster the rate of new product introduction, the more unfamiliar are the tasks being performed.

Managers are, therefore, less able to make precise estimates concerning resource allocations, schedules, and priorities. During the process of new product introduction, these same decisions are made repeatedly. The decisions concern tradeoffs among engineering, manufacturing, and marketing. This means there must be greater product influence in the decision process. The effect of diversity and change is to create a force to locate the organization farther to the right in Figure 23-3.

FIGURE 23-3.

THE RANGE OF ALTERNATIVES

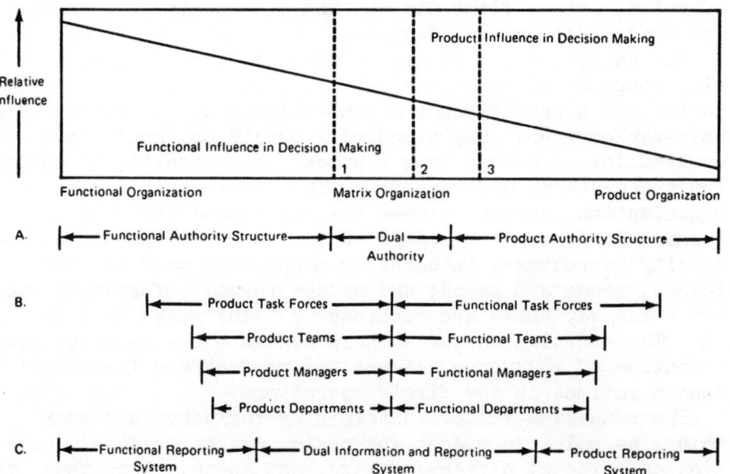

INTERDEPENDENCE

The functional division of labor in organizations creates interdependencies among the specialized subunits. That is, a problem of action in one unit has a direct impact on the goal accomplishment of the other units. Organizations usually devise mechanisms that uncouple the subunits, such as in-process-inventory and order backlogs. The degree to which inventories and backlogs develop is a function of how tight the schedule is. If there is a little slack in the schedule, then the functional departments can resolve their own problems. However, if rapid response to market changes is a basis of competition, then schedules are squeezed and activities run in parallel rather than series.[7] This means that problems in one unit directly affect another. The effect is a greater number of joint decisions involving engineering, manufacturing, and production. A greater need for product influence in these decisions arises due to the tight schedule. Thus the tighter the schedule, the greater the force to move to the right in Figure 23-3.

Although the tightness of the schedule is the most obvious source of interdependence, tight couplings can arise from reliability requirements and other design specifications. If the specifications require a more precise fit and operation of parts, then the groups designing and manufacturing the parts must also "fit and operate" more closely. This requires more coordination in the form of communication and decision making.

LEVEL OF TECHNOLOGY

If tight schedules and new products were the only forces operating, every organization would be organized around product lines. The level of technology or degree to which new technology is being used is a counteracting force. The use of new technologies requires expertise in the technical specialties in engineering, in production engineering, in manufacturing, and market research in marketing. Some of the expertise may be purchased outside the organization.

However, if the expertise is critical to competitive effectiveness, the organization must acquire it internally. If the organization is to make effective use of the expertise, the functional form of organization is superior, as described earlier in the article. Therefore the greater the need for expertise, the greater the force to move to the left in Figure 23-3.

ECONOMIES OF SCALE AND SIZE

The other factor favoring a functional form is the degree to which expensive equipment in manufacturing, test facilities in engineering, and warehousing facilities in marketing are used in producing and selling the product. (Warehousing introduces another dimension of organization structure, for example, geographical divisions. For our purposes, we will be concerned only with product and function dimensions.) It is usually more expensive to buy small facilities for product divisions than a few large ones for functional departments. The greater the economies of scale, the greater the force to move to the left in Figure 23-3. Mixed structures are always possible. That is, the capital intensive fabrication operation can organize along functional process lines, and the labor intensive assembly operation can organize along product lines.

The size of the organization is important in that it modifies the effect of expertise and economies of scale. That is, the greater the size of the organization the smaller the costs of lost specialization and lost economies of scale when the product form is adopted. Thus while size by itself has little effect on organization structure, it does moderate the effects of the previously mentioned factors.

THE CHOICE

While research on organizations has not achieved a sophistication that would allow us to compute the results of the above factors and locate a point in Figure 23-3, we can still make our subjective weightings. In addition, we can locate our present position and make changes in the appropriate directions as product lines, schedules, technologies, and size change during the normal course of business. The framework provides some basis for planning the organization along with planning the strategy and resource allocations.

If the organization's present structure is on the left side of the figure, many of the symptoms occurring in the Standard Products example signal a need for change. To what degree are communication overloads occurring? Are top executives being drawn into day-to-day decisions to the detriment of strategy development? How long does it take to get top level decisions made in order to continue work on new products? If the answers to these questions indicate an overload, then some movement toward a matrix is appropriate. Probably a sequence of moves until the bottlenecks disappear is the best strategy; this will allow for the proper attitudinal and behavioral changes to keep pace.

If the organization is product organized, then movements to the left toward a matrix are more subtle. They must be triggered by monitoring the respective technological environments.

An example from the aerospace industry may help. In the late fifties and early sixties the environment was characterized by the space race and missile gap. In this environment, technical performance and technology development were primary, and most firms adopted organizations characterized by the dotted line at "1" in Figure 23-3. The functional departments had the greatest influence on the decision-making process. During the McNamara era, they moved to point "2". The environment shifted to incentive contracts, PERT-cost systems, and increased importance of cost and schedule considerations.

Currently, the shift has continued toward point "3". Now the environment is characterized by tight budgets, a cost overrun on the C-5 project, and Proxmire hearings in the Senate. The result is greater influence by the project managers. All these have taken place in response to the changing character of the market. A few firms recently moved back toward point "2" in response to the decreasing size of some firms. The reduction in defense spending has resulted in cutbacks in projects and employment. In order to maintain technical capabilities with reduced size, these firms have formed functional departments under functional managers with line responsibility. These changes show how changes in need for expertise, goals, and size affect the organization design choice.

Many organizations are experiencing pressures that force them to consider various forms of matrix designs. The most common pressure is increased volume of new products. Organizations facing this situation must either adopt some form of matrix organization, change to product forms of organization, or increase the time between start and introduction of the new product process.

For most organizations, the matrix design is the most effective alternative. Managers must be aware of the different kinds of matrix designs and develop some basis for choosing among them.

FOOTNOTES

[1]See John F. Mee, "Matrix Organization," *Business Horizons* (Summer, 1964), p. 70.

[2]For a more detailed explanation, see Jay R. Galbraith, *Organization Design* (Reading, Mass.: Addison-Wesley Publishing Co., Inc., 1971).

[3]See Paul R. Lawrence and Jay Lorsch, "Differentiation and Integration in Complex Organizations," *Administrative Science Quarterly* (June, 1967).

[4]Paul R. Lawrence and Jay Lorsch, "New Management Job: the Integrator," *Harvard Business Review* (November-December, 1967).

[5]Jay Lorsch, "Matrix Organization and Technical Innovations," Jay Galbraith, ed., *Matrix Organizations: Organization Design for High Technology* (Cambridge, Mass: The M.I. T. Press, 1971).

[6]For product line diversity, see Alfred Chandler, *Strategy and Structure* (Cambridge, Mass.: The M. I. T. Press, 1962); for product change rate, see Tom Burns and G. M. Stalker, *Management and Innovation* (London: Tavistock Publications, 1958).

[7]For a case study of this effect, see Jay Galbraith, "Environmental and Technological Determinants of Organization Design" in Jay Lorsch and Paul R. Lawrence, eds., *Studies in Organization Design* (Homewood, Ill.: Richard D. Irwin, Inc., 1970).

STUDENT REVIEW QUESTIONS

1. Compare the functional organizational structure with the project form of organization. Give the benefits and limitations of each as discussed by Galbraith.
2. Why did Standard Products begin to change their organizational structure?
3. Briefly discuss Standard Products' evolution from a functional organizational structure to a matrix organizational structure.
4. Diagram a matrix organization. What distinguishes the pure matrix organization from other forms of organizations?
5. What are the major factors that determine the type of organizational structure the firm will have? Explain each briefly.

24

Reorganize Your Company Around Its Markets*

MACK HANAN

THROUGHOUT THE 1960s, market orientation was such a dominant business concept that it is surprising to find, a decade later, that few companies have found a way to organize themselves so that their customers' needs consistently come first. In most companies, the divisional structures are still determined by regions, organized around products, or structured to commercialize a process technology. It has been only over the past few years that a small number of companies have come to realize that:

- There is no substitute for market orientation as the ultimate source of profitable growth.
- The only way to ensure being market-oriented is to put a company's organizational structure together so that its major markets become the centers around which its divisions are built.

Some leading companies are emphasizing growth by gearing their organizational structures to their markets' needs instead of to their product or process capabilities. IBM's data-processing operations are segmented organizationally according to key markets, such as institutions like hospitals and retail establishments like supermarkets. Xerox Information Systems Group, which sells copiers and duplicators, has converted from geographical selling to vertical selling

*From *Harvard Business Review*, (November-December, 1974),

by industry. General Foods has adopted a market-targeting organizational style. Even the strict product orientation of some scientific companies is gradually giving way to a combined product and market orientation. In its electronics product marketing, for example, Hewlett-Packard has created a sales and service group that concentrates separately on the electricl manufacturing market while another group serves the market for aerospace. Still other groups sell to the markets for communications or transportation equipment.

In other companies steps are being taken to orient businesses to their markets. At Mead, broad market clusters are coming into being to serve customer needs in home building and furnishings, education, and leisure. PPG Industries has been examining the benefits of systematizing the marketing of its paint, ceramics, and glass divisions through a home environment profit center whose product mix could resemble the pattern shown in Exhibit 24-1. Monsanto has organized a Fire Safety Center that consolidates fire safety products from every sector of Monsanto and groups them according to the market they serve: building and construction, transportation, apparel, or furnishings. Revlon is engaged in "breaking up the company into little pieces": as many as six autonomous profit centers are being created, each of which is designed to serve a specific market segment.

General Electric is well along in constructing strategic business groups for its major appliance and power-generation businesses. For GE, the process of reorganizing from a product to a market orientation has been especially difficult. An average department contains three and one half product lines and may serve more than one business or, more frequently, only a part of a major business. Electric motors, for example, are divided among eight departments. Home refrigerators are split between two departments, even though the only significant product difference is the way the doors open. In such a setup, department managers have understandably become oriented to specific product lines rather than to the needs of a total market.

I use the term *marketcentered* (or marketcentering) to describe the wide range of corporate organizational forms that make a group of customer needs, rather than a region, a product line, or a process, the center of a business division. These forms include General Foods' "strategic business units," National Cash Register's "vocations," the "customer provinces" that some high-technology manufacturers are organizing as company-like units to concentrate on serving the needs of specific market groups, and the "financial need groups" through which some progressive banks serve the common financing needs of manufacturers of electronic systems, drugs, cosmetics, household products, and other items.

Marketcentering also describes the way some railroads are grouping their services around the common distribution needs of major customers so that they can provide a unique user-

EXHIBIT 24-1.

PRODUCT MIX OF A BUSINESS MARKETCENTERED ON THE HOME

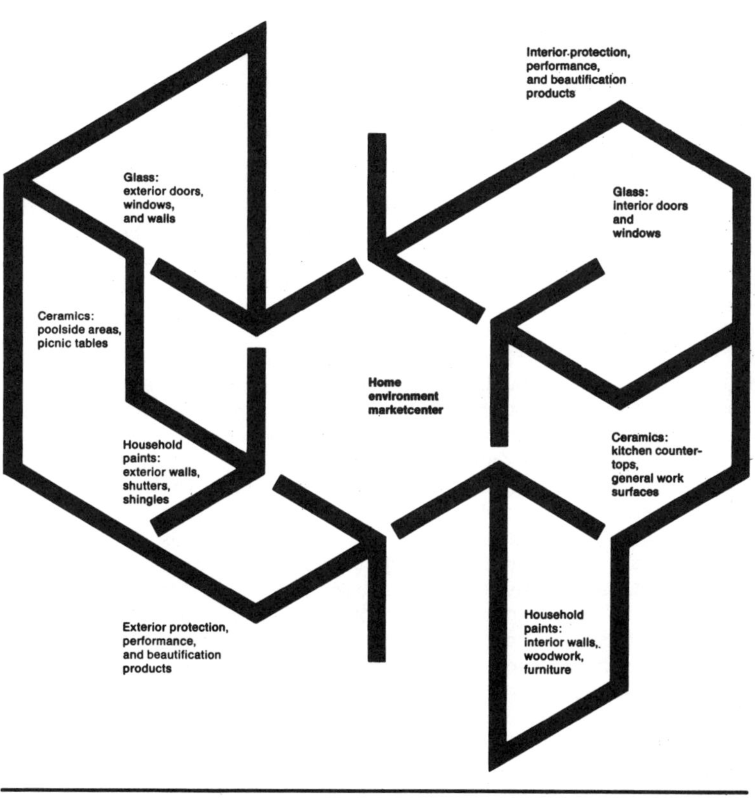

oriented service system for oil, chemical, and fertilizer shippers and a different system for grain shippers. These organizational formats are working so well that more railroads can be expected to adopt them.

WHEN SHOULD AN ORGANIZATION BE MARKETCENTERED?

Marketcentered describes an organization that is decentralized by markets--markets define the business. Organizing an enterprise in this way, which some companies think of as working backward from the points where they deal face to face with their customers, can yield many of the same benefits as decentralizing by processes, materials, or product lines. A marketcenter forms a natural profit center just as readily as does a materials center, such as Continental Can's Metal Operations group. A marketcenter may also be able to dominate the heavy users in its market to such an extent that it becomes the preeminent supplier, like such product centers as The Ansul Company's former Fire Protection Products division.

But marketcentering is not without some costs and inefficiencies. For example, when Coca-Cola was reorienting to its markets in the early 1960s, some of its veteran managers were moved to lament the passing of one of the most cost-efficient mass businesses of all time. Formerly, the company had manufactured a single product, made according to one basic formula and sold at one retail price, which was marketed with great economies in an internationally recognized bottle that conveyed instant product awareness. The managers saw this business give way forever to a diversity of sizes and prices and even to various companion products, all of which bore a considerable burden of their own administrative, operating, and marketing expenses.

Marketcentering an organization may incur other additional costs. In order to zero in on its market, management generally requires its own information bank of customer needs and its own exclusive sales force, which is intensively schooled to apply the data bank's resources to the center's customers. A company that has employed a single sales force before marketcentering may find itself recruiting, training, developing, and fielding several separate sales forces whose compensation plans and support services--to say nothing of product lines and channels of distribution--may be totally dissimilar.

CONDITIONS FAVORING CHANGE

When, then, does marketcentering become an appropriate form of decentralization? Executives of companies that have been reorganizing around their markets suggested five particular situations that especially favor a marketcentered approach:

1
When market leadership is threatened by a competitor who has achieved sufficient product parity to deprive the leader of price superiority. Marketcentering can restore a competitive advantage with the more creative marketing techniques it develops from improved knowledge of customer, distributor, and retailer needs.

2
When new-product famine has afflicted the product-development function so that nothing, or only a crop of lemons, is being delivered, or when R&D has been foundering in its resource allocation because of a lack of market direction. Marketcentering can stimulate new-product winners by transmitting current knowledge of market life-styles or emergent needs to technical management. Marketcentering also enables innovative breakthrough thinking to replace a preoccupation with generating only marginal extensions of established product categories.

3
When a product manufacturer desires either to diversify into higher-margin services as a means of broadening his profit base or to market systems of correlated products and services in order to gain a lock on key customers. Marketcentering can group market needs into highly visible targets for systems, enabling the marketer to operate as a one-stop supplier to each center.

4
When a manufacturer who has been selling product-performance benefits shifts his marketing strategy to feature the financial benefits of customer profit improvement. Marketcentering makes it easier to amass the required knowledge of how customers make their profits. Each marketcenter is made responsible for compiling its own data resource.

5
When a marketer desires to attract a more entrepreneurial type of manager. Marketcentering offers candidates an enlarged scope of supervisory duties and full profit responsibility. In a multimarket company, a mobile young manager can often tackle diverse challenges by moving from one marketcentered division to another. He does not have to go to another company in order to obtain variety.

EASING INTO A MARKETCENTERED FORM

A major organizational change like marketcentering can be a shock to any company--especially to the traditional product manufacturer (who, paradoxically, may benefit the most from it). Companies have been experimenting with several ways of easing themselves toward a marketcentered approach, since the change is often best implemented by degrees. Along the way, a company can learn how much marketcentering it can stand at any given time and what particular form it should ultimately have. Three ways of beginning the transition have emerged thus far.

Marketcentering a sales force is the first way. It requires the least up-front commitment and the least alteration in the basic structure of a business. In addition, it succeeds in establishing the central relationship that earmarks all forms of marketcentered organizations: contact between customers with many varying needs and a sales force that can prescribe the most beneficial systems for those needs. In the romantic version of marketing, this interface takes place on a prolonged person-to-person basis in the marketplace. The reality, however, is that customer information is collected and analyzed at a data bank.

This is the approach that NCR has taken. Each sales staff is assigned a well-defined industry group to serve. The company's salesmen are trained to sell systems of different but interrelated products and services in a consultative manner. They consider market knowledge, rather than product knowledge, to be their principal resource.

General Foods has chosen a second way to ease into marketcentering. It has created a separate marketing division to serve each major market. This approach involves reclassifying major markets into new, more comprehensive groups and consolidating similar but differently manufactured products into product families to be marketed to each group. While the NCR sales-centered approach requires a single salesman to serve most or all of a customer's needs with many different products and services, the General Foods approach coordinates a wide range of products that are essentially alike for a single user segment.

The third way is to begin with either the first or second step and then proceed to achieve a thoroughly marketcentered structure by integrating manufacturing and all marketing functions, including sales, into a single division. Both the NCR and General Foods examples lend themselves to this end result, which IBM and Xerox have perhaps most fully achieved.

In the following sections, I shall examine some of the major characteristics of the NCR and General Foods approaches. Then I shall describe the key criteria of a marketcentered organization, the role of the business manager, and the service systems needed to support that role.

NCR's APPROACH--SEPARATE SALES FORCES

NCR has been reorganizing its traditional product-line sales approach into a strategy of "selling by vocation" on an industry-by-industry basis. Each vocation is a broad industry grouping which forms a specific market definable by reasonably cohesive needs. NCR is focusing a separate sales force on each of the following vocational markets: financial institutions, retailers, commercial and industrial businesses, and computer customers in medical, educational, and government offices.

NCR's marketcentered sales organization is enabling the company to be more competitive, especially in the marketing of systems. In each market, the NCR salesman assigned to it can sell coordinated systems of numerical recording and sorting products. Previously, each salesman could sell only his own product line. Also, the decision maker in the customer company could be involved with several NCR salesmen, no one of whom could know the sum total of the customer's numerical control needs, let alone serve them. Under the new system, the same retail industry salesman who sells an NCR cash register to a department store can also search out and serve the store's needs for NCR accounting machines, data entry terminals, and a mainframe computer. If he needs help, he can organize a team with other NCR salesman that can bring the required strength to his proposal. The product groups he sells are still manufactured separately; the centralized sales approach is the innovation that makes the difference.

By selling groups or systems of products through a single salesman or sales team, rather than selling individual products through many uncoordinated salesmen, NCR believes it can help customers achieve greater profit improvement. It can prescribe systems that solve comprehensive problems which would otherwise remain immune to single product solutions. Management also believes it can expand its profitable sales volume by selling larger packages and insulating its position against competition.

Each vocational market's full range of recording and sorting needs is becoming better known to NCR personnel. In turn, by specializing in seeking out and serving these needs, each of NCR's vocational sales organizations can become known for expertise in its market, almost as if it were an independent specialist company. Moreover, every sales group can utilize the total financial and technical resources of the company for professional counsel and support in developing, prescribing, and installing product systems.

OPERATIONS AND OPTIONS

A vice president of marketing directs NCR's sales organization. The four vocational vice presidents report to him. Regional vocational directors supervise several states, giving a geographic underlay to the organization.

NCR's next step in marketcentering through its sales force is to specialize more precisely. This can logically lead to the appointment of retail specialists within the financial industry sales force, to mention one possibility. As additional ramifications of the new approach become apparent, NCR will be able to reorganize many other aspects of its corporate structure and operations, increasing its market orientation. Among the major options which will be open to the company are decentralizing staff services, bringing R&D and product development activities into closer vocational alignment, adding profit-making services to existing product systems, consolidating advertising and other promotional activities to appeal specifically to vocational needs, and combining the appropriate manufacturing and selling activities in marketcentered divisions.

GENERAL FOODS'S APPROACH--SEPARATE MARKETING DIVISIONS

While NCR has been stimulated to reorganize by the increasing preferences of its customers for systems and by the relentless competitive pressures of IBM, General Foods revised its approach because of internal strains and frustrations. In the early 1970s new product winners either stopped coming out of product development at their former rate or carried an unreasonable cost. Better knowledge of the needs of its consumers was obviously required if the company's product developers were to harmonize their technologies with the new life-styles influencing the demand for processed foods. At the same time, the needs of the company's customers at the retail level required new responses. Competitive brands were proliferating, clamoring for shelf and display space, while an increasingly attractive profit on sales was making private-label products more acceptable to the major supermarket chains.

These events combined to place unprecedented strains on the company's divisional structure, which was the legacy of a generations-old policy of acquisition. General Foods's major food divisions--Birds Eye, Jell-O, Post, and Kool-Aid --had evolved historically, each according to the process technology which it brought into the company. As the scope of each division's product categories grew, it was inevitable that one division's consumer provinces would be impinged on by other divisions, and that any given market would be served in a fragmented rather than a concentrated manner. Divisional sovereignties frequently made it impossible for the company to dominate a market that was served by two or more divisions with related product categories but with different styles and degrees of commitment.

Often more damaging for new-product development was the way in which division managers respected a no-man's-land between their provinces, leaving gaps in product categories that could give competitors a clear shot or deny the company a chance to establish a position of category leadership. Beverages are a case in point. They were marketed by three divisions. If they were frozen, they were marketed by Birds Eye. If they were powdered mixes, the Kool-Aid division marketed them. Breakfast drinks had to come from Post. No centralized attack on consumer beverage needs could be made. In a similar fashion, puddings were marketed by two divisions: Birds Eye had jurisdiction over frozen puddings while Jell-O was the steward division for powdered mixes. The pudding market as such had no general representative within the company.

RELATING PRODUCTS TO MARKET NEEDS

The General Foods approach to marketcentering has been to reorganize its process-oriented divisional structure into separate marketing organizations known as "strategic business units" (SBUs). Each SBU concentrates on marketing families of products made by different processing technologies but consumed by the same market segment. As Exhibit 24-2 shows, the Food Products division coordinates the marketing strategy for all desserts whether they are in frozen, powdered, or ready-to-eat form. The exhibit also shows how the Beverage and Breakfast Food division markets breakfast drinks of three different processing techniques and how the Pet Food division centers the marketing of freeze-dried, dry pellet, and semimoist dog foods.

This scheme allows each SBU to take an overview of how an entire product family can best be related to the needs of both end users and retailers. Each SBU functions like a division and draws on the full range of corporate technologies. It also derives support services from a corporate pool where market research, production, personnel, new-product development, and sales are consolidated for use by all SBUs. A small amount of product-connected market research and new-product development is still left to the individual SBUs. But their primary mission is to engage in "pure marketing" as much as possible and to concentrate their resources on cultivating the market segments to which they have been assigned.

Among the benefits that General Foods believes it has gained so far from its form of marketcentering are an increasingly productive trade merchandising capability and improved ability to dominate a full consumer-need category at the point of sale--the supermarket. The company has also

EXHIBIT 24-2. STRATEGIC BUSINESS CENTERS AT GENERAL FOODS

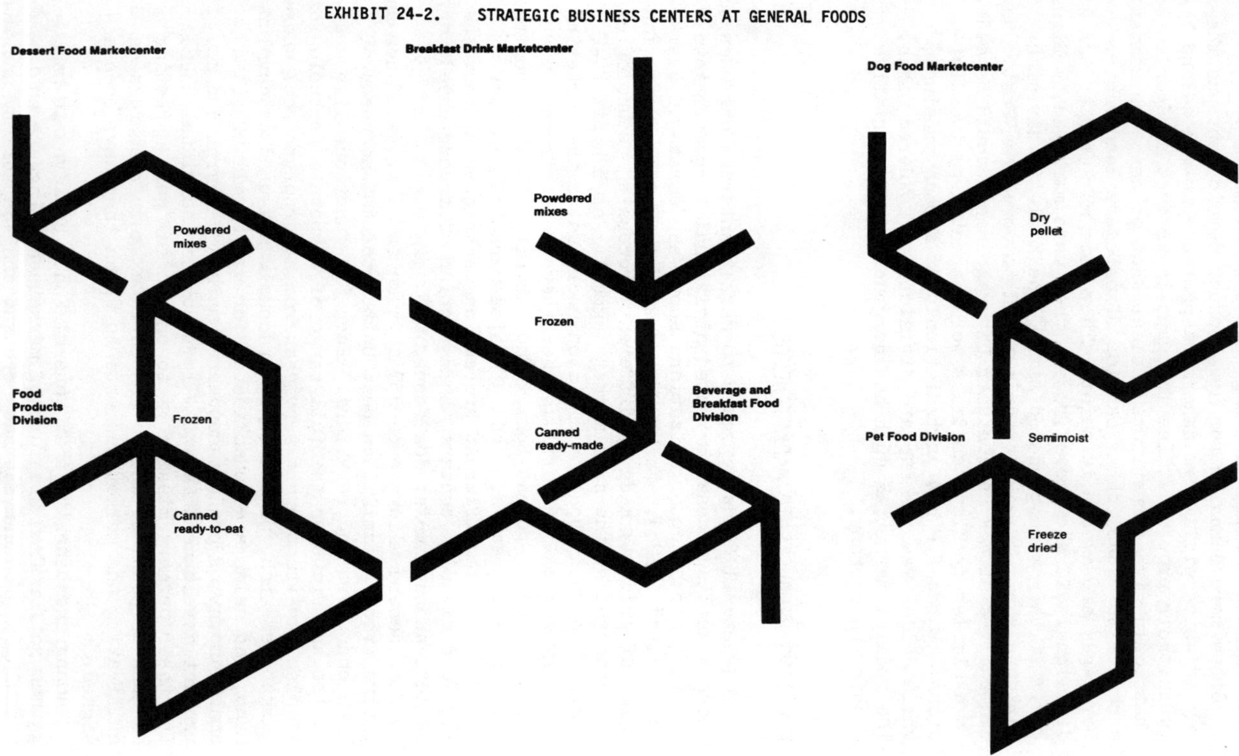

had better opportunities to aim multiple-product advertising at a single market, with the result that preferences for company brands have risen in certain product categories.

Another benefit has been that new products can be launched with fewer problems of stewardship than before. To take a hypothetical example, suppose that skin care products were to become part of the corporate growth scheme. If one proposed item were to be packaged in frozen form, it would not have to start its market life in the Birds Eye division, as presumably would have been necessary in the past, and therefore labor under the potentially negative connotations of having vegetable origins. Or, if the new skin care product were to be premoistened patty or a water-soluable pellet, it would not have to be marketed under the umbrella of the Gaines pet food division.

GUIDELINES FOR DEVELOPMENT

In sketching the main guidelines that product- or process-centered companies can use to change to a marketcentered approach, I shall place special emphasis on two areas. One is the key criteria of marketcentering. The other is the role of the manager who runs a marketcenter and the unique aspects of his supportive service system.

KEY CRITERIA

When an organization is fully marketcentered, a market becomes the focal point of every one of the company's major operations. The objective of each business is to become its market's preferred center for fulfilling one or more principal needs. Such a business is the sum of its marketcentered divisions and should meet these five criteria:

1
It must be chartered to serve a market which is defined according to a system of closely related needs. This permits the market to be served by a diversified package of products and services that, taken together, supply a combination of closely related benefits. The business may market two or more related products in a single sale or market a package composed of products and their related services.

2
Because a marketcenter is operated as a profit center, it should be administered by an entrepreneur. I like to call this executive the *business manager* of the organization. Unlike most product managers or brand managers, or even market managers who are merely profit-accountable, a business mana-

ger is fully profit-responsible. He enjoys considerable authority in running his business. He commands the key decisions. He sets prices, controls costs, and is charged with operating his marketcenter for a satisfactory profit.

3
Business managers are the chief line officers in their marketcentered organizations. All other corporate functions must be repositioned as satellite supply services that support the business managers' operations. Business managers employ corporate staff services on a contractual basis, which gives them authority to refuse to do business with any service that cannot be competitive in pricing, quality control, or delivery.

4
Once a division is marketcentered, its storehouse of market information quickly becomes its key asset. Through marketcentering, a company grows by basing its future expansion on knowledge about its existing markets. A corporatewide market information center can be set up to store and give access to the market knowledge required by each division, or marketcentered divisions can create their own information centers.

5
Top management must position itself as a holding company or, as it is sometimes called, a central bank. This central bank acts as a council of portfolio managers who centralize corporate policy making and investment funding for their decentralized businesses. Top management's prime concern is usually to manage a balanced portfolio of businesses in which no single investment accounts for more than 50% of total corporate profit, or at least not for long. The business managers consult the central bank when they want money or need advice.

HOW THE BUSINESS MANAGER OPERATES

A business manager may head up a single, large marketcenter or, if the operations are small or closely related, two or more such centers. His job is to manage the corporate investment in a center so that it will yield the maximum rate of return. At Textron, for example, a minimum pretax return on investment of 25% is mandated for every one of the company's businesses. At ITT, the manager's contribution must fall within the 10% to 12% annual range of increase in earnings.

As a result of his concentration on financial bogeys, a marketcenter's business manager tends to view himself as a profit creator rather than a curator of specific products or processes. He resists becoming addicted to any particular product line or acquiring a reverence for any technological process. "In my marketing mix, I recognize no such thing as an eternal product," one business manager told me. "Nor do I cherish any perpetual promotional appeals for them. Even the customer needs that I serve today will probably prove to be transient. Only my commitment to maximize the long-range profit of my marketcenter is everlasting."

SUPPORTIVE SYSTEMS

While marketcentering decentralizes the management of operations, it centralizes many of the staff services which business managers use. As Exhibit 24-3 shows, up to four consolidated service functions may revolve around each business manager.

Development services combine new-market research and development with new-product R&D under a single director. In this way, the market orientation of R&D--historically one of the chief stumbling blocks in raising a company's level of consciousness to its customers--is accomplished organizationally. New-market needs, new-process technology, and new-product development are able to interact harmoniously rather than competitively. With marketcentering, the traditional vice presidential functions for marketing and R&D can be subsumed under the director of development's functions. There is generally no need for a vice president of marketing in such an organization because the entire corporate structure is market-oriented and each business manager must act as his own chief marketing officer.

Control services do the basic research to evaluate the effectiveness of established product and service-system marketing. They also provide the necessary recruitment, compensation and motivation, training and development, legal, and financial functions. *Production services* coordinate engineering and manufacturing operations. And *promotion services* combine sales, advertising, and publicity.

These four groups of services are supplied by top management on an elective basis. Whether and when they are used depends on the business manager. Should he elect to contract with the internal services, he negotiates with the service managers as if they were outside suppliers.

CONTRACTING FOR SERVICE

Any one, or all four, of his company's internal services may be retained, either in whole or in part, by a business manager. As the following position description indicates, the business manager is also chartered to employ outside services whenever he feels they can better help him meet his

EXHIBIT 24-3.

SUPPORTING SERVICES AVAILABLE TO A BUSINESS MANAGER

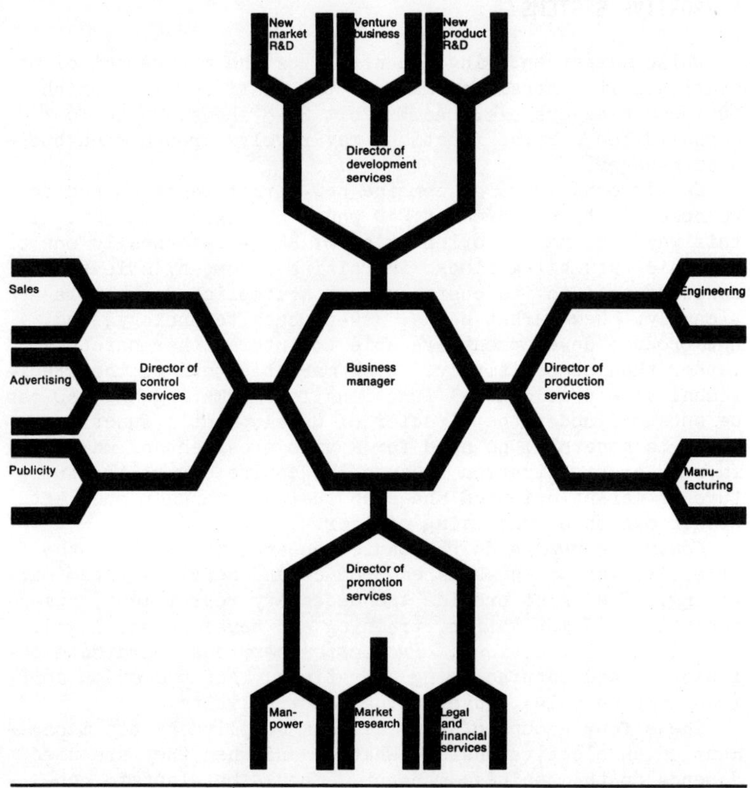

objectives:

"Through an annual contractual relationship with the director of production services, the business manager acquires a product supply to market. The business manager must, at minimal cost, negotiate for a dependable and sufficient supply of products, manufactured according to marketable specifications, that maintain maximum economies in production without impairing either market acceptance or corporate image."

Since the business manager has ultimate responsibility for profit, he must be free to negotiate with any strategic service that meets his product and market specifications at minimal cost. Much, if not most, of the time, these services will come from inside the company. But he can also buy them from outside and use them interchangeably with, or independently of, internal functions. In either case, the contractual form of doing business acts as his principal instrument of cost and quality control.

The service contract can also be an instrument of top management control. Making the use of internal services optional puts them squarely on their mettle. They must perform for the business managers, competing with alternate sources of supply in cost and quality terms, or be bypassed. If internal services are consistently selected by most business managers, top management can comfortably assume that they are competitive; if the services are rejected, that is a sign that they are not doing the job.

ENSURING CONTINUED SERVICE

From each business manager's point of view, being on the receiving end of a demand-feed schedule with contracted services is an almost ideal situation. Best quality at lowest price, every manager's dream, seems assured. But will there be chaos among the suppliers of services? To discourage an endless series of requests for custom-tailored variations in services, especially in production and promotion, a variance-request control system can be installed. Under this system, market-based justification can be required for all significant departures from contracted specifications.

However, it may be necessary to go further. What can be done to protect an internal supplier of services from having to react simultaneously to short-term strategy changes by several business managers? While a predictable problem area such as seasonal production peaks can be rather simply ironed out in advance, no service can fully anticipate a business manager's midcycle decision changes. He may need to alter his product mix in the face of sudden raw materials shortages. New corporate policies on allocating scarce ingredients or components may shut off his supply. Demand variations among his key customers may dry up one or more markets and force him to shift his product specifications to meet the needs of a previously less important customer group. Such stresses can disrupt R&D priorities, throw off manufacturing runs, scuttle cost estimates, and upset sales and advertising appropriations.

TWO-WAY GROWTH OPPORTUNITY

Some corporate executives feel that marketcentering may come to rank with Alfred Sloan's decentralization of General Motors along market-segmented lines. They see themselves regaining a customer focus that often became blurred by Procter & Gamble's brand management system. While contemporary with Sloan's market awareness, brand management directed the styles of many corporate formats away from customers and back to products. When product and brand management were imposed on the traditional organization of the manufacturing division and on the pyramidal organization chart, which was adapted for the needs of commercial business from Von Möltke's general staff concept, progress toward marketcentering slowed for half a century.

In the mid 1960s, the beginning of a new thrust toward the customer was signaled by the advent of free-form marketing groups. They were allowed to cut across corporate pyramids whenever unusual market sensitivity was demanded in an operation. A variety of problem-solving task forces and project management teams came into being for much the same reason; they represented jerry-built improvisations to defeat a product-oriented or process-centered organizational system. In other instances, managers have had to depart from the accepted corporate framework and to create highly decentralized conglomerates of market-targeted businesses.

Since it is probably that these dislocations will be with us for some time to come, methods for coping with them are under experimentation. Some companies are establishing resource allocation groups, composed of the directors of development, control, production,and promotion services, who recommend to top management the most favorable distribution patterns in times of materials short-falls. Their suggestions are based on the central criterion of close-in contribution to profit but are naturally conditioned by short- and long-term considerations, such as maintenance of the traditional market position, potential for future growth, and possible preemptive reactions from competitors.

Because a marketcentered company expands chiefly by serving new needs in established markets where it is well franchised, its growth is relatively safe. By asking and reasking the key question, "What *other* needs of the markets we know so well can we serve profitably?" management can develop new business on the basis of the strength of its existing businesses.

Marketcentering a company can give it two-way flexibility for growth. Each of its major markets can be served *intensively*, once it is established as the center of a business. When growth on a broadened profit base becomes desirable, the same markets can be served more *extensively* by searching our their closely related needs and centering new businesses around one or more of them. Through these two approaches, the basic growth strategy of a marketcentered company can be defined as meeting the greatest number of interrelated needs of every market segment it serves.

STUDENT REVIEW QUESTIONS

1. Explain what Hanan means by the terms "marketcentered" and "marketcentering".
2. What situations does Hanan say favor a marketcentered approach?
3. Describe the approach to marketcentering used by
   a. NCR
   b. General Foods
4. What are the "key criteria" that Hanan considers essential for marketcentering?

25

Strategy and Structure: The Italian Experience*

ROBERT J. PAVAN

IN 1962, ALFRED D. CHANDLER, JR. documented the trend of American industry toward increased diversification followed by adoption of the multidivisional structure [1]. He observed that growth in American firms has occurred by way of three strategies:

> Growth came either from an expansion of the firm's existing lines to much the same type of customers, or it resulted from a quest for new markets and sources of supplies in distant lands, or finally it came from the opening of new markets by developing a wide range of new products for different types of customers [1, p. 42].

The first strategy led to the adoption of an explicit functional organization. The latter forms of expansion led to new types of administrative problems. At first, firms attempted to manage these problems with the functional structure or with the holding company structure composed of almost autonomous subsidiaries with little central control. The functional form generally attempted too much central control; and the holding company form, too little. Primar-

---

Bracketed numbers throughout this article refer to the alphabetized list of references at the end of the article.

*From the *Journal of Economics and Business*, Vol. 28, No. 3 (Spring-Summer, 1976), pp. 254-260. Reprinted by special permission of the author.

ily, a strategy of diversification led to the development of the multidivisional form which permitted greater variation on the centralized-decentralized spectrum of control.

Of major importance was Chandler's calling attention to growth in complexity, not growth in size per se, as the critical element in the growing trend toward the multidivisional structure. Diversification produced greater complexity in administrative problems than did sheer growth in volume. Wrigley, studying 100 firms from the 1967 *Fortune 500*, found ninety diversified and eighty-six with a divisional structure [11]. Later, Rumelt reported that the 1969 *Fortune 500* contained 93.8 percent diversified companies and 88.8 percent with a structure other than functional [7]. Clearly, the earlier trend reported by Chandler had accelerated.

Scott, building upon the Chandler work and his own case studies of American firms, developed a model of organizational development [8]. In his model Scott described the managerial characteristics which tended to be associated with each of three stages of growth. The three stages are summarized in Table 25-1.

The Scott model does not attempt to explain why growth occurred nor why a firm should grow, nor why growth should occur via a strategy of diversification. It does state that empirical evidence indicates that if a firm follows a particular growth strategy and its business activities exhibit certain internal operational requirements and external distribution characteristics then the organizational structure for managing those business characteristics tends to follow certain patterns.

Inasmuch as the reported relationship of diversification and divisionalization was based on empirical research within the American environment, one may ask, "Is this relationship strictly an American phenomenon or do the managerial requirements of diversity among the largest industrial enterprises in the technologically advanced industrial societies of the Western world lead to a converging trend in the adoption of the divisional structure to manager diversification?" A study of the 100 largest manufacturing firms in France [6], Germany [10], Italy [5], and the United Kingdom [3] was coordinated by Scott to seek an answer. The basic hypotheses were, one, there are no patterns or regularities to the way the largest companies have developed over time, and there are no such similarities across industries; two, there are no such similarities or patterns among the major industrial nations of the West. Evidence rejecting these hypotheses would support the view that the patterns observed in the United States are not unique.

This article reports on the study of the 100 largest manufacturing firms in Italy. The evidence tends to reject the hypotheses.

TABLE 25-1. THREE STAGES OF ORGANIZATIONAL DEVELOPMENT

Co. Characteristics \ Stage	I	II	III
Product line	1. Single product or single line.	1. Single product line	1. Multiple product lines
Distribution	2. One channel or set of channels	2. One set of channels	2. Multiple channels
Organization structure	3. Little or no formal structure—one man show	3. Specialization based on function	3. Specialization based on product-market relationships
Product-service transactions	4. N/A	4. Integrated pattern of transactions A → B → C → Market	4. Not integrated A ↓ B ↓ C ↓ Markets
R & D	5. Not institutionalized—oriented by owner-mgr.	5. Increasingly institutionalized search for product or process improvements	5. Institutionalized search for new products as well as for improvements
Performance	6. By personal contact and subjective criteria	6. Increasingly impersonal using technical and/or cost criteria	6. Increasingly impersonal using market criteria (return on investment & market share)
Rewards	7. Unsystematic & often paternalistic	7. Increasingly systematic with emphasis on stability & service	7. Increasingly systematic with variability related to performance
Control system	8. Personal control of both—strategic and operating decisions	8. Personal control of strategic decisions with increasing delegation of operating decisions based on control by decision rules (policies)	8. Delegation of product-market decisions within existing businesses, with indirect control based on analysis of results
Strategic choices	9. Needs of owner vs. needs of firm	9. Degree of integration Market share objective Breadth of product line	9. Entry and exit from industries Allocation of resources by industry Rate of growth

Source: See [8].

DATA COLLECTION AND DEFINITIONS

The post World War II history of the 100 largest manufacturing firms operating in Italy in 1970 were studied to determine if diversification had occurred.[1] Selznick in discussing the value of studying organizational histories states:

> ...Taken as a total experience, each such history is, of course, unique. Nevertheless to the extent that similar situations summon like responses from similar groups, we may expect to find organizational evolutionary patterns [9, p. 103].

The use of the historical approach was encouraged further by the Chandler research. The approach permitted the observation of change in diversification and organization structure.

Published materials (annual reports, magazine and newspaper articles, manufacturers' catalogs, company histories) were used primarily for data on diversification. All of these materials were not available for all companies, but companies were cooperative in providing annual reports, often for the full period from 1945 through 1970. Diversification was classifed in 1950, 1960, and 1970 using the scheme developed by Wrigley when he found diversification definitions based on the standard industrialization classification (SIC)code were not meaningful in terms of the managerial needs of a firm [11]. His single business, dominant business, related business, and unrelated business classes were defined in terms of the degree (percent of sales) and kind (relatedness to previous markets and/or technologies and/or integration) of diversification. The boundary limits of the degree of diversification are based on empirical observations. The concepts of kind of diversification are developed from the earlier work of Edwards and Townsend [2]. Classification of firms at the end of three time periods provides a dynamic view of changes in diversification, either in degree or kind.

The organizational structure used by the firm for its worldwide operations was determined for 1950, 1960, and 1970. Originally, it was intended to classify structure as functional, multidivisional, and holding company. A variant of the holding company was observed wherein the parent firm was organized functionally; and it provided advice, on an ad hoc basis, to subsidiary firms; this form was termed a functional/holding company structure. In addition, the multidivi-

---

[1]Of the 100 companies, ninety-four were present in Italy in 1960; and eighty-four, in 1950.

sional form was divided into multiproduct divisions, multigeographic divisions, and international divisions. In some forms a combination of multidivisional forms was found; for example, a firm might be organized by product divisions in its home country but might be organized by geographical divisions beyond the borders. For testing the hypotheses a firm was classed as multidivisional whether it used one or more divisional variants; similarly, a firm was classed as a holding company when it used the functional/holding company variant. It should be noted that the terms functional/holding company and holding company refer to management structure and not to legal structure.

TABLE 25-2. DEGREE OF DIVERSIFICATION

SINGLE BUSINESS Firms which grow by the expansion of one main product line so that at least 95 percent of sales lie within the single product area.
DOMINANT BUSINESS Firms which grow primarily by the expansion of one main product line but which in addition have added secondary product lines making up to 30 percent or less of the total sales volume. These secondary activities can be related to the primary activity or can be unrelated.
RELATED BUSINESS Firms which grow by expansion by means of entry into related markets, by the use of a related technology, by related vertical activities, or by some combination of these so that no one product line accounts for 70 percent of the total corporate sales.
UNRELATED BUSINESS Firms which grow by expansion into new markets and new technologies unrelated to the original product-market scope so that no one product line accounts for 70 percent of the total corporate sales.

Data on organizational structure was obtained primarily from personal interviews with top managers in Italy. The interviews provided an opportunity to classify structure on more than published data (which were limited) and also to validate diversification data. Interviews were conducted at eighty-eight companies.

Diversification was used in the sense of products sold to the market and not in terms of products made within the firm. A firm which produced metal screws might have consid-

TABLE 25-3. FIRM ORGANIZATIONAL STRUCTURE OF A FIRM FOR WORLDWIDE OPERATIONS

FUNCTIONAL
Specialized functional managers (sales, production, purchasing, etc.) who report hierarchically to a chief executive office which acts as coordinator and general manager. The Scott Stage II organization, expected to be found with low product diversity which corresponds to the Wrigley single or dominant business categories.
MULTIDIVISIONAL
Division managers who control the functions (at a minimum, their own production facilities, and sales force) necessary to manager a business day-to-day within a policy outlined by the general office to which they report. The general office usually is divorced from operations and services, and it monitors the operating divisions and oulines policy.
Product Division: Multidivisional by product.
Geographic Division: Multidivisional by area.
HOLDING COMPANY
A parent company with financial control of a number of subsidiaries who are largely autonomous. Control is exerted essentially through the parent's man serving as chief executive officer or director. No overall strategy formulation, coordination, or uniform accounting or control procedures.
Functional/Holding Company: A parent company which is managed functionally, with the parent acting as staff on an ad hoc basis for the subsidiaries; otherwise, similar in form to the holding company.

ered that it had diversified by increasing the number of types of metal screws it produced; but for our purposes if the firm sold its expanded production to similar customers as before, it had not diversified. Further, diversification could be seen both as a strategy and the results of a strategy. There was no attempt to prove the existence of an explicit strategy of diversification in a firm. The research assumed each firm had a strategy in the sense of a concept of how to compete in the market whether it was expressed explicitly or not. It was noted only if diversification had occurred over time.

POPULATION STUDIED

The population of companies studied are the 100 largest manufacturing companies, by sales volume, operating in Italy in 1970. The list of companies include gruppi and societa. A gruppo is a totality of corporations or societa under one control. It is the equivalent of what is meant in the United States when one speaks of a company as though it were one legal entity when in reality it has numerous legal entities. Our interest is the totality and diversity of assets under the control of top management and how this diversity is managed; thus, when a company is referred to, it means the group if the company is part of a group.

Unfortunately, data on gruppi and societa are somewhat scarce, arbitrary, and commingled. There is no requirement that groups publish consolidated data or even that listed companies (whether or not part of a group) publish sales figures. The financial press reports published data for societa and gruppi as though each entry were independent, and further the published data for the same entry varies from list to list. The population studied was determined by combining lists published by *II Sole-24 Ore,*[2] Mediobanca in *Le Principali Societa Italiane,*[3] *and L'Impressa*[4] plus five other firms not on any list.

The final list includes three state companies, twenty-six listed Italian companies, thirty-two unlisted Italian companies, and thirty-nine foreign companies. Sales of the state companies represent 29 percent of sales for the 100 companies; while listed, unlisted, and foreign companies represent 42 percent, 12 percent, and 17 percent, respectively. If the readily identifiable nonmanufacturing revenues are removed--for example, banking, airlines, shipping lines, etc.--then the state, listed, unlisted, and foreign companies represent, respectively, 23 percent, 44 percent, 13 percent, and 19 percent. The figures undoubtedly are not absolutely correct; but they do illustrate three important characteristics of Italian industry--namely, the importance of state and foreign companies, the concentration of industry represented by the relatively few listed companies, and the continued presence of unlisted companies among the top 100 companies.

If family companies are defined as those having family members on the Consiglio di Amministrazione and in operating positions, having a history of at least two generations of

---

[2] *II Sole-24 Ore* is a financial and economic newspaper.

[3] *Le Principali Societa Italiane* is an annual publication limited to companies who respond to Mdeiobanca's survey.

[4] *L'Impressa* is a bimonthly management journal published by the Scuola Di Amministrazione Industriale, Torino.

family control, and having a minimum of 5 percent of the voting stock held by the family or trust interests associated with it, then the population studied reflects the strong presence of family companies in Italy. Of the thirty-two unlisted companies, twenty-nine were family companies; while seventeen of the twenty-six listed companies also so qualified. In contrast, only eight of the thirty-nine foreign companies showed a continued tendency to be managed by the founding family or families.

Sales value is used to determine the 100 largest companies. Sales values also are used as one criterion for classifying diversification. There are certain difficulties with ranking by sales--some difficulties are inherent in the criterion and others primarily are peculiar to Italy. Sales figures of companies within and across industries are affected by the value of the raw materials used, by the rate and the method of imposing and collecting taxes, and by the method of crediting sales, to mention but a few inherent distortions. In addition, in Italy the presumption of the tax collector that the amount of profit to be taxed is related to the sales level provides an incentive to reduce the apparent sales level by not invoicing all sales. Sales not invoiced also escape the payment of the *Imposta Generale sul Entrata* (IGE) tax, a turnover tax since replaced by the Value Added Tax which has reduced but has not eliminated the practice. Avoidance of the IGE also results in some sales being invoiced only for the value added with the customer purchasing and retaining title to the raw materials processed. No single criterion for ranking is without defects, and the sales criterion reduces the output of each company to a common denominator. There is no reason to doubt that the sales criterion performed its function which is to identify most of the major companies which should have been included in the study.

RESULTS

The results show that by 1970, 90 percent had diversified over 5 percent of sales; and 57 percent had diversified by 30 percent or more (Table 25-4). The proportion of single business companies had decreased dramatically in twenty years, dropping from 30 percent in 1950 to 10 percent in 1970. Clearly, manufacturing companies in Italy had become more diversified as had the American companies studied by Chandler [1], Wrigley [11], and Rumelt[7].

The data permitted an analysis of the path companies tended to follow in increasing their diversity (Table 25-4). As it might be expected, companies tended to increase their diversity gradually--i.e., over a twenty-five-year period, when changes occurred, the tendency was for the single busi-

TABLE 25-4.

CLASSIFICATION OF STRATEGY AND STRUCTURE IN 1950, 1960, AND 1970

Classification	No. Co's 1950	New Co's 1950-60	No. Co's Changing to Adopt S	D	R	U	No. Co's 1960	New Co's 1960-70	No. Co's Changing to Adopt S	D	R	U	No. Co's 1970
Single	25	4	—	5	2	—	22	2	—	13	2	—	10
Dominant	20	2	—	—	8	—	19	2	—	—	3	—	33
Related	36	4	—	—	—	—	50	2	1	2	—	2	52
Unrelated	3	—	—	—	—	—	3	—	—	—	—	—	3
	84						94						100

	No. Co's 1950	New Co's 1950-60	No. Co's Changing to Adopt F	H	MD	No. Co's 1960	New Co's 1960-70	No. Co's Changing to Adopt F	H	MD	No. Co's 1970
Functional	55	5	—	2	4	54	4	—	2	21	36
Holding[1]	23	4	—	—	5	24	1	1	—	10	16
Multidivisional	6	1	—	—	—	16	1	—	—	—	48
	84					94					100

1. Functional/holding and holding companies have been combined in this table.

ness company to become a dominant business company and the dominant business company to become a related business company. It could be that managers were comfortable with gradual change. It also must be noted that considerable diversification was required to move a firm more than one classification. Also, an environment such as the Italian postwar period when a nation was rapidly becoming industrialized and when per capita consumption while increasing rapidly was in almost all areas of output below that of other Western industrialized nations, the opportunity for growth in a company's present activities lessened the pressures for diversification as a means for additional growth.

Further, investment required to supply the demand in the existing businesses reduced the ability to finance diversification. Limits of other resources such as availability of managers also would tend to limit diversification. Another bit of evidence supporting this view on the gradual increase of diversity is not evident in the classification scheme used. A company in two different but related businesses would qualify as a related business company if neither of the businesses represented 70 percent of total sales, as would a company in 102 related businesses. In qualitative comparison of diversified Italian companies and diversified American companies, it was evident that Italian companies while diversified were engaged in fewer businesses than were the American companies. It would be expected that as the Italian market approached per capita levels of consumption comparable to other Western industrial nations and as managers gained experience in managing diversity that available resources for growth would be used to reduce this qualitative difference in diversification.

When the population of companies was classified by industry and when the industries were classified according to the demonstrated movement of the member firms toward diversity, three groups emerged: low diversification (vast majority of firms classed as S or D); wide diversification (vast majority of firms classed as R or U); and mixed diversification (almost equal numbers of S and D firms versus R and U firms).

Within the drink, oil, paper, and power machinery industries, companies have tended to remain as single or dominant companies or to move only from single to dominant. Firms have tended to choose to use their resources to maintain market share in the face of increasing of expected industry concentration. Industry growth has been sufficient to absorb the available resources as the industries are largely capital intensive. In addition, the companies have little transferrable technological or marketing skills.

The food and metal and mineral industry companies have shown no clear tendency relative to diversification. Founded largely under the protection of tariffs and developed often with cartel agreements, there has been some tacit attempt by food companies to continue to avoid competing in each other's industry sector. The sugar companies continue under legal cartel quotas. The ferrous metal companies have adopted a strategy of shifting production to finished products requiring capital investment to avoid competition with the state producer of basic metal and with small regional producers of semifinished and finished products. The nonferrous metal companies with little or no raw material supply advantages have adopted a similar strategy, while the cement companies with few transferrable skills have remained undiversified or have diversified into unrelated businesses through acquisitions.

Diversification into related businesses clearly has been the strategic tendency in the ceramic, chemical-pharmaceutical-toiletry, rubber, textiles, electric-electronic, engineering, and printing-publishing industries. The companies in these industries have transferrable technological and/or marketing skills. In general, diversification has not been as wide as the skills might permit. Financial resources which might have been used for diversification have been used to maintain market-share and to update technologies in existing businesses.

As the prevalence of diversification has grown, there has been increased adoption of the multidivisional form of organization. This structural form, virtually absent in 1950 among the firms studied, has been adopted by 48 percent of the firms by 1970. Among Italian companies only one of the sixty-three firms had the multidivisional form in 1950; whereas in 1970, fifteen of the sixty-one companies had introduced the structure. Considering only related and unrelated business companies with Italian ownership, the proportion with the multidivisional form has increased from 4 percent to 35 percent in the same period.

Despite the increased introduction of the multidivisional structure, a large number of diversified firms have continued to use the functional or the holding company structure. Where the functional structure remains, there has been an increase in committees seeking to control and to coordinate the multiplicity of decisions arising from being in more than one business. Top management's task is complicated by the need to allocate resources among businesses, not functions. The holding company form can serve as a transition from the functional structure by providing for the separation of operations by businesses, but it lacks adequate controls to permit top management to monitor and to measure performance against a priori goals; it encourages centralized decision-making with insufficient information or decentralized decision-making bordering on anarchy.

Where the Italian companies have introduced the multidivisional structure, significant differences remain from American multidivisional firms in internal characteristics. There appears to be no use of rewards or punishments for division managers based, at least in part, directly on the

TABLE 25-5. STRATEGY CLASSIFICATION BY INDUSTRY

	1950				1960				1970			
	S	D	R	U	S	D	R	U	S	D	R	U
Industries with Low Diversification												
Drink	2	—	—	—	2	—	—	—	2	—	—	—
Oil	5	3	—	—	6	5	—	—	4	9	1	—
Paper	1	—	—	—	1	—	—	—	—	1	—	—
Power machinery	4	2	1	—	4	2	2	—	1	8	—	—
	12	5	1	0	13	7	2	0	7	18	1	0
Industries with Wide Diversification												
Ceramics	1	—	1	—	1	—	1	—	—	—	2	—
Chemical, pharmaceutical, & toiletries	1	1	8	—	—	1	13	—	—	—	15	—
Electric & electronics	—	—	5	—	—	—	7	—	—	1	7	—
Engineering	1	2	2	—	1	—	4	—	—	—	5	—
Rubber	1	—	2	—	1	—	2	—	1	—	2	—
Printing & publishing	—	1	1	—	—	—	2	—	—	—	2	—
Textiles	1	2	1	—	1	2	1	—	—	2	2	—
Unrelated	—	—	2	3	—	—	2	3	—	—	—	5
	5	6	22	3	4	3	32	3	1	3	35	5
Industries with Mixed Diversification												
Food	4	5	7	—	3	3	10	—	1	5	10	—
Metal & minerals	3	5	6	—	2	6	6	—	1	7	6	—
	7	10	13	0	5	9	16	0	2	12	16	0
Total	25	20	36	3	22	19	50	3	10	33	52	5

performance of their division. Division managers are involved in corporate policy determination in a manner which increases the subjectivity of performance measures and resource allocation. Further, top management in many firms are concerned to a large degree with daily operations. Interdependence of divisions appears to be encouraged to attain greater corporate self-sufficiency at the expense of more accurate measurement of division performance. Greater divisional interdependence dampens internal competition for resources and reduces the ability to discontinue an unprofitable business activity.

Analysis of the differences concerning diversification and divisionalization tendencies among the three state, twenty-six listed, thirty-two unlisted, and thirty-nine foreign firms was undertaken. These results are not reported here, except to note that the state companies included a dominant, a related, and an unrelated business firm. The related and unrelated firms had adopted a divisional structure, while the dominant firm used a functional structure. Among private Italian firms, family companies, when diversified, have tended not to divisionalize. It is intended to publish these results at a later date.

SUMMARY AND IMPLICATIONS

Large companies in Italy have grown by expanding their original business in size, by geographic expansion, and by diversification. Those companies who have remained in a single business or who have diversified to a limited degree--less than 30 percent of total sales--beyond a single business have tended to develop a functional form of organization. Companies who have diversified more widely have tended to introduce the multidivisional structure. These results support the hypothesis that there are patterns to the way the largest companies develop over time, and these similarities cut across industries and exist among major Western industrial nations.

It may be expected that the differences in the degree of diversification and in internal characteristics of management between Italian and American firms will decrease as industrialization in Italy increases, as management acquires greater experience with the multidivisional structure, and as market competition increases the need for greater performance. The most obvious implication is that firms undertaking to diversify must prepare to alter their organizational structure. The likely direction of the change is toward the multidivisional structure which implies the need for generalists as division managers. As per capita consumption approaches levels of more industrialized nations, growth opportunities in existing businesses will decrease, and Italian firms can be expected to feel the need to diversify. Those who have developed a structure to manage diversity will have an advantage.

Countries, such as Italy, will need business schools to help train generalists. Business schools in Italy are a very recent phenomenon--few in number and small in size. Their growth will require increased numbers of trained management educators. Churchill, Frederick, and Holton present a recent analysis of needs [4].

The diversified, divisionalized firm implies more than a new strategy and structure. It is a system which internalizes in the firm external market competition. External market competition has increased in Italy with the abandonment of the policy of autarky after World War II, with the formation of the Common Market, with increased free international trade, and with the growth of multinational corporations. The multidivisional structure with performance measures, rewards related to performance, and with more internal competition for middle level general managers implies more respect for economic performance and for promotion based on ability than often has characterized Italian companies in the past.

REFERENCES

1. A. D. Chandler, Jr., *Strategy and Structure*, Cambridge, Ma., The M.I.T. Press, 1962.

2. R. E. Edwards, and H. Townsend, *Business Enterprise*, London, MacMillan and Co., Ltd., 1958.

3. D. F. Channon, *Strategy and Structure of British Enterprise*, unpublished doctoral dissertation, Cambridge, Ma., Harvard Business School, 1971.

4. N. C. Churchill, W. C. Frederick, and R. H. Holton, *Management Education in Italy: Analysis and Recommendations*, study sponsored by the Ford Foundation for the Programma di Formazione Manageriale, August, 1973.

5. R. J. Pavan, *Strategy and Structure of Italian Enterprise*, unpublished doctoral dissertation, Cambridge, Ma., Harvard Business School, 1972.

6. G. Pooley, *Strategy and Structure of French Enterprise*, unpublished doctoral dissertation, Cambridge, Ma., Harvard Business School, 1972.

7. R. P. Rumelt, *Strategy, Structure, and Economic Performance of the Fortune "500"*, Division of Research, Cambridge, Massachusetts, Harvard Business School, 1974.

8. B. R. Scott, *Stages of Corporate Development*, Case Clearing House, Cambridge, Ma., Harvard Business School, 1971.

9. P. Selznick, *Leadership in Administration*, New York, Harper and Row, 1957.

10. H. Thanheiser, *Strategy and Structure of German Enterprise*, unpublished doctoral dissertation, Cambridge, Ma., Harvard Business School, 1972.

11. L. Wrigley, *Divisional Autonomy and Diversification*, unpublished doctoral dissertation, Cambridge, Ma., Harvard Business School, 1970.

STUDENT REVIEW QUESTIONS

1. How did Pavan select the population to be sampled for his study? What types of sources did he utilize to obtain information?
2. Explain the degree of diversification represented by the following:
   a. Single business
   b. Dominant business
   c. Related business
   d. Unrelated business
3. What were the various organizational structures employed by the firms in the study?
4. Does the evidence indicate that the increase in the amount of diversity was gradual or rapid? Explain.
5. What does the research evidence show about the different industries involved in the population? Do different industries move toward diversity at different rates?
6. Is the Italian experience of industrial strategy and structure unique? Explain.

26

Diversification Strategies and Organizational Policies of Large Diversified Firms*

ROBERT A. PITTS

THE RAPID AND EXTENSIVE diversification of major corporations in recent decades has been well documented. Rumelt has found that in a sample of 100 firms selected at random from the 500 largest U. S. industrial companies listed annually by *Fortune* magazine the proportion of firms whose major single business activity accounted for less than 70 percent of total corporate sales had increased from 30.1 percent in 1949 to 64.6 percent in 1969 [20]. Other studies have discovered a similar trend among large British [6], French [18], German [22], and Italian [15] firms.

Organizational change accompanying diversification also has been documented well. Chandler in his landmark study has shown that diversifying firms tend to abandon their original functional organizations (see Figure 26-1A) and to adopt instead a product-division form of structure (Figure 26-1B) which assigns to each of several relatively autonomous organizational units responsibility for a separate business [5]. The extent to which diversified firms have adopted this organizational form has been documented well. Wrigley [24] has estimated that by 1967, 86 percent of the 500 largest industrial U.S. firms had adopted the product-division form of organization, while Fouraker and Stopford [9] found that 89.4 percent of 170 large U. S. firms with substantial investments abroad were organized along division

Bracketed numbers throughout this article refer to the alphabetized list of references at the end of the article.

*From the *Journal of Economics and Business*, Vol. 28, No. 3 (Spring-Summer, 1976), pp. 181-187. Reprinted by special permission of the author.

lines. Rumelt, tracing organizational change in the largest 500 U. S. industrial companies over a twenty-year time span, found that the percentage of firms having product-division organizations increased from 20.3 percent to 75.9 percent from 1949 to 1969 [20]. Similar studies of British [6], French [18], German [22], and Italian [15] firms indicate that divisionalization has accompanied diversification in these countries as well.

FIGURE 26-1.

A--FUNCTIONAL ORGANIZATION

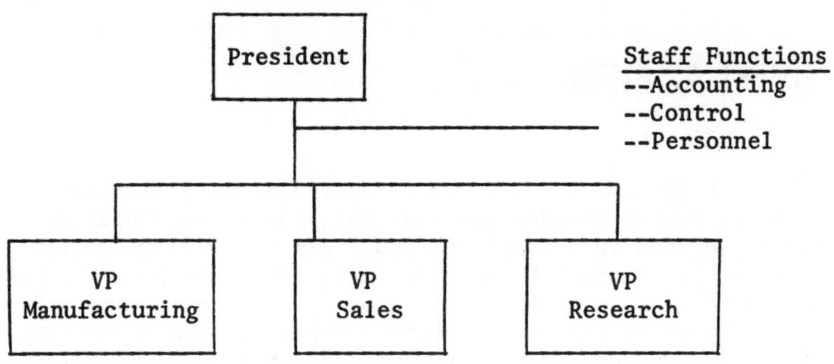

B--PRODUCT-DIVISION ORGANIZATION

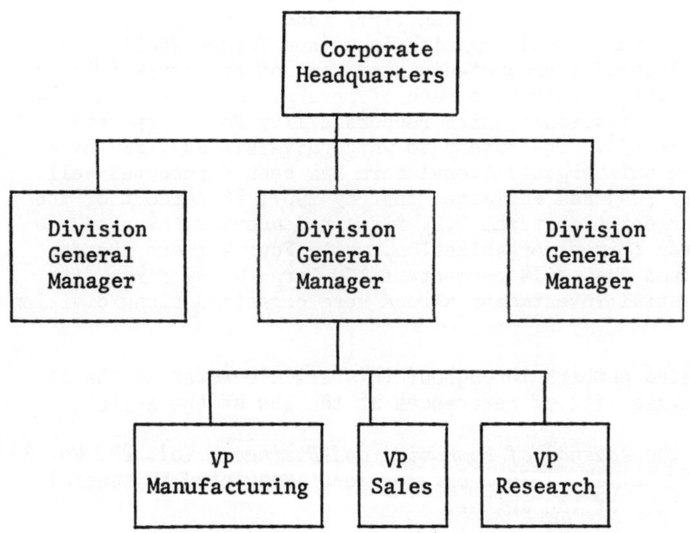

ADVANTAGES OF DIVERSIFICATION AND DIVISIONALIZATION

A variety of advantages of the multibusiness divisionalized organization over its predecessor, the single-business functionally-organized firm, has been cited. By enabling an enterprise to operate in a variety of diverse areas, it reduces overall business risk [13]. For this reason, failure in one business area rarely threatens the entire organization. It also provides for more efficient utilization of scarce financial, technical, and managerial resources. For example, it permits easy shifting of funds from divisions in mature, low-growth business to divisions in newer, more dynamic areas [4]. It also provides an opportunity to commercialize more broadly the benefits of technological developments [5, pp. 42-43] and by vastly expanding the number and variety of promotion opportunities for management personnel, to improve significantly utilization of this critical organizational resource [16].

FIGURE 26-2.

POLICY QUESTIONS AND ALTERNATIVES

Policy Questions	Range of Policy Alternatives
1. Diversification strategy	Internal diversification/ diversification by acquisition
2. Location of activities	Primarily at corporate level/ primarily at division level
3. Interdivisional transactions involving products, services, and people	Extensive corporate policies strongly encouraging such transfers/permit each division to determine for itself the extent of its participation in such transfers
4. Performance measurement of division executives:	
a. Impact of organizational performance	Corporate, group, and division performance/division performance only
b. Degree of discretion	Highly discretionary/based on quantitative measures of organizational performance only

POLICY QUESTIONS AND ALTERNATIVES

From the standpoint of top corporate management, these new enterprises pose some very difficult questions.

One, **diversification strategy.** How should a firm attempt to achieve diversification? Should it stress internal gen-

eration of new businesses or the acquisition of firms already operating in attractive new fields? If both, then in what combination and with what relative emphasis?
Two, **location of activities.** Which of a firm's major activities--manufacturing,marketing, research, finance, etc.--should be conducted, respectively, at the corporate and division levels? Should some activities be split between the two? If so, in what proportion?
Three, **interdivisional transactions.** To what extent and by what means should interchange among divisions--of products, services, and people--be encouraged? For example, should a division be permitted to purchase outside the company a product which can be supplied from within? At what price should a product be transferred across division lines? What policies are appropriate with respect to interdivisional transfer of personnel? When a position opens up in a division, for example, should the division in filling it be obliged to consider candidates from other divisions? If so, how should corporate management respond to a refusal by a candidate's superior to release a candidate for transfer to another division?
Four, **performance measurement.** How should performance of division managers be assessed? Should it be measured, on the one hand, entirely in terms of the performance of their respective divisions; or should it reflect corporate performance as well? In either case, should it be measured strictly objectively on the basis of accounting data; or should it reflect subjective, judgmental assessments?

DISCUSSION OF POLICY ALTERNATIVES

A fairly persuasive case can be made for either side of each of these questions.
One, **diversification strategy.** Diversification by acquisition offers two main advantages over internal diversification. First, it can be accomplished much more rapidly. Second, if payment is made in stock and if the acquiror's stock commands a higher price earnings multiple than that of the acquiree, it results in an immediate earnings per share gain for the acquiror. Internal diversification, on the other hand, has the advantage of being less risky. A firm has time to develop gradually experience in a new field. Internal diversification also provides a firm the opportunity before fully committing itself to test its capabilities against those of competition and to withdraw without large losses if the comparision proves too unfavorable.
Two, **location of activities.** In light of the considerable diversity existing, by definition, among the products and the markets of a diversified firm, production and sales activities are likely to be carried out more effectively at the division level. Conversely, financial, accounting, le-

gal, and public relations functions are likely to be performed most efficiently in a centralized fashion at the corporate level.

The proper location of technological research activities presents a real problem. If research is conducted independently by each division, costly duplication may occur. Funds available to individual divisions can be insufficient to underwrite significant research efforts. Centralizing research at the corporate level, on the other hand, while perhaps avoiding these difficulties, raises some others. Corporate research personnel may not understand really the true needs of divisions. This very possibility increases the difficulty of measuring managerial performance since, when research is centralized, a division's performance no longer will depend solely on the achievements of its management team but also on developments occurring in corporate research laboratories.

Three, **interdivisional transactions.** Just a single kind of interdivisional transaction--those involving managerial personnel--will be considered here. On the one hand, policies to encourage such transactions would appear beneficial. They would enable a division to draw upon the best management talent available throughout the company when an opening is filled. They also would expand each manager's promotion opportunities well beyond the confines of his immediate division, thereby reducing the likelihood of his leaving the company because of feeling blocked in his career progression.

The main disadvantage of policies in this area is their potentially detrimental impact on division autonomy. To achieve the benefits described above, divisions must be required to submit information on a fairly uniform basis regarding both available managerial candidates and job openings when they occur within their operations [14]. Policies for handling intransigent divisions--divisions unwilling to look elsewhere in the company for a candidate to fill a job opening or those refusing to give up managers to sister divisions--also would have to be developed [21].

Four, **performance measurement.** These policies detract from a frequently-voiced advantage of the multidivisional over the functional form of organization--namely, the relative ease of measuring managerial performance in the former [10]. When each division management team controls all functions needed to operate its business, it can be held fully accountable for divisional results. When it lacks control over key factors influencing divisional performance, accountability is much more difficult to establish. For example, when technological research is centralized at the corporate level or when divisions are required to give up valued managers to other divisions, divisional performance inevitably becomes a less valid measure of the true accomplishments of division management. Under such circumstances, a more subjective, judgmental performance assessment system would appear desirable.

These considerations suggest that the approach a firm takes to measuring performance of division managers probably should depend on the level of autonomy enjoyed by its division. Where autonomy is high, a quantitative measure of division performance would appear to be a quite appropriate measure of managerial performance. When autonomy is low, a more subjective approach would seem to be required.

These four questions provide the focus of the inquiry in this article. The discussion will proceed as follows. First, findings will be presented from three recently completed studies suggesting substantial differences in the way top managements of large diversified firms are answering these questions. Two of the studies have previously been reported elsewhere; the third is reported here for the first time.

The findings indicate that firms pursuing primarily internally generated diversification tend to answer these questions quite differently from those diversifying mainly by acquisition. These differences are explained as the outcome of organizational constraints imposed by diversification strategy. Finally, the implications of these constraints for scholars of business management, practicing executives, and public policy makers are explored.

RESEARCH FINDINGS

Berg 1973. The first systematic attempt to determine how these questions are being answered was that of Berg [3]. He examined the size and the composition of the corporate staffs in nine large, growing, highly-diversified firms. Recent diversification activity of four of them which he called diversified majors had been generated primarily internally while that of the remaining five conglomerates had been based importantly on outside acquisitions. His findings which are based on detailed staffing information obtained through personal interviews with corporate-level executives in each of the nine firms studied are reproduced in Table 26-1. As shown, the diversified majors supported much larger corporate staffs--particularly in research and development--than the conglomerates. While limited to just nine firms deliberately chosen to represent opposite extremes with respect to diversification strategy, Berg's findings suggest that the way a firm responds to question one may constrain severely its response to question two, and vice versa.

Pitts 1974. Berg's findings stimulated the author to question whether a firm's answer to question one also might constrain its response to question four. Existing evidence on incentive compensation practices in large diversified

TABLE 26-1. SIZE AND COMPOSITION OF CORPORATE STAFFS

Companies / Functions	Diversified Majors						Conglomerates						
	Company				Four Cos:		Company					Five Cos:	
	A	B	C	X	Total	Avg.	F	G	H	I	J	Total	Avg.
General executives	5	5	4	2	16	4	4	1	4	3	14	26	5
Finance	28	61	101	144	334	84	8	22	29	91	106	256	51
(of which control)	(10)	(36)	(78)	(107)	(231)	(58)	(6)	(12)	(8)	(38)	(49)	(113)	(23)
Legal-secretarial	4	10	22	42	78	20	1	7	5	6	66	85	17
Personnel adm.	11	6	20	25	62	16	1	2	3	10	20	36	7
Research & dev.	54	130	139	232	555	139	0	0	0	0	0	0	0
Marketing	5	0	34	0	39	10	0	0	0	0	0	0	0
Manufacturing	5	1	0	5	11	3	0	0	0	0	0	0	0
Public relations	1	6	9	16	32	8	5	3	5	6	9	28	6
Purchasing & traffic	10	1	33	4	48	12	0	0	0	2	0	2	0
Corporate planning	3	3	2	6	14	5	5	4	1	7	9	26	5
TOTALS	126	223	364	476	1,189	297	24	39	47	125	224	459	92

Note: Numbers shown indicate professional personnel in corporate functions as determined from field research.
The following firms participated in this study:

Diversified Majors
Bendix
Borg-Warner
Ingersoll-Rand
Company X (unidentified)

Conglomerates
Gulf + Western
Walter Kidde
Lear-Siegler
Litton
Textron

firms, while extensive, shed no light on this question since data in each case were aggregated in a way which precluded distinguishing among firms pursuing different diversification strategies (see, for example, [23 and 8]). In an effort to generate data which would permit this kind of distinction, the author investigated incentive compensation practices in eleven large diversified firms deliberately selected as representatives of extreme positions along the internal diversification-acquisition diversification spectrum [17]. All eleven which were included in *Fortune's* 1972 directory of the 500 largest U. S. industrial enterprises were operating at the time of the research in at least twelve different three-digit Standard Industrial Classification industries, had operated profitably each year since 1961, and had experienced substantial sales growth since 1961; six of the eleven had achieved recent diversification almost exclusively by internal developments; five, mainly by acquisition. The former were designated internal growth diversifieds (IGDs); the latter, acquisition growth diversifieds (AGDs). These terms were operationalized by computing the dollar sales acquired by each firm between 1961 and 1970 as a percent of its 1970 sales. IGDs were designated as firms meeting the aforementioned four criteria for which the percentage of acquired sales was less than 5 percent; AGDs as those firms for which it exceeded 50 percent.

Information on incentive compensation practices was obtained through personal face-to-face interviews followed up in many cases by telephone and mail communication with the corporate executive in charge of administering the incentive compensation plan in each of the eleven firms studied. Both formal procedures and less formal practices were studied. In firms employing a formula for computing incentive awards, computed awards were compared with amounts actually paid to participating executives during the year immediately preceding the study.

FIGURE 26-3.
PERFORMANCE AFFECTING INCENTIVE AWARDS
FOR DIVISION GENERAL MANAGERS

Performance	Company Type
1. Division, group, and corporate	3 IGDs
2. Division and corporate only	3 IGDs, 1 AGD
3. Division only	4 AGDs

IGD = Internal Growth Diversified
AGD = Acquisition Growth Diversified

FIGURE 26-4.
TOP MANAGEMENT DISCRETIONARY INFLUENCE OVER INCENTIVE AWARDS FOR DIVISION GENERAL MANAGERS

Means of Influence (In order of decreasing influence)	Company Type
1. Subjective judgments influence allocation of corporate bonus pool to groups, divisions, and individuals	3 IGDs
2. One or more variables in bonus formula determined subjectively	2 IGDs
3. Paid award frequently very different from amount computed by bonus formula	1 AGD
4. Revisions of bonus formula made frequently (more often than once a year)	1 IGD
5. None of the above	4 AGDs

The following firms participated in this study:

IGDs:	AGDs:
Borg-Warner	AMF
Corning Glass Works	Gulf + Western Industries
General Electric	ITT
Honeywell	Midland-Ross
3M	Sybron
Westinghouse	

The results of this investigation are summarized in Figures 26-3 and 26-4. The IGDs and AGDs studied did tend to answer question four very differently. While all six IGDs based division general manager incentive awards in part on corporate performance, corporate performance affected divisional general manager awards in only one of the five AGDs examined. In addition, considerably more discretion generally was employed in determining executive performance in IGDs than in AGDs. For example, in all six IGDs, one or another of the four mechanisms for exercising such discretion shown in Figure 26-4 was being employed; while in all but one of the AGDs, awards were determined by formula based entirely on quantitative measures of divisional performance.

Pitts 1976. These systematic differences in the responses of IGDs and AGDs to questions two and four prompted the author to speculate whether further systematic differences might exist with respect to question three. Investigation of this question was simplified in two respects. First, research was limited to a single aspect of interdivisional transactions--those involving managerial personnel. Second, the extent to which firms had in fact experienced such transactions, rather than the policies encouraging them, were studied.

Ten firms were selected for study. Each had 1973 corporate sales between $500 million and $1 billion dollars, derived less than 60 percent of corporate sales from its largest product-market area, operated in at least five other product-market areas each of which generated more than 5 percent of corporate sales, and reflected this diversity by an organization structure consisting of six or more operating divisions. As in the studies described above, each firm had achieved recent diversification almost wholly by a single route--either by internal expansion or by acquisition. While the IGD-AGD terminology was retained, definitions of these terms were modified slightly. Cumulative dollar sales, at the time of acquisition, of diversifying acquisitions made between 1964 and 1974 was computed as a percentage of each firm's 1964 sales. For IGDs this percentage was set at 5 percent or less; for AGDs at 50 percent or more.

Information on interdivisional managerial transfers was obtained through either a face-to-face or a telephone interview with a corporate executive in each of the nineteen firms studied--generally with the corporate vice president of personnel or with his equivalent. For research purposes, a division was defined as the lowest-level organizational unit having responsibility for manufacture and sale of a product line. Two data were obtained on each of a firm's division general managers: first, whether he had ever worked previously in another division of the same company and, second, whether he had done so within the three-year period immediately preceding the research. The percentage of a firm's division general managers falling into either category then was computed. These percentages are shown in Table 26-2. As it can be seen, interdivisional transfer of management personnel had been far more frequent in all four IGDs than in any of the six AGDs studied.

EXPLANATION OF RESEARCH FINDINGS

Any generalizations from the findings of these three studies must be qualified in several respects. First, only a small number of firms relative to the population of all diversified firms were examined in each study. Second, investigation was in each case limited to large firms only. Third, because data on dependent variables were not publicly available, accessibility to company management was an important consideration in choosing firms for research. Sample

TABLE 26-2.

PERCENTAGE OF DIVISION GENERAL MANAGERS WHO HAD WORKED IN ANOTHER DIVISION OF THE SAME COMPANY

Internal Growth Diversifieds	At Any Time During Their Careers	Within the Past Three Years
A	66%	0%
B	100	62
C	100	44
D	100	56
Average for IGDs	92%	41%
Acquisition Growth Diversifieds		
M	26%	0%
N	04	03
O	16	16
P	0	0
Q	0	0
R	0	0
Average for AGDs	08%	03%

The following firms participated in this study:

IGDs:	AGDs:
Corning Glass Works	Alco Standard
Ethyl	Dart Industries
Owens-Corning Fiberglass	Indian Head
Rohm & Haas	Walter Kidde
	Northwest Industries
	SCM

selection was not strictly random. On the other hand, with one or two minor exceptions, firms were selected for study without prior knowledge of their practices with respect to the dependent variables of interest.

In spite of these limitations, these findings do point out some interesting patterns in the way large U. S. firms currently are managing diversity. More specifically, they indicate that successful pursuit of internal diversification may require a quite different set of policies with respect to location of major activities, interdivisional transfer of personnel, and measurement of managerial performance than diversification by acquisition. The purpose here is to speculate on the nature of this requirement.

A useful point of departure is consideration of the competence upon which successful diversification by either avenue is based. One perceptive student of corporate strategy has pointed out that, "the strengths of a company which constitute a resource for...diversification occur primarily through experience in making and marketing a product line" [1]. Yet, diversifying firms by our definition of this term move into businesses involving entirely new products and customers. Product and market experience gained from their original businesses is likely to be of little direct use in these new ventures. In light of this fact, how can the "distinctive competence" of diversified firms be characterized?

INTERNAL GROWTH DIVERSIFIEDS

IGDs first are considered. Their substantial corporate research staffs relative to AGDs suggest that they may possess a primarily technological "distinctive competence." It would appear, for example, that Corning Glass Works' primary competitive advantage when they move into a new business area is its unique technological capabilities in glass manufacture. Similarly, Rohm and Haas' successful diversification appears to have been based importantly on its superior technological competence in several specialty chemical areas. But why centralize this competence at the corporate level rather than dispersing it among divisions? Two factors may account for this. First, an IGD's divisions are likely to be similar technologically since they generally will have been spawned from the same technology. Under such conditions centralization of research avoids costly duplication which would occur if this activity were conducted independently by divisions. Second, centralization permits underwriting of much larger research efforts than could be supported by divisions doing research independently.

Concentrating research at the corporate level involves a cost because it takes away from divisions an activity which vitally can affect their performance. With division autonomy thus substantially reduced, additional reduction in autonomy resulting from policies to encourage interdivisional personnel transfers is perhaps modest and poses few additional costs. With division autonomy relatively low, division management cannot be held entirely accountable for divisional result. This fact helps to explain why IGDs avoid measuring division general manager performance strictly on the basis of quantitative measures of division performance and prefer instead to employ multiple performance measures determined in part subjectively.

ACQUISITION GROWTH DIVERSIFIEDS

AGDs may have considerably more at stake in preserving high division autonomy than IGDs. In fact, an AGD's continued growth may depend to a large extent on its ability to do so. Consider for a moment the difficult situation an AGD faces as it moves into a new business area. Its corporate management, like its counterpart in IGDs, generally will lack experience with respect to the new business' products and markets. AGD top management will suffer an additional handicap. Unlike its IGD counterpart whose unique technological skills can compensate frequently for product and market inexperience AGD corporate management generally will possess no technological competence applicable to a newly acquired business. Consequently, it will be forced to rely much more heavily on the skills and the capabilities residing within its acquired businesses.

This necessity has two important consequences. First, when making an acquisition, an AGD cannot simply acquire the assets, product rights, and distribution channels of a company. It also must secure a company's management talent. Furthermore, in order to ensure the continued success of acquired businesses, it must retain and must motivate acquired managers.

These consequences impose fairly rigid organizational constraints upon AGDs. A manager of an acquired division accustomed typically to many years of operating an independent company is likely to resent infringement upon autonomy --to such an extent, in fact, that he very well may resign rather than subject himself to any appreciable diminution in autonomy. The resignation of key managers in several divisions is likely, in turn, to deal two devastating blows to an AGD. First, performance of the affected divisions is likely to suffer since corporate management--limited to a small number of general managers with lean staffs in finance, accounting, law, and public relations--will generally not itself have sufficient experience in an acquired division's business to manage it successfully. Equally important, any wholesale resignation of top division managers increases an AGD's difficulty in attracting future acquisition candidates, since top management of the latter are likely to scrutinize carefully any acquiror's organization policies and to shun those which do not guarantee divisions of high autonomy following acquisition.

While others have concluded that the unique competence of AGDs is their ability to obtain and to allocate efficiently financial resources, the findings presented here lead to quite a different view [11]. They suggest that equally critical may be their capability to attract, to retain, and to motivate acquired managers. AGDs may be sacrificing deliberately the potential benefits of centralized research and interdivisional transfer of personnel precisely to maintain the extremely high level of division autonomy upon which this capability is based. This view helps to explain the much more objective approach to assessing managerial performance in AGDs as compared with IGDs. Because autonomy of AGD divisions tends to be high, an objective measure of divisional performance becomes a quite valid index of the true accomplishments of their division managers.

IMPLICATIONS

Confident conclusions about the way diversified firms are answering these four questions must await further research of a more statistical nature. Even the preliminary studies reported here may be useful to several groups, including students of business management, business practitioners, and public policy makers. For the former, they provide some initial groundwork for building theory relevant to the management of diversity. For example, they represent an initial effort to define such key variables as extent of diversification, diversification strategy, divisionalization, and autonomy. They attempt, further, to trace important relationships among these variables. This effort results in the identification of two very different species of diversified firm--IGDs and AGDs--suggesting a rudimentary classification for diversified firms. These are, after all, the initial steps required in building theory in any area.

Clarification of the organizational constraints imposed by diversification strategy is of potential use to top managers of multibusiness firms as well. For example, a better understanding in this area might prevent IGDs and AGDs already possessing organizational characteristics appropriate for their type from making ill-advised shifts in growth strategy. Consider for a moment the plight of an IGD whose stock price is high relative to earnings. Top management of such a firm understandably may be tempted to supplement internal diversification by an occasional bargain acquisition. Yet, the findings presented here suggest that unless the prospective acquisition is operating in an area to which the IGD can apply its technological skills, succumbing to this temptation can result in serious difficulties. Top managers of the acquired firm, for the reasons described above, can be expected to react quite negatively to an IGD's organiza-

FIGURE 26-5.

SUMMARY OF RESEARCH FINDINGS

POLICY QUESTION	POLICY RESPONSE	
	IGD	AGD
1. Diversification strategy	Internal	Acquisition
2. Location of activities	Large corporate staff	Small corporate staff
3. Interdivisional transfer of executives	Extensive policies, procedures, and practices to encourage	Few policies, procedures, and practices to encourage
4. Measurement of division general manager performance		
a. Organizational performance affecting awards	Corporate, group and division	Division only
b. Top management discretionary influence over awards	Considerable	Little or none

tional policies. If dissatisfaction results in their resignation, then the performance of the acquired division can be threatened seriously, since corporate management whose competence is building strong businesses around its technological skill will be unlikely to have much to offer a business unrelated to these skills.

AGDs also might benefit from a better understanding of these constraints--particularly those eager to realize the synergistic potential inherent in the merger of previously independent firms [2]. Realization of this potential requires at least some departure from high division autonomy, since synergy can be achieved only by increasing interdivisional coordination and interdependence. Unfortunately, any departure from high autonomy is likely to make it difficult for an AGD to continue both to attract healthy acquisition candidates and to retain and to motivate managers following acquisition. The unexpected and dramatic profit declines posted by Litton Industries, originally an AGD, in the late 1960s may be directly attributable to such a departure as that company shifted its emphasis from high division autonomy to a synergistic systems organization [19].

Finally, the research can provide useful insights for public policy makers. Spokesmen for this group have long been concerned over the increased opportunities for reciprocity attendant upon diversification [12]. Reciprocity is described as occurring whenever one unit of a company improves its competitive position by utilizing the resources of another. For example, reciprocity is said to occur when a division threatens not to purchase from a supplier unless the supplier purchases from a sister division or when a division uses revenues earned in one division to underwrite predatory pricing activities in another. Interestingly, in trying to stamp out such arrangements, public policy makers have focused their energies mainly against AGDs [7]. Yet, the findings presented here suggest that reciprocity is actually much more likely to occur among IGD divisions because they are typically far more interdependent. The findings suggest that policies to discourage acquisitions can do little to reduce reciprocity; and to be effective in this area, public policy makers will have to tackle the much more difficult task of modifying the internal behavior of IGDs whose diversifying acquisition activities are minimal.

REFERENCES

1. K. R. Andrews, *Business Policy Text and Cases*, eds. Learned, Christensen, Andrews, and Guth; Homewood, Il., Irwin, 1969, p. 179.

2. H. I. Ansoff, *Corporate Strategy*; New York, McGraw-Hill Book Co., 1965, pp. 75-102.

3. N. A. Berg, "Corporate Role in Diversified Companies," *Business Policy: Teaching and Research*, eds. B. Taylor and K. MacMillan; New York, Halsted Press, 1973.

4. N. Berg, "Strategic Planning in Conglomerate Companies," *Harvard Business Review*, 43; 79-92 (May/June,1965).

5. A. D. Chandler, *Strategy and Structure*; Cambridge,

Ma., The M.I.T. Press, 1962.

6. D. F. Channon, *Strategy and Structure of British Enterprise*, unpublished doctoral dissertation, Cambridge, Ma., Harvard Business School, 1971.

7. *Conglomerate Mergers and Acquisitions: Opinion and Analysis*, St. John's Law Review, Special edition, Spring, 1970.

8. W. L. Davidson, "Executive Compensation in Diversified Companies," *Compensation Review*; New York, American Management Association, Fourth Quarter, 1971, p. 25.

9. L. E. Fouraker and J. M. Stopford, "Organization Structure and the Multinational Strategy," *Administrative Science Quarterly*, 13; 47-64 (June, 1968).

10. J. C. Kensey, "Dividing the Incentive Pie in Divisionalized Companies," *Financial Executive*, 38; 52-67 (September, 1970).

11. H. H. Lynch, *Financial Performance of Conglomerates*, Division of Research, Cambridge, Ma., Harvard Business School, 1971.

12. J. W. Markham, *Conglomerate Enterprise and Public Policy*, Division of Research, Cambridge, Ma., Harvard Business School, 1973.

13. Markowitz, *Portfolio Selection: Efficient Diversification of Investment*; New York, John Wiley & Sons, 1959.

14. A. T. Martin, "Skills Inventories," *Personnel Journal*, 46; 29 (January, 1967).

15. R. J. Pavan, *Strategy and Structure of Italian Enterprise*, unpublished doctoral dissertation, Cambridge, Ma., Harvard Business School, 1972.

16. R. A. Pitts, "Interdivisional Rotation of Middle Managers in Large Diversified Firms," *Academy of Management Proceedings*, New Orleans, La. (August, 1975).

17. -----, "Incentive Compensation and Organization Design," *Personnel Journal*, 53; 340-48 (May, 1974).

18. G. Pooley, *Strategy and Structure of French Enterprise*, unpublished doctoral dissertation, Cambridge, Ma., Harvard Business School, 1972.

19. W. S. Rukeyser, "Litton Down to Earth," *Fortune* 77;

138 (April, 1968).

20. R. P. Rumelt, *Strategy, Structure, and Economic Performance of the Fortune "500"*; Cambridge, Ma., Harvard Business School Division of Research, 1974.

21. R. D. Smith, "Information Systems for More Effective Use of Executive Resources," *Personnel Journal*, 48; 454 (June, 1969).

22. H. Thanheiser, *Strategy and Structure of German Enterprise*, unpublished doctoral dissertation, Cambridge, Ma., Harvard Business School, 1972.

23. *Top Management Survey*; New York, American Management Association, 1970.

24. L. Wrigley, *Division Autonomy and Diversification*, unpublished doctoral dissertation, Cambridge, Ma., Harvard Business School, 1970.

STUDENT REVIEW QUESTIONS

1. What advantages does Pitts say the divisionalized organization has over the functionally organized firm?
2. List and briefly explain the four policy questions that must be answered by firms pursuing a growth strategy.
3. What are the diversification strategy alternatives available to management? Discuss some of the advantages of each.
4. Summarize briefly the findings of the three studies cited by Pitts.
5. Compare the policy responses of IGDs to AGDs as indicated by the research findings.

REFERENCES FOR ADDITIONAL STUDY

Allen, Stephen A. III, "Management Issues in Multidivisional Firms," *Sloan Management Review*, Spring, 1972.

Daniel, D. Ronald, "Reorganizing for Results," *Harvard Business Review*, November-December, 1966.

Davis, Stanley, "Trends in the Organization of Multinational Corporations," *Columbia Journal of World Business*, Summer, 1976.

Davis, Stanley, "Two Models of Organization: Unity of Command Versus Balance of Power," *Sloan Management Review*, Fall, 1974.

Fouraker, Lawrence R., and John M. Stafford, "Organizational Structure and Multinational Strategy," *Administrative Science Quarterly*, Vol. 13; 1968.

Helbriegel, Don, and John P. Slocum, Jr., "Organizational Design: A Contingency Approach," *Business Horizons*, April, 1973.

Lorsch, Jay W., and Arthur H. Walker, "Organizational Choice, Product Vs. Function," *Harvard Business Review*, November-December, 1968.

Lorsch, Jay W., and Paul R. Lawrence, "Organizing for Product Innovation," *Harvard Business Review*, January-February, 1965.

Mazzolini, Renato, "The Influence of European Workers Over Corporate Strategy," *Sloan Management Review*, Spring, 1978.

Pitts, Robert A., "Strategies and Structures for Diversification," *Academy of Management Journal*, June, 1977.

Scott, Bruce R., "The Industrial State: Old Myths and

New Realities," *Harvard Business Review*, March-April, 1973.

Thain, Donald H., "Stages of Corporate Development," *The Business Quarterly*, Winter, 1969.

SECTION E.

TOP LEVEL LEADERSHIP AND MOTIVATION

27

Management by Cooperation: The Views of Seven Chief Executive Officers*

STEVEN H. APPELBAUM

> *The executive functions are thus to provide a system of communication, to maintain the willingness to cooperate, and to ensure the continuing integrity of organization purpose.*
>
> *Chester I. Barnard*

ORGANIZATIONAL competition has long been accepted as an easy method for improving a company's profitability and productivity. By setting one division against another in "friendly" competition, management has attempted to stimulate employee motivation and at the same time fulfill corporate goals. Competition is symbolic of American business and has been hypothesized as the stimulus responsible for the effectiveness, aggressiveness and success of dynamic corporations.

Perhaps the most extensive studies of variations in group goals are those dealing with "cooperation and competition." A competitive social situation is one in which the goal domains of each group member are such that if the domain is entered by any individual, other group members will, to some degree, be unable to reach their respective goals. A cooperative social situation is one in which the goal domains of each group member are such that if a goal domain is entered by any individual, all other group members are facilitated in reaching their respective domains. In a competitive

---

*Reprinted by permission from the November, 1977, issue of the *University of Michigan Business Review*, published by the Graduate School of Business Administration, The University of Michigan.

situation, goal achievement by one group member to some extent hinders the goal achievement of other members, whereas in a cooperative situation, goal achievement by one member facilitates goal achievement by all others.

While it is difficult to assess and measure the quantitative value of a cooperative management philosophy, the testimony of top cooperative-style managers indicates that qualitative productivity does increase, as this study will show. However, solid management structure is a prerequisite to a high degree of cooperation. This structure must include:

- on-the-job satisfaction built into jobs,
- individuals matched with jobs,
- a clear, unambiguous organization,
- effective communication networks,
- realistic and workable policies and procedures,
- consistency and participation, and approval and support.

To determine the congruency or fit of these factors to management structure, seven major corporations were selected for study. In-depth interviews were conducted with CEO's of these corporations because they demonstrate their endorsement of an open climate, participative management and supportive leadership. It is reasonable to conclude that a system of management by cooperation prevails as well. In every instance, the CEO provided all the relevant data for this undertaking. The companies studied are: American Telephone and Telegraph; ARA Services, Inc.; Sun Oil Co.; Penn Mutual Life Insurance Co.; Dean Witter and Co.; Amchem Products, Inc.; and First Pennsylvania Bank. The executives interviewed contributed contemporary perspectives concerning the state of the arts in the management of their organizations and their styles as well.

THE IMPACT OF MANAGEMENT STYLES

The CEO does not operate in a vacuum. While he must make the current climate effective and the future promising, he is also a captive of the past. The patterns of management styles practiced by the CEO's interviewed were affected by the leadership styles of their predecessors who had managed the organizations along a continuum from extreme authoritarianism to laissez faire and by systems of management ranging from cooperation to competition.

John D. deButts, CEO of American Telephone and Telegraph, indicated that management styles practiced by previous CEO's at AT&T have been uniquely different. He traced his predecessors to demonstrate that the current style is the result of a blend developed from the firm's history:

> The first [CEO] was very definitely the authoritarian type. He issued instructions. The CEO who followed him came up through the personnel department and spent a great deal more time on the human side of business--kind of pulled the group together. The next CEO was a hard, two-fisted line guy who came up through the plant department on the operating side of the business. He was demanding and yet he was extremely understanding. Under my leadership, if you will, we attempt to use a combination of what we call cooperation and what I would call natural competitiveness in any business.

William S. Fishman, CEO of ARA Services, Inc., (formerly Automated Retailers of America, Inc.), a 65,000-employee company with sales in excess of $1.5 billion, feels the management style practiced at ARA, Inc., has perpetuated itself. The reason for this is that the firm acquired numerous corporations which were merged into ARA and which brought with them varied style, character and personality. Fishman stated:

> We had a lot of merging to do with people as well as companies. More particularly people. I think my own style has changed over the last sixteen years from a more direct action-oriented authoritarian management style to a style of more delegation of authority and responsibility. The fact that we grew so rapidly precluded me from relying on the direct orders of authoritarian management if I had wished.

H. Robert Sharbaugh, president and top administrator of Sun Oil Co. indicates the management styles at Sun Oil at all stages of the managerial history of the firm have been consistent with the philosophy or organizational structure as well. He stated:

> Our management philosophy was aimed at building efficiency through integration; efficiency through what you might call sacrifice on the part of any part of the organization on behalf of the whole. Common goals were set up; they were very centrally organized, very functionally identified by activity. I don't believe there is such a thing as a totally decentralized or a totally centralized organization. Total decentralization is

no organization at all.

Charles R. Tyson, the Chairman of the Board of Penn Mutual Life Insurance Co., a 128-year-old mutual corporation with over one million policyholders, chose to approach management on the basis of objectives. He stated that at Penn Mutual:

> We have peer groups together who embrace and discuss various philosophical and actual problems at hand. We have a free and open exchange among these peer groups with little if any rancor involved in the individual rapprochement of the groups. So that the one thing I think that we are blessed with in this company is a lack of internal political activity. And with that we are able to discuss problems and personalities openly, frankly and go home feeling fine.

James F. Bodine, president of First Pennsylvania Bank, described all the management styles experienced during his relationship with the bank:

> I've been here over 25 years and I believe I served under five different presidents and so I have seen a number of different styles. At the outset this was a small one-man shop; I guess you would have to say an autocratic kind of arrangement where everything came to the top, absolutely everything. We had a benign management for a while that inherited a pretty gung-ho organization. It became clear to us after five years that this was the surest way to the graveyard.
>
> In a sense, everybody was working for the same end which was the bottom line of the corporation, which is cooperation--at least it's the ultimate resting place of all that was cooperation, working toward a common end. A problem occurs when individuals are going too far off on their own without guidance or some kind of parameters from the very top.

THE COMMITMENT FOR MANAGEMENT BY COOPERATION

In addition to planning, organizing, staffing, directing, coordinating, budgeting, and other leadership functions, the CEO must have a basic personal philosophy concerning the type of climate he desires within his firm. He has the option to select a climate ranging from competition to cooperation since, conceptually, trends and styles originate at the peak of the organizational mountain. The personal feelings of the CEO concerning an atmosphere of cooperation or competition are essential since the trend and commitment should originate within his office and by his example.

John D. deButts, CEO at AT&T, does not think there is such a thing as managing by competition:

> If you're talking about managing by directive that's different--I don't believe in that. I believe in managing by objectives with such objectives established after cooperation, if you will, and full discussion with all the factors involved. This is the responsibility of the CEO at all times.

Another view of commitment was shared by James Bodine, CEO of First Pennsylvania Bank who stated that he is not supportive of a management by cooperation system:

> Too much cooperation can lead to a very collusive kind of arrangement in which you develop such a team spirit that ultimately people tend to turn off completely. They get too comfortable. And, therefore, I would think that a proper mix is some kind of both. Obviously, I think that too much competition, on the other hand, is destructive. It can completely destroy the organization.
>
> Well, I believe commitment begins in the office of the chief executive. I think that's the fountainhead of the style. I believe that the chief executive is paid to direct from the top. I don't think he's paid to let the rest of the organization run over him.

ARA's CEO, William Fishman, described his personal feelings concerning top level commitment and the managerial climate within his firm:

> Well, we've tried from the very beginning to discourage competition among our senior people or in the vanacular of some companies, corporate politics. We try to discourage company politics and try to encourage a team or what you would call a cooperative approach. This is my responsibility at my level.
>
> The previous owner managed by competition, pitting one man against the other, so in that organization we inherited quite a

> lot of personal politicking and vying for the favor and attention of the top executive. Because I came in the company from the very beginning, as one of the founders, I apparently didn't have the same feeling of insecurity the other corporate executives seemed to have.

Robert W. Swinarton, Vice-Chairman of Dean Witter and Co., leans toward competitive climates as managerial strategies since the nature of his business lends itself naturally to this system:

> Well, of course, we live in a very intense competitive climate, firm to firm. Our competition is not just something that we know is there and we compete with on a silent basis.
>
> The entrepreneurial character of our business and the fact that if you don't like to compete you better not be in this business, is something you can't erase from the internal environment. It's going to be there, and I like it, and I want some of it and feel that it is essential to the nature and type of our business. However, it's got to be a controlled competition and it can't be destructive.
>
> We all have so much trouble dealing with competition on the outside that we don't have to look inside for competition.

H. William Sharbaugh of Sun Oil feels there is a dualism existing between the climates of cooperativeness and competition.

> I believe there needs to be an element of competitiveness (incentive rewards) even in a system that is primarily based on a cooperative element, management cooperation. There are two levels of cooperation which I am interested in building into the organization; one I would characterize as a vertical element which is the sense of mutuality and cooperation in any boss/subordinate relationship, that focuses heavily on the management by objectives concept. There is a horizontal level of cooperation, which I would characterize as a need for recognition on the part of separate parts of an enterprise, the degree to which their performance is to be evaluated in terms of their contribution to the success of the whole. And I think that ought to be related

> to the compensation systems.
>
> The trend and commitment for this system does begin in my office as CEO. In fact it begins by example here and it begins by the degree to which you are willing to admit the deep degree of interdependence that there is. The more sense of interdependence that you can build the more likely you can maintain an atmosphere of cooperation while you have a part of the compensation systems admittedly operating on the basis of competition.

TRIANGULAR RELATIONSHIP I:

COOPERATION, COMMUNICATIONS AND INTERPERSONAL RELATIONSHIPS

At all times within the corporate structure, a direct relationship exists consisting of management by cooperation, communication and interpersonal relationships. This relationship can be viewed within the scope of the organization and its boundaries.

Cooperation and communication will occur with greater frequency between members of a corporation when all are aware of the common goals to be pursued and achieved. Corporate objectives must be fully communicated and take precedence over individual goals or a competitive climate will prevail, aborting the mission. This relationship was explored with the CEO's understudy. In addition, when cooperation and interpersonal relationships are in accord, corporate members feel they have a more favorable effect upon fellow departmental members under this system.

All seven CEO's generally agreed that a relationship existed between a cooperative management philosophy and the interpersonal relationships within the organization.

As John D. deButts of AT&T explained:

> You can't have cooperation without communications. The only way you're going to get cooperation is if everybody understands exactly what the problem is, what the alternatives are, and is in general agreement that the road that the company selects or I select, because I'm the one that has to make the final decision, is the best.

H. Robert Sharbaugh, Sun Oil's Chief Executive, indicated he felt an extremely tight relationship should exist between all three. He indicated this by stating Sun Oil intentionally and purposefully spends extra money to protect the re-

EXHIBIT 27-1. TRIANGULAR RELATIONSHIP

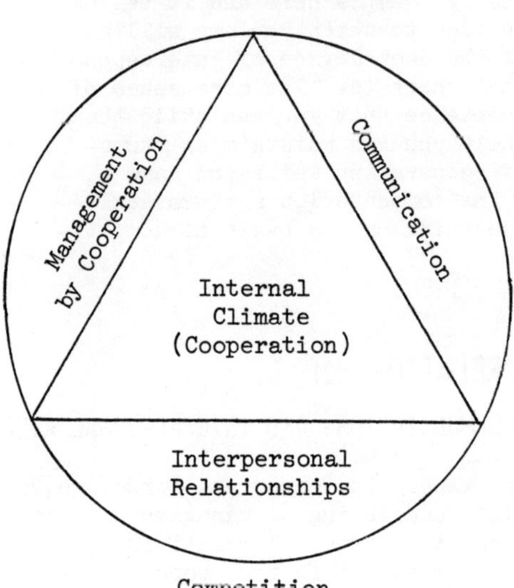

lationship:

> [We] built into our system a direct telephone communications network throughout the U. S. operations from desk to desk. We felt it important that any person in the organization whether hourly, salaried, supervisory, management or whatever, be able to go get information wherever it was, by phone. I also feel interpersonal relationships encompass much more than "good feelings" but actually could be evaluated in terms of productivity. In the sense of mutuality and cooperation, it is an essential part of a cooperative style. In my way of thinking it enhances productivity. Productivity is best achieved when there is a clarity of understanding that an individual is not all alone, so to speak, in his or her efforts to achieve that purpose.

TRIANGULAR RELATIONSHIP II:

COOPERATION, DECISION-MAKING AND PRODUCTIVITY

Another relationship was quite apparent as a result of the CEO's philosophy and style. Within the corporate structures studied, cooperation, decision-making and productivity effectiveness were all related. This triangular relationship can be envisioned within the scope and boundary of the companies examined.

The measurement of cooperation, as an alternative management style, is difficult. However, managerial studies and testimony from CEO's highlight the fact that the qualitative productivity of an organization increases with the merging of management by cooperation commitment, the decision-making process and productivity effectiveness.

EXHIBIT 27-2. TRIANGULAR RELATIONSHIP

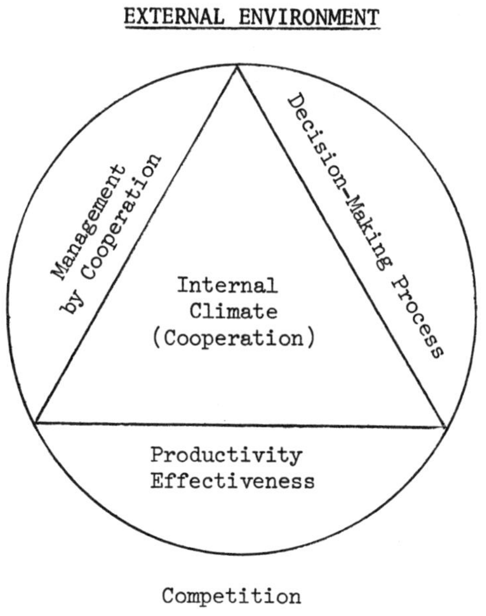

John D. deButts of AT&T examined the three key elements and concluded:

> I don't think you can have proper decision-making unless you have cooperation in order to get the input from those who know what the answers are.

> If you're talking about productivity improvements in an operating department within a company, their ability to improve productivity could depend to a large extent on the cooperation they're getting from other departments--who impact on their departmental operations. And so we spend a great deal of time talking about interdepartmental operations.

William S. Fishman, ARA's chief decision-maker, indicated his organization's style is a combination of varied systems in which participation is a key element:

> In our meetings we have people who represent the whole company and they understand that it's a forum and not a decision-making body. There's no question that our chairman and I always have made the final decisions. We have accepted recommendations. We'll use the committee for advice and counsel, for review, for criticism of part operations, our own decisions included. But when they come in with a recommendation which I don't approve I say to them: "It's your organization, you run it. I don't like your choice." And then they'll come back to me if it works and tell me so and if it doesn't they'll come back and tell me I was right.

TRIANGULAR RELATIONSHIP III:

COOPERATION, CONSISTENCY AND PARTICIPATIVE MANAGEMENT

Consistency within management structure is extremely significant to the organization seeking dependability, reliability, and a degree of homogeneity. The individual within the corporation seeks a degree of consistency in order to determine his role and status so that a counterproductive ambiguous situation will not occur. Closely associated with the need for consistency and cooperation is the degree and level of participation permitted by the organization for its members. There are relationships which exist between an individual's participation in decisions, cooperation, traumas and successes and his level of satisfaction with his corporation. It is essential that these three factors--cooperation, consistency and participation--are considered integral parts of a management by cooperation system and commitment. This relationship is presented in Exhibit 27-3.

EXHIBIT 27-3. TRIANGULAR RELATIONSHIP

EXTERNAL ENVIRONMENT

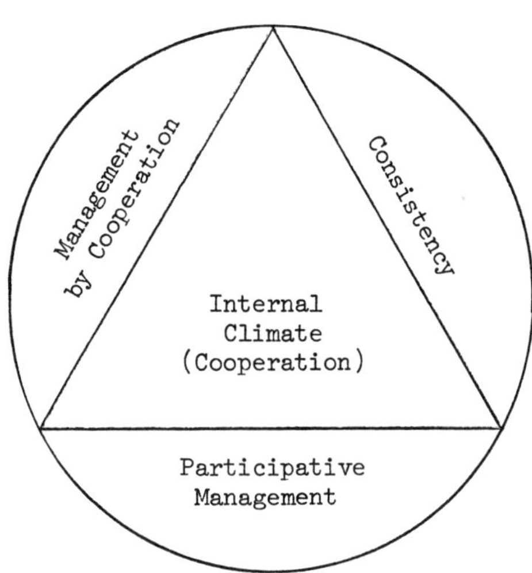

Competition

William Fishman stresses the need for participation, feedback and a consistent climate necessary to insure corporate stability and satisfaction:

> We are in 23 different kinds of service businesses; they vary and we have to adjust. We look upon ourselves not as an organization in the strict sense of the word but as a problem-solving group--almost as a consultants' group.
>
> We print score cards or report cards, as they are, to keep people informed of their performance. We print nearly 4000 computer profit and loss statements every month and each unit manager who manages [only] a cafeteria in a plant gets his own P & L statement. So he knows.

H. Robert Sharbaugh endorsed both a need for a corporate commitment to maintaining internal consistency and for a participative climate to enhance human resource involvement:

> I feel there is an essential need for consistency between the strategic planning process and the operational manage-

ment process.

> Participation works extremely well in a growing organization that's always adding things. But it has no effective way to cope with subtraction. You can't really ask a part of an organization to participate in a decision to subtract itself.

Charles R. Tyson envisions a direct relationship between these elements as part of the cooperative management strategy:

> We try to be consistent with the goals that we have established and the establishment of goals in a pretty tough assignment to begin with.
>
> When the goals are written and produced, they go right through the whole management system. This necessitates participation and we participate to the greatest degree within the firm.
>
> We practice participative management, through cross-fertilization, I guess you might call it, whereby we take an actuary and a salesman and an underwriter and we kick around the problem--through teams. We find that the other side of the fence usually begins to realize that they too have problems. But, cooperation helps to beat the band on all scores, there's no question about it.

James F. Bodine described his managerial philosophy concerning these related elements to be one of being "consistently inconsistent!" This is one way of insuring equilibrium in a dynamic climate:

> Now the world in which we're operating is an inconsistent world--interest rates are going up and down, the economy is up and down, and everything else. And therefore, we are consistent in tying ourselves to that inconsistent world, that changing world. The philosophy at the bank is to encourage a considerable amount of participation in our decision-making processes. We need their sense of participation in order to get their cooperation. On the other hand, we say that our philosophy is never to go so far in the practice of participation as to permit top management to give up its decision-making responsibility.

TRIANGULAR RELATIONSHIP IV:

COOPERATION, APPROVAL AND SUPPORT

Traditional management theories and practices have suggested organizations recognize an employee's contribution by rewarding him via systems of approval and support. However, this process usually takes the form of financial remuneration (bonus, perks, etc.) which is actually given on a one-time basis. The intrinsic value of compensation has some merits but, as a distinct motivation, it is as limited as a vague "slap-on-the-back." Support and approval systems are component parts of a management by cooperation strategy and must also be interrelated with the previous elements described--consistency and participation for total individual and organizational effectiveness. This unique yet important "soft" triad is presented in Exhibit 27-4.

EXHIBIT 27-4. TRIANGULAR RELATIONSHIP

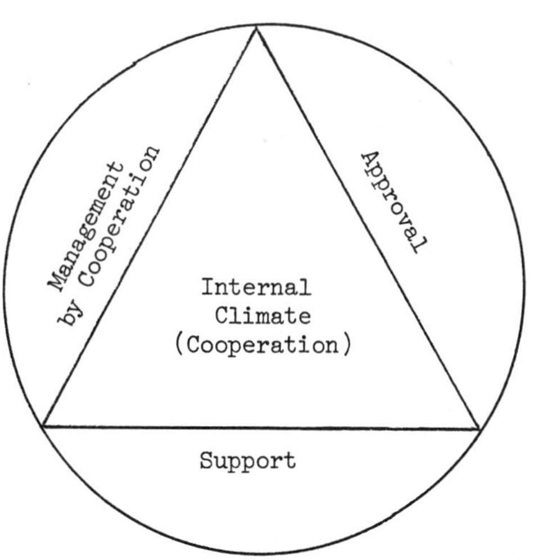

H. Robert Sharbaugh utilizes a systems approach at Sun Oil to integrate the three elements successfully:

> You actually handle support primarily through the recognition and emphasis of

> the two-way nature of a management by objectives team. [Such as] when you reinforce the idea that when you delegate the right to make a decision you delegate the right to be wrong. And you emphasize the two-way nature of a management by objectives process so that your managers have to be addressing the question to those whom they manage, "What can I do to support you in achieving what it is you're trying to achieve? What can I do that would get more information for you, to support, to back you up, to take your part in whatever dialogue is taking place surrounding a decision to be made?" The support systems have to be, I believe, internal to management. You do this through internalizing a sense that, as supervisor, you're accountable for providing the support necessary to hold another supervisor accountable to use the authority that has been delegated to him.

Eugene A. Snyder, CEO of Amchem Products, Inc., also utilized financial measures to demonstrate approval and support of his personnel. His system is a bit softer but focuses upon performance as a basis for effectiveness:

> We show our approval in the marketing area by obviously paying the going rate at the very least, the competitive rate; then we have a compensation incentive plan which rewards individuals in terms of individual performance.
>
> Performance is always the very least budget consideration and in just about all cases, if possible, [rewards are] premised on and based on improvement in the sales area (for people who have no profit responsibility) and profit improvement, incremental improvement over the prior year, by way of example. This is our method of rewarding.
>
> With the obtainment of objectives, both sales and profits, we can support the organization with something that is probably important to everybody--job security. We can support the various individuals and various functions with cash--certainly with competitive wages and competitive compensation plans.

ROLE OF THE CEO:

ARBITRATOR, MEDIATOR OR JUDGE?

Hypothetically, the CEO is expected to demonstrate patterned behaviors which can be anticipated by his subordinates. These expectations actually shape the role he is to play within his corporation. Roles are expected behaviors and help to decrease the frustration, anxiety and ambiguity felt by subordinates. It is not entirely clear whether the CEO must be an arbitrator, a mediator, or even judge in managing the fiscal, physical and human resources of the firm. He will assume varied roles and styles along the leadership continuum based upon the corporate and CEO philosophy of management by cooperation as opposed to management by competition. Systems of cooperation are strengthened when all win-lose competitive situations are discouraged by the CEO who cognizantly attempts to eliminate this one-reward, win-lose value dilemma. Collaborative efforts and cooperative systems maximize organizational effectiveness and should be employed with an equal distribution of rewards contributing to the achievement of organizational goals. This can, in addition, clarify the often enigmatic role of the CEO, who may be an arbitrator, mediator and/or judge in balancing the sensitive components of his corporation.

John D. deButts assumes a multiple role in which he occupies all positions:

> Sometimes you're a listener, trying to get all the facts you can as to why the problem is there, what's behind it, what the positions are of the people. Sometimes you attempt to, through discussion, get them to reach the conclusion themselves. You can call that mediation. Sometimes it gets around to the point where you get a head-on collision and somebody's got to make a decision and I make the decision, and that's arbitration.

William S. Fishman feels he is actually a mediator as the CEO of ARA:

> In the last analysis, I'm a judge, because when there is a conflict that can't be resolved by the people working with each other, then it has to be settled. But for the most part I'm a mediator, I bring people together to work through their problems with each other rather than through me. Very rarely does anybody make an appointment to see me. The door's open mostly, and they walk in.

Robert W. Swinarton, of Dean Witter and Co., feels the CEO must assume a multiple role within his firm:

> Maybe the CEO has to be all of those things. Every conflict has its different routes. I

> think you have to pick the one that suits the particular problem. Basically I think I would like to have those conflicts brought to the surface so that they don't fester, and then be resolved by the parties that are involved in an amicable and satisfactory way, looking at the ultimate objectives of the firm. Cooperation within the firm and competition outside this firm must be achieved since rewards are limited.

MEASURING MANAGEMENT BY COOPERATION

In addition to the difficulties arising out of the attempt to determine the role of the CEO, corporations are equally puzzled in attempting to measure a management by cooperation program.

It is difficult for management in general, and the CEO in particular, to be expected to commit the technical, managerial and human resources of the firm to a contemporary leadership philosophy without being able to evaluate and measure the success, effectiveness and impact of this management by cooperation system upon the organization. The development and implementation of a goal-oriented approach based upon a human resource blueprint must be qualitatively accountable in its quest to achieve viability, effectiveness and perpetuation. These human resource/behavioral science efforts basically fail because they are over generalized and faddish, while the "real-world" requirements stress valid evaluation and feedback.

William D. Fishman evaluates management by cooperation by applying some financial measures to a broad-based objective approach:

> Well, we do it by budgets and planning--both money budgets and people budgets. And we reward and motivate senior management, all the way down the line, on the number of people they develop each year. We work from a goal system, I guess you would call it MBO. In this type of business, people are our greatest asset and while they're not on our balance sheet, we believe (and we suffered the consequences sometimes of not believing) that if we don't manage our people and develop them and lead them and nurture them, the numbers on the balance sheet will change so fast that it'll make the company look like it's gone from one form to another overnight.

H. Robert Sharbaugh does not feel pure quantitative indices can accurately evaluate the impact of a program. Rather, management must rely on qualitative elements as they reflect the process of a program in operation:

> In effect, when you begin concentrating on the management processes that you're building rather than the procedures and you intend for those processes to reinforce the sense of cooperation, then you measure whether or not you're achieving it through, in effect, the sense of compatibility there is between what's occurring in an organization--are the processes being used in the way they were designed, and the purposes for which they were designed.

James F. Bodine, CEO of First Pennsylvania Bank feels competitive systems actually reflect a firm's ability to be more precise in evaluating a system. He further commented that cooperation was somewhat too soft to employ as an index in this evaluation of the success-impact of a program:

> I would like to also have a certain amount of banging heads. I'll use the word conflict as opposed to competition. I think a certain amount is necessary. I think it creates a certain amount of insecurity, which is good.
>
> If the chief executive makes it clear that the principal thing that is going to motivate him in terms of individual decision-making is performance, and if conflict produces greater performance, then I think the firm is ahead of the game. He's the boss and it's his game!

THERE ARE REMEDIES

While there is not an abundance of blueprints to encourage management by cooperation and discourage management by competition, there are procedures and value systems which can be utilized by the CEO and other top leadership to avoid counterproductive situations which are difficult to remedy while trying to balance organizational goals and individual objectives. One of the key elements to employ is a strategy of problem identification and prevention prior to applying the proverbial Band-aid to a tumor.

There are four conditions essential for the establishment of a cooperative relationship based on trust. First, each individual must be committed to reaching some goal where the commitment is such that failure to achieve the goal would cost him more than he would be willing to risk in an uncertain venture. Second, each individual must know that he cannot reach the goal without the help of other persons. Third, each individual must know that other persons are similarly dependent upon him for their rewards; that is, that all the members of the association are interdependent. Fourth, each individual must know that the others are each aware that the members are all mutually interdependent.

Chief executive officers must adopt some measures which will be able to minimize interdepartmental competition and emphasize the importance of managerial contributions. To prevent debilitating and wasteful competitive pressures, the CEO should consider:

> High priority to improving communications between department within an organization, thus increasing interaction and teamwork.
>
> Rewards allocated on a proportionate (rather than a simple win-lose) basis, with the lion's share going to those departments that do the most to further corporate goals.
>
> Regular rotation, where feasible, of departmental personnel to create mutual awareness of other persons' problems, thus furthering understanding and reducing conflict.
>
> Clear and understandable corporate goals; confusion because of ambiguous and unusual goals can only increase misunderstanding and distrust.
>
> Positioning corporate goals in such a way that in attaining them, individual goals are fulfilled at the same time.
>
> Availability of management courses stressing techniques in conflict resolution and interpersonal peace-making.

The foundations upon which American corporations have been founded, namely aggressiveness, competitiveness and the spirit of winning are not working within contemporary firms examined by this and other studies. An alternative management strategy and philosophy based on cooperation should be considered.

When the CEO has lucidly defined the purpose of his corporation, he has, at the same time, made a commitment to an alternative management strategy as well.

> *An organization is a system of cooperative human activities the functions of which are (1) the creation, (2) the transformation, and (3) the exchange of utilities. It is able to accomplish these functions by creating a cooperative system.*
>
> *Chester I. Barnard*

REFERENCES FOR STUDY

Appelbaum, Steven H. "An Experiential Case Study of Organizational Suboptimization and Problem Solving," *Akron Business and Economic Review,* Vol. 6, No. 3, Fall, 1975, pp. 13-16.

Appelbaum, Steven H. "Changing Attitudes: A Path to the Management of Conflict," *The Personnel Administrator,* Vol. 19, No. 4, June, 1974, pp. 23-25.

Barnard, Chester I. *The Functions of the Executive.* Cambridge, Massachusetts: Harvard University Press, 1938, p. 334.

Brickman, Philip (ed). *Social Conflict.* Lexington, Massachusetts: D. C. Heath & Co., 1974, p. 529.

Cathcart, Robert S. and Larry A. Samovar. *Small Group Communication: A Reader,* 2nd ed.; Dubuque, Iowa: Wm. C. Brown Publishers, 1974, p. 415.

Coleman, James C. and Constance L. Hammen. *Contemporary Psychology and Effective Behavior.* Glenview, Illinois: Scott, Foresman and Co., 1974, p. 562.

Deutsch, Morton. "An Experimental Study of the Effects of Cooperation and Competition Upon Group Processes," *Human Relations,* July, 1949, pp. 199-231.

Filley, Alan C. *Interpersonal Conflict Resolution.* Glenview, Illinois: Scott, Foresman and Co., 1975, p. 180.

Newman, William H., Charles E. Summer and E. Kirby Warren. *The Process of Management,* 3rd ed.; Englewood Cliffs, New Jersey: 1972, p. 748.

Porter, Lyman W. "Organizational Patterns of Managerial Job Attitudes," *American Foundation for Management Research,* 1964, p. 61.

Rhenman, E., L. Stromberg and G. Westerlund. *Conflict and Cooperation in Business Organizations.* London, England: Wiley Interscience, 1970, p. 116.

Shaw, Marvin E. *Group Dynamics: The Psychology of Small Group Behavior.* New York: McGraw-Hill Co., 1971, p. 414.

STUDENT REVIEW QUESTIONS

1. Explain what a cooperative social situation is.
2. What was the impact of past management styles on the present managers interviewed by Appelbaum?
3. Discuss the relationships among cooperation, communication and interpersonal relationships (Triangular Relationship I).
4. What should be the role of the CEO in a system of management by cooperation?
5. What are the conditions that are essential for the establishment of a cooperative relationship based on trust?

28

How to Motivate Corporate Executives to Implement Long-Range Plans*

JACOB NAOR

TOP MANAGEMENT IS showing a renewed interest in corporate long-range planning.[1] The periodic shortages of energy and other basic materials in recent years have underscored the need for improvements in the planning process.

A major problem in corporate long-range planning is that these plans generally are focused on the short run, and thus are not truly strategic.[2] For long-range planning to become or remain an effective managerial tool, changes in managerial attitudes and behavior are necessary. It is argued that the corporate incentive structure, centered on bonuses and promotions, is one of the most fundamental factors underlying managerial behavior.[3] Therefore, if top managers want changes in long-range planning practices of division managers, changes in the incentive structure *as it applies to long-range planning* will be necessary.

This article expands on the issue of tying the incentive structure (bonuses and promotions) to corporate long-range plans. Current practices and problems regarding incentives and long-range planning will be examined, and on them will be based proposals for change. Emphasis will be placed on planning by divisions, focusing primarily on growth-division planning, because the need for improvements in planning by such divisions will be greater than that for no-growth divisions.[4] The article will conclude with some problems that may be encountered with the proposed approach and suggestions for their solution.

---

*From *MSU Business Topics*, Summer, 1977, pp. 41-45. Reprinted by permission of the publisher, Division of Research, Graduate School of Business Administration, Michigan State University.

In order to assess corporate long-range planning problems, extensive interviews were conducted during the summer and fall of 1974 in ten midwestern capital goods and consumer goods companies.[5] The net sales of the participating companies ranged in 1973 from under $100 million to somewhat over $1 billion, averaging for all companies $428 million. Six of the companies served capital goods markets; the remainder manufactured consumer nondurable goods (three) and industrial nondurable goods (one). Twenty-eight executives were interviewed, ranging from top level functional headquarter executives to division heads and corporate planning directors. The proposed approach concerning the tying of the corporate incentive structures to long-range plans crystallized in the course of these interviews.

CRITERIA FOR THE IDENTIFICATION OF LONG-RANGE PLANNING PROBLEMS

An examination of planning problems requires at the outset the establishment of criteria for identifying such problems. Following are three suggested criteria, the violation or nonimplementation of which will be considered a planning problem.

The goal of long-range planning. Achieving the basic goal of long-range planning is seen as the main criterion. There is wide support in the planning literature for the proposition that the basic goal of long-range planning is to assure the continuing health and vitality of firms.[6] This stresses the aim of maintaining both the life of firms *and* their growth on a continuing basis. The viability and growth of the *entire* organism are stressed, not specifically those of any of its separate components (divisions). Thus, failure to contribute toward the continuing health and vitality of the firm will be considered a basic planning problem.

Plan implementation. Effective implementation is recognized as a test of the entire planning process. Allowances must be made here for those portions of the plan for which implementation becomes undesirable due to changes in the plan environment. Effective plan implementation of the *remaining* portions of the plan is, however, critical to the viability of the process. Thus, failure to implement such portions of the plan will be considered a planning problem.

Control. Control will be thought of as involving the following activities: (1) comparison of actual performance to planned targets; (2) evaluation of differences; (3) feed-forward of the results of the evaluation into the formulation or reformulation of targets. Failure to effectively control long-range plans through these activities will be considered a planning problem.

CURRENT USE OF THE INCENTIVE STRUCTURE

Bonuses. It was found that the practice of tying division managements' bonuses to the fulfillment of the annual budget targets of such divisions is common.[7] The gross profit of the division, before general overhead allocation, typically is used for such bonus calculations. It provides top management with a readily available, objective measure of performance to which bonuses can logically and easily be tied.

Promotions. Promotions, however, were in no case tied to the budget. Nor, for that matter, were they tied directly to the achievement of long-range plans by any company interviewed. Promotions commonly were tied to past performance over a number of years. In all cases, the evaluation included subjective criteria such as experience, talent, ability to handle people, and so forth.

There seems to be no direct link between long-range (or five-year) plan achievement and the incentive systems of companies.

PROBLEMS RESULTING FROM THE CURRENT INCENTIVE STRUCTURE

Based on the preceding criteria, several planning problems can be traced to the current structure of incentives.

Problems caused by bonuses. Tying the yearly bonus paid to divisional managers to the *budget performance* of the division is seen to:

- Strengthen the emphasis on the short term by these divisional executives.[8]
- Encourage a myopic view of the future because current products, markets, and technologies will be stressed in planning, rather than those that should now be developed for future market needs. In the words of one executive interviewed: "Most of the emphasis [of top management] is on the next year. Top people don't worry much about years two to five." Or as a business analyst said: "The executive [typically] stresses the short-term future, two years out."
- Encourage suboptimization of overall corporate goals, since achieving the goals of

the division (which may conflict with corporate goals) will receive prime attention.[9]

- Discourage risk taking for which the payoff is delayed; encourage preference for the relative certainty of the near future; and delay important decisions requiring long lead-times. As an executive of a major consumer goods manufacturing firm said: "Management does not worry about problems [due to excessive stress on short-term results] until they are tough."

In situations where division bonuses are tied to the budget performance of the entire company, all preceding points apply but the third. There is some improvement here in terms of our problem criteria, since the incentive to engage in flagrant suboptimizing activities (such as reducing or completely interrupting divisional research and development activities toward the end of the budget period) will have been blunted. The other points remain, however.

All the enumerated consequences of current bonus policies are seen to violate the goal of assuring the health and vitality of firms. Similarly, the bonus system does not encourage implementation of long-range goals. Instead, it encourages and rewards implementation of short-term goals. As to control, since bonuses are not tied to long-range goals, there is no incentive to compare and evaluate long-term performance, and typically such functions are not performed. There is, then, no feed-forward either. None of the companies sampled used the long-range plan for control. This may have been due in large measure to the lack of an effective tie-in of the incentive structure.

Problems caused by promotions. In contrast to bonuses, which generally are based on objective measures of performance (such as reaching or exceeding a predetermined target), promotions mostly were based on subjective performance criteria. The findings on promotions parallel the findings on bonuses to this extent: None of the companies sampled tied promotions *directly* to the achievement of long-range targets. The impression gained from interviews with planning executives was that the evaluation of a division manager's *planning ability* (a subjective criterion) entered only marginally into promotion decisions. The reluctance of top management to use long-range planning ability as a criterion for promotion may reflect the previously described workings of the bonus system, which counters serious efforts at strategic planning. Top management may feel unable to evaluate long-range planning ability, even if it wishes to do so.

The objective criterion of promotion decisions in the firms studied was "long-run" performance, which usually meant meeting the budget targets several years in a row. This procedure theoretically could have been used by top management as a proxy measure of divisional management planning ability. As used, it measures only the success of a series of short-run operational plans. It fails to reflect the strategic content of such plans, which is clearly at the heart of planning ability.

The findings that promotions are not directly tied to planning ability or to long-range plan implementation and control point to a planning problem, according to our criteria. Also, promotions are not seen as contributing appreciably to the long-run health and vitality of firms.

TYING THE CORPORATE INCENTIVE STRUCTURE TO THE LONG-RANGE PLAN

Since the primary purpose of long-range planning is to assure the continued existence and growth of firms, how can managements' attention both at the top and the divisional levels be shifted from the short run to the long run? The importance of achieving short-run results clearly must not be ignored. They must, however, contribute to the attainment of corporate long-range goals, and not be substituted for them. The danger of stressing the short run at the expense of the long run is ever present. Resisting and counteracting this danger may represent one of the biggest and possibly most urgent challenges confronting management. Since it is argued here that incentive structures as currently constituted, tend to reward short-run accomplishments at the expense of long-run accomplishments, changes with regard to the reward system clearly are needed. Specifically, in order to achieve more effective plan control and implementation, companies should tie managerial bonuses and promotions to the implementation of long-range targets. By proceeding along this line companies could be expected to accomplish the following:

- Bonuses and promotions tied to long-range targets will contribute to the continuing existence and growth of firms. Thus, their application will be in line with accepted goals of long-range planning.
- Plan implementation will improve, since the incentive structure will be tied to meeting or exceeding long-range targets.
- The control aspects--comparison, evaluation, and feedback of results--will be used effectively. They will, in fact, form an essential and indispensable part of planning, thereby completing the planning process and turning it into a closed-loop system.

For all three problem criteria, it appears that tying the

incentive structure to long-range targets will act in the desired direction. It will allow the use of the long-range plan as a strategic control instrument, a use to which it is not now being put. (The budget, of course, will remain the operational control instrument.) It will, as stated, improve plan implementation, since incentives will be tied to long-range plan targets. And long-range planning will be able to contribute more effectively toward assuring the continued existence of firms.

To achieve increased motivation and commitment, long-range planning, particularly in growth divisions, should be carried out interactively by teams including top management and divisional management. The advantages resulting from effective participation are many. They include, for example, greater readiness to accept change, increased motivation, greater sense of responsibility, better decision making, and increased loyalty and innovativeness.[10] These advantages are seen as crucial to the success of the approach advocated here; they will be referred to in the discussion of problems that are likely to arise with the implementation of the approach.

Hypothetical bonus-promotion scheme. The following will serve to illustrate one possible strategy for dealing with the effects of incentives on long-range planning. Other strategies are of course possible. In each case strategies will have to be adapted to the circumstances and to the types of problems encountered.

Exhibit 28-1 on Pages 442-443 presents a hypothetical example of a bonus scheme tied to the long-range plan targets of a growth division. Targets are yearly percentage improvements over a base period, year one. The rationale behind this scheme is as follows:

- The scheme is designed to encourage the *setting and achievement* of higher plan targets (percentage improvements) in later plan years. This is in line with the aim of moving managerial stress from the short run to the long run. (Targets and performance floors in later plan years are thus higher than those in earlier years.)
- Minimum floors for market share, gross return on investment, and gross profit for the division are set. The achievement of such floor targets should indicate average managerial performance, for which no bonus is received. The targets may be set by agreement, interactively, between top corporate management and divisional management.
- Two sets of achievable targets are indicated for each target year, A and B. The lower percentage improvements (A) may be set inter-

actively by divisional management and top management. These targets should be achievable with above average managerial effort and be compensated by a bonus. The higher percentage improvement figures (B) indicate maximum stretching, or estimates of what is achievable with a major effort (outstanding performance). It may be desirable to leave the setting of maximum targets, which require generation of extra effort, entirely to the initiative of the manager concerned. The achievement of profit targets (B) will be compensated by higher bonus rates than profit targets (A).[11]

- Bonus calculation will follow a preset schedule. Bonuses will be paid only if all division performance floors are met and achieved gross profit meets gross profit targets (A) or (B).[12] Higher bonus rates (B) will apply to later plan years and, in each of those, to the portions measuring extra managerial effort (that is, *outstanding performance* less *above average performance.)* The rationale here, again, is to shift managerial stress to later plan years by rewarding the extra managerial effort that will bear fruit in later plan years *more* than that of earlier plan years. The bonus rate schedule may be set interactively by agreement between divisional management and top management. It is likely to represent a compromise between the desire of divisional management for higher initial rates and that of top management for higher delayed rates. Bonuses as calculated here are for the entire divisional management team. The determination of how to distribute the bonus to individual team members may be left up to the teams. It may be arrived at interactively, with one possibility being that of distributing the bonus in proportion to the salaries of team members. Other solutions are of course possible. In all cases it is foreseen that this would be done interactively by all team members rather than by imposition from above.
- Bonus *rates* eventually will flatten out after a series of plans. Growth in the *absolute* amount of the bonus then will occur only through growth in the absolute target amounts. Thus, the scheme is basically a profit-sharing incentive device. This recognizes that promotion of managers generally will occur prior to the flattening out of the bonus rates.

EXHIBIT 28-1.

EXAMPLE OF A BONUS SCHEME APPLICATION TO LONG-RANGE PLAN TARGETS

(YEAR ONE = 100, OTHER YEARS SHOW PERCENTAGE IMPROVEMENT)

	DIVISION PERFORMANCE FLOOR			*GROSS PROFIT TARGETS*		*BONUS*
Year	Market shares[a]	ROI[b]	Gross profit	A	B	Schedule[c] In percentage
1	100	100	100	100		0
					100	0
2	100	100	100	102		10
					104	10
3	100	100	100	104		10
					107	10
4	102	101	102	107		10
					112	10
5	105	102	104	112		12
					118	15
6	109	105	107	118		15
					125	20

7	114	108	112	125		20
					133	26
8	120	111	118	133		26
					145	34
9	127	115	125	145		34
					170	45
10	135	120	133	170		45
					190	55

[a]These will apply to one or more of the main products of the division.

[b]Total gross profit of division over total assets of division.

[c]Bonus percentages of a particular year, for column (A), apply only if gross profit targets (A) have been achieved and are computed on the excess of actual achieved gross profit over the gross profit floor. Bonus percentages for column (B) apply only if gross profit targets (B) have been achieved and are computed on the difference between targets (B) and (A). Any excess of actual gross profit over target (B) will be compensated at rates applicable to target (B). No bonuses will be paid unless all appropriate performance floors for that year are met.

A major criterion for promotion in the growth division will be long-range planning ability. Since planning in such a division will occur interactively with top management, a continuous basis for evaluation will be available.

Top management may want to keep the criteria for promotion completely subjective and may include, in addition to planning ability, previously used criteria such as ability to get along with people, and so forth. It may, however, wish to tie promotions *directly* to long-range plan achievement, thus acquiring an objective criterion base. For example, top management may tie the achievement of a 25 percent improvement in divisional gross profits *in either the sixth or seventh plan year* to the promotion of some or all divisional managers.[13] Or it may want to retain the entire management team for the duration of the original plan. In that case promotions may be tied to the last plan year. Top management does retain some flexibility for rotation of managers, since it can either (1) not tie promotions directly to the plan or (2) tie promotions to any plan year except early years when plan effectiveness is not yet visible.

IMPLEMENTATION PROBLEMS AND POSSIBLE SOLUTIONS

Following are problems that are likely to arise when the proposed approach is applied. Some of them, in particular the thorny problem of uncertainty regarding future occurrences, are met whenever planning is attempted. The problems become more critical, however, when commitments tied to future bonuses and promotions, such as are suggested here, are undertaken. At our present stage of knowledge, suggested solutions must perforce represent a blend of the desirable and the possible. Therefore, the emphasis here will be on the *directions* in which solutions may be found rather than on definitive solutions. Reasonable compromises will be suggested for the present. More satisfactory solutions can be hoped for as our planning ability increases.

Effect of uncertainty on target setting and bonus determination. Uncertainty exists both with regard to the level of all targets included in the scheme and with regard to the probability of attaining those levels. Attempting to tie bonuses to long-range targets whose attainment is uncertain presents a formidable problem indeed. Yet targets must be set if control is to be exercised. Solutions may lie in two directions: use of past experience and use of alternative plans.

Past experience may be used to set the floors, or minimum targets, of the scheme. Alternative plans may be used to isolate and, if possible, eliminate fluctuations *external* to the company's operations. Ideally, these should not enter the bonus calculation. Switching to an alternative plan with its attached bonus schedule when major environmental changes occur could reduce this problem, although losses in bonus accrual still may occur.

Procedure designed to reduce the effects of uncertainty. A procedure such as the following may be used to arrive at a workable solution to the uncertainty problem:

- A series of alternative long-range plans, based on differing sets of assumptions with regard to the environment (inflation, unemployment, growth rate of the economy, and so forth), is worked out *interactively* by teams from top management and from divisional management. Agreement is reached on changes in objectives as assumptions change. Realistic and achievable gross profit growth rates and performance floors are agreed on for each plan.
- Bonus schedules are prepared jointly for the plans. Bonus rates may be held constant across plans, or may vary depending on the projected assumptions. If, for example, a high rate of inflation is forecast in one plan, its bonus rates may be set lower in order not to remunerate increases in expected demand (and gross profit) due to expectation of further inflationary pressures, and vice versa. Upper and lower floors may be set for bonus amounts that can be achieved. Again, this should be done interactively and not by imposition. Companies should strive to maintain bonus amounts in real terms by tying them, for instance, to the general price index. Companies should attempt to reward equal planning and execution effort equally across plans.
- A plan is chosen for implementation. Consensus with regard to the assumption base's probability of occurrence will determine the choice of plan.
- Agreement is reached on the degree of change in assumptions that will necessitate a shift to an alternative plan. Since planning teams will meet periodically to review the results of the plan, the need for a shift to another plan could be reexamined periodically.

  It may be expected that executives will resist switching to alternative bonus plans, since new plans will have lower initial bonus rates. This could result in a tendency to continue old plans beyond their desirable life. Flexibility must be maintained here to avoid such a dysfunctional effect of the scheme. Therefore, incentives should not be curtailed abruptly with the discontinuation of old programs.

The problem will depend in each case on the degree to which the new plan differs from the old. If, for example, all or most programs started in the old plan are continued in the new plan, albeit with reduced growth projections, it may be decided to continue the previous bonus rates. If, however, most old programs are scrapped, a gradual phase-out from the old schedule to the new one may be necessary. It clearly makes no sense to continue to pay bonuses for extended periods for discontinued programs, even if the discontinuation did not result from faulty planning or execution. A reasonable extension during which existing rates will apply may be agreed upon in such cases, allowing the executive team to refocus its attention on the future profitability of the new programs. The transition period may be longer or shorter, depending on the number and extent of new and discontinued programs. The essential point is that changes must be discussed and agreed upon by all team members and should not be abrupt or too frequent. Some reasonable stability with regard to the assumption base may be needed for the success of the approach. Also, the degree to which the earlier cited advantages of team participation will be forthcoming will, to a large extent, determine its success or failure. It may be advisable to proceed gradually and implement those portions of the scheme requiring sacrifices only after a considerable amount of team cohesion and cooperation has developed.

Transfer or promotion of managers. *Managers leaving the growth division*--The problem here is how to remunerate departing managers for past efforts for which delayed fruits should continue to accrue to them. One possibility would be to continue their bonus payments for a reasonable period. The length of this period should be determined by the particular contribution of the individual managers, which will have to be judged separately in each case.

Since it has been suggested that planning will be carried out by joint top management-divisional management teams, judgments as to the particular contribution of candidate managers for transfer could be arrived at to the mutual satisfaction of all sides. Top management will in any event have to exercise skill and sensitivity in its judgment to avoid offending the remaining members of the team.

One positive side effect of the scheme may emerge from tying top divisional management in a semi-contractual manner to the achievement of key portions of the plan. Divisional managers will have an incentive to see such key programs carried through to fruition. This will enhance their ego involvement in the success of the plan, while reducing their incentive for a quick rotation. Greater stability in job tenure, so important for long-range plan implementation, will result. Top management nevertheless retains a degree of flexibility to rotate managers when necessary. It too will be motivated, however, to reduce the rotation of those managers who are in the midst of promising programs.

Managers entering the growth division--Such managers will start at the bottom of the bonus schedule. Their contribution is seen to bear fruits in future plan years. This may cause some problems of administration, since several bonus rates may apply to the same plan year. Operating on different bonus schedules, however, may be quite acceptable to managers as long as such differences are justifiable on the basis of planning tenure.

Top level prerogatives. Top management may be reluctant to surrender some of its power over bonus and promotion decisions. The proposal does indeed move in the direction of a more objective determination of both, limiting the flexibility of top management. The scheme should nevertheless be more effective in achieving long-run improvements in performance than current incentive schemes applied to short-run plans. The negative aspects of using bonuses to reward short-run performance have been pointed out. The positive effects of applying bonuses to long-range targets seem to outweigh by far any undesirable reduction in top management flexibility. The problem of a reduction in top-management flexibility with regard to rotation of managers is more serious. The advantages inherent in the scheme may be considered to outweigh this difficulty.

Postponing rewards. The final issue is that of postponing rewards. Rewards that promptly follow efforts are no doubt more effective than delayed rewards. A lag between effort and reward in the proposed scheme results, however, from the nature of the planning process, since the rewards are tied to the *benefits* of the planning activity and its implementation. Some loss in reward efficiency seems unavoidable. This question is of great importance since a bonus delayed too long may be ineffective as an incentive.

The loss in reward efficiency, however, is not as severe

as it may seem. The improvement index presented should reflect both planning ability and managerial implementational effort. Rewards based on this index do accrue to divisional management, often fairly early. Thus, management is rewarded in reasonable proximity to its effort. Also, the relative *setting* of the bonus rates remains a managerial tool. Levels can be set so as to prevent too great a loss in reward efficiency. It may be desirable to establish limits to the lag between effort and reward, regardless of when the benefit accrued. Postponing the rewards too far into the future will weaken the scheme, while awarding the bonus too soon will negate the basic purpose of the scheme. Here, too, a compromise solution may become necessary.

CONCLUSION

Bonuses and promotions of growth divisional managers should be tied to the fulfillment of long-range plan targets. Such a change in the incentive system is expected to produce desirable changes in managerial behavior. These will include greater stress on the long run by divisional managers, as well as improvements in implementation and control of long-range growth division plans.

FOOTNOTES

[1]Murray T. Grode, "Corporate Planning: A Fact of 'Life,'" *Best's Review* 75 (April, 1975), 83-84; "The Return of the Long-Range Planner," *Dun's Review* 104 (July, 1974), 87; and Joel E. Ross, *Modern Management and Information Systems* (Reston, Virginia: Reston Publishing Company, 1976), pp. 56-57.

[2]E. Kirby Warren, *Long-Range Planning: The Executive Viewpoint* (Englewood Cliffs, N. J.: Prentice-Hall, 1966), chapter 2.

[3]*Ibid.*,p. 59.

[4]A growth division is defined here as one in which most products are in the growth stage of their product life cycle.

A no-growth division will have most of its products in the mature stage of their product life cycle.

[5]Jacob Naor, "Long-Range Planning: An Analysis of Planning Problems and Practices of Medium-Sized U. S. Capital Goods and Consumer Goods Companies," Ph.D. diss., University of Wisconsin, 1976, pp. 52-144.

[6]See, for example, Brian W. Scott, *Long-Range Planning in American Industry* (New York: American Management Association, 1965), p. 21.

[7]Out of seven divisionalized companies at which interviews were conducted, five tied bonuses of divisional management to the division's budget.

[8]For a detailed presentation of this and the following problems within the context of management by result, see Warren, *Long-Range Planning*, pp. 59, 62-70; and George A. Steiner, *Top Management Planning* (New York: Cromwell-Collier and MacMillan, 1969), pp. 101-102.

[9]In organizations that use the profit center concept, performance measurements of divisions (particularly if they are in different types of businesses) often can become dysfunctional. Through maximizing of personal payoff, the behavior of managers can actually run counter to the goals of the organization. See Paul L. Stonich, "Formal Planning Pitfalls and How to Avoid Them, Part 2," *Management Review* 64 (July, 1975), 33-34.

[10]See, for example, Alex Bavelas, "Some Problems of Organizational Change," *Journal of Social Issues* 4 (Summer, 1948), 48-52; and Robert Tannenbaum, Irving R. Weschler, and Fred Masarik, *Leadership and Organization: A Behavioral Science Approach* (New York: McGraw-Hill Book Co., 1961), p. 94.

[11]See Exhibit 28-1, footnote c.

[12]*Ibid.*

[13]Achieving a 25 percent improvement in gross profit *earlier* than the sixth or seventh plan year, however, will not be rewarded by promotion. The aim here is to prevent the increase of current profit streams at the expense of future ones.

STUDENT REVIEW QUESTIONS

1. What is the basic goal of long-range planning?
2. Discuss some of the problems caused by bonuses that Naor identifies.
3. What factors are promotions generally based on? Does this cause any problems?
4. Develop a hypothetical bonus-promotion scheme that will tie them to long-range planning.
5. Explain how the postponing of rewards could be a problem for the new system of bonuses and promotions tied to long-range planning. Discuss ways to alleviate the problem.

29

Increasing Organizational Effectiveness Through Better Human Resource Planning and Development*

EDGAR H. SCHEIN**

INTRODUCTION

IN THIS ARTICLE I would like to address two basic *questions*. *First*, why is human resource planning and development becoming increasingly important as a determinant of organizational effectiveness? *Second*, what are the major *components* of a human resource planning and career development system, and how should these components be *linked* for maximum organizational effectiveness?

The field of personnel management has for some time addressed issues such as these and much of the technology of planning for and managing human resources has been worked out to a considerable degree [24], [10]. Nevertheless there continues to be in organizations a failure, particularly on the part of line managers and functional managers in areas other than personnel, to recognize the true importance of planning for and managing human resources. This paper is not intended to be a review of what is known but rather a kind of position paper for line managers to bring to their attention some important and all too often neglect-

---

Bracketed numbers throughout this article refer to the alphabetized references at the end of the article.

*From *Sloan Management Review*, Fall, 1974, pp. 41-56. Reprinted by permission.

**Much of the research on which this paper is based was done under the sponsorship of the Group Psychology branch of the Office of Naval Research. Their generous support has made continuing work in this area possible. I would also like to thank my colleagues Lotte Bailyn and John Van Maanen for many of the ideas expressed in this paper.

ed issues. These issues are important for organizational *effectiveness,* quite apart from their relevance to the issue of humanizing work or improving the quality of working life [13], [21].

The observations and analyses made below are based on several kinds of information:

- Formal research on management development, career development, and human development through the adult life cycle conducted in the Sloan School and at other places for the past several decades [20], [6], [24], [29], [36], [4], [18];
- Analysis of consulting relationships, field observations, and other involvements over the past several decades with all kinds of organizations dealing with the planning for and implementation of human resource development programs and organization development projects [5], [6], [28], [12], [19], [1].

WHY IS HUMAN RESOURCE PLANNING AND DEVELOPMENT (HRPD) INCREASINGLY IMPORTANT?

THE CHANGING MANAGERIAL JOB

The first answer to the question is simple, though paradoxical. Organizations are becoming more dependent upon people because they are increasingly involved in more complex technologies and are attempting to function in more complex economic, political, and sociocultural environments. The more different technical skills there are involved in the design, manufacture, marketing, and sales of a product, the more vulnerable the organization will be to critical shortages of the right kinds of human resources. The more complex the process, the higher the interdependence among the various specialists. The higher the interdependence,the greater the need for effective integration of all the specialties because the entire process is only as strong as its weakest link.

In simpler technologies, managers could often compensate for the technical or communication failures of their subordinates. General managers today are much more dependent upon their technically trained subordinates because they usually do not understand the details of the engineering, marketing, financial, and other decisions which their subordinates are making. Even the general manager who grew up in finance may find that since his day the field of finance has outrun him and his subordinates are using models and methods which he cannot entirely understand.

What all this means for the general manager is that he

cannot any longer safely make decisions by himself; he cannot get enough information digested within his own head to be the integrator and decision maker. Instead, he finds himself increasingly having to manage the *process* of decision making, bringing the right people together around the right questions or problems, stimulating open discussion, insuring that all relevant information surfaces and is critically assessed, managing the emotional ups and downs of his prima donnas, and insuring that out of all this human and interpersonal process, a good decision will result.

As I have watched processes like these in management groups, I am struck by the fact that *the decision emerges out of the interplay.* It is hard to pin down who had the idea and who made the decision. The general manager in this setting is *accountable* for the decision, but rarely would I describe the process as one where he or she actually makes the decision, except in the sense of recognizing when the right answer has been achieved, ratifying that answer, announcing it, and following up on its implementation.

If the managerial *job* is increasingly moving in the direction I have indicated, managers of the future will have to be much more skilled in how to:

1. Select and train their subordinates,
2. Design and run meetings and groups of all sorts,
3. Deal with all kinds of conflict between strong individuals and groups,
4. Influence and negotiate from a low power base, and
5. Integrate the efforts of very diverse technical specialists.

If the above image of what is happening to organizations has any generality, it will force the field of human resource management increasingly to center stage. The more complex organizations become, the more they will be vulnerable to human error. They will not necessarily employ more people, but they will employ more sophisticated highly trained people both in managerial and in individual contributor, staff roles. The price of low motivation, turnover, poor productivity, sabotage, and intraorganizational conflict will be higher in such an organization. Therefore it will become a matter of *economic necessity* to improve human resource planning and development systems.

CHANGING SOCIAL VALUES

A second reason why human resource planning and development will become more central and important is that changing social values regarding the role of work will make it *more complicated to manage people.* There are several kinds of research findings and observations which illustrate this point.

First, my own longitudinal research of a panel of Sloan School graduates of the 1960s strongly suggests that we have put much too much emphasis on the traditional success syndrome of "climbing the corporate ladder" [31]. Some alumni indeed want to rise to high-level general manager positions, but many others want to exercise their particular technical or functional competence and only rise to levels of functional management or senior staff roles with minimal managerial responsibility. Some want security, others are seeking nonorganizational careers as teachers or consultants, while a few are becoming entrepreneurs. I have called these patterns of motivation, talent, and values "career anchors" and believe that they serve to stabilize and constrain the career in predictable ways. The implication is obvious--organizations must develop multiple ladders and multiple reward systems to deal with different types of people [32].

Second, studies of young people entering organizations in the last several decades suggest that work and career are not as central a life preoccupation as was once the case. Perhaps because of a prolonged period of economic affluence, people see more options for themselves and are increasingly exercising those options. In particular, one sees more concern with a balanced life in which work, family, and self-development play a more equal role [4], [22], [38], [25].

Third, closely linked to the above trend is the increase in the number of women in organizations, which will have its major impact through the increase of dual career families. As opportunities for women open up, we will see more new life-styles in young couples which will affect the organization's options as to moving people geographically, joint employment, joint career management, family support, etc. [39], [3], [2], [17].

Fourth, research evidence is beginning to accumulate that personal growth and development is a life-long process and that predictable issues and crises come up in every decade of our lives. Organizations will have to be much more aware of what these issues are, how work and family interact, and how to manage people at different ages. The current "hot button" is *mid-career crisis*, but the more research we do the more we find developmental crises at *all* ages and stages [33], [35], [16], [23].

An excellent summary of what is happening in the world of values, technology, and management is provided in a recent text by Elmer Burack:

> The leading edge of change in the future will include the new technologies of information, production, and management, interlaced with considerable social dislocation and shifts in manpower inputs. These developments are without precedent in our industrial history.
>
> Technological and social changes have created a need for more education, training,

> and skill at all managerial and support levels. The lowering of barriers to employment based on sex and race introduces new kinds of manpower problems for management officials. Seniority is coming to mean relatively less in relation to the comprehension of problems, processes, and approaches. The newer manpower elements and work technologies have shifted institutional arrangements: the locus of decision making is altered, role relationships among workers and supervisors are changed (often becoming more collegial), and the need to respond to changing routines has become commonplace....
>
> These shifts have been supported by more demanding customer requirements, increasing government surveillance (from product quality to anti-pollution measures), and more widespread use of computers, shifting power bases to the holders of specialized knowledge skills [10 pp 402-403].

In order for HRPD systems to become more responsive and capable of handling such growing complexity they must contain all the necessary components, must be based on correct assumptions, and must be adequately integrated.

COMPONENTS OF A HUMAN RESOURCE PLANNING AND DEVELOPMENT SYSTEM

The major problem with existing HRPD systems is that they are fragmented, incomplete, and sometimes built on faulty assumptions about human or organizational growth.

Human growth takes place through successive encounters with one's environment. As the person encounters a new situation, he or she is forced to try new responses to deal with that situation. Learning takes place as a function of how those responses work out and the results they achieve. If they are successful in coping with the situation, the person enlarges his repertory of responses; if they are not successful the person must try alternate responses until the situation has been dealt with. If none of the active coping responses work, the person sometimes falls back on retreating from the new situation, or denying that there is a problem to be solved. These responses are defensive and growth limiting.

The implication is that for growth to occur, people basically need two things: *new challenges* that are within the range of their coping responses, and *knowledge of results,* information on how their responses to the challenge have worked out. If the tasks and challenges are too easy or too hard, the person will be demotivated and cease to grow. If the information is not available on how well the person's responses are working, the person cannot grow in a systematic, valid direction but is forced into guessing or trying to infer information from ambiguous signals.

Organizational growth similarly takes place through successful coping with the internal and external environment [29]. But since the organization is a complex system of human, material, financial, and informational resources, one must consider how each of those areas can be properly managed toward organizational effectiveness. In this article I will only deal with the human resources.

In order for the organization to have the capacity to perform effectively over a period of time it must be able to plan for, recuit, manage, develop, measure, dispose of, and replace human resources as warranted by the tasks to be done. The most important of these functions is the *planning* function, since task requirements are likely to change as the complexity and turbulence of the organization's environment increase. In other words, a key assumption underlying organizational growth is that the nature of jobs will change over time, which means that such changes must be continuously monitored in order to insure that the right kinds of human resources can be recruited or developed to do those jobs. Many of the activities such as recruitment, selection, performance appraisal, and so on presume that some planning process has occurred which makes it possible to assess whether or not those activities are meeting *organizational needs*, quite apart from whether they are facilitating the individual's growth.

In an ideal HRPD system one would seek to match the organization's needs for human resources with the individual's needs for personal career growth and development. One can then depict the basic system as involving both individual and organizational planning, and a series of matching activities which are designed to facilitate mutual need satisfaction. If we further assume that both individual and organizational needs change over time, we can depict this process as a developmental one as in Figure 29-1.

In the right-hand column we show the basic stages of the individual career through the life cycle. While not everyone will go through these stages in the manner depicted, there is growing evidence that for organizational careers in particular, these stages reasonably depict the movement of people through their adult lives [11], [34], [14], [32].

Given those developmental assumptions, the left-hand side of the diagram shows the organizational planning activities which must occur if human resources are to be managed in an optimal way, and if changing job requirements are to be properly assessed and continuously monitored. The middle column shows the various matching activities which have to occur at various career stages.

The components of an effective HRPD system now can be de-

FIGURE 29-1.

A DEVELOPMENTAL MODEL OF HUMAN RESOURCE PLANNING AND DEVELOPMENT

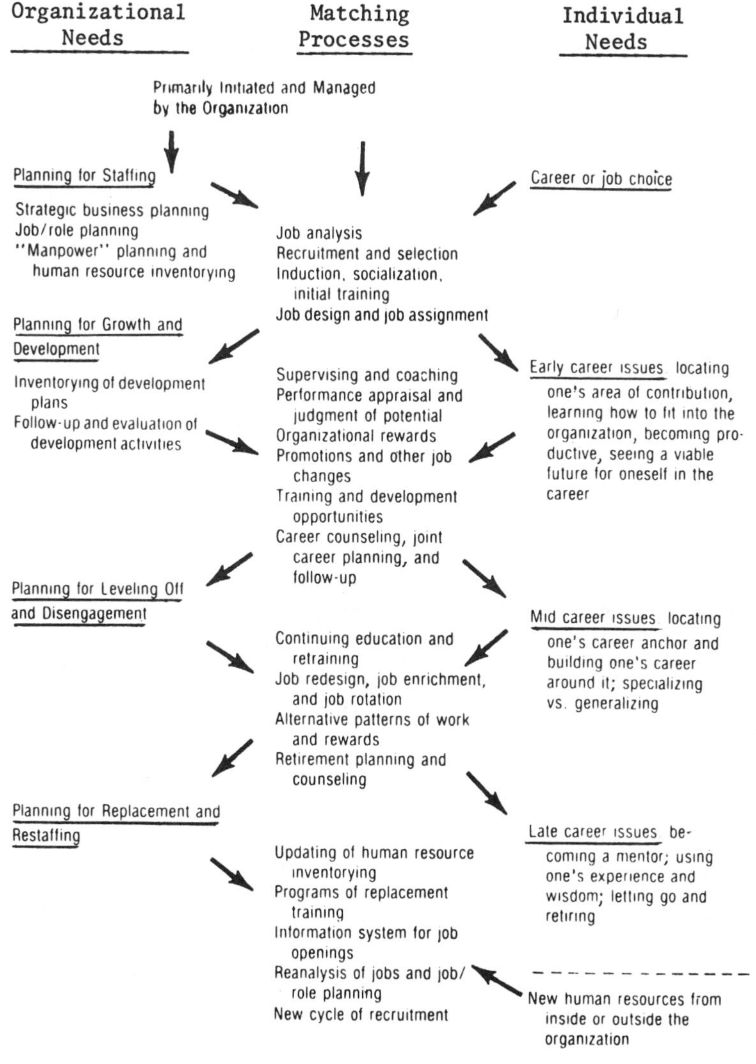

rived from the diagram. *First,* there have to be in the organization the overall planning components shown on the left-hand side of Figure 29-1. *Second,* there have to be components which insure an adequate process of staffing the organization. *Third,* there have to be components which plan for and monitor growth and development. *Fourth,* there have to be components which facilitate the actual process of the growth and development of the people who are brought into the organization; this growth and development must be organized to meet *both* the needs of the organization and the needs of the individuals within it. *Fifth,* there have to be components which deal with decreasing effectiveness, leveling off, obsolescence of skills, turnover, retirement, and other phenomena which reflect the need for either a new growth direction or a process of disengagement of the person from his or her job. *Finally,* there have to be components which insure that as some people move out of jobs, others are available to fill those jobs, and as new jobs arise that people are available with the requisite skills to fill them.

In the remainder of this article I would like to comment on each of these six sets of components and indicate where and how they should be linked to each other.

OVERALL PLANNING COMPONENTS

The function of these components is to insure that the organization has an adequate basis for selecting its human resources and developing them toward the fulfillment of organizational goals.

- *Strategic Business Planning.* These activities are designed to determine the organization's goals, priorities, future directions, products, markets growth rate, geographical location, and organization structure or design. This process should lead logically into the next two planning activities but is often disconnected from them because it is located in a different part of the organization or is staffed by people with different orientations and backgrounds.
- *Job/Role Planning.* These activities are designed to determine what actually needs to be done at every level of the organization (up through top management) to fulfill the organization's goals and tasks. This activity can be thought of as a dynamic kind of job analysis where a continual review is made of the skills, knowledge, values, etc., which are presently needed in the organization *and will be needed in the future.* The focus is on the predictable consequences of the strategic planning for managerial roles, specialist roles, and skill mixes which may be needed to get the mission accomplished. If the organization already has a satisfactory system of job descriptions, this activity would concern itself with how those jobs will evolve and change, and what new jobs or roles will evolve in the future [32].

This component is often missing completely in organizations or is carried out only for lower level jobs. From a planning point of view it is probably most important for the highest level jobs--how the nature of general and functional management will change as the organization faces new technologies, new social values, and new environmental conditions.

• *"Manpower Planning" and Human Resource Inventorying.* These activities draw on the job/role descriptions generated in job/role planning and assess the capabilities of the present human resources against those plans or requirements. These activities may be focused on the numbers of people in given categories and are often designed to insure that under given assumptions of growth there will be an adequate supply of people in those categories. Or the process may focus more on how to insure that certain scarce skills which will be needed will in fact be available, leading to more sophisticated programs of recruitment or human resource development. For example, the inventorying process at high levels may reveal the need for a new type of general manager with broad integrative capacities which may further reveal the need to start a development program that will insure that such managers will be available five to ten years down the road.

These first three component activities are all geared to identifying the *organization's* needs in the human resource area. They are difficult to do and tools are only now beginning to be developed for job/role planning [32]. In most organizations I have dealt with, the three areas, if they exist at all, are not linked to each other organizationally. Strategic planning is likely to exist in the Office of the President. Job/role planning is likely to be an offshoot of some management development activities in Personnel. And human resource inventorying is likely to be a specialized subsection within Personnel. Typically, no one is accountable for bringing these activities together even on an ad hoc basis.

This situation reflects an erroneous assumption about growth and development which I want to mention at this time. The assumption is that if the organization develops its *present* human resources, it will be able to fill whatever job demands may arise in the future. Thus we do find in organizations elaborate human resource planning systems, but they plan for the present people in the organization, not for the organization per se. If there are no major changes in job requirements as the organization grows and develops, this system will work. But if jobs themselves change, it is no longer safe to assume that today's human resources, with development plans based on *today's* job requirements, will produce the people needed in some future situation. Therefore, I am asserting that more job/role planning must be done, independent of the present people in the organization.

The subsequent components to be discussed which focus on the matching of individual and organizational needs all assume that some sort of basic planning activities such as those described have been carried out. They may not be very formal, or they may be highly decentralized (e.g., every supervisor who has an open slot might make his own decision of what sort of person to hire based on his private assumptions about strategic business planning and job/role planning). Obviously, the more turbulent the environment, the greater the vulnerability of the organization if it does not centralize and coordinate its various planning activities, and generate its HRPD system from those plans.

STAFFING PROCESSES

The function of these processes is to insure that the organization acquires the human resources necessary to fulfill its goals.

- *Job Analysis*. If the organizational planning has been done adequately, the next component of the HRPD system is to actually specify what jobs need to be filled and what skills, etc., are needed to do those jobs. Some organizations go through this process very formally, others do it in an informal unprogrammed manner, but in some form it must occur in order to specify what kind of recruitment to do and how to select people from among the recruits.
- *Recruitment and Selection*. This activity involves the actual process of going out to find people to fulfill jobs and developing systems for deciding which of those people to hire. These components may be very formal including testing, assessment, and other aids to the selection process. If this component is seen as part of a total HRPD system, it will alert management to the fact that the recruitment selection system communicates to future employees something about the nature of the organization and its approach to people. All too often this component sends incorrect messages or turns off future employees or builds incorrect stereotypes which make subsequent supervision more difficult [26], [32].
- *Induction, Socialization, and Initial Training*. Once the employee has been hired, there ensues a period during which he or she learns the ropes, learns how to get along in the organization, how to work, how to fit in, how to master the particulars of the job, and so on. Once again, it is important that the activities which make up this component are seen as part of a total process with long-range consequences for the attitudes of the employee [27], [36]. The goal of these processes should be to facilitate the employees becoming productive and useful members of the organization both in the short run and in terms of long-range potential.

• *Job Design and Job Assignment.* One of the most crucial components of staffing is the actual design of the job which is given to the new employee and the manner in which the assignment is actually made. The issue is how to provide *optimal challenge,* a set of activities which will be neither too hard nor too easy for the new employee, and which will be neither too meaningless nor too risky from the point of view of the organization. If the job is too easy or too meaningless, the employee may become demotivated; if the job is too hard and/or involves too much responsibility and risk from the point of view of the organization, the employee will become too anxious, frustrated, or angry to perform at an optimal level. Some organizations have set up training programs for supervisors to help them to design optimally challenging work assignments [26].

These four components are geared to insuring that the work of the organization will be performed. They tend to be processes that have to be performed by line managers and personnel staff specialists together. Line managers have the basic information about jobs and skill requirements; personnel specialists have the interviewing, recruiting, and assessment skills to aid in the selection process. In an optimal system these functions will be closely coordinated, particularly to insure that the recruiting process provides to the employee accurate information about the nature of the organization and the actual work that he or she will be doing in it. Recruiters also need good information on the long-range human resource plans so that these can be taken into account in the selection of new employees.

DEVELOPMENT PLANNING

It is not enough to get good human resources in the door. Some planning activities have to concern themselves with how employees who may be spending thirty to forty years of their total life in a given organization will make a contribution for all of that time, will remain motivated and productive, and will maintain a reasonable level of job satisfaction.

• *Inventorying of Development Plans.* Whether or not the process is highly formalized, there is in most organizations some effort to plan for the growth and development of all employees. The planning component that is often missing is some kind of pulling together of this information into a centralized inventory that permits coordination and evaluation of the development activities. Individual supervisors may have clear ideas of what they will do with and for their subordinates, but this information may never be collected, making it impossible to determine whether the individual plans of supervisors are connected in any way. Whether it is done by department, division, or total company, some effort to collect such information and to think through its implications would be of great value to furthering the total development of employees at all levels.

• *Follow-up and Evaluation of Development Activities.* I have observed two symptoms of insufficient planning in this area--one, development plans are made for individual employees, are written down, but are never implemented, and two, if they are implemented they are never evaluated either in relation to the individual's own needs for growth or in relation to the organization's needs for new skills. Some system should exist to insure that plans are implemented and that activities are evaluated against both individual and organizational goals.

CAREER DEVELOPMENT PROCESSES

This label is deliberately broad to cover all of the major processes of managing human resources during their period of growth and peak productivity, a period which may be several decades in length. These processes must match the organization's needs for work with the individual's needs for a productive and satisfying work career. The system must provide for some kind of forward movement for the employee through some succession of jobs, whether these involve promotion, lateral movement to new functions, or simply new assignments within a given area [30], [32]. The system must be based both on the organization's need to fill jobs as they open up and on employees' needs to have some sense of progress in their working lives.

• *Supervision and Coaching.* By far the most important component in this area is the actual process of supervising, guiding, coaching, and monitoring. It is in this context that the work assignment and feedback processes which make learning possible occur, and it is the boss who plays the key role in molding the employee to the organization. There is considerable evidence that the first boss is especially crucial in giving new employees a good start in their careers [26], [9], [8], [14], and that training of supervisors in how to handle new employees is a valuable organizational investment.

• *Performance Appraisal and Judgment of Potential.* This component is part of the general process of supervision but stands out as such an important part of that process that it must be treated separately. In most organizations there is some effort to standardize and formalize a process of appraisal above and beyond the normal performance feedback which is expected on a day-to-day basis. Such systems serve a number of functions--to justify salary increases, promotions, and other formal organizational actions with respect to the employee, to provide information for human resource inventories or at least written records of past accomplishments for the employee's personnel folder; and to provide a basis for annual or semiannual formal reviews between boss and subordinate to supplement day-to-day feedback and to facilitate information exchange for career planning and counseling. In some organizations so little day-to-day feedback occurs that the *formal* system bears the burden of providing the employees with knowledge of how they are doing and what they can look forward to. Since knowledge of results, of how one is doing, is a crucial component of any developmental process, it is important for organizations to monitor how well and how frequently feedback is actually given.

One of the major dilemmas in this area is whether to have a single system which provides both feedback for the growth and development of the employee and information for the organization's planning systems. The dilemma arises because the information which the planning system requires (e.g., "how much potential does this employee have to rise in the organization?") may be the kind of information which neither the boss nor the planner wants to share with the employee. The more potent and more accurate the information, the less likely it is to be fed back to the employee in anything other than very vague terms.

On the other hand, the detailed work-oriented, day-to-day feedback which the employee needs for growth and development may be too cumbersome to record as part of a selection-oriented appraisal system. If hundreds of employees are to be compared, there is strong pressure in the system toward more general kinds of judgments, traits, rankings, numerical estimates of ultimate potential, and the like. One way of resolving this dilemma which some companies have found successful is to develop two separate systems--one oriented toward performance improvement and the growth of the employee, and the other one oriented toward a more global assessment of the employee for future planning purposes involving judgments which may not be shared with the employee except in general terms.

A second dilemma arises around the identification of the employee's "development needs" and how that information is linked to other development activities. If the development needs are stated in relation to the planning system, the employee may never get the feedback of what his needs may have been perceived to be, and, worse, no one may implement any program to deal with those needs if the planning system is not well linked with line management.

Two further problems arise from this potential lack of linkage. One, if the individual does not get good feedback around developmental needs, he or she remains uninvolved in their own development and potentially becomes complacent. We pay lip service to the statement that only the individual can develop himself or herself, but then deprive the individual of the very information that would make sensible self-development possible. Two, the development needs as stated for the various employees in the organization may have nothing to do with the organization's needs for certain kinds of human resources in the future. All too often there is complete lack of linkage between the strategic or business planning function and the human resource development function resulting in potentially willy-nilly individual development based on today's needs and individual managers' stereotypes of what will be needed in the future.

• *Organizational Rewards--Pay, Benefits, Perquisites, Promotion, and Recognition.* Entire books have been written about all the problems and subtleties of how to link organizational rewards to the other components of a HRPD system to insure both short-run and long-run human effectiveness. For purposes of this short paper I wish to point out only one major issue--how to insure that organizational rewards are linking *both* to the needs of the individual and to the needs of the organization for effective performance and development of potential. All too often the reward system is neither responsive to the individual employee nor to the organization, being driven more by criteria of elegance, consistency, and what other organizations are doing. If the linkage is to be established, line managers must actively work with compensation experts to develop a joint philosophy and set of goals based on an understanding of both what the organization is trying to reward and what employee needs actually are. As organizational careers become more varied and as social values surrounding work change, reward systems will probably have to become much more flexible both in time (people at different career stages may need different things) and by type of career (functional specialists may need different things than general managers).

• *Promotions and Other Job Changes.* There is ample evidence that what keeps human growth and effectiveness going is continuing optimal challenge [11], [18]. Such challenge can be provided for some members of the organization through promotion to higher levels where more responsible jobs are available. For most members of the organization the promotion opportunities are limited, however, because the pyramid narrows at the top. An effective HRPD system will, therefore, concentrate on developing career paths, systems of job rotation, changing assignments, temporary assignments, and other lateral job moves which insure continuing growth of all human resources.

One of the key characteristics of an optimally challenging job is that it both draws on the person's abilities and skills and that it has opportunities for "closure." The employee must be in the job long enough to get involved and to see the results of his or her efforts. Systems of rotation which move the person too rapidly either prevent initial involvement (as in the rotational training program), or prevent closure by transferring the person to a new job before the effects of his or her decisions can be assessed. I have heard many "fast track" executives complain that their self-confidence was low because they never really could see the results of their efforts. Too often we move people too fast in order to "fill slots" and thereby undermine their development.

Organizational planning systems which generate "slots" to be filled must be coordinated with development planning systems which concern themselves with the optimal growth of the human resources. Sometimes it is better for the organization in the long run not to fill an empty slot in order to keep a manager in another job where he or she is just beginning to develop. One way of insuring such linkage is to monitor these processes by means of a "development committee" which is composed of both line managers and personnel specialists. In such a group the needs of the organization and the needs of the people can be balanced against each other in the context or the long-range goals of the organization.

• *Training and Development Opportunities.* Most organizations recognize that periods of formal training, sabbaticals, executive development programs outside of the company, and other educational activities are necessary in the total process of human growth and development. The important point about these activities is that they should be carefully linked both to the needs of the individual and to the needs of the organization. The individual should want to go to the program because he or she can see how the educational activity fits into the total career. The organization should send the person because the training fits into some concept of future career development. It should not be undertaken simply as a generalized "good thing," or because other companies are doing it. As much as possible the training and educational activities should be tied to job/role planning. For example, many companies began to use university executive development programs because of an explicit recognition that future managers would require a broader perspective on various problems and that such "broadening" could best be achieved in the university programs.

• *Career Counseling, Joint Career Planning, Follow-up, and Evaluation.* Inasmuch as the growth and development which may be desired can only come from within the individual himself or herself, it is important that the organization provide some means for individual employees at all levels to become more proactive about their careers and some mechanisms for joint dialogue, counseling, and career planning [15]. This process should ideally be linked to performance appraisal, because it is in that context that the boss can review with the subordinate the future potential, development needs, strengths, weaknesses, career options, etc. The boss is often not trained in counseling but does possess some of the key information which the employee needs to initiate any kind of career planning. More formal counseling could then be supplied by the personnel development staff or outside the organization altogether.

The important point to recognize is that employees cannot manage their own growth development without information on how their own needs, talents, values, and plans mesh with the opportunity structure of the organization. Even though the organization may only have imperfect, uncertain information about the future, the individual is better off to know that than to make erroneous assumptions about the future based on no information at all. It is true that the organization cannot make committments, nor should it unless required to by legislation or contract. But the sharing of information if properly done is not the same as making commitments or setting up false expectations.

If the organization can open up the communication channel between employees, their bosses, and whoever is managing the human resource system, the groundwork is laid for realistic individual development planning. Whatever is decided about training, next steps, special assignments, rotation, etc., should be jointly decided by the individual and the appropriate organizational resource (probably the supervisor and someone from personnel specializing in career development). Each step must fit into the employee's life plan and must be tied into *organizational needs*. The organization should be neither a humanistic charity nor an indoctrination center. Instead, it should be a vehicle for meeting both the needs of society and of individuals.

Whatever is decided should not merely be written down but executed. If there are implementation problems, the development plan should be renegotiated. Whatever developmental actions are taken, it is essential that they be followed up and evaluated both by the person and by the organization to determine what, if anything, was achieved. It is shocking to discover how many companies invest in major activities such as university executive development programs and never determine for themselves what was accomplished. In some instances, they make no plans to talk to the individual before or after the program so that it is not even possible to determine what the activity meant to the participant, or what might be an appropriate next assignment for him or her following the program.

I can summarize the above analysis best by emphasizing the two places where I feel there is the most fragmentation and violation of growth assumptions. First, too many of the activities occur without the involvement of the person who is "being developed" and therefore may well end up being self-defeating. This is particularly true of job assignments and performance appraisal where too little involvement and feedback occur. Second, too much of the human resource system functions as a personnel *selection* system unconnected to either the needs of the organization or the needs of the individual. All too often it is only a system for short-run replacement of people in standard type jobs. The key planning functions are not linked in solidly and hence do not influence the system to the degree they should.

PLANNING FOR AND MANAGING DISENGAGEMENT

The planning and management processes which will be briefly reviewed here are counterparts of ones that have already been discussed but are focused on a different problem--the problem of the late career, loss of motivation, obsolescence, and ultimately retirement. Organizations must recognize that there are various options available to deal with this range of problems beyond the obvious ones of either terminating the employee or engaging in elaborate measures to "remotivate" people who may have lost work involvement [2].

• *Continuing Education and Retraining.* These activities have their greatest potential if the employee is motivated and if there is some clear connection between what is to be learned and what the employee's current or future job assignments require in the way of skills. More and more organizations are finding out that it is better to provide challenging work first and only then the training to perform that work once the employee sees the need for it. Obviously for this linkage to work well continuous dialogue is needed between employees and their managers. For those employees who have leveled off, have lost work involvement, but are still doing high quality work other solutions such as those described below are more applicable.

• *Job Redesign, Job Enrichment, and Job Rotation.* This section is an extension of the arguments made earlier on job changes in general applied to the particular problems of leveled off employees. In some recent research, it has been suggested that job enrichment and other efforts to redesign work to increase motivation and performance may only work during the first few years on a job [18]. Beyond that the employee becomes "unresponsive" to the job characteristics themselves and pays more attention to surrounding factors such as the nature of supervision, relationships with co-workers, pay, and other extrinsic characteristics. In other words, before organizations attempt to "cure" leveled off employees by remotivating them through job redesign or rotation, they should examine whether those employees are still in a responsive mode or not. On the other hand, one can argue that there is nothing wrong with less motivated, less involved employees so long as the quality of what they are doing meets the organizational standards [2].

• *Alternative Patterns of Work and Rewards.* Because of the changing needs and values of employees in recent decades, more and more organizations have begun to experiment with alternative work patterns such as flexible working hours, part-time work, sabbaticals or other longer periods of time off, several people filling one job, dual employment of spouses with more extensive childcare programs, etc. Along with these experiments have come others on flexible reward systems in which employees can choose between a raise, some time off, special retirement, medical, or insurance benefits, and other efforts to make multiple career ladders a viable reality. These programs apply to employees at all career stages but are especially relevant to people in mid and late career stages where their own perception of their career and life goals may be undergoing important changes.

None of those innovations should be attempted without first clearly establishing a HRPD system which takes care of the organization's needs as well as the needs of employees and links them to each other. There can be little growth and development for employees at any level in an *organization* which is sick and stagnant. It is in the best interests of both the individual and the organization to have a healthy organization which can provide opportunities for growth.

- *Retirement Planning and Counseling.* As part of any effective HRPD system, there must be a clear planning function which forecasts who will retire, and which feeds this information into both the replacement staffing system and the counseling functions so that the employees who will be retiring can be prepared for this often traumatic career stage. Employees need counseling not only with the mechanical and financial aspects of retirement, but also to prepare them psychologically for the time when they will no longer have a clear organizational base or job as part of their identity. For some people it may make sense to spread the period of retirement over a number of years by using part-time work or special assignments to help both the individual and the organization to get benefits from this period.

The counseling function here as in other parts of the career probably involves special skills and must be provided by specialists. However, the line manager continues to play a key role as a provider of job challenge, feedback, and information about what is ahead for any given employee. Seminars for line managers on how to handle the special problems of pre-retirement employees would probably be of great value as part of their managerial training.

PLANNING FOR AND MANAGING REPLACEMENT AND RESTAFFING

With this step the HRPD cycle closes back upon itself. This function must be concerned with such issues as:

1. Updating the human resource inventory as retirements or terminations occur;
2. Instituting special programs of orien-

tation or training for new incumbents to specific jobs as those jobs open up;

3. Managing the information system on what jobs are available and determining how to match this information to the human resources available in order to determine whether to replace from within the organization or to go outside with a new recruiting program;
4. Continuously reanalyzing jobs to insure that the new incumbent is properly prepared for what the job *now* requires and *will* require in the future.

How these processes are managed links to the other parts of the system through the implicit messages that are sent to employees. For example, a company which decides to publicly post all of its unfilled jobs is clearly sending a message that it expects internal recruitment and supports self-development activities. A company which manages restaffing in a very secret manner may well get across a message that employees might as well be complacent and passive about their careers because they cannot influence them anyway.

SUMMARY AND CONCLUSIONS

I have tried to argue in this article that human resource planning and development is becoming an increasingly important function in organizations, that this function consists of multiple components, and that these components must be managed *both* by line managers and staff specialists. I have tried to show that the various planning activities are closely linked to the actual processes of supervision, job assignment, training, etc., and that those processes must be designed to match the needs of the organization with the needs of the employees throughout their evolving careers, whether or not those careers involve hierarchical promotions. I have also argued that the various components are linked to each other and must be seen as a total system if it is to be effective. The total system must be managed as a system to insure coordination between the planning functions and the implementation functions.

I hope it is clear from what has been said above that an effective human resource planning and development system is integral to the functioning of the organization and must, therefore, be a central concern of line management. Many of the activities require specialist help, but the accountabilities must rest squarely with line supervisors and top management. It is they who control the opportunities and the rewards. It is the job assignment system and the feedback which employees get that is the ultimate raw material for growth and development. Whoever designs and manages the system, it will not help the organization to become more effective unless that system is *owned* by line management.

REFERENCES

1. Alfred, T. "Checkers or Choice in Manpower Management," *Harvard Business Review*, January-February, 1967, pp. 157-169.

2. Bailyn, L. "Involvement and Accommodation in Technical Careers," in *Organizational Careers: Some New Perspectives*, edited by J. Van Maanen, New York: John Wiley & Sons, 1977.

3. Bailyn, L. "Career and Family Orientations of Husbands and Wives in Relation to Marital Happiness," *Human Relations* (1970); 97-113.

4. Bailyn, L., and Schein, E. H. "Life/Career Considerations as Indicators of Quality of Employment," in *Measuring Work Quality for Social Reporting*, edited by A. D. Biderman and T. F. Drury. New York: Sage Publications, 1976.

5. Beckhard, R. D. *Organization Development: Strategies and Models*. Reading, MA: Addison-Wesley, 1969.

6. Bennis, W. G. *Changing Organizations*. New York: McGraw-Hill, 1966.

7. Bennis, W. G. *Organization Development: Its Nature, Origins, and Prospects*. Reading, MA: Addison-Wesley, 1969.

8. Berlew, D., and Hall, D. T. "The Socialization of Managers," *Administrative Science Quarterly* 11 (1966); 207-223.

9. Bray, D. W.; Campbell, R. J.; and Grant, D. E. *Formative Years in Business*. New York: John Wiley & Sons, 1974.

10. Burack, E. *Organization Analysis.* Hinsdale, IL: Dryden, 1975.

11. Dalton, G. W., and Thompson, P. H. "Are R&D Organizations Obsolete?" *Harvard Business Review,* November-December, 1976, pp. 105-116.

12. Galbraith, J. *Designing Complex Organizations.* Reading, MA: Addison-Wesley, 1973.

13. Hackman, J. R., and Suttle, J. L. *Improving Life at Work.* Los Angeles: Goodyear, 1977.

14. Hall, D. T. *Careers in Organizations.* Los Angeles: Goodyear, 1976.

15. Heidke, R. *Career Pro-Activity of Middle Managers.* Master's Thesis, Massachusetts Institute of Technology, 1977.

16. Kalish, R. A. *Late Adulthood: Perspectives on Aging.* Monterey, CA: Brooks-Cole, 1975.

17. Kanter, R. M. *Work and Family in the United States.* New York: Russel Sage, 1977.

18. Katz, R. "Job Enrichment: Some Career Considerations." in *Organizational Careers: Some New Perspectives,* edited by J. Van Maanen, New York: John Wiley & Sons, 1977.

19. Lesieur, F. G. *The Scanlon Plan.* New York: John Wiley & Sons, 1958.

20. McGregor, D. *The Human Side of Enterprise.* New York: McGraw-Hill, 1960.

21. Meltzer, H., and Wickert, F. R. *Humanizing Organizational Behavior.* Springfield, IL: Charles C. Thomas, 1976.

22. Myers, C. A. "Management and the Employee," in *Social Responsibility and the Business Predicament,* edited by J. W. McKie, Washington, D. C.: Brookings. 1974.

23. Pearse, R. F., and Pelzer, B. P. *Selfdirected Change for the Mid-Career Manager.* New York: AMACOM, 1975.

24. Pigors, P., and Myers, C. A. *Personnel Administration,* 8th ed. New York: McGraw-Hill, 1977.

25. Roeber, R. J. C. *The Organization in a Changing Envi-*

ronment. Reading, MA: Addison-Wesley, 1973.

26. Schein, E. H. "How to Break in the College Graduate," *Harvard Business Review,* 1964, pp. 68-76.

27. Schein, E. H. "Organizational Socialization and the Profession of Management," *Industrial Management Review.* Winter, 1968, pp. 1-16.

28. Schein, E. H. *Process Consultation: Its Role in Organization Development.* Reading, MA: Addision-Wesley, 1969.

29. Schein, E. H. *Organizational Psychology.* Englewood Cliffs, N. J.: Prentice-Hall, 1970.

30. Schein, E. H. "The Individual, the Organization, and the Career: A Conceptual Scheme," *Journal of Applied Behavioral Science* 7 (1971); 401-426.

31. Schein, E. H. "How 'Career Anchors' Hold Executives to Their Career Paths." *Personnel* 52, No. 3 (1975); 11-24.

32. Schein, E. H. *The Individual, the Organization and the Career: Toward Greater Human Effectiveness.* Reading, MA: Addison-Wesley, forthcoming.

33. Sheehy, G. "Catch 30 and Other Predictable Crises of Growing Up Adult," *New York Magazine,* February, 1974, pp. 30-44.

34. Super, D. E., and Bohn, M. J. *Occupational Psychology.* Belmont, CA: Wadsworth, 1970.

35. Troll, L. E. *Early and Middle Adulthood.* Monterey, CA: Brooks-Cole, 1975.

36. Van Maanen, J. "Breaking In: Socialization to Work," in *Handbook of Work, Organization, and Society,* edited by R. Dubin. Chicago: Rand McNally, 1976.

37. Van Maanen, J., ed. *Organizational Careers: Some New Perspectives.* New York: John Wiley & Sons, 1977.

38. Van Maanen, J.; Bailyn, L.; and Schein, E. H. "The Shape of Things to Come: A New Look at Organizational Careers," in *Perspectives on Behavior in Organizations,* edited by J. R. Hackman, E. E. Lawler, and L. W. Porter. New York: McGraw-Hill, 1977.

39. Van Maanen, J., and Schein, E. H. "Improving the Quality

of Work Life: Career Development," in *Improving Life at Work*, edited by J. R. Hackman and J. L. Suttle. Los Angeles: Goodyear, 1977.

STUDENT REVIEW QUESTIONS

1. Why does Schein say human resource planning and development is becoming increasingly important?
2. Explain "human growth" as described by Schein.
3. What is job/role planning?
4. What does Schein mean when he says that the issue in designing the job is "how to provide the optimal challenge"?
5. Discuss briefly what Schein calls "Career Development Processes."
6. What are some of the ways organizations can plan for and manage the disengagement of employees?

REFERENCES FOR ADDITIONAL STUDY

Bailey, J. C., "Clues for Success in the President's Job," *Harvard Business Review*, May-June, 1967.

Brown, Courtney C., "Restructuring the Board: A Director's Perspective," *Management Review*, September, 1976.

Chandler, George A., "A Top Manager in the Middle: A Group President Looks at His Job," *Management Review*, October, 1975.

Daniel, D. Ronald, "Team at the Top," *Harvard Business Review*, March-April, 1965.

Dolmatch, Theodore B., "The Top Manager as Personnel Man," *Personnel*, January-February, 1964.

Groobey, John A., "Making the Board of Directors More Effective," *California Management Review*, Spring, 1974.

Hall, Jay, "To Achieve or Not: The Manager's Choice," *California Management Review*, Summer, 1976.

Katz, Robert L., "Skills of An Effective Administrator," *Harvard Business Review*, January-February, 1955.

Kotter, John P., "Power, Dependence and Effective Management," *Harvard Business Review*, July-August, 1977.

Osmond, Neville, "Top Management: Its Tasks, Roles and Skills," *Journal of Business Policy*, Winter, 1971.

Tilles, Seymour, "The Manager's Job: A Systems Approach," *Harvard Business Review*, Winter, 1971.

Thackray, John, "The Dilemma With Directors," *Dun's Review*, 1967.

SECTION F.

PROCESSES AND SYSTEMS FOR STRATEGY IMPLEMENTATION

30

The Social Response Process in Commercial Banks: An Empirical Investigation*

EDWIN A. MURRAY, JR.

WHEN FIRMS SEEK to interject novel initiatives related to their larger responsibilities to society into traditional, economically-oriented business activities, there may be a need to modify their administrative systems and procedures. These modifications and their implications are the subjects of this paper. They might include new management information systems, changes in organization structure, modified managerial job responsibilities, and revised reward and penalty systems.

THE STUDY

The objectives of the research were: to explore organizational adaptations occasioned by the implementation of corporate social policies in the commercial banking industry; to identify similarities and differences among approaches taken by banks as they responded to various social pressures; and to determine ways in which the structural characteristics of banking organizations influenced their response to social pressures.

In the course of field research involving large decentralized manufacturing firms organized by product divisions, Ackerman (1, 2) observed a fairly distinct pattern of corpo-

---

Numbers in parentheses throughout this article refer to the alphabetized references at the end of the article.

*From the *Academy of Management Review*, July, 1976, pp. 5-15. Reprinted by permission.

rate reactions to social demands which he described as the "social response process". Basically a top-down phenomenon extending over six to eight years, the process consisted of three phases (policy, learning, and organization) roughly corresponding to those organizational levels of management primarily involved (chief executive, staff specialists, and operating line managers, respectively). Problems were posed by the inherent structure and administrative systems of the decentralized firms. A high degree of divisional autonomy, management's reliance upon abstract financial reports, and the evaluation of managerial performance based largely on the results of financially oriented information systems all tended to impede the implementation of social policy. In addition the third, or "organizational", phase was accompanied by some form of trauma--either organizational or personal.

Lank (10) later described and analyzed several different roles that were required on the staff specialist in helping to successfully form, develop, and administer corporate social policy--again for decentralized manufacturing firms. By contrast, little was known about the social response characteristics of firms organized along more functional lines and exhibiting greater centralization in their administration. If such companies could be studied in a single industry, responses to economic versus social issues as well as comparative performance (economic and social) could be documented.

Selection of the Banking Industry

The commercial banking industry was uniquely suitable for such a study. Organized by fairly distinct yet interdependent functions and characterized by relatively strong centralized managements, major commercial banks represent an industry population within which one might expect the administrative barriers associated with decentralized companies to be non-existent or more easily overcome. Moreover, most large commercial banks--and urban ones in particular--are highly visible because of their size, economic power, and generally large number of retail branch offices within a relatively small geographic area. These banks often are called upon to participate in efforts designed to address social needs. Several senior bank executives have been declared a need to exert leadership in responding to social demands. Consequently many chief executives have committed their organizations to ambitious community programs and social policies.

In this research, the term "social policies" was interpreted broadly to include activities such as affirmative action programs for minorities and women and commercial lending programs for minorities. Other endeavors to meet rising social expectations were also counted, especially those which involved basic bank operations and which had significant impacts on the organization in terms of dollars spent, managerial resources committed, and strategic importance.

A number of studies have dealt with the social policies of commercial banks. Thieblot, in a study of 47 commercial banks, found that the banking industry had "delayed longer than most [industries]" in hiring and providing meaningful jobs for blacks, but after it began to act, there was evidence of a top-down management commitment in implementing more aggressive hiring policies (11, pp. 141, 162). In a 1970 case-study of employment policies at six large New York City banks, Corwin noted that with regard to the promotion of minorities,

> the policy maker who can align the directional thrust of [the use of threat, appeals to self-interest, and appeals to morality] is most likely to succeed in the introduction of new policies (5, p. 105).

In a study of 18 major commercial banks in six different cities, the Council on Economic Priorities found wide variations in the employment and promotion patterns for minorities and women among the individual banks, but there was:

> no significant correlation between female and minority employment statistics and (a) the size of an individual bank; (b) percentages of women and minorities in the city labor force; or (c) percentages of women and minorities in the city population (9, p. 156).

Most of this research focused on statistical relationships among banks over time in an effort to portray the relative progress or lack of progress made by banks in hiring and promoting minorities and women. The studies all purported to show "what hurt", but none appeared to probe satisfactorily the organizational processes by which social policy is actually effected in large banks.

From a listing of the 100 largest U. S. commercial banks as ranked by deposits in *American Banker*, seven banks were selected as research sites for a closer examination of their management of social policy. Through structured interviews with executives at each research site, an understanding was sought of administrative issues and problems encountered in managing social programs, and opinions were solicited about major variables affecting implementation of social policies. These interviews led to the following observations:

1. All sample banks appeared to respond to social demands with a fairly standard repertoire of programs. This was not entirely unexpected given the existence

of legal requirements for some (affirmative action programs); intra-industry coordinating efforts for others (the American Bankers Association's $1 billion minority lending program and clearinghouse sponsorship of certain programs); and the extensive dialogue among banks that goes on about still others (via public affairs conferences and similar meetings).

2. Despite generally similar forms of response, sufficient differences among banks were found to warrant further indepth investigation. The differences were not so much in the types of programs being administered as in the rapidity with which the programs were implemented and the extent to which they affected regular bank operations.
3. The rates and degrees of social responsiveness among banks appeared to depend upon whether top management utilized--individually and collectively--corporate policies, organizational structure, measurement and control systems, long-range planning, incentive systems, and organizational culture to achieve social objectives. This, in turn, was largely a function of the chief executive's commitment to social policy and the forcefulness and effectiveness of the executive's leadership.

These observations prompted intensive research in two banks, Jefferson National Bank and Trust Company and Continental Bank and Trust Company (pseudonyms)--designated "key banks". Within the industry, each key bank was considered to be competitively innovative and aggressive and at the same time socially responsive. Of the seven sample banks, the two key banks ranked first and second in terms of five-year compound annual growth rates of loan volume, net operating income (before securities gains and losses), and earnings per share. Both were considered by other bank executives to be leaders in the area of corporate social responsibility. For example, both had been pioneers in emphasizing commercial lending to minorities--a purely discretionary response to social needs. Although minority lending activities were in evidence at the other sample banks, the two key banks represented organizations in which the minority lending programs had matured to the point of being absorbed into regular bank operations.

Research Methodology

Through in-depth interviews with management at three levels of the organization (corporate general executives, corporate staff specialists, and division line officers), the historical development of each key bank's commercial lending programs for minorities was traced from its inception until early 1974. This entailed a nine-year period in the case of Jefferson National and a span of seven years at Continental. Particular attention was paid to the degree of commitment to the program by various levels of management, major policy shifts, and changes in executive job responsibilities as they affected the banks' minority lending efforts.

Whereas the viewpoints of several recent and current participants in these programs proved to be a valuable means of cross-checking the sequence and nature of events, corporate files were often consulted to document and clarify certain points. Insofar as possible, managers were observed as they operated within the organizational settings of the banks. Internal documents were analyzed, and where possible, management meetings such as credit committee meetings, urban affairs committee meetings, budget planning sessions, and informal executive conferences were attended.

CORPORATE RESPONSIVENESS AS A PROCESS

Despite some minor differences, the banks and their approaches to minority lending and other social programs were strikingly similar. This is not to assert that all banks or all organizations undertake social initiatives in exactly the same way, but simply that between the two key banks there was enough similarity to suggest the feasibility of mapping corporate responsiveness into a reasonably systematic framework. In both instances, the evolution of social policy appeared to constitute a process comprising three distinct, yet overlapping phases with the second phase consisting of two sub-phases.

Phase I

Phase I, the *policy* phase, encompassed the chief executive's growing concern about a social issue and its impact on the organization. In response to a combination of externally imposed demands and internalized personal values, the executive developed commitment to the issue and communicated this to the organization. Initial reaction varied considerably, but over time through persistent reiteration of personal feelings on the topic, the chief executive increased the awareness of the organization and began to broaden the corporate purpose to include this concern. For example, the president of Jefferson National stressed that the chairman had spent several years "marinating" the organization in rhetoric about corporate social responsibility, thus preparing the way for implementation of a social policy calling for increased commercial lending to minorities.

Perhaps for the first time, more than conventional financial performance was being called for, and the challenge for the organization was to respond effectively to the call for a new social initiative while preserving the bank's traditional and important economic functions. Efforts simply to articulate and disseminate policy did not suffice. Line management was reluctant to proceed on faith alone and consequently nothing happened. In fact, the novelty and imprecision of early social policy caused its complete development to take a considerable length of time. In both key banks, the social policy tended to become fully explicit only as the early stages of its implementation took place.

Phase II-A

The initiation of Phase II, the *learning* phase, was marked by senior management's designation of specialists to head a separate unit designed to institute a minority lending program. This actually turned out to be a stage of *technical learning*, denoted by Phase II-A, in that the staff of the special unit viewed its task as developing a viable, self-contained program of limited dimensions in order to deliver service to a specific target market. Emphasis was placed on the development of new knowledge and skills related to minority lending to permit the formulation of new credit procedures (or modification of existing procedures). There was direct feedback to the "top of the house" regarding the program's progress, but the program remained essentially a small show of good faith, organized and administered as a separate entity within the bank.

In light of senior management's continuing commitment, this arrangement was inadequate for the long term. It was apparent to minority lending specialists and top management that a genuinely effective and lasting minority lending policy for the bank would be effected only upon the active and ongoing participation of all relevant areas of the bank. Primarily this called for the inclusion of the bank's branch offices.

Phase II-B

In an effort to elicit a response from the branches, newly developed procedures were promulgated, and the staff of the special unit offered its technical assistance as needed. Lending officers and branch managers who participated did so on the basis of either their perception of top management's wishes (and expectations) or, as was more likely, their own personal proclivities. They received no distinguishing praise or rewards. Those who were cautious in their reaction, indifferent, or actually antagonistic to the program could avoid participation with relatively little concern about adverse consequences. With reporting and control systems non-existent or rudimentary at best, there was little likelihood of being singled out for either praise or censure. As a result, the decentralization of minority lending met with only limited success.

Nevertheless, this attempt to institutionalize social policy (and subsequent failure to meet expectations) ultimately proved to be of value. It formed the first part of a second sub-phase of *administrative learning* (Phase II-B) in which an improved understanding of the organization itself was acquired. At the time there was little appreciation of the way in which existing policies, information and control systems, and career pressures exerted a strong inhibiting influence on office managers and lending officers. On the basis of novel and somewhat simplistic appeals to their sense of fairness, they were being asked to make what all formal and informal credit guidelines indicated to be unacceptable, risky loans. Numerous bank policies involving lending standards, credit training, collection procedures, loan administration, and so forth had served to institutionalize the lending process, and few, if any, of those policies made provision for what were classified as essentially "unbankable loans".

To deal with this problem, senior management realized a need to expand the scope of its approach in order to attack organizational resistance on a more comprehensive basis. Staff specialists were asked to identify and highlight those aspects of the bank's administrative systems and procedures which required modification in order to bring them into congruence with and support of professed social objectives. In effect, what Bower (3) has described as the "organization context" was to be reshaped. If the performance of managers and lending officers was expected to change, it was insufficient merely to exhort them to behave differently. Incentives would have to be restructured in a manner which would mesh realistically with regular job responsibilities. An important staff activity in this regard was the development of data systems with which to track and analyze the social performance of the organization. These systems provided new sources and types of information which top management could use to monitor the implementation of social objectives as integral aspects of annual business plans.

Phase III

This renewed initiative of top management represented the beginning of Phase III, the *institutionalization phase*. For the chief executive, the issue was instilling a sustained

FIGURE 30-1. THE SOCIAL RESPONSE PROCESS SUMMARIZED

Level of Organization	**Phases**			
	I Policy	II-A Technical Learning	II-B Administrative Learning	III Institutionalization
Chief Executive Officer	Issue: Policy problem	Obtain knowledge	Seek organizational involvement	Institutionalize organizational commitment
	Action: Formulate and communicate corporate position	Designate staff specialists; establish special unit	Expand staff responsibilities; engage organization	Change performance expectations
	Outcome: Enriched purpose; increased awareness			
		Issue: Technical problem	Provoke response of operating units	Transfer knowledge and skills to operating units

Minority Lending and Staff Specialists		Action: Acquire new knowledge/skills; develop new procedures Outcome: Minority lending program	Promulgate procedures	Provide technical staff support
			Issue: Administrative problem Action: Decentralize program; design data systems Outcome: Limited response; new organizational information	Sustain response of operating units Apply data systems to performance evaluations
Branch Management				Issue: Management problem Action: Modify procedures and commit resources Outcome: Increased responsiveness

organizational commitment to a specific issue. Performance expectations had to be changed to explicitly take into account managerial performance relative to specific, measurable social objectives. To aid in meeting these new performance expectations, the specialized assistance of the minority lending unit was available. Its task was to provide adequate staff support to the operating units through the transfer of its particular knowledge and skills.

The brunt of this third phase was borne by operating unit managers. For the first time, they were expected to produce, on a continuing, systematic basis, results fulfilling socially-oriented policies. At the same time, they continued to be held responsible for their regular financial goals. In this context, the matter became a managerial problem in which the broad objective was to modify operating procedures and reallocate resources so as to increase social responsiveness of the sub-unit while preserving its historic economic productivity.

This discussion is summarized in Figure 30-1 which illustrates the involvement of different organizational levels during the various phases of the process.

DISCUSSION

A notable feature of the response process was the amount of direct involvement by the chief executives. In both key banks, members of top management interjected themselves personally to establish lending units. Intra-organizational boundaries were crossed readily, and other sub-units offered no observable resistance. Perhaps the most credible reason for this is that the chief executive's role in a commercial bank often requires participation in substantive business decisions. Therefore, the establishment of a special unit was not an unusual operating procedure. Certainly, those within the organization who were aware of the chief executive's strong personal commitment would not be likely to oppose the lending unit. For others who viewed the venture as capricious and ill-conceived, the unit hardly warranted serious consideration, much less criticism. In any event, the direct and visible participation of the chief executive officer was of primary importance not only in initiating the bank's response, but also in managing it over time.

Also important was the appearance of a two-part learning phase--a technical sub-phase followed by an administrative sub-phase. Although it would be tempting to fuse these two together, there appeared an important phenomenon that argues for their separation. In each bank the first effort to decentralize minority lending met with only limited success. There followed a de facto recentralization in which the original specialized unit again exercised leadership in minority lending. These "false starts" in decentralization marked the beginning of the administrative learning phase in which the organizational dynamics of the banks themselves were analyzed to identify areas of organizational resistance and methods of flanking or overcoming them.

This suggests that even in functionally oriented corporations with relatively centralized management, organizational learning plays a crucial role. The responsiveness of any firm to social pressure is probably more a function of its capacity for organizational learning than legislative edicts, regulatory pressures, or outside interest groups. Even well-intentioned senior executives committed to a social policy cannot be expected to reshape a complex and highly routinized organization instantaneously. Careful and often time-consuming adjustment of internal procedures is needed, but such a change will be effective only if it is based on a thorough analysis of existing administrative systems and organizational processes.

Remarkably, no major instance of organizational trauma was found. In neither Jefferson National nor Continental did top management forcefully intercede to overturn decisions of line subordinates for the purpose of enforcing social policy. This was primarily attributable to the lack of need for any such action. Because of the banks' functionally-oriented organizational structures and their own personal coordinating roles, chief executives were in a position to know about substantive business operations in considerable detail. Moreover, because of their personal interest and participation in the formation of the minority lending programs, chief executives had direct lines of communications to the special units. There were relatively few opportunities for surprises.

An exception to this may have been the substantial minority loan losses experienced by Continental in 1972 which were followed by a reorganization. That particular situation bordered on organizational trauma--albeit a trauma that was constructive in nature. In that instance, a detailed analysis subsequently was undertaken as part of a general reassessment of the minority loan program, but the resulting recommendations led to a general strengthening of the program.

It could be argued that some form of trauma might have hastened the social response process. That is, the sooner (and more severe) the trauma, the swifter might have been the corporate response. But there can be serious and undesirable consequences associated with the precipitation of such an event. Purposely creating organizational trauma carries with it great risks; the very social policy sought might be sabotaged, and even the performance of the organization or the careers of individual managers could be needlessly jeopardized.

There was a notable similarity between the social response process of the banks and that found in decentralized manufacturing firms. In both cases, three phases representing the successive commitments of different levels of management were observed. The involvement of several layers of management as well as the large size and complexity of the organizations contributed to long lead times and numerous problems in communication and coordination. Undoubtedly, this explains in part why the banks, as well as Ackerman's diversified manufacturing companies, took up to eight years to institutionalize social policies.

Organizational structure did not seem to be as dominant a variable in social policy implementation as first hypothesized. Instead, the banks' many administrative systems and procedures appeared to govern the nature, degree, and speed of response. It was not until management information systems, control reporting formats, credit training programs, loan review procedures, and managerial reward and penalty systems were modified that significant and lasting results could be achieved in the branch offices.

By viewing corporate responsiveness as a three-phase organizational process, many of the issues discussed above and their relationships to one another can be illuminated. The concept of a social response process is a new way of looking at social policy implementation in large corporations because it permits the systematic mapping of organizational phenomena by issues at several organizational levels over time. (For example, Figure 30-2 is a schematic representation of the sequence of major milestones and the changes in managerial commitment associated with the development of minority lending programs at the two key banks.) The corporate response process provides a conceptual framework to aid in the observation and analysis of corporate actions and the prediction of future events. It is particularly useful to the manager because it makes explicit and operational the critical steps necessary in social policy implementation. This enables him or her to monitor the execution of policy. It also allows the manager to pinpoint and even anticipate administrative problems, thus enabling allocation of time and resources to areas of greatest need. Generally, the social response process can serve as a descriptive model of policy implementation--regardless of whether the policy is economic, social or political in nature.

The findings reported above underscore the feasibility of methodically tracing and analyzing corporate responsiveness as an organizational process which can be both understood and managed. Furthermore, the process was managed so as to effect an accommodation with the banks' more traditional business activities. A progression of organizational adaptations helped transform what was at the outset essentially a "social issue" into a more routine form of banking activity. In each bank, as the minority lending program became more business-like in its objectives, planning, and adminis-

FIGURE 30-2. THE EVOLUTION OF MINORITY LENDING PROGRAMS AS A SOCIAL RESPONSE PROCESS

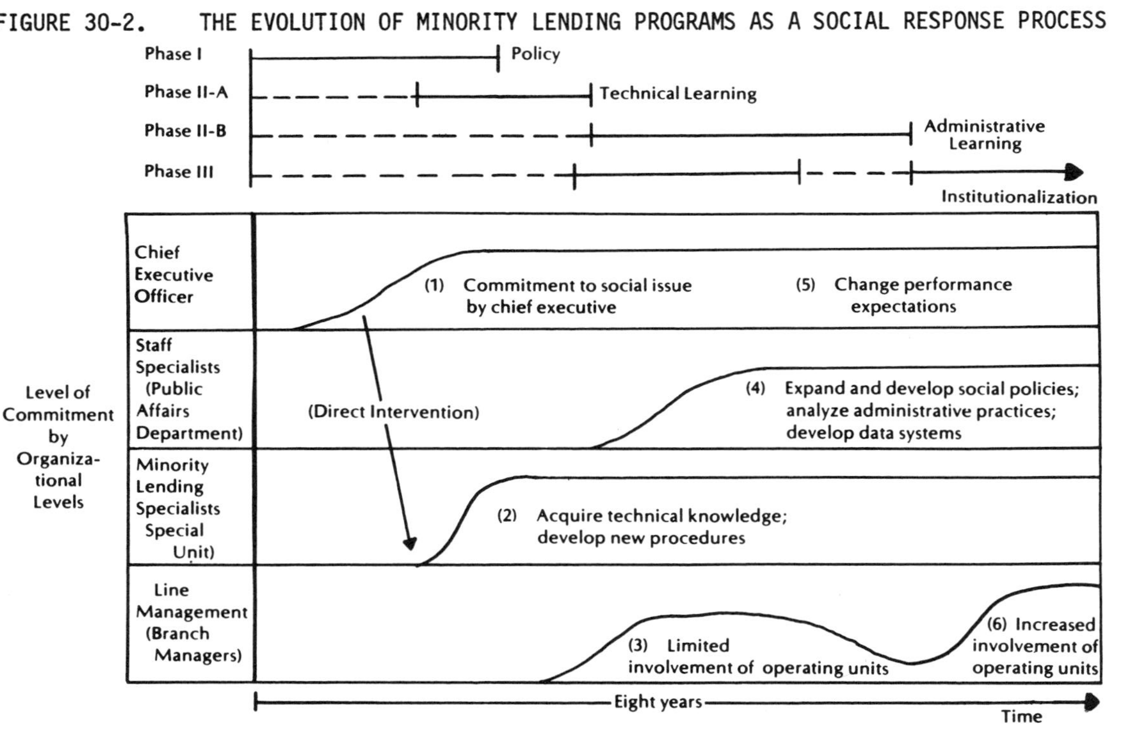

tration, it also became more effective. In both key banks, loan volume climbed at an accelerating rate while charge-offs and delinquencies were controlled with improved effectiveness. This suggests that corporate responsiveness to social demands may have elements in common with successful competitive behavior and that both may be characteristic of progressive management.

IMPLICATIONS FOR FURTHER RESEARCH

1. *Are only the most profitable companies socially responsive?*

Insufficient data were available to determine correlations between profitability and social performance, nor was it an intended objective of this research. The two key banks showed superior performance in both financial and social terms, but the more significant relationship may be the one which exists between competitive aggressiveness and social responsiveness.

Presumably, among participants in any industry there are distinguishable differences in social performance just as there are distinct differences in financial performance. Industry studies by The Council on Economic Priorities (6, 7, 8, 9) lend support to this proposition. If a positive correlation between social performance and financial performance could be substantiated, it would have profound policy implications. (Bragdon and Marlin (4), for example, have posited such a relationship based on their analysis of firms in the pulp and paper industry.)

Although a definitive resolution of this issue seems unlikely (because of the high percentage of indirect costs in large corporations, accounting differences, and the managed nature of costs and profitability), some notion of a general relationship might be sketched out based on a carefully designed questionnaire survey of a large number of banks. But Thieblot, using only employment data as a measure of social performance in his study of 49 banks, found "no relationship...between a gross measure of the performance of banking firms and the relative level of Negro employment" (11, p. 134). More detailed analysis of a greater number of appropriate variables will be needed to shed light on this issue.

2. *Does social responsiveness correlate with competitive responsiveness, and more importantly--if it does--why?*

Such a finding may not imply that "better" managers are more socially conscious so much as it may indicate that managers who are astute competitively also tend to be sensitive and competent along other strategic dimensions.

One obvious way in which social responsiveness could contribute to a firm's financial performance is through an improvement in its competitive posture. By promoting social policies some banks, for example, claim to be seeking an increase in their share of the retail market, particularly in minority neighborhoods. Conversely, a concern for corporate responsiveness may dilute management's time and an organization's resources. In the case of the banks, if efforts to hire and promote minorities led to the assimilation of less skilled tellers, service representatives, and so forth without any compensating improvement of their skills through training, a decrease in the quality of customer service serious enough to adversely affect market share could result.

Comparative in-depth case studies of the major competing banks and their retail market performance in a single metropolitan area would provide a rich source of data with which to address this issue.

3. *How can business enterprises effectively administer innovation?*

It is not enough to say that banks can manage novel, and in many instances risky, social programs simply because they have handled risky projects before. Managers are by and large accustomed to handling certain types of risk (credit risk, liquidity risk, etc.), but social policy represents the introduction of genuine change in basic values, assumptions, and potentially, the bank's very structure and operations.

Fundamentally, this study has dealt with the institutionalization of organizational change. The challenge is to determine how the effectiveness of change can be preserved without disrupting traditional economic efficiency. For example, even if the objectives of top management and staff specialists in a corporation include the institutionalization of social policy, what is to prevent the onset of stultifying bureaucratization? How can a major business institution be kept continually alert and responsive to new ideas, risks, and opportunities--whether social or economic in nature?

Comparable case studies of the ways in which individual firms in other industries have responded to changing competitive, regulatory, environmental, and technological conditions would be helpful in developing further insights into this important aspect of management.

Although the social policies examined in this article commanded only a small proportion of any bank's total resources and resulted in modest levels of bankwide involvement, they were of strategic significance. Insofar as they reflected the chief executive's commitment and influenced traditional, financially oriented business policies, they contributed to the shaping of corporate purpose. Moreover, they were instrumental in the adaptation of the firm's strategy to a changing social environment. This was particularly important to the chief executives because ultimately, the unique responsibility of top level management is the overseeing and guiding of organizational change to meet new environmental threats and opportunities.

REFERENCES

1. Ackerman, Robert W. "How Companies Respond to Social Demands," *Harvard Business Review* (July-August, 1973), 88-98.

2. Ackerman, Robert W. *The Social Challenge to Business* (Cambridge, Mass.: Harvard University Press, 1975).

3. Bower, Joseph L. *Managing the Resource Allocation Process* (Boston: Division of Research, Graduate School of Business Administration, Harvard University, 1970).

4. Bragdon, Joseph H., and John A. T. Marlin. "Is Pollution Profitable? Case of the Pulp and Paper Industry," Speech delivered to the Financial Management Association, Denver, Colorado, October 8, 1971. Mimeographed.

5. Corwin, R. David. *New Workers in the Banking Industry: A Minority Report* (New York: New York University, 1970).

6. The Council on Economic Priorities. *Paper Profits: Pollution in the Pulp and Paper Industry* (New York: The Council on Economic Priorities, 1971).

7. The Council on Economic Priorities. *The Price of Power: Electric Utilities and the Environment* (New York: The Council on Economic Priorities, 1972).

8. The Council on Economic Priorities. *Short-Changed: Minorities and Women in Banking* (New York: The Council

on Economic Priorities, 1972).

9. The Council on Economic Priorities. *In Whose Hands? Safety, Efficacy, and Research Productivity in the Pharmaceutical Industry* (New York: The Council on Economic Priorities, 1973).

10. Lank, Alden G. *The Implementation of Corporate Social Policies* (D.B.A. dissertation, Graduate School of Business Administration, Harvard University, 1974).

11. Thieblot, Armand J., Jr. *The Negro in the Banking Industry* (Philadelphia: The Industrial Research Unit, University of Pennsylvania, 1970).

STUDENT REVIEW QUESTIONS

1. Why did Murray choose to study commercial banks?
2. Briefly describe the three phases of the social response process Murray identifies.
3. Explain the distinction Murray makes between "technical learning" and "administrative learning".
4. How important was the involvement of the chief executives in the banks studied?
5. What role does organizational learning play in the social response process?

31

Management by Objectives: A Critical View*

GEORGE STRAUSS

MBO--Management by Objectives--has achieved great recent popularity in management circles [1], not only in private industry but increasingly in hospitals, school districts and the like, General Mills, Minnesota Mining and Manufacturing, Honeywell, PPG, Kimberly-Clark, these are but a few of the companies which have experimented with this promising new technique [2]. But there are numerous organizations which have tried it out and then abandoned it--and probably many more in which the program never really got off the ground or, after quick initial success, was gradually allowed to become moribund [3]. Too many managers look upon MBO either as a gimmick or a cure-all, without giving careful thought to the objectives they want MBO to accomplish--or the adjustments which must be made if these objectives are to be achieved. In other words, there is too little MBO-type thinking to the concept of MBO itself. This failure to recognize the fuzziness in MBO's own objectives has contributed to the ambiguity of MBO's results.

MBO is too useful a concept to be accepted blindly. Its difficulties must be squarely faced if management is to take full advantage of its strengths. Let me start out with the question of objectives, then describe the major problems which arise from MBO in practice, and finally suggest the

---

Bracketed numbers in the context of this article refer to the list of Footnote References at the end of the article.

*From *Training and Development Journal*, Vol. 26, No. 4 (April, 1972), pp. 10-15. Reprinted by special permission from the April, 1972 *Training and Development Journal*.

realistic limits to MBO's use.

CONFUSION AS TO OBJECTIVES

MBO is an umbrealla concept covering a multitude of objectives. For some it is a means of introducing a Theory-Y oriented form of autonomy in which managers are given freedom to set their own goals. Others approach it in terms of Theory X--as a means of tightening managerial control and getting subordinates to do exactly what management wants.

> The personnel director of an industrial laboratory looked upon it as a form of individual performance appraisal; the lab manager hoped it would get "the lab moving together as a team"; but for the majority of managers it seemed merely an additional contribution of their paperwork. One man said, "MBO, I do that. That's management by exception. If a man gets out of line you straighten him out." [4]

What did the originators of the concept want MBO to accomplish? Here we find little real agreement either.

PERFORMANCE APPRAISAL

As much as anyone, Douglas McGregor was responsible for the MBO concept, although he never used the term himself [5]. McGregor was looking for a method of performance appraisal which was superior to the traditional rating system [6]. Critics argued that the traditional system:

> ...stressed personality traits, which were subjective and difficult to measure or change;
> ...provided that ratings be determined in a unilateral fashion with the supervisor "playing God" and judging the subordinate's personal worth (as opposed to his performance);
> ...tended to emphasize past mistakes rather than future performance.

MBO sought to overcome all these problems by basing appraisal on (a) quantitative, measurable (or at least concrete) performance goals (b) set jointly by superior and subordinate. Thus the subordinate is judged by standards he helped determine.

PLANNING AND CONTROL

Soon it became apparent that MBO was useful, not just as a personnel tool, but as a means of planning and control [7]. MBO's new use was as an improved form of budgeting.

In too many companies, planning consists merely of adopting short-run cost budgets and setting sales targets. Global objectives may be set, but relatively little thought is given to how these goals are to be reached. And with the primary emphasis placed on *this* period's costs, profits and sales, there is a tendency to ignore other variables which may contribute to profits over longer periods, variables such as equipment maintenance, employee and product development, and customer relations.

MBO (at least when it works as it should) requires management to define exactly what it wants to accomplish and to specify all important objectives, especially those commonly ignored. It reduces the emphasis on short-run profits [8], increases the number of managerial goals and forces the explicit consideration of exactly what steps must be taken if these goals are to be fulfilled. In this way, it helps subordinates learn what is required of them, thus reducing their need for guesswork. As a result, it makes decision-making more rational, both for boss and subordinate. In sum, MBO can become a coordinated process of planning which involves every management level in determining both the goals which it will meet and the means by which they are to be met.

A DECISION-MAKING TOOL

Some companies go even further. MBO is viewed as a tool to help top management reevaluate whether the organization's present activities contribute to the organization's real objectives. MBO here is looked upon not as a means of evaluating individuals or of communicating management priorities, but as a tough-minded approach to problem-solving. (It is in a sense analogous to PPBS at the governmental level.)

As I will argue below, the autonomy and self-direction implied by the first objective runs somewhat counter to the coordinated control inherent in the second, and neither are entirely congruent with the decision-making approach of the third. Unfortunately, these inconsistencies have been insufficiently recognized by those who would make MBO a multipurpose remedy. Further, both literature and practice today seem to be giving greater emphasis to MBO-as-planning and playing down its role in evaluation [9]. And yet the rhetoric inspired by the early emphasis of self-direction at times leads to false hopes that MBO will democratize the organization.

SOME TYPICAL PROBLEMS

So much for objectives. What sorts of problems arise under MBO in practice? Here are some typical comments:

"There is a lot of paperwork in MBO. All sorts of goals are set and we talk big. But on a day-to-day basis, nothing changes. We are all too busy fighting fires for me to get involved in those extra things which I promised to do in MBO. And so is my boss."

"I could meet all my goals in training my men and developing new accounts, but in so doing I would lose $1,000,000 in bread-and-butter sales. MBO emphasizes fringes over the main objectives."

"MBO doesn't work where there is job rotation. My predecessor expected to be transferred soon. He accepted some unreasonable goals and I just don't feel bound by them."

"There is no follow up in my organization: They set goals with a big flourish, but no one pays any attention to them six months later."

"Things move so fast that by the time the review period comes around the goals are no longer relevant."

"If you don't meet goals in my company you can always find excuses. MBO just teaches you to lie better."

The above may imply only that the bosses of the managers who made these comments have failed to understand or accept the MBO philosophy. But more is involved. There are inherent conflicts between MBO and other management policies and, as suggested earlier, inconsistencies between the goals of MBO itself.

SUBORDINATE PARTICIPATION IN GOAL SETTING

As long as the subordinate is judged in terms of how well he does in terms of goals he himself sets, there is a danger that he will set his goals just as low as he can so as to give himself greater leeway in case of trouble. After all, his apparent success is a function of initial goals. If his goals are modest, it is easy to look good. And so--where MBO is working poorly--the subordinate tries to set a low initial goal and sell his boss that the goal is really hard.

I suspect that only in a minority of cases do subordinates feel really free to set goals as they wish. MBO may work where the managers' everyday style of management is participative and nondirective. But it is too much to expect the ordinary hard-bitten manager, who is directive and decisive, to transform himself suddenly into a participative manager when he engages in MBO [10]. In any case, knowing that his boss is the one who hands out rewards, the typical subordinate may look anxiously for some indication of what the boss thinks are proper goals. Once these become clear, he will quickly adopt them with "enthusiasm." Indeed, some subordinates might prefer that their boss indicate his wishes frankly from the start, instead of putting them through guessing games.

Actually the freedom of the subordinate to set his own goals is highly restricted whenever any kind of common plan is required [11]. It makes little sense for production to plan 15 percent more output if marketing plans only 10 percent more sales or for a plant manager to decide to rebuild a production bay if top management has decided to curb capital expenditures. Individual goals have to be consistent with organizational goals [12]. Thus organizational demands may conflict with individual desires, raising problems which I will discuss later on.

OBJECTIVE STANDARDS

MBO involves setting objective standards. Instead of telling a foreman he should exert more forceful leadership, he is setting the goal of increasing production by 17 percent or introducing a new line of equipment by November 1.

The trouble with such goals is they often force the subordinate to *look* good rather than *be* good and to emphasize the measurable rather than the unmeasurable. To be sure, some MBO systems make provision for unmeasurable goals, but exact numbers inevitably speak louder than vague descriptions. Production, which is measurable, is emphasized over employee development, which is not. Or, if employee development is to be measured, it is in terms of such superficial measures as the gross number of employees sent to training classes, not how this training changes behavior on the job [13]. Creative work, such as research, personnel or advertising, is often difficult to evaluate, as indeed is most staff work. Because of this difficulty, quality may be sacrificed for sheer quantity.

> A laboratory director set as his goal the enhancement of his laboratory's professional prestige, but since prestige is difficult to measure, he set as his performance target a certain number of papers to be read at professional meetings. And to fill this quota he "encouraged" individual subordinates to accept the writing of papers as goals for themselves. The result, as might be expected, was that the required number of papers were read, but that they were of such poor quality as to lower rather than raise the laboratory's prestige. (The story might have been less tragic, however, if the director's subordinates had felt really free to reject their assignments.)

Overemphasis on measurable data may also encourage the covering up of poor performance or the actual falsification of data. Long-run improvement may be slighted to look good during the current evaluation period. Since each individual is anxious to make himself look good, cooperation is discouraged. In addition, to the extent that a manager's overall performance is evaluated on the basis of a relatively few measures, there is always the danger that accidental factors outside of his control may distort the picture. A good manager with bad luck may look worse than a bad manager with good luck.

Unless an endless number of factors are measured, some significant items may be ignored or fall into the chinks between measured goals. And when one goal can be achieved only at the potential expense of another, the manager often has only imperfect standards for choice. He may easily emphasize side goals over the main show. ("I could meet all my goals in training my men and developing new accounts, but in so doing I would lose $1,000,000 in bread-and-butter sales.")

An important question relates to the assigning of responsibilities. For example, if a new product flops, who is held responsible: product development, for not doing its homework? manufacturing, for poor quality? or marketing, for insufficient sales effort? Some authors suggest that managers should be held responsible merely for factors under their direct control. Others argue for joint goals, with joint responsibility. Both approaches encourage buckpassing.

Staff effort is particularly difficult to measure, because staff, of course, has to achieve its results through others.

ORGANIZATION REWARDS

How is MBO to be tied into the organizational reward system? There are those who say that MBO and salary appraisal should be two separate processes, but this is difficult to work in practice.

Of course, there are real problems in integrating the two systems. If a man's pay depends on how well he meets the goals he sets for himself, he has every incentive to set these goals low and to blame his failure on someone else. Certainly the greater the emphasis we place on MBO in terms of determining salaries, the more likely subordinates are to emphasize short-run measurable results over longer-run intangibles.

But in a money-oriented society, if MBO isn't tied into the reward system, why should anyone pay attention to MBO at all? If MBO sets one set of goals and compensation rewards another, we get nothing but confusion.

So the two have to be integrated. But this means not only that goals have to be accepted by the individual and be consistent with the overall organizational plan, but also that they must be fair and equitable, so that one manager is not setting a goal which is harder than another's. To satisfy all these conflicting objectives is far from easy.

Finally, and certainly complicating both MBO and reward systems, is the fact that the organization exists in a turbulent environment. A company's sales record may be more a function of what happens in Washington than the effectiveness of its individual sales managers.

PARTICIPATION

MBO today has two primary objectives, individual performance appraisal and managerial planning and control [14]. The first objective implies that each manager will participate in setting his own individual goal, the second that these individual goals will be consistent with those of the organization as a whole. If these two objectives are not to clash, individual managers must participate in setting not only their own goals but those of the organization generally. In theory this means that there is a great deal of consultation, crossing all managerial levels, until a master plan is developed which everyone *freely* accepts.

Followed to its logical conclusion, MBO is a means of introducing participative (Theory Y, System 4, Argyris's YB) management on an organization-wide basis. The revolutionary implication of this is that each individual manager will do more than determine the details of how to carry out organizational goals; he will participate in determining the goals themselves. If meant seriously, MBO could be an organization development technique more potent than, say, sensitivity training or the Grid. It would threaten the corporate power structure and transform the traditional hierarchical structure of decision-making into something closer to Likert's System 4 interlocking chain of highly participative work groups.

Whether such a drastic change would be desirable is beside the point. Corporate democracy is more than most managements bargained for when they agreed to accept MBO. Over the last 10 years, the MBO literature has played down and redefined the concept of subordinate goal setting, so that the idea today differs considerably from that originally proposed by McGregor. In practice, MBO today is often viewed as means of tightening, not loosening, top management controls. Despite some trimmings of participation, top management typically sets the *basic* goals. Subordinates may have some freedom to set secondary goals (with regards to housekeeping or training, for example, but not with regards to production levels or capital outlays), to voice objectives and to determine how to *carry out* basic goals. Essentially the freedom is one of means, not ends. At Minneapolis Mining and Manufacturing,

> the process starts with the department manager sitting with each of his immediate subordinates to get across the general idea of what is to be required, based on objectives established at the top of the corporation.... Then each of these men sits with his subordinates, until the lowest man involved has been brought into the picture. At this point, the process reverses direction and specific objectives come up from the bottom, along with detailed plans for attaining them. The objectives are so set that the requirements will be met; if not, they are changed. *A boss cannot accept a subordinate's requirements unless he knows that they will produce what is required* [15].

The trouble is that those who view MBO primarily as a means of increasing individual participation may raise expectations which are inconsistent with organizational realities.

> To introduce a program of objectives may be to change the subordinate's expectations about participation and involvement....There seems to be a clear implication that he will have something to say about the factor or problem in which he is involved. The most serious human relations problems probably occur in organizations where there is an incongruity between the verbalized level and actually level of subordinate influence; that is, participation may be a stated policy, but in practice does not occur [16].

A REALISTIC VIEW

If any arguments are valid, it would be wrong to view MBO either as an all-purpose cure for every management ill or as a Trojan Horse which can be used to insinuate full-fledged Theory Y concepts of management throughout the organization. MBO can play a useful role, even if it isn't the star of the show.

1. As suggested just above, it is misleading and unrealistic to suggest that MBO can permit subordinates to set goals just for themselves, except in secondary areas. MBO in fact requires more communications, perhaps more mutual influence, but probably less autonomy and individual freedom. Group participation may increase, individual discretion may not. Where MBO is viewed as an exercise in subordinate motivation, the subordinate may "own" the goals, but the boss feels little commitment to them. The reverse may be true

where the goals are imposed by the boss in conformance with a master plan. It is extremely difficult to develop joint ownership or commitment.

2. Hard-nosed as managers are supposed to be, many find it difficult to operationalize their goals--to be really specific as to what they want either their subordinates or themselves to obtain. The research studies to date suggest that it is the setting of clear, concrete goals which is important, not the sense of participation [17]. Concrete goals direct performance, reduce uncertainty and serve as an instrument of communications--and do so whether the goals are introduced directively or participatively.

3. MBO may point out where greater coordination between managers is required. The goal setting process may be particularly useful in facilitating what has been called "bargaining" between boss and subordinate, line and staff, or departments tied together in the work flow (especially when such bargaining is confined to the details relating to goals set by higher levels). Department A may agree to cut scrap losses by 10 percent, but insists Department B must tighten tolerance by a given amount, personnel must recruit better trained employees, and that the boss obtain a capital authorization to purchase two new machines by April 15. Where there is joint responsibility, individual inputs should be specified in advance. The process of hammering out agreements on matters such as this may be MBO's most valuable by-product [18].

4. Effective MBO may permit and even require structural changes. Cases have been reported where MBO has led to broader spans of control and the elimination of organizational levels. As various studies have shown rules and goals can serve as substitutes for close supervision [19].

5. Reasonable care should be taken to insure that the right goals are set: the measures of success should measure what is really important to achieve, not trivia; the short run should not be emphasized over the long run, the measurable over the subjective, or the performance of single units at the expense of the organization as a whole. There is room for some experimentation with "contingency goals" (if Product X is released by April 15, we will raise sales level to 30,000 units by July 1) or "variable goals" (for every one percent increase in production, unit costs will be reduced by .2 percent). MBO can discourage flexible response to unexpected happenings; hopefully it can be designed to do the reverse.

6. Goals, however, can be overstressed. Ingenuity in solving problems is what counts, not ingenuity in measuring performance. It would be hopelessly unproductive to try to seek to develop a concrete goal for every aspect of performance. Goals may highlight special areas of emphasis. But managers should be rewarded on their overall performance, not just aspects specifically measured. Judgment and discretion

are required in interpreting performance data. Results do not "speak for themselves."

7. MBO must solve the problem of its relationship to reward systems. I think salary appraisal should be a fairly explicit procedure in which individuals are (in most cases) told the basis for pay decisions. MBO results should perhaps be the major input into this process, but the reward system should take into account a broader set of variables than does MBO, including many nonmeasurable.

8. Individual contributions should not be overemphasized. Some companies now base their rewards not just on the individual's own performance but also on the performance of his department and the organization as a whole, and this would seem to be a desirable move.

9. To a considerable extent the effectiveness of an MBO program depends on how the superior reacts when a subordinate fails to meet his goals. If the superior acts in a punitive manner, the subordinate will fear to take risks in the future and will seek to be given only the most conservative goals. Thus the boss must permit failure. On the other hand, if the boss completely ignores the failure, the subordinate may decide the entire MBO program is meaningless. Obviously the middle ground is preferable: the superior should use the failure as a springboard for a discussion of how performance in the affected area may be improved in the future.

CONCLUSION

MBO has a number of attractive features. Its emphasis on specific goals makes performance appraisal more objective, and even limited subordinate involvement in goal-setting tends to make "goals more realistic and palatable to the individual....No small accomplishment" [20]. MBO is a step toward a systems view of management, linking individual goals to those of the organization as a whole, strategies to objectives and facilitating coordination (bargaining) between departments. Ideally, it forces management at each level to specify exactly what it is seeking to accomplish, and it can be an effective means of communication, at least downward.

MBO's main limitations are of two sorts:

1. As the quotations previously presented illustrate, in many companies MBO is viewed as a gimmick or a slogan rather than as a method of management. Impractical goals are established without considering the likelihood of their being realized, and, once the going gets tough, they are forgotten.

2. MBO is not very realistic if looked upon entirely or primarily as a method of performance appraisal or subordinate goal-setting. Unless they deal with trivia, individ-

ual goals must mesh with those of the organization. At the most MBO can permit (a) greater individual control over how broader goals are met and (b) perhaps, within narrow limits, some greater influence regarding the level of these goals themselves.

Of the two fathers of the MBO concept, McGregor emphasized participation, Drucker goal-setting. The Drucker approach seems to be winning out. In many companies MBO is viewed chiefly as a means of communicating top management's goals. MBO is increasingly achievement rather than human relations-oriented.

Most companies which have experimented with MBO have treated it as a personnel technique (or even a gimmick), on the order of T-groups, brain storming, employee counseling or the case method approach to training. Given management's propensity to abandon old programs of this sort whenever a new fad comes along, I suspect that by 1980 the term MBO will be something of an anachronism. And yet, in a number of companies it will have left a legacy of more systematic planning, tighter, more realistic controls and better communications.

For those companies considering the adoption of MBO, I would say, "Try it. It is a fail-safe device which (compared, for example, to T-groups, which can do real harm) at worst will merely arouse false hopes."

FOOTNOTE REFERENCES

1. See, for example, John P. Campbell and others, *Managerial Behavior, Performance, and Effectiveness*. McGraw-Hill, New York, 1970, pp. 62-67. In Britain, too, it is "the current management top fashion," *The Economist*, April 25, 1970, p. 60.

2. According to a 1964 survey, 23 percent of the 141 companies surveyed made "much use" of "appraisal against specific objectives." W. S. Wickstrom, *Developing Management Competence: Changing Concepts--Emerging Practices*. National Industrial Conference Board, Studies in Personnel Policy, No. 189, 1964, p. 26. A similar 1964 study reported but five percent of the companies responding utilized MBO. Bureau of National Affairs, *Managerial Ap-*

praisal Programs, Personnel Practices Forum, Survey No. 74, September, 1964. It seems reasonably likely that the percentages are considerably higher today.

3. Recently I polled the participants in a management course of mine as to the experience of their companies with MBO. These managers came from a broad range of manufacturing firms. Of the approximately 25 percent who came from companies which had tried MBO, about one-third said the experience had been bad; in most of these companies MBO had been either formally dropped or, more commonly, it had just faded away. In another third, MBO was judged a success, and in the final third the experience was mixed. This is hardly my idea of rigorous research, but I suspect more careful studies would come to roughly the same conclusions.

4. I am indebted to Raymond Miles for this case. For other suggestions, I owe a debt to David Bowen, Joseph Robinson, Charles Snow, and John Sims--as well as to the Berkeley Organizational Behavior-Industrial Relations Ph.D. Seminar.

5. Perhaps equally responsible was Peter Drucker. See his *The Practice of Management*, Harpers, New York, 1954.

6. See Douglas McGregor, "An Uneasy Look at Performance Appraisal," *Harvard Business Review*, Vol. 35, No. 3, May-June, 1957.

7. George Odiorne was to a large extent responsible for popularizing this approach to MBO. See his highly influential *Management by Objectives*, Pitman, New York, 1964.

8. In Likert's terms, MBO places emphasis on intervening as well as on end-results variables. Rensis Likert, *The Human Organization*, McGraw-Hill, New York, 1967, MBO can also take advantage of "human assets accounting."

9. The changing emphasis means that MBO is less the property of the personnel department (or individual managers at all levels) and more the property of top management.

10. According to one study, subordinate goal setting leads to higher goal achievement than does goal setting by the boss only when the boss's usual pattern of management is participative. John R. P. French, Jr., Emanuel Kay, and Herbert H. Meyer, "Participation and the Appraisal System," *Human Relations*, Vol. 19, No. 1, 1966, p. 14.

11. According to one study of a single company, higher level managers feel greater freedom to set their own objectives

in the MBO process than do those at lower levels; greater freedom is also felt by managers in areas, such as marketing, where top management control is relatively difficult and the need for close coordination with other departments relatively little. Henry L. Tosi, Jr., and Stephen J. Carroll, "Some Structural Factors Related to Goal Influence in the Management by Objectives Process," *MSU Business Topics*, Spring, 1969, pp. 45-50.

12. Some companies distinguish between *personnel development* and *performance* objectives. Such a personal development objective for a design engineer might be to spend more time with the marketing staff, so that his product design might better anticipate changes in consumer preferences--or to attend a leadership training program to improve his relations with subordinates. Individual managers have considerably greater freedom to set their personal objectives than their performance objectives. Indeed there is tie-in between freedom to set personal objectives and what has been called the "open system" approach to management development. Theodore M. Alford, "Checkers or Choice in Manpower Management," *Harvard Business Review*, Vol. 45, January-February, 1967. By and large personal goals are secondary to performance. And so, MBO permits substantial subordinate participation only in relatively unimportant areas.

13. In other words, where output variables cannot be measured, the tendency is to measure input.

14. The decision-making objective, as yet, is running a poor third, though it is rapidly closing the gap.

15. National Industrial Conference Board, *Managing By and With Objectives*, Studies in Personnel Policy, No. 212, 1968, p. 58. Emphasis added.

16. Tosi and Carroll, *op. cit.*, pp. 50 and 45.

17. French, Kay, Meyer, *op. cit.*, and Stephen L. Carroll, Jr., and Henry Tossi, "Goal Characteristics and Personality Factors in a Management-by-Objectives Program," *Administrative Science Quarterly*, Vol. 15, No. 3, September, 1970, pp. 295-303.

18. That bargaining of this sort is common among departments I have suggested elsewhere. George Strauss, "Tactics of Lateral Relationship," *Administrative Science Quarterly*, Vol. 7, September, 1962. MBO merely formalizes and legitimizes the process. This bargaining should not be confused with unrestricted autonomy. The bargaining occurs within constraints provided by higher management.

19. Strauss, George, and Leonard R. Sayles, *Personnel*, 3rd ed., Prentice-Hall, Englewood Cliffs, N. J., 1972, Chap. 7.

20. Rothstein, William G., "Executive Appraisal Programs," *ILR Research*, Vol. 8, No. 2, 1962, p. 17.

STUDENT REVIEW QUESTIONS

1. Have all attempts to use MBO been successful? Why?
2. Explain what is involved in good MBO systems.
3. How free does Strauss say subordinates actually are when setting their objectives?
4. Is it feasible to keep the MBO and salary appraisal systems separate?
5. As MBO is practiced today is it a means of tightening or loosening top management controls?
6. What are the two major limitations of MBO that Strauss identifies?

32

Utilizing Operating Budgets for Maximum Effectiveness*

RALPH L. BENKE, JR.

DURING THE PAST DECADE we have witnessed a substantial change in the attitudes of employees toward their organizations. As employees have become better educated and more affluent they have demanded and received a greater voice in the activities of their organization. In response to this, management has had to give more consideration to the well-being and feelings of their subordinates when making decisions. The effective manager today is one who can properly combine concern for his employees with concern for production.

This change has affected the operating budget process. Traditionally, the operating budget process has been viewed as two dimensional. The first dimension is the use of budgets as a planning device; the second the use of the budget as a feedback device to insure that the employees of the organization are adhering to the plan. The assumption underlying the two dimensional view is that if planning has been properly done, and strict control maintained thru feedback, the operating budget process would be successful.

With the attitude of today's employees, this traditional two dimensional view is outmoded. Employees are no longer willing to passively accept plans made for them by their superiors. They are intelligent, well educated and capable of adding significantly to the effectiveness of planning. The tight controls utilized in the past can cause considerable dissatisfaction among employees today. At best tight controls will result in a steady exodus of creative personnel.

Thus, the effective operating budget process of today is

*From *Managerial Planning*, September/October, 1976, pp. 33-39.Reprinted by permission of Planning Executives Institute.

three dimensional. Along with the dimensions of the traditional view of the operating budget process, i.e. planning and feedback, we must add a third--behavioral considerations. Today, the effective operating budget is one that devises plans in a manner that brings about a commitment of the employees to the successful execution of the plans, and establishes feedback that encourages the continuation of the commitment. (See Diagram 32-1).

DIAGRAM 32-1.
EFFECTIVENESS OF THE OPERATING BUDGET PROCESS

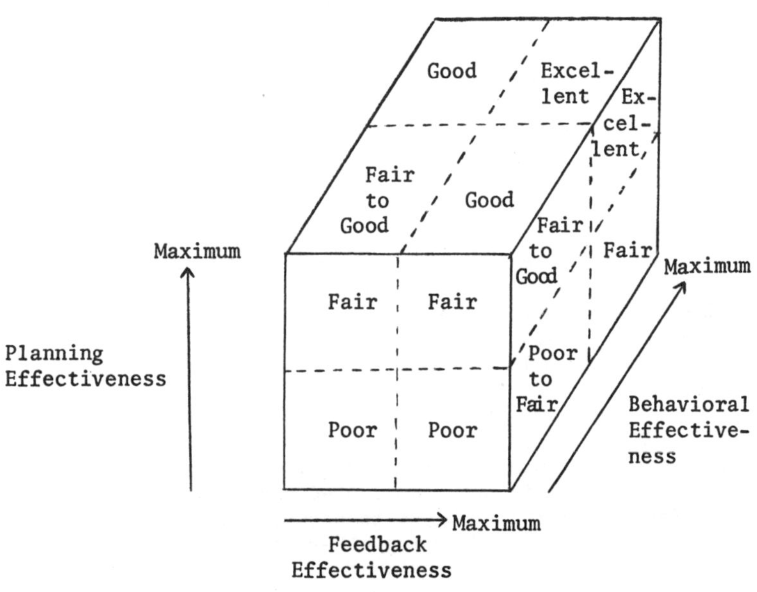

This diagram shows that when planning effectiveness, feedback effectiveness and behavioral effectiveness are at their maximums, the operating budget's effectiveness is "excellent." The best effectiveness that can be achieved with a two dimensional operating budget process is "fair."

If we ignore this third dimension--behavioral implications--of the operating budget process, one or all of the following problems may occur:

1. Budgets, as a planning device, will not be as effective as they could be.

2. Reports comparing actual performance to budgeted performance will not accurately reflect the extent to which plans are being accomplished by departments of the organization.
3. The budgets may not be prepared or utilized in a manner that motivates employees to take actions that are in the best interest of the organization.
4. In extreme instances, improper preparation or utilization of budgets may cause severe internal problems, such as depressed morale, that affect the overall well-being of the organization.

The purpose of this paper is to examine the operating budget process to determine how these problems occur, and to suggest means of coping with them. However, none of the problems is entirely avoidable, and we cannot construct a problem-free budgeting system. In any event it is unnecessary. Just as organizations need not be perfect in order to make a profit, budgets need not be perfect in order to be effective.

As noted in Diagram 32-2, the budgeting process for any period is composed of four stages. Ideally, those with budget responsibility would be able to remain in the loop between the decision and information stages, where evaluations are favorable. When forced out of this loop, the actions taken are designed to return to this loop.

The information stage, unlike the other stages, is primarily mechanical. The physical process of comparing actual performance to budgeted performance, whether it is done by hand or machine, is not complicated and allows little latitude for behavioral problems to occur. Our examination will, therefore, be confined to the other three stages.

THE PLANNING STAGE

There are a number of questions with behavioral implications that are faced in the planning stage. How sophisticated[1] should the process of setting standards be? Who should participate in establishing the standards? Who should have final determination of the standards? Should the standards be difficult or easy to reach or somewhere in

[1]Sophistication refers to efforts to make standards more objective. Thus, any technique that is employed to reduce subjectivity in setting standards is considered sophisticated.

DIAGRAM 32-2.

DIAGRAM OF OPERATING BUDGET PROCESS

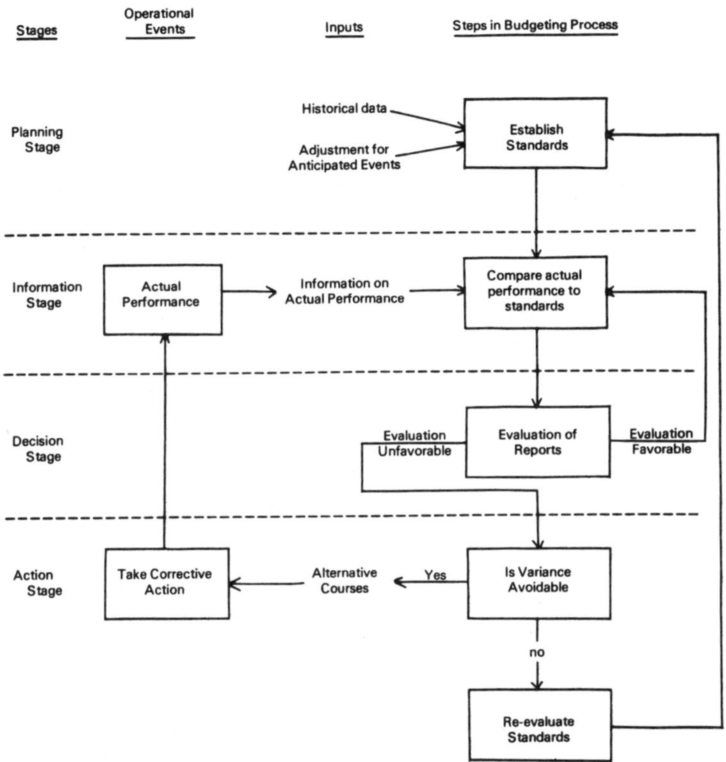

between?

The goal of the planning stage is two-fold. First, and quite obvious, is to establish standards whose accomplishment promotes the well-being of the organization, which in most cases means making a profit. Second, and an often overlooked goal, is to establish standards that are acceptable to the manager responsible for reaching them. Acceptance of the standards by the manager is referred to as internalization of standards, and, as will be discussed later, has a significant impact on motivation. From the viewpoint of the organization, when internalization takes place, the probability of accomplishing the first goal increases significantly.

The more sophisticated the process of setting standards, the more it tends to interfere with the internalization of standards. There are at least two reasons for this interference. First, techniques that increase objectively, such as regression analysis, necessarily increase the complexity of deriving standards. However, if the process of deriving standards becomes so complex that the managers cannot understand it, the standards may not be internalized, and their enthusiasm for reaching these standards will be considerably diminished. Thus, a budget with standards set by regression analysis is more sophisticated, but will be effective only if the managers understand regression analysis.

Certainly, this problem can be at least partially overcome with sufficient training. Even so, there is a second problem stemming from sophistication that cannot be overcome so easily. Techniques that increase objectivity also reduce input from the managers. Thus, the standards become less representative of the manager's views. This is a key point.

People are rarely motivated to attain standards set for them by others, because they represent what someone else expects of the individual, rather than what the individual expects of himself. Standards set by regression analysis or probabilitistic techniques, or any other technique by an operations research department or accounting department, however conscientiously, will seldom become internalized because they fail to include the views of the manager. The manager will believe and argue that the standards are "ideal," that they fail to take into consideration how thin things operate in the field. This becomes an easy excuse to explain failure and is hard to refute.

However, if the manager participates in setting the standards, they are more likely to become internalized since he has influenced them to represent his views. His desire to attain them is increased by the realization that, if under normal circumstance he fails to attain them, he can blame only himself.

This does not suggest that sophisticated techniques for setting standards should not be used. On the contrary, standards computed by such means can be very effective *guides* for those engaged in establishing standards. They also can be useful in insuring that the standards set by a manager are not unnecessarily conservative.

When a manager participates in setting his own standards, one of his concerns is that the standards are set at a level he can attain. Therefore, he is motivated to set conservative standards, which results in slack being built into the budget. Slack occurs when the manager underestimates revenues and overestimates expenses. Thus, the manager creates a "margin of error" for himself.

From the viewpoint of the organization, all slack should be eliminated to maximize profit. Standards should be high, and perfection would be achieved when every manager was stretched to his maximum capability and every standard was reached but not exceeded. This is the extreme of the so-called "stretch" theory which advocates setting standards so that a manager must extend his capabilities to reach them.

However, the evidence suggests that too much stretch is not beneficial to the organization. People are motivated more by moderately difficult standards than by standards that they fall short of or accomplish only with great difficulty. Reaching a moderately difficult standard and exceeding it provides great satisfaction. It gives us confidence and reinforces our faith in ourselves. It creates an atmosphere of success rather than one of failure. This suggests that some slack is desirable, but excessive slack must be avoided. To avoid excessive slack final standards should not be set by the manager who must attain them, but by negotiation between the manager and his immediate superior. Schiff and Lewin have shown that this procedure will control excess slack if it is done in depth.[2]

The supervisor must be careful in the negotiation process not to impose his standards on the manager. Such actions as requiring a 10% across-the-board reduction in expenses may result in standards that are not internalized, thus, destroying the purpose of participation by the manager.

When the supervisor encounters standards he feels are substantially incorrect because of excessive slack, he should attempt to induce the manager to change them by cogent arguments and avoid heavy-handed methods.

A subtle way for the superior to avoid standards with excessive slack is to provide the manager with guideline standards that tend to be on the high side *before* the manager sets his standards. Stedry showed that high guideline standards tend to result in high standards being set by the manager and that these standards become internalized.[3] The key is to provide the guidelines before the manager sets his standards, rather than trying to influence him to change them after they have been set.

In summary, during the planning stage every effort should be made to avoid *imposing* standards on a manager. Rather, he should be an integral part of the process of establishing standards, thus, creating a sense of obligation for him to accomplish the standards he has set. This will probably result in establishing moderately difficult standards, but these standards will provide greater motivation than standards that are too easy or too difficult.

---

[2] M. Schiff and A. Y. Lewin, "The Impact of People on Budgets," *The Accounting Review*, Vol. XLV, No. 2 (April, 1970), pp. 259-268.

[3] A. C. Stedry, *Budget Control and Cost Behavior* (Englewood Cliffs, N. J.: Prentice-Hall, 1960).

THE DECISION STAGE

The decision stage is concerned with determining whether further action is needed. As Diagram 32-2 shows, if no action is needed, i.e. the evaluation is favorable, you return to the information stage. The question faced in the decision stage is what requires further action and what does not?

The report received from the information stage will compare actual revenues and expenses with budgeted revenues and expenses, item-by-item. Should the evaluation be concerned with the item-by-item comparisons or the overall comparison of budgeted profit with actual profit? To illustrate simply:

	Budgeted	Actual	Variance	
Annual Revenues	$200,000	$200,000	$ 0	
Annual Expenses				
Wages	130,000	170,000	40,000	Unfavorable
Vehicle Maintenance	50,000	10,000	40,000	Favorable
Total Profit	$ 20,000	$ 20,000	$ 0	

Does the end justify the means? It appears that the organization's goal and the manager's goal, a $20,000 profit, has been accomplished. However, appearances are often deceiving, as they are in this instance.

In order for the manager to accomplish his goal and, hence, his portion of the organization's goal, he suboptimized, i.e. took actions that tended to maximize this year's profit at the expense of future years. In the illustration the suboptimal act was drastically reducing vehicle maintenance in order to offset the overexpenditure in wages. This surely means that regular maintenance has been curtailed, which probably means that the life of the vehicle will be shortened.

The budgeting process tends to encourage suboptimization since managers are rarely commended for actions that decrease this year's profit and increases future year's profits. Thus, a manager might eliminate a training program, even though he knows this will create a deficit of qualified personnel to fill future vacated positions, or slash advertising expenses, even though he knows this means fewer new customers next year, or deceive the union into accepting a lower than average wage increase, even though he suspects that when they find out trouble will develop and next contract's demands will be substantial.

The organizational system also encourages suboptimization since a manager frequently does not have to face the consequences of his own suboptimization. Many organizations rotate their employees regularly, hence, a manager can sacrifice the future for the present with the knowledge that his successor will face the consequences, not he.

Therefore, concentrating the evaluation only on the end result may create the impression that the means is unimportant, when clearly it is not. At the same time evaluating each item may unduly restrict the manager.

A useful compromise is to establish boundaries on each item. The manager is free to operate without interference as long as he does not exceed the boundaries. Thus, a "floor" below which expenses cannot fall might be placed on such items as vehicle maintenance, advertising, charitable contributions and special promotions. Percentage boundaries or dollar boundaries might be placed on other items.

Another concern during the decision stage is the interdepartmental effect of budgets. The organization can maximize its accomplishments only when all departments work together, hopefully creating a synergistic effect. However, the budgeting process forces managers to place intradepartmental considerations before interdepartmental considerations. Rarely does one department assume responsibility for another department's failure. Thus, interdepartmental cooperation will,to some extent, depend on how much it benefits the individual departments. For example, hiring new clerical personnel to support a sales campaign is disadvantageous for the Administration Manager,as it is an expense for his operation, and advantageous for the Sales Manager,as it will expedite billing and commissions. Under these circumstances the Administrative Manager may be motivated to avoid as much of the expense as possible by delaying the hiring of the new personnel, regardless of the impact on the Sales Department.

In summary, the decision stage is concerned primarily with determining whether a variance is favorable or unfavorable, and this determination should be made item-by-item to discourage suboptimization. However, simply because a variance is negative does not mean it is unfavorable. In the day-to-day operation of an organization temporary negative variances can be expected to occur for a number of reasons. For example an expenditure might be made before it was anticipated it would be made when the budget was compiled. In order to allow the manager latitude, variances should not be considered unfavorable unless they are significant.

It was also noted that a positive variance is not necessarily favorable, particularly vehicle maintenace, advertising, etc. The Administrative Manager's action could have resulted in a positive variance in salaries and wages, however, because of its negative impact on the Sales Department, it may be unfavorable.

THE ACTION STAGE

The action stage consists of two categories: avoidable

and unavoidable variances.[4] (See Diagram 32-2) Avoidable variances are those that should and could have been avoided by the manager responsible for the budget. As the variance was avoidable, the manager is responsible for taking corrective action designed to eliminate the variance.

Unavoidable variances are those that couldn't have been avoided by the manager responsible for the budget. The circumstances leading to the variance were completely beyond his control. When avoidable variances occur they are eliminated by revising the standards.

Many firms do not make a distinction between avoidable and unavoidable variances. They argue that standards should not be revised because: (1) revising standards is too expensive; (2) it creates conflict between the manager and his supervisor over what is avoidable and what is unavoidable; (3) managers will, as a matter of practice, ask that every unfavorable variance be considered unavoidable, because they have everything to gain and nothing to lose; (4) eventually the definition of what is avoidable will deteriorate and include almost everything; and (5) it all evens out. For every unavoidable occurrence that hurts the manager, there may be one that helps him.

These are persuasive arguments against a budgeting system that revises standards. Some of the arguments for it are: (1) a manager should not be held responsible for unfavorable variances emanating from occurrences over which he had no control; (2) a manager can do an outstanding job, yet still have an unfavorable variance because of an occurrence beyond his control; (3) if an unavoidable occurrence causes an unfavorable variance near the end of the budgeting period, the manager does not have time to recover; (4) if the impact on the budget of an occurrence beyond the manager's control is large, the manager may simply give up; and (5) new ideas that cost now and pay off later are discouraged.

The arguments for a budgeting system that revises standards are also persuasive. However, the arguments against it concern mainly the mechanics of the system, while the arguments for it are primarily behavioral. Thus, the weight of the arguments is in favor of revising standards. Problems of mechanics can usually be overcome.

One way to accommodate both sets of arguments, yet have a system that can be revised, is to narrowly define an unavoidable variance, so that it covers very few instances. The definition could be simply "an occurrence caused by an exogenous variable." An exogenous variable is a variable

---

[4] We are, of course, concerned with unfavorable variances. Although some purpose might be served by dividing favorable variance into avoidable and unavoidable, the cost of doing so would probably exceed the benefit.

that is entirely external to the firm.

Thus, if a manager plans for a $1.00 raise for his employees, and the union strikes the industry, receiving a $1.50 raise, the variance is unavoidable. If sales are down industry-wide, the sales department could have an unavoidable. If the Sales Manager falls short of his sales goals because of unexpected heavy illness among his sales staff, it is not an unavoidable variance, as he is responsible for insuring he has adequate trained personnel.

This type of budget avoids many of the arguments against a budget that revises standards and incorporates some of those for it. A difficult problem that must be resolved is who determines whether a variance is avoidable or unavoidable.

There are a number of possible solutions the best choice of which will depend on the characteristics of the organization. One solution would be to allow the manager's immediate supervisor to make the determination. This would have the advantage of having the decision made by someone "on the scene" who has first hand familiarity with the situation. On the negative side is the fact that someone who has a vested interest in the budget would be making the decisions. This might be avoided by having the decision made by someone further up the organizational structure.

An alternative would be to assign the decision to a staff department, who would investigate each situation. Guidelines should be established by higher management so that the department investigates only situations with merit, and is not deluged with requests to investigate variances that were clearly avoidable.

Another possibility would be to form committees of ressponsible persons in each division. A little more unusual would be the possibility of having managers on the same level as the manager requesting the investigation make the decision.

In the event an unfavorable variance is avoidable, as the vast majority will be, it is necessary to take some corrective action to return the variance to zero. From the viewpoint of the manager the corrective action is, in part, behavioral. He must motivate his employees to take actions that will correct the variance. However, as this type of motivation concerns non-managerial employees and is outside the budgeting system, it is beyond the scope of this paper.

From the viewpoint of the manager's supervisor, the problem is also behavioral. How can he use the budgeting system to motivate the manager to take corrective action? This question can be broadened to how can the supervisor motivate the manager to reach the standards? If the manager is not motivated to reach the standards, he will lack motivation for corrective action.

Earlier it was noted that internalization of standards by the manager would increase his desire to reach the standards.

While this is important, it is not sufficient by itself to highly motivate a manager.

An additional factor is the supervisor's response to variances. What degree of importance does the manager believe his supervisor assigns to the variances? Every action taken by the supervisor, whether it is a reward or punishment, contributes to the perception the manager has of the importance of variances. If the supervisor's interest is active, the manager's interest is likely also to be active, and corrective action will be emphasized.

It is worth noting that threats are not a viable means for a supervisor to indicate his degree of interest, although, they may carry that message. In addition to creating a hostile atmosphere, they do not motivate an employee, they push him, and they do so only as long as the threat is maintained. Therefore, the threat must be renewed to remain effective. Also, the supervisor must be prepared to support the threat with action. The result is usually negative for the supervisor, manager and other employees.

In conjunction with the supervisor's response to variances and the internalization of standards, there are a host of personal motivations. These can result from a desire to do a better job than another manager, or a better job than a predecessor, or simply a better job than last year.

There is considerable reinforcing interaction between these sources of motivation. If the supervisor does not attach some importance to the variances, personal motivation is unlikely to occur, and internalization of standards will make little difference. On the other hand, demoting an employee for consistent unfavorable variances may well destroy personal motivation if the standards were imposed on the manager, or he was the victim of exogenous variables in an unrevised budget.

In summary, one of the objectives of the budgeting process is to construct it so that managers are highly motivated to reach the standards. However,the budgeting process cannot totally motivate a manager. The final factor is personal motivation, and personal motivation is more likely to occur if the budgeting process reflects, as accurately as possible, the manager's performance. Participation in setting standards, boundaries within which a manager can operate without question, and dividing unfavorable variances into avoidable and unavoidable variances contributes to this.

CONCLUSION

The operating budget is the principle means of controlling expenses and revenues within an organization, and is, therefore, more influential in the attainment of the organizational goal of profitability than any other single process. The organization with an effective operating budget process has a much higher probability of reaching its potential than a firm with a less effective process.

Behavioral scientists have shown that in order for an operating budget process to achieve its maximum effectiveness, the process must be considered three dimensional. Thru understanding the third dimension--behavioral considerations--the organization can improve the effectiveness of its operating budget process by designing it to encourage managers to take actions that are in the best interest of the organization.

STUDENT REVIEW QUESTIONS

1. Explain the traditional two dimension budget process.
2. What dimension does Benke add to the traditional model of the budgeting process? Why?
3. What are the goals of the planning stage?
4. Why does Benke say "The more sophisticated the process of setting standards, the more it tends to interfere with the internalization of standards"?
5. Why does the budgeting process tend to encourage suboptimization? Does Benke suggest any remedies for this problem?
6. How does Benke recommend solving the problem of differentiating between avoidable and unavoidable variance?

33

Zero Base Budgeting as a Management Tool*

SCOTT S. COWEN

BURTON V. DEAN

ARDESHIR LOHRASBI

THE USE OF ZERO BASE budgeting as a management tool has become increasingly popular in the private and public sectors since the early 1970s. Recent surveys have indicated that ZBB is used by fifty-four of the largest one thousand companies in the United States, by eleven state governments, and by many municipalities.[1] It is an integral part of the fiscal 1979 federal budget process.[2]

The concept of ZBB, that is, building a budget from ground zero, is not new. What is new is the methodology used to set up a ZBB system. One of the earliest applications of the technique in the private sector was at Texas Instruments, in 1970. The company had considerable success with ZBB, and its experiences have been well documented in the literature.[3] As a result of Texas Instruments' success, the use of ZBB began to expand rapidly in the 1970s. In 1971, the state of Georgia introduced ZBB into its formal budget process. This served as the impetus for other state and local governments to follow suit.

The use of budgeting as a management tool has long been accepted in the fields of management and accounting. The

*From *MSU Business Topics,* Spring, 1978, pp. 29-39. Reprinted by permission of the publisher, Division of Research, Graduate School of Business Administration, Michigan State University.

budgeting system integrates the key managerial functions of planning, control, and performance evaluation. The effectiveness of budgets in assisting management depends on the type of activity in which they are used. For example, budgets are best used as a control device in those activities that are directly related to the final output of the organization. The reason for this is that the resources used by these activities are often a direct and observable function of the firm's output. Thus, a more accurate budget can be developed once the relationship between input and output has been specified. This specified relationship becomes the standard by which to develop budgets and exercise control.

In those units performing activities not directly related to the company's output, for example, legal staff and personnel office, budgeting serves a different purpose. It represents a statement of what the unit would like to do and a summary of the resources required to accomplish the tasks. Because the tasks and resources required are not related to the firm's output, it is difficult to determine whether the budget is realistic and reflective of efficient operations. ZBB is an appropriate tool to employ in controlling these support areas.

The traditional approach to budgeting in the support areas of an organization is based on the concept of incrementalism. Prior year cost levels are assumed given, and budget units focus their efforts on determining what changes from the prior year are required. In presenting proposed budgets, justification is provided for the incremental changes from last year's funding level. The use of incremental budgeting is more prominent in the evaluation of existing programs than in the planning and review of new ones. In the latter case, most organizations will justify new activities on the basis of cost-benefit analysis, which virtually necessitates building up costs and benefits from a zero base. An incremental approach to budgeting does not promote operational efficiency as a result of the following:

- Since last year's levels often are assumed, prior year inefficiencies are carried forward.
- The approach leads to continual growth in the budget. This is particularly true in the public sector.
- It is difficult to determine trade-offs between existing programs.
- The approach does not require a rigorous analysis of all proposed costs and benefits, that is, incremental as well as prior year; therefore, management has a lack of information for rational decision making.
- It is difficult to discern the impact of eliminating programs or reducing program

funding levels.

- The approach does not encourage managers to identify and evaluate alternative means of accomplishing tasks.

Management is usually aware of the shortcomings of incrementalism and often reacts to them outside the budget system through internal reviews and management audits. ZBB is a process by which internal management can eliminate incrementalism and build into the formal budget process periodic and comprehensive program review.

THE ZERO BASE BUDGETING PROCESS

Zero base budgeting has been defined as

> an operating planning and budgeting process which requires each manager to justify his entire budget request in detail from scratch (hence zero base). Each manager states why he should spend any money at all. This approach required that *all* activities be identified as "decision packages" which will be evaluated by *systematic analysis* and *ranked in order of importance.*[4]

The process requires managers to justify an entire budget request rather than just the incremental changes from the prior year's budget. A typical ZBB system would involve several steps.

Identification of decision units. A decision unit is a discrete entity within an organization for which a budget request is prepared. Decision units can revolve around cost centers, projects, programs, budget units, or any other entities which can be analyzed and for which budget decisions must be made.

An illustration of a statement and description of a decision unit is presented in Figure 33-1. The primary purpose of this statement is to force decision unit managers to describe departmental objectives and alternative ways to accomplish these objectives. As part of this process the manager stipulates alternative funding levels and the goals to be accomplished at each level.

Formulation of decision packages. The decision unit manager formulates, in priority order, a number of decision packages which altogether equal the sum of the budget request for the decision unit. Each decision package consists of a discrete set of services, activities, or expenditures. Figure 33-2 contains an illustration of a typical package.

A decision package should contain: (1) an identification of the decision package as a decision unit increment; (2) a description of the services to be provided or activities to

FIGURE 33-1. DECISION UNIT SUMMARY

(1) DECISION UNIT NAME	(2) ORGANIZATION	(3) PREPARED BY	(4) DATE	(5) COST CENTER

(6) OBJECTIVE OF DECISION UNIT

To manage the personnel in Central Accounting Services, to furnish direction, control and support so CAS functions can be accomplished efficiently and to furnish necessary secretarial support so that required statements and reports can be reported on a timely basis.

(7) CURRENT OPERATIONS AND REQUIRED RESOURCES

Seven employees manage, control, analyze, audit and furnish typing support for the accounting departments which pay employees, process vendors invoices, etc.

(8a) LIST ALTERNATIVE WAYS WHICH COULD ACCOMPLISH OBJECTIVES AND, IF APPROPRIATE, REASON FOR NOT USING IN 1978

1. Departments could be decentralized; this would be more costly as it would require more personnel at the operating division and training of division personnel.
2. Sections could be combined. Control and support would be weakened, etc.

(8b) DESCRIBE THE EFFECTS OF TRANSFERRING THIS FUNCTION TO OPERATING DIVISIONS

Several effects are described under (8a)1. In addition, current accounting operations are centralized, in one data processing operation (Work-In-Progress, Payroll Operations, Budget and Expense Systems). Extensive programming and systems changes would be required, etc.

(9) CRITICAL OPERATIONAL LINKAGES TO OTHER ORGANIZATIONAL UNITS

Group Controller — Information interchange. MC-CAS Manager — Same. Operating Division Accounting — Furnish information to and receive from operating results and forecast information, etc.

(12) INCREMENTAL IMPACT SUMMARY

1 of 3 — Combine two departments under one manager, no staff acct.

2 of 3 — Eliminate staff acct.

3 of 3 — Provide 100% of current service.

(10) SUMMARY OF INCREMENTS FOR 1978 / **(11) WORK LOAD/PERFORMANCE SUMMARY (CUM)**

(a) SERVICE PROVIDED (Identify current level in brackets)	INCREMENT NUMBER	INCREMENTAL EXPENSE	INCREMENTAL EMPLOYEES	CUMULATIVE EXPENSE	% (b)	CUMULATIVE EMPLOYEES	% (b)	Work Demand: Manage Five Departments	Work Demand: Staff Acct. Supporting MC-CAS	Quality: Est. No. of Complaints	Quality	Quantity	Quantity	Quantity
Combine depts. and eliminate staff acct.	1 of 3	212,300	5	212,300	81	5	71	4	0	3				
Eliminate staff acct.	2 of 3	29,000	1	241,300	92	6	86	5	0	2				
Maintain current level of operations	3 of 3	29.000	1	270,300	100	7	100	5	1	1				
(b) 1977 FORECAST EXPENSE AND EMPLOYEES				260,750		7		5	1	1				

FIGURE 33-2. DECISION UNIT INCREMENT

(1) DECISION UNIT NAME	(2) ORGANIZATION	(3) PREPARED BY	(4) DATE	(5a) RANK	(5b) INCREMENT
					1 of 3

(13) RESOURCES REQUIRED	1978 PLAN					
Five employees	INCREMENT		CUMULATIVE			
	EXPENSE	EMPLOYEE	EXPENSE	% (b)	EMPLOYEE	% (b)
(a) Increment Resources Required	212,300	5	212,300	81	5	71
(b) Decision Unit Resources Used in 1977 (Forcast)			261,000		7	
(c) Decision Unit Resources Used in 1976 (Actual)			240,000		7	

(14) OPERATIONS PERFORMED AND SERVICES PROVIDED BY JUST THIS INCREMENT PLUS IMPACT ON OTHER DEPARTMENTS:

Four department managers and one secretary would furnish guidance and support for the MC-CAS operation.

(15) CHANGES IN SERVICE BETWEEN EXISTING OPERATIONS AND PLANNED OPERATIONS THROUGH THIS INCREMENT:

Two departments (Accounts Payable and Inventories) would be combined under one manager. Control and direction would be weakened for the operations of the departments involved, etc.

(16) IF THIS IS INCREMENT 1, WHY WASN'T A LOWER LEVEL OF EFFORT DOCUMENTED?
IF NOT INCREMENT 1, WHAT WOULD BE THE CONSEQUENCES OF NOT FUNDING THIS INCREMENT?

Other departments within MC-CAS are not compatible enough in their efforts to make combinations practical. Each section requires skills and knowledge gained from extensive experience, etc.

(17) PLANNED WORK LOAD AND PERFORMANCE MEASURES:		1977 Actual	1978 Plan Increment	1978 Plan Cumulative
Work Demand				
Quality	Est. no. of complaints.	1/Mo.	3/Mo.	3/Mo.
Quantity	Time available to examine and improve operations, etc.	Est. 8 Mo.	—0—	—0—

be performed if the package is funded; (3) the resource requirements of the package and their costs; (4) a quantitative expression of workload output or results anticipated if the package is funded; and (5) an evaluation of the effects of changes if the package is funded.

A minimum level decision package is initially prepared representing the activity program--or a funding level below which it is not feasible to continue the decision unit because no constructive contribution can be made toward fulfilling its objectives. This package normally has a requested funding level significantly lower than in the prior year's budget. Once a minimum level decision package has been identified, the manager can propose additional packages which represent additional levels of activity and funding for the unit. The total of all the unit's decision packages equals its budget request.

Ranking. In the ZBB process, ranking has a key role in selecting the most effective decision package for funding. The ranking process provides management with a technique to allocate budget resources. It requires managers to assign priorities to budget increments by asking the following two questions:

- What purposes or objectivee should we attempt to achieve?
- How much should we spend in this attempt?

The decision packages are ranked in order of decreasing benefits to the organizational decision unit. The ranking process establishes priorities on the basis of functions described in the decision packages.

The managers at successively higher levels review rankings with lower level decision unit managers, using these rankings as a guide to produce a single consolidated ranking of *all* the decision pakcages presented to the higher level for review. The consolidated ranking uses all information available at both levels to evaluate alternative decision packages. This process is repeated at each succeeding higher level of the organization, as indicated in Figure 33-3.

The initial ranking occurs at the basic cost center or decision unit level, where the decision packages are developed originally. Each manager evaluates the relative importance of his or her own activities and ranks the specific decision unit's packages accordingly.

As is shown in Figure 33-3, rankings are first conducted by the individual decision unit (or section) managers, with the initial consolidation being made at the program level (P_2 in the figure). At the department level (D_1), program manager P_2 and program managers P_1 and P_3 form a committee to consolidate decision package rankings in a committee chaired by the head of the department (D_1). This process continues up to division, group, or even corporate levels. An example of a ranking table is given in Figure 33-4.

Allocation of organizational resources. The final step

in ZBB is to allocate organizational resources to decision units based on the consolidated ranking of decision packages and a projection of funds available. Once top management has a consolidated ranking of decision packages, a cutoff point is established for accepting packages based on funds available. All packages within the funding ceiling are accepted; others are rejected.

Accepted packages are translated into decision unit budgets by specifying what types of costs (salaries, supplies, utilities, and so forth) will be incurred to perform the activities identified in the package. This conversion process is illustrated in Figure 33-5. In this example, top management has decided that six decision packages requiring $55,000 will be accepted for funding for decision unit A. Decision package #1 requires $10,000, with $5,000 being used for wages, $1,000 for travel, $2,000 for supplies, and the remaining $2,000 for miscellaneous expenses. This crosswalk from decision package format to line item of expenditure format would be accomplished for each decision package funded in the decision unit. The sum of each column in the

FIGURE 33-3.

SEQUENTIAL RANKING OF DECISION PACKAGES

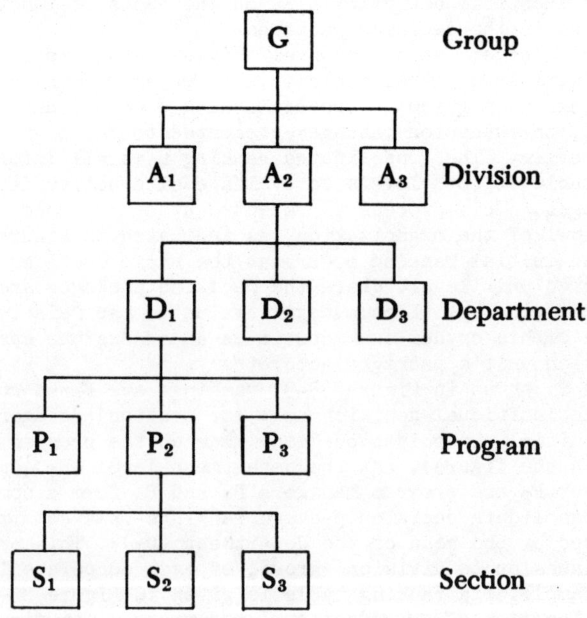

FIGURE 33-4. RANKING TABLE

(1) ORGANIZATIONAL UNITS BEING RANKED:							(2) PREPARED BY:		(3) DATE:		PAGE OF
(4) RANK	(5) DECISION UNIT INCREMENTS	INCREMENT NUMBER	(6) 1978 PROPOSED (a) EXPENSE	(6) 1978 PROPOSED (b) EMPLOYEES	(7) 1978 CUMULATIVE (a) EXPENSE	(7) 1978 CUMULATIVE (b) EMPLOYEES	(8) 1977 FORECAST (a) EXPENSE	(8) 1977 FORECAST (b) EMPLOYEES	(9) PERCENTAGE CHANGE 1978 ÷ 1977 × 100 (a) EXPENSE	(9) PERCENTAGE CHANGE 1978 ÷ 1977 × 100 (b) EMPLOYEES	(10) NOTES
1	Payroll	1 of 6	207,800	11	207,800	11	241,000	15	15.8	13.9	Pay salary monthly
2	Accounts Payable Invoices	1 of 5	143,000	12	350,800	23	191,000	17	26.6	29.1	No. invoice verification
3	A/P Freight and Claims	1 of 4	61,300	4	412,100	27	82,000	6	31.3	34.2	No. freight bill verification
4	Customer Billing	1 of 3	119,700	7	531,800	34	133,000	9	40.4	43.0	Minimal billing service
5	Administration	1 of 3	212,300	5	744,100	39	261,000	7	56.5	49.3	4 Mgrs./ No Staff
6	Capital, Exp. and Gen. Ledger	1 of 5	106,500	5	850,600	44	240,000	13	64.6	55.6	Basic reports only
7	Inventory	1 of 4	72,000	4	922,600	48	103,000	7	70.0	60.7	Part. Analysis/ No Cont.
8	Cashier	1 of 2	18,500	1	941,100	49	39,000	3	71.4	62.0	Do not pay Hrly. Claims
9	Personal Acct.	1 of 4	13,400	1	954,500	50	29,000	2	72.4	63.3	Record only/ No Control
10	A/P Invoices	2 of 5	18,000	2	972,500	52	1,319,000	79	73.8	65.8	Check invoice terms
11	Payroll	2 of 6	15,500	1	988,000	53			74.9	67.1	Semi-Monthly Salary
12	A/P Freight and Claims	2 of 4	9,000	1	997,000	54			75.7	68.3	Minimum verification
13	Administration	2 of 3	29,000	1	1,026,000	55			77.8	69.6	5 Mgrs./ No Staff
14		of									
15		of									
16		of									

FIGURE 33-5.

CROSSWALK FROM ZBB FORMAT TO LINE ITEM OF EXPENDITURE BUDGET FORMAT FOR DECISION UNIT A

Decision Packages \ Item of Expenditure			Wages	Travel	Supplies	etc.									Total
#	Amount ($000)	Cumulative													
1	10	10	5	1	2	1	1								10
2	15	25													15
3	7	32													7
4	8	40													8
5	9	49													9
6	6	55													6
All packages below this are unacceptable.															55

crosswalk matrix is the total amount to be funded by type of input. The column totals--$55,000--represent the total budget of the decision unit by type of expenditure, whereas the row totals would be the total budget of the unit by type of activities to be performed.

CRITERIA FOR RANKING

The ranking approach used should be adapted to organizational needs. There is no ranking system that is universally valid. The following are general types of approaches.

Single Criterion. All packages (projects/programs) are evaluated on the basis of one and only one criterion. Examples of economic criteria include return on investment, cost savings, net present value, discounted cash flow, cost-benefit ratio, and payback period.

The ranking procedure would involve the following steps:

- Agree on the single criterion to be used.
- Rank all packages from top to bottom, using the criterion agreed upon.
- Determine the cutoff point, based on available funds and/or personnel.
- Approve and fund all packages above the cutoff level, and defer or eliminate all others.
- Communicate the decision to the appropriate managers.

Voting System. Although the single criterion approach is conceptually sound, problems associated with several conflicting objectives make it inapplicable.[5] Peter Phyrr developed a voting system for use by a committee in ranking a large number of packages as follows:

- Each committee member is provided with a complete set of decision packages and ranking sheets.
- The committee discusses each package to obtain a thorough understanding of it, then votes on a fixed scale, with either the average or the total points determining the ranking.
- The ranking is reviewed and discussed by the committee, followed by resolution of principal differences and reordering of the packages.
- Final ranking is achieved and passed on to the next higher level for consolidation.[6]

Major Categories. One concern is that it might be possible to obviate the purposes of ZBB by ranking poorer packages higher than worthwhile packages, so as to increase the budget. To prevent the likelihood of this happening, it is worthwhile to classify packages by major categories, in order of importance.[7] For example:

- All efforts that are explicitly required by law.
- All efforts that pay for themselves in the first year.
- All packages that require a core management group.
- All packages that have a substantial long-term economic impact.
- All other packages.

Multiple Standards. Logan M. Cheek has applied a multiple standard approach to Xerox personnel and planning areas.[8] Five criteria are used to rank order packages.[9]

- Is the package legally required? (legal requirement)
- Does the organization have the necessary technical skills? (state of the art)
- Will line management accept and execute the package? (ease of implementation)
- Is the package cost-effective? (net economic benefits)
- Can the organization afford not to select the package? (economic risks)

The process of decision package ranking becomes more difficult when benefits cannot be quantified in dollar terms. Comparability among decision packages on the basis of benefits is compromised because of the differing units of measurement; thus, the ranking procedure becomes more complex. Instead of ranking packages on the basis of cost-benefit ratios, or return on investment ratios, other criteria must be used. As previously mentioned, these include: (1) perceived importance of service, (2) potential consequences of not providing service, (3) statutory or contractual agreements, (4) informal assessments, and (5) political reasons. The rigorousness of the ZBB methodology begins to deteriorate when these other ranking criteria are employed. Also, a major feature of ZBB--the setting of priorities--is undermined, and the benefits of ZBB are not fully realized.

Another critical problem in developing and ranking decision packages is the paperwork generated. The number of decision packages to be developed and ranked in an entity is contingent on the size of the organization, span of control, and nature of activities being performed. In a large corporation the number of decision packages can conceivably be in the hundreds. Quite naturally, management needs to develop techniques to control the volume of decision packages at each consolidation level in the organization.

A typical means of accomplishing this control is to establish cutoff limits at each consolidation level. For example, the first consolidation level may have a cutoff target of 50 percent. This means that the manager at this level will provide a cursory review of the decision packages handed up to him or her by the decision unit managers; extract the highest ranked ones until the expenditures represented by the extracted packages add up to 50 percent of last year's budget for the decision units under review; and then focus his or her attention on an intensive review of the other packages.[10] The cutoff target increases at each higher consolidation level, thus forcing management to review only those packages at the margin. Unfortunately, this volume control technique undermines the zero base review concept. Packages ranked high by decision unit managers are almost guaranteed acceptance because of the lack of time for a thorough review of all packages. As a consequence, the zero base standard is replaced by a 70 percent or 80 percent standard which minimally ensures that most decision unit activities will be funded at a level equal to about 70 percent or 80 percent of last year's level. Thus, the problem of controlling the paperwork, which is particularly acute in the public sector, can transform zero base budgeting into a quasi-incremental approach.

MONITORING THE ZBB SYSTEM

Organizations using ZBB must continually evaluate the effectiveness of the system. It is necessary to conduct periodic reviews of the performance of ZBB after its implementation period. Such a review should include an evaluation of the impact of ZBB on the organization in light of original expectations.

It must be remembered that ZBB is not merely a budget cutting system, rather, it is a comprehensive management tool for integrating planning, control, and performance evaluation. Thus, possible consequences of the system could include: (1) more efficient resource allocation, (2) more active participation by managers, (3) better information for decision making, (4) improved communication among all levels of management, (5) closer linkage between objectives setting, budgeting, and performance evaluation, and (6) elimination of duplicate activities and improvements in product/service quality. The ZBB system should provide an answer to the basic questions of whether the intended benefits for the system were achieved and whether they exceeded the incremental costs realized. If it is decided that ZBB is to be continued, the review process should include evaluation of procedures and practices and a mechanism for recommending appropriate changes in the system.

The following questions are relevant.

When should the ZBB system be evaluated? This is best done prior to the budgetary preparation cycle.

Who should evaluate the ZBB system? ZBB should be evaluated by the planning and budgetary group (ZBB task force).

FIGURE 33-6.

FLOW DIAGRAM FOR ZBB EVALUATION AND CONTROL PROCESS

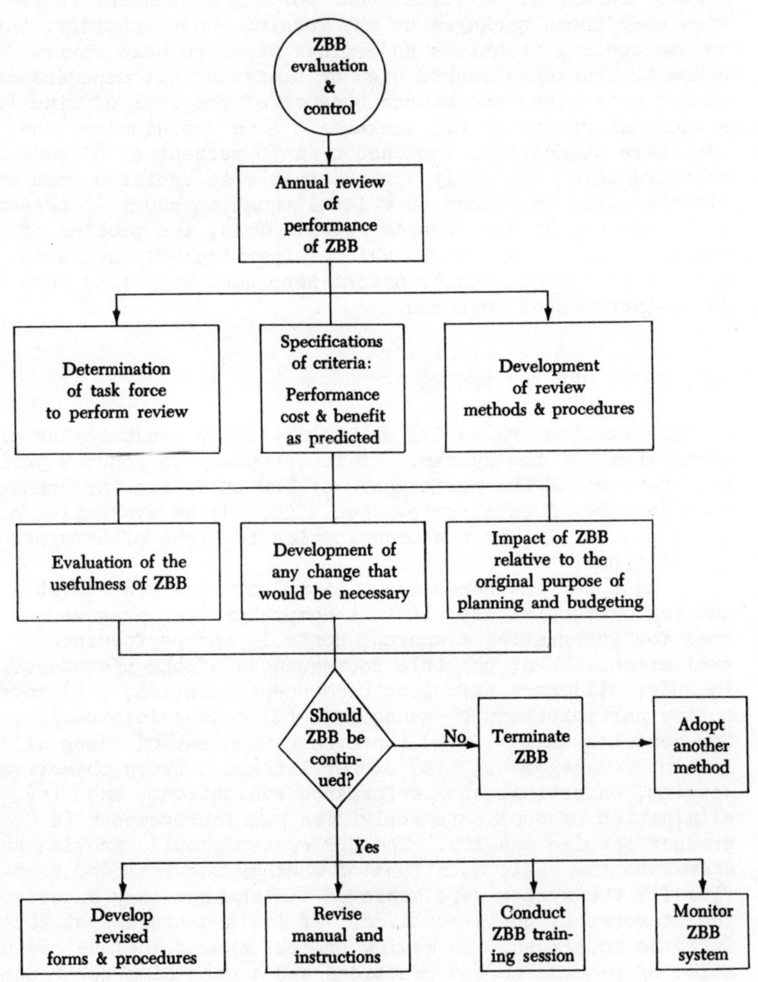

How should ZBB be evaluated? It is necessary to contact and obtain information on a sample or census basis from decision unit managers. In firms where ZBB is used, it is generally obtained on the basis of a survey of these managers.

The steps involved in a ZBB review are outlined in Figure 33-6. All information related to the costs and benefits of the ZBB system are evaluated by the ZBB task force group. This analysis often results in a modification of procedures and practices.

Example 1: In one firm, subsequent use of ZBB resulted in an increasingly detailed description of the decision packages.

Example 2: In another firm, subsequent use of ZBB involved both operating funds and a number of employees. Both resources were considered in the allocation process.

CONCLUSION

ZBB has come a long way since its origins at Texas Instruments. The popularity of the tool stems from its usefulness in closing the loop between strategic planning and results. It serves as an effective method of controlling areas within a firm which, by their nature, have been difficult for top management to control through the traditional budget process.

The primary responsibility for the succeesful implementation of a ZBB system lies with decision unit managers. The ability of these managers to develop and rank decision packages ultimately determines the effectiveness of ZBB as a management tool. Nonetheless, staff and line personnel at all levels of the managerial hierarchy can help ensure that the ZBB system is properly implemented and operated. Specific areas which deserve considerable attention prior to implementation are noted below.

- Determine the appropriate areas within a company in which to apply ZBB. As previously mentioned, ZBB is most effective in controlling discretionary cost centers where there is leeway in funding levels.
- Integrate the ZBB system with the firm's existing budget system. For example, will ZBB replace, complement, or be totally separate from the existing system? The most common situation is one in which a ZBB system is installed to complement and improve upon an existing budget system. Since operating budgets are normally prepared on the basis of line items of expenditures, ZBB would improve upon this by indicating how each line item of expenditure relates to final goods or services provided by the organization. Since ZBB is compatible with the traditional approaches to

budgeting, it can be integrated with these other systems with certain modifications. Of course, this integration of ZBB with traditional budget systems could also have significant implications for the way in which variance analysis is conducted and managerial and organizational performance is measured.

- Develop procedures and forms for use in system implementation.
- Train decision unit managers and assist these managers in operating the ZBB system.
- Monitor and recommend improvements to the ZBB process after its initial implementation phase.

ZBB is not a panacea for curing management ills. However, if properly implemented and operated, it can assist management in more effectively controlling operations. Its ultimate usefulness depends on where it is applied and on the effort expended to develop and implement the system.

FOOTNOTES

[1]Graeme M. Taylor, "Introduction to Zero-Base Budgeting," *Bureaucrat* 6 (Spring, 1977): 33.

[2]"*Zero-Base Budgeting,*" Bulletin No. 77-9 (Washington, D. C.: Office of Management and Budget, 19 April 1977), pp. 1-25.

[3]Peter A. Phyrr, *Zero-Base Budgeting* (New York: John Wiley & Sons, 1973).

[4]Peter A. Phyrr, "Zero-Base Budgeting," speech delivered at the International Conference of the Planning Executives Institute, New York, New York, 15 May 1972.

[5]Burton V. Dean, *Evaluating, Selecting and Controlling R&D Projects*, Research Study 89 (New York: American Management Association, 1968).

[6]Peter A. Phyrr, "Zero-Base Budgeting," *Harvard Business Review* 48 (November-December 1970): 111-21.

[7]Logan M. Cheek, *Zero-Base Budgeting Comes of Age* (New

York: American Management Association, 1977).

[8]*Ibid.*, pp. 68-69.

[9]Burton V. Dean and Meir J. Nishry, "Scoring and Profitability Methods for Selecting Projects," *Operations Research* 13 (July-August 1965): 550-69.

[10]Phyrr, "Zero-Base Budgeting," *Harvard Business Review*, p. 118.

STUDENT REVIEW QUESTIONS

1. What is zero base budgeting?
2. Explain the concept of incrementalism as an approach to budgeting. How is ZBB superior?
3. Explain what decision units and decision packages are and how they are used in the ZBB process.
4. What role does ranking have in the budgeting process?
5. The authors state "that ZBB is not merely a budget cutting system...." Do you agree? Why?

REFERENCES FOR ADDITIONAL STUDY

Ackerman, Robert W., "How Companies Respond to Social Demands," *Harvard Business Review,* July-August, 1975.

Anderson, Theodore A., "Coordinating Strategic and Operational Planning," *Business Horizons,* Summer, 1965.

Barrett, M. Edgar and LeRoy B. Frazer, III, "Conflicting Roles in Budgeting for Operations," *Harvard Business Review,* July-August, 1977.

Bofenkamp, Larry, "Effective Compensation: Today and Tomorrow", *The Personnel Administrator,* October, 1975.

Coleman, Bruce P., "An Integrated System for Manpower Planning," *Business Horizons,* October, 1970.

Hobbs, John M. and Donald F. Heany, "Coupling Strategy to Operational Plans," *Harvard Business Review,* May-June, 1977.

Howell, Robert A., "Managing by Objectives--A Three State System," *Business Horizons,* February, 1970.

Humble, John W., "Corporate Planning and Management by Objectives," *Long Range Planning,* June, 1969.

Monroe, Willys H., "Strategy in the Management of Executives," *Business Horizons,* Spring, 1963.

Phyrr, Peter A., "Zero-Base Budgeting," *Harvard Business Review,* November-December, 1970.

Tosi, Henry L., Jr., "The Human Effects of Budgeting Systems on Management," *MSU Business Topics,* Autumn, 1974.

Tosi, Henry L., John R. Rizzo, and Stephen S. Carroll, "Setting Goals in Management by Objectives," *California Management Review,* Summer, 1970.

SECTION G.

STRATEGIC CONTROL AND EVALUATION

34

The Domain of Management Control*

RAYMOND M. KINNUNEN

ROBERT H. CAPLAN, III

NUMEROUS ARTICLES have addressed certain issues that fall within the purview of management control systems. Examples of some of these issues include interdivisional pricing,[1] implementing the profit center concept,[2] financial control of decentralized divisions,[3] and incentives for performance.[4] Other notable work in the area focused on formulating principles for management control[5] and identifying a framework for classifying generalizations about planning and control systems.[6] More recently other authors have offered useful direction as to how control systems might be modified to increase effectiveness focusing primarily on the planning and measurement elements of management control.[7] The basic intent of this article is to build upon and extend previous work by identifying the elements and concepts of management control and including these in a conceptual scheme that will add both structure and understanding to the area.

With this basic intent in mind, the primary objectives, are, first, to clarify the meaning of the term management control and, second, to offer a comceptual scheme that clearly sets forth the domain of management control, forming the basis for a discussion of the elements included within this domain and how they relate to one another. The purpose is to bring into focus the concept of management control and

*Reprinted by permission from the May, 1978, issue of the *University of Michigan Business Review,* published by the Graduate School of Business Administration, the University of Michigan.

offer both scholars and practitioners a more universal conceptual reference.

THE CONCEPT OF MANAGEMENT CONTROL

At a high level of abstraction, management control may be defined as the process by which management translates the organization's *objectives* and *strategy* into specific *goals* for attainment by a specific time, and secures the *effective* accomplishment of these goals in an *efficient* manner. In more concrete terms, management control is the process employed (as part of the managing function) to:

Specify the goals it wants the organization to achieve at each management level;
Formulate the plans for achieveing these goals;
Allocate resources among organizational units responsible for implementing these plans;
Communicate these goals and plans, as approved, to personnel responsible for their accomplishment;
Influence individual managers to lead their organization units in achieving these goals as efficiently as possible;
Maintain balance and coordination in the activities of these organizational units;
Evaluate the degree to which these goals have actually been realized, and with what efficiency; and
Identify areas of unsatisfactory performance for management attention, and action where appropriate.[8]

A substantial portion of the planning activities of an organization constitute an integral part of the management control process. Planning is clearly involved in the first three activities listed above. However, not all forms of planning are considered part of management control. These forms which are an integral part will be identified shortly, together with the principal ones deemed to be outside the domain of management control.

It should be made clear that properly conceived, planning and control are inseparable concepts operating within the management control process. Separating planning from control does violence to the symbiotic relationship between these two closely inter-related concepts. Control, considered separately from the plans in terms of which control is to be exercised, is meaningless and fought with danger. Similarly, the design of control mechanisms without careful integration with applicable systems of planning is bound to cause trouble.

Koontz, an acknowledged authority on management and organization, agrees with this viewpoint. He argues that "...the two functions of planning and control are so closely interconnected as to be singularly inseparable...certainly, no manager can control who has not planned, for the very concept of control incorporates the task of keeping the operation of subordinates on course by correcting deviations from plans."[9]

PRINCIPAL ELEMENTS IN THE PROCESS

The basic process of management control may be conceptualized as shown in Figure 34-1. The advantages of the scheme are the identification of the principal elements in the overall process, and an indication of the important ways in which these elements relate to each other. Each of the important elements of the process will be described briefly to facilitate an understanding of the overall process.

GOAL SETTING

One of the elements of the management control process is goal setting. A goal may be defined as an aim that has been made specific as to magnitude and time. The principal functions of goals are (1) to provide focal points around which to develop plans and to allocate resources, and (2) to provide benchmarks against which to assess progress and to evaluate performance. Examples of goals that might be used in the management control process are (1) profits after taxes of $1.2 million in 1978, (2) return on net assets of 18 percent for the fiscal year 1978, (3) market share of 25 percent by the end of 1978, (4) establish two new branches in Western region by July, 1978, and (5) increase productivity by 5 percent by 1978.

The concept of a goal should be clearly distinguished from the concept of an objective. An objective may be defined as a broad aim or desired end which continues year after year with little change. A goal may be viewed as an objective that has been made specific as to magnitude and time. The crucial characteristic of a goal is its measurability, in contrast, an objective is not susceptible to measurement directly. An objective is enduring, timeless, never fully achieved. By their nature, objectives constitute a key element of corporate strategy. They are formulated as an integral part of the process of strategic planning, and are often made explicit as one of the tangible outputs of the strategic planning process. Goal setting, as part of the management control process, is involved with translating the objectives set forth in strategic plans into something more

FIGURE 34-1.

CONCEPTUAL SCHEME MANAGEMENT CONTROL PROCESS

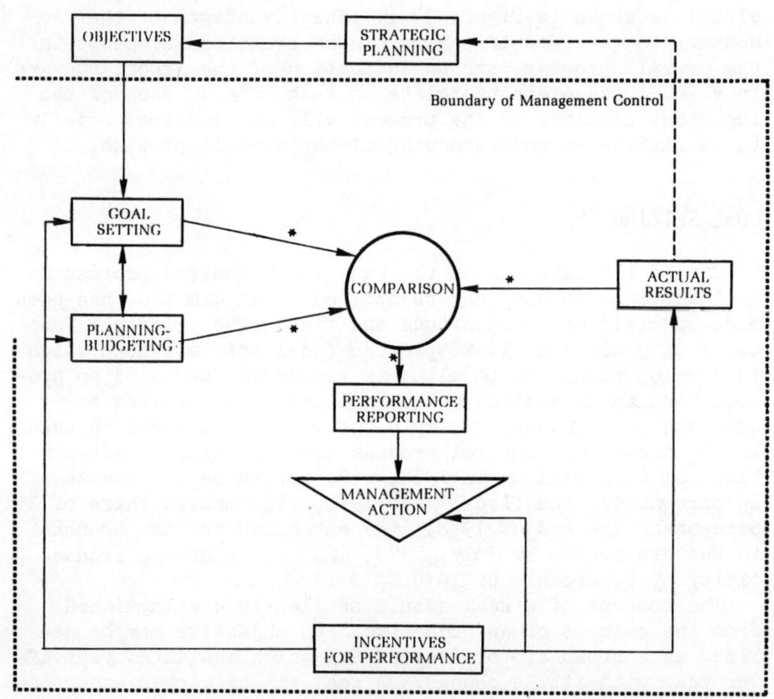

*Measurement involved; requires performance yardsticks.

tangible and meaningful for all management levels to achieve.

Goal setting represents a principal component in the planning portion of the management control system for activities and resource allocation have significance only when related to specific goals being sought. In principle, goal setting consists of establishing for each responsibility center, a point on each yardstick of performance. Consequently, goal setting is directly related to performance evaluation and contributes to the clarification of superior subordinate expectations from top to bottom in the management hierarchy.

PLANNING/BUDGETING

The broad domain of planning can be characterized as the conscious determination of actions designed to reach specific goals and thereby advance toward realization of organizational objectives. Planning involves decision-making about actions to be taken in the future. In general, planning involves a consideration of alternative courses of action for reaching a given goal. Part of this decision-making involves the allocation of the organization's resources (e.g., people, equipment and funds) among the competing planned activities.

Planning is not synonymous with budgeting or forecasting. Strictly speaking, budgeting constitutes the transalation of an organization's plans into financial terms. Operational planning/operating budget; facilities planning/capital budgeting; financial planning/cash budgeting, and manpower planing/budgeting are examples of plans and corresponding budgets. Thus, budgeting is only *part* of the planning process. A forecast represents an estimate of what is likely to happen in the future; no attempt is made to influence or to change the future as is the case with planning. Forecasts play an important role in the planning process, but they do not constitute planning as such.

A large number of formal processes can be identified within the broad domain of planning. Those considered part of the management control domain are programming, operational planning and budgeting. Each of these types of planning is defined briefly to facilitate an initial understanding of the full domain of management control.

> *Programming:* Systematic process for translating organizational strategy into specific implementing programs covering an intermediate period of time (e.g., two to six years) which provide the basis for developing the annual operating plan.
>
> *Operational Planning:* Systematic process for converting programs (cross-functional) into specific plans for accomplishment by

each organizational unit during the planning period--normally one year.
Budgeting: Systematic translation of operating plans for each organizational unit into financial terms including the resource allocation decisions associated therewith.

In the conceptualization presented here, strategic planning is considered to be outside the domain of management control. This concept of planning can be viewed as organized efforts directed at deciding in what businesses the company will engage, formulating corporate objectives, and developing ideas, major policies and broad plans for achieving these objectives. This involves viewing the relationship between the firm and its environment--an external orientation. In contrast, the focus of management control is internal. Strategy provides the interface between the firm and its environment and management control provides an interface between strategy and the internal organization.

The exclusion of strategic planning from the domain of management control follows from the view that the management control system is a major tool for implementing a chosen strategy. It is closely related to another tool, the design of an organizational structure, which has been discussed at some length by Chandler.[10] The major point to be made is that an organization's system of management control must follow from, and be tailored to, its chosen strategy. Just as structure follows strategy so should the management control system. Management control is a major vehicle for translating the organization's strategy into elements that are understandable and attainable by all levels of management. This view is depicted in Figure 34-1 by placing strategic planning and the setting of corporate objectives outside the boundary of the management control system. The feedback loop connotes that actual results are important inputs to planning future strategy.

PERFORMANCE REPORTING

The display of actual performance in comparison with planned performance and the reporting of this performance to the affected managers constitutes a critical link in the management control process. The element performance reporting is critical in the sense that its basic role is to provide meaningful accountability for the performance of managers, thereby enhancing the likelihood that desired results actually materialize. This basic role includes both providing information needed for control by managers of the respective responsibility centers, and providing meaningful accountability between these managers and their superiors. As Drucker has observed, "...every manager should be held strictly accountable for the results of his performance."[11]

Two of the principal purposes of performance reporting are scorekeeping and attention directing. The former adds insight in determining how a particular responsibility center stands in relation to what it had *planned* to accomplish within a specific period of time. The latter purpose of performance reports refers to indicating the existence of a problem that should be investigated. In this sense, performance reports (1) indicate the likely existence of a problem in a timely manner, and (2) stimulate the initiation of an analysis/decision/action sequence.

From the perspective of systems theory, performance reporting fulfills the feedback function in the control process of an organization. Deviations in actual performance from desired performance constitute the signals transmitted to the analyzer and motor functions (e.g., the responsible managers). In other words, performance reporting represents the closing of the loop on the delegation of responsibility for a specific domain of performance.

The existence of this feedback function requires benchmarks against which to compare actual performance. One type of benchmark is a predetermined goal that is generated during the planning process. Other types of benchmarks can be based upon the past performance of the particular responsibility center or current performance of others engaged in similar activities.

In terms of designing the performance reporting system, a basic principle is that the reports should be tailored to meet management control needs at each management position. Key determinants of these needs include the strategy of the organization; the nature of the business; the organizational structure; the mission of a particular responsibility center; the personal preferences of managers, and the opportunity for effective use of informal more personalized feedback techniques. In general, these needs tend to change as one moves from the lowest responsibility center up through an organization to top management.

The information in the performance reports should be limited to those dimensions of performance for which a given manager is responsible. In general, this means the yardsticks of performance established for the particular responsibility center and variances from budgeted expenses that are controllable by the particular manager. This is due to the argument that accountability (and thus performance measurement) must reflect as closely as possible the real responsibility of a particular position and the authority delegated to that position for fulfilling this responsibility. A manager should not, therefore, be held accountable for factors he is not able to "control"--that is, not in a position, by virtue of organizational limits, to influence significantly. To do otherwise opens the way for management behavior with dysfunctional consequences.

In their mildest forms, these dysfunctional consequences take the form of negative attitudes towards the management control system: a feeling that the evaluation of performance is arbitrary, unfair and lacking validity as an indicator of performance. Such attitudes erode the capacity of the management control system to influence the behavior of managers in the direction desired by top management (i.e., the goal congruence of the system is attenuated). In their more severe manifestations, these dysfunctional consequences take the form of attempts to influence and control activities beyond the legitimate boundaries of authority delegated to the responsibility center.

MANAGEMENT ACTION

Management response to reported deviations from planned performance is also vital to the effective functioning of the management control process. Responses can take many forms: renewed efforts at the points of substandard performance; shifting or adding of resources; adjustments or revisions to plans and, in the extreme, modification of goals and the plans associated therewith. At times, the appropriate response may be to wait and do nothing.

Seldom is action of the sort outlined above initiated *directly* on the basis of performance reports. In general, the appropriate response cannot prudently be determined until the causes of the reported deviations have been determined, alternative courses of action have been identified and evaluated, and a choice made from among these alternatives. In short, decision-making does not proceed directly from these performance reports, but only indirectly after the intervening steps of fact-finding and analysis.

INCENTIVES FOR PERFORMANCE

Incentives related in some visable manner to performance are an integral part of management control. They provide the driving force which energizes the whole process, eliciting the expenditures of energy and effort required by all participants to bring about the desired results. Without incentives for performance of any kind, the process would be sterile exercise at best.

There exists a rich, almost unlimited array of incentives which can be related to performance. At this introductory level of presentation, the principal categories of incentives need only to be identified: those incentives dispensed by the formal organization (e.g., bonuses, salary increases, promotions and demotions); those dispensed by the informal or social organization (e.g., status, prestige influence); and those incentives generated within the self (e.g., satisfaction with a job well done). The complete array of incentives includes penalties along with rewards. The best results are obtained when a carefully designed, well reasoned blend of these incentives are employed.

The basic purpose of having these incentives tied in some direct manner to performance is to encourage management effort directed at realizing specified goals and at taking timely corrective action where appropriate. This function is suggested conceptually in Figure 34-1 by the arrows moving outward from "incentives" to the affected elements in the management control process.

MEASUREMENT

The process of management control is aided immeasurably by the quantification of performance variables. Such measurement enters into both the planning phase and the performance evaluation phase of the overall process. These key points of measurement are identified in Figure 34-1. The principal benefits contributed by measurement to the management control process may be summarized as follows:

Greater meaningfulness of the vital comparative function between actual results and desired results (i.e., goals);

Establishment of meaningful accountability for performance;

Objectivity in stating goals and assessing degree of accomplishment; and

Better communication between superior and subordinate regarding expectations on one hand, and performance against these expectations on the other.

In order to carry out this measurement task, some kind of measuring instrument must be employed. The generic form of such measuring instruments is the "performance yardstick" (sometimes referred to as a performance index or performance indicator). Such performance yardsticks are used both for the purpose of expressing goals in measurable terms and for the purpose of measuring actual performance. The performance yardstick is the measuring instrument. Goals referred to earlier are the points along these yardsticks selected during the planning process. Yardsticks of performance determine the way in which the measurement of performance is to be carried out.

It is important to point out that each performance yardstick (e.g., return on assets employed) must be directly related to a performance dimension (e.g., profitability). Identification of the dimentions of performance which are relevant for a particular responsibility center must precede the selection and design of the yardstick used to measure the particular performance dimension. In addition, choice

TABLE 34-1.

PERFORMANCE DIMENSIONS AND YARDSTICKS

Performance Dimension	Performance Yardstick
Quantity of Output	
-Total output	-No. units completed -No. good units delivered to warehouse
-Throughput rate	-thous. gals/hr. processed
-Schedule fulfillment	-% units scheduled for period actually produced
Quality of Output	
-Reject rate	-No. units rejected/no. units tested
-Customer returns	-No. units returned/no. units sold
Timeliness	
-Delivery to customer	-% deliveries made in accordance with customer specifications
-Backlog management	-No. of items on backlog -No. of production days represented by backlog
Productivity	
-Manpower	-No. units/man-hr. -No. lbs./man-hr.
-Machines	-No. units/machine hr. -No. lbs./machine hr.
Cost Control	-Variances between actual cost and standard allowances
Profitability	-Profits before taxes but after all corporate charges -Profit margin (% sales) after taxes -Return on assets employed (net) -Residual income

of performance dimension should not be limited to monetary terms. For proper accountability to exist, every significant dimension of performance expected from a responsibility center should be reflected in the performance yardsticks used for this purpose. Examples of yardsticks matched with their corresponding performance dimensions, are shown in Table 34-1.

As the activities of organizations become more complex, the time lag between the performance of subordinate units and the reflection of this performance (both good and bad) in the end results for which the organization is in business, becomes longer and longer. As a consequence, there is a growing need to incorporate intermediate performance dimensions into the formal accountability system. This need for yardsticks to measure intermediate performance dimensions is heightened by the following long term trends: the increasing importance of human resources to the success and even survival of any organization and the increasing demands placed on an organization by the social system of which it is a part. Examples of intermediate performance dimensions associated with each of these broad trends are set forth in Table 34-2.[12]

RESPONSIBILITY CENTER

Every management control system is built around the basic unit of organization known as a responsibility center. A responsibility center is any organizational unit within a larger organization, charged with a well-defined mission or function, and headed by a manager who is responsible for insuring that the unit accomplishes its mission in an efficient manner and *accountable* in some systematic way for this performance. Every responsibility center has certain essential characteristics or attributes which follow from the foregoing definition: (1) a well-defined mission or function; (2) a set of activities by means of which resources are converted into desired outputs; (3) a manager or supervisor who is responsible for the performance of the unit; and (4) accountability of this same manager or supervisor for this performance to a higher level of management.

Responsibility centers constitute the primary building blocks for management control. They are created through the organizing process and, therefore, are directly related to the design of an organizational structure. Consequently, the design of responsibility centers represents a major point of interface between the process of organizing and the process of control.[13]

There exist certain specific types of responsibility centers that fall within the domain of management control: expense centers, profit centers and investment centers. The first of these (expense center) is a responsibility center

TABLE 34-2.
INTERMEDIATE PERFORMANCE DIMENSIONS

Human Resources	-Employee Attitudes -Management Development -Technical Competence
Environment	-Social Responsibility
Renewal of Mission	-Innovation -Product (service) Development -Product Leadership

in which the output cannot properly be measured in monetary terms. Only the inputs (i.e., resources consumed by the responsibility center) can be measured in monetary terms.

This type of responsibility center can further be categorized according to the specific nature of these inputs. The first is where inputs respond directly to the level of activity of the particular responsibility center. Examples of this type of expense center include production operations (manufacturing, service organizations, financial institutions, non-profit agencies); clerical activities (accounting, sales), and corporate service units (data processing, purchasing). The second category of expense center is where inputs do not respond to volume stimuli in the short run and are established largely through the exercise of management judgment. Research and development and corporate staffs (legal, public relations, corporate development) are examples of expense centers in this category.

The second type of responsibility center noted above is the profit center. A profit center is a responsibility center in a profit-seeking organization in which the manager is responsible for the profits generated by his center. Strictly speaking, the manager of a profit center is not responsible for optimizing the utilization of the assets employed by his center. If this latter situation does prevail, the responsibility center is really an investment center. Examples of organizational units frequently structured as profit centers include the following: individual stores in a retail chain; branch sales offices for an industrial company or insurance company; branches of a commercial bank; the entire sales organization of a company or division.

The last type of responsibility center noted above is the

investment center. The investment center is a responsibility center in a profit-seeking organization in which the manager is responsible for the profitable employment of the assets (i.e., capital invested) utilized by his center as well as the level of profits generated by his center. In general, the formal accountability of the center is expressed in some specified relationship between profits and assets employed. Organizational units frequently structered as investment centers include the following: operating divisions; a group of operating divisions; a subsidiary (i.e., a unit with its own legal identity), and units with essentially the same mission as a division but carrying a different designation (e.g., departments in the duPont company).

EFFECTIVENESS AND EFFICIENCY

In thinking about organizational performance and its measurement, two additional concepts are needed: effectiveness and efficiency. Effectiveness may be defined as the extent to which the *results desired* from a responsibility center are *actually achieved*. Efficiency, on the other hand, is the extent to which resources are used economically in generating whatever results are actually achieved. Every responsibility center is responsible, by definition, for *both* its effectiveness and its efficiency. It follows, therefore, that every responsibility center should be accountable--through the management control process--for its level of efficiency and effectiveness. This is implemented through the identification of dimensions of performance, design of yardsticks of performance, and setting goals that relate to effectiveness as well as efficiency.

SUMMARY

The basic intent of this article has been to add structure to and enhance understanding of the area of management control by (1) conceptualizing the elements of the process; (2) explaining how these elements relate to one another; (3) placing limits on the boundary of the management control system, and (4) viewing the total process of control from a total firm or strategic perspective. It is also intended that the scheme presented here be of value to the practicing manager toward determining both strengths and weaknesses in their management control systems. The following questions and comments are offered with this view in mind.

1. Have the goals of responsibility centers been set in a manner consistent with the strategy and objectives of the corporation?

(Nonconsistency here may lead to the responsibility centers achieving the goals set before them while the total corporation may not be fulfilling their objectives and desired strategy.)

2. Have programs, plans, and budgets been developed for responsibility centers that are also consistent with and contribute toward achieving a desired strategic posture?

(A formulated strategy is achieved via the efforts of the various organizational units. Consequently, programs, plans, and budgets not consistent will also lead to the corporation falling short of the strategy set forth by top management.

3. Have performance reports been designed with a view toward the mission of the particular responsibility center and the personal preferences of the managers responsible?

(Performance reports not designed in this manner will, in most cases, contain information that is of limited use for the responsible managers in identifying problem areas.)

4. Has the information in the performance reports been limited to (a) those dimensions of performance for which a given manager is responsible and (b) variances from budgeted expenses that are controllable by the particular manager?

(Information in performance reports that is not limited to that which a manager is responsible and that which he can control may lead to an improper portrayal and subsequent evaluation of the unit followed by negative attitudes by responsible managers toward the management control system.)

5. Has management taken appropriate steps in response to reported deviations from planned performance?

(Responses that have not appeared to be appropriate could be due to a number of reasons including: management haste and lack of adequate analysis or inadequacies in the reports themselves directly related to (3) and/or (4) above.)

6. Have incentives been related in some visible manner to the performance of the managers?

(Incentives not related in some visible manner may result in unsatisfactory performance by managers toward achieving specified goals and taking corrective action where appropriate.)

7. Have performance dimensions and corresponding yardsticks been chosen to reflect every significant dimension of performance expected from each responsibility center?

(If not, it is possible that the particular center may be performing inadequately along dimensions that will adversely affect the corporation in the future, e.g., poor customer service or inadequate hiring and training of future managers.)

8. Do the responsibility centers have the following attributes (a) a well-defined mission or function: (b) a set of activities by which resources are converted into outputs; (c) a manager or supervisor who is responsible for the performance of the unit, and (d) accountability of this same manager or supervisor for this performance to a

higher level of management?

(If a particular center does not possess the above attributes it could be that a restructuring of organizational units may be more desirable, e.g., combining the particular unit with another that produces a similar output.)

9. Is each responsibility center responsible for both its effectiveness and efficiency?

(An organizational unit that is running efficiently and at the same time falling short of desired results may not be contributing to overall corporate objectives.)

Before concluding, it should be emphasized that human beings occupy crucial positions in any system of management control. Without proper and skillful use of this formal apparatus by humans, the desired outcomes of the process--both management control and the larger process of management--will not be forthcoming. Thus, behavioral considerations must play a crucial role in thinking about management control systems and their proper design, implementation, and administration.[15] Behavioral concepts such as motivation, influence, incentives and commitment have direct relevance and are of primary importance to a proper understanding of management control.

In summary, then, the basic purpose of a management control system is to guide the efforts and actions of managers at all levels of the organization toward the achievement of organizational objectives with the greatest effectiveness and efficiency. The formal apparatus of a management control system owes its existence to the benefits it provides to management in their conduct of the management control process. The more important of these benefits may be summarized as follows:

Provide needed discipline to the whole process;
Facilitate understanding by all participants;
Stimulate action in a more timely manner;
Facilitate the establishment of meaningful accountability, and thereby the delegation of responsibility;
Enhance the visibility of performance; and
Conduct the whole process more effectively and efficiently.

In addition, a major contention of this article is that the management control system is a major vehicle for the effective implementation of an organization's strategy. Thus, the design and administration of an organization's management control system in a matter that requires top management involvement.

FOOTNOTES

[1]John Dearden, "Interdivisional Pricing," *Harvard Business Review* (January-February, 1960), pp. 117-125.

[2]John Dearden, "Problems in Decentralized Profit Responsibility," *Harvard Business Review* (May-June, 1960), pp. 79-86.

[3]John Dearden, "Problems in Decentralized Financial Control," *Harvard Business Review* (May-June, 1961), pp. 72-80.

[4]Arch Patton, "Why Incentive Plans Fail," *Harvard Business Review* (May-June, 1972), pp. 58-66.

[5]Harold Koontz, "Management Control: A Suggested Formulation of Principles," *California Management Review* (Winter, 1959), pp. 47-55.

[6]Robert N. Anthony, *Planning and Control Systems: A Framework for Analysis* (Boston: Division of Research, Harvard Business School, 1965).

[7]Peter Lorange and Michael S. Scott Morton, "A Framework for Management Control Systems," *Sloan Management Review* (Fall, 1974), pp. 41-56.

[8]It is proposed that this definition more adequately suggests the broad range of activities involved in the management control process and explicitly recognizes the relationship between the process of management control and corporate strategy. For another definition see, for example, Robert N. Anthony and John Dearden, *Management Control Systems: Text and Cases* (Homewood, Illinois: Richard D. Irwin, Inc., 1976), p. 8.

[9]Harold Koontz, "A Preliminary Statement of Principles of Planning and Control," *Journal of the Academy of Management* (April, 1958), p. 48.

[10]Alfred D. Chandler, Jr., *Strategy and Structure: Chapters in the History of the American Industrial Enterprise* (Cambridge, Mass.: The M.I.T. Press, 1962), p. 14. This close relationship exists due to the fact that both management control and organizational structure involve lines of authority and communication as well as the flow of information and data through these lines.

[11]Peter F. Drucker, *The Practice of Management* (New

York: Harper and Row, 1954), p. 133.

[12]A large proportion of General Electric's eight key result areas can be viewed as intermediate performance dimensions. See "General Electric" case, in Robert N. Anthony and John Dearden, *Management Control Systems: Text and Cases* (Homewood, Illinois: Richard D. Irwin, Inc., 1976), pp. 159-167.

[13]For a more detailed discussion of the relationship between organizational structure and management control see Richard F. Vancil, "What Kind of Management Control Do You Need?" *Harvard Business Review* (March-April, 1973), pp. 75-86.

[14]Robert N. Anthony, "Note on Responsibility Centers," in Robert N. Anthony, John Dearden, and Richard F. Vancil, *Management Control Systems* (Homewood, Illinois: Richard D. Irwin, Inc., 1965), pp. 165-171.

[15]For a more in-depth discussion of behavioral aspects of management control systems see, for example, Cortlandt Cammann and David A. Nadler, "Fit Control Systems to Your Managerial Style," *Harvard Business Review* (January-February, 1976), pp. 65-72.

STUDENT REVIEW QUESTIONS

1. What is the purpose of a management control system?
2. Discuss goals and objectives as defined by Kinnunen and Caplan. What part does goal setting play in the control process?
3. Should planning be considered to be synonymous with budgeting? Discuss briefly the three types of planning identified in the article.
4. What element in the control process fulfills the feedback function? Explain briefly.
5. Why do authors say that "There is a growing need to incorporate intermediate performance dimensions into the formal accountability system."
6. What is a responsibility center? What are the three types of responsibility centers identified by Kinnunen and Caplan?
7. Distinguish between organizational effectiveness and organizational efficiency.

A Strategic Framework for Marketing Control*

JAMES M. HULBERT

NORMAN E. TOY

THE DECADE OF THE 1960's led many companies down the primrose path of uncontrolled growth. The turbulence of the 1970's has drawn renewed attention to the need to pursue growth selectively, and many companies have been forced to divest themselves of businesses which looked glamorous in the 1960's, but faded in the 1970's. Simultaneously with this re-appraisal has come a much more serious focus on problems of control--a concern with careful monitoring and appraisal to receive early warning on businesses or ventures that are suspect.

Yet, despite the extent to which control is stressed by authors,[1] there does not exist a generally agreed upon strategic framework for marketing control, and there has been little successful integration of concepts in marketing strategy and planning with those of managerial accounting. In particular, the work of the Boston Consulting Group,[2] the results of the PIMS study,[3] and a variety of other sources[4] have stressed the importance of market share objectives in marketing strategy, coincidentally emphasizing the need to know market size and growth rate and thus the importance of good forecasts. Typically, however, procedures for market-

Footnotes are listed at the end of the article.

*Reprinted from *Journal of Marketing*, Vol. 41, No. 2 (April, 1977), pp. 12-20, published by the American Marketing Association.

ing control have not been related to these key parameters. (Incredibly, market size is sometimes even omitted from marketing plans, according to one knowledgeable author).[5]

In this article we seek to remedy that state of affairs by outlining a strategic framework for marketing control. Using the key strategic concepts discussed above, we first present a framework for evaluating marketing performance versus plan, thus providing a means for more formally incorporating the marketing plan in the managerial control process.

The plan, however, may well provide inappropriate criteria for performance evaluation, especially if there have been a number of unanticipated events during the planning period. A second stage of this article, therefore, is to provide a means of taking these kinds of planning variances into account, so as to provide a more appropriate set of criteria for performance evaluation. Two conceptual developments are shown as Part I and Part II in the Appendix.

PERFORMANCE VS. PLAN

In Exhibit 35-1 we show the results of operations for a sample product, *Product Alpha,* during the preceding period. In the analysis which follows, we shall focus on analysis of variances in profit contribution. As we discussed elsewhere,[6] an analysis of revenue performance is sometimes required; the procedure here is analogous. Organizationally, one of the results we would like to achieve is to be able to assign responsibility, and give credit, where due.

A variety of organizational units were involved in the planning and execution summarized in Exhibit 35-1, and an important component of control activity is to evaluate their performance according to the standards or goals provided by the marketing plan. We should also note, however, that the type of analysis we shall discuss has limited potential for **diagnosing** the causes of problems. Rather, its major benefit is in the **identification** of areas where problems may exist. Determining the factors which have actually caused favorable or unfavorable variances requires the skill and expertise of the manager.

The unfavorable variance in contribution of $100,000, for *Product Alpha* could arise from two main sources:[7]

1. Differences between planned and actual quantities (volumes).
2. Differences between planned and actual contribution per unit.

Differences between planned and actual quantities, however, may arise from differences between actual and planned total market size and actual and planned market share (penetration) of that total market. The potential sources of varia-

EXHIBIT 35-1.

OPERATING RESULTS FOR PRODUCT ALPHA

ITEM	PLANNED	ACTUAL	VARIANCE
REVENUES			
Sales (lbs.)	20,000,000	22,000,000	2,000,000
Price per lb ($)	0.50	.4773	0.227
Revenues	10,000,000	10,500,000	500,000
Total Market (lbs.)	40,000,000	50,000,000	10,000,000
Share of Market	50%	44%	(6%)
COSTS			
Variable Cost per lb ($)	.30	.30	--
CONTRIBUTION			
Per lb ($)	.20	.1773	.0227
Total ($)	4,000,000	3,900,000	(100,000)

tion between planned and actual contribution, then, are:

1. Total market size.
2. Market share (penetration).
3. Price/cost per unit.

This format for variance decomposition permits assignment into categories which correspond to key strategy variables in market planning.[8] The analysis proceeds as follows.

PRICE-QUANTITY DECOMPOSITION

In order to measure volume variance with the standard yardstick of planned contribution per unit, actual quantity is used to calculate the price/cost variance. (This procedure is standard accounting practice.) To be more concise, we utilize the following symbols:

S -- share of total market
M -- total market in units
Q -- quantity sold in units
C -- contribution margin per unit

We use the subscript "a" to denote actual values, and "p" to denote planned values. The subscript "v" denotes variance. Thus the price/cost variance is given by

$$(C_a - C_p) \times Q_a = (.1773 - .20) \times 22{,}000{,}000$$
$$= -\$500{,}000;$$

and the volume variance is given by

$$(Q_a - Q_p) \times C_p = (22{,}000{,}000 - 20{,}000{,}000) \times .20$$
$$= \$400{,}000.$$ [9]

The sum of these contribution variances therefore yields the overall unfavorable contribution variance of -$100,000 shown in Exhibit 35-1.

PENETRATION--MARKET SIZE DECOMPOSITION

The second stage of the analysis is the further decomposition of the volume variance in contribution into the components due to penetration and total market size. Exhibit 35-2 is helpful in the exposition of the analysis.

EXHIBIT 35-2.
VARIANCE OF TOTAL MARKET SIZE VS. SHARE

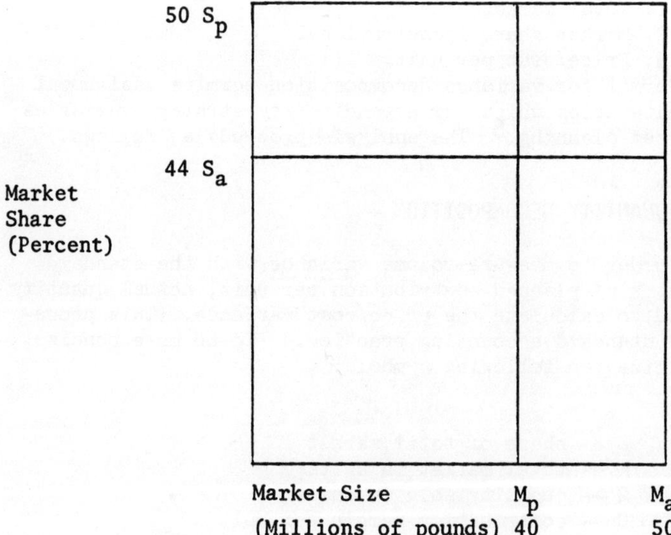

As a first step, we should like to explain differences in quantities sold ($Q_a - Q_p$), where actual and planned quantities are the product of the market size times share ($Q_a = S_a \times M_a$, and $Q_p = S_p \times M_p$). From Exhibit 35-2, rectangles I and II are clearly assignable to share and market size, respectively. Rectangle III, however, is conceptually more complex.

We argue that discrepancies in forecasting market size should be evaluated using the standard yardstick of planned share, just as the dollar value of the quantity variance is measured using the standard of planned contribution. Thus, actual market size is used to calculate share variance, while both share and forecast components (which together comprise the quantity variance) are measured using planned contribution. This procedure is also consistent with recommended accounting practice.[10]

Then the variance in contribution due to share is given by

$$(S_a - S_p) \times M_a \times C_p$$

$$= (.44 - .50) \times 50{,}000{,}000 \times .2$$

$$= -\$600{,}000 \ ;$$

and the market size variance is given by

$$(M_a - M_p) \times S_p \times C_p$$

$$= (50{,}000{,}000 - 40{,}000{,}000) \times .5 \times .2$$

$$= \$1{,}000{,}000 \ .$$

The sum of the market size and share variances yields the overall favorable volume variance in contribution of $400,000 derived in the previous section.

We may now summarize the variances which in total constitute the overall variance as follows:

Planned profit contribution		$4,000,000
Volume variance		
Share variance	(600,000)	
Market size variance	1,000,000	
		400,000
Price/cost variance		(500,000)
Actual profit contribution		$3,900,000

INTERPRETATION

Conceptually, variances may occur because of problems in

forecasting, execution, or both. In using the results of the analysis for performance evaluation, however, responsibility will have to be assigned. Generally, variances in total market size, for example, will be viewed as the responsibility of the market forecasting group.

Share or penetration variances present a more difficult case. They may arise due to incorrect forecasts of what "expected performance" should be, or due to poor performance itself. Apportioning responsibility in this case clearly necessitates managerial judgment. However, where marketing and sales personnel participate in the development of market share objectives, or where share declines relative to previous performance, the burden of proof is more likely to fall on the operating unit rather than on a separate planning or forecasting group.

Responsibility for price variances may also be difficult to assign. For example, prices may be seriously affected by changes in market or general economic conditions beyond the control of the operating group but which should have been foreseen by forecasters or planners. On the other hand, prices are an integral part of the marketing mix, and variances may well indicate problems in marketing or selling tactics.

With these considerations in mind, we may now review the results of the variance analysis:

First, *the favorable volume variance of $400,000 was in fact caused by two larger variances cancelling each other out. And while one of these variances was positive, the other negative, both are undesirable! By not achieving planned share of market, we lost $600,000 in profit contribution.*

The loss of market share may be due to poor planning, poor execution, or both...and managerial judgment is the key factor in diagnosing the causes of this discrepancy.

This unfavorable share variance was more than compensated for--or so it appears--by the $1,000,000 positive contribution variance due to the fact that the market turned out to be much larger than was forecast. This variance is unequivocally the responsibility of the forecasting group, though whether or not they should have been able to foresee the expansion is an issue which the manager must decide.

However, this nominally favorable variance is, in fact, a danger signal. We *seriously underestimated the size of the market, which was 25% greater, at 50 million pounds, than the forecast (40 million pounds).* As the dominant competitor, we have lost market share in what is apparently a fast-growing market, the kind of error which can soon lead to loss of competitive position.[11]

In this instance, then, the share/size decomposition of the volume variance serves to emphasize the importance of good planning--and good information for planning--in terms directly related to two crucial variables in strategy design.

This form of decomposition, we submit, generates considerably more useful insight into issues of marketing control *than isolation of only the volume variance, which is much less clearly interpretable.*

The final variance component is the unfavorable price variance of $500,000. Again, interpretation is the job of the manager. However, we should note that the accounting procedures used here (and generally) treat price and volume variances as if they were separable. *Yet, for the vast majority of products and services, demand is price-elastic to some degree so that variances in total revenue are the combined result of the interaction, via the demand function, of unit prices and quantities.*

In this example, for instance, the lower levels of prices may well have been an important factor in expanding industry and company demand. Nonetheless, the fact remains that failure to attain planned price levels led to a $500,000 decrease in actual versus planned profit contribution. The reasons for this variance may lie with performance (e.g., poor tactics) or planning (e.g., inaccurate forecasts).

Diagnosis and responsibility assignment procedures will be explored in more detail in the following section.

MONDAY MORNING QUARTERBACKING

A crucial issue, which we have thus far skirted, is the appropriate criterion for performance evaluation. This is a basic yet nagging problem underlying the whole area of strategic control. In the foregoing analysis, for example, we assumed that the marketing plan provides an appropriate set of criteria. The objectives therein are usually derived after considerable participation, discussion, and negotiation between interested parties,[12] and may well represent the most appropriate set of criteria that are available, at least at the beginning of the planning period.

In many companies, however, performance during the previous planning period serves as an additional set of evaluation criteria. In fact, the search for more "objective" criteria for performance evaluation led to the origins, at General Electric, of the PIMS project and the subsequent "par" criterion.[13]

The facts are, of course, that the marketing plan--which we used as our criterion--is generally based upon the best information which is available on an *ex ante* basis. The conditions which are manifest during the planning period, however, may be vastly different from those envisaged at the time of plan development. In some company planning systems, some of these changes may be encompassed by contingency planning, while in others the plan is updated when major environmental changes occur.[14] In many other instances the plan is not updated--at least in any formal way.[15]

Nonetheless, irrespective of the comprehensiveness of systems to provide flexibility in plans, when the time arrives to review performance, most marketing managers use some *ex post* information. In other words, the criteria of evaluation--implicitly or explicitly--are generally "what performance should have been" under the circumstances which actually transpired. Nor is this "Monday morning quarterbacking" undesirable, for it is eminently more sensible than blind adherence to a plan which is clearly outdated by violation of planning assumptions.[16]

For example, supply may be affected unexpectedly; a major competitor may drop out of the market--or an aggressive new competitor may enter; or demand may have an unexpected change--e.g., because of weather. Either of these would likely change the appropriate par market share for the company. The purpose of this second stage of the analysis, therefore, is to provide a variance decomposition which permits comparison of performance versus the criterion of "what should have happened under the circumstances."

Naturally, there are inherent dangers in such a process. Re-opening the issue of what constitutes an appropriate criterion for performance evaluation may mean opening a Pandora's Box. Equally clearly, however, there are frequently occasions when unforeseen events can significantly affect what target performance should be. In such instances, it is surely preferable that any adjustment process by systematic and orderly, explicit and visible.

USING "EXPERT" INFORMATION

Continuing with our previous operating results, then, let us construct the scenario which occurred during the planning period, using the *ex post* information which would be available to the marketing manager at the time of performance review:

1. A new competitor--Consolidated Company--entered the market early in the year. The competitor was a large, well-financed conglomerate, which used an aggressive promotional campaign and a lower price to induce trial purchase.
2. A fire in the plant of a European manufacturer led to totally unforeseeable foreign demand for one million pounds of *Product Alpha*.

With a small amount of additional work by the manager, we may now develop an appropriate *ex post* performance analysis. For example, the fact that the new competitor was quite prepared to subsidize his entry into our market out of his other operations was an important cause of the price deterioration, and also guaranteed that he would "buy" a share of market sufficient for him to run his new plant at close to standard capacity. At the same time, this aggressive entry and the price competition which ensued was an important factor in further expanding total industry demand.

In quantitative terms Consolidated's effective mean selling price for the year was $0.465 per lb. We had forecast an industry mean of $0.495 and a price for our own product of $0.475, and we realized $0.4773 per lb. Competitive intelligence informed us that Consolidated's new plant had a capacity of only 1.33 million pounds so that its inability to supply more set a lower limit for market prices, above that of Consolidated's introductory price.

We now reconstruct the discrepancy between conditions forecast at the time of planning and the conditions which subsequently prevailed.

MARKET SHARE

As noted, our intelligence estimates indicated that Consolidated's capacity would be 1.33 million pounds. Our historical market share had hovered around 50% for some time, so that *everything being equal*, we might expect that 50% of Consolidated's sales would be at our expense. However, knowing that we were (a) the dominant competitor and (b) the premium-price competitor, we also know that we were the most vulnerable to a price-oriented competitive entry. Consequently, we used as a planning assumption the supposition that 60% of Consolidated's sales would be at our expense. That is, we assumed that .6 x 1.33 million pounds, or 800 thousand pounds of sales volume which we would otherwise have obtained, would be lost to Consolidated. Thus, we had the following two conditions:

If no entry: forecast market share equal to
$20.8 \div 40 = 52\%$
With entry: forecast market share equal to
$20 \div 40 = 50\%$

Since we were certain that Consolidated would enter early in the year, we used the latter assumption. However, while our intelligence estimates on the size of Consolidated's plant were excellent, we did not glean the information that they would use 3-shift operation rather than two shifts which have been standard practice for the industry. As a result Consolidated's effective standard capacity was raised from 1.33 to 2.0 million pounds. Under these conditions, then, assuming the 60% loss rate holds, we should have expected to lose .6 x 2.0 or 1.2 million pounds to Consolidated, rather than 800,000 lbs. Thus, with perfect foresight we *should have* forecasted a market share of $19.6 \div 40$, or 49%.

PRICE

We had forecast an industry mean price of $0.495 per pound, and planned for a net price to us of $0.50 per pound. This $.005 per pound premium had been traditional for us because of our leadership position in the industry, with slightly higher quality product and excellent levels of distribution and service.

The actual industry mean price was $0.475 per pound, and our net mean price was $0.4773, so that we only received a premium of $0.0023 per pound.[17] Here, then, we have some basis for separating the planning variance from the performance variance.

Although the basis for this distinction again involves managerial judgment, for present purposes we assume that the planning group should have foreseen that Consolidated's entry would be based on a low price strategy which would lead to an overall deterioration in market prices. On the other hand, our selling and marketing tactics were responsible for the deterioration in our price premium.

MARKET SIZE

Finally, there was no possibility that our planning group could have foreseen the European fire, and it would be demonstrably unfair to hold them responsible for this component of the variance.

On the other hand, the remainder of the market expansion should have been foreseen, and the responsibility should be assigned to them. Their failure in this regard was no doubt related to the oversight in the pricing area, for it seems entirely plausible that demand was more price elastic than we had realized, and the price decrease brought a whole new set of potential customers into the market.

VARIANCE DECOMPOSITION

The full *ex post* decomposition using this information is displayed in Exhibit 35-2.[18] To simplify the exposition, we employ a third subscript, "r", which indicates the standard which "should have been"--in other words, the plan as revised by *ex post* information. A number of useful insights are generated by the tableau.

The first issue is the nature of planning variances, which is somewhat counter-intuitive. Consider, for example, the planning variance in market share--a negative $98,000. What this is really telling us is that, considering only this factor in isolation, our planned market share was set unrealistically high, and that adjusting for this factor alone would have implied planning for a total contribution of $4,000,000 less the $98,000, or $3,902,000. Conversely, however, positive (or favorable) planning variances are in fact undesirable and represent, potentially, opportunity losses.

For example, the $900,000 favorable planning variance in market size, which is responsible for the fact that overall variance is favorable, represents lost profit contribution due to the fact that we had not correctly anticipated the market growth rate (given, of course, that there were no short-run capacity constraints). The $88,200 performance variance in market size is viewed as unassignable in this instance. We have decided that the planners could not have foreseen the foreign demand, and that we don't feel it should be assigned to sales.

Similar issues arise with the price variance. The planning group's failure to correctly predict market prices is responsible for the bulk of the price variance. However, there is no way that this component might have been recovered; it simply indicated the fact that our plan was subsequently shown by events to be unrealistic in its price expectations. In contrast, the failure of the marketing department to maintain our traditional price premium is reflected in the unfavorable performance variance in price of $60,000.

Again, however, we should point out that the most important element of the analysis is the market size/market growth rate issue. Picture the poor salesmen as they operate during the planning period. They know they are feeling some price pressure, to which, as we have seen, marketing responded. However, they also know that their quantity of sales is up--22 million pounds of product versus a planned amount of 20 million pounds.

Thus, it is entirely feasible that our salesmen were not pushing that hard, since they appeared to be having a banner year, handsomely exceeding their monthly volume quotas and prior periods' performance. In fact, during this period we were frittering away our market position through our ignorance of the rate at which the market had expanded.

However, accurate and timely industry sales statistics, in combination with a flexible planning system which could readily incorporate these data in a revised plan and set of sales quotas, would preempt a problem which, by the time we recognized it, had developed into a fair-sized disaster. While market information is always important, it truly takes on new meaning for the company competing in a high-growth market.

Finally, we would note that the aggregate variances for quantity (including share and market size) and price/cost shown in Exhibit 35-3 do not agree with those developed in

EXHIBIT 35-3.

EXPOST PERFORMANCE EVALUATION: ANALYSIS OF CONTRIBUTION

Item	Composition	Type of Variance		Variance Totals	Reconciliation
		Planning Variance	Performance Variance		
PLANNED CONTRIBUTION					$4,000,000
QUANTITY VARIANCE					
SHARE					
Planning Variance	$(S_r - S_p) \cdot M_r \cdot C_p = (.49 - .50) \times 49{,}000{,}000 \times .20$	(98,000)			
Performance Variance	$(S_a - S_r) \cdot M_a \cdot C_r = (.44 - .49) \times 50{,}000{,}000 \times .18$		(450,000)		
Total				(548,000)	

MARKET SIZE					
Planning Variance	$(M_r - M_p) \cdot S_p \cdot C_p$ = (49,000,000-40,000,000) × .5 × .20	900,000			
Performance Variance	$(M_a - M_r) \cdot S_r \cdot C_r$ = (50,000,000-49,000,000) × .49 × .18		88,200		
Total				988,200	
TOTAL QUANTITY VARIANCE					440,200
PRICE VARIANCE					
Planning Variance	$(C_r - C_p) \cdot Q_r$ = (.18-.2) × 24,010,000	(480,200)			
Performance Variance	$(C_a - C_r) \cdot Q_a$ = (.1773-.18) × 22,000,000		(60,000)		
Total				(540,200)	
TOTAL PRICE VARIANCE					(540,200)
TOTAL PLANNING VARIANCE		321,800			
TOTAL PERFORMANCE VARIANCE			(421,800)		
TOTAL VARIANCE				(100,000)	
ACTUAL CONTRIBUTION					$3,900,000

the first part of the article. The reason is, of course, that there are now two possible criteria or yardsticks against which to compare actual results: the original plan (subscripted "p") and the revised plan (subscripted "r").

Following the conceptual development of Part II of the Appendix, therefore, we have used what we believe to be the soundest analysis. Alternative decompositions, which permit the retention of identical aggregate variances to the preliminary "versus plan" comparison are possible, but their conceptual framework is less defensible.

SUMMARY

To be useful to the marketing manager, a framework for control should be related to strategic objectives and variables and, whenever possible, should permit assignment of responsibility for differences between planned and actual performance. The procedures described in this article utilize the key strategic variables of price, market share, and market size as a framework for marketing control.

The framework was first used to analyze marketing performance vs. plan, decomposing quantity variance into components due to under- or over-achievement of planned market share and over- or under-forecasting of market size. Then, recognizing that the plan may well not constitute an adequate criterion for evaluation, we extended the example to illustrate how *ex post* information might be utilized to develop more appropriate evaluative criteria, which permitted isolation of the planning and performance components of the variance.

While there is evidently a considerable amount of managerial judgment involved in the decomposition procedure, marketing planning and control has never been exactly bereft of managerial judgment. There is nothing radical about the procedure, which simply recognizes that it is not always possible to update and modify plans to reflect changing conditions, but that such changes may nonetheless be taken into account in appraisal and evaluation via *ex post* revision of the plan.

The example we worked with also indicates the dangers of not continuously monitoring markets and revising plans and objectives, particularly when market conditions are fluid. In such markets, good tracking procedures[19] and responsive tactics are essential for any company seeking to maintain or increase its market position. The importance of marketing control--so long a stepchild--will surely increase in the years ahead. The markets of the late 1970's will differ considerably from those of the 1960's, and pressures of costs and competition will force companies to be more effective in performance appraisal and evaluation.

APPENDIX
Part I: Variance Decomposition—Comparison with Plan

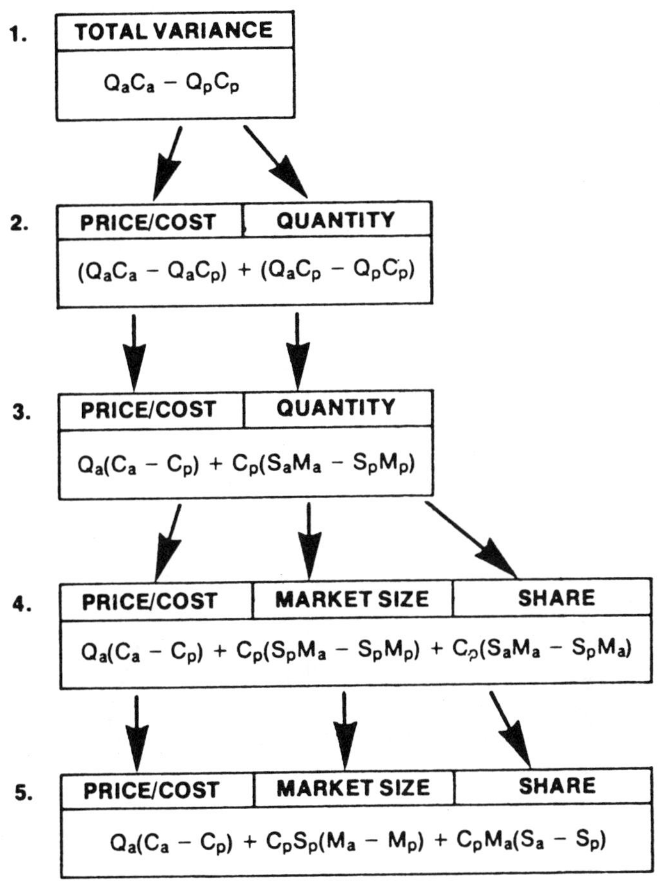

LEGEND

Subscripts
a = actual
p = planned

Variables
Q = Quantity
C = Contribution Margin
S = Share
M = Market

APPENDIX
Part II: Variance Decomposition—Use of *Ex Post* Information

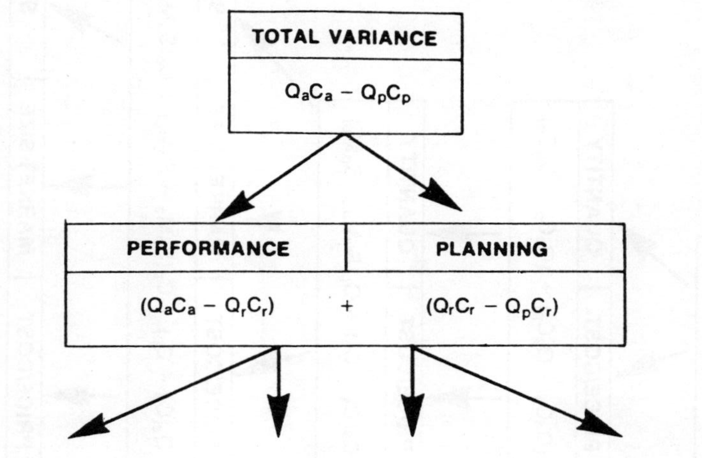

PERFORMANCE				PLANNING		
PRICE/COST		QUANTITY		PRICE/COST		QUANTITY
$Q_a(C_a - C_r)$	+	$C_r(Q_a - Q_r)$	+	$Q_r(C_r - C_p)$	+	$C_p(Q_r - Q_p)$

PERFORMANCE						PLANNING				
PRICE/COST		MARKET SIZE		SHARE		PRICE/COST		MARKET SIZE		SHARE
$Q_a(C_a - C_r)$	+	$C_rS_r(M_a - M_r)$	+	$C_rM_a(S_a - S_r)$	+	$Q_r(C_r - C_p)$	+	$C_pS_p(M_r - M_p)$	+	$C_pM_r(S_r - S_p)$

Legend

Subscripts
a = actual
p = planned
r = revised

Variables
Q = Quantity
C = Contribution margins
S = Share
M = Market

FOOTNOTES

[1]See, for example, V. H. Kirpalani and Stanley S. Shapiro, "Financial Dimensions of Marketing Management," *Journal of Marketing*, Vol. 37, No. 3 (July, 1973), pp. 40-47; David J. Luck and Arthur E. Prell, *Marketing Strategy* (Englewood Cliffs, N. J.: Prentice-Hall, Inc., 1968); Philip Kotler, *Marketing Management: Analysis, Planning and Control* (Englewood Cliffs, N. J.: Prentice-Hall, Inc., 1972).

[2]Boston Consulting Group, *Perspectives on Experience* (Boston: Boston Consulting Group, 1968); see also, Patrick Conley, "Experience Curves as a Planning Tool," in S.H. Britt and H. W. Boyd, eds., *Marketing Management and Administrative Action* (New York: McGraw-Hill, 1974), pp. 257-68; William E. Cox, "Product Portfolio Strategy: A Review of the Boston Consulting Group Approach to Marketing Strategy," in *Proceedings*, 1974 Marketing Educators' Conference (Chicago: American Market Association), pp. 465-70.

[3]Sidney Schoeffler, Robert D. Buzzell and Donald F. Heany, "Impact of Strategic Planning on Profit Performance," *Harvard Business Review*, Vol. 52 (March-April, 1974), pp. 137-45; Robert D. Buzzell, Bradley T. Gale and Ralph G. M. Sultan, "Market Share--A Key to Profitability," *Harvard Business Review*, Vol. 53 (January-February, 1975), pp. 97-106.

[4]See Bernard Catry and Michel Chevalier, "Market Share Strategy and the Product Life Cycle," *Journal of Marketing*, Vol. 38, No. 4 (October, 1974), pp. 29-34; C. Davis Fogg, "Planning Gains in Market Share," *Journal of Marketing*, Vol. 38, No. 3 (July, 1974), pp. 30-38.

[5]F. Beaven Ennis, *Effective Marketing Management*, (New York: Association of National Advertisers, 1973), p. 11.

[6]James M. Hulbert and Norman E. Toy, "Control and the Marketing Plan," paper presented to the 1975 Marketing Educators' Conference of the American Marketing Association.

[7]To simplify this example, no variances in either variable costs or marketing program costs are included.

[8](For algebraic exposition, see Appendix, Part I.)

[9]Algebraically, we have:

$$(C_a - C_p)\ Q_a + (Q_a - Q_p)\ C_p$$
$$= C_aQ_a - C_pQ_a + C_pQ_a - C_pQ_p$$
$$= C_aQ_a - C_pQ_p$$

[10]"Report of the Committee on Cost and Profitability Analyses for Marketing," *Accounting Review*, Supplement to Vol. XLVII (1972), pp. 575-615.

[11]Boston Consulting Group, *Perspectives on Experience*, same as reference 2 above.

[12]John A. Howard, James M. Hulbert and John U. Farley, "Organizational Analysis and Information System Design: A Decision Process Perspective," *Journal of Business Research*, Vol. 3.

[13]Schoeffler, Buzzell and Heany, same as reference 3 a ove.

[14]Ennis, same as reference 5 above, p. 57.

[15]Noel Capon and James M. Hulbert, "Decision Systems Analysis in Industrial Marketing," *Industrial Marketing Management*, Vol. 4, 1975, pp. 143-60.

[16]Joel S. Demski, "An Accounting System Structured on a Linear Programming Model," *The Accounting Review*, Vol. 42 (October, 1967), pp. 701-12.

[17]Some judgment is evidently involved here. Percentage differentials might well be used instead of absolute differentials.

[18]For algebraic exposition, see Appendix, Part I.

[19]John U. Farley and Melvin J. Hinich, "Tracking Marketing Parameters in Random Noise," in *Proceedings*, 1966 Marketing Educators' Conference.

The authors acknowledge the support of the Faculty Research Fund of the Columbia University Graduate School of Business, and the helpful comments of Professors Masai Nakanishi and Gordon Shillinglaw. Early drafts of this article were written while Prof. Hulbert was visiting at the Graduate School of Management, University of California, Los Angeles.

STUDENT REVIEW QUESTIONS

1. What are the three potential sources of variation between planned and actual results identified in the article?
2. What do Hulbert and Toy say about assigning responsibility for variances?
3. Explain the statements "most marketing managers use some *ex post* information" and "nor is 'Monday morning quarterbacking' undesirable".
4. Explain briefly the operating results and some probable causes for the variances of *Product Alpha*.

36

Toward a Concept of Managerial Control for a World Enterprise*

M. Y. YOSHINO

ONE OF THE MOST significant business trends today is the emergence of many American firms in the world market. The U. S. Department of Commerce reports that direct private investments overseas have almost tripled in the last decade, reaching $44 billion in 1964. In the same year, moreover, these investments earned $5.1 billion, of which $3.7 billion has been repatriated to the United States.[1] Over 3,300 American firms have some interest in overseas production either through licensing agreements or direct investments. For a substantial number of these firms, international business represents over 50 percent of earnings.

High profit potentials in the world market have also drawn a large number of firms from other industrially advanced nations into international business. As a result, competition in promising markets throughout the world is rapidly taking on a multinational character. Though international business continues to offer good profit potentials, there is mounting evidence that the return on foreign investment for many leading American firms, though still higher than on domestic investment, has been continuously declining over the last several years.[2] The increasing competitive pressure, coupled with the inherent difficulties in managing a worldwide enterprise, points to a need for ensuring effective managerial arrangements.

One of the critical tasks of managing multinational operations is to design an effective managerial control system

---

*Reprinted by permission from the March 1966 issue of the *Michigan Business Review*, published by the Graduate School of Business Administration, The University of Michigan.

to allow top management to coordinate and guide activities of a large number of far-flung foreign affiliates into a unified whole. Since entirely new variables enter into the calculus of decision making in international business, the mere extension of a domestic control system is inadequate in meeting the demands of multinational operations.

This article seeks to identify major problems faced by corporate management in exercising managerial control over foreign operations and to offer some basic suggestions toward development of a more meaningful way of viewing managerial control in multinational and cultural contexts.

ALLOCATION OF DECISION-MAKING AUTHORITY

Though it is by no means unique to international business, one of the recurring issues raised by corporate management is the division of authority between headquarters and foreign affiliates. Some firms choose to centralize practically all decision making at corporate headquarters and to require from foreign units extremely detailed operating plans and reports with great frequency. As one would expect, this arrangement tends to dampen the enthusiasm and initiative of the management overseas and to limit its flexibility and freedom in meeting local problems and opportunities.

Excessive demand for information and reports not only has a demoralizing effect upon local executives, but it also diverts them from more pressing operating problems. Frequently, the headquarters staff are paralyzed by the sheer volume of information coming from foreign affiliates and fail to make effective use of it. Decisions are likely to be delayed, leading to losses in operating effectiveness.

Interestingly, tight control does not necessarily guarantee that local management will adhere strictly to the policies of the home office. I have observed some local executives who ostensibly comply with the requirements of headquarters but in reality deviate substantially from the policy directives of the home office.

Some firms go to the other extreme by almost completely delegating decision-making authority to local management. My recent field research has revealed that corporate headquarters of some international firms exercise virtually no control over their foreign operations, as long as the foreign units somehow meet the minimum sales or profit goal established by the headquarters. This approach is observed to be particularly prevalent among manufacturers of consumer products with many years of international experience. Some do it out of a conviction that it is impossible to manage daily affairs of overseas units from a headquarters located several thousand miles away, while others follow this practice out of negligence.

WEAKNESSES OF LAISSEZ-FAIRE APPROACH

Though the laissez-faire approach gives maximum flexibility and freedom to local management, it suffers from two major weaknesses. Foreign affiliates which are virtually autonomous tend to generate subgoals not necessarily consistent with those of the headquarters. Also, extreme decentralization limits use of wide variety of resources and experiences available at headquarters which are of potential value to foreign units. There seem to be nearly always some elements of a company's managerial competence that can be applied overseas. The latter point is particularly important inasmuch as the real strength of a world enterprise derives from its ability to integrate the activities of widely scattered affiliates.

Obviously, the optimum pattern lies somewhere between the two extremes described. Since the effectiveness of a particular pattern depends on such factors as nature of products, stage of organizational envolvement, size of the company, and availability of executive talents, it is impossible to prescribe a pattern that is equally suitable under any circumstances. However, it appears that distance, complexity, and instability in operating environments overseas tend to favor maximum decentralization of decision making. Only the very critical decisions should be reserved for corporate management. These are likely to be decisions involving such elements as major capital investments, selection of top managerial personnel, important governmental negotiations, and introduction of new products. This approach tends to maximize contributions that both headquarters and local management are best qualified to make. It must be noted, however, that such an approach is effective only when the following conditions are satisfied: (1) The headquarters-foreign affiliates relationship must be examined in terms of the allocation of specific responsibilities. (2) Corporate headquarters must be properly informed by local units on major decisions that are made by the latter. (3) Finally, headquarters must design an effective system of control over those areas of responsibility that are delegated to the local units.

ESTABLISHING MEANINGFUL STANDARDS OF PERFORMANCE

A critical problem in planning managerial control for multinational operations is the determination of standards against which to evaluate the performance of foreign affiliates. In this regard, two points deserve careful consideration. They are (1) the appropriateness of reported profits as a measurement criterion, and (2) the need for multiple performance criteria. In multidivisional domestic operations, reported profit is generally accepted as the critical measure of managerial effectiveness. Each division is relatively self-contained, and interdivisional transactions can be adjusted through the mechanism of transfer pricing. Since general operating environments among various divisions are relatively homogeneous, top management can make some meaningful comparisons. In multinational operations, however, reported profit alone is quite inadequate as the measure of performance.

In the first place, the reported profit of a foreign operating unit is likely to be distorted by a number of external and internal variables that are absent in domestic operations. Because political and economic risks vary widely from country to country, what appears superficially to be high profit may, in fact, be quite unsatisfactory when risk factors are properly weighed. Foreign exchange regulations, legal restrictions, foreign tax structures, or unexpected political developments can have a decided impact upon the profit performance of a foreign affiliate. Yet the local management has virtually no control over these external factors.

Profit performance of a foreign affiliate can also be affected by intrafirm decisions that are beyond the control of local management. A worldwide enterprise has a wide range of alternatives in allocating its corporate resources. Hence, within the broad constraints of political and economic risk, a network of logistics can be developed on a global basis to maximize comparative advantages of each area. Obviously, companywide logistics decisions can only be made at headquarters. Nevertheless, these decisions can affect profitability of foreign units rather markedly. Some financial decisions made centrally to expand worldwide profits may also lead to an increase of profits in one or more individual country affiliates and a decrease in others. These factors provide convincing evidence that the reported profit-and-loss data must be carefully scrutinized and adjusted by removing various extraneous influences on the operations of a local unit. In so doing the following guidelines are important.

ENVIRONMENTAL VARIABLES

The most serious problem is determining the degree of controllability of the environmental variables. It is evident that local management can exercise no control over such developments as galloping inflation in a foreign economy or a surge of nationalistic feelings. However, it is possible to minimize the impact of these developments on the particular firm through careful planning and judicious actions. Corporate management must somehow determine the degree to which local management should be held accountable for these environmental variables.

Obviously, there is no hard-and-fast rule that is applicable to every situation. It must be noted that there is an inherent tendency for management of most foreign affiliates to attribute poor performance mainly to hard-to-measure environmental variables or arbitrary decisions made by headquarters. Hence, each case must be reviewed carefully. Careless or arbitrary decisions in this respect contribute to poor morale among local management and relaxed control.

The next step involves technical adjustments of reported data. Here, two considerations are important. Since adjustments of profit-loss data of a host of foreign affiliates are highly complicated, time-consuming, and costly, they should be limited to major items large enough to make significant differences. Also, adjustments should be made only on a memorandum basis without entering into the formal accounting records.[3] Furthermore, it is important that the criteria and methods of adjustments be explicitly defined and understood by the management of foreign affilitates.

EVALUATING PERFORMANCE

Removing distortions from the reported profit is only one step. Performance of all foreign units must be evaluated on a comparative basis. This is essential not only for the purpose of managerial control but for future decisions on allocation of corporate resources on a global basis. Establishing a comparative criterion of profit performance is extremely difficult because of a wide diversity in operating environments overseas. It is obvious that an investment in a high-risk country should earn a greater return than one in a stable economy. But is it possible to quantify the rather elusive political and economic risks?

One solution has been suggested by Millard Pryor, Jr., in a recent article in the *Harvard Business Review*. Pryor proposes to establish "compensatory" financial goals for operations outside the United States. Such goals are constructed by adding to the basic financial goals established for domestic operations factors which quantify the long-range overseas political and monetary risks and the extra costs of absentee management.[4]

Another promising concept that needs further exploration is the development of a classification scheme to group various operations into a number of clusters on the basis of key environmental variables. Common performance criteria may then be set for these operations in the same classification. For example, an important variable for a particular type of business may be the level of economic development. The firm's operations throughout the world may be classified into several categories on the basis, regardless of their geographic locations; and common performance criteria may be set within each level. Relative homogeneity in operating environments would presumably allow more meaningful comparison.

PERFORMANCE CRITERIA

Now let us turn to the second basic issue. This involves the question of the relative importance to be attached to profitability as a performance criterion. Though other standards are by no means insignificant, profitability is widely accepted as the final performance standard in multidivisional domestic operations. In view of added environmental dimensions, should the management of multinational operations rely predominantly or even exclusively on this single criterion in measuring managerial effectiveness of foreign affiliates? The answer is clearly negative when the following factors are considered. (1) Multinational operations are conducted in sovereign nations with diverse national goals and interests. (2) Foreign enterprise induces a potential conflict of interest between the American parent company, its local associates, and the governments of the host countries.

Any foreign enterprise that must rely heavily on local resources cannot expect to survive, let alone succeed, over the long run unless it is so structured and managed as to make the maximum contributions to the host country. This is particularly true in developing countries where productive resources are scarce and nationalistic feelings are rampant. Satisfaction on this requirement, however, may well conflict with the profitability criterion, at least in the short run. This conflict of interests must be recognized by top management in setting performance criteria for foreign affiliates.

Some may object to inclusion of such a consideration in performance criteria on the ground that it is beyond precise measurement. While very precise measurement is admittedly difficult, some imaginative approaches are being developed. For example, Professor Robinson has developed a conceptual framework to approximate the political and economic impact of a foreign enterprise on the host country.[5]

There is another area of potential conflict that must be recognized in establishing performance criteria. Many multinational operations involve joint ownership with local interests. Local investors can participate only in profits of the foreign enterprise, not those of the parent company located in the United States. Hence, performance criteria must be established in such a manner as to optimize the interests of different ownership groups. Otherwise, local management is likely to find itself subject to conflicting pressure groups in an atmosphere of indecision and confusion. Such a situation may lead to the ultimate emergence of one dominant group, which in turn enforces its own performance standards.

DESIGNING AN EFFECTIVE INFORMATION SYSTEM

The critical role of information in planning a managerial control system has been repeatedly emphasized in management literature. Distance, diversity, and instability in environments overseas place a premium on an effective information system in multinational operations. Information processing and analysis are much more complex and, correspondingly, more expensive in international business than in domestic operations. Top management, therefore, must balance comprehensiveness and speed on the one hand and the cost of information on the other.

Three basic considerations are important in designing an information system for a world enterprise. They are (1) the types of information sought, (2) the flow of information between headquarters and foreign affiliates, and (3) analysis of information for managerial planning and control.

The types of information sought must be determined by careful examination of the requirements of planning and control. The informational needs of a firm ultimately depend on corporate strategies and goals. This basic consideration, however, is often ignored. Though the exact requirements vary from company to company, basically three types of information are needed by the management of multinational operations. They are environmental data (political, social, and economic), competitive data (real and potential), and internal operating data (both quantitative and qualitative). In many multinational firms, the only type of data systematically and regularly gathered is that related to internal operations. Even those data are primarily designed for accounting purposes rather than for decision making.

Since international operations are much more vulnerable to external variables than domestic operations, data on environmental and competitive conditions become all the more critical. Moreover, much internal data are meaningful only in the perspective of the general environment and in the light of competitive activity.

In view of their importance, it is dangerous to delegate overall intelligence functions solely to foreign affiliates. Though foreign affiliates are unquestionably an important source of vital information for management, local executives are usually preoccupied with daily operating problems, and they may overlook subtle developments with far-reaching implications. Furthermore, there are other equally important sources of environmental and competitive data available to headquarters. For example, United Nations, U. S. government agencies, and trade associations can provide useful information.

THE FLOW OF INFORMATION

The second factor in designing a global information system is facilitating the flow of information between corporate headquarters and foreign affiliates. Two media of communication--written reports and personal visits--are available for this purpose. Though both serve useful functions, the balance between the two must be carefully considered. As noted earlier, excessive reliance on written reports tends to aggravate the already difficult and sometimes strained headquarters-foreign affiliates relationship. Action-oriented local executives find it time-consuming and difficult to prepare reports. Furthermore, foreign nationals are placed at a disadvantage because of language and cultural barriers. For these reasons, written communication should be kept to the minimum level. Headquarters must also standardize reporting procedures and methods to facilitate reporting and subsequent analysis.

Personal visits are used extensively by the management of most multinational corporations, though the character of personal visits varies widely as does their effectiveness. Too frequently, personal visits are used as a tool for trouble-shooting--to solve immediate problems occurring unexpectedly. Viewed in this fashion, personal visits have very limited educational value. Since face-to-face contacts can be useful in bridging the distance and cultural gaps that exist between headquarters and foreign affiliates, they must be well planned and made on a regular basis. Personal visits, if appropriately conducted, are useful in developing an insight into local problems, communicating policies of headquarters, discussing long-term plans, and sharing valuable experiences.

The most challenging area in designing an international intelligence system lies in analysis of data by headquarters staff for effective control and planning. Thus far, in many international firms relatively little has been done beyond the traditional accounting analysis. Comparative analysis of internal data is complicated by diverse environmental factors, as noted earlier; but this step is critical in identifying weak spots and unrealized opportunities. Some progressive firms have begun to make imaginative use of these ideas. For example, labor productivity, efficiency of logistics system, and effectiveness of a given marketing mix are analyzed and evaluated on a global basis.

UNDERSTANDING CULTURAL VARIABLES

Perhaps the most difficult and elusive aspect of managerial control in international operations is that control functions must be performed in a multicultural context. This is particularly significant when affiliates are managed by foreign nationals. Cultural variables affect managerial control in several ways.

First, culture may block effective communication between

foreign affiliates and headquarters. Particularly serious from the viewpoint of managerial control are distortions introduced in reporting as a result of certain cultural values prevalent in some societies. Some cultures tend to emphasize politeness and agreeableness in superior-subordinate reporting relationships, even at the expense of accuracy and directness. Thus, local management may ignore or distort data deemed unpleasant to corporate headquarters.

Second, to a large degree culture prescribes the standard of achievement and dictates the concomitant system of rewards. Not every culture rewards what is considered to be productive achievement in advanced industrial societies, nor is the reward for similar achievements the same. For example, some traditional cultures place the ultimate reward upon loyalty, devotion, and contribution to the group rather than upon outstanding individual achievement. Thus, a system of motivations and incentives--an essential ingredient in managerial control--must be meaningful in terms of the local culture.

Culture also affects superior-subordinate relationships in an organization. As Professor Fayerweather concludes from his pioneering research, some cultures are prone to produce interpersonal relationships characterized by distance, distrust, and hostility; while others are more conducive to group-oriented, collaborative interpersonal relationships.[6] He further notes that the former type is relatively prevalent in more traditional societies, whereas the latter is predominant in Western societies, particularly in American culture. Though each pattern is meaningful and effective in its own cultural environments, difficulties are likely to emerge when control functions must be performed among men of diverse cultural backgrounds and orientations.

Finally, there is the problem of sensitivity often manifested by national executives toward control exercised by American executives. This is particularly prevalent among those in underdeveloped and former colonial countries.

The only permanently effective way to overcome these cultural gaps is to view managerial control as an educational process rather than a superior-subordinate authority relationship. Continuous educational effort is the only feasible way to provide management of foreign affiliates with the necessary background to understand the headquarters' points of view. With this background, local management could intelligently interpret policy directives from the home office as well as effectively participate in the formation of such policies. Such an educational approach would also minimize the sensitivity problem mentioned above.

CONCLUSION

Managerial control in multinational operations is complicated by a number of external as well as internal variables unique to multinational operations. Clearly, it is impossible to rely solely on comfortable assumptions and generalizations developed out of domestic experience. A need is apparent for developing a conceptual framework for managerial control of multinational operations.

At the risk of oversimplification, this article has singled out four basic considerations as a step toward development of a useful way of viewing managerial control for a world enterprise. The task is by no means easy, but the undeniable facts of the tremendous potential of the expanding world market and increasing competition should provide sufficient incentive for American management to meet this challenge effectively.

FOOTNOTES

[1]U. S. Department of Commerce, Office of Business Economics, *Survey of Current Business*, September, 1965, p. 24.

[2]For example, see Walter P. Stern, "U. S. Direct Investment Abroad," *Financial Analysts Journal*, January-February, 1965, p. 98; C. Wickham Skinner, "Management of International Production," *Harvard Business Review*, September-October, 1964, p. 125.

[3]*International Enterprise: A New Dimension of American Business* (New York: McKinsey & Company, Inc., 1962), p. 30.

[4]Millard Pryor, Jr., "Planning in a World Business," *Harvard Business Review*, January-February, 1965, p. 134.

[5]Richard D. Robinson, *International Business Policy* (New York: Holt, Rinehart & Winston, Inc., 1964), pp. 99-145.

[6]John Fayerweather, *The Executive Overseas* (Syracuse, N.Y.: Syracuse University Press, 1959), pp. 15-40.

STUDENT REVIEW QUESTIONS

1. When does Yoshino advocate a completely decentralized decision-making structure for international businesses?
2. Why is reported profit often an inadequate measure of performance in multinational operations?
3. Whay types of information are needed by the managers of multinational operations?
4. How does Yoshino recommend that the flow of information between headquarters and the foreign affiliate be improved?
5. In what ways do cultural variables affect managerial control in multinational corporations?

REFERENCES FOR ADDITIONAL STUDY

Buchele, Robert B., "How to Evaluate a Firm," *California Management Review,* Fall, 1962.

Cammann, Cortlandt and David A. Nadler, "Fit Control Systems to Your Managerial Style," *Harvard Business Review,* January-February, 1976.

Dearden, John, "The Case Against ROI Control," *Harvard Business Review,* May-June, 1969.

Dearden, John, "Limits on Decentralized Profit Responsibility," *Harvard Business Review,* July-August, 1962.

Koontz, Harold and Robert W. Bradspies, "Managing Through Feedforward Control," *Business Horizons,* June, 1972.

Kotler, Philip, William Gregor and William Rodgers, "The Marketing Audit Comes of Age," *Sloan Management Review,* Winter, 1977.

McGregor, Douglas, "Do Management Control Systems Achieve Their Purpose?", *Sloan Management Review,* February, 1967.

Sherwin, Douglas, "The Meaning of Control," *Dun's Review and Modern Industry,* January, 1956.

Tilles, Seymour, "How to Evaluate Corporate Strategy," *Harvard Business Review,* July-August, 1963.

Vancil, Richard F., "What Kind of Management Control Do You Need?", *Harvard Business Review,* March-April, 1973.

Weston, J. J. Fred, "ROI Planning and Control," *Business Horizons,* August, 1972.